AS LONG AS THE GRASS SHALL GROW AND RIVERS FLOW

A History of Native Americans

Clifford E. Trafzer

*University of California
Riverside*

HARCOURT COLLEGE PUBLISHERS

Fort Worth   Philadelphia   San Diego   New York   Orlando   Austin   San Antonio
Toronto   Montreal   London   Sydney   Tokyo

Publisher:	Earl McPeek
Executive Editor:	David C. Tatom
Developmental Editor:	Margaret McAndrew Beasley
Market Strategist:	Steve Drummond
Project Editor:	Travis Tyre
Production Manager:	Diane Gray
Art Director:	Burl Sloan

Cover: "Red No. 6" by Fritz Scholder

ISBN: 0-15-503857-5
Library of Congress Catalog Card Number: 99-73311

Address for orders:
Harcourt, Inc.
6277 Sea Harbor Drive
Orlando, FL   32887-6777
1-800-782-4479

Address for editorial correspondence:
Harcourt College Publishers
301 Commerce Street, Suite 3700
Fort Worth, TX   76102

Web site address:
http://www.harcourtcollege.com

Printed in the United States of America

9 0 1 2 3 4 5 6 7 8   039   9 8 7 6 5 4 3 2 1

For Lee Ann, Tess Nashone,
Hayley Kachine, and Tara Tsaile
For the Henry and Sioui families and all descendants of the
Wyandot, Wendat, Wyandotte, Neutral, Erie, Tobacco, and Huron

HARCOURT BRACE

soon to become

Harcourt College Publishers

A Harcourt Higher Learning Company

Soon you will find Harcourt Brace's distinguished innovation, leadership, and support under a different name . . . a new brand that continues our unsurpassed quality, service, and commitment to education.

We are combining the strengths of our college imprints into one worldwide brand: Harcourt Our mission is to make learning accessible to anyone, anywhere, anytime—reinforcing our commitment to lifelong learning.

We'll soon be Harcourt College Publishers. Ask for us by name.

**One Company
"Where Learning
Comes to Life."**

PREFACE

THE STORY BEHIND THE BOOK

"As long as the grass shall grow and rivers flow!" That is the way my mother put it. "They said that as long as the grass shall grow and rivers flow, you can have your land." Actually, President Andrew Jackson used a similar phrase when he instructed Major David Haley to tell the Choctaws and Chickasaws that as a friend, the president planned to move the people to the trans-Mississippi West to a "land of their own, which they shall possess as long as grass grows or water runs." It is likely that the phrase originated from white negotiators making statements similar to that of Jackson, but I have preferred the way my mother remembered the phrase. Many Native Americans understood the essence of what had been said, and they also knew that the government forced the removal of thousands of native people from their ancient homelands. President Jackson and other policymakers lied to the people, and American Indians have not forgotten the duplicity and misrepresentation they discovered in the phrase ". . .as long as the grass shall grow and rivers flow."

Wherever you travel in the Americas, you are on Indian land. Tribes, clans, bands, and families did not own every part of the earth in the modern sense of the word, but they knew the land and often used it. They considered some lands too sacred to use in a secular fashion, and only medicine people visited those lands. Other areas of earth could not be approached at all by anyone. This was the law—Indian law. Some Native Americans believed that they emerged out of the earth and into their homelands or fell from the sky into a new land that was brought alive through the power of song, spirit, and story. Other tribes believed that they moved from place to place until they settled on a particular spot that had meaning to them. In any case, tribes knew the importance of place, and they hallowed these lands with their blood and the bones of their people. Europeans, and later white Americans, were never satisfied with the lands they took. They always wanted more land, more resources. The white people made agreements with Native Americans, saying that they would never move onto Indian lands again. But they repeatedly broke their word, and even their own laws. Throughout this book, both Indians and whites offer their voices and thoughts on the phrase ". . . as long as the grass shall grow and rivers flow."

THE COSTS OF EUROPEAN CONTACT

On a Greyhound bus traveling from Tucson to Yuma, Arizona, in 1967, I overheard a Quechan Indian telling a white man that the United States should accelerate its space program to the moon so that whites could colonize it and return this country to Indian people. The Quechan represented the views of many Native Americans, and his comments reflected an attitude shared by many people who feel that something terrible happened in American history as a result of Euro-American subjugation, conquest, and, in some cases, outright extermination of native peoples. This book attempts to interpret segments of that past—of conquest and resistance, of death and survival. For the past twenty-seven years, I have explained to students in my courses in Native American history that given European history, we could hardly have expected anything else of the Spanish, French, English, or Russians in their dealings with American Indians. European market economies encouraged agricultural growth, trade developments, and colonialism. Economic successes in Europe generated greater demand for exploitable lands, peoples, and natural resources. European nation-states had developed centralized governments and strong, authoritarian leadership. Decisions affecting large numbers of people that often affected economic growth were made without their consent. By the time of the European conquests of Native America, Europeans had already suffered biological scourges of plague, measles, smallpox, and other contagious diseases that actually provided the *survivors* of these endemic diseases a few natural immunities. Europeans used gunpowder, horses, cannons, ships, and strategies of warfare unknown to Native Americans. Their development of other technologies such as metal fishhooks, pots, pans, traps, knives, axes, and the like significantly affected the balance of power in these relationships. In addition, European and Christian attitudes of superiority influenced encounters with native peoples throughout the world, including those of the present-day United States.

American Indian civilizations and cultures had developed much differently than those in Europe. No utopia existed in the Americas prior to 1492 because Indian groups fought with each other and vented their prejudices toward one another. These tribes and bands largely employed decentralized governments with a great deal of political and economic autonomy. Some native nations had centralized governments with authoritarian leaders, but the vast majority were composed of autonomous groups that tended to be politically fluid. Power was concentrated in spiritual and military leaders, and it was not generally based on economic wealth. Indians fought and traded with each other, but most did not develop market economies or nation-states like those found in Europe. Agriculture existed throughout much of Native America, but it usually did not result in huge surpluses intended for export markets.

For the most part, Native Americans living in the United States did not encourage economic exploitation of other people and imperialism. Native Americans had endured conflicts and wars prior to European contact, but they had experienced only a few of the contagious diseases known to exist in Europe. Native Americans had few natural biological immunities, a fact that created a calamity when Europeans brought micro-organisms to the Americas. Diseases decimated thousands of men, women, and children simply as a result of trading. American Indians knew little about European diseases until they had suffered directly from epidemics, and by then it was too late. Although Native Americans shared a strong oral tradition, most did not have a written language with which to communicate information about whites to other Indians. Knowledge of the animals, warfare, diseases, and designs brought by whites never reached many, and certainly not in time for them to be proactive and avoid contact. Native leaders had little experience with Europeans, and contact between them came rapidly, often too quickly for Native Americans to assess their positions in a concerted, unified manner.

The result of the European invasion and colonization of America was disastrous for Native Americans, and American Indians acted in a variety of ways to preserve their cultures, protect their peoples, and defend their lands. Native American agency and resistance are legendary, and many Native American leaders are well-known in American history for their patriotic stance on behalf of their people. Conflict, resistance, and survival are powerful themes of this book. For Native Americans, the history of the United States is a tragedy that left thousands of people dead—the result of disease, war, starvation, and exposure. In addition, white expansion left thousands of people homeless and hopeless, and it contributed to anomie among the people who had lost their loved ones and lands they held most sacred, the lands that held the bones and blood of their ancestors. A few reviewers who assisted in the preparation of this book commented that they were disturbed by the book's tone. I believe that readers *should* be disturbed by the narrative and moved to think and rethink American history.

APPROACH: THE PAST IS PRESENT

In many ways, the past is the present in native history. Some native historians believe that historical events are part of the present and will be part of the future because these events did not simply occur and vanish, but they retain their meaning today. Wyandot elder and Huron spiritual mother Eleanore Sioui explained that First Nations people are never separated from the past because they are at once part of two worlds: the physical and the spiritual. My Choctaw friend Donna Akers recently told me that when she was a child in the 1950s and 1960s, her family talked about President Andrew Jackson as if he had recently left office. Choctaws call Jackson the Devil and speak of him today as if his orders to remove the people happened yesterday. When Akers was in grade school, she was shocked to learn that Jackson had been dead for more than 100 years and asked her grandmother about this. The answer was simple, for Choctaws and many other people, Jackson's forced removal of people from the eastern portion of the United States to present-day Kansas and Oklahoma may as well have happened yesterday. The wound is still open, the pain is still fresh. Removal is not simply a thing of the past, but it continues to influence the present. And so it is for Kiowas, Comanches, Arapahos, Cheyennes, and Plains Apaches in Oklahoma who fought the United States Army or the Lakota, Cheyenne, and Arapaho who fought Custer. The wars and policies of the past are not artifacts, but they have meaning today and will influence the future. This non-linear way of thinking is an approach taken in this book.

Native Americans are real people, not the imaginary or particularly noble characters portrayed in films and books. There are no "generic" Indians presented in the volume, although it is difficult to synthesize and interpret so many people, years, and topics without generalizing. American Indian history is complex and difficult to analyze because a variety of forces, opinions, peoples, and actions have influenced the past. Like most groups, Native Americans are rarely unified about issues. At various times, tribes, bands, villages, and individuals divide over issues, making it dangerous to claim that all people within a nation, tribe, band, or village acted in one way or another. For example, some Wyandots opposed Tecumseh and the Indian movement while others under Roundhead joined Tecumseh. Native Americans were and are diverse people with many divisions of opinion and action. They enjoy many languages, cultures, traditions, and values. All American Indians have their own histories and stories to tell. Only a few are provided chronologically and topically in this volume, but the number is sufficient to encourage readers to seek more information and to grow in their knowledge of native history. Each scholar will also approach this work in different ways, but it is my sincere hope that this book will provide students of Native American history with a general survey of important social, political, medical, military, and cultural history.

As Long as the Grass Shall Grow and Rivers Flow is a survey of Native American history with an emphasis on resistance, religion, survival, native voices, and native agency. These themes are developed throughout the work. In addition, Native American history is presented as an integral part of American history, and Western expansion and civilization cannot be fully understood apart from it. The book offers various interpretations of native history, but it also provides students with basic information assembled from many diverse sources. Finally, it is intended to encourage scholars to delve deeper into topics not developed comprehensively within the text. The early periods of American history are presented in a logical and flowing manner so that readers may learn the broader spectrum of Native American history. However, greater emphasis is provided on the twentieth century—a significant portion of the book deals with the years between 1900 and 2000.

CHAPTER-BY-CHAPTER OUTLINE

Ancient stories are not "fish tales that grow with the telling" but living histories that influence people today. The importance of creation as a process informs the historical narrative presented in writing. The relationship of the past in the lives of American Indians has been shared from generation to generation through oral narratives that communicate tribal histories involving communities that are at once composed of plants, animals, peoples, monsters, mountains, and spirits. Although the archaeological and historical record of scholars provides an understanding of the Native American past, another voice is offered through the oral tradition of tribal elders. **Chapter 1** offers a way of thinking about Native American history, sovereignty, religion, law, and place. The use of oral narratives and oral histories provided by tribal elders is presented in much the same manner that elders present their tribe's past in classes, homes, and lectures today.

Tribal historians recorded the coming of Europeans, and native interpretations of the Spanish invasion and conquest is presented in **Chapter 2,** including the impact of gold, slavery, laws, disease, population, and policies. **Chapter 3** provides a discussion of Native American interaction with the French, Dutch, Swiss, and Russian traders who significantly influenced Native Americans by introducing new technologies and served as the vanguard of white resettlement of native lands. The Pamunkey and other tribes of the Chesapeake Bay as well as the Wampanoags, Pequots, and Massachusetts of the Massachusetts Bay are the peoples discussed in **Chapter 4,** which examines the English invasion and resettlement of the southern and northern colonies and focuses on the ways in which Native Americans attempted to deal with the English and to resist European influences.

Chapter 5 examines Native American agency during the Colonial Wars, including King William's War, Queen Anne's War, King George's War, and the Seven Years' War, also known as the French and Indian War. The aftermath of the latter war brought many changes for Indian people who had allied so closely with the French. Ottawa Chief Pontiac's resistance and the subsequent Proclamation Line of 1763 are presented. **Chapter 6** offers an analysis of Native American involvement in the Revolutionary War and the significance the war had in the lives of many American Indians who were living east of the Mississippi River (including Mohawk leaders like Joseph and Molly Brant). The history of Cherokees, Iroquois, Wyandots, Shawnees, Delawares, Miamis, and many other tribes changed as a result of the American Revolution and the early Federalist period.

Chapter 7 examines the Indian movement during the early nineteenth century, before and during the War of 1812 when many tribes rose up against the United States to preserve their cultures. The chapter features many resistance leaders, including Muscogee Chief Hildas Harjo, Choctaw leader Pushmataha, Ho-Chunk Red Bird, and Sac-Fox Chief Black Hawk. The military defeat of many tribes by the United States led to disgraceful ethnic cleansing and the forced removal of most eastern tribes, along with the theft of their lands. **Chapter 8** interprets the mass removal of the tribes and the resistance of some to remain in their eastern homes. **Chapter 9** offers both general and specific information on the Native American reactions to the Lewis and Clark expedition, the expansion of the fur trade among the far western tribes, the opening of the Oregon Trail, and the introduction of American Indian policies in the Pacific Northwest. Native American resistance continues to be a theme developed in Chapter 9, with details about the Indian wars of the Northwest, Texas, New Mexico, and California. The chapter ends with a discussion of the California Gold Rush and its meaning to native people who resisted white encroachments and faced genocide. **Chapter 10** offers an overview of many Native Americans during the American Civil War. The war and reconstruction affected the lives of all Indians in Indian Territory, including those who fought for the Union and Confederacy. The past of these and other tribes flows into a discussion of war, peace, and confinement. **Chapter 11** offers details about the resistance movements of Kickapoos, Kiowas, Arapahos, Cheyennes, and Comanches. Particular emphasis is placed on Lakota resistance along the Bozeman Trail, the Treaty of Fort Laramie, the invasion of the Black Hills, and the efforts of Crazy Horse and others to defend their people.

Resistance was not confined to the Great Plains. In **Chapter 12,** readers will learn about the Modoc War, Shoshoni-Bannock-Paiute War, and Apache War. Details are provided about the Nez Perce War. **Chapter 13** deals with that transitional period-from the nineteenth to early twentieth century-with discussions about reservations, allotment, assimilation, education, and diseases such as tuberculosis and pneumonia, the great killers of Native American infants, children and young adults. **Chapter 14** offers some Native American responses to wars, diseases, reservations, and government policies in general that sought to destroy native cultures. In order to survive, American Indians turned inward to their own religious leaders who offered solace at a time when the people faced anomie, starvation, disease, and death. The chapter presents glimpses into the significance of Native American religions, spiritual leaders, songs, and dances.

Chapter 15 deals with white entrepreneurs and corrupt bureaucrats exploited timber, coal, oil, water, and other natural resources on Indian lands. Helen Hunt Jackson, Yavapai doctor Carlos Montezuma, Albert Smiley, John Collier, Yankton Sioux Gertrude Bonnin, and many other reformers organized and spoke out against the detrimental government and business policies. The result was a comprehensive investigation into the Office of Indian Affairs called the *Meriam Report* of 1928. The report led to concrete reforms during the New Deal era of American history, and this is the focus of **Chapter 16.** The chapter also examines the creation and execution of the Indian Reorganization Act, the importance of various economic recovery programs, educational reforms of the 1930s, and the Indian Claims Commission.

The Great Depression and World War II were watersheds in American history and Native American history. **Chapter 17** deals with World War II and its significance to Native American communities and peoples. It offers the experiences of only a few Native American soldiers, sailors, and flyers as well as women who worked in defense plants and served in the armed forces. A brief discussion is offered about the famous Navajo Code Talkers and the Japanese internment camps on the Colorado River Indian Reservation and Gila River Indian Reservation, in Arizona. **Chapter 18** focuses on the government's policy of terminating Indian tribes and relocating Indians from the reservations to urban areas during the 1950s and 1960s. In addition, the chapter surveys the years of the Johnson and Nixon administrations and provides information on Indian education, health, and politics. **Chapter 19** deals with American Indian resistance movements of the 1960s and 1970s, a common thread in Native American history. Fish-Ins, the takeover of Alcatraz Island, and the rise of Red Power are analyzed in the chapter, as are the Trail of Broken Treaties, the takeover of the Bureau of Indian Affairs building, and Wounded Knee (1973). The American Indian Movement, self-determination, tribal sovereignty, and Indian gaming are also discussed.

Chapter 20 provides a look at the development of Native American fine arts and includes information on architecture, pottery, painting, sculpture, carving, basketry, beads, textiles, silver smithing, ribbon work, and other art forms. Fine art developments and changes are noted as are some of the Native American artists who have influenced the course of American history. **Chapter 21** offers an examination of Native American writers and performing artists with a discussion of specific people who have influenced American history through their novels, short stories, satire, essays, songs, poetry, theater, film, histories, and other creative forms. The continuing circle of Native American history and the close relationship of the past to the present is presented in the last chapter.

Chapter 22 deals with contemporary efforts by Indian people to repatriate Native American remains and grave items, particularly through the Native American Graves Protection Act and the Native American Heritage Commission. In addition, the chapter offers a discussion of the important efforts of the National Museum of the American Indian to offer museum programs that accurately represent Native American peoples and their material culture. The chapter ends with a circular approach to thinking, because Native American stories have no beginning and no ending. Like a circle, Native American history strongly influences the present and future. It is not a static, linear history but one that comes alive with each telling because the events and people of the past affect events and people today.

A **Selected Readings and Bibliography** section is listed at the end of each chapter. When a work is mentioned for the first time in a given chapter, a full citation is provided. However, when the same work is used in a subsequent chapter, it will be listed only briefly in the bibliography introduction.

ACKNOWLEDGMENTS

Many people have made this book possible, particularly the men and women who have shared their knowledge with me through the written and spoken word. Whenever I think seriously of historical study, I remember my mother, Mary Lou Henry Trafzer, of Wyandot and German ancestry, who instilled in me a love of our native past and taught me its relationship to the present. I thank my mother for giving me an understanding of place, people, story, plants, animals, and community. I am indebted to Wendat-Huron spiritual leader Eleanore Sioui, Wendat-Huron historian Georges Sioui, Palouse-Nez Perce Andrew George, Cahuilla-Luiseño Edward Castillo, Palouse Mary Jim, Richard D. Scheuerman, Chemehuevi Dean Mike, Lummi Theresa Mike, Cahuilla Luke Madrigal, Cahuilla Anthony Madrigal, James Sandos, Cheyenne Rick West, James Rawls, Fred Bohm, Cherokee David Edmunds, Shawnee-Muscogee-Sac-Fox Don Fixico, Frederick Hoxie, Ojibwa Monte Kugel, Choctaw Donna Akers, Ajumawe Darryl Wilson, Cherokee Charlotte Heth, Laguna Lee Francis, Quechan Lee Emerson, Terence Winch, Chemehuevi Joe Benitez, Mohawk Richard Danay, Cahuilla Katherine Siva Saubel, Collin Calloway, Anishinaabe Duane Champagne, Joel Hyer, and Troy Johnson. The stories, books, and articles of these individuals have enriched my life and work.

I thank the editors of Harcourt, Inc. for making this book possible, particularly Margaret McAndrew Beasley (developmental editor) and

Travis Tyre (project editor). Carl Tyson and Drake Bush, both former colleagues at Harcourt, originally encouraged me to research and write this book, and I thank them sincerely for the confidence they had in me. Additional thanks go to David C. Tatom, executive editor, for seeing the project through to completion; Steve Drummond, market strategist; Diane Gray, production manager; and Burl Sloan, art director. Sapna Patel, Mehrdad Alemozaffar, and Nilufar Alemozaffar helped me with the final stages of this book, and I thank my colleagues and the outside reviewers who read the work and offered constructive criticism: Monte Kugel, University of California, Riverside; Fred Hoxie, Newberry Library; Donna Akers, Purdue University; Collin Calloway, Dartmouth College; Edward Castillo, Sonoma State University; Margaret Connell-Szasz, University of New Mexico, Albuquerque; Steven Crum, University of California, Davis; Vine Deloria, Jr., University of Colorado; Donald Grinde, University of Vermont; Peter Iverson, Arizona State University; and Thomas Wessel, Montana State University. My deep appreciation is extended to descendants of Wyandot, Wyandotte, Wendat, Huron, Neutral, Erie, and Tobacco peoples who have survived. I am most indebted to Lee Ann and our three girls, Tess Nashone, Hayley Kachine, and Tara Tsaile who patiently waited and gave me time to research and write.

Clifford E. Trafzer
Yucaipa, California

CONTENTS

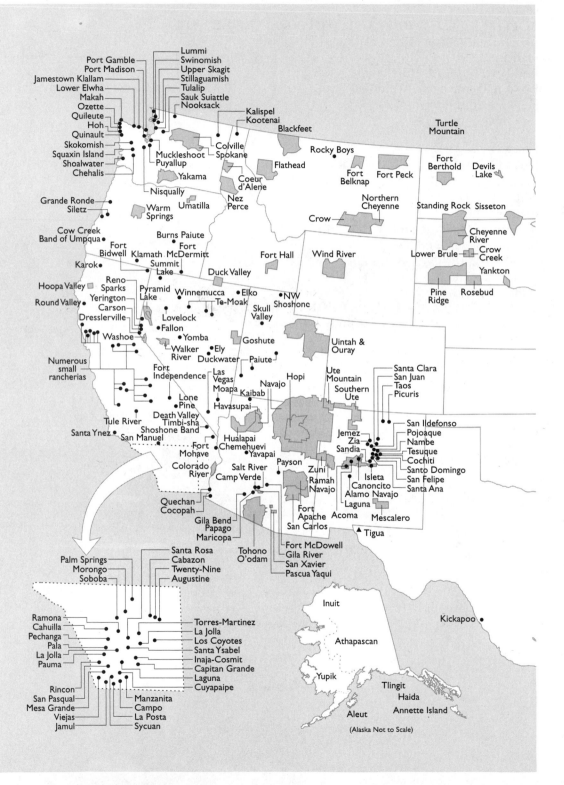

Lummi
Swinomish
Port Gamble
Upper Skagit
Port Madison
Stillaguamish
Jamestown Klallam
Tulalip
Lower Elwha
Sauk Suiattle
Makah
Nooksack
Ozette
Kalispel
Quileute
Kootenai
Hoh
Blackfeet
Quinault
Turtle
Mountain
Skokomish
Colville
Rocky Boys
Squaxin Island
Spokane
Shoalwater
Muckleshoot
Fort
Chehalis
Puyallup
Flathead
Berthold
Devils
Yakama
Fort
Lake
Belknap
Fort Peck
Coeur
Nisqually
d'Alene
Grande Ronde
Nez
Siletz
Warm
Umatilla
Perce
Northern
Standing Rock Sisseton
Springs
Cheyenne
Cow Creek
Burns Paiute
Crow
Cheyenne
Band of Umpqua
Fort
River
Fort
Bidwell
Klamath McDermitt
Lower Brule
Crow
Karok
Summit
Fort Hall
Wind River
Creek
Lake
Yankton
Hoopa Valley
Reno
Duck Valley
Sparks
Pyramid
Pine
Rosebud
Round Valley
Yerington
Lake
Winnemucca
Elko
Ridge
Carson
Te-Moak
NW
Dresslerville
Skull
Shoshone
Lovelock
Valley
Washoe
Fallon
Goshute
Uintah &
Yomba
Ouray
Numerous
Walker
Ely
Santa Clara
small
River
Duckwater
Paiute
San Juan
rancherias
Fort
Hopi
Taos
Independence
Las
Ute
Picuris
Vegas
Mountain
Moapa
Kaibab
Southern
Lone
Navajo
Ute
Pine
Havasupai
San Ildefonso
Tule River
Death Valley
Jemez
Pojoaque
Timbi-sha
Zia
Nambe
Santa Ynez
Shoshone Band
Hualapai
Sandia
Tesuque
San Manuel
Chemehuevi
Cochiti
Fort
Yavapai
Isleta
Santo Domingo
Mohave
Payson
Canoncito
San Felipe
Colorado
Zuni
Alamo Navajo
Santa Ana
River
Salt River
Ramah
Laguna
Camp Verde
Navajo
Acoma
Mescalero
Quechan
Fort
Cocopah
Apache
Gila Bend
San Carlos
Tigua
Papago
Maricopa
Fort McDowell
Palm Springs
Santa Rosa
Tohono
Gila River
Morongo
Cabazon
O'odam
San Xavier
Soboba
Twenty-Nine
Pascua Yaqui
Augustine
Inuit
Kickapoo
Ramona
Torres-Martinez
Cahuilla
La Jolla
Athapascan
Pechanga
Los Coyotes
Pala
Santa Ysabel
La Jolla
Inaja-Cosmit
Pauma
Capitan Grande
Yupik
Laguna
Tlingit
Rincon
Cuyapaipe
Haida
San Pasqual
Manzanita
Aleut
Annette Island
Mesa Grande
Campo
Viejas
La Posta
(Alaska Not to Scale)
Jamul
Sycuan

Federal Indian Reservations ▢
Federal Indian Reservations ●
State Indian Reservations ▲

Deer Creek
Bois Forte
Vermillion Lake
Leech Lake
Red Cliff
Bad River
Red Lake
L'Anse
White Earth
Fond du Lac
Grand Portage
Lac Vieux Desert
Sandy Lake
Ontonagon
Hannahville
Bay Mills
Sault Ste. Marie
Grand Traverse
Sokaogan Chippewa
Mille Lacs
St. Croix
Lac du Falmbeau
Upper Sioux
Prairie Island
Potawatomi
Shakopee
Menominee
Oneida
Lower Sioux
Winnebago
Isabella
Flandreau
Stockbridge-Munsee
Potawatomi

Micmac
Houlton Maliseet
Indian Township
Pleasant Point
Penobscot
St. Regis
Ganienkeh
Pennocock
Oneida
Shagticoke
Paugusett
Abnaki
Onondaga
Nipmuk-Hassanamisko
Tuscarora
Tonawanda
Wampanoag
Narragansett
Cattaraugus
Mashantucket Pequot
Oil Springs
Allegheny
Paucatuck Pequot
Shinnecock
Poosepatuck

Santee Sioux
Winnebago
Sac and Fox
Omaha
Sac and Fox
Iowa
Kickapoo
Potawatomi
Cheyenne
Shawnee
Pawnee
Quapaw
Peoria
Ottawa
Kaw
Wyandot
Osage
Seneca Cayuga
E. Shawnee
Miami
Modoc
Cherokee
Wichita
Caddo
Creek
Seminole
Choctaw
Chickasaw
Shawnee
Potawatomi
Sac and Fox
Shawnee
Kiowa
Arapaho
Kickapoo
Alabama-Coushatta
Coushatta
Chitimacha
Tunica-Biloxi

Mattaponi
Pamunkey
Cherokee
Catawba
Mississippi Choctaw
Poarch Creek
Brighton Seminole
Big Cypress Seminole
Dania
Miccosukee

BREATHING LIFE
INTO BEING

At certain times and for all times, creative forces put the earth into motion. Wind stirred the world into creation, breathing life into the earth. Movement set the world into motion, expanded that which was first created and contributed to the continuance of the creative power. Clouds, fog, and water developed when the earth was young, providing elements of the creative process. Beings of many names and sorts, some familiar and some unfamiliar, some seen and some unseen, interacted with each other in great drama. Animate and inanimate presence within the sky, land, and air joined together in this drama to create laws by which all life was to function. Creative forces differed from place to place, just as laws differed from group to group. Duality emerged on earth. There was night and day, male and female, good and evil, love and hate, cooperation and murder. The world contained much that was good and beautiful, but it also had its problems and perils. Monsters and evil forces emerged at the beginning of time as a counter to positive forces. Tension and confusion developed at the beginning of time, along with the ability to counter these forces to create calm resolutions. Through stories filled with meaning and symbolism, Native Americans tell of the creation, which is at once historical and contemporary, a process that continues to this day.

ORAL NARRATIVE AS HISTORY

Wolf walked through the woods bumping into trees as he moved along. Not far away, a tiny gray mouse ambled along until he spotted Wolf. Mouse hid behind the trunk of a great oak tree and watched Wolf. The animal continued to have problems as he moved forward, running headlong into a tree trunk, then backing up and moving forward until he ran into another tree. Courageously, the small gray mouse walked forward in front of Wolf, who sniffed the air.

"I see you have a problem," Mouse announced.

"Yes, I do," Wolf responded. "I have gone blind and can see nothing, and so I will die. I can no longer hunt, and without my eyes, I will perish."

Without a word, Mouse moved his tiny forepaws to his own eyes, reached up, and removed them. Mouse then reached up to Wolf and gave him his eyes. With Mouse's eyes, Wolf could now see. Wolf wept with joy at the magnanimous gift and thanked Mouse profusely.

"But what of you, Little Brother," Wolf said, suddenly realizing that Mouse would now be blind. "You cannot see and must have eyes in order to live."

"You are a great and wonderful animal, and you should live," Mouse replied. "As for me, I am small and insignificant. There are many like me, but you are a large and powerful creature that must live."

Wolf thanked Mouse again and again for the gift of sight and told Mouse they would be brothers. Wolf placed Mouse on the back of his neck and explained that from that day forward they would forever be friends. They traveled that way through life, hunting together and eating together. In fact, for years Wolf and Mouse camped, sang, prayed, and sweated together as brothers. One day as they traveled along, Mouse felt a change come over him. His tiny nose elongated and became hard like a beak, and his forearms spread out and became great feathered wings. His hind legs straightened out, and talons formed where his toes had been. And his eyes—his eyes grew back into his noble head, and he could see again. Mouse became Eagle, the all-seeing one, and he flew from Wolf's back directly into the sun, becoming like Eagle from the Light. Elders say that the Master of Life saw the good that Mouse had done and returned the gift of sight that he had so unselfishly shared with Wolf.

Native American history did not begin with the arrival of Vikings or Spaniards. According to tribal historians, Native American history began with creation, a time when the first movement took place and set creative powers afoot on this land. Archaeologists maintain that Native Americans did not originate in this land but rather moved across the frozen tundra through a land bridge linking Siberia with Alaska. Native American traditionalists look to their oral narratives for their origins. For tribal elders and young people who think in the old way, traditional native stories are sacred texts filled with meaning for the past and present. They tie the people to the natural world as well as to certain places that have meaning to native peoples. Such places are marked by rivers, hills, forests, swamps, prairies, mountains, valleys, deserts, and rock formations. They contain specific varieties of plants and animals that are part of the Native American community. The redwoods of northern California have no place in the oral texts of Plains Indians, and the buffalo of the Plains are not a part of the sacred narratives of California's native people. The places of Native America are distinguished by certain weather patterns and natural phenomena such as earthquakes, hurricanes, tornadoes, thunderstorms, lightning storms, drought, floods, fires, and other calamities. Oral narratives are the cultural foundations of native people, providing life's lessons and explaining who the people are and what they are obligated to do in this life.

Native American history began before humans, when plants, animals, and places of nature interacted with each other to make the world ready for humans. Stories weave this time together, establishing laws by which all things should function. Such laws include those detailing which foods could be eaten or used for medicine as well as those prescribing times and methods for the foods' use. Laws included songs of thanksgiving and prescribed ceremonies that had to be conducted at specific times and in particular ways to ensure the success of the ceremonies and continuance of the community. In many stories, animal people, plant people, mountain people, or spirit people act out a drama that teaches the law. Among the Yakama of present-day Washington, there is a story about Pahto (Mount Adams) and the other volcanoes of the region, including Mount Hood, Mount St. Helens, and Mount Rainier. According to the story, Sun married five great Mountain Women in the Northwest, and each day when he chose to appear, he embraced his wives with his light. The wives grew jealous of Mount Adams because she received her husband's embrace earlier than the others, so the other wives plotted against her. They caused this beautiful Mountain Woman to explode and disfigure herself. But the Creator saw this jealousy and caused her to re-create herself. It took years, but this wife received a new face and beauty. She is still a favorite wife who receives her husband's first embrace each morning.

Among the Chinook, Clatsop, Klickitat, Wasco, Yakama, and other people of the Northwest, it is against the law to dam rivers. The Creator established this law long before the arrival of whites at a time when five giant monster women known as the Tah Tah Kleah dammed the Columbia River to create a fish dam. In this way, when the salmon made their annual runs up the Columbia, the salmon could not break through the fish dam. In this way, the Tah Tah Kleah could take as many fish as they wanted. The story is about greed taking over the minds of the monsters, people more concerned about themselves than the well-being of many others who lived upstream and depended on the salmon. It is also about a hero—in this case, Coyote—who works for the benefit of the people rather than for his own glorification, although he cannot help but bask in his own glory. He has a right to do so, because he reestablished the law broken by the five monster women who were selfish and shortsighted. By establishing the fish dam, they would destroy the salmon runs altogether within a few years when the salmon could no longer travel up the river to spawn.

Of course, animal people living upstream from the fish dam knew that the dam was against the law, but no one wished to fight the dangerous monsters. Coyote agreed to challenge the monsters, and to this end, he dressed like a baby, climbed into a basket, and floated down the Columbia to the fish dam. In this story, Coyote is a hero, a person who worked on behalf of the community and taught people an important lesson that has not been forgotten. When he arrived at the lake created by the dam, the five Tah Tah Kleah saw him and thought he was a baby. Enamored by the baby, the four oldest sisters wanted to fish Coyote from the water and raise him as their own child, but the youngest sister sensed danger in the situation. She warned her older sisters not to adopt Coyote, but her older sisters did not heed her warning. They adopted Coyote as their own baby and took care of him. Each day, while the monsters went forth to fish, hunt, and gather great quantities of food—because they had voracious appetites—they tethered Coyote to a pole with a rope tied around his waist so that he would not fall into the river and drown. Each day when they left, Coyote untied himself and used five digging sticks to dig out the dam. The first day he made five digging sticks and five ladles made from the horn of bighorn sheep. He set the ladles to his side and worked furiously digging out the dam for five days.

On the fifth day, the monsters left the village as usual, leaving their baby tied to the rope. When they had gone, Coyote went to work on the dam. During the course of the day, a digging stick used by a Tah Tah Kleah broke, which was a sign to them that something was wrong. They hurried back to camp to check on the baby, only to find that the child was Coyote and that he was digging out their dam. Coyote had almost dug out the dam and could not stop, so he kept digging while the monsters used clubs to beat his head. Before they got to him, Coyote used a ladle as a helmet to protect his head and continued digging. When the first ladle broke, he used another one and kept digging. The monsters kept beating him on the head, which is why Coyote is still a little crazy, but the hero continued his work until he broke through the dam. The waters of the Columbia rushed out to the Pacific, and the salmon raced inland in great numbers, following their new chief. Coyote led the salmon people up the river systems of the inland Northwest, allowing the fish to swim near those villages where the people generously gave him wives and food. He prohibited salmon from going by the villages of stingy people, forcing them to travel some distance in order to get salmon at their fisheries. According to the law, no one could place dams on the river.

Like many people, Coyote is an unusual hero. In this story, Coyote acted when no other person wanted to face the Tah Tah Kleah. And he faced his challenge in an innovative, if not provocative, manner, dressing as a baby and floating down the Columbia River. Although other animal people thought him a fool, he used this method to disarm his adversaries. Coyote demonstrated great courage in going down the river to face five monsters, and he was wise to dress as a baby in order to get the monsters to take him in as their own. Certainly babies are disarming, except to the youngest Tah Tah Kleah, who warned her sisters that something was not right about the baby. Often, older siblings scoff at the ideas of younger members of the family, even when they would do well to consider their opinions. After Coyote was accepted by the monsters, he planned ahead by making five digging sticks and five helmets. He had the forethought to create these items and took time to do so before he launched into his job. As for the monsters, they heeded the sign when a digging stick broke, returning to the village early and finding their baby busy breaking their dam. By breaking the dam, Coyote freed the waters of the river, allowed the salmon to enter the rivers to spawn, and corrected the law that the Creator had established. For many native people, dams violated ancient tribal law and were built by monsters bent on disturbing the earth to benefit themselves. Such selfishness is still a violation of native laws, because people were supposed to act for the common good of communities.

IROQUOIS, MAIDU, AND CHOCTAW STORIES

Iroquoian peoples of the Northeast–including Wyandot-Huron–believe in a Sky World above the earth, a place where life began while the earth was filled with sea water. Before there was land on earth, great sea animals inhabited the endless ocean, and birds lived in the sky. Many people lived in the Sky World, including a demanding woman who was pregnant and insisted that her husband provide her with a variety of foods and medicines. In the middle of the Sky World, a huge and unusual sacred tree grew. It was against the law for anyone to disturb the sacred tree in any manner. But the woman did not care, because she wanted bark from the roots of the tree for herself and ordered her husband to bring her some bark. He dug around the base of the tree, exposing some of its roots. Much to his surprise, he opened a hole in the sky and could look down upon the endless sea on earth. Without disturbing the great tree, he went home to tell his wife about the great hole in the Sky World. His curious wife went to the tree, peered down at the earth, and fell through the opening. In her hand, she had grasped plants and parts of the sacred tree.

As she fell toward the ocean, the birds in the sky used their wings to catch her. They sat Aataentsic (Her Body Is Magic), commonly known as The Woman Who Fell from the Sky, on Turtle's back. Muskrat dove to the bottom of the ocean and brought up soil that they used to begin earth on Turtle's back. Endlessly, the woman walked sunwise around Turtle's back, which made the earth expand out and form valleys, mountains, lakes, and prairies. With the plants and debris she had brought down from the Sky World, the woman created the first plants on earth. One day, she gave birth to a girl, who helped her mother walk upon Turtle's back, helping the earth grow and prosper. When the girl was older, a man appeared to her, a man likely from the Sky World, and the sight of him made her faint. While she was asleep, the man placed two arrows on her chest, a blunt arrow and sharp one. When she awoke, she was pregnant with twins who quarreled endlessly with each other in utero. One son, the right-handed one, was straight minded, but his brother, the left-handed one, was of a crooked mind. The right-handed son, called Sapling, was born in the normal fashion, but the left-handed son, called Flint, came out of his mother under her left arm, which killed her.

The boys buried their mother, and from her head came corn, squash, and beans—the Three Sisters. From her heart grew tobacco, a sacred plant used in sending prayers into the sky. Aataentsic was the first "mother" of Iroquois people and established the pattern of female leadership that has so characterized the people ever since. The strong role of women emerged among the people at the time of creation, and over time women became the clan mothers who chose the male chiefs. They give and take power, exerting a powerful influence in Iroquois life to this day. Her two sons symbolize the tension within families, clans, and tribes. The boys continued their feud with each other outside their mother's body, creating tensions between positive and negative powers and manifesting their competition through creation of different plants and animals. At this time, Sapling created the first humans, molding them from clay and baking them in a fire. Flint may have helped create humans, because the forces of both characters are in all people. The boys dueled with each other until Sapling defeated Flint and tossed his body off the edge of the world, where he controls the night while his brother sustains the daylight. Their grandmother had always favored Flint, perhaps because she was of a selfish nature, and when she learned that Sapling had killed Flint, she became enraged. In his own anger against his grandmother, Sapling killed her, cut off her head, and tossed it into the sky, where at night she looks over her beloved Flint in the form of the moon. Both Sapling and Flint influence life on earth to this day, but they do not live on the same plane of being as humans. Iroquois refer to Sapling as the Master of Life, Creator, or He Holds Up the Skies, and they call Flint the Devious One, Old Warty, or One Covered with Boils. Both are important figures in Iroquois history as well as contemporary society. The people pray, sing, dance, and burn tobacco in remembrance of creation, ritual acts that tie the past to the present and ensure the future.

Throughout American history and in many tribal communities, Native American women have played a significant role. Women continue to hold a special place, and their lives are integrally tied to traditional stories that explain the leadership role of women. In her book, *The Sacred Circle,* Laguna scholar Paula Gunn Allen has demonstrated the continued power of Pueblo women in the Southwest, drawing on oral narratives to illustrate the connection between past and present. Laguna writer Leslie Silko accomplishes a similar point by using Yellow Woman stories to explain the powerful position of women in Laguna society. Throughout the native past, oral stories have provided a framework for understanding the rich and varied place of women within diverse communities, and these stories continue to illustrate the power of women today in the hearts and minds of Indian people.

Some years ago, Maidu Indian elder Dalbert Castro of northern California related a portion of the Maidu creation story. In a shortened version of a complex narrative, there was a time when a great ocean enveloped the entire earth. Earthmaker and Coyote floated on a raft in an endless sea. For an extended period of time, they were content with this life, until Earthmaker had a vision of solid ground with an earth made of mountains, rivers, valleys, forests, and meadows. In his vision, Earthmaker saw clouds, rain, thunder, lightning, plants, and animals. So he sang his song of creation, calling on his mountains and valleys, his fog and rain to appear. He sang day and night until he became tired and asked Coyote to continue his song. And so Coyote sang until he became tired. Earthmaker continued the song of creation until one day he heard Robin singing, and he saw a round nest bobbing in the water. Earthmaker told Coyote that he would make his Little World from the nest and took ropes, stretching them out in many directions. Earthmaker brought mud from the bottom of the ocean and packed it on the nest and ropes, forming the earth and sculpting mountains, valleys, prairies and meadows. Coyote painted some of the earth red, the color of blood.

All Native Americans enjoy a rich oral tradition detailing the creation of the earth, plants, animals, sky, sun, moon, stars, and other elements of the universe. People, places, leadership, migrations, settlements, warfare, and times of peace are chronicled in this oral tradition. Choctaws believe that for generations their people traveled in the vast American West, some say for forty-three years. Choctaw men, women, and children carried the bones of their ancestors, including those of ancient people whom none of them had known. Over the years the bundles of bones became so numerous that the people left some bundles behind, carried others forward, and then returned to bring forward the bundles they had left behind. Tribal law required them to fulfill this obligation until they reached a sacred place where they were to settle. Each evening the leader planted the Leaning Pole into the ground, which bent in the direction the people would move the next day.

For years the Choctaws traveled on foot, crossing the Mississippi River into present-day Mississippi. One day the Leaning Pole remained perfectly upright, signifying that the people had arrived at the special place. Choctaws buried the remains of their dead in a great mound called Nanih Waiya, the Mother Mound of the people, which nourished and re-created them. Tribal law required that they never leave Nanih Waiya and the

George Catlin captured this painting of a Choctaw ball game, which required players to have great skill and agility. Indians from many regions attended these ball games, including people from the Great Plains who erected their tepees as seen in the background.

remains of their people, a violation that would cause them starvation and death. Stories about Nanih Waiya encompass both positive and negative forces, and they are as alive today as they were when Choctaws built their sacred mound. In most native stories of creation, animate and inanimate objects are infused with positive and negative powers, even human beings (who have the ability to use their creative powers to do good for their communities or to do evil by satisfying their own selfish will). Such negative powers may manifest themselves in a number of ways, depending on the tribe, but they always involve powerful and harmful forces.

Among the Hupa of northern California there is a belief that people who wish to gain prominence and power may use their creative abilities to transform themselves into Bear People who do great harm to others, including murder. Diné (Navajo) people believe that destructive and greedy individuals may use their power to become "witches," who may turn themselves into Coyote People or skin walkers. Hopis believe that there are people within their communities who become part of the negative forces that kill others or do harm in order to live longer. They call such people Two Hearts. Wyandots and other Iroquoian peoples also believe in such negative power and individuals within the nations who use their power to harm others or even kill enemies. Most native peoples–if not all–have traditional beliefs about individuals who use negative power to benefit themselves, a dangerous subject in contemporary society that emerged at the time of creation.

Several traditional stories deal with the issue of negative power and the misuse of power to benefit oneself over communal good. An old Wyandot story tells of a young man who grew up in a village along the St. Lawrence River. Elders greatly admired this young man because he was courteous, athletic, generous, smart, and eager to learn from them. He knew how to listen and learn. As the years passed, elders often told other young people that they should be more like this young man, which created tension between the young man and his peers. When the young man was in his early teens, the other boys of the village hatched a plan to kill him and be done with him forever. They invited him to join them in a great hunt in the river between Hochelaga and Lake Ontario, and the young man naively accepted. The boys canoed a great distance to a large island in the river, an island inhabited by numerous wildcats, bears, and other animals. The boys had come to prove themselves great hunters of the most dangerous beasts, so when they arrived, they split up to go in several directions, agreeing to meet back at the river's edge to make camp that night. The young man walked off alone with his bow and arrow, but found no scat, no sign of animals. As the sun began dropping quickly in the west, he returned to camp. The boys had abandoned the place, taken the canoes, and left the young man on the island alone to die.

By this time, the sun had set, and night began to fall. So the young man climbed an old tree and slept in the folds of a large branch. He slept restlessly and awoke feeling someone breathing on his neck. It was the time of gray light in the morning, but as the young man opened his eyes, he saw steam in the air, felt the heavy breath upon his neck. He slowly turned to see what was there. Wildcat was right beside him with his right paw raised as if to strike. The young man turned his head and waited for the blow, but it did not come. He waited and turned again to look. Some storytellers say that the small wind in his ear spoke to him, telling him to look again. And so he did. Wildcat's paw was still raised, and his claws were fully extended, gleaming in the morning's light. This time, the young man did not turn away but rather studied the great paw and saw a thorn stuck deep into the furry flesh between the pads. Again he heard the small wind in his ear tell him to pull out the thorn, and so he did. Bravely, he reached up and carefully took hold of the paw in one hand and used his fingers to grasp the thorn with his other hand. In a mighty tug, he pulled out the thorn. When he did, Wildcat spoke to him.

"Thank you, grandson," the Wildcat said. "I have tried for four days to pull the thorn out with my teeth and paw, but I could not. You have saved my life, for the splinter would have turned my paw bad and poisoned me. You have been very brave and kind to help me, so I wish to give you something in return. From this time forward, you will have my power as a hunter. You will always do well hunting, and your family and friends will never be without meat because you will have my power as a hunter."

The young man thanked Wildcat for his gift, a lifelong gift that he would use to feed his family and village. The young man and Wildcat spoke for some time, getting to know each other before Wildcat gave the young man another gift.

"I know that the other boys brought you here and left," Wildcat announced. "I watched you leave on the hunt and saw all of the boys get back into the canoes and leave you here. I know they wanted you dead, so I watched. They have returned to your village to announce your death to your parents and the elders. Don't be afraid. The elders do not believe you are dead, and they are already on their way back here to find you."

Wildcat paused momentarily to lick his sore paw and allow his cold words to melt in the young man's mind. He knew that the young man was angry at the treachery exhibited by the boys. He wanted revenge, so Wildcat gave him time to think about what he had said.

"When the villagers return to this island, the boys will be with them," Wildcat continued. "But you should not set your mind on them and the harm they intended for you. Rather, you should train your mind on the gift I have given you, the ability to hunt and provide. Whenever your mind turns to revenge, push the thoughts aside and remember the good that has come of our meeting. If you do this, you will do well. If you allow yourself to dwell on the jealously and hate they have for you, then you will harm yourself and never be well."

Wildcat and the young man came down out of the tree, and Bear jumped up on her hind legs to attack the young man. Wildcat jumped between Bear and the young man, threatening Bear if she attacked. When Bear learned that Wildcat was a friend of the young man, she withdrew. Wildcat turned to the young man.

"They are coming for you now," he said. "They will be here soon, and I will watch from the trees. Remember my words but do not tell them that we have met or the things I have told you. These things are between us. Carry my words in your heart."

And so it was that the villagers canoed to the island, where they found the young man patiently waiting for them. His parents were overjoyed to find him safe, but the boys were not. They fully expected the young man to tell his story, but he did not have to say a word. Some of the people understood what had happened, whereas others did not think about it. The young man said nothing against the boys. The people returned to their village, and over the years, the young man became a hunting leader, a man respected by many people for many abilities.

Through the years he never told his story until he was dying. Before he left this world, he summoned his children, grandchildren, and great-grandchildren, telling them his story of Wildcat and the lessons this grandfather had taught. They listened to the story and remembered. They told their children and grandchildren, who, in turn, told their children and grandchildren. And so the story of Wildcat is still alive, a small part of Wyandot history that lives with each telling, a reminder to keep one's mind focused on the positive things of life, not the negative, even when an event could cost a person life or limb. This is Indian law, taught through story.

NATIVE STORIES AS HISTORICAL NARRATIVE

When native storytellers share these stories, they are filled with colorful descriptions and minute details that have been handed down from generation to generation. Often storytellers make animal sounds or those of thunder, thrashings, waterfalls, winds, and wild excitements. Stories of creation often last several nights, and storytellers may vary the accounts, emphasizing a particular episode at the first telling and another episode at a later telling. Some stories originated thousands of years ago and have been kept alive with each telling, whereas other stories are more recent. Stories have life, and native people consider them a part of their history. Traditional stories lay the foundation for understanding particular native nations, tribes, bands, villages, and people. The stories are interdisciplinary, offering information about religion, medicine, economics, literature, politics, psychology, biology, and many other fields of study. Stories explain the relationship of Native Americans to geographical places, geological formations, and biological features of regions. Within a body of stories there are actions and reactions, transitions and continuance, but always survival. And survival is a central theme of this book. After a long and dangerous journey that began with first contact with Europeans, Native Americans survived and recovered from the American holocaust. The theme is much like that found in an ancient story of the North Wind and Chinook Salmon shared by many tribes of the Columbia Plateau.

During the time of the Wah-tee-tash or animal people, the five Cold North Wind Brothers invaded the Pacific Northwest from Alaska to California. They swept the entire region with cold winds, snow, sleet, and ice, which froze the lakes and rivers. In the spring, the Cold North Wind Brothers fought off the Warm Chinook Winds from the Ocean and would not allow them to enter the region. When the salmon came up the Columbia River to spawn in the spring, the great fish could not go far upstream or pass through the frozen river. Salmon Chief challenged the five Lalawish (Wolf Brothers) to a wrestling match, and if Salmon Chief won, the Cold North Wind Brothers would withdraw to their original home and thaw out the snow and ice. The Wolf Brothers agreed, but if Salmon Chief lost the match, Coyote would slit his throat. Salmon Chief wrestled the Wolf Brothers, defeating the first and second brothers but losing to the third. When the third Wolf Brother threw Salmon Chief to the ground, Coyote raced over to kill him.

When Coyote slit Salmon Chief's throat, a great bloodletting began as the allies of the Wolf Brothers and Cold North Wind Brothers killed all the salmon people. They cut open the stomachs of all the females, including the wife of Salmon Chief, and ripped out their fish eggs. The Wolf Brothers and allies smashed every one of the eggs in order to stamp out the people. But the Wolf Brothers and their allies missed an egg belonging to Salmon Chief's wife. It had fallen between rocks and could not be reached easily. They knew where the egg was lodged, and they painstakingly tried to dislodge it. But they could not, and so they left the area, believing that the sun and wind would dry it. But the Creator had watched the entire scene and sent a warm rain to wash the egg into the water at the point where the river began to freeze. The egg attached itself to the sand, and semen floating in the water fertilized it. A small smolt was born in this way and swam backward to the ocean with its head upstream. When Young Chinook Salmon reached the Pacific, his paternal grandmother embraced him and took care of him.

Grandmother Salmon did not originally tell Young Chinook Salmon what had happened to his parents, but she began training the young boy to face future challenges. Grandmother Salmon put Young Chinook on a strict diet and trained him to wrestle. She had him lift heavy weights such as trees and rocks, building his muscles and stamina. Grandmother Salmon symbolized the power of native women in the Northwest, the keepers of traditions and the mothers of large, extended families. Like many women past and present, Grandmother was a caretaker of children, a nurturer, and a teacher. When he was older, Grandmother Salmon told Young Chinook Salmon stories about his mother, father, and people. She told him how the Cold North Wind Brothers had broken the law by freezing the inland Northwest, which prevented the salmon from spawning. She told him how his father had fought the Wolf Brothers and had lost. She told him that Coyote had slit his father's throat and helped kill all the Salmon People. Grandmother Salmon explained how he had been born through a holy act of the Creator. Through the story, Young Chinook Salmon realized what he had to do and why his grandmother had expected so much of him. He trained for another year, and when he was prepared, Young Chinook Salmon led the people up the Columbia River to challenge the five Wolf Brothers.

Young Chinook Salmon faced the five Wolf Brothers in a wrestling match, just as his father had a few years before. Two women who had been forced into slavery spilled fish oil on the ice to help Young

Chinook Salmon. He wrestled the five Wolf Brothers, throwing each one in succession to the ice, where Coyote killed them with his knife. After years of ice and snow, Coyote had changed sides and supported the Salmon People. When Young Chinook Salmon threw the last Wolf Brother, the Chinook Wind began to blow into the Northwest, melting snow and ice. However, the sister of the Wolf Brothers ran off to the north. From that day forward, there has been a time of winter and spring, with the warm Chinook Wind coming from the west to melt snow and ice. Each year She Wolf (winter) returns to the Northwest, but only for a few months.

THEMES OF NATIVE AMERICAN HISTORY

The story above is a metaphor for Native American peoples who faced years of near-death resulting from successive invasions, conquests, wars, epidemics, and government policies brought to Turtle Island by Europeans. In large part, the history of early America is a history of a holocaust, a tragic era in which nonnative peoples overran Native American lands, stole valuable resources, and forced many native people to move from their former lands. During this era, non-Indians forced many native people into the interior, forever pressuring them to get out of the way of white expansion and settlement. Freedom-loving whites continually denied Native Americans their freedom of movement, settlement, and permanent control of their lands and property. They also denied Native Americans their freedom of religion, because whites considered native peoples to be heathen and Satan's children. For nonnative people, it was never enough. No amount of land or resources was ever sufficient to satisfy their desire for land, even if it meant killing the original inhabitants or driving them from their homes. It was never enough, or so it seemed to Native Americans.

White settlers and their representatives at various governmental levels continually demanded more native lands. City, county, state, and federal governments acted on behalf of white citizens, not American Indians. The premise that governments act "for the people" and "by the people" meant that the government acted for, by, and on behalf of white citizens (white males), not Native Americans, who were not citizens. American Indians were sovereign peoples, separate from whites, but nonnatives extended their power over tribes, forcing many Eastern Woodlands peoples into the trans-Mississippi West. Even the eastern portion of the country was not sufficient for whites, as the United States created its own Indian Territory, forcing tribes from many regions of the country onto smaller lands within the territory. Everywhere the United States expanded, government agents sought to control, Christianize, and civilize Native Americans as if it were their manifest destiny and God-given right to take from Native Americans and justify their greed.

The United States forced tribes out of northern Indian Territory (Kansas) into the southern part of the territory (Oklahoma). The government found several reasons to shrink Indian Territory further and to deprive tribes of lands that had once been promised to them "as long as the Grass shall grow and water runs." The government made agreements when to do so suited its representatives and broke agreements when to do so it benefited white settlers, businessmen, politicians, soldiers, and other nonnative interest groups. After creating the Indian Territory and reducing its size after the Civil War, the government destroyed it altogether, first establishing Oklahoma Territory in 1889 and then the state of Oklahoma in 1907. Through all of this, Native Americans lost millions of acres of land and billions of dollars' worth of resources.

Throughout the American colonial period and nineteenth century, Native American populations plummeted in numbers and power. The decline of native populations is far more than numbers. It is the loss of infants, children, and young adults. It is the loss of one's mother, father, brothers, sisters–people, real people, human beings. Diseases, starvation, wars, removals, reservations, and allotments all contributed to population decline, as did social anomie, cultural depression, and feelings of hopelessness. During different times, some native people felt despair, dislocation, and depression, which contributed to mortality and morbidity. These are factors that cannot be quantified, but anyone who has studied native communities can attest to their existence. Since the twentieth century, native populations have increased in strength, numbers, and vitality. However, problems of poverty, ill health, unemployment, infant mortality, disease, drug abuse, suicides, and poor education still exist. Yet, native history in the twentieth century is also a story of rebirth.

During the century, many native nations, tribes, bands, villages, rancherias, groups, and individuals recovered. It has been an era of renewal when native people have preserved portions of their cultures, including languages, songs, stories, music, dance, and ceremonies. Like the small salmon egg, native people have survived and sustained themselves, growing in numbers during the twentieth century with the help of elders like the grandmother of Young Chinook Salmon. This is an important era of Native American history and a time period often overlooked by historians. It is also an era that consists of many changes and important transitions, many of which have been skillfully detailed by author-historian James Rawls in his cutting-edge book, *Chief Red Fox is Dead: A History of Native Americans since 1945* (1995). Because the twentieth century is so important and so often ignored, approximately half of this book deals with native peoples from 1900 to the present, including a good deal of cultural history that focuses on literature, theater, film, art, and other fine arts. Less emphasis has been placed on the colonial and early national periods because so much is readily available on these eras.

This book emphasizes the relationship of native people to place and the biological elements of their homelands. Native American history is a subject of place and time, the relationships of humans to the larger community, which to native people includes trees, rocks, rivers, mountains, hills, valleys, and other elements of the natural world. These relationships are described in detail in oral narratives, and the relationships between humans and their environments have historical, spiritual, sociological, biological, and philosophical meanings that are generally not well understood. Some attempt is made in this book to provide an understanding of the important relationship of humans to the earth, particularly the soil that holds the remains of ancestors.

In addition to the relationship between American Indians and the things of nature, there is a continual relationship between native peoples and the bones of their people. This relationship remains an issue among several tribes from the East that presently live in Oklahoma and Kansas. As remains are unearthed in Ohio, Kentucky, Pennsylvania, Georgia, Mississippi, and other eastern states, tribes that once lived in these areas wish to have a say in the disposition of their ancestral remains. The same is true of Native Americans throughout the Americas. The remains of their ancestors are often stored in boxes by various museums and universities in the East, where "scientists" claim dominion over them in spite of the Native American Graves Protection Act. Tribal members and elders have a spiritual relationship with the dead, and tribal laws dealing with the dead are not generally understood by non-Indians. But, this relationship is one that ties contemporary people with named and unnamed ancestors. These and other spiritual beliefs are powerful factors in Native American culture, past and present.

This book also recognizes the diversity of social, political, and economic institutions among Indian people and the fact that some of these cultural elements change over time. Historically, tribes in California were more closely tied to village or regional identities than they were to a "tribal" identity. Most of the people of the Great Plains identified with their bands and considered themselves Oglalas, Brules, Miniconjous, or Hunkpapas. Although native peoples of the Southeast share cultures based on agriculture, hunting, fishing, and gathering, they identified themselves by their languages and villages. This was no less true on the Northwest Coast and Columbia Plateau, although people also associated themselves with regions where related people lived and worked. Many Iroquoian and Algonquian nations had stronger tribal identities in the Northeast and Great Lakes region, but Senecas, Mohawks, Onondagas,

Wyandot-Huron elder Eleonore Sioui is "keeper of the council fire" and a First Nations scholar who preserves oral traditions through the written and spoken word. She was the first native woman in Canada to receive a Ph.D.

Cayugas, and Oneidas also had strong clan affiliations. Native Americans had many distinct social, political, and economic ways of life with several variations, because theirs was never a single cultural form that could apply to all Indian people.

This book provides a voice for some Native Americans who participated in past events as well as native scholars who have provided interpretations about the past. Of course, the book is intended as a survey history, and no work of this nature can provide sufficient detail and analysis of specific events that are such a part of the past. Little is provided about discussions at Council Fires regarding tribal decisions to move west or face the Long Knives in a protracted war. Still, the fact that people discussed such issues and made their own decisions is central to this book. Many times divisions arose within Native American nations, tribes, communities, villages, rancherias, clans, and families over such important issues. Some of these divisions remain to this day. However, the divisions among native people are not always as clear as historians have contended in past writings. Convenient categories such as full bloods and mixed bloods, Christians and non-Christians, or progressives and conservatives are not easily deconstructed. This is a simplistic way of conceiving native history, and it belies basic human nature.

Even the term *traditional*, which is used in this book, is highly suspect and difficult to use. The term *traditional* might have a given meaning at one point in time and another meaning at another point in time. Usually people were not totally traditional or nontraditional. It all depended on the context and time period. Wyandots in Ohio who sang and prayed in their own language may have also attended church services at the Methodist Mission in Upper Sandusky. These same people may have been more pro-American at a particular point in time and still watched their Delaware neighbors torture to death Colonel William Crawford. Such people are not easily identified as traditional or progressive, pro-American or anti-American. Throughout this book an attempt has been made not to simplify such divisions among the nations and tribes, telling the reader some of the issues involved and the leadership of particular sides whenever appropriate. In the larger scheme of things, no attempt is made to portray all native people as good and all nonnatives as evil. Native American history is composed of a variety of people who acted in many ways and for many reasons, some of which are presented in this book.

Every Native American community contains tribal historians, men and women who enjoy the past and preserve elements of tribal memory. These are the real Native American historians, and scholars have much to learn from them. Wendat Eleonore Sioui is a Keeper of the Council Fire as well as a scholar and teacher who keeps Huron traditions alive, while her son, Georges, carries on these traditions as a professor, author, and tribal member. Quechan historian Lee Emerson received his calling to be a historian through his dreams, whereas Cahuilla scholar and historian Katherine Saubel received her training from her father. She has preserved portions of her tribe's history through her writings, stories, and songs. Some of her knowledge is too sacred to share outside the Cahuilla community, and because no one has asked her to teach the sacred songs that she learned as a young woman, they will die with her one day. As she says, "the book will close on that chapter of Cahuilla history when I pass away." The book has been closed on many aspects of native history, but other chapters are waiting to be preserved and written. Such chapters are to be found through the teachings of elders all across Indian country, among men and women who know the stories of their families, clans, tribes, and nations. Other chapters will be found through written documents that provide another voice for native history. In any case, there is much work yet to be done.

Although Native American history began with creation, the focus of this book is on contact with nonnative peoples, that era from roughly the 1400s to the present. Long before Francis Jennings published his significant study, *The Invasion of America: Indians, Colonialism, and the Cant of Conquest* (1975), Native Americans knew that there had been an invasion and conquest. American Indians had known for generations that something terrible had happened, which they referred to in English as "invasion" and "conquest"–and worse. Native people had done their best to oppose the invasion and conquest, using a variety of strategies, but they had not prevented it. They had not stopped the multiple consequences of invasions, deaths, wars, diseases, removals, reservations, or poverty. Contemporary native people also know they survived invasion and conquest. The invasion of America marks the beginning of this book, but it is also a theme found throughout the work. Contemporary native people still cope with the effects of the invasion and conquest, a theme that links the past to the present. The invasion began over five hundred years ago. Turtle Island was not a utopia at the time of the first invasion. Native people knew about war and death, hatred and greed, slavery and conquest. But there was something markedly different in the invasion of America by the Spanish, something more systematic and institutional, something more dangerous and long-term than anything native people had known before or since.

Selected Readings and Bibliography

Some of the information in this chapter stems from oral histories by Mary Lou Henry-Trafzer, Eleonore Sioui, Georges Sioui, Donna Akers, Anna Puzz, Mary Jim, Andrew George, Ray Winnie, Lee Emerson, Henry DeCorse, Joe Benitez, Dean Mike, Theresa Mike, Chancellor Damon, Harding Big Bow, Luke Madrigal, Anthony Madrigal, Darryl Wilson, Larry Myers, Jane Dumas, Henry Rodriquez, and David Whitehorse.

Akers, Donna. *Living in the Land of the Dead.* East Lansing: Michigan State University Press, forthcoming.

Beavert, Virginia. *The Way It Was: Anaku Iwacha.* Toppenish, Wash.: Johnson O'Malley Consortium, 1974.

Bierhorst, John. *The Red Swan: Myths and Tales of the American Indians.* New York: Farrar, Straus and Giroux, 1976.

Cajete, Gregory. *Look to the Mountain: An Ecology of Indigenous Education.* Durango, Colo.: Kivaki Press, 1994.

Erdoes, Richard, and Alfonso Ortiz. *American Indian Myths and Legends.* New York: Pantheon Books, 1984.

Fitzhugh, William W., and Aron Crowell. *Crossroads of Continents: Cultures of Siberia and Alaska.* Washington, D.C.: Smithsonian Institution Press, 1988.

Francis, Lee. *Native Time: A Historical Time Line of Native America.* New York: St. Martin's Press, 1996.

Jennings, Francis. *The Invasion of America: Indians, Colonialism, and the Cant of Conquest.* Chapel Hill: University of North Carolina Press, 1975.

Margolin, Malcolm. *The Way We Lived: California Indian Stories, Songs, & Reminiscences.* Berkeley: Heyday Books, 1981.

Marriott, Alice, and Carol K. Rachlin. *American Indian Mythology.* New York: Mentor Books, 1972.

Mourning Dove. *Mourning Dove's Stories.* Clifford E. Trafzer and Richard D. Scheuerman, eds. San Diego: San Diego State University Press, 1991.

Nabokov, Peter, ed. *Native American Testimony: An Anthology of Indian and White Relations, First Encounter to Dispossession.* New York: Thomas Y. Crowell, 1978.

Nashone. *Grandmother Stories of the Northwest.* Newcastle, Calif.: Sierra Oaks, 1987.

Penn, W. S. *The Telling of the World.* New York: Stewart, Tabori and Chang, 1997.

Rawls, James J. *Chief Red Fox Is Dead: A History of Native Americans since 1945.* Fort Worth: Harcourt Brace & Company, 1996.

Smith-Trafzer, Lee Ann, and Clifford E. Trafzer. *Creation of a California Tribe.* Newcastle, Calif.: Sierra Oaks, 1988.

Thompson, Stith. *Tales of the North American Indians.* Bloomington: Indiana University Press, 1968.

Trafzer, Clifford E. "Masked Gods of the Navajos." *Gods Among Us: American Indian Masks.* Ross Coates, editor. San Diego: San Diego State University Press, Publications in American Indian Studies, 1989, pp. 52–71.

——. "Grandmother, Grandfather, and the First History of the Americas." Arnold Krupat, ed. *New Voices in American Literary Criticism.* Washington, D.C.: Smithsonian Institution Press, 1993, pp. 474–487.

Trafzer, Clifford E., ed. *Grandmother, Grandfather, and Old Wolf: Tamánwit Ku Súkat and Traditional Native American Narratives from the Columbia Plateau.* East Lansing: Michigan State University Press, 1998.

Trigger, Bruce G. *The Children of Aataentsic: A History of the Huron People to 1660.* Kingston: McGill-Queens University Press, 1976.

Viola, Herman J., and Carolyn Margolis. *Seeds of Change.* Washington, D.C.: Smithsonian Institution Press, 1991.

Yazzie, Ethelou. *Navajo History.* Many Farms, Ariz.: Navajo Community College Press, 1971.

INVASION

Since their first contact with Europeans, Native Americans have considered the colonization of their homelands to be an invasion and conquest. Oral histories today abound with stories of first contact between native nations and various Europeans. At times, first contact was benign, even positive, with a good deal of trading. At other times, first contact between peoples was hostile and dangerous, leading to deaths and enslavement that set the tone for poor relations in the future. Although the Norse invaded America long before the Spanish, their significance to Native American history is minor because of the great impact the Spanish had on American Indians over a huge area from the tip of Tierra del Fuego in South America to the Nootka villages of western Canada. The Age of Discovery and European colonization of Native American lands and peoples initiated a holocaust that lasted for centuries and continues in some parts of the Americas. The invasion of America also gave rise to native resistance movements that have lasted for centuries and are alive today. Native Americans have survived and live in nearly every parts of the hemisphere in spite of a conquest that began inauspiciously on October 12, 1492.

From their homes, Taino (Island Arawak) men, women, and children watched three ships approach their island in the Bahamas. According to Taino scholar José Barriero, the people questioned the meaning of these creatures that flew over the waters with white sails and large wooden hulls. The three caravels were the *Niña, Pinta,* and *Santa María.* Admiral, Viceroy, and Governor Christopher Columbus landed on the island of San Salvador (modern Watlings Island). Columbus had traveled about three thousand miles, but the distance between the two lands was small in comparison to the cultural and social distance between Europeans and Native Americans. Columbus and his men brought biases and assumptions from Europe that would forever change the lives of millions of tribal people, whom the foreigners labeled *Indios* or Indians. Like other Christians of his time, Columbus was significantly influenced by a wellspring of racial hatred that pitted white Christians against non-Christian people of color. Columbus and Spanish *conquistadors* were influenced by nearly eight hundred years of bloody warfare, religious bigotry, and cultural intolerance between Christian people of the Iberian Peninsula and African Moslems. Racial and religious intolerance traveled with the Spaniards to America and contributed significantly to the genocide of thousands of Native Americans.

RECONQUISTA, RESETTLEMENT, AND SLAVERY

In 711, African soldiers had invaded the Iberian Peninsula, sweeping into southern France until Charles Martel defeated them. Moslem soldiers retreated over the Pyrenees Mountains but controlled portions of the Iberian Peninsula for centuries until 1492, when King Fernando and Queen Isabella's armies defeated the Moors at the Battle of Granada. It is no coincidence that when the Reconquista ended, the conquest of America began. During the Reconquista and Crusades, Christians developed deep racial hatreds for dark-skinned non-Christians, whom they characterized as evil, primitive, and savage. Christians portrayed Moslems as Satan's children, licentious subhuman counterimages whom God intended for Christians to exterminate. While Christians from the Iberian Peninsula fought and killed Moslems, other European Christians launched the Crusades into the Middle East to kill Moslems in the name of Christ and recapture the Holy Lands. Racial and religious hatred, born during the Middle Ages, was transferred to Africa and Asia by Portuguese expeditions and to the Americas by the Spanish and Portuguese.

America was not a virgin land in 1492, and it was not a wilderness to native populations. The research of Lakota scholar Vine Deloria, Francis Jennings, and Gary Nash has aptly demonstrated this fact. Approximately ten million Native Americans lived in present-day Canada and the United States, whereas between twenty and thirty million American Indians lived in Mexico. And between sixty-five million and one hundred million native people lived in Central and South America. Yet, by "right of discovery" and "right of conquest," Spaniards claimed the right to control the lands and people of any regions they were colonizing, demanding that other European nations not intervene. Nevertheless, the Spaniards overran lands long settled by American Indians, refusing to recognize native sovereignty, land rights or resources, or freedom of religion. Spaniards exploited native labor and land in order to benefit themselves and Spain, stealing gold, silver, and other raw materials while enslaving peoples by the thousands and killing them through punishments and excessive work. Most conquistadors cared nothing about permanently resettling America but wanted only to accumulate wealth and return to Spain. Conquistadors were ruthless individuals who believed themselves superior in every way to American Indians. They reflected the arrogance of Queen Isabella, King Fernando, and Pope Alexander VI, who divided the "heathen world" between Spain and Portugal through the Treaty of Tordesillas (1494), permitting Portugal to resettle Brazil and Spain to claim the rest of America.

Spaniards brought with them European institutions through which to accomplish the conquest of Native America. When Columbus established Navidad, the first Spanish settlement on the northern coast of Hispañola (present-day Haiti and Dominican Republic), he ordered his soldiers to build a *presidio* or fort. The major thrust of the Spanish conquest was military, and presidios would support soldiers throughout North, South, and Central America. When Columbus returned to Hispañola in 1493, Indians had killed his forty-four soldiers for committing rape, theft, and other abuses. Columbus founded a new settlement called Isabella and planned a *pueblo* or town, another key institution of the Spanish empire. His brother, Bartolomé, later established Santo Domingo, the first permanent European pueblo in America. Columbus and other Spaniards enslaved Native Americans on Hispañola and throughout Latin America, forcing thousands of natives to work and die for the crown. Slavery became an early institution used by the Spanish to control and exploit native labor, and when Indians fought as patriots against exploitation, forced labor, sexual abuses, and oppression, presidio soldiers ruthlessly destroyed native opposition by hanging prisoners, burning people alive, and flaying the skin of their victims. Between 1493 and 1500, approximately five hundred thousand Native Americans—perhaps more—died in the Caribbean Islands.

Spaniards murdered and tortured men, women, and children if they did not produce their quota of one small bell full of gold dust every three months. Soldiers cut off fingers, hands, feet, legs, noses, and genitals of recalcitrant men, women, and children who would not pay homage and tribute, and they set their war dogs on native people to tear them to shreds. Spaniards burned caciques (leaders) and their followers to death in rows of thirteen in honor of Christ and the Twelve Apostles. Spaniards enslaved and sold thousands of native people after 1503, particularly those Indians living under the rule of a Spaniard who was given an *encomienda* or a specific number of Indians who were entrusted to an *encomendero* for labor and in return were supposed to receive Spanish civilization and Christianization. After 1550, Spaniards enslaved Indians through *repartimiento,* whereby the Spanish uprooted Indians and forced them to work in mines, plantations, and public works. Many Indians died from forced labor, brutal punishments, lack of food, and poor housing. Throughout the conquest, soldiers and officials indiscriminately raped mothers, wives, and daughters, creating a reign of terror in Native America.

Some natives fought as patriots against the Spanish, whereas others fled into the mountains. Native Americans resisted the conquest as best they could but were hampered by the systematic, experienced, and ruthless manner in which Spaniards dealt with "others." Thousands of Native Americans in the islands and on the mainland died of European diseases to which they had no immunities. Over many centuries, Europeans had developed immunities to common diseases, but native populations had not known smallpox, chickenpox, cholera, typhoid, influenza, measles, and many other maladies until whites arrived. Indians died in far larger numbers than did Europeans during the Black Plague. Soon after the invasion began, Arawaks called Spaniards Yares or Demons. Spaniards sold Indians into slavery or forced them to work as beasts of burden because Europeans had few horses.

Some Indians committed suicide or killed their children rather than have them live in a world controlled by the Spanish. Birth rates dropped to zero, and the native population declined radically. According to the Cakchiquel Maya who kept a chronicle of an epidemic: "Great was the stench of the dead. After our fathers and grandfathers succumbed, half of the people fled to the fields. The dogs and vultures devoured the bodies. The mortality was terrible." The Maya realized that with the passing of the grandfathers, the "son of the king and his brothers and kinsmen," his people became "orphans," and it appeared to the people that they had been "born to die!" Noted scholar Alfred Crosby carefully addressed the effects of disease in his pathbreaking book, *The Columbian Exchange.* Although Columbus was not responsible for the conquest, he remains a symbol of the deaths, destruction, and atrocities. As the Dominican father Bartolomé de las Casas pointed out, Columbus "started the bloody trail of the Conquest."

The long-term effects of the invasion of America have been graphically illustrated by a number of contemporary Native Americans. In 1992, Anishinaabe writer Kimberly Blaeser composed a letter to Christopher Columbus in an anthology of native writers entitled *Dear Christopher: Letters to Christopher Columbus by Contemporary Native Americans.* In her fictional letter, Blaeser tells a story of a Wisconsin native fisherman who had been arrested by state authorities many times for exercising his treaty rights to fish, but after a series of Supreme Court cases in favor of Indian fishing, he could not get arrested until one day while fishing in an area designated for nonnatives:

> "You're fishing on the wrong side of the imaginary line," declared the game warden. "Well, god dammit," he replied in understandable frustration, "I imagine it's over here!" And this, Christopher, is a parable for our time. It might say that life is absurd and we shouldn't take it too seriously. It might say it's time that Indian people began to imagine clearly their own lines, against all authority. Or it might be just a story that is told.

From the outset Spaniards condemned Native Americans to conquest, exploitation, and an inferior status that tied Catholic dogma with Spanish legalism. Spaniards exploited Native American labor and resources, and

American Indians were derided as objects of scorn by Europeans who imagined themselves superior because of their birth and religion. Spaniards had preconceived notions about Native Americans as uncivilized savages, the lowest forms of humanity. Based on information presented as "facts in writing" by Father Pedro de Cordoba, one Spanish soldier characterized Indians as "more stupid than asses" who "refuse to improve in anything." Furthermore, the Spaniards reported that:

> On the mainland they eat human flesh. They are more given to sodomy than any other nation. There is no justice among them. They go naked. They have no respect either for love or for virginity. They are stupid and silly. They have no respect for truth, save when it is to their advantage. They are unstable. They have no knowledge of what foresight means. . . . They are incapable of learning. Punishments have no effect upon them. Traitorous, cruel, and vindictive, they never forgive. Most hostile to religion, idle, dishonest, abject, and vile, in their judgments they keep no faith or law. . . . Liars, superstitious, and cowardly as hares. They eat fleas, spiders, and worms raw, whenever they find them. They exercise none of the humane arts or industries. When taught the mysteries of our religion, they say that these things may suit Castilians, but not them, and they do not wish to change their customs.

Although no Catholic priests accompanied Columbus on his first voyage, they traveled with him in 1493 and soon after arriving in the Caribbean Islands began to set up missions and defend Indian rights. In 1511, Antonio de Montesinos created a stir when he preached that he was "a voice crying in the wilderness." He denounced his Spanish congregation: "You are in mortal sin . . . for the cruelty and tyranny you use in dealing these innocent people." He concluded by condemning conquistadors, saying that "in such a state as this, you can no more be saved than the Moors or Turks." The words of Montesinos affected future American Indian policies proclaimed by the crown. For the first time and in a dramatic fashion, a non-Indian spoke out forcefully against the murder and enslavement of native men, women, and children. Montesinos brought light where there had been darkness, and the light of his reform movement had a long-lasting but limited impact on the relations of Spaniards and native peoples. Eventually the crown responded to the call for reforms and created laws governing Spanish and Indian relations. However, the laws carried little force in the Americas, where Spaniards continued their killings and enslavements in spite of protests.

Although Spanish military and civil officials successfully forced Montesinos to return to Spain, Las Casas began his fifty-two-year fight on behalf of native peoples. King Charles I and the Council of the Indies lent a sympathetic ear to Las Casas and passed the Laws of Burgos and other measures to ensure humane treatment of Indians. Under Spanish law, Spaniards were to permit Native Americans the opportunity to swear allegiance to the crown and church, laying down their arms in submission and becoming subjects of the king. Native American slavery ended, except for those who refused to become subjects and those who resisted Spanish soldiers. Spain's reforms did not stop slavery, murders, and mistreatment of Native Americans by "ravenous wolves." However, the laws led to creative new devices used by Spaniards to ensure the implementation of the reforms. One such reform was the use of the Requerimiento, which was a document—written in Spanish—outlining Christian creation, God's law, crown authority, papal rule, and the requirement of natives to surrender or face utter devastation. The document demanded that Native Americans accept Spanish rule so they would do well:

> But if you do not do this, and wickedly and intentionally delay to do so, I certify to you that, with the help of God, we shall forcibly enter into your country and shall make war against you in all ways and manners that we can, and shall subject you to the yoke and obedience of the Church and of their Highnesses; we shall take you and your wives and your children, and shall make slaves of them, and as such shall sell and dispose of them as their Highnesses may command; and we shall take away your goods, and shall do all the harm and damage that we can, as to vassals who do not obey, and refuse to receive their lord, and resist and contradict him. . . .

Often Spaniards read the Requerimiento aboard ships, to mountains, or to sleepy villages before engagements. Like so many laws designed to protect Indians, the Requerimiento was a farce. In reality, the document meant nothing and was not truly a reform, because the excesses of the early Spanish colonial period continued unabated in spite of the requirement to give native peoples a chance to surrender before being annihilated by soldiers and war dogs. Slavery of Native Americans continued in one form or another throughout the colonial period and expanded to the enslavement of Africans as well. Freed Africans were likely part of Columbus's first voyage but were brought to America as slaves as early as 1512. Five years later, Las Casas encouraged the crown to use African slaves over Native American slaves because African Moslems had had an opportunity to become Christians and had rejected Christ. Las Casas later renounced his stand on African slaves, but trafficking in millions of African slaves to work in mines, sugar, cotton, and coffee fields accelerated.

Las Casas greatly influenced Spanish and Indian relations by encouraging priests to Christianize Native Americans throughout America by establishing *reducciones* or missions. Spaniards used missions to control American Indians. Missionary activities in America grew as a result of passionate men like Las Casas, and Christianization expanded greatly after Las Casas published his most famous account, *Very Brief Recital of the Destruction of the Indies* (1552). The book detailed Spanish atrocities against American Indians and had a long-term effect on perceptions of the conquest. Although exaggerated and misleading in terms of statistics, the narrative graphically depicted the bloody conquest of Native Americans and laid the foundation for the Black Legend. Spanish armies annihilated Native American populations throughout the islands and extended their killing fields to the mainland. In addition to fighting for Christ, Spaniards fought for slaves and gold. They believed themselves to be the lords of native people and native lands, regardless of prior occupancy by Native Americans on the islands or in Mexico.

CONQUEST OF MEXICO

From the islands of the Caribbean Sea, Spanish *entradas* traveled to the mainland of South, Central, and North America. Wherever they traveled, Spaniards claimed native lands and proclaimed native peoples to be subjects of the crown. *Adelantado* Hernán Cortes led a significant expedition in 1519, when he commanded 550 men, sixteen horses, and eleven ships, which weighed anchor in Yucatan and Tobasco before arriving in Veracruz. In Yucatan he picked up a shipwrecked Spaniard named Aguilar who spoke Maya, and in Tobasco he was given la Malinche (Marina), an Aztec who spoke Maya and Aztec. Through them, Cortes had interpreters and an Aztec mistress who understood the cultural beliefs of Aztecs. She knew that Moctezuma was a god-king leader who ruled a vast empire, rich beyond belief. Moctezuma was at war with surrounding native people who would welcome the conquest of Aztecs. She knew that Aztecs feared that one day the sun would no longer appear and life on earth would end. In order to keep the sun alive, Aztec priests offered human sacrifices, generally taking victims from surrounding tribes. Moctezuma feared that recent thunderstorms, earthquakes, and volcanic activities as well as a comet and frightening prophecies foretold doom for the Aztecs. Moctezuma also worried about the return of a legendary and powerful Toltec king-god named Quetzalcoatl, the Feathered Serpent.

When Moctezuma learned of Cortes, he was convinced that the Spaniard was Quetzalcoatl, a god that Huitzilopochtli, the Toltec god of war, had banished from Mexico long before the time of the Aztecs. When Quetzalcoatl had left the region and moved east, he told the people he would return one day. According to famed Latin American scholar Miguel Leon-Portilla, Moctezuma believed that the signs all around him indicated that Cortes was Quetzalcoatl, which crippled the Aztec king because he believed he could do nothing about the invasion of his country by these strange men. Immediately before the Spanish arrival, a comet foretold events. The Valley of Mexico erupted with volcanoes, earthquakes, and severe thunderstorms, which native scholars interpreted as signs that

The Spanish invasion of the Southwest affected the lives of all Pueblo Indians including those living at Acoma in present-day New Mexico.

something momentous was about to happen. The stone figure of an Aztec god broke, and advisors of the king warned that they had received psychic messages that a catastrophe was about to occur. In the wake of all this, informants told Moctezuma that Cortes and his men had landed near present-day Veracruz and were making their way inland with the help of hundreds of native allies.

Moctezuma tried to negotiate with Cortes, sending him gold, jewels, feather art, and colorful cotton cloth. Some Spaniards wanted to retreat, but Cortes burned his ships and marched through the mountains toward Tenochtitlan (Mexico City). Along the way Cortes created an alliance with the Tlaxcalans and slaughtered five thousand Cholulans. Many Indians, enemies of Aztecs, joined Cortes in the conquest. In November 1519, Moctezuma invited Cortes and his men into the heart of Tenochtitlan, a city described by Bernal Díaz as having "palaces magnificently built of stone, and the timber . . . with spacious courts and apartments . . . gardens . . . beautiful and aromatic plants . . . and a lake of the clearest water." Tenochtitlan had a population of approximately three hundred thousand–larger than that of Paris, London, or Madrid. Aztecs excelled in architecture, with magnificent buildings, temples, dams, and aqueducts. They skillfully created art out of stone, feathers, gold, and silver. They irrigated fields of corn and took tribute from surrounding people. As Díaz noted, Mexico "was the garden of the world." But the garden turned to hell as disease and death spread among the native populations. Throughout the conquest, Aztecs and their neighbors suffered from a devastating epidemic of smallpox, which significantly weakened the population, contributing to the Spanish successes.

Not long after entering Tenochtitlan, Cortes arrested Moctezuma, held him prisoner, executed Aztec leaders who had killed the Spanish garrison in Veracruz, and collected a ransom of gold, silver, and jewels. Over eight hundred Spaniards arrived in Mexico and joined Cortes. They held sway over Tenochtitlan until Aztecs lost faith in Moctezuma, stoning and mortally wounding him when he made a public appeal. When Moctezuma died, Aztecs followed their leader Cuitláhuac until his death eighty days later of smallpox. Then Cuauhtémoc assumed command and led a successful resistance against the Spanish, driving Cortes from Tenochtitlan on June 30, 1520. Cortes fled Tenochtitlan to Tlaxcala, suffering great losses from native attacks, but he regrouped, built thirteen small ships with cannons, and returned to Tenochtitlan with nearly six hundred Spaniards and thousands of Tlaxcalans to launch a land and naval battle. In December 1520, Cuauhtémoc and his Aztec warriors met Cortes, fighting to preserve their culture and city. But a deadly smallpox epidemic had swept through Tenochtitlan, crippling the Indian fighters and helping the Spanish destroy the native population. Cortes captured, tortured, and hanged Cuauhtémoc. In August 1521, Tenochtitlan became the capital of New Spain and Cortes the governor and captain-general. The Aztec empire vanished with the Spanish conquest of Mexico, but Aztec people survived and continue to be an integral element of Mexican culture. The blood of Aztecs, Mayas, Olmecs, Zapotecs, and hundreds of other Native Americans flows through the veins of thousands of people of Mexican descent, who know of their enduring heritage.

INVASION ALONG THE BORDERLANDS

Spanish entradas moved out from Mexico City like the spokes of a wheel, journeying into the present-day Southeast, Southwest, and Pacific Coast. Conquistadors invaded native peoples, spreading terror and claiming native lands. Spaniards brought institutions of conquest to Florida, Georgia, Louisiana, Texas, New Mexico, Arizona, and California: presidios, missions, pueblos, ranchos, repartimiento, and slavery. Although the details of the invasion, conquest, and resettlement differed from place to place, the basic institutions of the invasion remained relatively constant. Native Americans sometimes received Spaniards with friendship and curiosity, but sometimes with hostility, particularly if they learned from neighbors and travelers about Spanish treatment of other Indians. In 1528, for example, Apalachee people near Tampa Bay, Florida, killed Pánfilo de Narváez and nearly four hundred soldiers, but Alvar Núñez Cabeza de Vaca and four survivors traveled along the Gulf Coast, through Texas to the Gulf of California, and into Mexico City. Estevánico, a Moroccan slave, was one of these survivors, and in 1539, he led Fray

Marcos de Niza into present-day Arizona and New Mexico, where the Ashiwi (Zuni) executed the troublesome Estevánico. Niza hurried back to Mexico City to report to Viceroy Antonio de Mendoza that he had seen the first of "Seven Golden Cities of Cibola."

Zunis at the village of Hawikuh believed they were rid of the invaders, but in 1540, Francisco Vásquez de Coronado returned. Zunis defended their home, fighting a fierce battle before losing. Spanish soldiers occupied Hawikuh, while Coronado led others from pueblo to pueblo in northern New Mexico, brutally crushing every overt native resistance. Branches of the expedition led by Pedro de Tovar met the Hopi of northern Arizona, and Hernando de Alarcón and Melchoir Díaz met the Cocopa, Quechan, and Tohono O'odham (Papago) of Sonora, Arizona, and California. With initial help from two native guides, Coronado traveled through Texas, Oklahoma, and Kansas in search of the fabled golden cities. Neither Coronado nor any branch of his expedition found them, and in 1542, Coronado returned to Mexico a mentally, physically, and financially broken man. Although Coronado claimed dominion over Native Americans and their lands by right of discovery, he did not inhabit the region or establish crown rule. Like Hernando de Soto, who led another expedition (1539–1542) through lands belonging to many sovereign native nations from Florida to the Mississippi River, Spanish conquistadors invading north of present-day Mexico left a legacy of death, destruction, and invisible enemies–diseases. However, they did not resettle Indian lands until the end of the sixteenth century.

After the first Spaniards left, Native Americans recorded their historical relations with white men through pictographs, paintings, and oral traditions. They passed down historical accounts from generation to generation through the spoken word, teaching their youth to memorize and recite accounts accurately so that tribal memories would be preserved. Pueblo Indians in New Mexico later recorded the invasion of their lands by Don Juan de Oñate in 1598. Earlier that year, the Council of the Indies in Spain ordered the viceroy of New Spain to settle present-day New Mexico, believing the land was filled with gold. With 139 men, women, and children, including soldiers and priests, Oñate entered several pueblos along the Rio Grande. In 1598, approximately forty thousand Indians lived in sixty-six pueblos, but by 1800, disease and death reduced the population to about ten thousand. Cherokee scholar Russell Thornton and researcher Henry Dobyns have demonstrated that their numbers continued to decline until the nineteenth century.

When Oñate arrived, he informed the people that their lands belonged to Spain and that they were subjects of the crown. Spaniards ordered Native Americans to abandon their "pagan" religions and submit to Christianity and Spanish domination. When the people of Ácoma resisted, killing thirteen soldiers, the Spanish retaliated in January 1599 by launching a fierce three-day attack in which the conquistadors killed eight hundred people and captured five hundred women and children as well as eighty men. After a "trial," the Spanish sentenced all males twenty-five years of age and older to have a foot chopped off and to serve twenty years of slavery. Young people from Ácoma between the ages of twelve and twenty-four served as slaves for twenty years but were spared amputations. Spanish priests kidnapped all children under twelve, keeping them as their own. Spanish soldiers found two Hopis at Ácoma, so they cut off their hands and sent them off to spread the word among Native Americans: Do not resist Spanish rule.

Spanish rule within the present boundaries of the United States extended from Florida to California. San Juan Pueblo scholar Alfonso Ortiz and Jemez Pueblo historian Joe Sando have shown in their works that Pueblo peoples resisted Spanish occupation, laws, and institutions, and they continued to stand against the invasion by foreign powers throughout the colonial period. Native Americans who resisted Spanish rule often faced treatment as harsh as that faced by the people of Ácoma. Spanish soldiers, missionaries, and settlers often removed Indians from lands that the newcomers desired. Spaniards demanded tribute in the form of food and regulated native access to water, timber, foods, and other resources that belonged to Indian groups. Spaniards actively sought to destroy native religions and supplant them with Christianity. Spaniards forced their laws and punishment on Native Americans who continued to resist by quietly practicing their religions and following their own governance. The Spanish, and later Mexican, government imposed a foreign political structure on the Pueblos, establishing secular government among the natives while ignoring religious leadership. This created tension between secular and religious leaders that has characterized Pueblo history since the colonial era. As a result, the Pueblos (along with other Native Americans) developed a two-tiered system in which they outwardly followed Spanish religious and secular laws and inwardly adhered to their own leaders, both religious and secular. Such survival strategies sustained the people and have continued to function.

PUEBLO REVOLT

In seventeenth-century New Mexico, Spanish soldiers and priests raided Pueblo Indian ceremonial lodges known as *kivas*, destroying altars, paintings, and kachina masks, which represented a pantheon of spirits. In 1661 alone, the Spanish burned nearly two thousand kachina masks and religious objects, destroying several kivas. Pueblo Indians resisted and organized. Finally, in 1680, a leader named Popé from San Juan pueblo led a revolt against Spanish oppression. During the fighting, Pueblo Indian resistance fighters killed over four hundred Spaniards and drove Governor Antonio de Otermín out of Santa Fe to El Paso del Norte. After the fighting, Indians reestablished some of their autonomous pueblos and lived without Spanish interference until 1689, when Spanish troops invaded Zia pueblo, killing approximately six hundred people and enslaving seventy others.

The attack on Zia was the beginning of the Spanish *Reconquista* of New Mexico, which began in full measure in 1692, when Governor Diego de Vargas led Spaniards from El Paso to Santa Fe to reestablish Spanish rule through negotiations and war. Pueblo Indians resisted in many ways, but by 1710, Spain dominated much of the Rio Grande Valley. Some Pueblo people moved to avoid Spanish rule, living with Diné or Navajos. Apaches, Navajos, Comanches, Kiowas, and Utes resisted Spanish rule and relieved some of the pressure on Pueblo peoples. Bands of these Indians swept across New Mexico, raiding ranchos for horses, cattle, sheep, and mules. Some bands and individuals established rich economies based on raiding, developing herds of livestock and trading them for goods, including guns, ammunition, metal, pots, pans, beads, cloth, hats, and a host of items. Sometimes they kidnapped children and women, enslaving them or inviting them into their families. However, through a study of Catholic mission records by noted scholar David Brugge, it is clear that the Spanish stole hundreds of Indian children, enslaving them to work as domestics, cowboys, and field hands in towns and on ranches throughout the Rio Grande Valley. Stealing native women and children was common among Spanish populations throughout America, including those in present-day California, New Mexico, Texas, Louisiana, Florida, and Arizona.

Spanish conquistadors under Coronado's command claimed Arizona in 1540, but they did not settle the *Pimería Alta* (upper lands of the Pima Indians) until 1687, when Italian-born Eusebio Francisco Kino built Mission Dolores on the San Miguel River in Sonora. In 1691, the Jesuit began mission work with Ak-mul Au-authm (Pima) and Tohono O'odham (Papago) living along the Santa Cruz and Santa Pedro valleys of Arizona. Kino established sites for Mission Guebavi, Tumacacori, and San Xavier del Bac, although the native people of southern Arizona were not enthusiastic about missions. Like missionaries everywhere, Kino introduced Indians to new varieties of fruits, vegetables, and livestock. Catholic missionaries taught the people to plant wheat and make flour tortillas and bread. Fry bread developed from this tradition. Missionaries introduced grapes and made wine, and they brought fruit trees of peaches, plums, apples, and citrus to the borderlands. Father Kino brought to Arizona sheep, goats, cattle, mules, and horses, animals that enriched native culture but helped destroy the natural environment by grazing on native plants and introducing new pathogens.

Following quickly in the wake of missionaries were Spanish settlers, eager to claim "free" lands for ranchos. Like Kino, they introduced livestock to the region, allowing their animals to graze on mesquite, screw beans, chilla, cactus fruit, and other native plants that Indians used for food and medicine. Spanish settlers overran Indian lands and forcefully took control of water rights. They instituted new laws, including religious laws, that often conflicted with native beliefs, ceremonies, and rituals. Some settlers demanded tribute from Indians and enslaved Pimas, forcing them to work for periods of time. By 1695, Pimas living on Rio Altar in Sonora revolted, but Indians living in present-day Arizona remained peaceful until 1751, when they allied under the leadership of Luis Oacpicagigua, who fought as a patriot against Spanish rule. The revolt was not widespread or long-lasting, although Oacpicagigua and his followers killed eighteen Spaniards and native converts. Spanish soldiers defeated and executed him and his leaders.

The Pima struggle for independence encouraged Spanish military officials to establish the presidio of Tubac in 1752. However, a greater threat to Spanish rule came from Apaches who raided herds in southern Arizona. As a result of administrative reforms in 1763, presidio commanders assumed greater power over the *Provincias Internas* (New Mexico and Arizona; later, Texas and California). Ultimately, Spain established three presidios in Arizona, trading poor guns and bad liquor to Apaches, which contributed to the decline of Apache effectiveness from 1775 to 1790. As among other native populations, bacterial and viral diseases, a continual scourge among all American Indians, also diminished Apache power. Knowingly and unknowingly, Spanish settlers brought a host of pathogens that preyed upon Native Americans, working as invisible enemies. Disease harmed native people throughout the colonial period. It invaded Apache society but did not destroy it. Indeed, skilled Apache warriors and raiders kept Spanish settlement of Arizona at bay until the 1790s, when ranchers and miners moved into the region. By this time Spanish settlers moved onto native lands in other areas of the Southwest as well as the Southeast and California.

INVASION OF CALIFORNIA'S INDIANS

In 1542, the Kumeyaay Indians of San Diego, California, were the first Native Americans of Alta California to encounter Juan Rodríquez Cabrillo, a Portuguese sailing for Spain. After anchoring six days in San Diego Harbor, fighting and trading with the Kumeyaay, Cabrillo sailed north. His was the first of six European naval expeditions that interacted with Native Americans in California, but Spain showed little interest in Alta California until the 1760s, when Russian and Aleut traders from Alaska began taking furs along the coast of Alta California. In 1768, King Cárlos III instructed Viceroy Marqués de Croix to settle and secure San Diego and Monterey. As a result, José de Galvez traveled to Spanish religious, civil, and military settlements in Baja California to prepare for the invasion of Alta California. Spanish settlement of Alta California was motivated primarily by defensive expansionism–fear by Spain of Russian and British designs on California–but the Spanish also wanted to convert "heathens." The Kumeyaay and other Native Americans of California heard rumors of their coming, but the arrival of soldiers, missionaries, horses, and cattle into their homelands would forever change the first nations of California.

In 1769, the "sacred expedition" reached San Diego in three contingencies, including missionaries under Father Junípero Serra, professional soldiers or *solados de cuera* (leather jacket soldiers) under Captain Gaspar de Portolá, and supply ships under Juan Perez. The Spanish established their first settlement at Cosoy, a Kumeyaay village located in Old Town, San Diego, and not far away, Serra built the first Mission San Diego de Alcalá. This was the first of twenty-one missions near the coast and marked the beginning of Spain's invasion and conquest of Alta California, but Catholic missionaries baptized no Kumeyaay for two years after their arrival. Cahuilla-Luiseño historian Edward Castillo argues that "permanent colonization almost from the beginning raised native suspicions and ultimately led to violence." Within a month after Spaniards arrived in San Diego, Kumeyaay warriors attacked the Spanish, attempting to drive them away from their homelands. The Spanish prevailed, but Kumeyaay people resisted white settlement, including a major revolt involving eight hundred men in 1775 at the second site of the San Diego Mission, located in the valley of the San Diego River.

The Catholic Church, Catholic historians, and their supporters have offered a popular image of missions as benevolent institutions. People who wish to see the Church proclaim Father Serra a saint have portrayed missions as idyllic institutions of love, culture, civilization, and positive change. However, many Indian neophytes and contemporary Native Americans consider missions to have been prisons, where missionaries exploited Indian labor at the expense of many lives. In his book, *The Conflict between the California Indians and White Civilization* (1976), Sherburne Cook argued that in spite of "innumerable lamentations, apologies and justifications, there can be no serious denial that the mission system in its economics was built upon forced labor." In recent years, ethnohistorians such as Edward Castillo, Robert Jackson, George Phillips, James Rawls, Florence Shipek, and others have emphasized that missionaries and Spanish settlers forced Indians to work as farmers, masons, cowboys, and carpenters without compensation. Within the missions, the priests locked up unmarried women each night in barracks where bacteria and viruses multiplied rapidly and spread death among mission populations. Venereal disease, smallpox, measles, and a host of other scourges plagued mission Indians.

Spaniards and mission fathers raped native women and children, and native women strangled babies born of forced intercourse. Spanish concentration of Native Californians into missions created catastrophic declines in native populations, and if Indians tried to leave the missions, soldiers rounded them up and punished them for this and other infractions of Catholic moral codes. Most missionaries would have agreed with Father Fermín Francisco de Lasuen, who viewed California's Indians as "barbarous, ferocious and ignorant" people who required "more frequent punishment." As Castillo points out, "the California missions were coercive authoritarian institutions" where Serra and his missionaries punished Indian men, women, and children with barbed whips, branding irons, shackles, mutilations, stocks, work teams, and jails. Missionaries also executed native men and women. Unfortunately, the Catholic Church has closed its punishment books in its archives in Santa Barbara and will not permit scholars open access to documents that might further tarnish the Church or Serra's rise toward sainthood. A former tribal chairman of the Cuyapaipe Reservation in eastern San Diego County summed up the missions: "The Indians were slaves. They did all the work and after a day's work, the priests locked them up. . . . They fed them actually as little as possible. They beat them and killed them if they were sick, or couldn't work, or didn't agree to do certain work." This is a contemporary view of the mission system shared by many Indians in California.

In addition, Spanish introduction of nonnative plants and animals altered the environment and created many problems for California's native people. Longhorn cattle, horses, mules, pigs, and sheep ranged across California, grazing on native fruits and vegetables that composed the diets of native people. New plants brought by the Spanish, including fruit trees, grapes, and wheat, altered the environment as cultivation of these crops destroyed native foods. Forced confinement of California's Indians in the missions broke the seasonal food cycle and spiritual relationships with native plants and animals. Nutritious diets rich in game, fish, seeds, and acorns were replaced by diets consisting of a starchy gruel called atole. Malnutrition spread among Indians living within the missions as diets changed, and this factor lowered the resistance of Native Californians so that they could not fight infections effectively. Starvation and deaths resulted, not only in California but also among many native populations affected by Spanish missions.

In 1989, during an archaeological dig of Mission San Diego, archaeologists unearthed a "plague pit" or mass grave of several native people who died simultaneously or within a few days of one another. People were buried on top of one another with their heads facing west and their bodies lined up in neat rows. The bare white skeletons lay exposed to the sun for the first time in over a century, and small skeletons of infants and children made up a large portion of the burial. Whether from disease or

Edward D. Castillo, a Cahuilla man, is professor and chair of Native American studies at Sonoma State University. He is the foremost American Indian scholar on native relations with the Spanish.

starvation, these Native Americans died when they were very young as a result of conditions brought about by the mission system. The Catholic Church tried to prevent public disclosure of the archaeological dig by placing eight-foot-by-four-foot plywood fencing around the cemetery, but a member of the Native American Heritage Commission announced the desecration on commercial television through a news report and offered to discuss the matter publicly with Church officials, who never accepted the offer. But no amount of damage control could blot out the awful fact that many Native Americans died as a result of conditions introduced by the Church. However, Native Americans did not passively submit to the mission system, and over the years hundreds of people fled the missions to live as their ancestors before them or to find work on private ranches away from the missions.

Everywhere the Spanish traveled, Native Americans resisted conquest aggressively and passively. Many Indians continued to practice aspects of their old religion while also participating in Christian ceremony and ritual. They slowed their work and refused to help Spaniards locate other Indians to be forced into the mission system. Native Californians escaped the missions when they could, including over two hundred Ohlones who fled Mission Dolores in 1795. Indians incarcerated at Missions San Miguel and San Antonio poisoned priests, and in 1812, Ohlones at Mission Santa Cruz assassinated Father Antonio Quintana. In February 1824, Chumash and other natives living at Missions La Purisima and Santa Barbara rose in a major revolt. Fighting broke out initially when Spaniards whipped a neophyte at Mission Santa Ynez, and the Indians there burned several mission buildings. The same day, two thousand natives captured Mission La Purísima and were soon joined by Indians from Santa Ynez and San Fernando. Native American soldiers fortified the mission, cutting gun ports in the adobe walls and setting up cannons and swivel guns.

Other Indians in the area responded to the call, including Chumash at Mission Santa Barbara who armed themselves and prepared to die for their freedom. For several hours the Indians at Mission Santa Barbara fought Spanish soldiers but eventually gave up and retreated to the presidio of Santa Barbara. The Chumash sacked Mission Santa Barbara and moved into the mountains. In March 1824, hundreds of Spanish cavalry and infantry attacked the four hundred native defenders at Mission La Purisima, who fought with cannons, guns, bows, and arrows. After fighting several hours, a priest negotiated an armistice. California Indians from other missions joined the Chumash, but by May and June the revolt slowed, especially after some neophytes agreed to return to the missions—although four hundred refused to return. Spanish officials negotiated an end to the rebellion and then launched a criminal investigation that resulted in the execution of seven leaders and a sentence of ten-years, chain-gang labor, for four other leaders.

INDIANS, SPANIARDS, AND THE BORDERLANDS

Indian resistance to Spanish missions, presidios, pueblos, and slavery occurred from coast to coast. In Florida, the Gulf Coast, Mississippi River Valley, and Texas, tribes including Apalachees, Yamasee, Mikasukis, Calusas, Choctaws, Chickasaws, Cherokees, Muscogees, and many others resisted the Spanish invasion. One factor facilitating Spanish expansion northward was the fear of other European nations—particularly the French and English—who threatened Spain's hold on Caribbean islands and Mexico. Expanding defensively, Pedro Menéndez de Aviles founded the presidio of St. Augustine in 1565. For over thirty years, Native Americans in Florida lived under the thumb of Spain until 1597, when they rebelled against Catholic missionaries. Spanish soldiers from the presidio of St. Augustine burned Indian villages and stores of food, bringing the overt rebellion to an end. As in California, Arizona, and New Mexico, Indians in Florida practiced other forms of resistance. Spanish soldiers, missionaries, and traders felt genuinely threatened after 1673, when Louis Joliet and Jacques Marquette followed the Mississippi River south to the Arkansas River, speculating that it ran into the Gulf of Mexico.

Acting on information gained by Joliet and Marquette, in 1682 Robert Cavelier, Sieur de la Salle, and a large band of Indians traveled down the Mississippi to the Gulf of Mexico. La Salle claimed the entire Mississippi River Valley for France and honored his king by calling the western lands Louisiana. French control of the Mississippi River meant that traders could extend their trade among many more native people and move their furs from trading posts in the western Great Lakes region down the Mississippi River to be shipped overseas through the Gulf of Mexico. In 1699, the French established the town of Biloxi and several other settlements along the Gulf Coast, but French control of the Gulf Coast was always tenuous. The French population was never great in this region, and American Indians held onto their traditional cultures and lands until after the French and Indian War. After the war, France ceded New Orleans and Louisiana to the Spanish in 1762. Because of the Napoleonic Wars and threats against the Spanish by the English and Americans, Spain transferred title of New Orleans and Louisiana back to France for safe keeping in 1800. Needing money to finance his wars, Napoleon sold Louisiana to the United States in 1803. The transfer and sale of lands belonging to a host of Native American nations occurred without the permission of American Indians and often without their knowledge. Such arrogance involving native lands was born of European traditions of chauvinism and self-proclaimed "superiority."

While France and England expanded their empires, Spain also moved defensively into Texas. Spanish priests established two missions along the Nueces River among the Hasinai Indians but abandoned these institutions after the native people revolted in 1702. However, Spanish missionaries returned in 1715 after French traders expanded their holdings in Louisiana. In addition to mission work with the Hasinai, Catholic missionaries moved among the Oamayas, Tawakonis, Tonkawas, Karankahuas, and others, attempting to convert these people to Christianity. At the same time, Spanish officials established presidios along the Texas-Louisiana border. Their largest settlement was at San Antonio de Valero, a pueblo that boasted a presidio and mission called the Alamo. As was true in all Indian missions, Spanish priests demanded that the Indians of Texas surrender much of their culture and way of life. Priests at the Alamo and other missions ordered native families to end their lives as hunters, gatherers, and independent farmers. They were to leave their villages and move into the mission compound, where they could live an orderly, systematic, sedentary life controlled by Spaniards who wanted them to work without compensation for the Church, presidio, and pueblo. Some Indians resisted, but all were influenced by foreign animals, plants, policies, and pathogens. As a result, American

Indians in southern and central Texas suffered a dramatic decline in population that psychologically affected Indian people for generations.

QUECHANS AND SPANIARDS

Spain spread its influence across a wide region of the Americas, including that controlled by Quechan Indians, who lived at the confluence of the Gila and Colorado rivers in the southeast corner of California. Powhatan-Lenape historian Jack Forbes has shown that the Quechans controlled an important area, because it contained the best crossing on the large and swift Colorado River. In 1771, Father Tomás Garcés followed a trail used by Native Americans for centuries down the Gila River to its junction with the Colorado. As a result of discussions with Quechans and personal observations of the mountains, the priest determined that the California coast was nearby and could be reached by a land route. In 1774, Garcés traveled with Captain Juan Bautista de Anza on his epic journey through the Quechan country to San Gabriel in the Los Angeles basin. Although Native Americans had made this journey many times, historians have heralded the trip because it opened a land route from Sonora to California by which people and goods could be transported to California. In 1775 and 1776, Anza returned to California with 240 emigrants who ultimately settled a small village that became San Francisco, thus opening California to further settlement by non-Indians.

Far more important for Quechans, the Spanish returned to their settlements in 1781 to establish missions, pueblos, and a presidio at La Purisima de la Concepcíon and San Pablo y San Pedro de Bicuñer, both located on the California side of the Colorado River. At first, Quechan leader Salvador Palma and his followers supported Spanish settlement, but after the settlers overran Quechan farms, destroyed native foods along the river, raped native women, and publicly whipped Quechan boys, the Indians turned against the Spanish. On July 17, 1781, Quechan warriors rose against Spanish tyranny, killing several people and capturing women and children. At Bicuñer, Quechans killed two priests and every settler, but at Concepcíon, the two priests and several women and children survived by moving down river to the Quechan villages near present-day Algodones, Mexico. According to Señora Yslas, the wife of the alcalde, Quechans appeared a few days later and told Fathers Garcés and Juan Barrenache to come out. When they complied, the Indians beat their heads with war clubs. According to Quechan oral history, the Tohono O'odham warriors, not Quechans, killed the priests, but both peoples say they watched the souls of the priests rise out of their bodies after the slayings.

The Spanish rescued most of the women and children from the Yuma Crossing, but the Quechans and thousands of other Native Americans remember the Spanish invasion of their lands as a devastating episode. Spain had claimed native lands by right of discovery and war, fighting any tribe or band that resisted Spanish rule. Native Americans often resisted Spanish rule overtly and passively, and although they could accommodate many aspects of Spanish rule, European diseases killed thousands of men, women, and children who had no immunities to foreign sicknesses such as smallpox, measles, colds, influenza, diphtheria, typhoid, and cholera. In order to survive, some Native Americans acculturated into Spanish society by eventually becoming Christians and speaking Spanish as their second or third language. Some wore European dress and worked as *vaqueros* (cowboys), farmers, cooks, and maids. However, they did not surrender that which was truly native, including their languages, religions, laws, kinships, and foods. Through radical change, most Native Americans did not assimilate into Spanish culture or lose all elements of their native cultures. They did not adopt everything that was Spanish. In the larger sense, Native Americans survived missions, presidios, pueblos, slavery, disease, and malnutrition, living through and with a myriad of radical changes that came with the Spanish invasion.

Selected Readings and Bibliography

Several works in this chapter deal with the invasion of America. Most helpful has been Jennings's, *The Invasion of America*, which deals with discovery and conquest. A Pueblo Indian interpretation of the Spanish invasion of the Southwest is found in Francis's, *Native Time*, and Margolin offers California Indian perspectives in *The Way We Lived*.

Anderson, H. Allen. "The Encomienda in New Mexico, 1598–1680." *New Mexico Historical Review* 60 (1985): 353–379.

Bancroft, Hubert H. *History of California, 1542–1800*. 6 volumes. San Francisco: The History Company, 1886.

——. *History of Arizona and New Mexico, 1530–1888*. San Francisco: The History Company, 1989.

——. *History of the Northern Mexican States* and *Texas*. 2 volumes. San Francisco: The History Company, 1989.

Bannon, John F. *The Spanish Borderlands Frontier, 1513–1821*. New York: Holt, Rinehart and Winston, 1971.

Billington, Ray Allen. *Westward Expansion: A History of the American Frontier*. New York: Macmillan, 1967.

Bishop, Morris. *The Odyssey of Cabeza de Vaca*. New York: Century Company, 1933.

Bolton, Herbert E. *The Spanish Borderlands*. New Haven: Yale University Press, 1921.

——. *Rim of Christendom: A Biography of Eusebio Francisco Kino.* New York: Macmillan, 1936.

——. *Coronado: Knight of Pueblos and Plains.* Albuquerque: University of New Mexico Press, 1949.

——. *Pageant in the Wilderness.* Salt Lake City: Utah State Historical Society, 1950.

Bolton, Herbert E., ed. *Spanish Exploration in the Southwest, 1542–1706.* New York: Charles Scribner's Sons, 1916.

Bolton, Herbert E., and Thomas M. Marshall. *The Colonization of North America, 1492–1783.* New York: Macmillan, 1920.

Brandon, William. *Indians.* Boston: Houghton Mifflin, 1961.

Brebner, John B. *The Explorers of North America.* Cleveland: World Publishing, 1955.

Castillo, Edward D. "The Impact of Euro-American Exploration and Settlement." *Handbook of North American Indians, California,* 8. Washington, D.C.: Smithsonian Institution Press, 1978.

Castillo, Edward, and Robert Jackson. *Indians, Franciscans, and Spanish Colonization.* Albuquerque: University of New Mexico Press, 1995.

Chapman, Paul H. *The Norse Discovery of America.* Atlanta: One Candle Press, 1981.

Cook, Sherburne. *The Conflict between the California Indians and White Civilization.* Berkeley: University of California Press, 1976.

Cook, Warren L. *Flood Tide of Empire: Spain and the Pacific Northwest, 1543–1819.* New Haven: Yale University Press, 1973.

Costo, Rupert, and Jeanette Henry Costo. *Natives of the Golden State: The California Indians.* San Francisco: Indian Historian Press, 1995.

——, eds. *The Missions of California: A Legacy of Genocide.* San Francisco: Indian Historian Press, 1987.

Crosby, Alfred W. *The Columbian Exchange: Biological and Cultural Consequences of 1492.* Westport, Conn.: Greenwood Publishing Company, 1972.

——. *Ecological Imperialism: The Biological Expansion of Europe, 900–1900.* Cambridge: Cambridge University Press, 1986.

De las Casas, Bartolome. *A Short Account of the Destruction of the Indies.* New York: Penguin, 1992. Originally published in 1552.

Dobyns, Henry F. *Their Numbers Become Thinned.* Knoxville: University of Tennessee Press, 1983.

——. "Indians in the Colonial Spanish Borderlands." *Indians in American History.* Frederick Hoxie, ed. (Arlington Heights, Ill.: Harlan Davidson, 1988) pp. 67–93.

Dozier, Edward P. "The Pueblo Indians of the Southwest." *Current Anthropology* 5 (1964): 79–97.

Drinnon, Richard. *Facing West.* Minneapolis: University of Minnesota Press, 1980.

Faulk, Odie B. *Land of Many Frontiers: A History of the American Southwest.* New York: Oxford University Press, 1968.

——. *Arizona: A Short History.* Norman: University of Oklahoma Press, 1978.

Gibson, Arrell M. *The American Indian: Prehistory to the Present.* Lexington, Mass.: D. C. Heath, 1980.

Gibson, Charles. *Spain in America.* New York: Harper and Row, 1966.

Hackett, Charles W. *Revolt of the Pueblo Indians of New Mexico and Otermin's Attempted Reconquest.* Albuquerque: University of New Mexico Press, 1942.

Hafen, Leroy R., and Ann W. Hafen. *Old Spanish Trail: Santa Fe to Los Angeles.* Glendale, Calif.: Arthur H. Clark, 1954.

Hall, Thomas D. *Social Change in the Southwest, 1350–1880.* Lawrence: University Press of Kansas, 1989.

Hallenbeck, Cleve. *Alvar Nunez Cabeza de Vaca.* Port Washington, N.Y.: Kennikat Press, 1970.

Hammond, George P. *Don Juan de O'ate and the Founding of New Mexico.* Santa Fe: El Palacio Press, 1927.

Haring, Clarence H. *The Spanish Empire in America.* New York: Oxford University Press, 1947.

Herring, Hubert. *A History of Latin America.* New York: Alfred A. Knopf, 1955.

Hollen, W. Eugene. *The Southwest: Old and New.* New York: Alfred A. Knopf, 1967.

Hoxie, Frederick, ed. *Indians in American History.* Arlington Heights, Ill.: Harlan Davidson, 1988.

John, Elizabeth A. H. *Storms Brewed in Other Men's Worlds: The Confrontation of Indians, Spanish, and French in the Southwest, 1540–1795.* College Station: Texas A&M University Press, 1975.

Kelsey, Harry. "European Impact on the California Indians, 1530–1830." *Americas* 41 (1985): 494–511.

Kessell, John L. *Kiva, Cross, and Crown: The Pecos Indians and New Mexico, 1540–1840.* Washington, D.C.: National Park Service, 1979.

Knaut, Andrew L. *The Pueblo Revolt of 1680: Conquest and Resistance in Seventeenth-Century Mexico.* Norman: University of Oklahoma Press, 1995.

Koning, Hans. *The Conquest of America: How the Indian Nations Lost Their Continent.* New York: Monthly Review Press, 1993.

Leon-Portilla, Miguel. *Broken Spears.* Boston: Houghton Mifflin, 1962.

Margolin, Malcolm, ed. *Monterey in 1786, Life in a California Mission: The Journals of Jean Francois de La Perouse.* Berkeley: Heyday Books, 1989.

McNickle, D'Arcy. *They Came Here First.* New York: Harper and Row, 1949.

Morison, Samuel Eliot. *The European Discovery of America: The Northern Voyages, A.D. 500–1600.* New York: Oxford University Press, 1971.

Nash, Gary. *Red, White and Black: The Peoples of Early America.* Englewood Cliffs, N.J.: Prentice-Hall, 1974.

——. "The Hidden History of Mestizo America." *The Journal of American History* 82 (1995): 941–962.

Ortiz, Alfonso, ed. "San Juan Pueblo." *Handbook of North American Indians, Southwest 9.* (Washington, D.C.: Smithsonian Institution Press, 1979) pp. 278–295.

Parry, John H. *The Age of Reconnaissance: Discovery, Exploration, and Settlement, 1450–1650.* Cleveland: World Publishing Company, 1963.

Phillips, George H. *Chiefs and Challengers: Indian Resistance and Cooperation in Southern California.* Berkeley: University of California Press, 1975.

——. *The Enduring Struggle: Indians in California History.* San Francisco: Boyd and Fraser, 1981.

Rawls, James J. *Indians of California: The Changing Image.* Norman: University of Oklahoma Press, 1984.

Russell, Jeffrey Burton. *Inventing the Flat Earth: Columbus and Modern Historians.* New York: Praeger, 1991.

Sale, J. Kirkpatrick. *The Conquest of Paradise.* New York: Knopf, 1990.

Sanford, Charles L. *The Quest for Paradise: Europeans and the Moral Imagination.* Urbana: University of Illinois Press, 1961.

Spicer, Edward H. *Cycles of Conquest: The Impact of Spain, Mexico, and the United States on the Indians of the Southwest, 1533–1960.* Tucson: University of Arizona Press, 1962.

Stannard, David E. *American Holocaust.* New York: Oxford University Press, 1992.

Thornton, Russell. *American Indian Holocaust and Survival.* Norman: University of Oklahoma Press, 1987.

Trafzer, Clifford E. *Yuma: Frontier Crossing of the Far Southwest.* Wichita: Western Heritage Press, 1980.

Wagner, Henry R. *Juan Rodriguez Cabrillo, Discoverer of the Coast of California.* San Francisco: California Historical Society, 1941.

Webb, Edith B. *Indian Life at the Old Missions.* Lincoln: University of Nebraska Press, 1952.

Weber, David J. *The Spanish Frontier in North America.* New Haven: Yale University Press, 1992.

Wilson, Darryl, and Barry Joyce, eds. *Dear Christopher: Letters to Christopher Columbus by Contemporary Native Americans.* Riverside, Calif.: University of California, Riverside, Publications in American Indian Studies, 1992.

Wise, Jennings. *The Red Man in the New World Drama.* New York: Macmillan, 1971.

Wright, Ronald. *Stolen Continents.* Boston: Houghton Mifflin, 1992.

Pocahontas, the Pamunkey daughter of Chief Powhatan, moved to England with her husband John Rolfe. While there, she was the subject of this portrait by an unknown artist. The painting reflects the European notion that Pocahontas was royalty, the daughter of a prince and emperor.

National Portrait Gallery, Smithsonian Institution/Art Resource, NY.

On the Virginia coast not far from Roanoke Island, Native Americans built the village of Secotan. John White made this watercolor, which De Bry engraved in 1590, depicting corn fields, ceremonial fire, dancing, and feasting. Note the style of houses.

The Granger Collection, New York.

Ohlone Indians of Mission San Jose in 1806 danced in colorful paints, dress, and headpieces. Music, dance, song, and body art were integral elements of California Indian culture, but such cultural elements clashed with the views of Catholic priests, who often depicted native culture as barbaric.

The Granger Collection, New York.

American Indians adopted the horse after the Spanish invasion. Horses transformed native life in many regions, including the Great Plains, where native hunters trained their horses to move in close to the great animals for the kill. Paul Kane painted this Assiniboine hunter, his horse, and his prey.
Corbis.

JOSEPH BRANT—THAYENDANEGEA

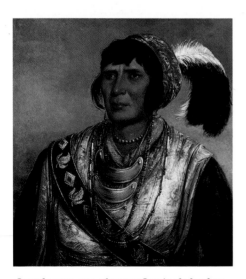

Osceola was one of many Seminole leaders who fought the United States and retreated into the Everglades, where many Seminoles live today. While negotiating under a flag of truce, soldiers of the U.S. government captured and imprisoned Osceola. George Catlin met the leader and painted this portrait in 1838.
National Museum of American Art, Washington D.C./Art Resource, NY.

Mohawk leader Joseph Brant led several Native American forces against the United States during the American Revolution. The younger brother of Molly Brant, a woman married to British agent William Johnson, Joseph often used intelligence (supplied by Molly) against the Americans. Wilhelm von M. Berczy painted this realistic likeness of Joseph.
Corbis.

CHAPTER 3

NATIVE AMERICANS AND NORTHERN EUROPEAN RESETTLEMENT

Long before the European "discovery" of America, Native Americans traded with each other, traveling great distances by sea, land, rivers, and lakes. American Indians dealt with the Norse adventurers who visited Newfoundland after the year 1000 and traded with nonnative sailors, possibly other Europeans as well as Africans, Pacific Islanders, and Asians. Native Americans residing along the entire length of the Atlantic, including the First Nations living near the mouth of the St. Lawrence River in present-day Quebec, New Brunswick, and Newfoundland Ocean, increasingly traded with European sailors during the sixteenth century. In 1534, French explorers, including Jacques Cartier, and two small ships sailed along the Newfoundland coast, through the Straits of Belle Isle, and into the Gulf of St. Lawrence. They made first contact with First Nations peoples of Canada. The French believed that the "Great Bay" might lead to the Straits of Anian or the Northwest Passage, a mythical water route linking the Atlantic and Pacific oceans. After exploring the Gulf of St. Lawrence and trading with many Wyandot-Hurons, Micmacs, Montagnais, and St. Lawrence Iroquois, the French returned home. Cartier made three voyages to North America. In 1540 and 1541, he sailed up the St. Lawrence River as far as Montreal and attempted to establish a colony, a venture that failed at first. The French believed they found gold in "New France" but soon learned it was iron pyrite–fool's gold.

FIRST NATIONS AND FRENCH RESETTLEMENT

Although there was no gold, Cartier recognized the financial benefit of the Indian trade. Native Americans of the wooded Northeast lived in a land filled with fur-bearing animals that Europeans prized for coats, capes, hats, gloves, and other apparel. Bruce Trigger and Arthur Ray have pointed out in their books that Cartier and other Frenchmen successfully traded with many tribes, establishing important relationships with First Nations peoples. While the Indians cured Cartier's sailors of scurvy, the French unintentionally introduced smallpox, measles, influenza, and syphilis, which quickly depopulated the First Nations peoples living near the St. Lawrence River, particularly Iroquois. The arrival of the French also coincided with the decline of the Wyandot-Huron and Montagnais populations. In European fashion, Cartier claimed present-day eastern Canada for France and popularized the region as rich in resources and filled with friendly natives eager to trade. According to Wendat-Huron scholar Georges Sioui, Cartier kidnapped seven prominent Wyandot leaders, who never returned to the people. When asked where they were, Cartier explained that the men had become prominent leaders in France. No one believed Cartier, because all knew that the men had perished.

Nevertheless, Wyandot-Hurons and their neighbors along the rivers and eastern Canadian coast established trade relations with the French, offering fine furs of beaver, sea otter, mink, and bear in exchange for knives, pots, pans, beads, blankets, tomahawks, and other manufactured items—but few firearms. In 1603, a group of adventurers and investors, including Samuel de Champlain and Sieur du Pontgravé, sailed to New France, where First Nations peoples offered their furs for trade goods. In 1605, the French established their first permanent settlement at Port Royal, Nova Scotia, and established Quebec in 1608. Wyandot-Hurons living between the Ottawa River and Lake Huron (present-day Ontario), Montagnais living near the Sagenay River, and Algonquian of the Ottawa River eagerly traded with the French and used their association with the Europeans to their advantage against the Haudenosaunee or the five tribes of the Iroquois Confederacy: the Onondaga, Seneca, Mohawk, Cayuga, and Oneida. During the sixteenth century, the Five Nations or Iroquois Confederacy lived south of Lake Ontario and were often enemies of Wyandots and their neighbors to the north. As a result of the French alliance with Wyandots (and other members of the Huron Confederacy), Montagnais, and Algonquians, French traders extended their influence and business over a huge area of the Great Lakes, Mississippi Valley, and Ohio River Valley.

Wyandot middlemen were key to the French fur trade during its first fifty years, and Champlain developed a trading empire based on an alliance with Wyandots, Neutrals, Tobacco People, Montagnais, and Algonquians. Most important, Wyandots enjoyed a friendly relationship with many western tribes from Quebec to Wisconsin as well as various tribes of the Old Northwest of present-day Ohio, Indiana, Illinois, and Michigan. The fur trade with the French was a natural extension of Wyandot trading that predated the arrival of Europeans, and it was lucrative to

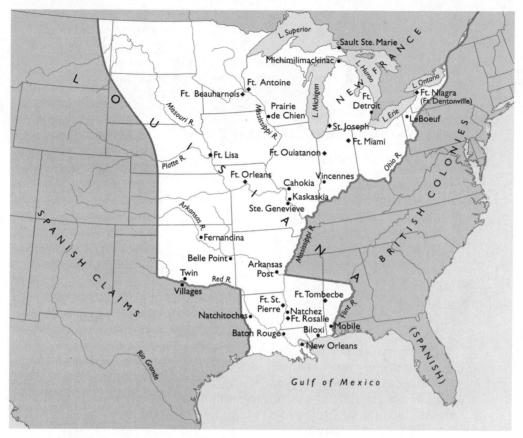

French Claims to Native American Lands

native traders who acquired French manufactured goods. Interest in acquiring trade items led prophets and elders to warn that dependency on French and other European manufactured goods would prove disastrous for the people, who would ultimately abandon elements of their old material culture. Adoption of manufactured goods had a significant impact on Native American cultures everywhere.

Over time the abandonment of bows for guns, wooden bowls and baskets for kettles, and skins for blankets had far-reaching effects for tribes, bands, and individuals. And the fur trade often took Native Americans out of their traditional environments, so that they sometimes lost their ties to clumps of trees, bodies of water, rock outcroppings, specific birds, and certain animals. Sometimes they left the lands of their parents and grandparents, leaving behind a home filled with spirit, marked with the blood, flesh, and bones of past generations. However, scholar William Fitzgerald has shown that the Neutrals persisted making lithic tools in

spite of the availability of manufactured goods, and the people maintained their use of traditional technologies until their populations declined so dramatically that they had to use manufactured items. The
preservation of material culture among Indians was a form of cultural
survival, one that was far more widespread than past scholars have
believed.

WYANDOT TRADERS AND NEW FRANCE

In *The Wendat Civilization*, Georges Sioui argues that during the first
four decades of the seventeenth century, Wyandots dominated the fur
trade in New France. Wyandot women raised fields of corn, tobacco, and
hemp, much of which they packaged for trade among their western
neighbors in the Old Northwest. In fleets of birch bark canoes, hundreds
of Wyandot traders traveled down the St. Lawrence River and across the
Great Lakes, trading with Potawatomi, Ho-Chunk (Winnebago), Anishinaabe (Ojibwe, Ojibwa, Ojibway, or Chippewa), Miami, Sac, Fox, and
other people. After the French arrived, Wyandot traders also carried
manufactured trade items such as kettles, beads, blankets, jewelry,
knives, tomahawks, axes, cloth, and others. Wyandots reigned supreme
as traders, and the French allied themselves with Wyandot traders to enhance their own economic designs. The French empire in America centered on the fur trade, not agriculture or mining, and the key to this trade
was friendship, cooperation, and alliance with Native Americans. In
sum, French traders needed native traders and worked closely with them
while always maintaining their view that French culture was superior to
that of any native nation's.

Some French became much a part of native communities. The French
coureurs de bois (wilderness trappers-traders) traveled deep into the
western reaches of the Great Lakes, establishing trading posts and living
much like Indians. They often married native women, learned tribal languages, and became integral parts of native communities. The *coureurs de
bois*, and most French for that matter, recognized Native Americans as
human beings and tribes as sovereign nations to be dealt with on a nation-
to-nation basis. Wyandots and their neighbors to the west generally dealt
with the French by diplomacy and goodwill rather than by war, although
French relations with Wyandots and others came at a price. In 1609, a
French army viciously attacked the Iroquois, killing men, women, and
children, which led to counterattacks by members of the Five Nations–
particularly Mohawks–against the French and their Wyandot allies. This
incident heightened hostilities between Wyandots and Iroquois, contributing to the ongoing hostilities between the two people and destruction of the Huron Confederacy during the seventeenth century.

Alliance with the French cost Wyandots dearly. It intensified the hatred between Wyandots and Iroquois, causing destructive warfare that

greatly reduced and ultimately destroyed Wyandot power. The fur trade also brought brandy and other alcohol into native communities, initiating a dependency that has been the bane of numerous native communities ever since. Contact with the French also led to increased diseases that indiscriminately killed men, women, and children. In addition, Recollects, Jesuits, Sulpicians, and Capuchins brought the mission system into Canada. Although the fur trade was not conducive to the mission system, because native trappers were required to travel vast distances, Catholic missionaries had great influence among the people. The French government required that Indians convert to Catholicism before they could possess guns. This was not the case among the Iroquois who dealt with Dutch traders. According to Wendat-Huron scholar Sioui, the first Wyandot to convert did so in 1640, primarily to obtain firearms, but by this time, it was too late. By 1643, the Iroquois had approximately four hundred guns, far more than Wyandots, and this factor contributed greatly in the defeat of Wyandots by the Five Nations.

In addition to disease and firearms, Wyandots suffered from the mission system. Jesuits were particularly adept at establishing missions and spreading the Christian gospel among the tribes. The introduction of Christianity split native communities into Christians and non-Christians, creating divisions that often pitted individuals against individuals, families against families, and elders against young people. Missionaries encouraged Indians to give up their "heathen" and "pagan" practices so that they could be saved in this world and the next. Native American spiritual beliefs, songs, stories, ceremonies, and rituals declined over time, in part the result of Christianity. While the Huron Confederacy declined, the Iroquois Confederacy gained great political, economic, and military power, extending its influence throughout the Great Lakes. The power gained by Iroquois in the seventeenth century helped enable them to maintain that power and neutrality until the middle of the eighteenth century. However, the decline of the Huron Confederacy was not based entirely on Iroquois power. The French contributed as well, signing a major peace treaty with the Iroquois in 1701 and opening the fur trade between the Iroquois and Indian nations of the Ohio Valley, including Chippewas, Ottawas, Miamis, Illinois, and others.

French trappers and administrators also contributed to the unsettling of native societies by removing Indians to the West, where they could be more beneficial to trading companies. Although Wyandots controlled the fur trade during the first five decades of the seventeenth century, their influence declined because of Iroquois hunters and traders working with the Dutch in New York. Iroquois and Wyandots fought a series of deadly wars from the 1640s to the 1680s, resulting in Iroquois dominance of the trade in the Northeast and beyond. As a result of overtrapping and the depletion of furs in the eastern forests, French officials moved some Wyandot allies west, where they could directly influence

French and Wyandot traders introduced Native Americans living near the Mississippi and Missouri rivers to manufactured cloth. This Wahzahzhe (Osage) girl wore colorful ribbon work titled "Hands that Love You to Your Hands" during the 1904 Louisiana Purchase Exposition in St. Louis.

the flow of furs into French hands and away from the British. The French encouraged some Wyandots to remove from Huronia in Ontario to Quebec to work more closely with French administrators bent on expanding and strengthening the western trade. They also relocated some Wyandots and other native allies to trading posts at Mackinac Island (1700), Detroit (1701), and Sandusky (1725) near the western shores of Lake Erie to better control the fur trade among the western tribes. Wyandots moved among the Chippewa, Ottawa, Sac, and Fox of the Great Lakes region, negotiating and trading on behalf of the French. Some Wyandots settled in the prairies and woodlands of northwestern Ohio from present-day Toledo to Upper Sandusky.

Generally, French relations with western tribes were nonviolent, but increased trade with the French accelerated cultural change as the tribes in the Northwest became increasingly dependent on manufactured goods. For the most part, French traders did not use force in dealing with native people but rather recognized Indian rights, dealing with them as sovereign nations. They respected linguistic and cultural diversities among the tribes, and they learned native languages, customs, ceremonies, songs, and stories. Often French trappers participated in Native American rituals and events, becoming part of the community rather than standing aloof, judging Indians as "the other." Nevertheless, the French never surrendered their belief in cultural superiority over all native people. During times of war, Indian and French trappers enslaved some people, but the French never participated in the Indian slave trade to the degree practiced by the Spanish.

In contrast to the Spanish, English, Dutch, Russian, and other Europeans, the French were more successful in their dealings with Native Americans, in large part because they truly needed native trappers for the success of New France. Each year French governors traveled among the tribes, visiting the people and maintaining friendly relations. Each May the governors hosted tribal leaders in Mobile, Alabama, and Montreal, Canada, where Indians and Frenchmen alike shared their views on a number of matters. The French encouraged the tribes to remain a part of the French alliance and sealed their friendships with gifts and parties. The Indians also intermarried with French trappers, forming lasting familial relationships that were mutually beneficial. Many Indians willingly joined the fur trade, but over time they became increasingly dependent on French goods. Alliances between the French and Native Americans were critical for the successful execution of the fur trade, because native hunters and trappers killed the animals, bargained for furs, tanned hides, preserved the furs, and transported them from the forests to docks.

Native Americans living in the Mississippi Valley from Minnesota to Louisiana were influenced by French traders. This was also true of American Indians living west of the great river, where Indian traders and

French trappers sold their goods to natives of the Great Plains. In 1673, American Indian scouts guided Father Jacques Marquette and Louis Joliet down the Fox and Wisconsin rivers, entering the "Father of All Rivers" and following it south to the Arkansas River. Learning that the Mississippi River flowed into the Gulf of Mexico rather than the Pacific Ocean, they returned to Quebec in 1674 and announced to Louis Count de Frontenac and Robert Cavelier, Sieur de la Salle their discovery of a river that connected the Great Lakes with the Caribbean Sea, a natural water route to take furs from the forests of the upper Mississippi River Valley to Europe. In 1679, La Salle launched his plan to establish a series of trading posts from Green Bay to the Gulf of Mexico, including St. Louis, Arkansas Post, Natchitoches, New Orleans, Biloxi, and Mobile. In 1682, La Salle reached the mouth of the Mississippi River, opening a new route for the French, although it had been known to Native Americans for centuries. Wichitas and Caddoes allied with the French, trading with numerous tribes west of the Mississippi, whereas Choctaws and Musco-gees cooperated with the French east of the great river. The Indians traded buffalo robes, bear skins, beaver pelts, and other furs for a host of manufactured goods. But not all Indians participated in the French fur trade, including the Chickasaws of northeastern Mississippi, the Fox of Wisconsin, and Natchez of Louisiana. Whereas the Chickasaws success-fully fought French domination, Fox and Natchez ultimately succumbed to French power.

NATIVE AND DUTCH TRADERS

Some native and colonial nations opposed the expansion of the French into the West. Because of their own interest in the Indian trade and furs, Dutch merchants and traders challenged the French and their Indian allies. In 1609, Dutch merchants hired Henry Hudson to find the fabled waterway through North America. Although he failed in this endeavor, he claimed the region from the St. Lawrence River to Virginia—present-day New York, Pennsylvania, and Delaware—for the Netherlands. Dutch fur traders in "New Netherlands" dealt primarily with the Lenape (Delaware), Canarsees, Esophus, Pequots, Pavonias, Wappingers, Hackensacks, Tappans, Raritans, Munsees, Manhattans, and Mohicans. All of them controlled lands along the Atlantic seaboard near the mouths of the Delaware and Hudson rivers, except the Pequots, who resided in the Connecticut River Valley, and the Mohicans, who lived in the upper Hudson River Valley. Mohicans and Pequots were key to the expansion of the Dutch fur trade inland, al-though Lenape men began their lengthy career serving as scouts and guides. The United New Netherlands Company operated the fur trade from Fort Nassau in the heart of Mohican territory until 1617, when independent traders took over the trade.

In the 1620s, the Dutch West India Company assumed the trade in New Netherlands, issuing a set of rules demanding peaceful relations with sovereign American Indian nations through negotiations and treaties. Although most Dutch traders were members of the Dutch Reformed Church, few of them were interested in supporting missions among the Indians, whom Reverend Domine Jonas Michaelius described as "devilish men, who serve nobody but the Devil." Dutch citizens were not permitted to sell firearms to Indians, but they could sell brandy and other spirits. The company allowed Dutch traders to fight Indians only as a last resort, and traders were not permitted initially to join in intertribal wars. At first the Dutch respected Native Americans, believing that they had a natural right to their land. However, title to native lands could be extinguished and acquired through purchase, a circumstance challenged by many Native Americans. Dutch relations with Mohawks and other tribes of the Iroquois Nations remained cordial and cooperative throughout the history of New Netherlands. In contrast, Dutch relations with Algonquian-speaking Indians were friendly only as long as the Europeans needed their cooperation, but after the Dutch (and other European traders) perceived that the Indians were no longer useful, the white men turned against the Lenape, Mohicans, Esophus, and others, killing them off and stealing their lands.

Algonquian and Iroquoian Indians watched with interest as traders of the Dutch West India Company penetrated their lands in 1623, establishing settlements and trading posts on Manhattan Island (New Amsterdam or New York), Long Island, Fort Orange (Albany), Beverwyck, Fort Nassau, and Fort Good Hope. Many Native Americans were familiar with European trade items, having traded for French goods. They were particularly keen on acquiring wampum beads (often made into belts), mirrors, vermilion, hatchets, knives, hoes, and cloth. At first the Indians received the Dutch with open arms, and native women intermarried with Dutch traders, giving birth to mixed-blood babies, which helped tie the tribes to the Europeans. The Dutch carefully nurtured their relationships with Algonquian and Iroquoian tribes, negotiating peace and trade agreements with delegations. However, the presence of European traders, regardless of their nationalities, created conflict among the tribes, who competed with each other over control of the fur trade. Prior to the arrival of Europeans, Native Americans had fought each other, but conflicts intensified as tribes competed for furs. They encroached on lands claimed by other people and resorted to killing, burning, and removing their opponents.

When the number of fur-bearing animals declined in Delaware and Mohican country, these tribes moved aggressively onto neighboring lands controlled by other tribes who resisted such encroachment because they,

too, were involved in the fur trade. Mohawks moved against their old adversaries, the Mohicans, triggering a war between the two tribes during
1626 and 1627. As the Dutch trade developed rapidly at Fort Orange,
Dutch officials determined that they needed Mohawk cooperation far
more than that of the Mohicans. In the 1630s, the Dutch West India Company revised its rules, permitting the sale of firearms, powder, and lead
to Mohawks while continuing its ban on the sale of guns to Algonquians.
Mohawks quickly armed their relatives among the Cayuga, Oneida,
Onondaga, and Seneca, who began their own aggressive expansion into
the lands of their neighbors. Iroquois bands invaded many tribes, including the Wyandot, Erie, Munsee, Lenape, Susquehanna, and others.
They expanded west, traveling throughout the Old Northwest taking
control of the fur trade. During the last half of the seventeenth century, Iroquois traders and their Ottawa allies held sway over the fur trade
throughout the Great Lakes region from the Atlantic Ocean to the
Mississippi River.

Iroquois and Algonquian Indians were very cognizant of the fact that
Europeans were invading from the east. It is likely that many tribes
viewed themselves as superior to the newcomers, believing that they
could handle any threat brought to their villages by white men. But as
the seventeenth century wore on, many tribes began to feel the pressures
of white colonization, expansion, and resettlement of their former homelands. In addition to the Dutch and French, English colonists had established themselves in Connecticut, Massachusetts, Rhode Island, and
Virginia. English farmers, merchants, and traders were expanding
rapidly into the interior, challenging the Dutch and French for more of
the fur trade and control of native lands. The Pequot of the Connecticut
River Valley had traded with the Dutch, but their association with the
West India Company ended in 1637 after fighting a disastrous war with
English colonists of Massachusetts Bay. Algonquian Indians also dealt
with Swedes, who established Fort Christina on the west side of Delaware
Bay in 1638. The New Sweden Company was organized as an economic
venture and was far more interested in conducting the fur trade than
spreading Lutheranism. The Swedish adventure was short-lived because
the Dutch West India Company forced the Swedes to flee in 1655.

Looking eastward, Native Americans faced a continual threat from
European nations eager to exploit natural resources found on native
lands. Although many early colonists focused on furs and the Indian
trade, they were also interested in exploiting lush American forests for
ship masts, lumber, tar, and pitch. It seemed to Indians that whites created friendships when it was to their advantage and broke off relations
with tribes and bands whenever it suited their needs. European colonists
were not content to settle on Indian lands along the Atlantic and soon
made incursions into the interior, moving up the river systems to establish new trading posts and towns. To some degree, all European colonists

desired to "own" native land, making formal agreements with Indians to extinguish their title to the land. The concept of real estate ownership was foreign to Native Americans, who believed that certain groups controlled and used particular areas but did not "own" land in the same manner in which Europeans owned land. To Native Americans, land was a sacred gift from the Creator, and the relationship of humans to land and resources was established at the time of creation and is known through oral texts that form the basis of Indian law. In the minds of Native Americans, the earth and all its bounty were set forth for use by all living things, and land could no more be bought and sold than could air. However, after the arrival of European colonists, Native Americans quickly perceived the danger posed by newcomers interested in owning the land and all upon it. Europeans intended to take the land, exploit its resources, and exclude Indians from their own estates.

From the outset, whites intended to exploit the minerals, water, plants, and animals of America for their own material gain. It seemed to many American Indians that European colonists would not be happy until they had taken every parcel of land and raped the earth of everything that might provide profit. Since the time of creation, Native Americans had also used the earth and its abundant resources. Indians had killed plants and animals for food, clothing, and housing. They had gathered roots, berries, seeds, shell fish, and other foods. Native Americans had cleared forests for villages and farms, used wood for homes and fuel. They had mined coal, copper, catlinite, obsidian, flint, silver, and gold, placing value on certain metals and shells. But they had done so with an understanding of their relationship to the natural environment and the creation. Before European contact, Native Americans had fought each other over many issues, including land and resources. Certain areas were known to be that of one group or another, and tribal groups fought each other to maintain their lands. However, Europeans brought a new law to the land, one born of European traditions, not American, one that emphasized land ownership in perpetuity. Europeans also believed land to be a commodity that could be broken up into parcels and sold by individuals, in contrast to native communal land ownership patterns. Conflict over the land and "ownership" of the earth weighs heavily in Native American history, and it is a paramount element of Indian-white relations that ties the past to the present in a never-ending circle that has yet to be reconciled.

In addition to the clash over land and resources, European colonists often maintained friendly relationships with Native Americans as long as it was to their advantage to do so. When European colonists no longer needed native peoples or desired to take their lands, the newcomers turned on American Indians in a deadly contest for property and power. As the Dutch population in New York grew, it resettled native lands and urged American Indians to move inland. Like other European settlers,

Dutch farmers desired Indian lands that had been previously cleared of thick woods. For generations Native Americans had cut trees to enhance range lands for animals, opening well-watered meadows so that animals would come to those places to graze. Native farmers had also cleared the land for agriculture, planting corn, squash, beans, melons, and other native foods. They also planted tobacco, a sacred plant they used in prayers, rituals, and ceremony. Native American men, women, and children also worked to clear lands for villages, opening tracts of land for communities throughout the Northeast. Clearing the forest was a good deal of work, and Dutch colonists (and other Europeans) wanted Indians to move inland so that they could take over vast amounts of land, including those previously cleared by Native Americans. What emerged was a contest for the land and justification for the theft of it. The Dutch and other Europeans began changing the public image of woodland Indians from farmers to hunters and gatherers. Europeans argued that because Indians lived by hunting and gathering, they should move inland where there were more resources. Besides, they argued, the lives of Native Americans living in the interior would be unfettered by Europeans.

Dutch policies of diplomacy and cooperation with the tribes ended in 1639, when Governor-General William Kieft arrived in New Netherlands. Kieft was a racist who advocated exterminating Indians who were of no use to the Dutch. Shortly after his arrival he levied a tax on Native Americans, requiring Indians to pay an annual tribute of corn to support the Dutch. Algonquian Indians did not submit to the tax, and they stood defiantly against Dutch farmers who allowed their livestock to graze on Indian gardens and outright stole native lands. Kieft retaliated against recalcitrant Indians, and he encouraged his Mohawk allies, enemies of the Algonquians, to kill Mohicans. In 1643, a war party of Mohawks killed seventy Mohicans and enslaved numerous women and children. Shortly afterward, Kieft sent eighty soldiers to attack the Pavonia (a branch of Lenape-Delaware), who killed native men and women, butchering infants and children in such a "manner to move a heart of stone." The Dutch returned to New Amsterdam to display eighty heads of the fallen Indians and to torture thirty prisoners.

The Dutch atrocity of 1643 spurred sporadic and immediate Algonquian attacks by small bands on Dutch and English settlements from the Connecticut River Valley to Delaware Bay. A joint troop of English and Dutch soldiers led by John Underhill retaliated, commencing a scorched-earth campaign against Algonquians that resulted in the killing and kidnapping of men, women, and children. Underhill's army also sold prisoners into slavery, sending them to the Dutch West Indies to work on plantations. In 1644, the Indians sued for peace, but uneasy tensions continued for twenty years between Algonquian-speaking Indians and the Dutch and English invaders. The quasi-peace disintegrated completely after 1665, when a Dutch farmer killed a native woman who was picking his peaches. The woman's family retaliated while a large band of Indians, who were sick at heart and resentful of the conquerors, prepared an attack on New Amsterdam. While the Dutch slept, Algonquian warriors attacked, killing several men, taking many prisoners, and burning homes, barns, and businesses. Peter Stuyvesant, the last governor-general of New Netherlands, struck back immediately, burning Indian towns and taking several captives. Another uneasy truce ensued, continually aggravated by Dutch expansion of farmers up the river systems of New Netherlands.

Facing the advance of Dutch farmers, Esophus Indians living midway between New Amsterdam and Fort Orange (Albany) made their last stand to preserve their culture and protect their home. In 1657, Esophus warriors struck Dutch farms and the village of Wiltwyck. The Indians agreed to meet Stuyvesant to discuss terms of peace, but while they slept the night before council, Dutch soldiers murdered the men. Esophus warriors retaliated, capturing and burning eight Dutch soldiers. Stuyvesant ordered all the Indians living in New Netherlands to send a delegation of children to New Amsterdam to be held as hostages, and because of their weakened condition, many tribes submitted. But not the Esophus, who flatly refused, causing Stuyvesant to launch a major campaign against the tribe. In addition to killing men, women, and children, Stuyvesant imprisoned several hundred Indians, sending them to the Dutch West Indies, where they died in slavery. The governor-general then invited his Mohawk allies to kill the Esophus, but the people continued to fight. In 1664, Stuyvesant concluded the last treaty between the Dutch and Esophus Indians, claiming all the lands previously held by the tribe by right of conquest. That same year, Charles II of England ordered his soldiers to take over New Netherlands, which they did, splitting the area in two and calling the northern part New York and the southern part New Jersey. The Esophus gained nothing in the bargain, because the English were just as ruthless as the Dutch. Thus, in spite of their gallant efforts to preserve their land and way of life, Esophus people lost everything to European expansion.

NATIVE ALASKANS AND RUSSIAN TRADERS

Whereas the numerous Algonquian- and Iroquoian-speaking Indians of the Northeast contended primarily with Europeans from France, the Netherlands, and England, native peoples of Alaska, western Canada, and the Aleutian Islands initially contended with only one Euro-Asian country—Russia. Like northern Indians to the east, Aleuts, Eskimos, Athabascans, Tlingits, Haidas, Kwakiutls, Tsimshian, Nootka, and other Indians of the far Northwest were invaded by Europeans with economic motives. The Russians were not seeking gold, oil, timber, or fish. Russians wanted millions of furs–sea otter, fox, beaver, bear, mink, sable, seal, and wolf–in large part because they had nearly exterminated fur-bearing animals in their country in the pursuit of profit. The Russians' invasion of the Aleutian Islands, Alaska, and Canada was a natural extension of their conquests of native peoples in Siberia. By the 1730s, *promyshlenniki* (Russian fur hunters) had set up trading posts at Kamchatka Peninsula and the Sea of Okhotsk. They were looking for new areas to exploit when the czar sent Vitus Bering, the Danish sailor, to explore the North Pacific. He plied the sea that bears his name today and on his expedition of 1741 discovered the Aleutian Islands and Alaska.

Bering claimed the vast region of the North Pacific for Russia and inaugurated the most brutal invasion ever faced by Native Americans. Independent Russian traders attempted to capitalize on his voyages of discovery, and in 1743, six Russian fur traders returned from the Aleutians with sixteen hundred sea otter furs worth 480,000 rubles, a huge sum of money for the time. The Russian rush for furs commenced after this voyage, with parties of traders moving from island to island in the Aleutian chain, taking many furs. From 1743 until 1765, these independent traders terrorized Aleuts by taking over their villages, kidnapping women and children, and demanding that Aleut men trap hundreds of animals while the traders lived comfortably in the villages, where they raped and tortured women and children. When the people resisted, Russians tortured and executed them in large numbers, but Aleuts and their Inuit neighbors persisted in their resistance. In 1762, Aleut and Inuit warriors launched large-scale attacks, killing several Russian traders and burning five ships. Nonetheless, this was the beginning of the end for Aleuts. Some of them died of European diseases that spread from the Aleutian Islands to the mainland. However, most Aleuts were slaughtered by Russians in a bloody conquest that easily rivals that of the Spanish in the Caribbean Islands.

Between 1762 and 1765, Russians under the leadership of Ivan Solovief launched the systematic extermination of Aleuts. Russians sailed from island to island with a small fleet of heavily armed men and ships, skirting the shores of Umnak, Unalaska, Kodiak, and other islands and blasting apart Aleut villages. Russian soldiers overran and killed hundreds of people, capturing Aleut woman and forcing them into sexual servitude. Russians set out to kill as many Aleuts as they could find, creating a much smaller native population that the traders could exploit and manage easily. Within a few years, Russians reduced the native population from roughly twenty-five thousand to twenty-five hundred.

With the Aleut population at a manageable size, several Russian trading companies vied for the Aleutian and Alaskan fur trade, impressing Aleuts into their service and extending the trade along the Alaskan

Aleut women were an integral part of Native Alaskan society when the Russians invaded. Russians spared neither women nor children in their ruthless campaign to reduce the Aleut population to a "manageable" size.

mainland. Small fleets of Aleuts in their *bidarkas* (seaworthy two-man crafts similar to kayaks) plied islands and inlets killing thousands of animals. During this era of Russian expansion, Gregory Shelikhov in 1784 founded Three Saints on Kodiak Island, the first permanent Russian village in North America. Aleuts resisted but were gathered into large groups to watch the Russians execute selected leaders. Soon the Aleuts on Kodiak succumbed to Russian brutalities, and their home became the hub of the Russian trade. In order to consolidate his business and gain a monopoly of the Russian fur trade, Shelikhov set out to buy out all his competitors, a feat that he accomplished in 1790. Shelikhov and his wife lobbied the czar for a royal monopoly of the Pacific fur trade in the Northwest, much like that of the British East India Company. In 1799, four years after Shelikhov's death, the czar issued a charter creating the Russian American Company.

While Shelikhov managed the overall affairs of his business, Alexander Baránov ran the everyday operations of the company. Baránov ruthlessly removed Aleuts from their villages, assigning them duty wherever he desired them to work and ordering them to do whatever he wanted. He forced men, women, and children to do his bidding by hunting furs, preparing them for shipping, making clothes for his workers, procuring and preserving food and fuel, and repairing boats, traps, and other equipment. Baránov meted out harsh punishment and death to any Aleut who defied him, and he forced Aleuts to accompany him great distances in search of furs. Under his direction, the company took millions of furs, rivaling other companies as one of the greatest trading adventures in the world. But Baránov did not go unchallenged by Native Americans or Europeans. In 1778, Captain James Cook of the British Navy explored the North Pacific, and during the 1780s, British and American traders invaded the region in search of furs. Traders from Britain and the United States posed minor threats to the Russian enterprise, but the mighty Tlingit Indians were a real and constant threat to Russian traders.

During the 1790s, Baránov extended the company to southeast Alaska and the many islands of the region. This was Tlingit Indian country, and these natives resented Russian and Aleut traders, particularly after Baránov established Sitka in the heart of Tlingit territory. Tlingits had their own commercial ties with British and American traders, and in 1802, they launched a major war with the Russians, burning their towns, stealing their furs, and killing 150 Aleuts and Russians. After a series of successful engagements, Tlingits negotiated a tenuous peace with Baránov. Some Tlingits continued to resist Russian encroachment and resettlement of their lands until the last days of the Russian American Company (1867), although the missionary efforts of Father Ivan Veniaminoff of the Russian Orthodox Church tempered relations between the two peoples after he began work among the tribe in 1834. Veniaminoff learned the Aleut, Inuit, and Tlingit languages, which he reduced to writing, using their native languages in books and other publications. In spite of the priest's efforts, Tlingit fighters remained a constant threat to Russian traders throughout the early nineteenth century.

American Indian resistance to European conquerors is a persistent theme in Native American history. As the Russians extended their influence throughout the Pacific Northwest, Native Americans willingly traded with them, but if Russians provoked American Indians, the native peoples resisted Russians who threatened their homes and families. This was no less true of Kashaya Pomos of northern California, who were forced to contend with Russian traders bent on exploiting their lands for furs and food. Russian trading vessels had ranged from Alaska to Baja California, trading mirrors, wire, cloth, beads, tools, and other items for furs. On their journeys down the California coast, Russians met several native peoples and marveled at the lush coast. In 1805, Chamberlain Nikolai Rezánof recommended that the Russian American Company establish a trading post in New Albion (California) and an agricultural settlement there to provide food for Russian settlements to the north. Supplying Russian and Aleut traders with nutritious food had always been a challenge for the Russian American Company, so in 1812, Aleut and Russian traders numbering 175 men invaded Pomos about eight miles above the mouth of the Russian River and ninety miles north of San Francisco Bay, where they built Fort Ross, the southernmost settlement of the company.

At first the Pomos traded and provided some labor, but Russians impressed some Pomos into their service, enslaving them to clear lands, till the soil, plant, harvest, and preserve foods. According to contemporary Pomo elders, Russians and Aleuts held Pomo women captive for sex and punished or killed Pomos who refused to cooperate. The Pomo community suffered from social and cultural dislocations, depression, and diseases, but Pomos also resisted Russian rule. Like other Native Americans who dealt with Russians, Pomos witnessed cultural and population decline, which harmed the people. This was not unlike the consequences suffered by the Pamunkeys, Pequots, Wicomocoes, Wampanoags, Narragansetts, Nanticokes, Wyandots, and other native peoples of the East who met the European invasion of America. Russian rule at Fort Ross continued until 1841, when the traders abandoned the post.

European traders introduced Native Americans to a wide variety of fascinating and useful trade goods, but these goods came at quite a high price. The onset of the trade brought profits for European traders, which encouraged other non-Indians to settle native lands in order to exploit the people and their resources. And with these Europeans came new laws, values, and ideas that challenged Native American culture, language, and religion. Furthermore, European traders exposed Indian people living along the Pacific Rim north of Baja California to smallpox, influenza, syphilis, gonorrhea, and a host of other diseases that devastated Native American populations. The trade enabled some nations to conquer others and to reign supreme in the trade for a time, but in the end, all tribes lost to European settlers. Trade with the French, Dutch, and Russians brought disaster to the tribes, just as it would to those that dealt with the English.

Selected Readings and Bibliography

Several volumes deal with Native American interactions with the French, Dutch, and Russians, including McNickle's *They Came Here First*, Gibson's *The American Indian*, Wise's *The Red Man in the New World Drama*, and Billington's *Westward Expansion*. However, *Native Time* by Francis offers an excellent comparative work. Trigger's *The Children of Aataentisic* is strong on the Wyandot trade. Brandon's *Indians*, and Spicer's *Cycles of Conquest* are helpful sources for the study of native relations with early Europeans.

Axtell, James. *The Invasion Within: The Contest of Cultures in Colonial North America*. New York: Oxford University Press, 1985.

Bancroft, Hubert H. *History of Alaska, 1730–1885*. New York: Arno Press, 1967.

Broadhead, John R. *History of the State of New York.* Volume 1. New York: Harper & Brothers, 1853.

Caldwell, Norman W. *The French in the Mississippi Valley, 1740–1750.* Philadelphia: Porcupine Press, 1974.

Chance, Norman A. *The Eskimo of North Alaska.* Volume 1. New York: Harper & Brothers, 1853.

Clarke, I. Wood. *The Bloody Mohawk.* New York: Macmillan, 1940.

Colden, Cadwallader. *The History of the Five Indian Nations of Canada.* New York: A. S. Barnes, 1904.

Debo, Angie. *A History of the Indians of the United States.* Norman: University of Oklahoma Press, 1970.

Dickason, Olive Patricia. *Canada's First Nations: A History of Founding Peoples from Earliest Times.* Norman: University of Oklahoma Press, 1992.

Eccles, William J. *The Canadian Frontier, 1534–1760.* New York: Holt, Rinehart and Winston, 1969.

——. *France in America.* New York: Harper and Row, 1972.

Edmunds, R. David, and Joseph L. Peyser. *The Fox Wars: The Mesquakie Challenge to New France.* Norman: University of Oklahoma Press, 1993.

Ennis, Harold, A. *The Fur Trade in Canada.* Toronto: University of Toronto Press, 1956.

Fisher, Raymond H. *The Russian Fur Trade, 1500–1700.* Berkeley: University of California Press, 1943.

Gibson, Charles, and Howard Peckham, eds. *Attitudes of the Colonial Powers towards the American Indians.* Salt Lake City: University of Utah Press, 1966.

Gibson, James R. *Imperial Russia in Frontier America.* New York: Oxford University Press, 1976.

Gubser, Nicholas J. *The Nunamiut Eskimos: Hunters of Caribou.* New Haven: Yale University Press, 1965.

Hagan, William T. *The Sac and Fox Indians.* Norman: University of Oklahoma Press, 1958.

Hulley, Clarence C. *Alaska, 1741–1953.* Portland, Ore.: Binfords & Mort, 1953.

Hunt, George T. *The Wars of the Iroquois: A Study in Intertribal Trade Relations.* Madison: University of Wisconsin Press, 1940.

Jaenen, Cornelius J. *Friend and Foe: Aspects of French-Amerindian Cultural Contact in the Sixteenth and Seventeenth Centuries.* New York: Columbia University Press, 1976.

Kenney, Alice P. *Stubborn for Liberty: The Dutch in New York.* Syracuse, N.Y.: Syracuse University Press.

Kessler, Henry H., and Eugene Rachlis. *Peter Stuyvesant and His New York.* New York: Random House, 1959.

Krause, Aurel. *The Tlingit Indians.* Seattle: University of Washington Press, 1956.

Lain, B. D. "The Decline of Russian America's Colonial Society." *Western Historical Quarterly* 7 (April 1976): 143–153.

O'Callaghan, Edmund B. *History of New Netherland.* 2 volumes. New York: D. Appleton, 1855.

Okun, Semen B. *The Russian-American Company.* Cambridge, Mass.: Harvard University Press, 1951.

Phillips, Paul C., and J. W. Smurr. *The Fur Trade.* 2 volumes. Norman: University of Oklahoma Press, 1951.

Sauer, Carl O. *Sixteenth Century North America: The Land and the People as Seen by Europeans.* Berkeley: Turtle Island, 1980.

Sioui, Georges. *The Wyandot Civilization.* Vancouver: British Columbia University Press, 1999.

Spicer, Edward H. *A Short History of the Indians of the United States.* New York: D. Van Nostrand, 1969.

Tompkins, Stuart R. *Alaska: Promyshlennik and Sourdough.* Norman: University of Oklahoma Press, 1945.

Tooker, Elisabeth. *An Ethnography of the Huron Indians, 1615–1649.* Syracuse: Syracuse University Press, 1991.

Trelease, Allen W. "Indian-White Contacts in Eastern North America: The Dutch in New Netherlands." *Ethnohistory* 9 (1962): 137–146.

——. "The Iroquois and the Western Fur Trade: A Problem in Interpretation." *Mississippi Valley Historical Review* 49 (1962): 32–51.

CHAPTER 4

AMERICAN INDIANS AND ENGLISH RESETTLEMENT

By the late sixteenth century, numerous Native Americans living on the Atlantic coast of North America had dealt with English sailors, traders, and fishermen. English pirates had sailed the Atlantic Ocean and Caribbean Sea, reaping rich profits from Spanish galleons. English traders and fishermen had also garnered profits along the Atlantic Coast and popularized the region through their writings and storytelling. European sailors had spread numerous diseases among the tribes of the Atlantic Seaboard, wiping out entire tribes and villages. Even before Europeans resettled Native Americans' lands and claimed them as their own, lethal diseases had depopulated Native American peoples. The crown and capitalists in England were acutely aware of the vast wealth Spain had taken from Indians in Mexico and Peru during the sixteenth century, and English businessmen were eager to take their share through colonialism in America. Hatred of Catholic Spaniards also encouraged English Protestants to plant a colony in North America to check the religious, social, economic, and cultural expansion of the Spanish Empire.

ROANOKE AND JAMESTOWN

Between 1584 and 1587, Sir Walter Raleigh established the first English colony on Roanoke Island, but the experiment resulted in failure when all the English men, women, and children disappeared and became the famed Lost Colony of Roanoke. Native Americans living near the coasts of present-day Virginia and North Carolina had their first experience with English colonists at Roanoke, but they would not fully understand the meaning of English resettlement for twenty years. In 1606, King James I issued the royal charter granting the Virginia Company the right to colonize Virginia. England claimed the vast region of the Chesapeake Bay by discovery, although no Native American group in the area would have recognized such a claim. Still, Chief Wahunsonacock (referred to in documents as Powhatan) of the Pamunkey tribe warmly welcomed the English in 1607 near the mouth of the James River, where the Europeans established James Fort. Powhatan (meaning "Falls of the River," the village where the chief lived) was born in 1550 and rose to become the head of a great Indian confederacy in the Chesapeake Bay.

Chief Powhatan was an Algonquian-speaking leader who held sway over two hundred towns and villages, encompassing a territory from the Tidewater to the Potomac River. Powhatan and his people lived in numerous towns filled with homes made of mats, poles, and bark. Powhatan's people enjoyed a rich woodland culture based largely on agriculture. Native Americans in the region cultivated the earth, farming corn, squash, beans, melons, sunflowers, and tobacco. Indians harvested the rivers, streams, and sea for many varieties of fish, oysters, clams, mussels, lobsters, and crabs. In the dense green forests near their homelands, Indians cleared hunting grounds, where they took deer, bear, buffalo, rabbit, squirrel, turkey, duck, geese, and other animals. The people had their own religion, rituals, and ceremonies, which were based on oral traditions handed down from generation to generation. They educated their young people through oral narratives, expecting children to memorize lessons and repeat them out loud. Each winter native teachers spent hours sharing tribal information about history, literature, art, medicine, music, agriculture, warfare, political science, sociology, economics, and religion. Like other Native Americans, the Pamunkey and their neighbors believed in the sacredness of the earth, plants, and animals. They believed that animate and inanimate objects have a spirit that ties people to place and the creative power. The Creator, Supreme Being, or Master of Life had set the world into motion with positive and negative forces that made life what it had been at the time of creation and what it continued to be at the time of first contact. In sum, these Native Americans had their own cultures, societies, and civilization.

English colonists at Jamestown came to Virginia with preconceived notions about Native Americans as "the other." Before meeting American Indians, many Europeans viewed native peoples as savage barbarians who were uncivilized children of Satan. Many Europeans believed that Native Americans were inferior, uncultured, unchristian–just like Africans, Asians, and other peoples of color. English colonists had firsthand experience perceiving Scots, Irish, and others as backward barbarians, and they applied this racial view to Native Americans. From past accounts provided by explorers and colonists, whites created a negative mental image of native people. And after Europeans arrived, they confirmed their racial views of Native Americans by observing native ceremonies, rituals, languages, music, customs, habits, housing, dance, and dress. At best, Europeans viewed Native Americans as noble savages and at worst as expendable dirty savages, counterimages of Christ.

Initially, the English recorded that Native Americans farmed large gardens and made a good portion of their living from agriculture. However, within a short time after arriving in America, English colonists argued that Indians made their livelihood primarily from hunting, fishing, and gathering: economic pursuits they could perform in the interior forests and mountains far from English settlements. English colonists soon expected Native Americans to move from their homes, farms, and hunting grounds. In this way, English settlers could resettle Indian lands and exploit the earth for material gain. The English argued that the earth was "virgin land" that primitive savages had hardly used and certainly had not made profitable. The English offered progress and economic opportunity through productive agriculture that would yield capital and stimulate a greater market.

Native Americans farmed and made economic use of the earth, but their relationship to the earth also involved a spiritual element that seventeenth-century European Christians did not understand. Several native ceremonies centered around agriculture, including planting, mid-season, and harvesting ceremonies. In addition, Native Americans in the East held ceremonies that featured drumming, dancing, and singing during the night by the light of fires. They used strange languages, which whites considered inferior and degrading. Native Americans sang of the sun, moon, sky, trees, wind, waters, and other wonders of the earth, raising their voices in thanksgiving and praise for many elements all around them. Europeans likened such beliefs to witchcraft and devil worship, often referring to Native Americans as red devils and Satan's children. In leather leggings and dresses, exposing unmentionable body parts, native people danced in "grotesque" manners unknown to the disapproving English.

Whites particularly loathed native medicine men and women, holy people who called on spiritual and medicinal means to direct their positive and negative powers. Christian Europeans denigrated Native American religion, art, music, dance, ritual, and ceremony, stereotyping them as savage. Whites portrayed American Indians as animals, not humans. Such negative perceptions created a dangerous climate for native peoples, because the English newcomers determined from the outset that they were superior lords and masters, the children of Christ, and that they had an obligation to destroy that which was evil and primitive. It was also to their economic advantage to kill Indians and displace them. Early on the English determined that Native Americans were obstacles to God's plan and Christ's gospel. And in such a climate as this, it was easier for English colonists to justify killing Native American men, women, and children while destroying native cultures. American Indians lived in jeopardy not only because they controlled land and resources desired by whites, but also because Europeans viewed them as dispensable beings who stood in the way of Christ, civilization, and economic progress.

During his explorations up the James River, Captain Christopher Newport wrote that he thought he would find vicious native people "naturally given to treachery" but instead found the Indians to be "a most kind and loving people." Although the English landed in Virginia in May 1607, they did not cut wood, build homes, or set up foods for the upcoming winter and spring. Instead, the English collected iron pyrite, believing it was gold. When winter came, the white men suffered a starving time, losing 58 of the 104 settlers by September 1607. More died of starvation and exposure during the early winter of 1607. George Percy, one of the colonists, wrote that "Our food was but a small can of barley, sodden in water, to five men a day. Our drink, cold water taken out of the river; which was at flood very salty; at low tide full of slime and filth." They lived on "the bare cold ground" until January 1608, when "God . . . put a terror in the savages' hearts" and directed these "wild and cruel pagans" and "our mortal enemies, to relieve us with victuals, as bread, corn, fish, and flesh in great plenty." Percy grudgingly noted that actions of the Pamunkeys were "the setting up of our feeble men; otherwise we had all perished." If Powhatan had not sent his people to help the English, the first permanent English settlement would have failed.

POWHATAN AND PAMUNKEYS

The English paid the Pamunkeys and their neighbors for their generosity in 1608 by taking a military stance against the Indians. Captain John Smith, a soldier who had fought "infidel" Turks, advocated a military solution to the so-called Indian problem, not the peaceful solution portrayed in Disney's *Pocahontas*. Smith's Indian policies encouraged many Pamunkeys and other Indians to keep their distance from Jamestown. In 1608 and 1609, Englishmen tried to force Native Americans to abandon their homes, gardens, and hunting grounds that were located near Jamestown by burning Indian crops and villages, destroying native fishing weirs and canoes, and generally keeping Native Americans at bay. Powhatan remarked succinctly in a speech to John Smith "that you are come to destroy my Country, so much affrighteth all my people as they dare not visit you." Powhatan responded to English attacks and determined to allow the English to starve, saying that he would not trade with the colonists or give them free corn. His people watched in horror as the English ate horses, dogs, cats, and mice. Some Englishmen "dug up the corpse of their own fallen fellows and ate them." One man "murdered his wife, ripped the baby out of her womb and threw it into the river, and after chopped the other in pieces and salted her for food." The Pamunkeys probably viewed the English as barbarians and believed that the colony would fail. Famine, disease, and exposure injured the colony, and its population dropped from roughly five hundred to sixty. However, in 1610, relief ships saved the colony, but its population did not grow steadily until the 1640s, when the white population in Virginia increased rapidly due to the growth of tobacco as a cash crop and English adaptation to Virginia. From 1609 until his death in 1618, Powhatan pressured the English with attacks and counterattacks in a general border conflict. Powhatan recognized that the English intended to take his lands, but he never launched a major offensive to extinguish the English colony. As early as 1609, Powhatan noted that the English posed a threat to Native American security and land, asking, "Why will you take by force what you may have quickly by love? Why will you destroy us who supply you with food? What can you get by war?" He mused that the English had only to ask, and his people would "give you what you ask, if you come in a friendly manner, and not with swords and guns."

In 1612, the English kidnapped Powhatan's seventeen-year-old daughter, Pocahontas, and two years later she married John Rolfe–not John Smith. Pocahontas had worked as a mediator between native and foreign peoples, but she ultimately supported English colonization. In 1617, Pocahontas died in England of a European disease while attempting to promote the Virginia Company. Her death strained the tenuous relationship between the tribes of the Chesapeake Bay and English settlers, and it is discussed thoroughly in Helen Roundtree's *Pocahontas's People*. The death of Pocahontas was certainly important to Indian and white relations in Virginia, but probably not as important as English expansion onto Indian lands away from Jamestown in order to clear lands for tobacco production. When Columbus returned to Spain from his first voyage, he introduced the first *tabacos*. In the 1580s, Sir Walter Raleigh popularized smoking, but "the barbarous and beastly manners of wild, godless, and slavish Indians" did not spread widely until 1612, when Pocahontas's husband, John Rolfe, developed a strain of tobacco that was "strong, sweet and pleasant as any under the sun."

In the southern colonies, tobacco provided a cash crop and rapidly accelerated large-scale agricultural production, which required new land and labor force. This was particularly true of colonial Virginia, which continually expanded its claim to western lands for the benefit of white growers. Englishmen stole American Indian lands for their tobacco plantations and used African slaves to develop their crops. In the South, an acre of ground produced approximately five hundred pounds of tobacco, which sold in England for £125. However, tobacco exhausted the soil within five to seven years, so English farmers expanded rapidly into the interior to extend their tobacco farming. This led to greater expansion, usually up the river system to the fall lines, so that white farmers could transport their crops to the ocean and export them. While the English prospered from tobacco, Native Americans suffered from white contact as a result of disease, war, the loss of thousands of acres, and forced removal.

Expansion of the tobacco culture onto Native American lands also increased and expanded African slavery. Originally the Spanish, Dutch, Portuguese, and English used Native Americans as slaves, but the Spanish and others forced Africans into slavery during the sixteenth century. Englishmen in Virginia began the African slave trade in the seventeenth century because of their demand for labor to work tobacco fields. Over the years many Africans formed friendly and familial relationships with Native Americans, particularly among the southern tribes. Today, many African-Americans have Native American blood from their family relations in the eastern part of the United States as well as in Kansas, Oklahoma, Missouri, and Arkansas. Tobacco—and later cotton—was a bane to Africans and Indians alike, because it increased the African slave population while destroying the native population and landed estates of native peoples. In 1608, approximately thirty thousand Indians lived in the Chesapeake Bay, but by 1669 about two thousand remained. Pamunkeys and their neighbors became strangers in a stolen land, but not without a fight.

OPECHANCANOUGH AND VIRGINIA

Opechancanough, Powhatan's brother and a Renapé leader, became head of the Powhatan Confederation in 1618. Although he had once been John Smith's friend, he turned against the English because of their exploitation of native peoples and lands. After Powhatan's death, Opechancanough planned to destroy the English colonists, who were expanding their tobacco farms and forcing native children into schools run by Anglican missionaries. In a surprise attack in 1622, Opechancanough's men swept through the English colony, killing about one-third of the white population (350 people) on the first day of the war and laying waste to farms, towns. and granaries. The colonists fought back to "root out" Native Americans "from being any longer a people." John Smith was absent when Opechancanough attacked but wrote that the Indian war "will be good for the Plantation, because now we have just cause to destroy them by all meanes possible." Another Englishman wrote that the colonists were "now set at liberty by the treacherous violence of the Sauvages. . . . So that we, who hitherto have had possession of no more ground than their waste . . . may now by right of Warre, and law of Nations, invade the Country, and destroy them who sought to destroy us: whereby wee shall enjoy their cultivated places, turning the laborious Mattocke into the victorious sword."

The attack provided colonists with a justification to launch a major and prolonged campaign against the Indians. It permitted colonists to proclaim that they were executing a "just war" that allowed them to enslave Indians and take land. During the conflict in 1622 and afterward, Virginians claimed Native American lands by right of conquest, particularly land previously cleared by Indians for farms and hunting grounds, "whereas heretofore the grubing of woods was the greatest labour." In response to the Indian attack in 1622, the English launched a scorched-earth campaign against Native Americans, attacking them "by force, by surprize, by famine in burning their Corne, by destroying and burning their Boats, Canoes, and Houses, by breaking their fishing Weares, by assailing them in their huntings, whereby they get the greatest part of their sustenance in Winter, by pursuing and chasing them with our horses, and blood-hounds to draw after them, and Mastives to tear them." By every means possible, whites sought to force Native Americans from their lands and their very existence on earth. In many areas, the war became one of extermination.

Between 1622 and 1644, the English moved aggressively against Native Americans, driving them from their homes and pushing them into the interior. They justified their continued attacks, arguing that they were clearing the land of Satan's heathens to make way for God's productive people. Rather than live oppressed, Opechancanough launched another attack on the colonists, killing about five hundred. The English fought back again, killing approximately one thousand Indians. The bloody conflict continued for two years until Indians and English negotiated a peace treaty establishing boundaries between the two people and Indian "reservations." The Indians agreed to serve as scouts for the Virginia militia and to pay an annual tribute in furs. For thirty years the Indians watched as the English expanded onto new farm lands, territory claimed by Native Americans. When the Susquehannas, Shawnees, and other tribes fought back, the English retaliated against all Indians, including those who had once been a part of Powhatan's confederacy. In 1715, the colonial government forcibly removed the remaining Indians from the Chesapeake Bay, relocating them to southwestern Virginia. By this time, Virginia had lost over 75 percent of its native population.

English invasions of other Native Americans in the southern colonies had similar patterns and results. The Yamasee and Tuscarora of the Carolinas and Georgia originally allied with colonists, hunting deer for hides and stealing captives for slaves from among each other as well as from the Cherokee, Catawba, Muscogee (Creek), Okanichi, Euchees, Timuca, Apalachee, and others. Some Indians willingly worked with white traders, but whites forced others to work. White traders exploited many Indians, including their allies, cheated them, addicted them to alcohol, stole their lands, and raped women and children. Yamasee, Tuscarora, Catawba, and other Indians rose in wars against the English, striking severe blows to colonial traders and settlers, but, like Opechancanough, they were unable to defeat the English. As a result of these conflicts, some Tuscarora moved north to New York to join the five Iroquois nations. The Muscogee, Cherokee, Choctaw, and Chickasaw remained independent of English rule, although they were influenced by English, Spanish, and French traders throughout most of the eighteenth century.

The decline of the native population as a result of white contact in the South also occurred in the North. By the time the Pilgrims landed, Indians of the North Atlantic had experienced "firesticks" and plague brought by white traders. Many tribes had been decimated by European diseases, including a deadly epidemic in 1616–1619. The population of New England natives declined from between seventy thousand and ninety thousand in 1600 to about twenty-five thousand in 1620, when Pilgrims first landed. Like the Virginians, Pilgrims came to America with preconceived notions that affected their relations with Indians.

PILGRIMS, WAMPANOAGS, AND MASSACHUSETTS

Before leaving the *Mayflower*, the Pilgrim men signed a pact among themselves to obey majority will (not including women or children). According to the Mayflower Compact, the men, women, and children who had separated from the Church of England had set out "for the Glory of God, and Advancement of the Christian Faith . . . to plant the first colony in the northern Parts of Virginia." From the *Mayflower*, William Bradford, leader of the Pilgrims, wrote "what could they see [from the *Mayflower's* deck] but a hideous and desolate wilderness, full of wild beasts and wild men." From the outset, Pilgrims viewed the land as a foreboding, dangerous place and the people of northern Virginia (present-day Massachusetts) as wild beasts who had to be tamed by "civilized" Christians. Wampanoag people chose to maintain relatively friendly relations with whites. However, Miles Standish, a professional soldier with the group, feared Indians, and Bradford likely offered the feelings of many when he wrote that whites were in "continual danger of the savage people, who are cruel, barbarous, and most treacherous."

On November 11, 1620, a party of Pilgrims went ashore at Cape Cod, and four days later they saw five or six Indians–Pamet or Nauset–and a dog walking along the beach. These Native Americans ran into the forest so that the Pilgrims did not meet them, but the white men found a hill near present-day Truro (Corn Hill) where the Pilgrims found and took baskets of corn. The Pilgrims returned some days later to take more corn, but they did not want to establish their colony on Cape Cod. Using a map made by John Smith in 1614, the Pilgrims sailed to a place marked

"Plymouth" but known to Algonquian-speaking Indians as Patuxet, a village stricken in 1617 by disease that killed the inhabitants. The white men landed on Plymouth Rock on December 11, 1620 (December 21 according to the Gregorian calendar).

The Pilgrims began the resettlement of Patuxet on Christmas Day 1620, although they were plagued by the "General Sickness" that killed many settlers. They eked out a living in the huts until March 16, 1621, when they met a remarkable man. Sentries prevented him from entering the Common House, so from the doorway the man said, "Welcome." He announced that his name was Samoset, an Abnaki, visiting from the Pemaquid band in Maine. He had learned English while sailing on trading vessels along Newfoundland. He told Pilgrims stories long into the evening, telling them that a Wampanoag chief named Ousamequin (Yellow Feather) was the most important leader in the region. He was also known as Massasoit (Big Chief) because of his stature among the tribes. Samoset introduced the Pilgrims to many things, including the fur trade, which became a major source of capital for the Separatist Pilgrims, people who had separated from the Church of England. He also introduced them to Tisquantum or Squanto, a Patuxet Wampanoag who spoke English. Squanto's Patuxet people had once inhabited Plymouth. He had been kidnapped in 1614, survived enslavement, life with Spanish friars, life aboard an English trading vessel, and reentry into native society. The meeting of the Pilgrims with Squanto was critical for the whites, because in Squanto they found a friend who helped them until his death in 1622. He taught them how and where to hunt, fish, and plant. He taught them to make maple syrup and use medicinal plants. He arranged a peace agreement between the Pilgrims and Massasoit and other Indians and acted as a mediator many times because he spoke Algonquian and English. Bradford wrote that Squanto was "a special instrument sent of God for their good beyond their expectation."

Like the Virginians, Pilgrims at Plymouth suffered a starving time, but in the spring of 1621, the Separatists worked hard to till the soil, fish, hunt, and preserve foods for winter. They traded for furs with Massachusetts and other tribes, and found much for which to give thanks. In October, Bradford asked Squanto to invite Massasoit to a thanksgiving feast and dispatched four men to shoot ducks, geese, and turkeys. The Pilgrims also provided venison, corn, corn bread, eel, lobster, plums, berries, and wine. Even with this horn of plenty, Pilgrims were not prepared to feed over ninety Indians whom Massasoit brought to the dinner. Sensing that his hosts were not prepared to feed so many, Massasoit sent hunters into the forest, and they returned with deer. The Wampanoag enjoyed the festivities so much that they remained at Plymouth three days. No doubt they appreciated the gesture, but Native Americans in Massachusetts and throughout the Americas had celebrated thanksgiving ceremonies prior to 1621. This thanksgiving held special significance for

Pilgrims who had survived in spite of death and hardship. Unknown to Wampanoags, the feast was the beginning of a destructive era for Native Americans, and the event would become a symbol of European duplicity that many Native Americans have never forgotten.

Pilgrims maintained good relations with Wampanoag, Pamet, Nauset, Massachusetts, Narragansetts, and other Indians of Massachusetts Bay, although the colonists feared that the Indians might rise up in a war like that led by Opechancanough in Virginia. Massasoit used the white men as allies, maintaining relatively positive relations with the Pilgrims to counter the influence of the Pequots and Narragansetts. The Indians did not attack the Pilgrims, but the colonists attacked a few Indians whom they claimed had plotted against whites. Standish and nine men found seven Massachusetts Indians at Wessagusset and stabbed six of them to death and hanged another, a medicine man named Wituwamat. Standish cut off Wituwamat's head and placed it on a pole at the top of Fort Plymouth. Standish made an example of these Massachusetts people, hoping to frighten other Indians into submission with his ruthless killings. However, the incident did little except earn whites the title *wotowquenage* (stabbers), a term used widely to identify all whites. Standish's murders encouraged Native Americans to resist white expansion, a feat the Indians accomplished until 1630, when fifteen hundred Puritans arrived.

PURITANS AND NATIVE AMERICANS

Unlike Pilgrims and Virginians, Puritans never had a starving time, and their colony succeeded from the outset. Whereas Puritan presence contributed to the decline of the native population in Massachusetts, the Puritan population increased rapidly, so that in 1640, a total of twenty-five thousand Puritans lived in New England and outnumbered all the Indians in the region. The Puritan population increased rapidly during subsequent decades, an indication, in Puritan minds, that God was watching over His people and increasing their numbers while simultaneously destroying the native population. In Puritan theology, God took care of His chosen people and used His wrath against the children of Satan. This theology included a covenant whereby Puritans joined hands with each other and excluded outsiders in large part because Puritans believed themselves to be on a mission from God. Under the leadership of John Winthrop, the Puritans set out to create a "City Upon the Hill." Puritans wanted to purify the Church of England by removing themselves from England to a place where they could set up a just and righteous society.

Like Christ's example, Puritans sought to establish a colony that would serve as a beacon to Christians everywhere. In order to set up this pure society, Puritans formed a covenant with each other, and as a group, with God. They had a sacred bond with each other and the Almighty to form a holy society. Covenant theology segregated people into those who were "in" and those who were "out." Although Puritans professed that a primary goal of their colony was to Christianize Indians and destroy Satan among them, they made little effort to include Indians in their world, because natives were positioned outside the body of God and squarely within that of the devil. Although most Puritans conceded that Indians could achieve salvation, they could do so only after years of training in Christian beliefs, the Bible, and English civilization.

Most Puritans believed that it was not likely that many Indians would ever be considered part of the "elect," that select group of people who would receive God's grace in this world and the next. The vast majority of Indians were outside the covenant and always would be. In the Puritan mind, evidence that Indians were Satan's children abounded, because native people knew nothing of Christ or the Christian religion, and Puritans said natives worshipped in a manner similar to that of witches and warlocks. Indian medicine people claimed to communicate with plants, animals, and invisible spirits. They met around fires in all-night ceremonies with dancing, singing, and offerings of tobacco that seemed satanic to Christians. Puritans claimed superiority over Indians, including their leaders, offering as proof the fact that whites died from disease far less frequently than did native peoples. In 1633–1634, smallpox ravaged New England, killing thousands of Indians but few French, English, or Dutch. One writer stated "without this remarkable and terrible stroke of God upon the natives, [we] would with much more difficulty have found room, and at far greater charge have obtained and purchased land." According to Winthrop, the Indians were also inferior because "they inclose noe Land, neither have any setled habytation, nor any tame Cattle to improve the Land by, and soe have noe other but a Naturall Right to those Countries, soe as if we leave them sufficient for their use, we may lawfully take the rest." Winthrop's statements ignored the fact that Indians farmed, lived in towns, and improved the land. Winthrop lied to justify theft.

Winthrop and the Puritan oligarchy believed that God had a right to all lands, and because Puritans were God's own agents on earth, they had a right to all native lands, "there being more than enough for them and us." Puritans purchased some Indian lands, including those not technically "belonging" to a particular tribe. Puritans also gained land by arresting Indians for offenses, trying and convicting them before magistrates, and fining them in land that whites desired—whether the land belonged to those Indians or not. In many ways, Puritans encouraged Native Americans to leave their homelands and seek new homes in the thick inland forests far from Boston, Salem,

Quincy, Marshfield, Gloucester, Exeter, Portsmouth, and other towns. In this way, Puritans physically forced natives outside their communities, and most Puritans agreed with this policy, but not all. Reverend Roger Williams wrote that "King James has no more right to give away or sell Massasoit's lands and cut and carve his country, than Massasoit has to sell King James' kingdom." But other ministers pointed out that Indians were not part of God's covenant and had no right to the land, because they had been "decoyed" to America by Satan "in hopes that the gospel of the Lord Jesus Christ would never come here to destroy or disturb his absolute empire of them." In 1643, the General Court—the legislative branch of Massachusetts—arrogantly recognized the right of natives to fish and hunt on unused areas of lands ceded to whites, but this right would soon vanish because American Indians were "the accursed seed of Canaan," and it became a Christian duty to "exterminate" haughty natives who opposed English rule.

WHITE WAR AGAINST PEQUOTS

Certainly the Puritans considered the defiant Pequot tribe of the Connecticut River Valley to be Satan's children and outside the covenant. Pequots had little interest in joining hands with Puritans, because they were an independent, sovereign people who distrusted the English. Other Algonquian Indians considered Pequots to be "Killers of Men" because of their aggressive fighting abilities. The Indians of New England were not unified in their approaches to English settlers. Each group was sovereign, independently deciding for itself how to deal with whites. And among themselves, they were often divided, fighting against each other. Most of the tribes disliked the Pequots, so when whites settled on an aggressive policy against the Connecticut peoples, other Indians either remained neutral or joined in the conflict against the Pequots. This was the case with Mohicans and Narragansetts who joined the white men. The Wampanoags remained fairly neutral.

Pequots often attacked white traders, and in 1634, a band of Indians (probably Narragansetts) killed nine slave traders under John Stone. Massachusetts's General Court used the killings to claim jurisdiction over the Pequot and sent John Endicott to negotiate with the tribe. Some Pequots agreed to surrender the killers and pay retribution in the form of forty beaver pelts, thirty otter furs, about one thousand feet of wampum, and a large tract of Connecticut. These Indians probably made this agreement in order to be rid of Endicott. For two years the Pequots refused to fulfill the terms of the agreement, but their delay fueled the passions of whites to punish the Pequots. In 1636, Indians (probably Narragansetts) attacked another group of traders and killed one white man. In reaction, on May 1, 1637, the General Court declared war on the Pequots and attacked them.

The Pequots retaliated, killing thirty whites and taking women and children captive. Sassacus, the foremost Pequot leader and war chief, led one group of Pequots, retreating to a palisade Indian fort on the Mystic River. On May 26, 1637, a combined force of five hundred Narragansett, seventy Mohigan under Uncas–a rival of Sassacus–and 180 Puritans/Pilgrims moved swiftly through the forest and surprised the Pequots at Mystic Fort. Whites and Indians alike attacked the native fort, setting fire to it and slaying men, women, and children as they fled the flames. Puritan minister Cotton Mather later wrote that "in little more than one hour, five or six hundred of these barbarians were dismissed from a world that was burdened with them." John Mason, Puritan commander of the troops, wrote that God made the Indians "a fiery oven" and "judged among the heathen, filling the place with dead bodies." John Underhill, second in command, wrote that "Many courageous fellows were unwilling to come out, and fought most desperately through the palisades, so they were scorched and burnt." Bradford was not present, but wrote that "It was a fearful sight to see them thus frying in the fire and the streams of blood quenching the same, and horrible was the stink thereof. But the victory seemed a sweet sacrifice, and they gave praise thereof to God, who had wrought so wonderfully for them, thus to enclose their enemies in their hands and give them so speedy a victory over so proud and insulting an enemy."

Underhill reported that many Pequots "were burnt in the fort–men, women, and children. Others forced out . . . twenty and thirty at a time, which our soldiers received and entertained with the point of the sword. Down fell men, women, and children." The earth was red with blood, and "many souls lie gasping on the ground, so thick, in some places, that you could hardly pass along." Narragansetts, longtime enemies of the Pequots, were so sickened by the savage attack that they left the field of battle. But some Puritans and Pilgrims likened their annihilation of the Pequots to David's wars as found in the first book of Samuel. Underhill wrote that "Sometimes the Scriptures declareth women and children must perish with their parents," but he was little concerned about killing noncombatants because the English had "sufficient light from the Word of God for our proceedings." In an hour, pious Christian soldiers and their allies nearly exterminated one group of Pequot people. Some people survived and escaped, but when Puritans captured Pequot survivors, they sold them into slavery or trolled with them in Massachusetts Bay, feeding them to the sharks. Some of the Pequots, including Sassacus, fled and lived with Mohawks and other tribes, but in one morning, Puritans crushed one of the most hostile and populous tribes in New England.

FORCED REMOVAL AND PURITAN RESERVATIONS

Native Americans throughout the region watched as Puritans consolidated their power in the years following the Pequot War. In 1638, the Puritans began a vigorous campaign to consolidate Indians onto "reservations" where they could be controlled, Christianized, and "civilized." Native leaders resisted white attempts to control their people, but among them, they had no unified policy to match that of the Puritans. Reverend John Eliot, pastor at Roxbury, missioned to Native Americans, whom he considered to be "the dregs of mankind" and people "so stupid and senseless" that they could be dealt with only in isolation on reservations. He and other paternal Puritans wished "to move Indians from the power of darknesse and the kindom [sic] of Satan, to the knowledge of the true and only God." The Puritans established their first of fourteen "plantations" or reservations of twelve hundred acres among the Quinnipiac tribe in present-day New Haven, Connecticut. The General Court appointed an English magistrate or Indian agent (usually a minister) to manage the "praying Indians," who were expected to accept Christianity, the only religion permitted on the reservation. Puritans forced Quinnipiac people to remain on the reservation and to seek permission of the magistrate to leave.

Puritan magistrates prohibited non-Quinnipiac Indians from entering Quinnipiac country so that they could not stir up trouble. Puritans also prohibited Indians from owning guns, lead, powder, or flints—even for hunting. And although Puritans drank beer and other spirits, they prohibited American Indians from drinking alcohol. Puritans also stripped reservation Indians of elements of their self-determination and sovereignty. Puritans did not permit Native Americans to openly practice self-rule, although Quinnipiacs and other Native Americans in New England did not surrender every aspect of traditional government or obey the Puritan laws. Initially, Puritans would not recognize the right of native peoples on the reservation to sell any portion of their land, but after 1652, the General Court permitted reservations to be divided into individual parcels called allotments to facilitate the "civilization" of the people. During the 1650s, Puritans created an Indian court system on the reservations, with Native American juries but Puritan judges. To coordinate the removal, relocation, and management of the new bureaucracy, the General Court appointed Daniel Gookin the first superintendent of Indian affairs for Massachusetts in 1656. All these policies foreshadowed forced removal to the reservation system adopted by the Office of Indian Affairs in the United States during the nineteenth century, the seeds of which were largely Puritan.

Relocation of Native Americans in New England onto reservations did not go unchallenged. Over the years several native groups in New England defied Puritan rule, refusing to become "praying Indians," but the most noteworthy leader to challenge Puritan policies was Massasoit's son, Metacom or King Philip. He led a protest against corralling, consolidating, and Christianizing Indians. He opposed the Puritan reservation system, claiming that whites initiated the system to control Indians and to steal more native land. He visited Indians throughout the region, including those living on reservations, and encouraged them to resist. Puritan officials arrested Metacom, fined him, and ordered him not to speak out against Puritans or their reservation system. When he was released, Metacom increased his protests and organized a federation primarily of Wampanoag, Nipmuck, Abnaki, and Massachusetts. He informed Native Americans that whites were not interested in Christianizing Indians. Rather, they were interested in stealing Indian lands, as evidenced by Puritans reducing the total number of reservations and consolidating several tribes onto fewer reservations. According to Pequot William Apess, Metacom traveled about in 1675, telling Native Americans throughout New England to rise up against whites because of the danger whites posed to native security.

> Brothers, these people from the unknown world will cut down our groves, spoil our hunting and planting grounds, and drive us and our children from the graves of our fathers, and our council fires, and enslave our women and children.

In June 1675, a white man shot an Indian for allegedly trespassing, and King Philip's War began. The General Court declared war on the Indians and reduced the number of reservations from fourteen to five, forcibly removing families and consolidating them onto smaller parcels of land. Puritans impressed native soldiers into service and forced them to work as scouts against other Indians. In the meantime, Metacom attacked Dartmouth, Taunton, Middleborough, and Scituate. Indians rallied against the Puritans to such an extent that Puritans rounded up and removed "praying Indians," set fire to their homes and fields, and executed some of them on mere suspicion. Then the Puritan armies systematically attacked Indian towns, butchering hundreds of men, women, and children—including Puritan allies like Narragansetts. In one battle, Puritans killed six hundred Indians and captured four hundred more, who were executed or sold into slavery. Metacom retaliated with vigor. In the summer of 1676, Captain Benjamin Church captured Metacom's wife and son and killed other members of his family near Sowams, Rhode Island, at Massasoit's old home. Caleb Cook and a praying Indian named Alderman set a trap for Metacom, and Alderman shot and killed Metacom during an ambush. Puritans left the body to be eaten by wolves but cut off Metacom's head and hands. They sent the hands to Boston to be displayed as trophies and placed the head on a pole at Plymouth, where it remained for twenty years.

Native Americans in New England resisted white rule, and some fought for their lands, cultures, and families. Some survivors moved away, whereas others remained to reorganize and assert themselves in the centuries ahead. Puritans and Pilgrims did significant harm to the first peoples of New England, but they did not exterminate them. However, Puritan policies toward Native Americans after 1640 are extremely important for the course of native history. Equally important was the fact that traditional tensions and divisions among the autonomous groups of native people in New England made it easier for whites to divide and conquer Indians, forcing some to remove to reservations or remote areas while encouraging others to leave the region forever. Conflicts between Indian people prior to white settlement aided whites in their conquest, and this pattern of intertribal and intratribal division was to emerge often in native history as whites expanded deeper into Indian country.

Selected Readings and Bibliography

Jennings offers an insightful interpretation of English colonization in *The Invasion of America*, and Nash's *Red, White and Black* provides a scholarly study that reveals racist views by English colonists. Also, Brandon's *Indians* is a useful volume for a study of early native/European relations during the colonial era.

Andrews, Matthew P. *The Founding of Maryland.* Baltimore: Williams & Wilkins, 1933.

Axtell, James. *The European and the Indian.* New York: Oxford University Press, 1981.

Barbour, Philip L. *Pocahontas and Her World: A Chronicle of America's First Settlement.* Boston: Houghton Mifflin, 1970.

Boorstin, Daniel J. *The Americans: The Colonial Experience.* New York: Random House, 1958.

Bourne, Russell. *The Red King's Rebellion: Racial Politics in New England, 1675–78.* New York: Atheneum, 1990.

Bradstreet, Howard. *The Story of the War with the Pequots, Re-Told.* New Haven: Yale University Press, 1933.

Bridenbaugh, Carl. *Jamestown, 1544–1699.* New York: Oxford University Press, 1980.

Brown, Douglas S. *The Catawba Indians: The People of the River.* Columbia: University of South Carolina Press, 1966.

Bruce, Philip A. *Economic History of Virginia in the Seventeenth Century.* 2 volumes. New York: P. Smith, 1910.

Canny, Nicholas P. "The Ideology of English Colonization: From Ireland to America." *William and Mary Quarterly* 30 (1973): 575–598.

Carroll, Peter N. *Puritanism and the Wilderness.* New York: Columbia University Press, 1969.

Corkran, David H. *The Cherokee Frontier, 1540–1783*. Norman: University of Oklahoma Press, 1967.

——. *The Creek Frontier, 1540–1783*. Norman: University of Oklahoma Press, 1967.

Craven, Wesley F. *The Southern Colonies in the Seventeenth Century*. Baton Rouge: Louisiana State University Press, 1949.

——. *White, Red, and Black: The Seventeenth Century Virginian*. Charlottesville: University Press of Virginia, 1949.

Cronon, William. *Changes in the Land*. New York: Hill and Wang, 1983.

Henderson, Archibald. *North Carolina*. Chicago: Lewis, 1941.

Hudson, Charles. *Four Centuries of Southern Indians*. Athens: University of Georgia Press, 1975.

——, ed. *The Southeastern Indians*. Knoxville: University of Tennessee Press, 1976.

Jennings, Francis. *The Ambiguous Iroquois Empire*. New York: Norton, 1984.

——. *Empire of Fortune*. New York: Norton, 1988.

Kawashima, Yasuhide. *Puritan Justice and the Indian*. Middletown, Conn.: Wesleyan University Press, 1986.

Kupperman, Karen Ordahl. *Settling with the Indians: The Meeting of English and Indian Cultures in America, 1580–1640*. Totowa, N.J.: Rowman and Littlefield, 1980.

Leach, Douglas E. *Flintlock and Tomahawk*. New York: Macmillan, 1958.

Lurie, Nancy O. "Indian Cultural Adjustment to European Civilization." *Seventeenth Century America*. James M. Smith, ed. Chapel Hill: University of North Carolina Press, 1959.

Miller, Perry. *Roger Williams: His Contribution to the American Tradition*. Indianapolis: Bobbs-Merrill, 1953.

——. *Errand into the Wilderness*. Cambridge: Harvard University Press, 1956.

Molony, Francis X. *The Fur Trade in New England*. Hamden, Conn.: Archor Book, 1967.

Morton, Richard L. *Colonial Virginia*. 2 volumes. Chapel Hill: University of North Carolina Press, 1960.

Nash, Roderick W. *Wilderness and the American Mind*. New Haven: Yale University Press, 1967.

Phillips, Paul C., and J. W. Smurr. *The Fur Trade*. 2 volumes. Norman: University of Oklahoma Press, 1961.

Porter, H. C. *The Inconstant Savage: England and the North American Indian, 1500–1660*. London: Duckworth, 1979.

Powell, William S. "Aftermath of the Massacre: The First Indian War, 1622–1632." *Virginia Magazine of History and Biography* 66 (1958): 44–75.

Reid, John Phillip. *A Better Kind of Hatchet: Law, Trade, and Diplomacy in the Cherokee Nation during the Early Years of European Contact*. University Park, Penn.: Pennsylvania State University Press, 1976.

Richter, Daniel. *The Ordeal of the Longhouse: The Peoples of the Iroquois League in the Era of European Colonization*. Chapel Hill: University of North Carolina Press, 1992.

Roundtree, Helen C. *The Powhatan Indians of Virginia: Their Traditional Culture*. Norman: University of Oklahoma Press, 1989.

———. *Pocahontas's People: The Powhatan Indians of Virginia through Four Centuries.* Norman: University of Oklahoma Press, 1990.

Salisbury, Neal. "Red Puritans: The 'Praying Indians' of Massachusetts Bay and John Eliot." *William and Mary Quarterly* 31 (1974): 27–54.

———. *Manitou and Providence.* New York: Oxford University Press, 1982.

Sheehan, Bernard. *Savagism and Civility.* Cambridge: Cambridge University Press, 1980.

Shuffelton, Frank. "Indian Devils and Pilgrim Fathers: Squanto, Hobomok, and the English Conception of Indian Religion." *New England Quarterly* 49 (1976): 108–116.

Silver, Timothy. *A New Face in the Countryside.* Cambridge: Cambridge University Press, 1990.

Thomas, G. E. "Puritans, Indians, and the Concept of Race." *New England Quarterly* 48 (1975): 3–27.

Trelease, Allen W. *Indian Affairs in Colonial New York: The Seventeenth Century.* Ithaca: Cornell University Press, 1960.

Vaughan, Alden T. "Pequots and Puritans: The Causes of the War of 1637." *William and Mary Quarterly* 41 (1964): 256–269.

———. *New England Frontier.* Boston: Little, Brown, 1965.

———. "'Expulsion of the Savages': English Policy and the Massacre of 1622." *William and Mary Quarterly* 35 (January 1978): 57–84.

Woodward, Grace S. *Pocahontas.* Norman: University of Oklahoma Press, 1969.

CHAPTER 5

NATIVE SURVIVAL AND EUROPEAN IMPERIALISM

In the aftermath of King Philip's War, Native Americans throughout the Eastern Woodlands had to face an ever-expanding white population during the colonial era of American history. Although the Spanish had settled parts of Florida with presidios, missions, and pueblos, they did not pose a major threat to Indian nations of the South. The French to the north expanded west to the Great Plains and moved down the Mississippi River Valley, establishing trading posts and small communities. The objective of most French expansion was control of the fur trade, and at its zenith, the French had no more than eighty thousand people in America. In marked contrast, English settlers sailed to the Atlantic Seaboard and resettled Native American lands in familial units and communities. English colonists expanded in every direction, not just westward.

ENGLISH EXPANSION

English expansion onto the Native American estate came at a high price for native peoples, who lost land and lives, societies and cultures. Many Native Americans died of diseases and wars, but others fought and survived. Some remained on the lands of their grandmothers and grandfathers, living in accommodation with whites. Others moved inland to escape white settlement and to live in freedom from white rule. Yet sooner or later, each tribe, band, clan, and family had to contend with whites. This expansion, so heralded in American history, literature, education, drama, and film as a positive enterprise that helped tame wild lands, civilize savage people, and build a nation, was costly for Native Americans.

The establishment of forts, ferries, farms, taverns, trading posts, and roads is a common element of local, state, and national history in the United States, but with expansion more settlers established their homes, farms, and businesses in Native America. And with these new people came their new institutions, cultures, languages, and prejudices. Many settlers from Virginia, New York, Massachusetts, Rhode Island, and other colonies had been involved in conflicts. Other settlers had heard stories of native outrages and had formed negative images of American Indians. Some white traders, soldiers, farmers, and merchants brought positive images of Native Americans with them into the forests of Maine, New York, Pennsylvania, Ohio, Kentucky, Tennessee, and the Carolinas, but others brought a destructive and deadly image of Native Americans.

Throughout the colonial period of American history, other themes emerged. Native Americans experienced radical change over short periods of time and acted-reacted to situations as best they could as tribes, bands, and groups. Thus, there was no single Native American response to white settlement and expansion but rather several, depending on circumstances and personalities involved. Mohawks reacted differently to English expansion above Albany than did the Oneida. In the eighteenth century, Delaware living in Pennsylvania and Ohio reacted differently to Moravian missionaries than did Wyandots living in the same region. Even before the arrival of Europeans, Native American societies had their divisions, but these divisions multiplied and intensified with white contact and expansion, often dividing families, clans, villages, and tribes.

Regardless of tribal actions or reactions, there was one constant among most native peoples. They perceived colonists as real threats to their lives and cultures. This was particularly true of Eastern Woodlands Indians who had to contend with an ever-increasing number of farmers bent on acquiring, clearing, and cultivating more and more land. French, Dutch, Russian, and English traders exploited fur-bearing animals, but the English differed from others by colonizing in familial units and farming large tracts of land. As William Cronin has shown, English settlers plowed the earth, eroding the soil and depleting its nutrients. They cut down trees and burned out stumps to make room for farms. They used large quantities of wood for lumber and firewood, forever altering the earth by creating farms where thick deciduous forests once stood. They allowed livestock to graze on natural foods eaten by Indians. The English altered water courses for mills, using the natural power of rivers to generate capital from saw and grist mills. In order for English settlers to be successful, they needed land, and they expanded up river valleys, establishing farms, towns, and communities on the Native American estate.

In addition to taking land, English settlers set in motion a condition that was detrimental to Native Americans. Expansion of whites onto Indian lands and the successful growth of the English population created social chaos or *anomie* among many tribes. Although most tribes continued to resist white rule, Pequots, Wampanoags, Narragansetts, and Massachusetts suffered some degree of anomie in the early seventeenth century, and later other tribes–Shawnee, Miami, Wyandot, Delaware, Cherokee, Creek, Choctaw, Chickasaw, and others–also suffered this internal anomie. It is impossible to measure the degree of chaos or its influence among the people, but anomie was present and affected Indian people. Societal chaos occurred among many Native Americans at different times and different places, depending on the group and its geographical proximity to whites. But Native Americans learned sooner or later that white colonial expansion threatened their existence as a people. Historically, this was a psychological factor that cannot be quantified, but one that developed and matured throughout American history. The effects of anomie among Indian people continue to influence native peoples to this day. In part, the anomie was tied to native spiritual beliefs, the very core of native societies. White expansion forced Native Americans to leave the lands of their mothers and fathers, grandmothers and grandfathers. White expansion and exploitation forced Native Americans from their sacred places, cemeteries, and bones of their ancestors. This fact alone threatened Native Americans, because the dead were among them and had power. Removal from the land threatened their spirit and their sacred link between the dead and living, the past and present–their paths to the future.

Native Americans also reeled from the effects of contagious diseases. In addition to killing large numbers of people, diseases threatened the power of holy men and women who had healed the people for generations and who often failed to cure smallpox, measles, cholera, influenza, pneumonia, meningitis, and a host of other invisible killers; the spread of European diseases added to social anomie among native peoples. Diseases destroyed elements of Native American life and culture far more than did guns and armies. Ever-present and ever-virulent bacilli and viruses traveled in the air, water, food, and material items from person to person, spreading and multiplying in the bodies of vulnerable hosts. Because Native Americans had little or no immunities to European diseases, they died in large numbers. Smallpox, measles, influenza, scarlet fever, plague, alcoholism, and many others killed thousands of Indians. Like social chaos, disease has been a continual problem among Native Americans since the colonial era, often reducing tribes during the colonial era by one-fourth, one-half, or more. During every period of American history, Native Americans have suffered the ravages of epidemics, and this was especially the case during the colonial era.

COLONIAL INDIAN POLICIES

In spite of diseases, racism, tribal divisions, and warfare, many Native Americans survived the seventeenth and eighteenth centuries. And although most native people were forced to move from their homelands, they maintained their tribal identity, language, culture, and sovereignty. Europeans dealt with Native Americans in nation-to-nation relationships, generally recognizing tribes as independent, sovereign nations and entering into treaties. Written treaties emerged from a European tradition, not a Native American one, and they were binding only as long as both parties agreed to maintain their formal relationships and honor their agreements. Thus, if one band of Shawnees, for example, retaliated against a white farmer for encroaching on its lands without permission, the Virginia House of Burgesses might ignore the treaty with all Shawnees and send the colonial militia to attack Shawnee people and their neighbors, regardless of whether or not they had been party to the original attack on the encroaching farmer. And if the Virginians were successful in their attack, they might claim all Shawnee country and create a new treaty requiring Shawnees to leave Virginia and move north of the Ohio River.

English newcomers usually had no unified Indian policy like the French had in Canada. Instead, each of the thirteen colonies had its own Indian policies, and the policies of any one colony might be different within its own borders. For example, American Indian policy of the Massachusetts General Court might not be followed by colonists in the Berkshires. A unified colonial American Indian policy did not emerge in the English colonies until the French and Indian War, and by that time, colonists were loath to follow England's policies. Still, the colonial era provided American colonists with many lessons from which to learn, and one of them was the difficulty in maintaining thirteen separate Indian policies. By the time of the American Revolution, many policy makers in the Continental Congress were more inclined toward a unified Indian policy to curtail confusion and ambiguity. In the same way, the colonial period provided Native Americans with ample lessons about pursuing autonomous tribal policies toward whites without pooling their wisdom in large councils and attempting to follow a unified white policy. There was nothing new about various tribes and bands meeting in councils to discuss policies, but the woodlands tribes learned much from their experiences with whites during the colonial period. During the late seventeenth and early eighteenth centuries, the tribes joined forces more often to stand against whites. At times, Native Americans broke down their own ethnocentric tribalism, cultural barriers, and linguistic differences to forge new alliances with old enemies to stand against whites. However, this usually did not occur in a well-planned, systematic manner. Still, at times tribes or segments of tribes came together because American colonists posed a serious threat to their lands and cultures, but they also came together because of powerful visions of religious leaders and prophets who warned them that the Master of Life or Supreme Power had directed native people to stand against English expansion. Not all Indians joined these native alliances, and often tribes or portions of tribes fought each other. Still, by the time of the French and Indian War of 1754, many Eastern Woodlands tribes were co-operating with each other, and they did so out of self-interest and self-determination, not because they were pawns of European nations.

KING WILLIAM'S WAR

At the end of the seventeenth century, Native Americans were drawn into a conflict that inaugurated an era that would greatly weaken them and advance the imperialistic designs of Europeans. However, at the time the colonial wars began, native people could not perceive the far-reaching effects these wars would have on their own well-being. Native Americans participated in King William's War (1689–1697), the first of four imperial wars. Wyandots, Iroquois, Abnakis, and other Indians, as well as English and French soldiers, killed and butchered men, women, and children throughout this war, setting a precedent for all of the colonial wars. The origin of the struggle began before the outbreak of war when, in 1684, Iroquois traders allied with the English and expanded into northern New York, New England, and to the St. Lawrence River, selling better goods at lower prices. Iroquois traders aggressively took English manufactured goods deep into forests, where the native people had long traded with native traders allied with the French. The Iroquois fought their way to Montreal, declaring that they had captured a portion of the French trade and would extend their influence to Wisconsin.

In 1687, in response to Iroquois incursions into Canada, the marquis de Denonville led a force of eight hundred men into Iroquois country, but the Iroquois retaliated two years later with fifteen hundred warriors in a destructive attack on the French town of La Chine, where they killed two hundred people and carried off over 120 prisoners. Comte de Frontenac responded with a three-pronged attack on New York and New Hampshire, during which Wyandot, Abnaki, and French soldiers attacked Schenectady, killing sixty men, women, and children. Troubles in Europe over the ascension of William of Orange led to King William's War between the French and English. In America, native allies of France eagerly launched attacks against the Iroquois and English colonists living in the upper Mohawk Valley, New Hampshire, and Maine, which the Iroquois and their English allies answered with equal severity and bloodshed. Both sides burned native and colonial farms and villages, killed and captured their enemies, and stole as many goods as they could carry away. The Mohawks remained the most ardent supporters of the English, but the Seneca, Cayuga, and Onondaga sought neutrality. The Oneidas stood alone among the Iroquois nations, suing for peace with the French and their native allies. In 1697, King William's War ended in a draw with the Treaty of Ryswick, and French officials met with Iroquois delegates to urge them to maintain neutrality. When English agents objected, proclaiming that the Iroquois were their subjects—an assertion vehemently denied by Iroquois leaders—native leaders pointed out that the Mohawk, Oneida, Onondaga, Seneca, and Cayuga were sovereign, independent nations, not vassals or children of any European nation.

QUEEN ANNE'S WAR

Although King William's War ended indecisively, it marked the beginning of three more bloody imperial wars that would conclude in a major victory for the English. The second imperial war, called Queen Anne's War (1707–1713), was the product of age-old rivalries between the English, French, and Spanish, although in America the fighting began in 1704 over the expansion of English trade in the North and South, where French traders had reigned supreme since the middle of the seventeenth century. In order to hold their control over the region, fifty French troops with two hundred Abnaki and Caughnawaga warriors attacked Deerfield, Massachusetts, killing fifty English settlers and taking over one hundred captives. The English retaliated with a raid on Acadia led by Benjamin Church and later tried to attack Port Royal but failed.

When Queen Anne's War began, the English assigned few troops to America and needed Indian allies so much that in 1710, they sent several Mohawk chiefs to London to impress them. That same year, English war ships transported colonial militia to Port Royal and Acadia, and Acadia became English-controlled Nova Scotia. However, English colonists failed to capture Quebec. For the most part, Native Americans fought and killed each other as well as colonists and traders in the forests, burning homes, destroying crops, killing livestock, and capturing prisoners. Like prior wars, this war was fought primarily in the North; but in the South, Muscogees and Choctaws sided with French troops against English traders and their effective Chickasaw allies.

The war had significant consequences for the Tuscaroras and Yamasee. In 1711, Swiss settlers under Baron Christoph von Graffenried forced a group of Tuscaroras to leave their native town in North Carolina. After meeting in council, the Tuscaroras attacked the Swiss settlement, killing almost two hundred men, women, and children. With reinforcements from South Carolina, a force of thirty-three whites and one thousand Indians attacked the Tuscaroras, killing several hundred and capturing over four hundred, who were sold into slavery for £10 each. Most Tuscaroras abandoned their homes in the South, moving north to join the Iroquois Confederacy, but others under Tom Blount signed a peace agreement with the English in 1715. Although most Tuscaroras live in New York today, some remained in the southern portion of North Carolina, living in Robeson County near Lumbee Indians—many of whom are still there today. Like the Tuscaroras, the Yamasee of South Carolina and Georgia suffered severely during the war. After the Yamasee attacked traders and settlers who had overrun their homelands, killing over one hundred people and setting fire to their homes, trading posts, and fields, the English launched two deadly attacks that killed several people and drove the Yamasee into Spanish Florida. Queen Anne's War concluded with the Treaty of Utrecht in 1713, which was more of a truce than a settlement. The conflict between Indians and European settlers was far from settled.

KING GEORGE'S WAR

Conflicts between England and France in America quieted considerably after 1713, except in parts of Maine, Massachusetts, and New Hampshire, where English farmers encroached on native lands and Abnakis retaliated. In 1724, Captain John Lovewell and eighty-seven colonial militia soldiers killed and scalped ten Indians, receiving a scalp bounty of £1,000. Later that year, Abnakis attacked Lovewell and his men, killing Lovewell and several of his men. Colonial officials had applauded Lovewell's attack on the Indians and viewed native retaliation as an act of treachery. The killings fueled racial hatreds on both sides, but the immediate conflict soon waned. The next year, the two parties agreed to peace, and all remained quiet in New England until King George's War (1739–1748). Although the war began in Europe in 1739, open warfare in America did not break out until 1744, when limited fighting ensued between the French and English from Maine to New York. A few Indians participated in these forays, but English and French militia and regulars did most of the fighting. Many Iroquois remained neutral, and members of the Iroquois nations claimed the Ohio River Valley until the Lancaster Council in 1744, when the Iroquois gave up their "claim," offering their consent for the English to settle the region. Actually, many Shawnees lived in the area, and Delawares were edging ever westward toward the Ohio River. Few Iroquois lived in the Ohio country, but the various tribes of the confederacy claimed domination over the rolling hills and deep green forests. In 1748, some Shawnee leaders—but not all—signed the Loggstown Treaty, authorizing the English to settle the Ohio River Valley. The Shawnees were likely concerned about French designs in the region and sought to ally with the English, fearing French advances into the area, a scenario that soon unfolded.

During King George's War, the English gave the Iroquois and other tribes tribute, promises, and hospitality, hoping to win native peoples to their side or neutralize them. Most tribes chose not to become deeply involved. The Iroquois remained neutral throughout the war, although some Mohawks, ardent supporters of the English trader and speculator William Johnson (Warraghiyagey or He-Who-Does-Much), agreed to harass the French near Lake Champlain. The major issue among colonial and European powers was the fur trade, which the English wanted to expand into western New York. By the time of King George's War, the English had built a series of defensive trading posts near Lake Ontario, including the stone fort of Oswego. Not to be outdone, the French moved south to Crown Point, building Fort St. Frederick on the western shore of Lake Champlain. Colonial militia and English regulars did most of their fighting against the French near Louisbourg on Cape Breton Island. In the South, Cherokees and Chickasaws allied with the English, cutting off the flow of French trade down the Mississippi River. Muscogees and Choctaws sided with the French, although their participation was not consequential to the outcome of the war. Like the earlier colonial wars, King George's War ended indecisively, but from this war emerged the last major conflict between France and England. As the next war approached, Native Americans in the North, South, and West made their own choices about the degree of their participation in the upcoming war. Their decisions were not unified, but collectively they were significant to their own fate and that of future generations of native people.

THE SEVEN YEARS' WAR

Just as it had been in the previous imperial wars, the fur trade was one cause of the Seven Years' War, better known as the French and Indian War (1754–1763). But it was not the most important cause. Far more important was European expansion. English settlers had expanded onto western lands, where land speculators and individual farmers had settled. Native Americans viewed the expansion of white farmers as a threat, particularly those native peoples living in the Great Lakes region and the Old Southwest. Fertile farmlands lured speculators and farmers to present-day Pennsylvania, Ohio, Indiana, Kentucky, Tennessee, and Georgia. White farmers and business interests also had their eyes on fertile lands farther west. Speculators wanted to control these territories, investing in these "undeveloped" lands first before breaking them up into smaller parcels and selling them to eager farmers at higher prices. In addition to the fur trade, the acquisition and sale of land to farmers from the East or Europe were primary motives. Neither governments nor speculators cared about the effect of economic development on the lives of native people. Whites generally viewed Indians as impediments to progress and expansion. Thus, economic development drove the English into the interior, and colonial and crown governmental bodies encouraged expansion as a way to challenge the French and several sovereign Indian nations.

English colonists outnumbered French, and their numbers increased yearly. By agreements made in the 1740s with the Iroquois at Lancaster and Shawnees at Loggstown, the English claimed the Ohio River Valley. This would have been news to Shawnees, Susquehannas, Delawares, and other Indians living in Pennsylvania. And the French believed they had a prior claim to the region and planned to strengthen their hold on the Ohio River Valley by building Fort LeBoeuf at present-day Waterford, Pennsylvania. Seeking to check the French, Governor Robert Dinwiddie of Virginia sent militia Colonel George Washington to inform the French that they were on English soil. The twenty-one-year-old Washington met the French commander, who told Washington that he was on French soil and ordered the English to leave.

Dinwiddie responded by sending a small force under Washington to build an English fort at the confluence of the Monongahela and Allegheny rivers, the head waters of the Ohio River at present-day Pittsburgh. In April of 1754, Washington led 120 men through the forests, hills, and mountains to reinforce the English troops. No Indians traveled with Washington until he met Mingo Chief Half King, who committed twelve men to the expedition. Washington learned that the French had ordered the English fort builders to abandon the region and that the French had established Fort Duquesne on the site. When Washington received this news, he took forty soldiers forward to reconnoiter. Half King and his Mingo warriors accompanied him, and this party clashed with thirty-three French troops. Half King and Washington's men killed ten Frenchmen and took twenty-three prisoners for a time before releasing them. This was the opening engagement of the Seven Years' War.

Washington retreated to Grand Meadows, where he built a small stockade named Fort Necessity. His forces totaled four hundred, but they were no match for nine hundred French troops and their native allies. On July 3, 1754, the French opened fire on Fort Necessity, pinning down the English and killing or wounding enough soldiers that Washington surrendered. The French allowed Washington and his men to return to Virginia while the French savored their victory. Although few Native Americans were involved in the opening salvos of the war, they soon chose to participate. Dinwiddie recognized the importance of Native American alliances and neutrality, so he wooed Delaware, Cherokee, and Chickasaw. Delegates from seven colonies met Iroquois leaders at the Albany Congress in 1754. Initially, the Iroquois refused to ally with the English because of pressure they had received from land speculators who wanted them to cede more lands to whites. However, with the encouragement of their friend, William Johnson, many Iroquois reluctantly committed themselves to an English alliance.

Although the Iroquois joined forces with England during the early part of the war, far more Indians joined with France. In the North, Abnakis and Caughnawagas (missionized Iroquois) allied with the French, and to the south, Choctaws and Muscogees did the same—just as they had during other imperial or colonial wars. In Pennsylvania, Delawares and Shawnees sided with the French, and Miamis, Wyandots, Ottawas, and Anishinaabe (Chippewas) of the Old Northwest above the Ohio River did the same. In most cases, not all members of any one tribe sided with the French or the English. Some chose to fight, whereas others refused, maintaining neutrality. Sometimes native alliances changed, but Indians acted out of their own self-interest—just as Europeans and colonists did. George Washington revealed his own frustration in dealing with Indians when he wrote that "every service of theirs must be purchased; and they are easily offended, being thoroughly sensible of their own importance." Native Americans fought for one side or the other when they deemed it to their advantage. For example, when the old but skilled General Edward Braddock set out in June 1755 with twenty-five hundred soldiers to crush the French at Fort Duquesne, not one Indian accompanied him. In part, the Indians did not support Braddock because he cared little for the fighting ability of the "naked Indians." Yet Delaware, Shawnee, and others reluctantly joined the French to face Braddock's force on July 9.

In the thick, green woods near present-day Pittsburgh, approximately two hundred Indians and two hundred French soldiers from Fort Duquesne surprised Braddock and 1,460 of his fast-moving forces. English regulars formed a skirmish line immediately, but Delaware, Shawnee, and other warriors raced on both sides of the English, firing, running, reloading, and firing again. They shot point blank at the redcoats from trees, hills, and ravines, causing pandemonium among the royal regulars. For three hours the Indians and their allies launched an offensive in which only 480 men survived. The Indians and their French allies killed or wounded 980 English regulars, including Braddock. George Washington, who was serving without pay as Braddock's aide, found a wagon and took Braddock from the field of battle. Two days later Braddock died, and Washington buried him in an unmarked grave in the heart of Indian country.

The Indian and French victory opened Pennsylvania, Virginia, and Maryland to native attacks against English colonial settlers, and it encouraged native supporters of the French to strike farms in New York and New England. In a preemptive strike, Superintendent of Northern Indian Affairs William Johnson asked his friend, Mohawk Chief Henrick, to lead an advance party of two hundred Mohawks and one thousand colonial militia troops to the French stronghold of Crown Point, located on the south shore of Lake Champlain. Before they arrived, Mohawks and English soldiers ran headlong into a French ambush that cost many lives, including that of Chief Henrick. The survivors fell back to Johnson's line of defense, where they fought off the French. Near the present-day town of Lake George, Johnson built the English stronghold of Fort William Henry. This fort challenged French dominion over the region south of Lake Champlain.

Indians supporting the French had much to celebrate, especially in 1756, when the French named Louis Joseph, the marquis de Montcalm, supreme commander of French forces. Shortly after taking office, Montcalm dispatched three thousand troops to take Fort Oswego, which they did handily. Indians in the Old Northwest rallied to the French after their victory at Oswego, including those who had leaned toward neutrality or the English. Even Washington worried that "our Friendly Indians are deserting Our Interests," and his concerns were justified when Montcalm recruited over two thousand Indians from the Great Lakes to support his attack on Fort William Henry, giving them prized wampum belts as tribute. With a force of eight thousand, Montcalm took and burned Fort William Henry while Wyandots, Ottawas, Abnakis, Anishinaabes, and other allies joined in the effort. In his book, *Betrayals,* Ian Steel has questioned whether the tribes butchered their old enemy or the English and Americans created the story for propaganda. No doubt, however, the tribes hated English expansion onto Indian lands. The attack on Fort William Henry marked a low point in the war for the English and the beginning of the end for the French.

Only a few Native Americans were involved when the English took Louisbourg and Fort Frontenac in 1758. Late that year General John Forbes won the support of Shawnees, Mingoes, and Delawares as he prepared to take Fort Duquesne. Moravian missionary Christian Frederick Post helped in the endeavor, telling the Delawares that after the campaign they could return safely to their former villages along the Susquehanna. The Delaware were naturally skeptical. Not long after, Forbes met over five hundred Indians near Easton, Pennsylvania, where they concluded a treaty that was later ratified by the crown, agreeing to return lands to Native Americans west of the Appalachians. The Easton Treaty reassured many western tribes that the English were not interested in expanding westward, but the treaty was made between English officials and selected tribes, not American colonists who had other plans for western lands. French agents tried to win back the Delaware and others with wampum belts, but on one occasion, a band of Delaware took a French wampum belt and kicked it about as if it was a snake, before throwing it away. In 1758, Forbes led an army of Indian, colonial, and regular forces to Fort Duquesne, which the French had evacuated, renaming the site Fort Pitt.

However, the capture of Fort Duquesne was not the crushing blow that ended French power in America. That occurred in September 1759 on the Plains of Abraham near Quebec when General James Wolfe fought French troops of Montcalm. Both commanders died in this short but decisive battle. Within a short time, the English also captured Montreal, and it was a matter of time before the French capitulated. On February 10, 1763, the French and English signed the Treaty of Paris, formally ending the war. It was a disastrous agreement for France, which ceded Canada and all its claim to lands west of the Appalachian Mountains, except New Orleans.

Native Americans from many geographical areas, representing numerous tribes, fought in the French and Indian War. Nearly all of them suffered as a result. English troops and colonial militia attacked Wyandot, Shawnee, Abnaki, Miami, and Ottawa villages. These tribes and their French allies killed hundreds of Iroquois from the Five Nations as well as other Indians and English settlers. Diseases, exposure, lack of food, and removal destroyed or weakened other tribes. Native populations declined, and their quality of life deteriorated as more white settlers moved onto native lands. The cultural and social fabric of the people was torn by warfare, and their economies were in shambles. Rather than hunting furs, farming, killing game, fishing, and gathering, the woodlands tribes throughout the eastern portions of Canada and the United States had spent seven years fighting each other. Their economies declined, and starvation resulted.

Although the tribes resisted, a general anomie hung over many Native Americans as they assessed their condition after the war. This anomie manifested itself in many ways as tribal and clan relationships broke down, people drank to drown their trouble, families abandoned their old religions, and individuals did not obey the old laws set forth in traditional oral narratives. Yet, although some Indians languished over radical cultural change and the fact that they had lost the war and their French allies, others rose to the challenge. New leaders emerged to speak strongly at the council fires, telling the people to be as tenacious as their grandfathers and grandmothers before them. They spoke of tribal and cultural survival and the revitalization of traditional beliefs and laws. In order to do this, some Indians remained on the lands of their ancestors, treasuring their relationship with the earth that held the bones of their ancestors. Others, however, could not remain. They moved north, south, or west, temporarily out of the reach of English settlements. Native Americans survived the French and Indian War and its aftermath, but survival came at a great cost.

CHEROKEES, SOVEREIGNTY, AND PONTIAC

American Indians drew on the strengths of their cultures and their past experiences with European nations to re-create their future. Most tribes fought for their sovereignty, culture, and lives on several fronts. During the war, six hundred Cherokees had fought for the English, including several who served with General Forbes in the Ohio River Valley. After taking Fort Duquesne, a band of Cherokees completed their military service and traveled homeward, south through present-day West Virginia. When they came across some unmarked horses running wild in the woods, they rounded them up to ride them home. White men–irregular Virginia militiamen eager to collect scalp bounties offered by their colonial legislature–claimed that the horses were theirs. They surprised the Indians and killed forty of them. The senseless killings triggered a major Indian war that lasted from 1760 to 1761. Cherokees attacked English settlers from Virginia to Georgia, burning homes, crops, and towns. Many Cherokees were led by the astute warrior Oconostota. English and colonial forces retaliated in 1761 with the help of their own Indian allies. The number of English regulars and Indian warriors swelled to three thousand, and they moved through the forests, destroying Cherokee villages and killing men, women, and children. The Cherokees fought gallantly, but they lacked sufficient guns, powder, and lead to continue. They sued for peace in 1761, agreeing to permit the English to occupy forts on native lands and to allow English officers at the posts to adjudicate differences between Indians and colonists. The agreement also established a boundary between Cherokees and white settlers, all of which limited the absolute sovereignty that Cherokees had enjoyed since the time of their creation.

In the aftermath of the wars, Lord Jeffrey Amherst, supreme commander of English forces in North America, announced his plan to punish the Indians for siding with the French. He ended the age-old practice of providing aid to the tribes in order to keep them loyal to the crown or neutral. Against the advice of more experienced and astute soldiers, Amherst ordered post commanders to end their aid in arms, ammunition, clothing, and other trade goods to Indians. For years Indians had received and expected such gifts from French and English troops–material items that tied the tribes to the foreigners. Ending gifts to Native Americans strained relations, but other developments were even more significant. Rumors circulated among many tribes that the redcoats planned to exterminate all Indians. White expansion and duplicity created a troublesome era in which many Indians, former allies of the French, wished to reassert their own power over western lands. In the midst of dramatic political changes, a native spiritual leader emerged with words from the Master of Life that brought hope and pride to the people. Neolin, the

Delaware Prophet, was a holy man who preached among the tribes in the 1760s, telling them to throw off white dependence and stand patriotically against whites. This, he said, was the wish of the Master of Life. Indians far and wide heard the message, which coincided with the feelings of many leaders and made good sense to native people. One chief who used the teachings of the Delaware Prophet to launch a stand against "those dogs clothed in red" was the great Ottawa leader Pontiac.

In 1760, Major Robert Rogers and two companies of his famed rangers traveled into the Old Northwest to take control of French posts. Near the mouth of the Detroit River, Rogers met a number of Wyandot, Potawatomi, and Ottawa leaders, including Pontiac, who "demanded my business in his country and how it happened that I dared to enter it without his leave." Rogers said that he had come in peace and gave Pontiac and the others wampum belts as signs of friendship. After smoking a pipe of peace, the native leaders allowed Rogers to pass through their country to take control of Fort Detroit and other posts. Unlike French leaders, native chiefs had not surrendered to the English or given up their lands. They maintained their sovereignty and continued their intercourse with French traders and settlers. Native Americans everywhere in the Eastern Woodlands soon learned that the English soldiers and colonists continued to regard them with contempt, ending foreign aid and forbidding them from entering the posts. More colonists crossed the Appalachian Mountains, moving onto Indian lands. Between 1761 and 1763, Wyandots, Ottawas, Delawares, Senecas, Shawnees, Miamis, Potawatomis, Sacs, Foxes, and Anishinaabes sent war belts to one another, encouraging all native people to strike the forts and force the English from their lands. Each tribe had its own leaders, but Pontiac rose as a central figure among them.

At a council fire by the Ecores River in 1763, Pontiac said that he had learned from the Delaware Prophet that the Master of Life had ordered his children to end their feuds among their native brothers and sisters, stop drinking alcohol, end the use of white manufactured goods, and drive the white man from their lands. Native peoples, he argued, had suffered too long from diseases, dependence on European trade, racism, alcoholism, land thefts, and foreign laws designed to destroy the First Nations. According to Pontiac, the Master of Life had said: "The land on which you live, I have made for you, not for others. Why do you suffer the white man to dwell among you? My children, you have forgotten the customs and traditions of your forefathers." Pontiac's articulation of the Delaware Prophet's message had a profound effect among northwestern Indians, who believed that their medicine men and women had the power to receive messages from the Creator. Although the message seemed of little significance to the English and colonists, Native Americans believed that the Delaware Prophet had received a divine message and that Pontiac was fulfilling the wishes of the Master of Life.

On May 7, 1763, Pontiac entered Fort Detroit with three hundred warriors with the intent of taking the post from within. Someone leaked the plan to Major Henry Gladwin and foiled Pontiac's initial attempt. Within a few days, however, war spread across the Great Lakes as warriors from a variety of tribes struck white settlements and captured English forts at Sandusky, Michilimackinac, Ouiatenon, Venango, and other places. Captain Simeon Ecuyer at Fort Pitt refused to surrender to the Delaware but gave them whiskey, cloth, and food, which helped ease tensions. The Delaware withdrew in October 1763, the same month in which Pontiac gave up his siege of Fort Detroit.

PROCLAMATION LINE, 1763

The next year, the English government pardoned Pontiac and pushed for an alliance with western tribes in order to foster better relations and save money. The Indian war in 1763 had one positive, if only temporary, consequence for native peoples. In response to Indian attacks on the English forts and settlements, the crown announced the Proclamation Line of 1763, prohibiting white settlement west of the Appalachian Mountains. English law required colonists to remain east of an imaginary line that ran down the middle of the mountains, in order to prevent further bloodshed and expenditures to pay for another Indian war. Nevertheless, Amherst hated Indians and was determined to destroy them by all means possible, including the use of smallpox and other diseases.

During the wars for Indian sovereignty following the French and Indian War, numerous Native American warriors attacked and killed English colonists and English regulars in an attempt to drive them into the Atlantic Ocean. Some accounts put the death toll at two thousand men, women, and children, and even more were taken captive. Whatever the correct number, some colonists continued to resettle native lands, including lands west of the Proclamation Line. They disregarded Indian rights and English law, believing they had the right to resettle wherever they wanted. Settlers in the western parts of Pennsylvania, Virginia, New York, and the Carolinas believed they had a legitimate right to move onto lands occupied by Shawnees, Delawares, Wyandots, Cherokees, Choctaws, Muscogees, and others because these tribes had fought American settlers and therefore had forfeited their land rights.

When English and colonial officials tried to rein in American frontiersmen and women, trouble resulted. Rumors of continued Indian fighting complicated the situation. In November 1763, rumors spread that peaceful Delaware and Susquehanna (Conestoga) Indians in Pennsylvania were supporting hostile Indians in the West. When crown and colonial officials in Pennsylvania refused to address Indian issues championed by western settlers, the people formed vigilante groups to deal with Indians directly. In December 1763, mobs from Paxton and Donegal twice attacked Susquehanna Indians who were under the protection of officials in Lancaster County. The "Paxton Boys" killed six Susquehannas and wounded several others. Historian Dawn Marsh suggests that remnants of the tribe melted into the forest away from whites or lived with Delawares, Wyandots, Iroquois, and Shawnees. Even Ben Franklin decried the murders and helped defuse the volatile situation. The killing of Susquehannas was one of many incidents that continued hostilities between Indians and whites.

Colonial conflicts between whites and Indians pointed out problems stemming from the whites having no unified Indian policy. Some observers had recognized this problem for over a century, but the English did not address the issue until the French and Indian War. In 1755, Edmond Atkin of South Carolina offered the *Atkin Report and Plan* to the South Carolina governor's council, arguing that England needed a unified Indian policy like that of France. The concept of a unified Indian policy offered by a centralized government emerged in 1763 at the close of the French and Indian War. Rather than permit each colony to execute its own Indian policy, the crown created royal policies to govern trade, land, immigration, treaties, and war. English officials dealt with the tribes as sovereign nations that made their own laws and executed their own justice in accordance with tribal traditions. English officials were not interested in assimilation–the attempt to make Indians into English men and women. English bureaucrats were interested in power and money, and they became the architects of a new Indian policy that would contribute to the growing unrest between England and its colonies.

Selected Readings and Bibliography

Vaughan's *New England Frontier* contains a great deal of useful information on colonial relations between Native Americans and English settlers. Reid's *A Better Kind of Hatchet,* Jennings's *The Invasion of America* and *Empire of Fortunes,* and Gibson's *The American Indian* all contain historical scholarship that informed this chapter. Other helpful sources are Brandon's *Indians* and Corkran's *The Cherokee Frontier* and *The Creek Frontier.*

Dowd, Gregory E. "The French King Wakes Up in Detroit: 'Pontiac's War' in Rumor and History." *Ethnohistory* 37 (1990): 254–278.

——. *A Spirited Resistance.* Baltimore: Johns Hopkins University Press, 1992.

Gibson, Arrell M. *The Kickapoos.* Norman: University of Oklahoma Press, 1963.

——. *The Chickasaws.* Norman: University of Oklahoma Press, 1971.

Gipson, Lawrence H. *The British Empire before the American Revolution.* 15 volumes. New York: Knopf, 1936–1972.

Hamilton, Milton W. *Sir William Johnson.* Port Washington, N.Y.: Kennikat Press, 1976.

Hatley, Tom. *The Dividing Paths: Cherokees and South Carolinians through the Revolutionary Era.* New York: Oxford University Press, 1993.

Jacobs, Wilbur R. *Diplomacy and Indian Gifts.* Stanford: Stanford University Press, 1950.

———. *Dispossessing the American Indian.* New York: Scribner, 1972.

Krech, Shephard, ed. *Indians, Animals and the Fur Trade: A Critique of Keepers of the Game.* Athens: University of Georgia Press, 1981.

Leach, Douglas E. *Arms for Empire.* New York: Macmillan, 1973.

Martin, Calvin. *Keepers of the Game: Indian-Animal Relationships and the Fur Trade.* Berkeley: University of California Press, 1978.

McConnell, Michael N. *A Country Between: The Upper Ohio Valley and Its Peoples, 1724–1774.* Lincoln: University of Nebraska Press, 1992.

Nammack, Georgiana C. *Fraud, Politics, and the Dispossession of the Indians.* Norman: University of Oklahoma Press, 1969.

Peckham, Howard H. *Pontiac and the Indian Uprising.* Chicago: University of Chicago Press, 1961.

———. *The Colonial Wars, 1689–1762.* Chicago: University of Chicago Press, 1964.

Philbrick, Francis S. *The Rise of the West, 1754–1830.* New York: Harper and Row, 1965.

Slotkin, Richard. *Regeneration through Violence.* Middletown, Conn.: Wesleyan University Press, 1973.

Sosin, Jack M. *Whitehall and the Wilderness.* Lincoln: University of Nebraska Press, 1961.

Utley, Robert M., and Wilcolm E. Washburn. *Indian Wars.* Boston: Houghton Mifflin, 1977.

CHAPTER 6

NATIVE AMERICANS, REVOLUTION, AND THE EARLY NATIONAL ERA

Between 1763 and 1774, most Native Americans in the Eastern Woodlands gravitated toward support of the British rather than the American colonists. Most native peoples approved of the Proclamation Line established by British officials and feared American designs on western land. The evidence seemed clear. In spite of British Indian policies to the contrary, American settlers moved west onto native lands without regard for Indian rights to the land. Colonies such as New York, Massachusetts, Virginia, the Carolinas, and others claimed western lands, sometimes all the way west to the Pacific Ocean. Most states encouraged white settlement of the West, regardless of the individuals involved in the migration. This included colonial and European families as well as a host of lawless men who hated Indians and had no respect for Indian rights, agreements, cultures, or peoples. Often these individuals stirred up trouble, creating crises that resulted in thefts, killings, rapes, removals, and racism.

The era between the French and Indian War and the American Revolution witnessed numerous bloody attacks on white settlers and settlements by Native Americans who sought to drive white people from western lands and to encourage them never to return. At the outset of the American Revolution, most Native Americans believed they could win back lost lands; but the conflict would result in the loss of native lands, destruction of homes, forced removal, and deaths of numerous Indians. The American Revolution was a watershed in Native American history, one that would set in motion local, state, and national policies that were detrimental to all native people, including full bloods, mixed bloods, Christians, non-Christians, and men, women, and children of African and European descent who came to live among the tribes and adopt their cultures. Among many tribes of the Eastern Woodlands, these people were considered Native Americans because of their allegiance to native peoples and their acceptance of native culture as a way of life.

WESTWARD EXPANSION

Indians and whites shared in the bloodshed that began between the French and Indian War and the American Revolution as more and more whites moved into present-day Tennessee, Kentucky, Ohio, and upstate New York, killing game, cutting trees, planting crops, and claiming native lands. "Land stealers"–surveyors and speculators who divided and sold land–took Indian lands and resettled them. Between 1771 and 1774, whites moved into present-day Kentucky, western Pennsylvania, and eastern Ohio. Shawnees claimed the region and attempted to enlist the help of Cherokees and Senecas to fight the whites. Sir William Johnson persuaded the Six Nations (formerly the Five Nations, but now including Tuscaroras) to remain neutral, and Cherokees were preoccupied with their own difficulties. When whites murdered numerous Indians in 1773, Shawnees showed restraint, but in 1774 they rose against the whites.

Without the aid of others, Shawnees under Cornstalk struck white settlements. Daniel Boone and Michael Stoner rushed west to warn other white settlers that war had commenced. Virginia Governor Lord Dunmore, part owner of the Illinois Land and Wabash Land companies, acted in his own self-interest as well as that of his constituents. He first dispatched Major Angus McDonald and four hundred men to destroy Indian villages along the Muskingum River of eastern Ohio. He ordered Colonel Andrew Lewis and one thousand Virginians to invade the Shawnee, while Dunmore moved eleven hundred volunteers down the Ohio River from Fort Pitt. When Cornstalk learned of the divided force, he moved quickly to attack Lewis in the Battle of Point Pleasant. Mistaking a flanking movement for reinforcements, Cornstalk withdrew, but before he reached his villages, he learned that Dunmore had moved his army dangerously close to Shawnee villages. Cornstalk sued for peace, and Dunmore forced the Shawnee to sign the Treaty of Camp Charlotte, whereby they surrendered their hunting rights in Kentucky and permitted whites to settle the region. As a result of Lord Dunmore's War, whites opened Kentucky for settlement and exploitation.

In 1774, white Americans often considered issues involving Native Americans who were powerful nations in many parts of the East. Indeed, when the First Continental Congress met in that year, it established a Committee on Indian Affairs and committed £40,000 so that American agents could buy gifts for western tribes and urge them to maintain peace with American colonists. The British were in a better position to deal with Native American affairs than American colonists. In addition to their years of experience in native affairs, the British had two Indian superintendents already in place who were closely allied with native people: Sir John Johnson (son of William Johnson, who died in 1774), head of the northern superintendency, and John Stuart, head of the southern superintendency. Whereas most native leaders advocated neutrality toward the British and Americans until the outbreak of war, Mohawk Chief Joseph Brant spoke strongly in favor of siding with the British. Brant had visited Britain with other chiefs and witnessed the strength of the British Army and Navy. He was convinced that in any war, the redcoats would win. He and many native leaders from numerous tribes quietly agreed that it was in their own best interest to proclaim neutrality and then side with the British in the event of war. Some Oneidas and Tuscaroras as well as small elements of other tribes sided with the Americans during the Revolution, but most openly sided with the British.

CHEROKEES AND THE REVOLUTION

Before the outbreak of fighting between British regulars and the Continental Army, most tribes did maintain neutrality. The Cherokees were one of the first tribes to proclaim their allegiance to King George III in April 1776. Henry Stuart, brother of British Superintendent of Indian Affairs John Stuart, was present at the pronouncement and recognized the immediate danger posed to American settlers at Nolichucky and Watauga. He warned American colonists, who were prepared to meet and defeat Cherokee Chief Dragging Canoe when his warriors approached Eaton's Station at the Long Island of the Holston River. Dragging Canoe retreated but attacked Fort Watauga the next day. Like the Americans at Eaton's Station, those at Watauga were forewarned and beat back the Cherokee attack. Rather than end the conflict, these losses helped unite Cherokee, Choctaw, and Muscogee warriors against American settlers. Volunteer militia forces from Virginia, North Carolina, and South Carolina struck the Cherokees who lived in villages on lands close to the western boundaries of each state.

North Carolina militiamen numbering twenty-five hundred swept down on the Middle Cherokee towns just east of the Tennessee River. The militia moved south to join the South Carolina force and strike the Lower Cherokee living near the upper reaches of the Savannah River. At the same time, an army from Virginia laid waste to the Overhill Cherokee, who lived east of the Middle Cherokee. Although Cherokee men, women, and children fought bravely, the American soldiers burned their homes, destroyed their crops, and divided the people. A few leaders of the Lower Cherokees signed the Treaty of DeWitt's Corner in May 1777, ceding their lands in South Carolina. In July 1777, leaders of the Overhill Cherokees signed the Treaty of Long Island, ceding their lands east of the Blue Ridge Mountains and lands already resettled by Americans at

Watauga and Nolichucky. Like the British and French, Americans continued the process of defeating Indians militarily and forcing them to surrender large tracts of land. Treaties resulting from conquests became the foundation of an American Indian policy that fed on "legal" theft of native lands. This process would continue for another century until the American government found other means to take the Native American estate.

For two years following these agreements, most Cherokees remained peaceful, but in 1779 they feared that the Americans, not the British, might win the Revolution. Cherokees reasoned that if Americans won the war, they would allow settlers to steal more lands and take over the rest of the Cherokee domain. Of course, American settlers had their eyes fixed on the Cherokee estate, and Cherokee resistance provided a just cause to invade their lands again. To counter the Americans while the war still raged, Cherokee war parties struck the Americans from their villages at Chickamauga and all along the Tennessee River. Colonel Evan Shelby retaliated with a combined force of militia from North Carolina and Virginia, moving through the Chickamauga villages in the spring of 1779, burning Indian towns and crops while forcing families to escape or be killed. In autumn, a group of volunteers from South Carolina torched six more villages and promised to return and kill any Indian who threatened whites in the United States. Although most Cherokees remained peaceful, white soldiers returned. In the autumn of 1780 and spring of 1781, militia soldiers from Virginia, Kentucky, and Tennessee traveled through the Overhill and Middle Towns of the Cherokee, wreaking havoc by burning, killing, and butchering the people. On July 26, 1781, Colonel John Sevier forced some Cherokee leaders to sign the new Treaty of Long Island in which the Indians ceded more lands to the whites. By the end of the American Revolution, many Cherokees believed they could not defeat the Americans militarily and had to find new avenues to resist American aggression.

IROQUOIS AND THE REVOLUTION

Indians living in New York and the surrounding region fared no better than Cherokees during the American Revolution, but they initially believed they could destroy American colonists and armies above Albany. Joseph Brant and his British allies counted on an aggressive war against the Americans to drive them from the region. The Indians controlled key areas around Niagara and Oswego, and they used them as their base of operation against the Americans. During the summer of 1777, Iroquois warriors worked in concert with British armies as General John Burgoyne marched from Canada down Lake Champlain, and General Barry

St. Leger left Oswego for the Mohawk and Hudson river valleys. When St. Leger reached Fort Stanwix with seventeen hundred men, he laid siege to the fort, but the 750 American soldiers fought brilliantly, fending off the Iroquois and their British allies and forcing them to retreat to Oswego. With advance knowledge of American movements, given to the Iroquois by Mohawk Molly Brant, the Iroquois met and defeated eight hundred troops, led by General Nicholas Herkimer, who were coming to the aid of soldiers at Fort Stanwix. On August 5, Iroquois and British troops ambushed Herkimer and his Tuscarora and Oneida allies eight miles from the fort, defeating the Americans and their allies in the Battle of Oriskany. However, the fight accentuated the divisions among the Iroquois, driving the nation into two camps—those favoring the British and those favoring the Americans. This was particularly important for the Oneida who sided with the Americans. Later, some Onedia moved to Wisconsin, where they live today.

The Battle of Oriskany cost Herkimer and his American troops two hundred lives and many more wounded. Although the Iroquois under Brant gave up their siege of Fort Stanwix, their victory at Oriskany encouraged them to strike American settlements again on May 30, 1778. With intelligence from his sister and other informants, Brant knew that many American farmers had left their homes to fight the British and that their settlements were made vulnerable by their departure. Three hundred Iroquois Indians from many of the Six Nations attacked American settlements all along the Mohawk River, killing and capturing many settlers and burning homes and crops. At the same time, one thousand Iroquois warriors followed British Colonel John Butler into the Wyoming Valley of Pennsylvania. Approximately five thousand Americans fled their homes for Forty Fort, and as the Iroquois advanced, three hundred Americans rushed forward in an offensive movement to meet Butler's forces. With rifles, arrows, knives, and tomahawks, the Iroquois cut down the attackers, ultimately killing approximately 360 people, wounding others, and forcing over 4,600 to escape into the woods, where some died of exposure. In late June 1778, Brant and Butler joined forces to take the war offensively to American settlers along the Mohawk and Schoharie river valleys.

Joseph Brant and the Iroquois rested a few months but rose again after an American army destroyed the villages of Unadilla and Oghwaga. In November 1778 the Iroquois retaliated, striking south of the Mohawk River at Cherry Valley, killing thirty people and wounding over seventy others. The Americans responded in 1779 when Colonel Daniel Brodhead marched north into western New York, burning a fiery path through Seneca country. While Brodhead cut north from Pittsburgh, American General James Clinton traveled west from Albany, and General John Sullivan moved east from Easton, Pennsylvania. They joined forces at Tioga Point, New York, with a force numbering thirty-two hundred men, as well as cannons to be used in case of a siege. They headed west along the Chemung River and soon learned that the Iroquois and British had dug in at an Indian village called Newtown. With cannons blasting and soldiers charging, the Americans overran Iroquois and British forces, driving them from the battlefield and pressing the attack far beyond Newtown.

The Iroquois and British lost only thirty men, but the fight proved disastrous as the Indians moved swiftly toward the Canadian border. Sullivan and his men moved pell mell through Iroquois country, killing and burning in scorched-earth fashion in order to cripple Brant and the Iroquois people. Some Iroquois moved west into Pennsylvania, Ohio, and Michigan, where they reestablished themselves. In 1780, Seneca war parties struck Brodhead at Fort Pitt, harassing Americans living in western Pennsylvania. In 1782, Brant led a war party from Detroit into Ohio and Pennsylvania, but these Iroquois strikes were not as lethal as those in the Cherry and Wyoming valleys. The Iroquois had lost their punch. As British fortunes waned, so did those of the Iroquois. Like the Cherokees and other southern tribes, the Six Nations failed to defeat the Americans, even with the aid of British allies. As a result, American soldiers and colonists posed a threat to their homes, land, culture, and sovereignty.

The war forced Molly Brant and many other Iroquois to flee to Canada. In 1783, she moved to Cataraqui in Ontario (present-day Kingston). For years she had served as a diplomat between her people and the British, keeping her younger brother informed about British and American plans, settlers, and troop movements. Her intelligence greatly helped the British and Iroquois during the Battle of Oriskany. She also supplied those fighting against the Americans with food and ammunition. She was born into a leadership family and was married to Sir William Johnson. She lived out her life dedicated to Iroquois people, and her family continues to influence the course of Iroquois affairs today. Mohawk Maurice Kenny recently honored Molly Brant with a book that emphasizes her courageous leadership during a detrimental era of American history.

TRIBES OF THE OLD NORTHWEST

Most Native Americans living in the Ohio River Valley during the American Revolution also believed it was in their best interest to side with the British. Although Delawares, Wyandots, Shawnees, Ottawas, Miamis, and others professed neutrality in 1774, they soon decided to use the British to help them drive the Americans from their homelands and hunting grounds. Driven from their homes, Shawnees and Delawares moved south of the Ohio River in 1776 to attack isolated American settlements or "stations" in Kentucky. White settlers responded either by returning east or removing to Boonesborough, St. Asaph's, or Harrodsburg. These were three palisade forts, designed to defend settlers against Indian attacks. Shawnee chief Blackfish launched the first major attack of Boonesborough on March 7, 1777, and laid siege to all the American forts for months. In August, Colonel John Bowman brought one hundred reinforcements, and fifty more arrived in September. By then, Blackfish and the Shawnees had accomplished their goal of penning up the Americans so that they had no provisions for winter. As Blackfish moved north to his villages above the Ohio River, American settlers faced a winter of near-starvation. Except for meat and water, they had little else.

In January 1778, Shawnees captured Daniel Boone, who led the war party to Blue Licks, where he convinced thirty white men to surrender in order to save the families back at the forts. The Shawnees took Boone and the other men north to their village at Chillicothe, Ohio, where the Indians adopted sixteen of the whites into the Shawnee nation. Blackfish adopted Boone as a son, and the Shawnees treated these whites as family, until Boone escaped and raced south into Kentucky to warn the Americans of an impending attack. In September 1778, Blackfish attacked Kentucky again, laying siege to Boonesborough until giving up and moving back to his villages in Ohio. Still, Shawnee, Wyandot, Delaware, and other native parties moved about Kentucky, taking advantage of settlers whenever possible. Throughout 1778, Shawnees and Delawares also attacked Americans in western Pennsylvania, as well as at Fort Henry on the east side of the Ohio River. In spring of 1778, American General Edward Hand left Fort Pitt, traveling north and west through Ohio to Sandusky, located on the western edge of Lake Erie. Although Hand burned villages and engaged a few native people, his expedition was a failure. It served to encourage Indians throughout Ohio to stand with the British against the "Long Knives."

While small parties of Shawnees, Delawares, Wyandots, and others moved throughout Kentucky harassing white settlers, the flow of American settlers into Kentucky increased in 1778 and 1779. In part, this was because most Indian villages were located north of the Ohio River or south, in Tennessee. Whites had to contend with Indians raiding in Kentucky, but only a few lived in the region. Equally important, whites could buy one hundred acres for about ten shillings, and if they chose lands farther west, they could claim four hundred acres for nothing. Farmers, ferrymen, trappers, tavern keepers, millers, hunters, loggers, bakers, smiths, and a host of other "frontier" types built new towns, like Louisville at the falls of the Ohio River, and Nashville on the Cumberland River. They built the "Wilderness Road" into Kentucky, which brought thousands of settlers west. Successful settlement of whites encouraged others from the East or Europe to resettle Indian lands. More whites arrived and demanded more land. And so it went in the West, threatening the existence of numerous tribes. Indians resisted, attacking settlers and attempting to drive them from their lands.

In response to Indian attacks throughout the western borders of the United States, young George Rogers Clark of Kentucky and 175 men struck out for the Illinois country in the summer of 1778. In July, he easily captured Fort Kaskaskia, and he quickly won over French farmers. Soon Cahokia and Vincennes fell to the Americans, and by August, Clark claimed control of Illinois. He called a conference at Cahokia, telling the chiefs and their people that the United States now held Illinois. Native Americans from many tribes listened to Clark and accepted his generous gifts of trade items. Some leaders from the upper Mississippi River Valley and the Ohio country accepted the Americans as their allies, but others returned to their villages still fearing the threat of American immigration. General Lachlan McIntosh followed up on Clark's victories in Illinois by leading one thousand men into Ohio, building Fort McIntosh on Big Beaver Creek, and marching through Ohio on an ill-fated trip to Detroit. McIntosh's expedition was not successful and had to turn back. Building Forts McIntosh and Laurens enraged Delawares, Shawnees, Wyandots, Miamis, Ottawas, and Chippewas, inciting war parties to strike the Americans whenever possible. McIntosh's expedition countered Clark's success in Illinois, as did Iroquois victories in New York.

When Captain Henry Hamilton, commander of Fort Detroit, learned of Clark's victory at Vincennes, he marched south with several hundred Wyandot, Delaware, Shawnee, Ottawa, and Miami Indians, as well as British soldiers. This force captured Vincennes in December 1778 and remained there for the winter. When Clark learned that the Indians and British had taken Vincennes, he marched through mud, icy waters, and cold rains with 172 men, who surprised Hamilton and forced him to surrender. Surviving Indians returned home defeated, but Clark sent the British officers to Virginia. Clark determined to augment his forces with Virginians and Kentuckians and attack Detroit. On his way to join Clark, Colonel John Bowman and his Kentucky rifles first moved north of the Ohio River to attack the Shawnee at Chillicothe. When the Kentuckians finished fighting Shawnees, nearly all of them returned to their homes, likely fearing reprisals. Only thirty men accompanied Bowman, and only 150 Virginians answered Clark's call for reinforcements to attack Detroit. With such a small force, Clark did not risk attacking Detroit.

Believing they had Clark at a disadvantage, in 1780, Captain Henry Bird marched from Detroit down the Miami River toward Kentucky in order to create a diversion for Emanuel Hesse, who was to attack south from Mackinac. Bird had 150 soldiers and one thousand Indian allies, as well as two cannons. They traveled south of the Ohio River into the Licking Valley of Kentucky. American settlers at Riddle's and Martin's stations surrendered to Bird, and with one hundred prisoners, Bird and his force returned to Detroit. In the meantime, Hesse moved south with one thousand Indian allies (including Sacs from Wisconsin) and British regulars from Mackinac along the western shore of Lake Michigan to the Mississippi River and south to Cahokia. The Indians attacked the Americans under Clark at Fort Cahokia, but the native warriors soon gave up the fight and moved south to attack the Spanish post at St. Louis. They were met there by cannon and gunfire, so they retreated, fearing all the while that Clark would strike them from the rear. American Colonel John Montgomery and a small force followed Hesse's footsteps north to the Sac villages in Wisconsin, where he attacked their villages and burned their crops.

While Montgomery moved north to the Sac villages, Clark hurried east to support the Kentucky settlers under attack by Bird and his native allies. At Harrodsburg he rallied one thousand Kentucky rifles, eager for revenge against the Indians for their recent attacks on the Kentucky stations. Clark and his army carved a destructive path north into Ohio, burning Chillicothe and laying siege to Piqua on the Big Miami River. Wyandots, Delawares, Shawnees, Ottawas, Miamis, and others fought with the help of a white man, Simon Girty, but Clark's cannon battered away at the Indian defenses, forcing the warriors to flee. Small raiding parties moved out of New York and Ohio into Kentucky and Pennsylvania, but these were few and ineffective in preventing white migration. Conflict between the Americans and Indians died down until 1782, when three hundred Pennsylvania militiamen crossed the Ohio River intent on taking Indian lands. They stopped at Gnadenhütten, a Delaware village in east-central Ohio inhabited by friendly Indians who were under the influence of the Moravian church. After being hosted for three days, the militia turned against the Delawares, murdering twenty-nine men, twenty-seven women, and thirty-four children. Descendants of Delawares and other Native Americans from the Old Northwest have not forgotten the unprovoked massacre of peaceful, Christian Indians at Gnadenhütten.

Delawares, Wyandots, Shawnees, Ottawas, Miamis, Chippewas, and others moved into action, attacking white settlements in the Ohio River Valley. In May 1782, Colonel William Crawford marched from Fort Pitt to the Sandusky River in central Ohio bent on punishing the Indians for their attacks. Near Upper Sandusky, Ohio, he met a combined force of Delawares, Shawnees, Wyandots, and others who fought a fierce one-day battle on June 4 that ended in Crawford's rout and the death of fifty Americans. The Americans ran from the battlefield, but pursuing Indians captured nine soldiers, including Crawford. Although various Indians asked for leniency, the Delawares refused because of their disdain for Crawford and the murders at Gnadenhütten. They stripped Crawford naked, tossed hot coals on him, poked him with sharp sticks, and slowly burned him to death. Brant followed up with attacks on western Pennsylvania, while a British force under Alexander McKee and William Caldwell moved from Detroit into Kentucky. Daniel Boone helped track McKee and Caldwell, and he warned his Kentucky cohorts of a possible ambush. The Americans ignored the old man's warnings and walked into a trap during the Battle of Blue Licks, which cost the lives of sixty Kentucky volunteers. Clark responded to the attack with another strike at Chillicothe and Piqua, but to no avail. In spite of the Revolutionary War and many attempts to dislodge the British and discourage Native Americans, Indians still held sway in the Old Northwest above the Ohio River.

ORDINANCES AND INDIANS

Most of the fighting of the Revolutionary War ended in 1781 when General Lord Cornwallis surrendered after the Battle of Yorktown. But more fighting seemed inevitable because the various states claimed western lands that belonged to Native Americans, and local, state, and national governments encouraged white immigration westward. Following the Revolutionary War and the signing of the Peace of Paris in 1783, Congress claimed all lands from the Atlantic to the Mississippi River–lands still claimed and inhabited by a host of tribes. In addition, various states also claimed lands in the West and continued to sell them to settlers until the states agreed to allow Congress to deal with western lands. However, even though the states gave up most of their claims to native lands in the West, many held on to "reserves" for state disposition. For example, Virginia retained a claim on 150,000 acres of land in Ohio on the north bank of the river as a reward for the service of George Rogers Clark and his men. Virginia also kept another huge segment of land between the Scioto and Little Miami rivers, while Connecticut kept the "Western Reserve" of almost four million acres in northeastern Ohio below Lake Erie. New York, New Hampshire, Massachusetts, North Carolina, South Carolina, and Georgia also claimed western lands, most of which they ceded to the Congress of the United States in the late eighteenth and early nineteenth centuries.

After the states ceded most lands to Congress, Congress formed a committee to recommend a mechanism by which the government would deal with western lands. The result was the Ordinance of 1785, whereby "government-owned" lands would be divided into six-mile squares called townships. The townships would be subdivided into thirty-six sections of one mile square, or 640 acres, and sold for $1 per acre. Congress kept four sections of each township as a future investment and set aside one section for a public school. This is the origin of township schools. Two years later, Congress passed the Ordinance of 1787, which created a Northwest Territory, which would be divided ultimately into three to five states. Congress would select a governor, secretary, and three judges to administer the territory. When the population of white males twenty-one years and older who owned property reached five thousand, the citizens could elect a legislature and work with an administrative council chosen by the governor. When the territorial population reached sixty thousand, the territory could adopt a constitution and apply for statehood. Although Congress prohibited slavery in the Northwest Territory, slavery of African-Americans, including those of mixed African-Native American blood, continued in the southern territories and states.

Through these two laws of 1785 and 1787, the United States found an orderly means to deal with the sale of western lands and transitional government from territory to statehood. The Ordinance of 1787 promised that the United States would provide "utmost good faith" in dealing with Indians, their lands, and property. The ordinance stated that "their land and property shall never be taken from them without their consent" and that "they shall never be invaded . . . unless in just and lawful wars." The government claimed the right to enact laws pertaining to native peoples that were just and humane in order to prevent "wrongs done to them." Additionally, the ordinance provided for Indian education but not the means to effectuate this grand proposal. The two ordinances were designed for the benefit of whites, not Indians, particularly white males, because white females—like Native Americans—were not citizens. White Americans did not include native peoples in their new nation, because Indians were considered sovereign but foreign and inferior nations that were outside the covenant of the United States. However, white Americans worried about angering the western tribes and triggering more warfare. But they generally saw Indians as a barrier to white expansion, progress, civilization, and national growth.

Between 1782, when the last fighting of the Revolutionary War ended in the Ohio Valley, and 1787, when the Constitution was framed, Indians ran their own affairs because they were independent nations. During the revolution and in its aftermath, Congress assumed power over many aspects of Indian relations and administered its Indian policies through a Committee on Indian Affairs. Under the Articles of Confederation, Congress had "sole and exclusive right and power of . . . regulating trade and managing all affairs with Indians, not members of any of the states, provided that the legislative right of any state within its own limits be not infringed or violated." Most states had their own Indian policies under the Articles, so native people had to contend with a dual system of American policies. At the same time that the national government set forth its policies toward Indians, so did state and local governments. Often these policies were at odds with each other, causing problems, conflicts, and resentment.

BUFFALO PARTY AND FEDERAL INDIAN POLICY

George Washington and other officials familiar with native peoples pushed for centralized control of Indian policy. State and local officials challenged the right of Congress to administer Indian policy on a national level, often arguing that national politicians–living far removed from Native Americans–were too soft on former enemies of the United States. In New York, hostilities toward most Iroquois ran so high that local politicians formed the Buffalo Party, which set forth an Indian policy of extermination of all Indians. The view of most members of the Buffalo Party was set forth by a New York editor named Brackenridge, who wrote that rather than whites acknowledging Indian title to any land, he believed that Native Americans had surrendered their claim to lands because "not having made better use" of the earth for hundreds of years, Native Americans "had forfeited all pretense to a claim." Brackenridge said he would much rather admit the land title of a buffalo over an Indian. He believed that all Native Americans were "fierce and cruel" and that whites should exterminate all Indians as an "honorable" objective to clear the United States of "the animals vulgarly called Indians." Such journalism swayed public opinion against Native Americans and helped elect a number of politicians from upstate New York who hated native peoples whether or not they had sided with the United States during the American Revolution. Not all Americans believed in extermination, but many acknowledged the right of states to take native lands and open them to white settlement.

Editors such as Brackenridge would have never acknowledged the fact that some Founding Fathers were influenced by the cooperative work of the Iroquois Confederacy. According to Yamasee historian Donald Grinde and Bruce Johansen, delegates to the Philadelphia Convention at Independence Hall in 1787 considered the Iroquois Confederacy as a model for a new government. The delegates heard numerous speeches by skilled politicians, including Benjamin Franklin, who urged his colleagues to study the Iroquois Confederacy, which had unified five woodland nations for years and more recently added the Tuscaroras. The Iroquois Confederacy had always stressed political equality, individual freedom, free speech, and a sense of a common political community. Some of these ideas were also in vogue during the Enlightenment and influenced many of the delegates during the convention. One of the important topics discussed by delegates was Native Americans, and most delegates favored a national Indian policy over thirteen separate state policies. The Commerce Clause of the Constitution is found in Article 1, Section 8, which states that the House and Senate shall "regulate commerce with foreign nations, and among the several States, and with the Indian tribes." Congress extended its authority to regulate other issues involving the tribes, while the Senate ratified Indian treaties with a two-thirds vote before sending the treaties to the president to be signed.

The Ordinance of 1786 had divided the United States west of the Appalachian Mountains into northern and southern agencies directed by two superintendents. Historian Paul Prucha has detailed how Congress considerably expanded its role in Indian affairs after the states ratified the Constitution. Congress enacted laws in 1790, 1793, and 1796, creating the Federal Factory System and regulating trade and intercourse with the tribes. The United States licensed Indian traders, tried unsuccessfully to prohibit liquor sales to Native Americans, and formally dealt with the tribes. Most important, the United States negotiated with Native Americans over treaties that were ratified by the Senate with a two-thirds vote and became law when signed by the president. Thus, the United States created national Indian policy by entering into formal agreements between the tribes.

Following the example established in the Articles of Confederation, the War Department handled most Indian policies of the government. However, territorial governors and special commissioners also acted on behalf of the government, making treaties and negotiating agreements between sovereign peoples. Although the United States promised good faith in dealing with the tribes, federal, state, and local governmental officials often acted in bad faith when dealing with the tribes. Secretary Henry Knox argued that "Indians being the prior occupants, possess the right of the soil. It cannot be taken from them unless by their free consent, or by the right of conquest in case of a just war." However, native title to the land could be liquidated with formal agreements. Treaties became a major vehicle through which the national government dealt with the tribes, particularly in relationship to their lands. Government officials wrote the treaties, convened treaty councils, and convinced some leaders among native peoples to cede lands to the United States for paltry sums of money often paid in goods rather than cash. Treaties became the basis of American Indian policy administered by the national government, while state governments such as those of New York, Virginia, North Carolina, South Carolina, and others seized native lands and claimed them outright.

After the states ratified the Constitution in 1789 and elected Washington president, Congress created the Department of War, empowering it to administer Indian affairs. Through superintendents, commissioners, agents, and military officers, the United States negotiated treaties with sovereign Indian nations. During the late eighteenth and early nineteenth centuries, many civilians working within the War Department and presidential administrations believed that Native Americans could be civilized and assimilated into American society. The government encouraged and provided funds to Christian organizations like the

Society for the United Brethren for Propagating the Gospel among the Heathen, the Missionary and Bible Society of the Methodist Episcopal Church in America, and the American Board of Commissioners for Foreign Missions to conduct mission work among Indians. Methodists, Moravians, Quakers, Baptists, Episcopalians, Congregationalists, Presbyterians, and others also established missions, but their views of native people and those of enlightened government officials, did not represent those of most whites in the western settlements.

The vast majority of white settlers wished to develop commercial agriculture, transportation systems, and urban areas. They viewed American Indians as impediments to white progress, civilization, and nation building. Settlers re-created political institutions they had known in the eastern states, which gave all white males twenty-one years of age and older who owned property the right to vote. Indians, women, and African-Americans did not have the right to vote. White men voted to send men of like mind to represent them at every governmental level. Town councils, territorial legislatures, and Congress were often filled with men who believed that Americans should liquidate Indian title to every acre of land and force Indians across the Mississippi River. No one typified this attitude more than William Henry Harrison, the twenty-six-year-old Jeffersonian elected to represent the Northwest Territory in 1799. Harrison used every opportunity to advocate and effectuate the cession of Indian lands to the United States and the removal of Indians from their homelands.

Most Indians remained peaceful from 1782 to 1785 but justifiably weary of the Americans who wanted to remove them so that whites could resettle their lands. Indian removal had always been a part of American history, and the United States decided on a policy of "voluntary" removal immediately following the Revolution, encouraging native peoples through any means possible to move away from American settlements. Americans continued the European tradition of dealing with the tribes through written treaties, even though most Native Americans could not read English and relied on translators hired by the government to explain details of such agreements. Americans, not Indians, created written treaties, and Americans constructed the treaties for their own benefit, not that of Indian people. This was the nature of American Indian policies.

Treaties became a foundation of American Indian policy after the Revolution, and the first treaties made by the United States with Indian nations were concluded prior to the Constitution. The first treaty with the Delaware allowed American troops to move unmolested through Indian country, but more important were the treaties negotiated after the Revolution. The United States took the position that it had defeated the tribes and so it could dictate policies to the vanquished. The vast majority of Indian people had nothing to do with the first treaties of the United States, but minority groups within the tribes often made agreements that the government then applied to all Iroquois, Delaware, Wyandot, Shawnee, Cherokee, and others. A sham to Indian peoples, the treaties became legal documents used by the government of the United States to dispossess the people of property and resources.

In 1784, Congress gave five Indian commissioners instructions to meet with the tribes, and to this end, three of them treated with representatives of the Iroquois at Fort Stanwix, pushing the leaders to relinquish their claim to the Old Northwest. Some Iroquois signed the Treaty of Fort Stanwix (1784), surrendering Iroquois claims in the Ohio River Valley. With the Iroquois out of their way, the commissioners turned south to treat with Wyandots, Delawares, Ottawas, and Chippewas (Anishinaabes). On January 21, 1785, some Indian leaders–including the famous Kelelamand or Colonel Henry–agreed to the Treaty of Fort McIntosh, ceding a portion of Ohio to the United States, except for lands in north central and western Ohio between the Cayahoga-Tuscarawas rivers and the Maumee River on the western edge of Lake Erie. Under the agreement, the United States could keep its posts on the Great Miami River, Maumee River, and mouth of the Sandusky River on Lake Erie. Leaders of the five groups of Shawnees refused to recognize the agreement, and others agreed with the Shawnee view.

WAR ALONG THE OHIO

Many Indians resented these treaties and hated white outlaws who flooded into Ohio, claiming lands and ignoring Indian rights. These white men stole lands from Ohio to Illinois still inhabited and used by Indians. Native warriors and women discussed the actions of these outlaws in councils that included their own tribes and leaders from other groups. American commissioners and military men became so alarmed about a possible war that they ordered Colonel Josiah Harmar to use American troops to remove the white invaders. Harmar moved through the Ohio River Valley, informing whites that they were trespassing on Indian lands, but white setters claimed they had a right to the land and would remain. Harmar refused to use his troops to remove whites by force, so Native Americans in western New York, Pennsylvania, and the Ohio country met in councils to discuss their situation. Major leaders among the tribes included Tarhe of the Wyandot, Blue Jacket of the Shawnee, Little Turtle of the Miami, Red Jacket of the Seneca, and Joseph Brant of the Mohawk. These men and many others spoke out against the Americans who claimed native lands by conquest. In response, Indian commissioners met some Wyandot, Delaware, and Shawnee leaders at a council on January 31, 1786, in southwestern Ohio at Fort Finney.

Rather than resolve conflicts, the Treaty of Fort Finney heightened tensions and helped trigger warfare. The new treaty extended the line of white settlement from the Great Miami River west to the White River in present-day Indiana. By means of this treaty, a few Shawnee agreed to the provisions of the Fort McIntosh Treaty. But no sooner had these few Indians agreed to the Fort Finney Treaty than they denounced it, organized for war, and fell upon illegal white settlers, settlements, and traders. Other tribes also became openly hostile. Miamis, Chippewas, Ottawas, Potawatomis, Kickapoos, Senecas, and other native peoples of the Great Lakes region joined in a confederacy with Wyandots, Delawares, and Shawnees. They repudiated the treaties at Forts Stanwix, McIntosh, and Finney, and they agreed by 1788 to cede no more land to the United States. They also agreed to ally with the British still occupying posts near the Great Lakes and to press for a new treaty that recognized native rights to all the Ohio country north of the Ohio River. Thus, Indians throughout the region responded with resistance and an armed confederacy to the white invasion and theft of native lands.

In July 1786, about five hundred Miami warriors threatened Vincennes, announcing they would kill all Americans in the area. Although they left without a fight, their appearance in the white settlement signaled heightened hostilities. Fearing future conflict, George Rogers Clark, the old veteran living in Kentucky, organized a force of twelve hundred men that moved north of the Ohio River before falling apart due to desertions. But another force under Colonel Benjamin Logan moved up the Great Miami River of western Ohio, destroying Indian villages and large quantities of corn. Clark's failure encouraged the tribes, and Logan's expedition angered them. In 1786 and 1787, the tribes held two large councils to denounce the treaties and whites, determining that no whites should be allowed above the Ohio River. This was at the very time Generals Rufus Putnam and Benjamin Tupper–as well as the government's land officer, Colonel William Duer–engineered a corrupt bargain to sell the Ohio Company and the Scioto Company millions of acres of land for as little as 8¢ an acre instead of the $1 prescribed by the Ordinance of 1785. The Indian councils had no idea about the land deals or the fact that Congress had created a new bureaucracy called the Indian Department with superintendents of Indian affairs in the North and South to execute Indian policies of the new nation. At the same time, Congress ordered more troops to western posts. Indians and Americans had set the stage for war.

Native Americans believed that the United States demonstrated its arrogance and disregard for Indian rights by allowing the Ohio Company to build a settlement called Marietta in the spring of 1788. Parties of native warriors struck fear into the hearts of many Americans, and Kentucky volunteers broke up into small parties to raid native people north of the Ohio. Governor Arthur St. Clair responded to the threat of Indian war by calling another council with the tribes in January 1789 at Fort Harmar. Wyandot, Delaware, Seneca, Shawnee, Kickapoo, Miami, and others of the united Indian nations attended the council. The Indians became divided over a permanent boundary line that would separate whites from natives. Joseph Brant had urged the tribes to designate the Muskingum River as their boundary, but Shawnees, Kickapoos, Miamis, and members of other tribes remained firm that whites should remove from all lands, posts, and communities north of the Ohio River. St. Clair created the Treaty of Fort Harmar, and some Indians signed it before returning to their villages more angry than before.

While the tribes sent war belts from village to village mustering men to stand against the Americans, Congress passed the first of four Trade and Intercourse Acts on July 22, 1790, designed to create economic, political, and legal relations between the government and the tribes. These acts have been skillfully analyzed by Paul Prucha, who established that the acts set forth the principle that ownership of Indian lands could be negotiated only by the federal government, not states, and this has become the basis of many land claims cases in the late twentieth century. It is doubtful that many Indians knew specifics about the Trade and Intercourse Acts or cared, because of the threat they felt from white encroachment on their lands. As a result, many tribes responded to the call, and many woodlands peoples sent their men to face the Americans. In the autumn of 1790, General Harmar organized an army to fight the Indians. He and his soldiers left Fort Washington near present-day Cincinnati for the Maumee River but could not find native warriors.

While Harmar's soldiers searched in vain for their enemies, the warriors had no trouble tracking the movements of the Long Knives. The tribes had gathered in the thick forests surrounding the Maumee River to challenge Harmar's troops but remained out of harm's way to watch the white men. Harmar marched up the Maumee and then turned about as if to move back to the Ohio River. Believing he could outsmart the Indians, Harmar sent some of his troops back to the Maumee River to surprise the unsuspecting warriors. Instead, the Indians were waiting for them, striking hard and killing 183 American soldiers. Harmar made a hasty retreat to avoid further casualties while the Indians celebrated their victory. However, the United States did not end its campaign with a single fight but instead ordered Arthur St. Clair to lead a force into the Ohio country. With a force of three thousand men, St. Clair reached the Maumee River in northwestern Ohio in November 1791. His men, tired after traveling some distance and building three log posts along the way, set up camp quickly to get much-needed rest. However, the Americans retired without posting guards. A combined Indian force, with many led by Little Turtle (Miami), surrounded and surprised St. Clair. The Indians killed 630 soldiers and wounded 283 more. This was the greatest military victory by Native Americans against the United States in all of American history, and one that propelled many young men into tribal prominence, including a young Shawnee leader named Tecumseh. St. Clair escaped with his life and rapidly retreated south. Native American patriots had won the day against a large American army, and many believed themselves invincible.

BATTLE OF FALLEN TIMBERS

In the wake of St. Clair's monumental defeat, Shawnees, Wyandots, Delawares, Miamis, Senecas, Mohawks, Potawatomis, and others joined in the raids against American settlers, traders, surveyors, and speculators. Tecumseh joined his older brother, Chiksika, who was living in Tennessee with Muscogees and Cherokees. Tecumseh's family was related to the Muscogees through his mother, so he had a long-standing relationship with the southern tribe. Tecumseh, his brother, and other Shawnees helped Muscogee and Cherokee warriors raid white settlements in the South. When Tecumseh's brother was killed in a fight with whites near Nashville, Tecumseh joined a party of Chickasaws to continue the fight against his enemy. Tecumseh moved throughout the South, visiting villages of several tribes and establishing diplomatic contacts that he would use in the future. Late in 1793 Tecumseh learned that American troops were gathering at Cincinnati, so he headed north to join Shawnees under Blue Jacket, the combined native force in western Ohio.

During the winter and spring of 1791–1792, native fighters threatened all settlements on both sides of the Ohio River. They also met agents with instructions from Lord Dorchester and John G. Simcoe—well-placed government officials in Canada—who encouraged the Indians to demand an Indian state north of the Ohio River and the complete withdrawal of all Americans from the region. American commissioners had planned to council with leaders of the united Indian nations at Sandusky, and Native American leaders planned to use this council as their opportunity to press their demand for an Indian state. However, before the council took place in 1793, American commissioners learned of the demand and did not travel to Sandusky. When President George Washington learned the nature of Indian demands, he ordered General Anthony Wayne to attack. In the autumn of 1793, Wayne advanced to Fort Jefferson, east of the present-day boundary of Ohio and Indiana, then a few miles north to the Greenville River, where he built a post. Indian scouts watched his movement but waited, patiently. Rather than risk a campaign that might be prolonged into the approaching winter, Wayne waited until the spring of 1794 to strike.

*Tecumseh was a Shawnee leader
and the architect of a pan-
Indian confederacy designed to
unite several native nations in
a political and military movement. A great orator, warrior,
and statesman, Tecumseh is considered by many Indians to be
a great native patriot.*

Throughout the winter, Wayne trained his troops and prepared for
the upcoming campaign. Indian warriors from many tribes assembled
at Fort Miami on the Maumi River near present-day Toledo, Ohio. In
February 1794, Lord Dorchester assured Indian leaders that British
soldiers would fight with them against the Long Knives and help
native peoples restore their claims to all of Ohio. Between fifteen
hundred and two thousand warriors prepared for war at or near Fort
Miami, while runners watched Wayne move north to Fort Recovery.
Wayne defeated the Indians in a small skirmish and marched forward
to the Maumee River. He built a preliminary fortification in the woods
by the river and told native allies that he would attack on August 17,
1794. Little Turtle had warned the Indians that Wayne had moved
through the woods like a blacksnake and that they should be wary of
him. The comparison gave rise to Wayne's native name, Blacksnake.
But the war leaders were determined to defeat Wayne at a place they
chose to defend. In the thick, green forest near Fort Miami, the Indians knew a place torn apart by a great whirlwind. Trees had been
uprooted and thrown into tangles. At this place where the timbers
had fallen, the native people set up their defenses and waited for
Wayne.

On August 17, Wayne moved his troops up the Maumee but
stopped ten miles short of Fallen Timbers. Already the warriors had

started their fast, cleansing their bodies, minds, and souls for the coming fight. They waited for Wayne and continued their fast for three days, not knowing exactly when the attack would come. When Wayne received word from his scouts that approximately five hundred Indians had gone to Fort Miami for food, he sent two columns forward to begin the attack. Approximately eight hundred Shawnees, Miamis, Wyandots, Delawares, and others fought from the dead and tangled trees, but Wayne's troops kept up a constant fire as they moved forward, using a frontal and left flank movement. After a two-hour fight, the warriors retreated into the forest, some escaping to Fort Miami. The British refused to fight with the Indians or aid them, as Lord Dorchester had promised. In fact, they locked the gates so the retreating warriors could not seek refuge in the fort. When the Battle of Fallen Timbers occurred, the British would not risk another war with the United States by engaging Wayne's troops or aiding the Indians in any way. About fifty Indians died during the battle, which was not a large number, but the fight was devastating for the tribes because it broke their spirit. Not only had they not effectively resisted Wayne, but also their allies had let them down. The future appeared bleak for the northwestern tribes who had to live under the ever-mounting stress of the white invasion.

Wayne marched west along the Maumee River after the battle, establishing Fort Wayne in present-day Indiana and wintering at Fort Greenville. In the spring of 1795, Wayne held a council with several leaders of twelve tribes, laying out the terms of the Treaty of Greenville, which forced the tribes to surrender a portion of eastern Indiana and all of Ohio, except for the northwest quadrant. Indian leaders promised to live peacefully with whites and end their alliance with the British. The treaty had far-reaching consequences for Native Americans living north of the Ohio River, because it opened millions of acres of Indian lands to white settlement. The treaty signing ignited a land rush unprecedented in American history through the eighteenth century as "Great Land Animals" swarmed over the Ohio River to lay claims and resettle territory once the sole domain of native peoples. The treaty and subsequent land rush also created more problems for the Indians, who regrouped and discussed the future of their sovereign nations. Although many Native Americans believed that they could still stand strong against the Long Knives and regain lost lands, others wondered and worried about which course of action they should take in their dealings with whites. Intertribal and intratribal discussions and arguments emerged, and societal stress and cultural tension became common among many native peoples in the wake of Wayne's treaty at Greenville.

SOUTHERN TRIBES

The troubles visited on the Indians of the Old Northwest between the end of the American Revolution and 1800 were repeated in the South, where whites continually and unlawfully seized native lands. White settlers claimed native lands as their own and resettled on choice parcels previously cleared by Native American farmers and hunters throughout the South. In the Northwest, many tribes had allied with the British, but in the South many allied with the Spanish. Choctaws, Muscogees, and Chickasaws feared American expansionists, and they well knew that the southern states extended their claims westward onto lands that were the sole domain of native peoples. These tribes watched as their Cherokee neighbors, who lived in close proximity to American settlers in Kentucky, Tennessee, North Carolina, and Georgia, were overrun by white settlers. In order to protect their own interests, Choctaws, Muscogees, and Chickasaws concluded a treaty of alliance with Spain, agreeing not to trade with anyone without a Spanish license.

Cherokees did not make a treaty with the Spanish, in part because they were busy dealing with a tide of white immigrants who proposed a new state of "Franklin" and negotiated the Treaty of Dumplin Creek with minor Cherokee leaders in 1785. Although the United States repudiated this treaty by an unauthorized "state," the government did not intervene with military support to force settlers off Cherokee lands. Instead, the United States instructed its Indian commissioners to meet Cherokees as well as Choctaws and Chickasaws at Hopewell on the Keowee River. Leaders of the Cherokee, Choctaw, and Chickasaw nations counciled with American negotiators at Hopewell off and on in 1785 and 1786, and all these tribes ultimately signed treaties with the Americans. For example, the Cherokees concluded the Treaty of Hopewell on November 18, 1785, agreeing to be under the protection of the United States and permitting the government to regulate trade and try any American criminal acting within Cherokee lands. The Cherokees secured their sovereignty under the terms of the treaty and agreed to maintain peace with the United States.

Although the United States acted in good faith after ratifying the Treaty of Hopewell, the government did little to prevent white settlers from crossing boundaries set forth in the treaty and stealing additional Cherokee lands. Under the terms of the treaties, whites had right-of-way through native lands as well as guaranteed sites for military and trading posts. Often whites settled along these roadways, establishing taverns, ferries, and other businesses. Others took their goods up navigable rivers to and through native lands. Minor problems arose between whites and Indians, so rather than wait until major hostilities erupted, forty Cherokee leaders, including war chiefs from the Chickamauga villages, met American negotiators at present-day Knoxville to negotiate the Treaty of Holston in 1791. The Indians lost the lands stolen by whites who had violated the Treaty of Hopewell. They agreed to allow whites to navigate the Tennessee River and have right-of-way through Indian lands. They hoped that these concessions and well-defined boundaries would end their difficulties with white settlers. Their hopes vanished soon after when white volunteers burned Cherokee villages, destroyed farms, and murdered innocent people. Cherokee warriors retaliated, attacking American settlements until the people received word of Wayne's victory at Fallen Timbers. Rather than continue the war and face strengthened American forces, Cherokee leaders negotiated a peace agreement with Governor William Blount at the village of Tellico in 1798.

Muscogees under the astute leader Alexander McGillivray, the son of a half-blood native Muscogee woman and a Scottish trader, refused to attend the council at Hopewell. Muscogees were angry over the theft of their lands by Americans and the inability of the southern states to hold back the tide of immigration. Besides, McGillivray was receiving an annual salary from Spain and was not interested in offending his allies. Not until 1790 did McGillivray and the Muscogees enter into the Treaty of New York with President Washington and General Knox, agreeing to "protection" by the United States and accepting an annuity of $1,500, livestock, and farm equipment for Muscogee lands stolen by Georgians.

The treaty did not end native difficulties with whites, as American settlers crossed Muscogee lands, burning, stealing, and killing. Muscogee warriors struck back but negotiated again after Wayne's victory in Ohio. In 1796, they signed the Treaty of Colerain, which recognized boundaries set in the Treaty of New York and restored some of the lands taken illegally by Georgians. Nevertheless, in years to come Muscogees had to surrender land claims on property already stolen from them by white settlers, which was like tearing out their hearts. Benjamin Hawkins, American commissioner, superintendent, and Indian agent, worked with the Muscogee from the 1790s to his death in 1816. During this period he watched whites overrun thousands of acres of Muscogee land while he urged the Indian nation to pursue peace through cultivation and commerce. Many Muscogees followed the path pointed out by Hawkins, whereas others rose against the Americans in the early nineteenth century.

During the first three decades of the nineteenth century, some groups within southern tribes acculturated some aspects of white culture into their own. Some Cherokees set up commercial farming, growing cotton and tobacco with the labor of African-American slaves. Others owned grist mills, saw mills, and cotton gins, selling their services and products to Indians and non-Indians alike. Cherokees and other south-eastern people adopted technologies of European and American origin, including spinning wheels, textile looms, wagons, and farm equipment. However, none of the southeastern Indians assimilated totally into white society. Indeed, the era gave rise to greater native nationalism, and many people sought to preserve and perpetuate selected elements of their culture, including their attachment to their lands. This development is evidenced by a genuine concern for language preservation among all the tribes, including the Cherokee, who developed a written language.

Sequoyah, the Cherokee genius unschooled in English, developed a Cherokee syllabary in 1821. Each symbol represented a consonant and vowel, and it was so basic and easy for Cherokee speakers to learn that thousands of people adopted the written language, translating the Bible into Cherokee and publishing a weekly paper, the *Cherokee Phoenix*, in the language. Other southern tribes developed their own written languages and adopted similar measures to include elements of white culture into their own. They did this to preserve their cultures and placate Americans. As a result of their efforts, white Americans began referring to five nations–Cherokees, Choctaws, Chickasaws, Seminoles, and Muscogees–as the "Five Civilized Tribes." These nations sent nonvoting representatives to Congress to monitor legislation that affected their nations and to lobby in behalf of their people. They learned to speak and read English so they could communicate better with Americans, and they sent their children to public schools. Rather than endear these people to Americans, these efforts often angered whites, who grew jealous of the southern nations. Many whites during the early national period of American history envisioned a day in the near future when they could force the Indians from their lands, steal their improvements, and cancel white debts to native businesses.

The federalist era of American history was a traumatic time for Eastern Woodlands peoples in the North and South. Although the United States offered educational benefits and recognized lands belonging to their former allies–Tuscaroras, Oneidas, and Stockbridges–other Indians lived in a state of anomie. Most Native Americans had sided with the British during the American Revolution and had lost lives, land, property, and cultural elements. Immediately after the war, various states opened western lands they claimed by conquest to white settlement. American and European immigrants poured into New York, Pennsylvania, Ohio, Kentucky, Tennessee, and other areas. Whites claimed native lands and resettled regions that had been the domain of Native Americans. Some tribes fought back, whereas others moved west to escape the conquest. Indians died of diseases, exposure, starvation, and war. Their worlds were torn apart, and the stress placed upon them due to the invasion is immeasurable.

HANDSOME LAKE

In the wake of the wars, treaties, removals, boundary disputes, and diseases, Native Americans turned inward to find solace in their own cultural beliefs. During the federalist era, many native peoples looked to holy men and women within their tribes for answers to their dilemmas. They listened to the words of native prophets, hoping for divine intervention in their troubled lives and clues to their future courses of action. Among many tribes, medicine men and women shared their wisdom and visions of how to deal with the Long Knives. One of these prophets was a Seneca clan leader, brother of the famed war chief Cornplanter, living in upstate New York. His name was Handsome Lake. In 1799, Handsome Lake was on the verge of death, so his family and friends gathered at his side. He passed away. They wept beside his death bed, and they were shocked when Handsome Lake revived to tell them that his spirit had left his body and gone outside to meet three Native American angels. The angels, he said, told him to end his drinking and begin preaching in accordance with thc old teachings and new ones to be taught him by the Master of Life. Handsome Lake was told to expect a fourth angel who would be the Creator.

In the autumn of 1799, Handsome Lake had his second and most significant vision when he "died" and traveled with the Creator to heaven and hell to discuss what native peoples must do to preserve their cultures in the wake of the American conquest. According to Anthony F. C. Wallace, Handsome Lake drew heavily on his experiences as well as the ancient beliefs of the Iroquois to revitalize the Longhouse Religion. By the 1830s, Iroquois called the faith the Handsome Lake Church, which teaches the *Gaiwiio* or good words of Handsome Lake. The religion emphasizes that native people are not white people, that they have to draw on the strengths of their own cultures to survive, but that Native Americans should live in peace with whites. By following the positive and constructive teachings of the Seneca Prophet, the people can retain their culture and have a future for their nations. Members of the Handsome Lake Church meet and pray together today, and in the summer during the Strawberry Festival, learned members of the religion stand and tell the story of Handsome Lake, his teachings, and his messages. The Gaiwiio still lives among members of the Haudenosaunee (People of the Longhouse, the Six Iroquois Nations).

Religious revitalizations among Native Americans throughout the East were common during the late eighteenth and early nineteenth centuries. Historian Gregory Dowd has analyzed many of these movements in *Spirited Resistance*, an important work that deals with the inner strength of the tribes as a result of their religions and their common search for a way to deal with the United States and westward expansion of white Americans.

Selected Readings and Bibliography

The American Revolution and federalist era are dealt with in Gibson's *The American Indian,* Francis's *Native Time,* and Debo's *A History of the Indians of the United States.* Kenneth M. Morrison provides an insightful essay, "Native Americans and the American Revolution: Historic Stories and Shifting Frontier Conflict" (pp. 95–115) in Hoxie, *Indians in American History,* while Charles F. Wilkinson provides "Indian Tribes and the American Constitution" (pp. 117–134) in the same volume. For the significance of the Revolution in the South, see Corkran, *The Carolina Indian Frontier,* and for native participation in the war, see Utley and Washburn, *Indian Wars.*

Berkhofer, Robert F. Jr. *The Salvation and the Savage: An Analysis of Protestant Missions and American Indian Response, 1787–1862.* New York: Atheneum, 1972.

Calloway, Collin G. *Crown and Calumet: British-Indian Relations, 1793–1815.* Norman: University of Oklahoma Press, 1987.

——. *The World Turned Upside Down: Indian Voices from Early America.* Boston: Bedford Books, 1994.

Champagne, Duane, ed. *The Native North American Almanac.* Detroit: Gale Researchers, 1994.

Fey, Harold E., and D'Arcy McNickle. *Indians and Other Americans.* New York: Harper, 1959.

Graymont, Barbara. *The Iroquois in the American Revolution.* Syracuse: Syracuse University Press, 1972.

Grinde, Donald A., and Bruce E. Johansen. *The Iroquois and the Foundation of the American Nation.* San Francisco: The Indian Historian Press, 1977.

——. *Exemplar of Liberty.* Los Angeles: American Indian Studies Center, University of California, Los Angeles, 1991.

Harmon, George D. *Sixty Years of Indian Affairs.* Chapel Hill: University of North Carolina Press, 1941.

Hatley, Tom. *The Dividing Paths: Cherokees and South Carolinians through the Revolutionary Era.* New York: Oxford University Press, 1993.

Higgenbotham, Donald. *The War of American Independence.* New York: Macmillan, 1971.

Horsman, Reginald. *Expansions and American Indian Policy, 1783–1812.* East Lansing: Michigan State University Press, 1967.

Kelsey, Isabel Thompson. *Joseph Brant, 1743–1807: Man of Two Worlds.* Syracuse: Syracuse University Press, 1984.

McLoughlin, William G. *Cherokee Renascence in the New Republic.* Princeton: Princeton University Press, 1986.

Mohr, Walter H. *Federal Indian Relations, 1774–1778.* Philadelphia: University of Pennsylvania Press, 1933.

O'Donnell, James Howlette III. *Southern Indians in the American Revolution.* Knoxville: University of Tennessee Press, 1973.

Peace, Roy Harvey. *Savagism and Civilization.* Baltimore: Johns Hopkins University, 1965.

Peake, Ora B. *A History of the United States Indian Factory System.* Denver: Sage Books, 1954.

Prucha, Francis Paul. *American Indian Policy in the Formative Years.* Cambridge: Harvard University Press, 1962.

Smelser, Marshall. *The Winning of Independence.* Chicago: Quadrangle Books, 1972.

Sosin, Jack M. *The Revolutionary Frontier, 1763–83.* New York: Holt, Rinehart and Winston, 1967.

——. "The Use of Indians in the War of the American Revolution: A Re-Assessment of Responsibility." *The American Indian: Past and Present.* Roger L. Nichols and George R. Adams, ed. (New York: John Wiley, 1971). pp. 96–110.

Sword, Wiley. *President Washington's Indian War: The Struggle for the Old Northwest 1790–1795.* Norman: University of Oklahoma Press, 1985.

Turner, Katherine C. *Red Men Calling on the Great White Father.* Norman: University of Oklahoma Press, 1951.

Tyler, S. Lyman. *A History of Indian Policy.* Washington, D.C.: U.S. Government Printing Office, 1973.

Wallace, Anthony F. C. *The Death and Rebirth of the Seneca.* New York: Knopf, 1969.

Washburn, Wilcomb. *Red Man's Land, White Man's Law.* New York: Scribner, 1971.

——. *The Indian in America.* New York: Harper and Row, 1975.

White, Richard. *The Middle Ground.* Cambridge: Cambridge University Press, 1991.

Wilkinson, Charles F. *American Indians, Time, and the Law: Historical Rights at the Bar of the Supreme Court.* New Haven: Yale University Press, 1987.

CHAPTER 7

NATIVE AMERICANS, JEFFERSON, AND JACKSON

Native Americans in the eastern part of the United States faced a difficult time following the Battle of Fallen Timbers and the Treaty of Greenville. The time was a positive one for most whites in the United States, particularly those who desired "free" or cheap land in the West where they could begin life anew. But Native Americans in the North and South had lost a series of important campaigns against the Long Knives and knew they faced enemies in the soldiers and civilian bureaucrats of the United States as well as state and territorial militia troops that could be quickly mustered into military forces in the Old Northwest and Old Southwest. Moving west across the Appalachian Mountains, white families flooded into the interior in search of more land. Many families had exhausted agricultural lands by planting tobacco and cotton in Virginia, North Carolina, South Carolina, and Georgia. White farmers did not use fertilizers, rotate crops, or allow lands to lay fallow for a span of time. So white farmers sought new lands to exploit in Kentucky, Tennessee, Alabama, and Mississippi.

WHITE EXPANSION AND INTERNAL IMPROVEMENTS

Other whites resettled native lands in Vermont, New Hampshire, and New York, leaving only remnants of land for the original inhabitants. Whites moved into the woods, hills, and meadows south of the St. Lawrence River where Iroquois and Abnaki had once ruled. After the Treaty of Greenville, other whites crossed the Ohio River to farm, and they used "internal improvements" such as land surveys, roads, bridges, and boats to move more rapidly into former native lands. Like their counterparts in the South, northerners resettled lands that Indians had previously farmed or cleared as hunting grounds. Like great land waves, they built small communities along the Muskingum, Scioto, and Great

Miami rivers, extending their trade, agriculture, and commerce. Whites built many roads to the West, including the Jonesboro, Knoxville, and Nashville roads into Tennessee, or the Richmond, Great Valley, and Wilderness roads into Kentucky. Whites built Braddock's Road west from Baltimore to Pittsburgh and Forbes Road linking Philadelphia with Pittsburgh. Settlers took the Greenwood and Catskill roads inland or the Mohawk Turnpike and Great Genesee Road into the heart of Iroquois country.

Whites used old Indian trails and created new roads, cutting their way into the forests to establish communities and taverns along the way. These internal improvements, so beneficial to whites, were detrimental to native peoples, who watched their former lands consumed by voracious, land-hungry settlers who ultimately prospered and attracted more whites. By 1796, seventy-seven thousand whites occupied Tennessee, and the territory prepared for statehood. By 1800, over 220,000 whites lived in Kentucky, and by 1812, 250,000 whites lived in Ohio. Many settlers prepared to move north from Steubenville, Marietta, Gallipolis, Portsmouth, Massie's Station, and Cincinnati on the Ohio River into Indian lands ceded by the Treaty of Greenville. Ravenna, Youngstown, Zanesville, Columbus, Xenia, Williamsburg, Dayton, and other towns emerged. Former Indian towns, like Chillicothe, became towns run by non-Indians, and settlers pushed ever closer to northwestern Ohio, where Wyandots, Miamis, Shawnees, Ottawas, Mohicans, Senecas, Ojibwes, Delawares, and others lived and pondered their futures.

Stress and tension characterized the era for tribes as they faced the nineteenth century, and their talks around the council fires inevitably turned to white migration, resettlement, and expansion. They had experienced all this before–at other times in other places. From the north, south, and east tribes had moved to Ohio seeking new lives and security from whites, but the lands they claimed in 1800 were coveted by others. The very presence of whites on their borders threatened Native Americans who well understood that white Americans had an insatiable desire for more native land. While trouble swirled all around them, some Indians voluntarily left their homes for Indiana, Illinois, Michigan, and Missouri. Others remained to cope with their problems and live in their homelands. Between 1802 and 1809, Indiana Territorial Governor William Henry Harrison concluded fifteen treaties with Delawares, Kickapoos, Piankeshas, Potawatomis, Miamis, Ottawas, Kaskias, and others.

As a result of these treaties, Native Americans lost millions of acres of their estates without settling ongoing disputes with white Americans. Although Indians wished to discuss a variety of grievances at the treaty councils, the topic always returned to lands that Harrison insisted had to be ceded to the United States. In his book, *The Shawnee Prophet*, Cherokee historian David Edmunds points out that Harrison believed that it was his patriotic duty to separate Indians from their lands. This was beneficial to speculators like Harrison as well as to white Americans eager to resettle Indian lands west of the Appalachian Mountains. Harrison lied to and cheated Indians of their estates for the benefit of non-Indians and land companies such as the Wabash Land Company, in which Harrison was an investor. With threats and bribes, the governor convinced a few native men to sign the treaties that ceded millions of acres. By 1809, many Indians were strangers in a stolen land.

TENSKWATAWA AND TECUMSEH

In the swirling milieu of Indian apprehension about the new century, a holy man emerged to lead native people of the Old Northwest. At Wapakoneti, a Shawnee village near Greenville, Ohio, lived a man named Lalawétheka. He was alcoholic, a poor provider, and epileptic. Lalawétheka lived in the shadow of his brothers, Chiksika and Tecumseh, who were both great Shawnee warriors and hunters, leaders among the people. He had only one eye and was overweight. One November night in 1805, Lalawétheka fell over dead in his lodge, and his family prepared his body for burial. On the way to the cemetery, he revived, saying that he had returned from the land of the dead, where he had spoken to the Master of Life. The transformation and significance of this holy man have been detailed by Cherokee historian Edmunds, who points out that Lalawétheka returned to life a new man with a new name, Tenskwatawa–the Open Door. The prophet told the people that the Master of Life wanted them to stand united against the Long Knives and not to sell any more land. Tenskwatawa's message from the Master of Life included the concept that no human or tribe owns the earth, because it is held in common for all native people.

Tenskwatawa's teachings earned him the respect of many Native Americans in the Old Northwest. He quickly became known as the Shawnee Prophet, and he preached to hundreds of diverse native people who eagerly accepted his doctrine of active resistance against white expansionists and institutions. He also urged his followers to turn inward to find strength in their own native cultures. He asked them to end witchcraft, alcohol consumption, and adoption of white culture. Tenskwatawa urged his followers to end their use of white material culture and return to the items made and used by their ancestors. Indians were to end their fighting and bickering with each other and face their common enemy. The Shawnee Prophet had epileptic seizures at times but could cure his people and offer prophecies. The one-eyed holy man made perfect sense to Native Americans living with the threat of white expansion, but he made little sense to Harrison and other whites. The Shawnee Prophet did not fit the white image of a great leader, particularly with his emphasis

George Catlin painted this portrait of Tenskwatawa, the Shawnee Prophet, in Kansas. The "Open Door" continued his ministrations to native people during his exile, but he is best known for originating the pan-Indian movement in the Old Northwest before the War of 1812.

on spiritual power as the means by which native people could ward off the white invasion and win back their lands. Tenskwatawa was not a great warrior, politician, or diplomat, and most whites in the region viewed him as a fake, fraud, and charlatan. But to many Indians, Tenskwatawa and his teachings fit well into the philosophy and experience of Native America.

The Shawnee Prophet spoke out against the white invasion and conquest, calling on power derived from the spirit world to cope with the white problem. White people, he claimed, were children of a great serpent that lived in the Atlantic Ocean. They were destructive and avaricious monsters who had extended their influence from the Atlantic to the Ohio country and would not be satisfied until they consumed all the land, leaving native stewards without a home to call their own. This was the monster that they faced, one that Shawnees, Wyandots, Miamis, Munsees, Potawatomis, Ojibwes, and others well understood. Native Americans from many regions of the Great Lakes region as well as the South and West came to hear the Shawnee Prophet. So many people visited Tenskwatawa that the native people used up available resources of game, wood, and fish near the Shawnee village in western Ohio. As a result, Tenskwatawa ordered the people to relocate the village to central Indiana at the junction of the Wabash River and Tippecanoe Creek. The new village became known as Prophetstown.

Even before the move into Indiana, the Shawnee Prophet's fame as a spiritual leader spread throughout the region, among Native Americans and whites alike. Indiana Territorial Governor Harrison had heard much about Tenskwatawa, so in 1806 he sought to diffuse the Shawnee Prophet's growing power by writing to the Delaware: "If he is really a prophet, ask him to cause the sun to stand still, the moon to alter its course, the rivers to cease to flow." Tenskwatawa accepted the challenge, appointing the day on which he would blot out the sun. After ample preparation for this holy rite, Tenskwatawa assembled numerous followers on June 16, 1806, and blotted out the sun. On that day a total eclipse of the sun occurred, and Tenskwatawa's stock as a spiritual leader soared. Some scholars claim that Tenskwatawa had learned of the eclipse from a *Farmer's Almanac,* and perhaps he had. But more important was the native interpretation of this significant event, because they believed that the Shawnee Prophet had cast a dark shadow over the sun—the giver of life. Any human who could stop the sun from shining had powers far beyond those of most people, powers that could be derived only from a superior spiritual source. Tenskwatawa proved himself to be an extraordinary human in 1806, and hundreds of native people joined his resistance movement.

While numerous native people flocked to Ohio and Indiana to hear the Shawnee Prophet's words, Tecumseh played a secondary role in the resistance movement. Tecumseh, dubbed the "greatest" Indian by some historians, was generally known to other Indians as the Shawnee Prophet's brother. However, Tecumseh's role grew with the passage of time. Although at first he doubted his brother's power, he soon joined the Shawnee Prophet's movement and began devising a plan to use the religious revitalization movement as the basis for his own cause. Tenskwatawa's crusade was built on a spiritual movement, whereas Tecumseh assumed the role of enlarging the movement to include political and military solutions to the white problem. To this end, Tecumseh traveled to Fort Malden, a British post on the Canadian side of the Detroit River, where Captain Matthew Elliott graciously received him. Tecumseh believed that the British would aid the Indians in the event of open conflict with the United States, but the time to strike had not yet come.

TECUMSEH'S RESISTANCE

In September 1809, Harrison called a council at Fort Wayne, and over one thousand Indians assembled to meet the governor. Representatives of the Delaware, Potawatomi, and Miami agreed to another treaty at Fort Wayne, but the Shawnee, Kickapoo, Wea, and others refused to attend.

Some leaders attending the council agreed to cede to the government an additional three million acres for $7,000 in cash and annuities for all tribes totaling $1,750. In terms of cash, not including annuities, the United States paid the tribes .0023¢ per acre for lands under the terms of the Treaty of Fort Wayne. This cession was over and above the 107 million acres already ceded to the United States by northwestern tribes since 1800. Although the amount paid to the Indians for their lands was obscene, the dollar amount was not at issue among Native Americans. Instead, at issue was ceding lands at all because the earth was held in common as a gift of the Master of Life. Through lies, tricks, and bribery, Harrison had convinced selected individuals among the tribes to sign treaties, but the Treaty of Fort Wayne was a watershed in Native American history, and it brought quick action by Tecumseh.

The ink on the treaty had barely dried when Tecumseh called on Harrison at Vincennes in 1810. As the outdoor meeting opened, Harrison invited Tecumseh to sit in a chair, but the Shawnee leader replied that "The Great Spirit is my father. The Earth is my mother–and on her bosom I will recline." He sat down on the ground, and the council commenced. Regarding the land Tecumseh explained that no Indian or "tribe has the right to sell, even to each other, much less to strangers." He said that land is held in trust by all Native Americans, saying that "this land that was sold, and the goods that was given for it, was only done by a few." In his own way, Tecumseh threatened Harrison, telling the governor not to cross into native lands because to do so would "produce great trouble between us." Tecumseh concluded, proclaiming: "Sell a country! Why not sell the air, the great sea, as well as the earth? Did not the Great Spirit make them all for the use of his children?" Then the Shawnee leader reminded Harrison that Native Americans had no faith in white actions. "When Jesus Christ came upon the earth," Tecumseh said, "you killed Him and nailed Him to the cross. You thought He was dead and you were mistaken." Any people who would kill their own savior could not be trusted.

Such blunt talk by an Indian enraged Harrison, who claimed that Americans had always been fair to Indians. Tecumseh jumped to his feet and called Harrison a liar. The governor pulled his sword, his men cocked their guns, and the warriors drew their weapons. Harrison dismissed the council until the next day, when Tecumseh apologized. The two men spoke again, taking a seat on a bench. During the conversation, Tecumseh kept moving close to the governor, who scooted away, only to have Tecumseh crowd him again and again. Finally, Harrison reached the end of the bench and asked the Shawnee what he was doing. Tecumseh explained that this was exactly what the white people were doing to Native Americans. Although the Shawnee leader laughed at his actions, he had made his point. Still, the point was lost on Harrison, who cared little about the Indian position and acted on behalf of his government and its manifest destiny to take the lands from Native Americans and resettle them with whites. Tecumseh left the council to prepare for war. Sporadic fighting occurred during 1810, as angry Indians passed their war belts. Major strikes on Harrison did not ensue because the governor did not try to survey the lands he had taken in the Treaty of Fort Wayne.

During this interim period in 1810 and 1811, Tecumseh visited Major General Isaac Brock at Fort Malden, located at Amherstburg, Ontario, to ask for arms and ammunition. Brock denied the request because Britain was not at war with the United States. Still, Tecumseh was encouraged that the British would eventually ally with those tribes willing to stand against the Americans. Even before the British became involved, bands of Indians attacked isolated white settlements in an attempt to encourage whites to leave the region. As momentum toward renewed warfare with the Long Knives increased, Tecumseh decided to strengthen his political and military confederacy by bringing other Indians into the cause. In July 1811, Tecumseh and a small band of Shawnees and Kickapoos visited Harrison at Vincennes to announce that they were on their way south to enlist the support of Cherokees, Choctaws, Chickasaws, Seminoles, Muscogees, and other southern tribes. The Shawnee pointed out that Harrison could avoid war if he remained off Indian lands, but the governor told the chief that he would have the lands surveyed. In the company of two Muscogees, including a holy man named Seekaboo, Tecumseh traveled south on August 5, 1811, to meet numerous native people and encourage them to join him in a pan-Indian confederacy designed to stand against the United States.

At various councils Tecumseh treated with the southern tribes. When he met the Choctaw, Cherokee, and Muscogee on the banks of the Tallapoosa River, Tecumseh encouraged his listeners to "War now. War forever. War upon the living. War upon the dead; dig their very corpses from the grave; our country must give no rest to a white man's bones." At this council and others, Tecumseh spoke of themes significant to Native Americans at the time. He continually told the Indians that whites are a "wicked race" because of their "continual series of aggressions." He pointed out that native "hunting grounds are fast disappearing, and they are driving the red man farther and farther to the west." This would be the fate of all eastern tribes if "the power of the whites is not forever crushed." Whiskey, disease, rapes, and ruin were the product of white expansion, so the "only hope of the red man is a war of extermination" against all whites.

During his orations, Tecumseh often asked: "Where today are the Pequot? Where are the Narragansett, the Mohican, the Pocanet, and other powerful tribes of our people?" He pointed out that many tribes "have vanished before the avarice and oppression of the white man, as snow before the summer sun." Tecumseh asked the southern Indians if they were willing to be destroyed without a fight. "Shall we, without a struggle, give up our homes, our lands, bequeathed to us by the Great Spirit?"

Pushmataha was a famous Choctaw leader who refused to follow Tecumseh. Like most Native American leaders living in the South, Pushmataha believed it was not to the advantage of Choctaws to fight the United States.

He prophetically pointed out that the "graves of our dead" were sacred places and that the "bones of our dead" would "be plowed up, and their graves turned into plowed fields." Tecumseh was right. The rich farm lands of Ohio, Indiana, Illinois, Michigan, Tennessee, Mississippi, Louisiana, Alabama, and many other states fell out of Indian hands and into private ownership of nonnative farmers, who have plowed up native graves, robbed grave goods for their own collections, and publicly sold and displayed Native American remains and funeral items. There has been no rest for the dead due to such desecration, a source of continued conflict between Indians and whites.

Pushmataha, one of the great leaders of the Choctaw Nation, urged his people not to join Tecumseh's confederacy, even "though our race may have been unjustly treated and shamefully wronged by them." He reasoned that it was not in the best interest of Choctaws to join in the coming fight, in part because members of the Choctaw Nation "now have no just cause to declare war against the American people." Furthermore, Pushmataha pointed out that the Americans had far more land than the Choctaws and were "far better provided with all the necessary implements of war, with men, guns, horses, wealth, far beyond that of all our race combined." The Choctaws chose not to join Tecumseh and fight the United States. This was the stance of the Cherokee, Chickasaw, Seminole, and many Muscogee, except for that part of the nation known as the

Red Sticks. Tecumseh had traveled south with two Muscogee, including Seekaboo, and he was related to the nation on his mother's side of the family. Hildas Harjo and Lamotachee (Red Eagle or William Weatherford), two prominent leaders who represented the prowar group of the Muscogee Nation, joined the confederacy, proclaiming that the great Shawnee leader would stamp his foot as a sign that he had arrived home. On December 15, 1811, a major earthquake centered in the Mississippi Valley shook the country from the river east to Georgia. For months the people felt aftershocks from the earthquake, all signs of significant change and Tecumseh's power.

BATTLE OF TIPPECANOE

While Tecumseh traveled to visit the southern tribes, Harrison assembled an army of one thousand seasoned soldiers. In late September 1811, Harrison marched north along the trail running parallel to the Wabash River toward Prophetstown. Harrison's army reached Prophetstown on November 6, and his men camped in a large, level area less than a mile away. The Indians showed little alarm at the arrival of the army, because Tenskwatawa told them that they had nothing to fear from the Long Knives since the Master of Life was with the native people and would protect them. Rather than rely on the advice, plans, and actions of Indian warriors with fighting experience, the Shawnee Prophet planned the attack and deployed the warriors. In the predawn hours of November 7, a cold rain fell on native warriors as they moved quietly through the woods and marsh to surround Harrison's army.

The governor's men slept on their weapons and were awakened when one of their guards fired at someone moving in the darkness. Pandemonium ensued as the Indians raced into the camp, moving from one tent to another, fighting at close range. The soldiers held their ground and fought back the first wave. When the native fighters moved back to regroup, the soldiers formed lines and fired thunderous volleys into them. While this was occurring, Harrison ordered his cavalry to attack the Indians from two directions. The cavalry attack broke the native offensive, and the Indians retreated in numerous directions. Rather than allow his men to continue the attack, Harrison had his men return to camp, ordering them to prepare breastworks in anticipation of the next wave of attack. It never came, and the next day he learned that the Indians had abandoned Prophetstown. The soldiers plundered the town and set it aflame, returning to Vincennes in victory. Approximately thirty-eight Indians and an equal number of whites lost their lives during the Battle of Tippecanoe. About 150 warriors and an equal number of whites were wounded.

In terms of dead and wounded the fight was a draw. However, it was significant for a few important reasons. The fact that the Indians had retreated and deserted their village was demoralizing, but the event was made worse by the burning of Prophetstown. But more important, the battle signaled the end of Tenskwatawa's approach to the white invasion and a rapid decline in his influence. The Shawnee Prophet had assured the Indians that they would win the fight because of divine intervention, but the people had not swept the Long Knives from the field of battle. Tenskwatawa's power among the people was diminished, and in the aftermath of the Battle of Fallen Timbers, Tecumseh's star rose higher and brighter. After 1811, Tecumseh became the most important native leader in the Old Northwest, and his approach of a political and military solution to the white problem became the dominant one. Native Americans continued to pray and sing to the Great Holy One, but they believed that their best hope of defeating whites and regaining their lost lands was through a political unification of Indians who would fight collectively to defeat their common enemy.

NATIVE AMERICANS AND THE WAR OF 1812

When Tecumseh returned to the Northwest, he chastised his brother for his folly and ordered the warriors to attack American settlements. Even before the War of 1812 began officially, the West was embroiled in a heated war between white Americans and Native Americans. Many whites in the West wanted war. As early as 1810, "War Hawks" such as Henry Clay of Kentucky went to Washington demanding that Congress become more aggressive in fighting Indians and removing the British from Canada. Clay, Harrison, and other leaders claimed that hostile Indians like Tecumseh were receiving guns, ammunition, goods, and intelligence from British agents in Canada. American politicos demanded action against both and were pleased in 1812 when the United States declared war on Britain. While Americans planned an invasion of Canada, British soldiers and Indian allies took Fort Mackinac in July 1812 without firing a weapon.

Shortly thereafter, General William Hull, governor of Michigan Territory, marched toward Fort Malden. In July 1812, Hull reached Detroit with two thousand soldiers and soon crossed the Detroit River into Canada on his route to Fort Malden. Tecumseh and his allies attacked Hull, and the Americans never made it to Fort Malden. They retreated into the United States to protect their supply lines but were too late. Tecumseh's warriors and British commander General Isaac Brock cut off Hull's supplies and forced the Americans to surrender. While the Shawnees and their allies fought Hull and captured Detroit, Potawatomis

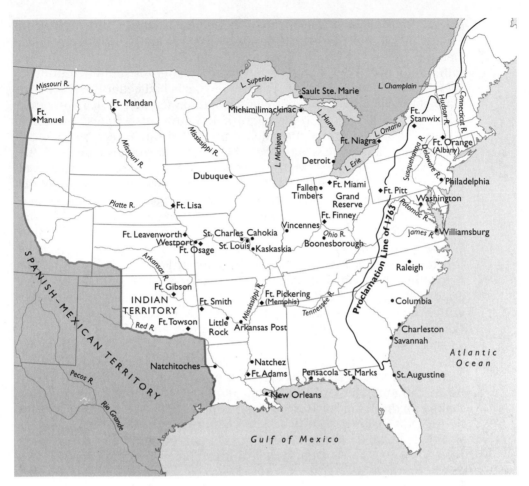

Native Americans and White Expansion, 1760–1830

captured Fort Dearborn at present-day Chicago. And when the American garrison from Fort Dearborn marched across the sand dunes on the lower end of Lake Michigan, Potawatomis and their allies attacked the Americans, killing twenty-six men outright and torturing to death nine others.

Throughout the first summer of the war, Native Americans attacked Fort Wayne and Fort Harrison, keeping General William Henry Harrison and the Americans pinned down. Numerous Native Americans fought without British support, taking the war to American settlers throughout the Old Northwest. Although some American Indians fought with the United States, most allied with the British or fought on their own against the Long Knives. Some Indians helped the United States invade Canada across the Niagara River, but their effort failed when Native American and British forces defeated American militia soldiers at Niagara Falls. General Henry Dearborn attempted to take Canada with five thousand militiamen via Lake Champlain but returned after his soldiers mutinied, refusing to cross into Canada. The United States had better luck invading Spanish Florida, but the American occupation led Seminoles and other native people living in Florida to cross into the United States and attack settlers. At the same time, President James Madison asked Congress for authority to annex East and West Florida. Madison also ordered the Tennessee militia under Andrew Jackson to prepare for an invasion of present-day Alabama and Florida. When Congress refused to annex the Floridas, Madison dismissed Jackson's army. The invasion and annexation of Florida by the United States would come after the War of 1812.

In the Northwest, Harrison prepared an army to take Fort Malden. In January 1813, Indians prepared to fight Harrison's army. Colonel Henry Procter had replaced Brock as commander at Fort Malden, and he enlisted the help of native peoples to fight the Americans. As historian John Sugden has shown in *Tecumseh's Last Stand,* Tecumseh worked closely with Procter, planning military strategy of an extremely high level. The Long Knives gave the Indians and British forces an excellent opportunity to strike when one thousand of Harrison's men disobeyed orders and moved forward to capture a small settlement on River Raisin. Indians and British soldiers surprised the Americans on River Raisin, cutting down 250 Americans and capturing another 500. Tecumseh did not participate in this fight, because he had traveled south to visit the Muscogees and recruit six hundred Indian fighters from Illinois. Harrison did not attack Fort Malden after the River Raisin fight, but built Fort Meigs near present-day Maumee, Ohio, and reinforced other forts in the Northwest. Between April 28 and May 7, 1813, Tecumseh and Procter attacked Fort Meigs but found the fighting difficult because of Harrison's well-placed fortifications.

Meanwhile, eight hundred Kentucky volunteers moved up to reinforce Harrison. Tecumseh's men intercepted the Kentuckians, killing several hundred and taking 150 prisoner. The Indians forced the Americans to run the gauntlet. Some were tomahawked, stabbed, or shot. Others were beaten and clubbed. Afterward some of them were tortured or slaughtered while the British watched. When Tecumseh learned of these excesses, he rode forward and ended the killing of prisoners. He also chastised Procter for not intervening. Tecumseh wanted to continue the siege on Fort Meigs, but Procter called it off after 350 American soldiers broke through the British lines to spike their cannons. In July, Tecumseh, fourteen hundred Indian allies from numerous tribes, and British regulars began the second Battle of Fort Meigs. This time Tecumseh led the attack without the use of heavy British bombardment. Confident that Fort Meigs could withstand the attack, Harrison withdrew to

Ohio to prepare for another attack on Fort Malden. Leaving Major George Croghan at Fort Stephenson near Sandusky Bay on Lake Erie, Harrison moved south along the Sandusky River to Fort Seneca. Tecumseh and his allies fought valiantly but could not take Fort Meigs. Indian and British forces fell back after the second Battle of Fort Meigs. Tecumseh and Procter moved southeast into Ohio to attack Fort Stephenson, commanded by the twenty-one-year-old Croghan and his 150 volunteers. Located below Sandusky Bay along the Sandusky River, Fort Stephenson was nothing more than a small log stockade with a dry moat surrounding it. But the fort proved to be invincible. Refusing to surrender, Croghan's men withstood a bombardment from Procter's six-pound cannons, which were not large enough to destroy the log walls. When Tecumseh and Procter ordered a two-pronged attack, Croghan waited patiently until a large number of soldiers were in the dry moat in front of the fort. Then the Americans blasted the British regulars with their only cannon, sending grapeshot into their faces. The redcoats retreated into the forest with a loss of nearly one hundred dead. There they met Harrison's soldiers moving north from Fort Seneca. Few Indians lost their lives in the attack because they were not foolish enough to risk a frontal assault.

The battles at Fort Meigs and Fort Stephenson signaled the beginning of the end for the Indian confederacy. British and Indian forces fell back to Fort Malden, but many Indians decided to return home, particularly the Sac, Fox, Chippewa, and Menominee from Wisconsin. Tecumseh tried to encourage the warriors to continue the fight, but more and more it appeared that Native Americans would not be able to regain Ohio, Indiana, or Illinois. It appeared to many Native Americans that the British had no commitment to take the fight to the Old Northwest and drive the Long Knives away forever. Wyandots from Upper Sandusky under Tarhe had opposed the war with the Americans, and elements of the Delaware, Seneca, and Shawnee refused to take up the tomahawk against the Long Knives. All these people had known battle before, and all of them had experienced warriors among them. Still, something whispered to them that the British would lose the war and that the best policy for the people was neutrality or friendship with the Long Knives.

Following the Battle of Fort Stephenson, Harrison asked representatives of the Wyandots, Delawares, Senecas, and Shawnees living near the Sandusky River to travel to Brownstown, Michigan, and encourage Walk-in-the-Water's Wyandots to end their alliance with Tecumseh and the British. Tecumseh, Tenskwatawa, Wyandot War Chief Roundhead, and British Indian Agent Matthew Elliott were in town when the delegation arrived. While Walk-in-the-Water said little, Roundhead admonished the delegation, calling Harrison a ground hog for barricading himself in Ohio. Tiring of the conference, Tecumseh, Tenskwatawa, Roundhead, Elliott, and pro-British native people left Brownstown. When they had gone, Walk-in-the-Water confided that he would abandon the Shawnee brothers and the British. Clearly he believed that Harrison and the Americans were in a stronger position and would defeat the British in the West. Walk-in-the-Water mirrored the pessimism of many Indians who had supported the British, and his view of the situation proved correct.

BATTLE OF THE THAMES

For the Americans, control of Lake Erie was a key to defeating the British in the West. To this end the United States assigned Oliver Hazard Perry, a twenty-seven-year-old captain, to build a fleet on Presque Isle. In late August 1813, Perry's fleet appeared suddenly off Barclay's Point at the mouth of the Detroit River. It remained at the site for two days, laying down a gauntlet that the British refused to run. Tecumseh and his allies witnessed the challenge and visited Procter to inquire why Captain Robert H. Barclay had not responded with his fleet. Tecumseh learned that the British ship, the *Detroit*, did not have sufficient firepower to meet Perry, but with armaments from Fort Malden, Barclay sailed out to meet Perry near Put-in-Bay. On September 10, the two forces engaged in a three-hour naval battle that was a stunning victory for the United States, sinking or capturing the entire British force.

Procter did not inform Tecumseh and his allies of the British defeat for nearly eight days, although the Indians suspected the outcome because the force never returned from the engagement. When Procter announced he had lost the fleet and Harrison was mounting an offensive, he also proposed a retreat to Niagara. Tecumseh rose to face Procter with a wampum belt in his hand and ostrich feather in his hair. He delivered a stinging speech, rebuking the idea of retreat. "You always told us to remain here and take care of our lands," Tecumseh proclaimed. "You always told us, that you would never draw your foot off British ground; but now we see you are drawing back, and we are sorry to see our father doing so without seeing the enemy." Tecumseh likened Procter to a "fat animal" that "carries its tail upon its back, but when affrighted, he drops it between his legs and runs off." The Shawnee chief reminded Procter that they had not been defeated by land and that the Indians "wish to remain here, and fight our enemy."

Tecumseh concluded his oration, saying that the Indians would put their trust in the Master of Life. "As for us," he said, "our lives are in the hands of the Great Spirit. We are determined to defend our lands, and if it be his will we wish to leave our bones upon them." Men, women, and children who were gathered at the council cried out in agreement, and those carrying weapons brandished them in the air with war cries and calls to the sky. The land was sacred to them, and many committed to standing their ground and fighting. But in a meeting with Tecumseh, Procter convinced the Shawnee leader that they had to pull back along the Thames River and fight Harrison from a position selected by the British and Indians. Tecumseh did not want to leave the Detroit area, but he needed British support and supplies if he was to have any chance of defeating Harrison and regaining lost lands in the Old Northwest.

So Tecumseh agreed to an orderly retreat up the Thames. Approximately three thousand native men, women, and children from the Wyandot, Potawatomi, Ho-Chunk, Kickapoo, and Shawnee nations accompanied Tecumseh and Procter. Other Indians from the Potawatomi, Ottawa, Chippewa, Sac, and Fox nations followed the Potawatomi Wabeno Main Poc into nearby Michigan, where they watched the advancing Americans from Amherstburg. If Tecumseh and Procter defeated the Americans, Main Poc and his followers would cut off the American retreat. They would also fall on American settlers and take what they could from those who had stolen native lands. In any case, these people would move into the woods of Michigan, as far from the Long Knives as possible. While the Indians and British pulled back, Harrison advanced across Lake Erie, making a landing three miles south of Fort Malden on September 27, 1813.

When Harrison learned that Procter was moving into Ontario by way of the Thames River, he pursued immediately. Tecumseh and some of his allies fought Harrison in a short skirmish at McGregor's Creek, but soon withdrew up the Thames to join Procter. Two miles west of Moraviantown on the north bank of the Thames, Tecumseh, his allies, and Procter made their last stand. In midafternoon on October 5, 1813, Harrison's troops advanced and soon collapsed the British lines, which caused the Redcoats to run. Tecumseh and his warriors stood their ground and fought hand-to-hand combat in the thickets, refusing to retreat. With the British on the run, the Americans concentrated their efforts against the Indians. Colonel Richard M. Johnson and his mounted infantry (soldiers who advanced on horseback, fought on foot, and were later known as dragoons) poured a deadly fire into the thickets. Infantry soldiers advanced into the thickets, and the warriors fought back courageously. During the heated fight, Tecumseh received a mortal gunshot wound in his chest and died. Surviving warriors fell back, but after the fight, some of them returned to secure Tecumseh's body, burying him in an unmarked grave.

MUSCOGEE PATRIOTS

While Harrison advanced on Tecumseh, General Benjamin Howard and fourteen hundred militiamen from Illinois and Missouri swept Illinois, burning Indian villages and killing native people. More important, troops under Andrew Jackson gathered at Fayetteville, Arkansas, to advance against the Muscogees. On August 30, 1813, Weatherford and Muscogees–known as Red Sticks–hostile to the United States had attacked a log blockhouse known as Fort Mims located a few miles above Mobile on the Alabama River. Over 500 Americans were crowded into the fort when Weatherford attacked, easily rushing through the opened gates and taking the site. The Muscogees killed 107 soldiers, 100 African American slaves, and 160 civilian men, women, and children. The killings outraged other Native Americans as well as whites in the South. Six hundred Cherokees joined Jackson as he advanced down the Alabama River, while Pushmataha and his Choctaw warriors augmented an army moving up the same river. Muscogees who opposed Weatherford and the Red Sticks joined a militia force of Georgians moving west against the Red Sticks.

The Red Sticks fought valiantly and effectively against their native and white enemies. They drove back Jackson's Tennesseans on two occasions and pushed the Choctaws and Georgians back as well. However, Jackson and his native allies proved persistent and effective, destroying the Muscogee towns of Tallushatchee and Talladega while killing hundreds of Muscogee men, women, and children. The Red Sticks regrouped at Tohopeka on the banks of the Tallapoosa River and from their fortifications waited for Jackson to attack. With three thousand soldiers and hundreds of Muscogee, Choctaw, Chickasaw, and Cherokee allies, Jackson began the Battle of Horseshoe Bend on March 27, 1814. While Jackson prepared a frontal assault, his native allies swam the Tallapoosa River and charged the Muscogees from the rear. Confusion reigned inside the Red Stick village as the Indians fought at close quarters.

Sensing the moment, Jackson ordered his soldiers to charge. His volunteers rushed the Muscogees already fighting other Indians behind the zigzag log fortifications. Within minutes the soldiers were inside the Indian fortification, slaughtering Muscogee defenders. The Americans and their native allies killed about eight hundred Native Americans who had opposed the United States and the theft of their lands. Nearly every Muscogee warrior fighting to defend Tohopeka lost his life. Some Muscogees survived the fight, lying wounded among the dead. Only a few Red Stick men, women, and children escaped the wrath of Jackson and his allies. Some of them met the general on August 9, 1814, at Fort Jackson, where the future president dictated a treaty that forced the Muscogee Nation to cede twenty-two million acres (about two-thirds of all Muscogee land) and confess their guilt. Furthermore, the Muscogee had to guarantee that they would never again raise arms against the Long Knives. While some Muscogee leaders signed the Treaty of Fort Jackson, others left the region for Florida to join former Muscogee patriots known as Seminoles. Among those escaping into Florida was Osceola, the great warrior who led the Seminoles against the United States in the Seminole Wars of 1833–1842.

RESISTANCE AND SURVIVAL

Elements of the Choctaw, Cherokee, Chickasaw, and Muscogee nations remained with Jackson after the Battle of Horseshoe Bend. They even fought for the Americans defending New Orleans in the famous battle that won Jackson national renown and helped him win the presidency. The fate of these native allies of the United States would be shared with the country's former native enemies. The Americans would turn on their former allies and force them from their lands. This was true of all the southern tribes, just as it was for those of the Old Northwest. Some Wyandots, Senecas, Delawares, Shawnees, and others had sided with the United States during the War of 1812, believing that it was to their advantage to oppose Tecumseh and the British. Many Indians had fought alongside American soldiers, giving of their blood in the fight. Indians from the North and South had died fighting for the United States, but their reward for loyal service was to be the same as that of those who had opposed the government. The United States would remove most of them across the Mississippi River. Native American understanding of this treacherous development would evolve rapidly during the years following the Treaty of Ghent, signed on December 24, 1814. However, many tribes remained confused about the best way to protect their lands and rights and remain in the homes of their ancestors in the face of American aggression.

Following the War of 1812, Native Americans in the eastern part of the United States continued to resist American expansion, exploitation, and rule. They asserted themselves by exercising their sovereignty, and various tribes sent nonvoting members of their native nations to Washington, D.C., and to state and territorial capitals to monitor proceedings, laws, and temperament. The tribes did not live passively in the face of great changes, but rather tried to stay informed so that they could determine the best course. This was extremely difficult for the Native Americans, most of whom could not speak English but had learned something about the many levels of American government through their own experience and that of their elders. In addition, the years following the War of 1812 were momentous for American Indians because of the tremendous expansion of white settlers into the West and the unprecedented flood of nonnatives who taxed the patience of native people and brought great political power to the new western states. Most Indians tried to cope with Americans through politics and diplomacy. Only a few turned to open hostilities against the United States.

During the 1820s, an era erroneously described by American historians as the "Era of Good Feelings," white farmers and miners moved into western Illinois and eastern Wisconsin. Miners rushed to the rich lead deposits in the region, while settlers claimed the fertile lands for their farms. Their success led other whites to move to the region as merchants, freighters, surveyors, and the like. Soon these newcomers moved onto lands belonging to Ho-Chunks (Winnebagoes). White miners stole lead from the Ho-Chunks, claiming that the Indians were not making good use of the resource. The invasion of Ho-Chunk lands by miners and farmers triggered a minor Indian war. In 1827, a prominent Ho-Chunk chief named Red Bird led his people against the miners, striking the whites on lightning raids and retreating rapidly. The Indian initiative was intended to force whites from the region, but the whites dug in harder. Farmers and miners joined forces against the Ho-Chunks and were soon joined by General Henry Atkinson and regular troops of the U.S. Army. Red Bird withdrew from the region, moving his people to the upper Wisconsin River, where he was forced to surrender. In spite of this defeat, the Ho-Chunks survived the American invasion and are still a force among native nations today.

BLACK HAWK'S RESISTANCE

Throughout the 1820s, white settlers pressured numerous Indians living in the eastern portion of the United States to surrender their lands and resources. In the spring of 1829, a mob bullied a group of Sac and Fox Indians from their own cornfields. Whites coveted Indian farms and hated the Indians, so they threatened them during the attack and "encouraged" them to move. Chief Keokuk loved his Illinois home but knew that if he remained, he would have to fight the Americans. He knew the history of Indians and whites; he knew that Illinois farmers would not be content until they drove his people across the Mississippi River into Iowa or killed them trying. To avert bloodshed, Keokuk moved, but Sac and Fox chief Black Hawk refused, remaining on his ancestral lands until 1831, when whites convinced themselves that the Sac and Fox posed a great danger. In June an Illinois force of fifteen hundred militiamen prepared to attack Black Hawk, but before they arrived, the people moved quietly across the Mississippi River. They reached Iowa too late to plant corn and starved during the bitter winter.

In the spring of 1832, one thousand Sac and Fox under Black Hawk returned to Illinois in full view of Fort Armstrong. This was not a war party, because it was composed of about four hundred men and six hundred women and children. Instead, the Indians returned to Illinois for spring planting, believing that whites would understand their need to be home

Black Hawk, the great Sac and Fox leader, resisted the American invasion of his beloved Illinois and was captured and imprisoned by the Americans. This portrait by John Jarvis (1833) features Black Hawk in the foreground with his son behind him and illustrates his great dignity and bearing.

where they could survive by farming. Whites panicked at the return of Black Hawk as rumors—so characteristic of whites who dealt with Indians—circulated in the Old Northwest, bringing over one thousand soldiers into action. Near Dixon's Ferry on Rock River, Black Hawk tried to surrender, but volunteers shot at his band and triggered a conflict. While women and children waited in the swamps of Lake Koshkonong, warriors fought the whites with loss of lives on both sides. General Atkinson moved against Black Hawk, who left the security of the swamps for a northwesterly route back to Iowa. Hotly pursued by soldiers, Black Hawk lost several people who died of hunger and exhaustion. When he arrived at the junction of the Bad Axe and Mississippi rivers, Black Hawk found an American gunboat waiting and an army pursuing him from behind.

Black Hawk was trapped. He could either chance the Mississippi and the gunboat or face certain death at the hands of the charging soldiers. He tried to surrender with a flag of truce, but soldiers aboard the gunboat answered with fire. His only chance was to make it to Iowa, so men, women, and children tried to swim the river. Soldiers from the gunboat and the Illinois shore shot down as many people as possible. Soldiers on the Iowa side of the river gathered the survivors, including Black Hawk. Of the one thousand Sac and Fox people who had entered Illinois, only 150 lived to tell their side of the Bad Axe tragedy. After his capture, Black Hawk said that he was "not afraid of death" and had "fought for his countrymen . . . against white men, who came year after year, to cheat them and take away their lands." Recounting the day of his surrender, he lamented, "The sun rose dim on us in the morning, and at night it sunk in a dark cloud, and looked like a ball of fire. That was the last sun that shone on Black Hawk. His heart . . . no longer beats quick in his bosom."

FORCED REMOVAL

The brutal killing of men, women, and children served notice to all Indians remaining in the East that they were not wanted and that they would be exterminated if they remained on the lands of their mothers and fathers. Resistance to American expansion by Red Bird and Black Hawk had led to military defeats, and both incidents served as reminders to other Native Americans that white settlers were willing to kill Indians for land and resources. During the early nineteenth century, most white Americans came to regard forced removal of eastern Indians to the trans-Mississippi West as a humane and necessary condition for the preservation of Native Americans. The alternative, they argued, was extermination. Removal had always been a part of American history. Even before the arrival of Europeans, tribes had forced other tribes to move from region to region. Spanish, French, Dutch, Russian, British, and other colonists had removed Indians. Indeed, the history of the United States between the 1770s and the 1820s was marked by voluntary and forced removals. But the aftermath of the War of 1812 brought new meaning to Indian removal, as American settlers expanded into the West.

American territories west of the Appalachian Mountains became states, sending congressmen to Washington to push a new agenda of forced removal of eastern Indians. The increased power of the West was apparent in all three branches of the national government, and Native Americans had no voice regarding their own fate. Echoing the paternalism and justifications of the day, Superintendent of Indian Affairs William Clark stated that all eastern Indians "should be removed to a country beyond" the Mississippi where whites could teach them to "live in houses, to raise grain and stock, to plant orchards . . . to establish laws for their government, to get the rudiments of common learning, such as reading, writing, and ciphering." The suggestions that Native Americans should be left in the East on smaller reserves or on individual allotments of 80 to 160 acres gave way to the concept of extermination or removal. And by the early nineteenth century, the Supreme Court ruled in *Johnson's and Graham's Lessee v. McIntosh* (1823) that the legal title of all lands within the boundaries of the United States belonged to the nation. By right of discovery, European nations had taken possession of the land, and by acquiring this same land, the United States had assumed the same right of discovery. This right overshadowed land rights of Native Americans.

American Indians, according to Chief Justice John Marshall, had a right to their land until the United States had extinguished their title. Indian nations, the court ruled, had a right of occupancy that the United States could extinguish. Advocates of Indian removal used the court's decision to support their claims to lands over those of native people, arguing that the government had an "absolute" right to the land and that the government could remove Indians from any lands "owned" by the United States. The *McIntosh* decision flew in the face of the previous view that Indians were the first occupants of the land, held a natural right to it, and could not be alienated from the soil without their permission. To do so had been a violation of "fundamental laws of nature," according to Washington's Secretary of War, Henry Knox. However, times had changed. After the War of 1812, the judicial, executive, and legislative branches of the government reflected the nation's growing power, particularly that in the West, and the national desire to take native lands and remove Indians from the East. All of this developed before the term *manifest destiny* appeared, but the national cry to expand onto sovereign Indian lands was every bit as vehement and violent as that of the 1840s and 1890s.

Thomas Jefferson was the first American president to propose removal of the tribes from the eastern portion of the United States, and James Monroe was the first executive to propose a plan for removal of the tribes. In January 1825, Monroe submitted his plan to Congress calling for voluntary removal so that tribes could decide whether they would move. By this time, elements of some tribes had already moved across the Mississippi River. Cherokees led by The Bowl had moved into Arkansas, while other groups of Cherokee had moved into Spanish Texas. Bands of Delawares, Kickapoos, and Shawnees also moved into Texas, sometimes serving as scouts for non-Indians chasing Comanches across the southern Great Plains. Some Kickapoos surrendered their lands in Indiana and Illinois, agreeing to move west, whereas other Kickapoos resolved to ignore the Treaty of Edwardsville and remain in Illinois. However, in 1824, Chief Mecina led his Kickapoo band across the great river, and in 1834, Kennekuk, the Kickapoo Prophet, did the same.

In a series of treaties concluded in 1825 at Prairie du Chien, Wisconsin, groups of Sac, Fox, Ho-Chunk, Potawatomi, and Sioux surrendered thousands of acres, and within ten years most of them had moved west of the Mississippi. Whites encroached on tribal lands in the East, but Indians had little recourse. They were forced onto smaller land areas, losing millions of acres. Most Indians knew that if they opposed the United States they would lose their last estates in the East by right of conquest and be forcibly removed to the West, and this view was verified when Red Bird and Black Hawk stood up for their rights. All the tribes were under horrendous pressure from white settlers and government officials to surrender their eastern lands and move west. Native Americans lived under the constant pressure of racism, rumors, threats, and war. Native families worried daily about their security and the lives of their children and grandchildren. They worried about the future of their nation and the likelihood of its survival in the East. Some Native Americans came to believe that the only chance for survival was to leave their ancestral lands. This was a terrible conclusion to reach but one much discussed by men and women whose hearts were broken by the prospect of removal.

In 1817, Cherokees under the leadership of Going Snake, Charles Hicks, and George Lowry met Commissioners Andrew Jackson, David Meriwether, and Joseph McMinn in Tennessee. They ceded one-third of the remaining Cherokee estate in the East to the United States for lands in northwestern Arkansas, but most Cherokees were not enthusiastic about removal. By 1835, about six thousand Cherokees had moved to Arkansas, while twenty thousand remained in the East. The Choctaw Nation also faced Commissioner Jackson at Doak's Stand on the Natchez Trace in 1817. Pushmataha, a former ally of Jackson in his fight against the Muscogees and British at New Orleans, led the Choctaw delegation. He had no interest in surrendering lands that held the bones of his ancestors, sacred lands given the Choctaw by the Creator, and he knew that Jackson misrepresented future Choctaw lands in present-day Oklahoma. The chief said that Jackson was "entirely ignorant of the geography of the country he is offering to swap [in present-day Oklahoma, where Pushmataha had hunted and visited many times], and therefore I shall acquit him of intentional fraud."

Pushmataha knew the land west of the Mississippi, and Jackson did not, except through reports. Never being one to allow facts to get in his way, Jackson protested Pushmataha's words but did not move the old leader. Still, Pushmataha did not want to be forced from his home without a place for Choctaws to live. He did not want the Choctaw to be gunned down or starved to death. He did not want his nation to suffer the wrath of white America. Jackson warned him to make an agreement or lose everything. With lives at stake, Pushmataha gave up one-third of lands in the old Choctaw Nation for lands in present-day Arkansas and Oklahoma as well as rifles, bullets, blankets, and kettles. In addition, Pushmataha sold fifty-four sections of land, the proceeds to be used to finance public education for Choctaw youths. Less than one-quarter of the Choctaw Nation of twenty-two thousand moved into Arkansas and Oklahoma. Many refused to leave present-day Mississippi and are still there.

Most had no stomach for surrendering their lands and the graves of their grandmothers and grandfathers. Whites already living in Arkansas were outraged when they learned that the federal government was removing Choctaws and Cherokees to their territory. On October 7, 1820, the *Arkansas Gazette* reported that "it is no doubt good policy in the states to get rid of all the Indians within their limits as soon as possible; and in doing so, they care very little where they send them, provided they get them out of the limits of their state." Not many years would pass before whites would force the government to remove Indians from Arkansas, repeating the ordeal again for the tribes.

By the 1820s, eastern Indians realized that the United States intended to force all of them onto lands west of the Mississippi River. This had become the objective of the nation as well as nearly every state and local government in the country, in spite of objections from well-meaning whites who pointed out the injustice of forced removal. Andrew Jackson, the great leader of the common people, had barely lost the presidential election of 1824 (because of a "corrupt bargain" in the House of Representatives when Henry Clay gave the election to John Quincy Adams) when he began campaigning openly in favor of forced removal. Jackson's racist rhetoric became more vehement in favor of Indian removal between 1824 and his ascendancy to the presidency in 1828. Eastern Indians well knew Jackson's position on Indian removal, and they resisted removal as best they could in the face of incredible odds.

Selected Readings and Bibliography

The history of American Indians during the early nineteenth century is contained in Washburn's *Red Man's Land, White Man's Law;* White's *The Middle Ground;* Gibson's *The Kickapoos;* and Prucha's *American Indian Policy in the Formative Years.* Other helpful sources are Utley and Washburn's *Indian Wars,* Berkhofer's *Salvation and the Savage,* Harmon's *Sixty Years of Indian Affairs,* McLoughlin's *Cherokee Renascence,* Hagan's *The Sac and Fox Indians,* and Tyler's *A History of Indian Policy.*

Ambrose, Stephen E. *Undaunted Courage.* New York: Simon & Schuster, 1996.

Berkhofer, Robert F. Jr. *The White Man's Indian.* New York: Knopf, 1978.

Clark, Jerry E. *The Shawnee.* Lexington: University of Kentucky Press, 1977.

DeConde, Alexander. *This Affair of Louisiana.* New York: Scribner, 1976.

Drake, Benjamin. *Life of Tecumseh.* New York: Arno Press, 1969.

Edmunds, R. David. *The Shawnee Prophet.* Lincoln: University of Nebraska Press, 1983.

——. *Tecumseh.* Boston: Little, Brown, 1984.

Foreman, Grant. *The Five Civilized Tribes.* Norman: University of Oklahoma Press, 1934.

——. *Indian Removal.* Norman: University of Oklahoma Press, 1942.

Green, James A. *William Henry Harrison.* Richmond, Va.: Garrett and Massie, 1941.

Greene, John C. *American Science in the Age of Jefferson.* Ames: Iowa State University Press, 1958.

McCluggage, Robert W. "The Senate and Indian Land Titles, 1800–1825." *Western Historical Quarterly* 1 (1970): 415–425.

Sheehan, Bernard W. *Seeds of Extinction.* Chapel Hill: University of North Carolina Press, 1973.

Tucker, Glenn. *Tecumseh.* New York: Russell & Russell, 1956.

White, Richard. *The Roots of Dependency.* Lincoln: University of Nebraska Press, 1983.

CHAPTER 8

FORCED REMOVAL

For many Native Americans living in the East, the prospect of removal to the West was abhorrent. Many eastern peoples believed that west was the direction of death, toward the land of the dead. It was bad enough that the United States planned to force the tribes from their native homes and sacred places where spirits abounded, but to move west in the path of the dead was troubling beyond words. The issue of removal transcended money and real estate. It involved leaving their sacred lands, because the earth was their religion, and their religion was the earth. It was unthinkable to leave the bones of mothers and fathers, grandmothers and grandfathers—bones of the recent dead or long dead. For native people, the dead are still alive and part of their communities. A portion of the dead spirit was always associated with their nation, and the bones of the dead provided a link between the living and past souls, protectors of future generations. This was a shared belief of many Native Americans and one that tied them to the lands, their places on this earth.

INDIAN LAW AND REMOVAL

It was against native law of most Indians to abandon the bones of ancestors. To do so was a wrong against the dead and the living, a wrong deeply felt by native peoples. This belief is also a common thread today, linking Native Americans with the past and present and one often developed by Choctaw historian Donna Akers and Pawnee scholar James Riding-In. To walk away from cemeteries and leave the bones of friends and relatives was beyond comprehension, and it was difficult for native people to deal with whites who did not understand the depths of their native beliefs. When Emigrating Agent John J. McRae urged Choctaws to remove, Choctaw Chief Colonel Cobb replied that "These are their graves, and in those aged pines you hear the ghosts of the departed. Their ashes are here, and we have been left to protect them." Cobb explained that "If the dead could but have been counted," the removal treaty would never have been made. The dead, Cobb said, "stood around, they could not be seen or heard," but when they learned of removal, "Their tears came in the rain-drops and their voices in the wailing wind."

It was also against Indian law to leave the lands of one's ancestors, lands that had been given to the people at the time of creation. It was against the law to leave the rivers, hills, valleys, lakes, oceans, forests, and mountains that were a part of native people. The land was new to whites, and they did not have the same attachments to it, and they did not think like Native Americans and did not share such deep and abiding attachments to the earth. But American Indians had been tied to certain areas for generations by ancient stories, songs, beliefs, arts, ceremonies, rituals, and religions. And even when they had moved from area to area over the years, they still had a relationship to selected areas where they had developed a history with animals, places, plants, and people. Their languages were part of the geography of the region that dated back to the beginning of time when the Creator put things into motion and set the world on its course. Language held the elements of tribal law, the highest of laws in which people were a part of life in accordance with the grand scheme, as related in oral narratives.

The people knew about such laws through stories and songs, lessons taught to them from childhood. Tribal elders taught the people of their strong relationship to place, plants, and animals, often referring to these "people" as sisters and brothers, their relatives in a real sense. Bears, bats, bobcats, wildcats, wolves, wolverines, deer, moose, eagles, hawks, turtles, toads, turkeys, and a host of other animals were relatives of native people and kin who had power. The people knew their special places. They knew the spirits living in rock formations, clumps of woods, and open meadows. Native Americans knew about seasons, climates, weather patterns, natural phenomena, and positions of the stars, sun, and moon. They had intimate knowledge of their places, and they could read the signs to know when to fish and hunt, plant and harvest, canoe a watercourse, and remain at home. The question of removal was a political and economic matter among white Americans, and it became a political matter to the tribes. Economic considerations, as understood by whites, had little bearing on removal among tribal communities. Far more important to American Indians were the religious ramifications of removal. Tribal lands were sacred, held in trust by tribes, gifts from the Creator.

ORIGINS OF FORCED REMOVAL

Secretary of War John C. Calhoun, a native of South Carolina, conceived the formal Indian policy of removal, and President James Monroe offered his removal plan to Congress on January 24, 1825. It took the generally slow-moving Congress just five weeks to approve the plan. As a result, the United States added removal to its formal Indian policies. Government agents used bribes, threats, and coercion to force Indian tribes to surrender their homes, or, as Pomo scholar Larry Myers put it, "they shoved those treaties down our throats and expected us to like the taste of their deceit." President John Quincy Adams continued the removal policy of Monroe, but Andrew Jackson, elected president in 1828, brought new meaning to the word *removal.* A hero among western settlers, Jackson pursued removal with unbounded vigor, either negotiating removal agreements himself or instructing commissioners to do his bidding. In either case, Jackson refined the use of threats, bribes, and lies used by William Henry Harrison in the North. He treated Native Americans like dependent children who were too ignorant and savage to know that the time had come for them to move out of the way of progress and civilization. Although well-meaning whites fought Indian removal, Congress passed the Removal Act in 1830, and President Jackson rapidly acted upon it.

The United States began its removal policy by taking its policies and procedures across the Mississippi to the Osage, Oto, Missouri, Quapaw, and Kansa tribes of present-day Nebraska, Oklahoma, and Kansas. In 1833, the Stokes Commission convinced some Kansa and Osage to surrender all of present-day Kansas and the northern part of present-day Oklahoma, except for two reservations for the two tribes. In addition, the Stokes Commission, with a military escort led by Major Henry Dodge, established new tribal lands for relocated Shawnees, Senecas, Cherokees, Muscogees, Caddoes, and others. The commission also treated with Kiowas, Comanches, Caddoes, and Wichitas in 1834, initiating a process that continued for three years. Colonel Dodge and his First Dragoon Regiment advanced their relations with Kiowas when they ransomed a Kiowa girl named Gunpandama from the Osage and returned her to her relatives. During the first phase of negotiation, Philadelphia artist George Catlin accompanied the commissioners and soldiers, painting memorable scenes of Kiowas, Comanches, and other Indians as well as horses and American bison. Through these extensive meetings with western tribes and Indians who recently arrived in Indian Territory, the government opened vast areas of the "Great American Desert" for native exiles from the East. This included Native Americans from the Old Northwest and the Southeast.

As a result of prior treaties, in 1817 and 1820, some Choctaws and Cherokees had removed to Arkansas. By 1825, southern cotton farmers and speculators determined that Arkansas was too valuable for Indians, so in 1825 and 1826, the government drafted new treaties that forced Choctaws and Cherokees into Indian Territory (present-day Oklahoma). The two tribes accepted millions of acres in Indian Territory but would have preferred to remain in their eastern homelands or Arkansas. The Muscogees of Georgia and Alabama as well as Seminoles of southern Georgia, Alabama, and Florida resisted removal. Federal, state, and local government officials pressured Indians to move from their ancestral lands, and various southern states passed laws discriminating against the Indians as a means of forcing them out. States claimed legal jurisdiction over the Indians, in spite of treaties that tied tribes to the United States, not state governments; but federal officials were no help in protecting Indians. Federal officials conspired with state and local officials to force tribes from their homes.

States abolished tribal entities and extended state laws over southern tribes. Federal and state officials threatened violence against the Indians, saying that troops would overrun their nations and push them west. "Under this threat," one Choctaw recalled, the people fled their homes, "even the women and children had fled to the swamps, and camped–determined to die there." For twelve years, Mississippi Choctaws hid out while the state made them "subject to laws they could neither read nor comprehend–annoyed with suits for misdemeanors of which they were unconscious ... growing poorer every day." Whites in the South "looked down upon [Indians] as too inferior for intermarriage or social intercourse; uneducated; unadvised; their claims unsettled; disregarded by the federal government, and obnoxious to the State authorities." Whites hunted down some Choctaws and shot them as wild beasts. Choctaws, like other native peoples of the East, were considered "intruders by a new people" who feared and hated them.

CHEROKEE RESISTANCE AND REPUBLIC

Although Choctaws, Chickasaws, Muscogees, and Cherokees had made many land cessions to the United States, the Cherokee were the first to sign an agreement that provided migration westward. By the Cherokee Treaty of 1817, about six thousand Cherokees moved to Arkansas, but over twenty thousand remained in the East. Of that number, most Cherokees were farmers and merchants, some operating extensive plantations with African-American slaves. Some Cherokees had made a conscious choice to acculturate, becoming more whitelike in lifestyle but retaining their Cherokee identity. In this way, Cherokees hoped to remain in their homes in the old Cherokee Nation. Approximately fifteen Cherokees owned two thousand spinning wheels, seven hundred looms, and eight cotton gins, the advanced technology of the day that allowed the Indians to compete in the budding cotton and textile industry. Cherokees owned and operated thirty-one grist mills and ten saw mills and sold their flour and forest products to Indians and non-Indians alike. Cherokees owned thirteen hundred African-American slaves and hired others who worked for Indian people and ultimately migrated west with them as slaves or free people.

Sequoyah, a Cherokee genius, created a syllabary of eighty-six characters that transformed a spoken language into writing. Sequoyah's alphabet was easy for Cherokee speakers to learn, and the nation soon published newspapers, notices, and books in Cherokee.

Cherokees and other eastern tribes valued formal education like that offered to many white Americans. Some of them had been formally educated in English, math, history, and government. Some Cherokees sent their children to one of the eighteen schools sponsored by the tribe and religious groups, and a few attended Christian churches sponsored by Moravians, Presbyterians, Baptists, Methodists, and Congregationalists. The Cherokee had their own rich language, which became a written language when Sequoyah created a symbol alphabet of eighty-six characters that was easily understood by Cherokee speakers. The Cherokee written language gained widespread use among the people and was taught in schools. Elias Boudinot, editor of the tribal newspaper, *Cherokee Phoenix,* first used Sequoyah's syllabary in an issue of the paper in 1828. The newspaper commonly ran bilingual issues, with one column in Cherokee and another in English. Between 1828 and 1833, the Cherokee Nation reached total literacy because Sequoyah's syllabary was so easily understood and commonly used by the newspaper, in letters, and as other means of written communication.

In many ways Cherokees became more "civilized" than many whites living in the South. This was a conscious strategy on the part of Cherokee leaders, in order to preserve their native culture and ancestral land. They wished to create an image that they had adapted and fit into the larger population. They did not assimilate into white culture and society, but elements of their lives and culture became more in tune with whites. This included a major change in their governmental system. For thousands of years, the Cherokees had successfully governed themselves through their villages, clans, and families. For years Cherokees had governed themselves through tribal chiefs, including Pathfinder, a hereditary tribal chief in the 1820s. On July 4, 1827, Cherokees met at New Echota, Georgia, to create a constitutional government called the Cherokee Republic. Charles Hicks was the principal author of the Cherokee Constitution, which established three branches of government, including an elected president. By August the Cherokee had ratified the constitution and elected Chief John Ross their first president.

Cherokees had believed that whites would respond positively to the progressive, new government, which was similar to that of the United States. They also felt that their constitutional government would give the Cherokee Nation greater political clout with which to fight removal. Whites in Georgia were outraged by Cherokee actions. They were angry and envious, having long coveted Cherokee lands and resources. Many southern whites hated Native Americans, and their racism greatly influenced their reaction to the Cherokee Republic. Georgia's government officials claimed that the Cherokee Republic was a violation of the Georgia and U.S. constitutions. They asked federal officials to punish Cherokees for their arrogance by removing them. Congress responded positively to Georgia's proposal, appropriating $50,000 for Cherokee removal. Even before the election of Andrew Jackson to the presidency, removal agents flooded the South, coercing tribes to migrate west. Agents promised Cherokees and others lands west of the Mississippi River, a travel package that included transportation, tour guides, tobacco, food, blankets, rifles, powder, lead, kettles, and other extras, including $50 cash for each emigrant.

Cherokees declined the offers, bribes, and threats. Agents told them to move or they would be forced westward with no compensation, but the Cherokees refused to move. In 1828, white males in the United States elected Andrew Jackson president, and he was inaugurated in March 1829. Cherokees and others had expected this election and, with it, increasing pressure to move. In his address to the nation, Jackson called for the removal of all Indians from the East and the right of states to design their own Indian policies. The president opened the door for state legislation to discriminate against Indians, and he did so by giving state and local officials opportunities to terrorize Native Americans into leaving their states and emigrating west. The state of Georgia quickly passed laws claiming jurisdiction over Indians and resources on Indian lands, extinguishing debts owed by whites to Indians, prohibiting legal testimony of

Indians against whites, demanding loyalty and silence from white missionaries working with the tribes, and in other ways discriminating against Indians. Andrew Jackson, known to Cherokees as Chicken Snake and to Choctaws as The Devil, spent over a decade advocating Indian removal. As president, and with Congress firmly behind him, Jackson set out to force the tribes from their lands. Matters became worse in 1829 after prospectors found gold in the mountains of northern Georgia. Within weeks, thousands of miners invaded the Cherokee Nation, trespassing, burglarizing, burning, bullying, rustling, and assaulting. Cherokees demanded the removal of whites and brought legal actions against the miners, but federal officials did nothing, and officals in the state of Georgia refused to bring charges against whites, claiming that Cherokees were incompetent witnesses and could not bring actions in Georgia's courts. Cherokees knew that the president and Congress had not and would not support them, so they turned to Supreme Court Chief Justice John Marshall.

CHEROKEE SUPREME COURT CASES

Marshall accepted the case, *Cherokee Nation v. Georgia* (1831). Cherokees argued that they had a legal relationship with the United States, not Georgia, and that the state had unlawfully extended state laws to the Cherokees. Although sympathetic to the Indians and unsympathetic to Jackson, the justices ruled that the Supreme Court lacked original jurisdiction because the Cherokee Nation was a "domestic dependent nation," not a foreign nation. Marshall decided not to rule on the case because Cherokees were not citizens of the United States. The chief justice all but told the Cherokees to return with a case involving a citizen of the United States, and the Cherokee soon complied. In essence, Marshall ruled that the Cherokee Republic was not a legal body under the Constitution and could not bring the lawsuit. *Cherokee Nation v. Georgia* was significant in that it changed the legal designation of tribes by the United States from foreign nations to domestic nations. Later, the Cherokees used the arrest of a missionary to challenge Georgia. In 1832, Samuel Worcester brought action against Georgia, and in *Worcester v. Georgia* (1832) Marshall ruled that the "Cherokee Nation . . . is a distinct community, occupying its own territory, with boundaries accurately described, in which the laws of Georgia can have no force, and which the citizens of Georgia have no right to enter, but with the assent of the Cherokees." Marshall asserted that through treaties and congressional laws the United States had a legal relationship with Cherokees and that the law under which Worcester was convicted "is consequently void, and the judgment a nullity." The court nullified all of Georgia's laws against the Cherokees.

Cherokee and other eastern tribes had followed the case with much interest, and they believed they had won a great victory that would preserve what was left of the Indian estate. The court had ruled that tribes had a legal relationship with the United States as a result of treaties and congressional laws as established by the Constitution. In addition, since its birth, the federal government had adhered to a national Indian policy. Thus, the states could not create Indian policies when the national government had done so. Indian observers and their supporters believed that the *Worcester* case ruled that Georgia could not pass laws pertaining to Indians and that Georgia, Mississippi, Alabama, and other states would have to follow this legal judgment. But they were wrong. Jackson ignored the court's ruling, encouraged states to continue forcing native people from their homes, prepared for forced removal, and ordered agents and military officers to prepare Indians for removal.

Short of another war with the United States–which would have been disastrous for the tribe–Cherokees had exhausted every avenue of resolution and were without recourse. They knew where Jackson and his democratic Congress stood on removal, and they knew that Congress would do nothing to force the president to enforce the court's decision. This was Jacksonian democracy for Cherokees and all the eastern nations. The tribes were like the trout, and Jackson was the eagle. Many Indians prepared for removal, selling off livestock and personal property before the ax fell. Georgians reacted quickly when they learned that Jackson ignored Marshall's ruling and championed states' rights over the tribes'. Any hesitation by Georgia came as a result of Jackson's fight with South Carolina, a state that defied federal law and threatened not to allow federal agents to collect tariffs on imports. South Carolina threatened secession, and Jackson threatened war. The state backed down. In a reversal, Jackson supported states' rights to destroy the tribes and force them to move, in spite of a Supreme Court ruling to the contrary.

In 1834, Georgia ordered the survey of Cherokee land so that it could be confiscated through a state lottery. White planters overran the large estates of successful Cherokee farmers like Chief John Ross, and others stole smaller parcels. Georgia militiamen invaded Cherokee land to harass natives. The soldiers took over New Echota and destroyed the press that printed the *Cherokee Phoenix*. As a result, prominent Cherokee leaders Major Ridge, John Ridge, Elias Boudinot, and Stand Watie decided that the best course of action was removal, and their followers became known as the Treaty Party. Chief John Ross and his followers opposed removal at any cost, and they became known as the Ross Party. The schism had finally emerged, and federal commissioners seized the opportunity of negotiating a removal treaty with Ridge and his followers. Previously, Cherokees had stood firm against removal and had agreed to enforce the death penalty against anyone who signed a removal treaty. Nevertheless, on December 29, 1835, Ridge and his cohorts signed the Treaty of New Echota, committing the entire tribe to removal. On June 22, 1839, Cherokees in Indian Territory executed Major Ridge, Elias Boudinot, and John Ridge for signing the Treaty of New Echota. Cherokees have not forgotten this era of their history, which affects tribal politics to this day.

Chief John Ross led those Cherokees who refused removal to Indian Territory. In spite of his efforts, the United States forced most Cherokees west, where Ross continued to lead the nation. This painting is by Charles Bird King.

FORCED REMOVAL

Only a minority of Cherokees agreed with the Treaty Party, but the U.S. Senate quickly ratified the treaty, and Jackson signed it without hesitation. It became law and committed Cherokees to ceding their entire estate of eight million acres for $5 million or about 63¢ per acre. The United States forced eastern Cherokees to move within two years, but the government promised to pay for emigration and to support the people with food and supplies for a year so they could adjust to their new home. Between 1835 and 1838, about two thousand Cherokees—mostly supporters of the Treaty Party—moved west, but the Ross Party staunchly refused to remove until 1838, when federal troops and Georgia militia invaded their homes and rounded up people, imprisoning them in stockades before driving them like cattle to Indian Territory. Many "squads of troops were sent to search out with rifles and bayonet every small cabin hidden away in the coves or by the sides of mountain streams." The soldiers seized Cherokee men, women, and children and beat them when they resisted. On their way to the stockades, "on turning for one last look as they crossed the ridge they saw their homes in flames, fired by the lawless rabble" who looted and pillaged Cherokee homes.

In Michael Green and Theda Perdue's edited work, *The Cherokee Removal: A Brief History with Documents,* Rebecca Neugin offers a first-hand account of soldiers forcing her family to leave its home when she was three years old. She reported that her "father wanted to fight, but my mother told him that the soldiers would kill him if he did." Soldiers forced them from their home, but Rebecca's mother "begged them to let her go back and get some bedding." Federal troops allowed her to do so, and she took blankets, pots, pans, and other incidentals. The family also secured its wagon and oxen, moving west with nine children, two or three widows, and their children. Rebecca's mother and father walked the entire distance, and her father hunted deer, turkey, and other game to supplement government rations of salt pork. Rebecca remembered that many people were ill, "and a great many little children died of whooping cough." Baptist minister Evan Jones remarked that "Our minds have, of late, been in a state of intense anxiety and agitation," and he reported that everyone wept, including "terrified children, without a friend to speak a consoling word."

In *American Indian Holocaust and Survival,* Cherokee scholar Russell Thornton characterized removal as "Exceptionally tragic" and an "ordeal that the tribe subsequently named Nunna daul Tsunyi" or "the trail where we cried." It is commonly called the Trail of Tears. And anthropologist James Mooney recorded that "this Cherokee removal of 1838, as gleaned by the author from the lips of actors in the tragedy, may well exceed in weight of grief and pathos any other passage in American history." Hundreds of Cherokees died in the stockades, and thousands died on the Trail of Tears from depression, disease, starvation, and exposure. Mooney estimated that "over 4000 Cherokee died as a direct result of the removal." The actual number will never be known, but some Cherokees feel that the number far exceeds the estimate. Chickasaw historian Arrell Gibson estimated that the Trail of Tears cost the Cherokees 25 percent of their population. Regardless of the numbers of dead, the Trail of Tears will continue to be a tragedy of immense significance to Cherokees, other Native Americans, and Americans from diverse backgrounds who have knowledge of the invasion, theft, and forced exile of the Cherokee and their neighbors.

Not all Cherokees experienced the Trail of Tears. Hundreds hid in the hills and forests north of Georgia. A few Cherokees moved into the fringes of white society, making new lives as laborers, merchants, and farmers in Tennessee, Kentucky, and North Carolina. Approximately one thousand Cherokees came together as a group in North Carolina, escaping removal with the cooperation of state officials. One white man, William H. Thomas (called Wil Usdi by Cherokees), purchased land in western North Carolina in his own name on behalf of the Indians. He also defended them in court and represented their case in Washington, D.C. There are about ten thousand Cherokees from western North Carolina today, of which half live on the reservation and half live and work off the reservation. This group of Cherokees constitutes the eastern band of Cherokee but maintains close contact with friends and relatives among Cherokees in present-day Oklahoma.

CHOCTAW REMOVAL

Choctaws fell victim to removal in September 1830, when unscrupulous agents convinced a minority of the nation to sell their eastern homes. Under the terms of the Treaty of Dancing Rabbit Creek, in return for surrendering millions of acres of prime land in Mississippi and Alabama, Choctaws secured an equal amount of land north of the Red River in southeastern Indian Territory (present-day border of Oklahoma and Texas). In addition, the government did not include all the lands inhabited and used by Choctaws, including lands in Alabama and West Florida. Futhermore, the government guaranteed to educate forty Choctaws each year and provide the nation $50,000 so it could establish public schools in Indian Territory. The government also agreed to provide Choctaws with annuities of $20,000 for twenty years, supplies, and moving expenses. Much of this money was never paid, although various sums of money trickled into the Choctaw Nation for years. However, when the people needed money most, between 1832 and 1840, the government did not provide the promised cash. Whereas some Choctaws began their treks west, others continued to resist removal, using a clause in the Treaty of Dancing Rabbit Creek to their advantage.

A provision of the Choctaw treaty permitted members of the nation to accept 640-acre allotments (or more) and remain in Mississippi. Immediately 540 adults announced their intentions to claim allotments, but this number swelled to approximately one-fourth of the tribe, who decided to be allotted rather than removed. However, Agent William Ward defrauded the allottees, never filing the proper papers to make these allotments a reality. In addition, he worked with state and local citizens as well as speculators to steal Choctaw lands. They swindled Choctaws out of the so-called floating claims before Indians officially registered them with the United States. The government of the United States and the state stood by and did nothing. By 1840, those Choctaws remaining in Mississippi were living in poverty, disease, and death—strangers in their own land. They lost their lands, homes, livestock, and property. However, they never lost their identity as Choctaw and have never been alienated from the earth they hold sacred. Descendants of these people are known today as the Mississippi Choctaw and are skillfully led by Phillip Martin.

The states of Mississippi and Alabama discriminated against Choctaws as a means of encouraging them to move to Indian Territory. Like Georgia, Mississippi and Alabama also passed a number of laws forcing Indians to obey state laws. As a result of state laws, Choctaws were prohibited from forming a tribal government within state boundaries, testifying in court against whites, and exercising tribal power as Indian leaders. Whites moved onto Indian lands, challenging native people to fight. Whites stole homes, crops, horses, cattle, and everything of value. A reign of terror unfolded in Mississippi, and when Choctaws asked for help from federal troops, they were always denied. Federal officials turned their backs to Choctaws, permitting state and county officials as well as white settlers to trample the Choctaw Nation. Agents, superintendents, commissioners, and soldiers did nothing to stop the mayhem, because the ultimate goal of President Jackson and the nation was removal. They ignored past treaties between the United States and Choctaws that provided protection from white incursions and guaranteed the supremacy of federal law over state and local ordinances. The consequences were deadly for many Choctaws.

Between 1832 and 1839, the Choctaws moved in waves to Indian Territory, suffering greatly as a result of forced removal across the Mississippi River. According to Choctaw historian Donna Akers, some six thousand men, women, and children perished during the Choctaw ordeal. Often soldiers forced the people to walk westward during the winter when "a heavy sleet [had] broken and bowed down all the small and much of the large timber." The people starved on the journeys and froze because they were "without any covering for their feet, legs, or body except a cotton underdress." They traveled through rain, mud, snow, and ice. Children died of malnutrition, and most everyone suffered from cholera, influenza, pneumonia, and other diseases. The head of the Office of Indian Affairs characterized removals as a "humane policy" that was producing "good effects." This was an easy statement to make from an office in Washington, D.C., far from the misery, disease, and death of Choctaw people.

CHICKASAW REMOVAL

Like Choctaws, the Chickasaws of northern Mississippi and northwestern Arkansas lost all their lands. Over the years, Chickasaws had ceded millions of acres to the United States, but these land cessions were never enough. When whites in Mississippi realized that Chickasaws would not move easily, settlers harassed them. Whites overran Indian lands, destroyed native homes and property, and allowed their animals to graze on Chickasaw crops. Mississippi's legislature followed Georgia's example, invalidating Chickasaw tribal government and subjecting the people to state laws that discriminated against Indians. After years of trying to retain their lands, the former allies of the United States signed the Treaty of Pontotoc in 1832. At the tribal council house at Pontotoc Creek, Chickasaws agreed to cede all tribal lands east of the Mississippi River and move west when the government and Indians agreed on suitable lands in Indian Territory.

In the meantime, the government agreed to survey Chickasaw lands and assign each family a homestead while the Indians waited for removal. In this way, Chickasaws could remain on their lands for a longer period of time, and satisfy white lust for their lands. Surplus lands not homesteaded by Indians in the old Chickasaw Nation would be opened for white settlement and sold at public auctions. Under the terms of the agreement, Chickasaws were to receive the money from this land sale. In addition, Chickasaws visited areas west of the great river, including those lands west of the Choctaw Nation in Indian Territory, between the Canadian and Red rivers. Chickasaw leaders did not rush to make a decision and did not select lands until January 1837, when they signed the Treaty of Doaksville with Choctaw leaders to settle west of the Choctaw Nation. Lands chosen by the Chickasaw were directly west of the Choctaws' and just east of lands claimed by Kiowas and Comanches. By selling these lands to the Chickasaw, the Choctaws created a buffer between themselves and the great fighters of the Southern Plains.

Almost immediately after making the agreement with the Choctaws, government officials pushed Chickasaws into removal. In the spring of 1837, the first Chickasaws made the trail westward. Members of the Chickasaw Nation had more time to sell their personal property, pack their household goods, and plan for removal. They moved west in an orderly fashion, although they were plagued by cholera and gastrointestinal diseases, some of which stemmed from consuming spoiled meat and rotten flour provided by the government. As with other southern tribes, Chickasaws moved to Indian Territory with African-American slaves as well as with freed men and women, many of whom were of mixed African and Indian blood, who chose to remain with the Chickasaw Nation and live in Indian Territory. According to African-American historian Nudie Williams, the first large number of African-Americans to enter present-day Kansas and Oklahoma came with the tribes who were forced west by the United States. By 1840, Chickasaws had completed their removal and were busy rebuilding their nation in Indian Territory. Like the other Indian nations from the South, Chickasaws lamented forced removal from their ancestral lands, sacred places, and cemeteries. Nevertheless, their removal progressed far better than those of the other southern Indian nations, including the Muscogees.

MUSCOGEE REMOVAL

Like the Cherokees, Muscogees split over the issue of removal, but their tribal division had occurred long before 1824–1825, when removal was demanded by the United States. In part, division among them was traditional, with villages grouped around those who favored war and those who did not. During the War of 1812, that segment of the nation known as Red Sticks favored war, whereas other Muscogees remained neutral or sided with the United States. Division within the Muscogee Nation continued after the war and led some Muscogees to decree death to any member of the nation who signed an agreement selling lands or exchanging eastern lands for western lands. Chief William McIntosh believed that the Muscogees would have to leave their ancestral lands or "be beaten like dogs" and left homeless in their own lands. He determined that the Muscogees "will go to a new home . . . till the earth, grow cattle and depend on these for food and life." Only through removal, he argued, could the Muscogee "grow and again become a great nation."

In 1825, McIntosh signed the Treaty of Indian Springs, a scandalous document committing every Muscogee to surrender all eastern lands. Shortly afterward, Chief Opothleyoholo ordered his followers to execute McIntosh and two of his associates, thus accentuating an old tribal division. With one hundred warriors, the nontreaty Muscogees surrounded McIntosh's home, set fire to it, and when the three stepped out, shot them to death. This event in Muscogee history is well recorded in the memory of the people today, who view the killings as a watershed in native history. Removal had caused a civil war within the nation and a division that is a part of Muscogee culture today. Within many native nations removal caused the same form of intense division, which sometimes resulted in violence, death, and long-term grudges. Hard feelings about removal remain today but are kept within the purview of the Indian nation and generally not shared with others. Clearly, a major schism emerged among the Muscogees as a result of the Treaty of Indian Springs, and this development found its way to the White House.

President John Quincy Adams acknowledged the fraud and injustice of the Treaty of Indian Springs and refused to sign it. He called a conference in Washington, D.C., in 1826 and negotiated a new treaty with Opothleyoholo. Months earlier, Opothleyoholo had opposed Muscogee removal, but after his visit to Washington, he determined that a major civil war would erupt among the Muscogee over removal if he did not sign. Furthermore, Adams called the conference to deal more fairly and directly with the Muscogees, but he supported Indian removal and made his views known to Opothleyoholo. As a result, removal was a part of the Treaty of Washington in 1826. Under the terms of this treaty, Muscogees surrendered a portion of their remaining eastern lands for lands in Indian Territory. The treaty allowed Muscogees until January 1, 1827, to move off their lands. Most Muscogees who had been loyal to McIntosh moved, but others under Opothleyoholo lingered in the old Muscogee Nation. White settlers pressured the remaining Muscogee mercilessly, stealing land, rustling horses and cattle, and creating as much conflict as possible.

Governor George M. Troups of Georgia protested the new treaty and concessions made to Muscogees. He announced his outrage and publicly stated that he would not recognize the Treaty of Washington and that Georgians could move onto Muscogee lands immediately. The federal government committed a lone U.S. marshal to hold back the tide of settlers, and he resigned in disgust. Adams sent no soldiers to protect Muscogees or their property from land-grabbing outlaws in Georgia and Alabama, who raped, murdered, and stole anything of value. To avoid whites in Georgia, some Muscogees had moved to Alabama and Florida–some living with Seminoles–but whites there also wanted to be rid of Indians. Most Muscogees moved to Indian Territory, but some hid in the forests of Alabama, Georgia, and Florida and squatted on lands that had once belonged to native people. Many Muscogees headed west beginning in November 1827, and for two years joined the stream of Indian refugees fleeing terrorism in their homelands. Those Muscogees reestablished the nation in the east-central portion of Indian Territory between the Choctaw Nation to the south and Cherokee to the north.

Meanwhile, a reign of terror–like that suffered by many tribes–developed in Alabama. McIntosh had warned that whites would beat Muscogees as punishment for being Indians and remaining on their own lands, and he had been correct. Lawlessness was sanctioned–if not ordered–by the state government, while federal troops, representatives, marshals, and commissioners did nothing. Muscogees had a legal relationship with the United States, not Alabama, through their treaties, but the United States did not execute its superiority but rather allowed the states to dictate Indian policy. The United States permitted murder, rape, and mayhem, because most whites wanted Muscogees banished from their ancestral homes. In 1832, Opothleyoholo agreed to the second Treaty of Washington, which called for Muscogee removal to Indian Territory, travel expenses paid by the government, an annuity of $12,000 for five years and $10,000 for the next fifteen years.

The treaty ended the nation in Alabama, although the United States assured individual Muscogees protection if they wished to take land allotments of 320 to 640 acres and try to survive under Alabama's laws. Only 630 Muscogees volunteered to move immediately, as most tried allotment. But individual ownership of land was as new to Muscogees as it was to most Native Americans, and whites in Alabama took advantage of the fact. They lied and cheated, swindling Muscogees out of the remainder of their domain. Whites settlers claimed false debts owed to them by Muscogees, and courts sided with land-grabbing whites, ruling in their favor against the Indians. Like the Ku Klux Klan of another era, white vigilantes attacked Muscogee farms and families, and when the Muscogees resisted, state and county law enforcement locked up Muscogees for assault. When the Creeks organized under Eneah Emothla, the U.S. Army intervened. Military protection of Muscogees against whites

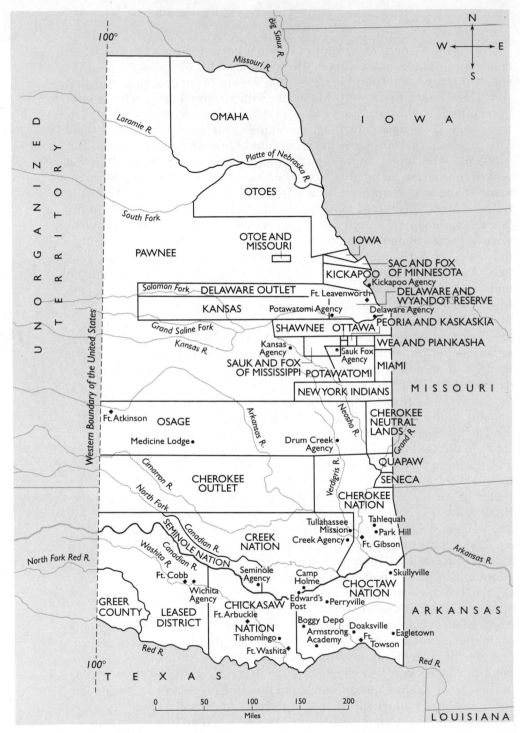

Indian Territory, 1850

had been codified in the second Treaty of Washington, but the army had remained invisible until whites claimed that a new Indian rebellion had begun.

Rumors and lies created by whites circulated about the coming "Creek war," so state and federal soldiers as well as state and local law enforcement personnel overran Muscogee homes and took people prisoner. Whites set up Muscogee concentration camps and forced about thirty-five hundred Muscogee men, women, and children to march under federal guard to Indian Territory. Heavily armed soldiers marched them along, many of them barefoot and heavily shackled. One group of three hundred Muscogee men, women, and children drowned when the government forced them to ride a rotting river boat that sank in the Mississippi River, killing all the native passengers. By 1837, a total of fifteen thousand Muscogees had reached Indian Territory, but another thirty-five hundred had perished from starvation, accidents, exposure, disease, and depression. The government that had agreed to protect Muscogee lives actually facilitated the death and destruction of thousands of Muscogee people. Some Muscogees resisted removal by moving south to live with their relatives, the Seminole. But the Seminole were to face the same pressures as those brought to bear on other native nations during the 1830s and 1840s.

SEMINOLE REMOVAL

The last of the southern tribes to move west were Seminoles, who lived in southern Georgia and Alabama as well as Florida. The Seminole Nation was composed of bands led by village chiefs and town councils. Many of the people had moved south into Spanish Territory to escape the strong arm of the United States, but after 1819, and the Adams-Onis Treaty, the United States claimed jurisdiction over them again. Seminoles knew exactly what the United States planned for all the eastern tribes, and they knew about the removal treaties and trails of tears of the other tribes. In 1823, the United States acted on the request of whites invading Florida, negotiating the Treaty of Tampa, which forced Seminoles to move into the swamps east of Tampa Bay. Before the ink was dry on the document, white settlers demanded the complete removal of the Seminole to Indian Territory. White newcomers kept up the chorus, claiming that Seminoles were a threat to property, persons, and civilization. They claimed that Seminoles stole their slaves and harbored runaway slaves.

In 1832, James Gadsden negotiated the Treaty of Payne's Landing with the Seminole, directing Seminoles to find a new home in the West and move within three years. In return for the Seminoles ceding all their lands in Florida, the government would pay Seminoles $15,400 and an annuity of $3,000 for fifteen years. The United States also agreed to pay for removal and a subsistence package for one year so that the tribe could adjust to the new home in Indian Territory. Some Seminoles agreed to move west, meeting Muscogees in Indian Territory and negotiating the Treaty of Fort Gibson, by which these Seminoles bought lands west of the fort along the north fork of the Canadian River, in present-day central and western Oklahoma. Approximately three thousand Seminoles left Florida for Indian Territory, reestablishing a portion of the Seminole Nation on the arid plains far from Florida and the land of trees, water, and ocean breezes. However, not all Seminoles took the Trail of Tears west.

Osceola, Jumper, Micanopy, Bowlegs, Alligator, and Coachoochee (Wildcat) led the Seminole resistance against removal. These leaders ordered the execution of one of the Seminoles who signed the Fort Gibson agreement, and they told the government they would rather die than move. Agent Wiley Thompson ordered the arrest of Osceola, who was captured, imprisoned, and placed in irons for a time before being released. Agent Thompson thought that he was teaching Osceola a lesson and that the chief would end his hostilities. Instead, the chief and his cohorts attacked the agent and several other people before ambushing and killing 107 American soldiers near Fort King. This triggered the Seminole War of 1835–1842, which spread across Florida to many areas. Seminole fighters fought from the swamps, striking settlements and soldiers before returning to their sanctuaries. In 1836, General Thomas Jesup met a group of Seminoles who had entered into negotiations under a flag of truce. Ignoring the flag, Jesup captured Osceola and imprisoned him in Charleston, South Carolina, at Fort Moultrie. The great chief died in a dank cell in January 1839.

In spite of Osceola's imprisonment and death, Seminoles fought under the skilled leadership of several war chiefs. They never surrendered in spite of setbacks, disease, and death. No one knows the number of Seminoles who died for their nation, but the war cost the United States fifteen hundred soldiers and $20 million. Like many other Indian nations, the Seminoles divided over the issue of removal. Some Seminoles remained in the East, whereas others made the trek westward. This latter group included some of the bands who had fought long and hard to retain their lands in Florida but who ultimately decided it was in the best interest of their people to move west. As a result of the war and forced removal, Seminole people live in Florida and Oklahoma.

Removal was not confined to Seminole and other southern tribes. The larger native nations in the Old Northwest, particularly those that still held title to land, suffered forced removal between the 1820s and 1840s.

REMOVAL OF OLD NORTHWESTERN TRIBES

Removal of Indians from the Old Northwest began immediately after the War of 1812 and continued into the 1840s. Over a period of several years, the United States forced many tribes into present-day Iowa and Missouri before pushing them farther west into present-day Nebraska, Kansas, and Oklahoma. By the 1840s, a large "Indian Territory" extended from the Missouri River in the North to the Red River in the South. The Indian Territory bordered the Missouri River to the east and south along the present state borders of western Missouri and Arkansas. It was bordered on the west by the hundredth meridian, the western border of the United States. Otoes, Missouris, Pawnees, Omahas, Iowas, and Minnesota Sac and Fox were situated in the northern segment of Indian Territory. The United States had removed Kickapoos, Delawares, Wyandots, Shawnees, Ottawas, Peorias, Chippewas, Kaskaskias, Weas, Piankeshas, Miamis, Potawatomis, Senecas, and Mississippi Sac and Fox to the middle segment of Indian Territory in what is principally Kansas today.

Other eastern Indians were forced to the West but did not have standing with the United States and had largely been absorbed by other tribes. The people preserved their own identity in tribal memory, but the names were not commonly used in the records because whites who created the records did not know an Erie from a Seneca or a Mohican from a Delaware. These included the so-called New York Indians, who included the Seneca but also other tribal remnants formerly from New York, Pennsylvania, Ohio, and other regions north of the Ohio River. These also may have included some Susquehannas or Conestogas who had joined with other tribes to survive the American holocaust. Immediately south of these eastern Indians were the Osage, and south of them the government forced Cherokees, Muscogees, Seminoles, Choctaws, and Chickasaws to relocate. However, even these lands were not safe and secure.

During the 1850s and 1860s, whites invaded the northern portion of Indian Territory, carving out the states of Kansas and Nebraska. They also convinced the government to shrink Indian Territory, so the tribes were uprooted once again, pushed onto smaller and smaller parcels. The tribes had little power with state and local governments or the national government. Indians could not vote and had no political or economic clout. So white officials on every level, including the so-called friends of Indians who pretended to have the best interest of native people at heart, took advantage of Indians. With such friends, Indians did not need enemies. As a result, whites continually reduced the Native American estate, including that of Indians who had already surrendered millions of acres in the eastern part of the United States and who had been forced to resettle west of the Mississippi River. This was as true for the Wyandots of Ohio as it was for Senecas, Ottawas, Ojibwes, Miamis, Mohicans,

Delawares, Shawnees, and many other tribal groups who had resisted removal and remained in their homes in northwestern Ohio.

WYANDOT REMOVAL

The history of Native American removal from the Old Northwest is similar from tribe to tribe, whether or not they were allies of the United States during the War of 1812. Some Wyandots under Roundhead had fought with Tecumseh, whereas others under Tarhe (Crane) had remained neutral or sided with the United States. Many Wyandots lived in northwestern Ohio along the Sandusky River, where they farmed the open prairies and hunted in the dense woods of present-day Wyandot, Crawford, and Richland counties. At one time or another, Delawares, Shawnees, Miamis, Chippewas, and Ottawas lived near the Wyandot villages of Upper Sandusky, Ohio. Some of these people intermarried with Wyandot and remained in the area, but most moved into Michigan or Indiana. Many Wyandots remained in Ohio after the War of 1812 or moved into Michigan to live with other Wyandots near Detroit. Both groups of Wyandots tried to live in harmony with white neighbors.

After the War of 1812, many Wyandots tried to acculturate into white society. Some farmed and traded, whereas others worked for non-Indians. Many gradually became Christians, particularly Methodists. In addition to preserving native spiritual beliefs, many Wyandots had been Catholics while under French influence, but in 1816, Reverend James B. Finley assigned Reverend John Stewart, an African-American minister (perhaps of mixed Indian blood) from Powhatan County, Virginia, to meet monthly with the Wyandot congregation in Upper Sandusky, Ohio. Then in 1821, Reverend Stewart established the Methodist Episcopal Mission at Upper Sandusky, a small stone structure and the first Methodist mission among any group of Native Americans. At the time, Wyandots, Delawares, and remnants of other tribes remained in the region, most living in a fashion similar to whites but maintaining their identities as Indian people.

Some of these Indians also became Christians, including Shawnees and Delawares who listened to Stewart and became Methodists. However, in spite of the Indians' efforts to become more whitelike in their outward dealings, whites wanted their land. This was particularly true of those tribes that retained title to thousands of acres. As in other times and other places, Wyandots, Delawares, Shawnees, Ottawas, and others became the target of white settlers who wanted control of all eastern land and removal of native people to Indian Territory. Because white settlers had a voice in Indian affairs through their elected officials, they demanded that the government respond to their desire for more Indian land. Indians were not citizens of the state or nation, and they had little voice in public affairs now that war was no longer an option for them. Native Americans knew that the political climate around them favored removal, and all, in their own ways, fashioned strategies to keep their homes for as long as possible.

All the tribes in the Old Northwest discussed removal among themselves and with other Indian tribes. Each waited its turn to deal with the American official assigned to negotiate removal treaties. After Commissioner James B. Gardiner negotiated removal treaties with Senecas, Shawnees, Ottawas, and mixed bands of Seneca-Shawnees, he turned his attention to the Wyandots who inhabited the Grand Reserve of 109,144 acres near Upper Sandusky, Ohio. For years Wyandots had lived in the region, farming the open prairies, fishing the Sandusky River, its tributaries, and lakes. Wyandots had hunted the thick deciduous forest of the area and the open prairies in present-day Wyandot, Crawford, and Richland counties. After the War of 1812, they had lived in relative harmony with Delawares, Shawnees, Ottawas, and other Indians as well as whites who pressed the boundaries of the Grand Reserve with their farms. Although Wyandots from Upper Sandusky and many of their native neighbors had remained loyal to the United States during the War of 1812, Commissioner Gardiner proposed to remove them from Ohio. In 1831, he organized an exploring expedition into the trans-Mississippi West that visited Missouri. Wyandot leader William Walker and four other representatives of the tribe traveled west but were unimpressed with the land and people. They recommended that the tribe remain in Ohio.

Although the Wyandots from the Grand Reserve refused removal in 1831, the Big Springs band of Wyandots ceded their title to sixteen thousand acres to the United States for $20,000, agreeing to relocate onto the Grand Reserve or the Huron River Reserve of Michigan or to move into Canada. Some of these people remained in the area, squatting on lands and farming in one place and then another. While the Big Springs people shifted for themselves, Wyandots living on the Grand Reserve received increasing pressure from the government and white settlers to remove. The tribe split over the issue of removal, with the "Christian Party" opposed to removal and the "Non-Christian Party" favoring it. In 1834, another delegation of Wyandots explored the West for a suitable home, visiting the Shawnees in Johnson County, Kansas, but the tribe refused removal. While the delegation was gone, Governor Robert Lucas–acting under orders from Jackson's secretary of war, Lewis Cass–pressured the Wyandots to sell their land. When Wyandots refused removal, the government changed its tactic by buying parcels of Wyandot lands and reducing the number of acres. Slowly, whites bled Wyandot people of their holdings, pushing them onto smaller and smaller land areas.

On April 23, 1836, Wyandot leaders signed the Treaty of Washington, ceding a five-mile strip of land from the easternmost portion of the Grand Reserve to the United States as well as two other parcels outside the reserve. Historian Robert Smith has worked with Leaford Bearskin and the tribe for years and has pointed out that Wyandots ultimately agreed to move because of intense and ever-increasing pressure from the government and settlers. In 1839, a Wyandot exploring party visited Delawares and Shawnees in Kansas, but still the tribe refused removal. Wyandot leaders negotiated with American commissioners for years and visited Cherokees, Senecas, Delawares, and Shawnees in 1841. They met Agent John Johnson on many occasions, trying to work out an agreement that would be acceptable. They knew the difficulties of removal, but they also knew the perils of refusing removal. On March 17, 1842, Chief Francis A. Hicks and six other Wyandot leaders agreed to surrender the Grand Reserve in Ohio and the Wyandot Reserve in Michigan for 148,000 acres in the West, an annuity of $17,500 for twenty years, and $500 per year for the tribe to operate a public school. In addition, the government guaranteed to pay $10,000 for removal costs. The Methodist Mission and the cemetery were deeded to Wyandots in perpetuity, and the burial ground and restored stone building remain in Upper Sandusky today. It stands as a somber and sacred place for Wyandot people, the burial place of men, women, and children.

On July 12, 1843, approximately 750 Wyandots from Michigan and Ohio congregated at the Methodist Church in Upper Sandusky, Ohio, to express their "strong attachment to the familiar scenes of their infancy, and in particular the burial places of their kindred." Men, women, and children cried and expressed "their great reluctance to leave" the graves of their people. Under the shade of the tall maple and oak trees, lay leader Squire Greyeyes preached a farewell sermon that ended in one of the most moving poems written by an American Indian during the nineteenth century.

Adieu to the graves where my fathers now rest!
For I must be going to the far distant West.
I've sold my possessions; my heart fills with woe.
To think I must leave them, Alas! I must go.
Farewell ye tall oaks in whose pleasant green shade
In childhood I sported, in innocence played;
My dog and my hatchet, my arrows and bow,
Are still in remembrance, Alas! I must go.
Adieu ye loved scenes, which bind me like chains,
Where on my gay pony I chased o'er the plains.
The deer and the turkey I tracked in the snow.
But now I must leave them, Alas! I must go.
Adieu to the trails which for many a year
I traveled to spy the turkey and deer,
The hills, trees and flowers that pleased me so.
I must now leave, Alas! I must go.
Sandusky, Tymochtee, and Brokensword streams,

Nevermore shall I see you except in my dreams,
Adieu to the marshes where the cranberries grow.
O'er the great Mississippi, Alas! I must go.
Adieu to the roads which for many a year
I traveled each Sabbath the gospel to hear,
The news was so joyful and pleased me so,
From hence where I heard it, it grieves me to go.
Farewell my white friends who first taught me to pray
And worship my Savior and Maker each day.
Pray for the poor native whose eyes overflow,
With tears at our parting, Alas! I must go.

Before beginning his journey south to Cincinnati to board two steamboats headed west, Squire Greyeyes and his family walked to the side of the Methodist Mission to the small plot marked by granite headstones. They bowed their heads, prayed, and bid adieu to the members of their family they were leaving behind. This included their infants and small children. They wept over these graves and in this way shared the tragedy of American Indian removal with all Native Americans from the eastern portion of the United States who were uprooted from their homes and forced to live in the trans-Mississippi West. In August 1843, William Walker and his family arrived in Missouri and Kansas, where the chief commented to a reporter of the *Western Star*. "You cannot imagine my feelings on landing," Walker lamented, "and hunting a shelter for the family—faces all strange—we feel truly like strangers in a strange land." Still, Walker and his family survived, as did members of many other eastern tribes who had been forced west.

Removal affected the lives of thousands of Native Americans, and the policy continues to affect native people everywhere. After the 1830s, forced removal of Native Americans became a common event in American history as the United States continued the contest for the land west of the Mississippi River. Government officials moved Native Americans from place to place without much thought about the consequences that the diaspora had on native people. Rather, the government's key concern was to effectuate the best policy for the benefit of white settlers. As a result, the government moved portions of nearly every tribe in the American West, and agents often commented to native people that in comparison to eastern tribes, the government asked western tribes to move only short distances. However, like the eastern tribes, western people removed by the United States often surrendered sacred places, streams, trees, mountains, and other elements of their communities. And in so doing, they lost a part of themselves. When Squire Greyeyes left the Methodist Mission in Ohio, he left the graves of his small children. Although he returned to Ohio before his death to say prayers over those graves, he carried thoughts of those graves in his heart while he lived out his days in Kansas.

Selected Readings and Bibliography

Forced removal of Native Americans from the eastern states to the trans-Mississippi West is analyzed in several works. Debo provides a survey of removal in her book, *A History of the Indians of the United States,* and Gibson offers excellent details of the creation of Indian Territory, Jackson's policies, removal, and adjustment to life in the West in *The American Indian.* Hoxie's edited volume, *Indians in American History,* provides well-written essays–Theda Perdue's "Indians in Southern History" and R. David Edmunds's "National Expansion from the Indian Perspective"–that deal effectively with removal. Both authors capture the emotion, conflict, and tension felt by Indian people because of their loss of power, threat of removal, and physical displacement from their homes. Previously cited, these books also deal with removal: Akers's *Living in the Land of the Dead,* Champagne's *The Native North American Almanac,* Gibson's *The Chickasaws* and *The Kickapoo,* Harmon's *Sixty Years of Indian Affairs,* Prucha's *American Indian Policy in the Formative Years,* and Washburn's *Red Man's Land, White Man's Law.* Also see Tyler's *A History of Indian Policy,* Hagan's *The Sac and Fox Indians,* and Utley and Washburn's *Indian Wars.*

Agnew, Brad. *Fort Gibson: Terminal on the Trail of Tears.* Norman: University of Oklahoma Press, 1980.

Debo, Angie. *Rise and Fall of the Choctaw Republic.* Norman: University of Oklahoma Press, 1934.

——. *The Road to Disappearance.* Norman: University of Oklahoma Press, 1941.

DeRosier, Arthur H. *The Removal of the Choctaw Indians.* Knoxville: University of Tennessee Press, 1970.

Eby, Cecil. *"That Disgraceful Affair": The Black Hawk War.* New York: Norton, 1973.

Edmunds, R. David. *The Potawatomis.* Norman: University of Oklahoma Press, 1978.

Ehle, John. *Trail of Tears.* New York: Doubleday, 1988.

Foreman, Grant. *The Five Civilized Tribes.* Norman: University of Oklahoma Press, 1934.

——. *Indian Removal.* Norman: University of Oklahoma Press, 1942.

Gibson, Arrell M. *America's Exiles.* Norman: University of Oklahoma Press, 1976.

Gittinger, Roy. "The Separation of Kansas and Nebraska from the Indian Territory." *Mississippi Valley Historical Review* 3 (1917): 442–461.

Green, Michael D. *The Politics of Indian Removal: Creek Government and Society in Crisis.* Lincoln: University of Nebraska Press, 1982.

Jahoda, Gloria. *The Trail of Tears.* New York: Holt, Rinehart and Winston, 1975.

Lancaster, Jane F. *Removal Aftershock: The Seminoles' Struggles to Survive in the West, 1836–1866.* Knoxville: University of Tennessee Press, 1994.

Mathews, John Joseph. *The Osages.* Norman: University of Oklahoma Press, 1961.

McLoughlin, William G. *After the Trail of Tears: The Cherokees' Struggle for Sovereignty, 1839–1880.* Chapel Hill: University of North Carolina Press, 1993.

McReynolds, Edwin C. *The Seminoles.* Norman: University of Oklahoma Press, 1957.

Nichols, Roger L. *General Henry Atkinson.* Norman: University of Oklahoma Press, 1965.

Ourada, Patricia K. *The Menominee Indians.* Norman: University of Oklahoma Press, 1979.

Perdue, Theda, and Michael D. Green, eds. *The Cherokee Removal: A Brief History with Documents.* Boston: Bedford Books, 1995.

Prucha, Francis Paul. "Andrew Jackson's Indian Policy: A Reassessment." *Journal of American History* 56 (December 1969): 527–539.

Rogin, Michael P. *Fathers and Children: Andrew Jackson and the Subjugation of the American Indian.* New York: Knopf, 1975.

Satz, Ronald N. *American Indian Policy in the Jacksonian Era.* Lincoln: University of Nebraska Press, 1975.

Smith, Robert Emmett Jr. "The Wyandot Indians, 1843–1876." Ph.D. dissertation. Stillwater: Oklahoma State University, 1973.

Unrau, William E. *The Kansas Indians.* Norman: University of Oklahoma Press, 1970.

Viola, Herman J. *Thomas L. McKenney, Architect of America's Early Indian Policy.* Chicago: Sage Books, 1974.

Whitney, Ellen M. *The Black Hawk War, 1831–1832.* 4 volumes. Springfield: Illinois State Historical Library, 1970–1978.

Woodward, Grace S. *The Cherokees.* Norman: University of Oklahoma Press, 1963.

Young, Mary Elizabeth. "Indian Removal and Land Allotment: The Civilized Tribes and Jacksonian Justice." *American Historical Review* 64 (October 1958): 31–45.

——. *Redskins, Ruffleshirts and Rednecks: Indian Allotments in Alabama and Mississippi, 1830–1860.* Norman: University of Oklahoma Press, 1961.

CHAPTER 9

NATIVE AMERICANS AND WESTWARD EXPANSION

Removal of Native Americans from one region to another did not end in the 1840s but continued throughout the nineteenth century. Proponents of forced removal had argued that relocation of the tribes would enable Native Americans to preserve their cultures from the vices of whites. By the 1840s and the expansion of American influence to the hundredth meridian, some whites felt that the United States was "complete," having expanded beyond the Mississippi River. Other Americans disagreed, pointing out that the nation should expand from shore to shore, extending its democratic ideals and equal opportunity from the Atlantic to the Pacific. Of course, the West was already inhabited by thousands of Indians, who claimed certain geographical areas and who had a lengthy history before meeting white people. This history tied the people to the earth, animals, and spirits of their land. This history also included friendly and hostile relationships with each other. As in other places among other native peoples, American Indians in the West lived in harmony with some Indian peoples and fought others.

NATIVE AMERICANS AND LEWIS AND CLARK

In Indian and white relations in the West, the whites had the advantage. The United States had a unified government system with a constitution that designated the national government to deal with Indian tribes through congressional acts, treaties, reserves, removal, and war. The government of the United States functioned through majority rule of white males over twenty-one years of age who owned property. Native Americans could not vote in matters dealing with whites. They did not write formal treaties or submit laws to Congress. American Indian policy was the domain of white men, not Indians, and it functioned for the welfare of the United States and white people, not Native Americans.

During the early nineteenth century, the United States had developed a great deal of experience treating with native nations, and representatives of the government and its citizens brought this experience with them when they entered the West. Native Americans had dealt with each other for years, and they had experience functioning through bands, villages, and tribes with other native people and some foreigners, such as traders. But dealing with non-Indians regarding trade was far different from dealing in foreign policy that could result in substantial political, military, and cultural change for the people. All of this would be learned rapidly by native nations in the West.

Long before the Stokes Commission traveled to the "Indian Country" west of the Mississippi River to negotiate agreements with tribes already living there and resettle some eastern Indians onto western lands, the United States was expanding beyond the Mississippi River. American citizens were also moving into the region before the War of 1812, leading the way for expansion into the vast domain. Even earlier in the nineteenth century, Thomas Jefferson was interested in exploring the American West, and as president, he would put his plan of exploration into action.

President Jefferson planned westward exploration before the Louisiana Purchase. Early in his first term, Jefferson appointed Meriwether Lewis and William Clark (the younger brother of George Rogers Clark) to lead the Corps of Discovery to explore, map, and describe the region of the upper Missouri River, Rocky Mountains, and Pacific Northwest. Lewis and Clark were instructed to travel to the Pacific Ocean, making notes about geography, geology, hydrology, flora, and fauna. They were to note exploitable resources and Native American people and populations, with close attention to tribal alliances and enemies. By their presence and evidence of their journey through the Northwest, Lewis and Clark claimed the vast region for the United States, particularly that area west of the Rocky Mountains beyond the borders of the Louisiana Purchase. They gave peace medals and American flags to native people and in this way marked the region for the United States. Lewis and Clark also wrote extensive reports about the region, resources, plants, animals, and people that popularized the area and encouraged whites to venture west to trade and trap furs, lay claim to these "virgin lands," and make new lives for themselves. According to James Rhonda, all these events would affect the life and culture of Native Americans, but they knew nothing of the Corps of Discovery until the arrival of Lewis and Clark.

St. Louis, Missouri, buzzed with activity in the autumn and early winter of 1803. Many Indians lived in or near St. Louis, and Indians and whites throughout the region were aware that Lewis and Clark were training forty-eight men for the arduous adventure west, including an African-American named York. In the spring of 1804, the Corps of Discovery traveled up the wide Missouri River in a keelboat and two dugout canoes. They traveled all year, enjoying good relations with native peoples. They arrived among the Mandans of present-day North Dakota, who treated the explorers with respect, helping them survive the cold winter of 1804–1805. Although Lewis and Clark built Fort Mandan and lived there throughout the winter, they spent a good deal of time visiting the Mandan villages and partaking of Mandan hospitality.

While Lewis and Clark wintered in Mandan country, they met a sixteen-year-old Shoshoni woman, Sacájewea, who had been kidnapped by Hidatsa Indians about the age of ten and traded to Dakota people who sold or traded her to Toussaint Charbonneau, a French-Canadian trader. Lewis and Clark hired Charbonneau as a scout but soon learned that Sacájewea was far more important to the success of their expedition. She spoke some French and learned English but was proficient in dialects of the Sioux and Shoshoni languages. She often acted as interpreter for the explorers, pointed out important landmarks and trails, and introduced them to medicinal and edible plants. When she gave birth to a boy called "Pomp," she added an important person into the expedition. Members of the Corps of Discovery became part of her family, treating the mother and each other with civility. Furthermore, women and babies rarely took part in war parties, and their presence with the expedition disarmed other Indians, helping the group treat in a friendly manner with other Indians. Sacájewea contributed in all of these ways and more, especially when they met the Lemhi Shoshonis.

The Corps of Discovery remained among the Mandans until April 1805, when the explorers continued up the Missouri River to Great Falls in present-day Montana. For years Indians had watched the water fall eighty feet, crashing into the river below on its way to the Mississippi, but now non-Indians witnessed the natural wonder. Portaging their boats and goods around the falls took a month, but the Corps of Discovery continued to a point where three streams formed the Missouri. Lewis and Clark named the streams the Jefferson, Madison, and Gallatin. Sacájewea pointed the way, telling them to take the northern branch, which they had named the Jefferson. The entire party moved forward until Lewis took a small party in search of Indians. He was interested in trading for horses and food. He also needed instructions about crossing the Rockies before winter. Lewis found two native women and through them met Lemhi Shoshoni Chief Kameawait.

Lewis convinced some Shoshonis to return to the main encampment and help the corps collect its goods and cross the mountains. When Sacájewea saw these Shoshonis, she danced and showed "every mark of extravagant joy . . . suckling her fingers to indicate that they were of her native tribe." These Shoshonis were her people, and Kameawait was her brother. As a result, the Lemhi Shoshonis could not do enough for the strangers who had returned Sacájewea. They provided horses and guides, taking the party across the Lemhi Pass of the Rockies and north into the Flathead Indian country of western Montana. Shoshonis and

Flatheads were enemies, so Shoshoni scouts returned to their mountain homes. Lewis and Clark passed through the Bitterroot Valley and met the Flatheads, who took them to the Lolo Trail that crossed the rugged Bitterroot Mountains of western Montana and eastern Idaho. The corps followed the trail through thick forests where rivers rushed through granite canyons. They followed the Clearwater River out of the mountains to the eastern slopes of the Bitterroots, where they met a band of Nee Me Poo or Nez Perce Indians under Chief Twisted Hair.

According to Nez Perce oral tradition, the people learned that Lewis and Clark were making their way out of the mountains, and some people wanted to kill the white men. Nez Perce prophecy spoke of the coming of strangers who would straighten the curvy places of nature and make them straight (highways, railroads, and tunnels) and who would bring buffalo with no beards to their country. When some Nez Perce suggested harming the suyapo (whites), an elderly woman, Watkuiis, spoke against the idea, telling everyone that the strangers meant no harm. Nez Perce men, women, and children took the Corps of Discovery into their villages, helped the whites build cedar canoes, grazed their broken-down horses, and fed them fish, game, roots, and berries. After the explorers had gained strength, the Nez Perce guided them down the Clearwater and Snake rivers into Palouse Indian country.

Lewis and Clark canoed past a number of Palouse villages, but it was October, the time when tamaracks turn yellow, and the people were hunting and gathering late roots and berries. The Palouse and their neighbors learned that the Corps of Discovery was traveling through their homeland, so they met it at Quosispah, a village located at the confluence of the Snake and Columbia rivers. Lewis and Clark flew the Stars and Stripes on a pole in the village and gave the flag to the headman. The Indians also received medals struck for the Corps of Discovery sporting an image of President Jefferson on one side and a pipe-tomahawk on the other with an inscription, "Peace and Friendship." Many Indian leaders received the medals, and they treasured them for years. Yakama, Wanapum, Walula, Walla Walla, Cayuse, Chinook, and others gathered at the village to sing all night. Lewis and Clark believed that the native people were singing in their honor, and they were, but they sang many prophecy songs that elders had taught them to perform when the strange men arrived in their country.

Provisioned with roots, venison, antelope, and salmon, the Corps of Discovery set out on the last leg of its journey, down the Columbia to the Pacific Ocean. By the time the explorers reached the lower Columbia, all of the Chinookan-speaking peoples were aware of their presence. Chinooks tried to get Lewis and Clark to spend the winter at Chinook Village on the north bank of the Columbia in present-day Washington, but because Chinooks had stolen some of their goods, Lewis and Clark accepted the invitation of Clatsop Indians, who enticed them south into present-day Oregon. The explorers spent a miserable winter of rain, fog, and cold among the Clatsop, who were as skilled as their Chinook neighbors in taking things from outsiders. In late March 1806, Lewis and Clark began their return trip home.

The Corps of Discovery had hoped to board a ship and return to the United States via the Straits of Magellan, but unable to connect with a trading vessel of any stripe, the men hurried up the Columbia, crossed the Columbia Plateau through Umatilla and Walla Walla Indian lands, and returned to the Nez Perce country. Twisted Hair and his people had given their word to take care of horses and supplies belonging to Lewis and Clark. True to their word, they returned everything, and the horses were in excellent condition. Lewis and Clark noted in their journals that the Nez Perce and their plateau Indian neighbors were outstanding people on horseback and raised high-quality horses. They also commented in their journal that the Indian country in the West would make a great settlement for whites. On September 23, 1806, Lewis and Clark returned to St. Louis after a momentous journey of thousands of miles and hundreds of meetings with Native Americans.

American Indians living on the Great Plains, in the Rocky Mountains, on the Columbia Plateau, and near the Pacific Coast had varying degrees of experience trading for manufactured goods of Americans and Europeans and most welcomed the opportunity for future trade with white men. Several American explorers, and some British explorers from Canada, traveled the West, mapping the region, establishing relations with the tribes, and introducing Indians to various trade items. The most notable American explorers included Lieutenant Zebulon Montgomery Pike, who in 1805 explored the Mississippi River Valley north of St. Louis to Leech Lake in Minnesota. The next year Pike explored the Great Plains between the Arkansas and Red rivers, traveling to Colorado before heading south into New Mexico. Pike viewed the Royal Gorge of the Arkansas River before a Spanish army out of Santa Fe captured the Americans. After questioning him in Chihuahua, Mexico, the Spanish escorted Pike to Natchitoches and permitted them to reenter the United States. Major Stephen H. Long and Colonel Henry Atkinson explored the Great Plains from Council Bluffs, Iowa, south to the Royal Gorge. Long explored along the Cimarron and Canadian rivers, producing a map of the Great Plains in the 1820s that indicated that the region "is almost wholly unfit for cultivation, and of course uninhabitable by a people depending upon agriculture for their subsistence." This region would become a suitable dumping ground for American Indians, described by Cherokee humorist Will Rogers in the early twentieth century as "a place where the rivers don't flow and the grass don't grow." Long labeled the region "the Great American Desert," and although a few white settlers inhabited the region, most moved over the Plains to California or Oregon. Many explorers mapped the West, siting places to water and graze livestock and to cross rivers and mountains. Explorers, traders, and surveyors recorded routes to take them from the East into the Northwest, Southwest, and California.

THE FUR TRADE

Exploration brought non-Indians to the West. These people trapped, traded, and in other ways exploited the region. Indeed, less than a year after Lewis and Clark left the Pacific Northwest, British trader David Thompson traveled down the Columbia River seeking an outlet for furs from the interior mountains of western Canada to the Pacific Ocean. Thompson was surprised when he found the flag of the United States flying over Quosispah. He left the Union Jack flying in the village and continued down the Columbia, opening the trading route for the North West Company. Although the British first developed the fur trade in the Canadian Rockies and Pacific Northwest, John Jacob Astor's Pacific Fur Company was not far behind. In 1811, American traders built Fort Astoria on the south side of the Columbia River in present-day Oregon and worked up the Columbia and Snake rivers, trading with Chinooks, Yakamas, Wanapums, Walla Wallas, Palouses, Nez Perces, Paiutes, and others. Whereas the coastal Indians had plenty of furs to trade, plateau Indians had few, and most refused to trap fur-bearing animals. Instead, they traded fine horses for trade goods. The Astorians failed to establish a firm footing in the Northwest, and news of a British warship moving to the Columbia River encouraged the Astorians to sell Astoria to the North West Company, which named the post Fort George. In 1821, the North West Company sold its interest to Hudson's Bay Company, which worked successfully among many diverse tribes for years.

Other fur companies operated in the Rocky Mountains, upper Missouri Valley, and Southwest. Manuel Lisa, William Clark, Pierre Chouteau, Auguste Chouteau, Major Andrew Henry, and others owned the Missouri Fur Company, which began trapping and trading in 1807. Several companies moved in and out of the mountains, taking bales of pelts and furs from many different animals that manufacturers turned into coats, hats, gloves, stoles, boots, belts, luggage, liners, and a host of other items. The fur trade had always been a part of American history. Native Americans traded in furs before white contact, and early European explorers from France, Russia, England, the Netherlands, and Sweden traded in furs. American Indians were drawn into the European fur trade during the colonial period, and some eastern Indians worked with white traders as they moved across the Mississippi River. The fur trade affected native peoples throughout the West in different ways.

In order to participate in the slaughter of animals for their furs but waste other parts of the animals, Roger Carpenter argues that Native

Americans had to overcome their spiritual relationship with the animals, which had been established at the time of creation. Many Indians believed that the Creator had made the earth, water, plants, and animals before human beings and that the "animal people" had put the world into motion for the benefit of humans. Animals sacrificed themselves so that humans could survive because that was the "law" of creation. But human beings had an obligation to deal with animals in accordance to native laws, which often included offering prayers and specified behavior or ritual on behalf of the animals so that the process of hunting, killing, consuming, and thanking would be fulfilled in accordance with the law. Indians did not consider animals to be lesser persons than themselves but rather relatives with full obligations to one another.

Oral narratives of Native Americans established the relationships between animals and humans. These narratives were told each winter so they could be transmitted from generation to generation. The narratives often focused on coyote, wolf, beaver, sea otter, cougar, deer, antelope, bear, and other fur-bearing animal people. The fur trade significantly harmed the relationship, ritual, and law as established at the time of creation. In order for Native Americans to participate fully in the slaughter, they had to turn their backs on traditional beliefs and accept a nonspiritual attitude toward animals as commodities to be exploited. Fur became the means of material wealth in trade items that dramatically changed native cultures. Some Indians participated in the slaughter, whereas others refused.

The fur trade affected Native Americans in other ways. It brought many native peoples into close contact with whites who brought diseases such as smallpox, measles, influenza, pneumonia, syphilis, whooping cough, tuberculosis, and gastrointestinal disorders. Diseases killed untold numbers of native people in the West, just as they had in other parts of the Americas. Traditional medicine men and women were almost powerless to fight the "white man's diseases," which usually would not respond to traditional Indian doctoring that incorporated medicinal plants and ritual procedures, including sweats, songs, prayers, dances, and sand painting. Disease disrupted native culture and life and was destructive far beyond decreasing the population. Of course, Native Americans did not understand germ theory–nor did whites until after the 1880s–but even if they had known that pathogens caused disease, they would not have known how to combat bacilli or viruses.

The fur trade introduced Native Americans to new technologies and goods that changed their lives. Traders brought guns, traps, powder, lead, pots, pans, cloth, beads, rope, knives, tomahawks, axes, and the like. Thousands of Native Americans became dependent upon the trade. Acceptance and use of the new material culture may have been inevitable, given the human propensity to use items that make their lives appear to be better and more efficient. For example, given the opportunity to cook in metal pots rather than in pits or baskets, many women chose pots. Men had successfully used stone knives and axes for years, but stone knives were fragile, breaking easily, whereas metal knives and axes were more durable and easily obtained from traders. During the nineteenth century, most Native Americans in the West became dependent upon firearms, which required maintenance and ammunition, both of which came from whites. Some Indians gravitated to the trade, whereas others–particularly holy men and women–warned against trading with whites and becoming dependent on goods as eastern Indians had done in years past.

In spite of divisions among the people over the issue of trade, most Native Americans entered into commerce with whites in one fashion or another. The fur trade flourished in the West during the first half of the nineteenth century, bringing new and interesting material items into the Native American world. For the most part, fur trappers or mountain men did not try to Christianize or civilize Indians. Sometimes trappers married native women and entered into familial and tribal relations through their wives, but most trappers were more interested in earning a living through the trade than converting and civilizing. A notable exception occurred among the Flatheads and Spokanes when in 1825 George Simpson of the Hudson's Bay Company sent two boys, Garry and Pelly, to be educated at the Canadian mission school at Red River. The boys returned to their people in 1829, speaking and reading English, preaching the gospel, and causing a stir among northwestern Indians.

MISSIONARIES, OREGON TRAIL, AND KILLINGS

The Nez Perces and Flatheads became interested in knowing more about the spiritual power of white men, so in 1831, they sent a delegation to St. Louis to inquire about the source of this power and about the book of knowledge used by Christians. In St. Louis the northwestern Indian delegation met Superintendent of Indian Affairs William Clark, Catholic Bishop Joseph Rosati, and Chief William Walker, who was in the West to find a suitable home for Wyandots from Ohio. A devout Methodist, Walker wrote G. P. Disoway about the Indian delegation from Oregon. Disoway, in turn, wrote an article in the popular *Christian Advocate and Journal and Zion's Herald* about the "wandering sons of our native forests." Disoway made a call for Christian missionaries to uplift the "inquirers after the truth." Protestants, not Catholics, were the first to respond. Jason Lee responded but, after a brief association with northwestern Indians, took up the real estate business in the Willamette Valley of Oregon and left the major missionizing work to Samuel Parker, Marcus and Narcissa Whitman, Henry and Eliza Spalding, and other zealots. Parker and Whitman traveled west in 1835, arriving in Wyoming at the annual rendezvous of fur trappers on the Green River.

Whitman returned to the United States for supplies and help, while Parker rode to the Northwest. A band of Nez Perce Indians and Jim Bridger escorted Parker across the rugged Nez Perce Trail of present-day Idaho. Parker nearly died, and by the time he reached the Hudson's Bay posts of Fort Walla Walla (formerly Fort Nez Perce) and Fort Vancouver (both located in present-day Washington), he gave up his mission and returned home on a ship. Before leaving, Parker told Chief Factor Dr. John McLoughlin of Hudson's Bay that the two best sites for missions were Waiilatpu (Place of the Rye Grass) among the Cayuse Indians and Lapwai (Place of the Butterfly) among the Nez Perce. After an arduous journey across the Great Plains, Rocky Mountains, Continental Divide, and Blue Mountains, the Whitmans, Spaldings, and William H. Gray arrived on the Columbia Plateau. When they reached Fort Vancouver in the autumn of 1836, across the Columbia River from present-day Portland, Oregon, Dr. McLoughlin told them that Parker had departed but had left his recommendation to build missions among the Cayuse and Nez Perce.

Without asking permission of the chiefs who controlled the use of land, the Whitmans began building their mission in the Walla Walla Valley, whereas the Spaldings built theirs on the Clearwater River near present-day Lewiston, Idaho. Both offered religious instructions and basic education. Both were largely failures at conversion, although Spalding had more followers than Whitman. Although some Cayuse, Nez Perce, and other plateau Indians demonstrated an interest in Christianity, many more remained loyal to their own holy men and women as well as their old faith. The two Protestants operated their missions from 1836 to 1847 with varying successes and growing suspicion on the part of Indians against white settlement, particularly after 1840, when Joe Meek, William Craig, Robert Newell, John Larison, Caleb Wilkins, and other former fur trappers opened the Oregon Trail across the Blue Mountains. These men encouraged white emigrants from the United States to resettle Indian lands in Oregon. Whitman joined the enterprise, leading wagon trains through the Columbia Plateau and into the Willamette Valley and selling food and supplies to emigrants.

During the late 1830s and early 1840s, white settlers in the Northwest continued a process started during the colonial era—expansion throughout the Far West from the Northwest to the Southwest and everywhere in between. All this would take time and occur during different eras of the nineteenth century, but every tribe was adversely affected by the "Winning of the West." The Clowwewalla, Atfalati, Ahantchuyuk, Alsea, Yamel, Yaquina, Luckiamute, Santiam, Siletz, and other Native Americans living in or near the Willamette Valley lost thousands of lives and acres of land. Whites stole Indian lands, harassed native families, and advocated the removal of all of Oregon's Indians east of the Cascade Mountains onto the Columbia Plateau.

Some Native Americans moved east across the Cascades to escape the white invasion. Others congregated into groups of confederated tribes and bands to protect themselves. Disease spread among them, killing indiscriminately. American Indians living near the Pacific Coast or inland valleys had more contact with whites, and they suffered the most because of their close proximity to whites who farmed, fished, logged, hunted, and settled native lands. Few whites settled on the Columbia Plateau near Waiilatpu or Lapwai, but emigrants off the Oregon Trail often visited the Whitman Mission, which was not far from the trail. The visitors purchased goods, got directions and advice, and inadvertently introduced the Cayuse and their neighbors to several diseases, including measles, which arrived in epidemic proportions in 1847.

Measles spread from tribe to tribe, but Cayuses, Walla Wallas, Umatillas, and Palouses died in particularly large numbers. Whitman had previously threatened to unleash a bottle of poison among the Indians if they continued stealing fruits and vegetables from his garden, and many Indians believed that Whitman had caused the sickness. According to Palouse oral tradition, Indians also believed that Whitman was dispensing poison to his patients. To test the theory, a Palouse elder took medicine from Dr. Whitman, became ill, and died. The Indians believed that this was sufficient evidence that Whitman, a medicine and holy man who could work his power in positive or negative ways, was killing the people. On November 29, 1847, a few Cayuses, including Tilokaikt, who claimed the land upon which the mission was situated, murdered Marcus and his wife, Narcissa Whitman. Tomahas struck Whitman in the head with a tomahawk, and Indians shot Narcissa. They killed eleven others at the mission, and three more people in the mission hospital died when they were unattended.

Relations between Spalding and many Nez Perce had deteriorated as well. Young men had threatened Spalding, and during the Whitman killings, some advocated murdering the preacher. Some Nez Perce accused Spalding of mistreatment, including whippings and sexual misconduct. William Craig, a former mountain man married to Chief Big Thunder's daughter, did not like Spalding. Still, he rescued and protected Eliza and Henry after the Whitman deaths. But Craig could not control events farther west, where Oregon volunteers under Colonel Cornelius Gilliam, a veteran of the Black Hawk War and Seminole War, prepared an attack. In the spring of 1848, Gilliam entered the Cayuse country bent on punishing the Indians for the Whitman killings, but finding the Cayuse gone, he pushed forward to find a huge horse herd and many cattle. The colonel ordered his men to round them up and drive them back to Oregon City, where they would sell them and share the profits.

The Oregon volunteers had just started driving the horses when four hundred Palouse warriors, well mounted and painted for war, appeared on the great rolling hills south of Snake River. The Palouse attacked, pouring a steady fire of arrows at the volunteers and forcing them to release the herd. They fought a spirited battle along the Tucannon and Touchet rivers, and when Gilliam retreated, Palouse warriors dogged him for an hour. Gilliam accidentally shot himself, but his volunteers scoured the region, looking for elusive Cayuses. The soldiers never found the Cayuses, but five prominent leaders surrendered to the whites so that they could negotiate an end to their conflict. Instead of negotiations, whites sentenced all five to death, including innocent men who had opposed the killings and had not participated in the Whitman killings. On June 3, 1850, whites hanged the Cayuse leaders, ending the Cayuse Indian War but initiating an era of great uncertainty for Native Americans. Indians had little idea that the United States had settled its boundary dispute with Britain and that the United States now claimed their lands, believing that the nation could bring peace to the Oregon country rocked by the Whitman killings.

Conflict between white Americans and Native Americans was widespread. Nearly everywhere that whites expanded, Indians resisted settlement, encroachment, and bullying by the newcomers. As Cherokee historian E. A. Schwartz has pointed out in *The Rogue River Indian War and Its Aftermath*, the native people of Willamette, Klamath, and Rogue rivers clashed with miners, soldiers, and settlers. Ajumawes, Atsugwes, Shastas, Umpquas, and Klamaths raided whites in northern California and western Oregon. In 1849, Ajumawe and Atsugwe attacked and killed Captain William H. Warner of the Corps of Topographical Engineers. In the early 1850s, Indians living on the Russian River had to contend with troops under Captain Nathaniel Lyon, who passed through Pomo country near Clear Lake, California, and made their way to the Russian River, where they killed over seventy-five Indians. Phil Kearny also fought Native Americans along Rogue River, and his engagement, like those of others, inflamed relations with the Indians.

Several tribes in Oregon and California were heavily influenced by the discovery of gold on or near their lands, and they fought to drive the invaders from their lands. In addition to attacking miners, Native Americans followed an age-old pattern of striking wagons, stages, mining camps, and way stations to discourage settlement. The army launched expeditions to protect its citizens, not Indians, and Oregon Superintendent of Indian Affairs Joel Palmer negotiated numerous treaties, including the Table Rock Treaty of 1853 with the Rogue Indians. This treaty precipitated the Rogue River War of 1853, which resolved nothing. Palmer negotiated treaties with Umpquas, Shastas, and Calapooyas, authorizing them to move onto the Rogue River Reservation. Conflicts between the tribes and among whites and Indians resulted from Palmer's fast actions designed to benefit whites.

More whites moved into Oregon, challenging Indians for land and resources. Some Indians struck back, whereas others remained peaceful. Tensions grew in 1855, when a general war swept the Northwest. Captain James Lupton attacked the village of Old Jake, killing twenty-three women, children, and elders. Volunteer troops attacked other villages of the Rogue River tribes, and the Indians retaliated swiftly, killing twenty-seven whites to settle the score. White volunteers and regular troops mobilized against the Rogues, Umpquas, Shastas, Klamaths, Scotans, Grave Creeks, and Cow Creeks. Editors of the *Oregonian* newspaper labeled all Native Americans "inhuman butchers and bloody fiends" who must be "EXTERMINATED." The Rogue River War lasted nine months and ended in disaster for Native Americans in northern California and southern Oregon. Troops attacked them repeatedly until various leaders surrendered, agreeing to move onto reservations.

Dr. Elijah White became the first Indian agent for the entire Northwest and began the process of Indian removal after passage of the Donation Land Law of 1850, which granted 320 acres to men over eighteen if they occupied or cultivated the land—and an additional 320 acres if they married before December 1, 1851. The law encouraged white migration and resettlement on Native American land and forced Indians out of their homes. White's role as agent was overshadowed after 1853, when the United States split the Oregon Territory, creating Washington Territory. Isaac I. Stevens became the first governor and superintendent of Indian affairs in Washington Territory, while Joel Palmer became superintendent of Oregon Territory. In 1854, both superintendents actively engaged northwestern Indians in treaty making, pushing the Indians of western Washington and Oregon into treaties that called for removal to well-defined reservations where several Indians would live together under an agent of the United States.

NORTHWESTERN TREATIES AND WARS

Most Indians opposed treaties and reservations proposed by the United States, but many believed that they would have to make an agreement or lose everything. Delawares, Iroquois, and other eastern Indians who worked for Hudson's Bay Company and lived in the Northwest whispered to the western tribes, telling them of their fate. Some western Indians believed they had no choice but to sell their lands, whereas others resolved to stand against whites and their policies. Rumors circulated that if they did not sign treaties and move to reservations, the government would remove them to the Arctic. By 1854, most tribes knew the general outline of American Indian policies of removal, treaties, and boundaries, but they had little experience dealing with such policies. Tribes, clans, and families split over white policies, and the effects of these divisions remain with several western tribes today.

Stevens negotiated the Treaties of Medicine Creek, Point No Point, and Point Elliott. At Point Elliott, Duamish Chief Sealth (Seattle) told Stevens that "the ashes of our ancestors are sacred and their resting place is hallowed ground. You wander far from the graves of your ancestors and seemingly without regret." Sealth said that "our dead never forget the beautiful world that gave them being." He reminded Stevens that "Every part of this soil is sacred in the estimation of my people. Every hillside, every valley, every plain and grove, has been hallowed by some sad or happy event." Sealth said that "the very dust upon which you now stand responds more lovingly to their footsteps than to yours, because it is rich with the dust of our ancestors and our bare feet are conscious of the sympathetic touch . . . even the little children who lived here and rejoiced here for a brief season, still love these somber solitudes and at eventide they grow shadowy with returning spirits."

Sealth prophesied that white men would "never be alone" because "these shores will swarm with the invisible dead" and that the region "will throng with the returning hosts that once filled them and still love this beautiful land." Sealth concluded by telling Stevens to "be just and deal kindly with my people, for the dead are not powerless. Dead–I say? There is no death. Only a change of worlds." On January 22, 1855, Sealth and other native leaders agreed to the treaty, which forever changed their lives and encouraged whites and others to resettle native lands surrounding Puget Sound. Stevens received far less cooperation when he dealt with Leschi, a Nisqually chief, who refused to sign the Medicine Creek Treaty of December 26, 1854. White and native observers claim that Leschi never signed the treaty and that Stevens forged his mark on the document. In any case, Leschi crossed the Cascade Mountains to inform his cousin, Chief Kamiakin, and other plateau Indians that Stevens intended to bring his treaty delegation to them. Stevens had reportedly told some Yakamas that if the Indians did not sign a treaty, they would lose all their land. Leschi verified this view and warned Kamiakin about the suyapo.

In March 1855, James Doty acted as an agent for Stevens, meeting Owhi, Teias, and other Yakama leaders on Ahtanum Creek at the St. Joseph Catholic Mission. Kamiakin reluctantly met Doty and chided his uncles, Owhi and Teias, and his brothers, Showaway and Skloom, for accepting gifts from Doty. When Doty offered Kamiakin some tobacco, the chief told Doty's interpreter "that he had never accepted from the Americans the value of a grain of wheat without paying for it" because whites "gave goods . . . then claimed that the Indians' lands were purchased by them." Doty denied the accusation, but Kamiakin was correct. Still, the fifty-five-year-old chief agreed to meet Stevens at the Walla Walla Council in May–June 1855. Some Yakama, Cayuse, Umatilla, Walla Walla, Wanapum, Nez Perce, and Palouse met Stevens to discuss treaties. Joel Palmer joined Stevens at the council ground and explained American Indian policies of treaties, reservations, rights of way through reservations, resources, civilization, education, and American control of native people, all of which seemed uninviting to most Indians.

Kamiakin received his power on Mount Rainier and as a boy learned that he would lead his people in a difficult resistance movement. Between 1855 and 1858, Kamiakin led Yakama, Palouse, and other northwestern Indians in a war against the United States.

Kamiakin said little at the Walla Walla Council, but his views were expressed by Walla Walla Chief Peopeo Moxmox (Yellow Bird), Stickus (Cayuse), Owhi (Yakama), and Young Chief (Cayuse). While Stevens and Palmer spoke about secular issues, the Indians talked about their religion, particularly their holy link with the earth. After all, the discussion centered around the earth, so the Indians reminded Stevens of this sacred relationship. Peopeo Moxmox listened to the discussion about surrendering the land and consolidating tribes onto the Nez Perce, Umatilla, and Yakama reservations. He told Stevens that he did not see the offer being made because it was like a post between them. Stevens had insulted Peopeo Moxmox, and the chief told Stevens he felt like a feather blowing in the wind. Stickus explained that the earth was his mother and presented his view to Stevens and Palmer in this way. "If your mothers were here in this country who gave you birth, suckled you and while you were suckling some person came and took your mother and left you alone and sold your mother, how would you feel then?"

In 1855, several Plateau Indians met Governor Isaac Stevens at the Walla Walla Council, where Americans dictated the terms of three treaties. Gustavus Sohon painted the arrival of twenty-five hundred Nez Perce as they galloped forward while singing, drumming, and firing their guns in a native demonstration of power.

Owhi pointed out that "God gave us day and night, the night to rest in, and the day to see, and that as long as the earth shall last, he gave us the morning with out breath; and so he takes care of us on this earth and here we have met under his care." Owhi asked those assembled: "Is the earth before the day or the day before the earth. God was before the earth, the heavens were clear and good and all things in the heavens were good. God looked one way then the other and named our lands for us to take care of." Owhi pointed out that it was Indian law to take care of the earth. Young Chief agreed, saying:

I wonder if this ground has anything to say: I wonder if the ground is listening to what is said. I wonder if the ground would come to life and what is on it; though I hear what this earth says, the earth says, God has placed me here. The Earth says, that God tells me to take care of the Indians on this earth; the Earth says to the Indians that stomp on the Earth feed them right. God named the roots that he should feed the Indians on: The water speaks the same way: God says feed the Indians upon the earth: the grass says the same thing: feed the horses and cattle. The Earth and water and grass says God has given our names and we are told those names; neither the Indians or the Whites have the right to change those names: The Earth says, God has placed me here to produce all that grows upon me, the trees, fruit, etc. The same way the Earth says it was from her man was made. God on placing them on the Earth, desired them to take good care of the earth and do each other no harm.

Yakama leaders negotiated until June 9, when they agreed to sign a treaty committing fourteen diverse tribes and bands who spoke dialects of three language families to relocate to the Yakama Reservation in central Washington Territory. Kamiakin signed the agreement under duress as "an act of peace and friendship" but not as the so-called head chief of these various tribes, a title he never accepted. The Umatilla, Cayuse, and Walla Walla agreed to settle on the Umatilla Reservation of present-day northeastern Oregon, while the Nez Perce retained much of their traditional lands. Not long afterward, Palmer left the Walla Walla Council and negotiated with Sahaptin and Chinookan-speaking Indians living along the Columbia River an agreement that forced them to surrender much of their land and remove to the Warm Springs Reservation of central Oregon, a land base they later shared with Paiutes.

The Walla Walla Council of 1855 created three treaties concluded in June, and by that summer white miners invaded the inland Northwest in a new gold rush. Stevens had assured the Indians that the treaties would not take effect for a few years, until the Senate ratified them with a two-thirds vote and the president signed them. However, before leaving the council grounds, Stevens wrote dispatches to newspapers opening eastern Washington and Oregon, as well as present-day Idaho, Montana, and Wyoming, to white settlement. When miners staked out claims along the Spokane River, stole Indian horses, and raped native women, the federal government did nothing. But when Owhi's son, Qualchin, executed a few outlaws, Agent Andrew Jackson Bolon investigated. While riding across Yakama country, Bolon fell in with a few people; two of them had grievances against whites and murdered the agent.

The United States declared war, and many plateau Indians gladly joined in the fight against the suyapo. Indians living along the Rogue River, Willamette River, and Puget Sound also rose against white rule. Many tribes participated in two attacks on Seattle, unsuccessfully attempting to drive whites from Indian lands. Native Americans from the Canadian border south into California joined a general Indian war triggered by settlers, miners, and soldiers, the theft of Indian lands, and establishment of American Indian policies. Perhaps the largest geographical area—containing most tribes affected by the war—was the Columbia Plateau. At first the Plateau Indian War of 1855–1858 went well for the Indians, particularly at the Battle of Steptoe Butte, where over one thousand warriors descended on 150 ill-prepared troops under Colonel Edward Steptoe and drove them from the region. Regular and volunteer troops and inter- and intratribal divisions brought the fighting to an end in 1858. At the Battles of Four Lakes and Spokane Plain, the army pushed the combined forces of Yakama, Palouse, Okanogan, Coeur d'Alene, Spokane, Flathead, and others from the battlefield. Kamiakin was wounded by an artillery shell and saved by his fifth wife, a warrior woman named Colestah. Colonel George Wright pursued the Indians, capturing and slaughtering nearly one thousand Indian horses east of present-day Spokane, Washington. He swung south along the present boundary between Idaho and Washington, where he hanged several Indians, including Qualchin, shot Owhi to death, imprisoned several men, and took women and children hostage. Kamiakin and his band escaped into Canada and later resettled in the Palouse country. Meanwhile, Wright threatened all of the Indians he met, telling them that if he ever returned to fight them again, he would kill every man, woman, and child. His orders to do all this have never come to light and were probably given orally, but shortly after the campaign, the army promoted Wright to general. In 1859, the Senate ratified the three treaties negotiated at Walla Walla, and the president signed them into law. Life would never be the same for the Indians.

TEXAS RANGERS AND NATIVE AMERICANS

While these events transpired rapidly in the Pacific Northwest, other momentous events between the United States and Mexico changed the course of Native American history. In 1835, Texas declared its independence from Mexico, and the Mexican Army responded by moving troops into the rebellious region. After winning important victories at the Alamo and Goliad, Mexican troops led by General Santa Anna lost the Battle of San Jacinto. Soon Texas became an independent nation with Samuel Houston as president. The new Texas government followed an Indian policy comparable to that of the United States, but from the outset Texas refused to recognize native title to any land. Texas Indian policy centered around forced removal from Texas or extermination, and the Texas Rangers executed this policy. The Texas Rangers–made famous by the cartoon, radio, and television versions of *The Lone Ranger* and more recently by Larry McMurtry in *Lonesome Dove*–were organized to kill Indians and hang horse thieves, cattle rustlers, and the more general varieties of outlaws.

At one time, several diverse tribes lived in Texas, including Jumanos of the Rio Grande Valley, Lipan Apaches of western Texas, the Hasinai tribal confederacy of the Sabine and Angelina rivers, Tonkawas, Karankawas, and others of the Gulf Coast, the Caddodacho tribal confederacy of central Texas, Wichitas and Caddoes of the Red River Valley, and Kiowas and Comanches who moved and lived throughout most of Texas. In addition, Cherokees, Delawares, Shawnees, Kickapoos, and remnants of other eastern tribes moved into Texas. Some of these people served as scouts for the Texas Rangers, particularly when the rangers operated against Kiowas and Comanches, people who once disliked most eastern tribes almost as much as they did the rangers. Yet, in spite of native loyalty to Texas, whites turned against the eastern tribes just as they did other native groups. The hatred of Indians that had characterized white-Indian relations in the East and in Mexico moved into Texas. Texans used racial hatred to justify the annihilation or forced removal of most Indians. Texas Rangers attacked and killed native men, women, and children, forcing most survivors to flee into Indian Territory or Mexico, where most of them live to this day.

In 1845, the United States annexed Texas as a state, but the agreement between the two nations included a clause allowing Texas to retain its public lands—including all lands claimed by Indians. Shortly after statehood, Texas enacted a bill denying the United States the right to extend its Indian policies, including treaties, to the state and denying the tribes rights to any lands within the boundaries of Texas. In 1846, the United States negotiated an Indian treaty and submitted it to the Senate, where the Texas delegation engineered its defeat. Without a treaty, the Texas tribes had no legal relationship with the United States and no lands accurately described in a federal document that would strengthen their claims. At best the tribes received guarantees of a boundary between Indians and whites, but both parties violated the boundary, and soon the agreement broke down.

North central Texas became a bloody battleground between Indians and whites during the 1850s, until the United States sent troops to monitor the region. But the United States was not impartial, because the army protected the "citizens" of the nation and state, not the tribes. Besides, federal troops and Texas Rangers reflected racial views of the country, which did not protect Indian lives, liberties, or rights. The United States allowed the Texas Ranger to ride roughshod over the tribes because rangers acted out the views of many white Americans regarding the Indian "savages." In 1854, the United States created two small reservations on the Brazos River of northwestern Texas but later forced over two thousand of their Indians into Indian Territory.

Increasingly, the U.S. Army worked in greater concert with the Texas Rangers to destroy Comanches and Kiowas. Racial hatred in Texas reached a heightened level against Comanches and Kiowas, and the Indians returned the favor, despising the invading whites and striking terror wherever and whenever they could. Like the Texans, Kiowas and Comanches killed and enslaved men, women, and children, which encouraged more Texas Rangers, and such Indian allies as Tonkawas, Tawakonis, Keechies, Ionies, Wacoes, Anadarkoes, and others to attack Comanche and Kiowa villages inside and outside Texas. Thus, numerous Indians in Texas died during the prolonged and bloody fighting. Texans also perished during the wars as Comanches and Kiowas killed and burned white settlers, threatening such large settlements as San Antonio. Indians struck Texas settlements and ranches before fleeing south into Mexico or west into the Llano Estacado (Staked Plains) of Texas and New Mexico. Comanches and Kiowas rode hard north into Kansas and Colorado, often disappearing like phantoms of the plains. On the Southern Plains, Kiowas and Comanches kept the armies on the run until the 1870s, during the Red River Wars.

INVADING THE NAVAJO

Many other tribes in the Southwest felt the effects of white expansion from the United States. As early as 1821, William Becknell and Thomas James entered the Southwest via the Santa Fe Trail, opening trade between white Americans and the New Mexicans. Indians also became involved in the trade, buying horses, mules, guns, ammunition, whiskey, cloth, and many other items from American and Mexican traders. However, contact between southwestern Indians and Americans increased dramatically after 1846, when the United States declared war on Mexico. The immediate cause of the war was the location of the southern boundary of Texas. However, the Texas boundary was just one of many issues precipitating the war. The war brought hundreds of American troops into the West, particularly the Southwest and California, and behind them were a host of merchants, farmers, ranchers, saloon keepers, prostitutes, ferrymen, and so forth. The war with Mexico had broad implications for Indians as white Americans moved into the West in ever-increasing numbers. When war broke out in 1846, Colonel Steven Watts Kearny and the Army of the West followed much of the Santa Fe Trail from Kansas into New Mexico. Kearny claimed this part of Mexico as American territory by right of conquest and pushed on to California by way of the Gila Trail, Yuma Crossing, and Colorado Desert. When he left New Mexico, Kearny left a large part of his army, including one portion under the command of Colonel Alexander W. Doniphan, who was ordered to deal with the Diné, or Navajos, who raided New Mexican villages, stealing cattle, horses, and sheep. Occasionally Navajos stole women and children, using them as slaves or selling them to other Indians. According to research by David Brugge, the Navajo slave trade was nothing in comparison to that practiced by New Mexicans, who used Indian slaves as domestics and ranch hands or sold them to slave buyers in Mexico.

By the time the United States invaded New Mexico, Navajos and other Indians in the Southwest had dealt with Spanish and Mexican citizens—or Nakai, as Navajos called them—for approximately 250 years. Navajos and Nakai had long warred against one another, stealing stock and slaves and creating a mutual hatred that continued the conflict. The same was true of various bands of Apaches, Comanches, Kiowas, and Utes, who raided the Rio Grande settlements and fought the New Mexicans for years. When the United States entered the region, government agents, soldiers, and settlers took the side of New Mexicans, not Indians, bringing with them their hatred of Native Americans. The government also brought its Indian policies, extending them to all southwestern Indians. Colonel Doniphan brought American politics to the Navajos when he divided his forces and invaded Dinétah (Land of the People) with the help of Sandoval and his band of Diné Ana'aíí (Enemy Navajos), who served as scouts for the army.

In 1846, Doniphan signed the Bear Springs Treaty with some of the autonomous bands of Navajos. But the treaty meant little, and Navajos even stole horses from Doniphan as he made his way back to the Rio Grande villages. Navajo relations with the United States were marked by periods of peace and war, largely short-term skirmishes between rancheros and warriors who stole livestock or fought slave traders who entered Navajo lands. As in other areas controlled by noncompliant natives, the United States built Forts Wingate and Defiance on Navajo soil without the permission of the Indians. Usually, patrols tried to prevent Navajo raiding parties from entering central New Mexico, but sometimes the army halted slave raiders attempting to steal Diné women and children. On April 30, 1860, Navajos attacked Fort Defiance in an attempt to drive the Bilagáana from the land of the people. After a lengthy battle, Navajo warriors retreated.

Colonel Edward Canby, veteran of the Seminole War, responded by launching a scorched-earth campaign against Navajo people. Canby's fast-riding troops moved more like Navajos, Apaches, Kiowas, and Comanches than bluecoat soldiers. Without fanfare, Canby's horse soldiers raced across Navajo country, killing and burning until most Navajos agreed to negotiate a peace with the Bilagáana. Even the famed Navajo Naa'tani Manuelito sued for peace at Fort Fauntleroy, and the peace struck between Navajos and Canby might have become permanent if the American Civil War had not erupted and if New Mexican volunteers under the command of Manuel A. Chavez had not murdered twelve innocent Indians and enslaved 112 more at Fort Fauntleroy in September 1862. The senseless incident triggered the last major conflict between the Navajo Nation and the United States.

QUECHAN, CAHUILLA, AND CUPEÑO RESISTANCE

When Colonel Kearny traveled to California in 1846, Kit Carson guided him to Yuma Crossing on the Colorado River. Carson knew that this was the best place to cross the river and enter California, and he knew this was land controlled by Quechan Indians. The river crossing was a strategic area, because its control regulated the east-west flow of transportation from Texas and New Mexico as well as Mexico. After the war, the United States and Mexico ended the conflict with the Treaty of Guadalupe Hidalgo, Mexico ceding millions of acres in present-day California, Arizona, Nevada, Utah, New Mexico, Texas, and Colorado to the United States. Lieutenants Amiel Weeks Whipple and Cave Johnson Couts surveyed the new Mexican-United States boundary in 1849, and the army planned a new post, Fort Yuma, to command Quechan country. By the time Major Samuel Heinzelman arrived to build Fort Yuma, the Quechans had already had some major conflicts with murderous Indian scalp hunters as well as volunteer troops from California, under Major Joseph G. Moorehead.

Heintzelman began building Fort Yuma in 1851, but the lack of supplies forced him to withdraw most of his troops to San Diego. The major returned in March 1852 to reestablish Fort Yuma, sending Major Edward H. Fitzgerald and his First Dragoons to receive supplies waiting for them aboard the *Sierra Nevada*, anchored at the mouth of the Colorado River on the Gulf of Baja California. Thirty miles south of the fort, near present-day San Luis, Mexico, Quechans attacked Fitzgerald, killing seven men and wounding another. Between March and October 1852, Heinzelman sent his soldiers in every direction to attack Quechans living along the Colorado and Gila rivers near Fort Yuma. Quechans fought when they could, but dragoons on horseback had the mobility to move quickly, strike, and retreat. Indians withdrew from the area, so the troops pursued them. By September, many Quechans had moved north along the Colorado River near Picacho, where Heintzelman engaged them in a firefight. In the end, several Quechan leaders, identified in Heintzelman's notebook as Antonio, Pascual, José María, Macedon, and Huttamines, agreed to peace with whites. According to Heintzelman, they also agreed to allow the United States to operate a military reservation on their lands, near the junction of the Colorado and Gila rivers.

The Quechan War was part of a pattern of unrest among California's Indians, due to the invasion by American troops and gold seekers. In the deserts east of Los Angeles and San Bernardino, the Serrano, Cahuilla, Cupeño, Kumeyaay, and Luiseño were upset at the violence that whites brought to their communities, threatening the well-being of their clans and families. This was particularly true for the Cahuilla and Cupeño, who lived along the main route of travel from the Colorado Desert east of Yuma Crossing to Los Angeles. A contest of leadership arose between Antonio Garra and Juan Antonio that resulted in a short-lived rebellion led by Garra, who hoped that disgruntled Californios of Mexican descent would join him in a war against Americans. The contest ended when Juan Antonio captured Garra and turned him over to Americans, who executed Garra and others. Garra is remembered by native peoples throughout southern California as a patriot who stood against the United States and the abuses of the newcomers. Juan Antonio is also seen as a patriot and pragmatist. According to Cahuilla historian Katherine Saubel, Antonio spent his life working to better relations between Indians and non-Indians, and he stood for justice. He protected ranchers from outlaws and rustlers, even putting his life on the line to fight ruthless gangs from Los Angeles. Cahuillas say that after he spent his life protecting non-Indians, whites sent him a load of army blankets infected with smallpox, from which Antonio became infected and died.

GOLD RUSH AND MURDERS

During the war with Mexico, the United States established military control of California. Under Spain and Mexico, California's Indians had experienced the oppressive mission system that enslaved them and forced them to work for the Catholic missions as masons, carpenters, cooks, cobblers, cowboys, wranglers, bakers, farmers, gardeners, dam builders, general laborers, and so forth. Many Indians resisted the mission system, fleeing into the interior to live as their ancestors had, raid horse and cattle herds of the mission fathers or Californios, or work on ranches owned by Californios. The invasion of California by Spain and Mexico proved harmful to Native Americans, but the effects of the American invasion were far worse. In *Exterminate Them: Written Accounts of Murder, Rape, and Enslavement*, Wyandot historian C. E. Trafzer and Joel Hyer point out that in addition to losing nearly all their extensive lands and vast resources, California's Indians lost their families to disease, murder, and mayhem. They lost their children and wives to slave traders. In 1800, there were between 200,000 and 250,000 Native Americans in California. By 1860, their numbers had dropped to 20,000 to 40,000. The takeover of California by the United States and the California gold rush were extremely deadly to the native people of the state.

On January 24, 1848, Maidu and Nisenan Indians working for James Marshall found gold while digging a mill race for John Sutter's saw mill at Coloma on the American River. In his book *Indians of California: The Changing Image*, historian James Rawls points out that one Native American, named "Indian Jim," found a gold nugget about the size of a quarter dollar while digging the mill race. Jim showed the nugget to Peter Wimmer and James Brown, who showed it to Marshall, who began panning. He soon found flakes and nuggets of gold and later admitted that he and Indians had found the color. Native Americans living in the Sierra Nevadas had seen gold before, but they did not value it as white people did. They had not collected and hoarded gold, and they had never killed one another for it. Within a year, California's Indians would learn what value non-Indians placed on gold and the high price Native Americans would pay for greed and gold.

By March 1848, word had spread that gold had been discovered on the American River; life would never be the same again for California's Indians. The first people to react to the gold rush were Californios who owned ranchos throughout California. These ranchers employed many Native Americans, so Californios took their employees into the foothills of the Sierra Nevada Mountains to pan for gold. Thus, the Stockton Cattle Company, operated by Charles M. Weber, became the Stockton Mining Company. Weber, and one thousand California Indians—most of whom were Yokuts—found gold at Dry Diggings, which became known as Hangtown and, later, Placerville. In the summer of 1848, Weber and another white man reported clearing $10,000 in a week. The Stockton Mining Company was just one of many companies that hired Indians and made thousands of dollars off Indian labor. In fact, when Colonel Richard B. Mason, ex-officio governor of California, made a tour of the gold mines in 1848, he reported that over half the miners were California Indians. Other Indians mined gold independently, using pans, rockers, or long toms. Sherburne F. Cook reported that "practically the entire native population of the Sierra foothills" panned for gold, and this included Native Californians living "from the Feather [River] to the Merced."

In 1850, the number of Indian miners working in the California gold fields declined, while some eastern Indians—Cherokees, Choctaws, Chickasaws, Wyandots, and others—participated in the gold rush. The number of California Indian miners declined, largely because of racism. New miners, traders, and others entering the gold fields hated Indians and thought they should be shot down like beasts. In addition, miners venturing into California believed that Californios (including Mexican-Americans) had an unfair advantage because they employed large numbers of Indians who could take more gold than a single white miner. Pierson B. Reading employed sixty Indians on the Trinity River, and Oregon miners ordered him to get rid of his Indian employees. Reading simply left the region, but more trouble developed on Weber's Creek, where other Oregonians attacked Indian miners, killing twelve and taking many others captive.

The Oregonians took eight of the Indian captives to Coloma, because they worked for James Marshall. After the Oregonians were at the Maidu

When Native Americans found gold at Coloma in 1848,
California ranchers brought their Indian employees to the
foothills to pan for gold. Women and children worked
alongside men, as depicted in this sketch of 1859.

village of Coloma, they released the Indians, telling them to join other
miners on the American River. When the Indians turned their backs and
began the short walk down to the river, the Oregonians opened fire, murdering them. This was the beginning of a bloody era that overshadowed
that faced by Indians in Texas. Shootings and murders of California Indians became commonplace as miners disregarded tribal lands and
fanned out in every direction, looking to make a strike. Miners set fire to
Indian villages, stole native property, and kidnapped children, enslaving
and forcing them to work in the mines. This was particularly true of
young girls who were stolen and raped or forced into a life of prostitu-
tion. Newspapers throughout California reported the violent events from
1850 to 1860, providing insightful articles detailing rapes, murders, and
kidnappings.

Robert Heizer, James Rawls, George Phillips, and Hupa Jack Norton
have detailed these abuses in their historical works. On May 5, 1855, the
Humboldt Times reported that Colonel T. J. Henley was "endeavoring to

discover persons engaged in the nefarious trade of stealing Indians" because a "large number of children have been brought down and sold in the agricultural counties." White slave traders sold native children for $50 to $250. In 1853, the district attorney for Contra Costa County reported that after they were captured, Indian children "are treated inhumanely, being neither fed nor clothed; and from such treatment many have already died, and disease is now threatening destruction of the remainder." In December 1861, Superintendent George M. Hansen wrote the commissioner of Indian affairs that he had found three men kidnapping Indian children, and when he inquired about the kidnapping, one of the three men explained that they were taking the children "as an act of charity . . . [to] provide homes for them, because their parents had been killed, and the children would have perished with hunger." When asked how they knew that the parents were dead, one man answered that he had "killed some of them myself."

CALIFORNIA'S LAW AND DISORDER

The accounts of kidnapping, slavery, rape, and murder demonstrate that these acts were widespread. Although many whites in California decried the situation, and editors, government officials, and military men called for action, they did little to end the problem. Thus, everyone knew what was happening, but the state and county officials did little to stop the slave trade, and the federal army and superintendent of Indian affairs did virtually nothing to end the rape and carnage. Kidnappers, slavers, and murderers accomplished the task that government officials could not–clearing California lands of Native Americans. There was no known conspiracy in the lack of action, no official plan to allow outlaws to exterminate California's Indians, but neither was there any concerted effort by the counties, California, or the United States to end the violence. White officials wrote a good deal about the violence but did virtually nothing. Thousands of Indians died, and millions of acres became available for nonnative settlement because California's Indians had no political clout.

California became a state in 1850, and in that year passed "An Act for the Government and Protection of Indians." California Statute 133 established state jurisdiction over Indians and outlined laws governing them. The statute allowed whites to indenture Indians into forced labor and services, stating that the right of custody of Indian children could be assumed by whites. Indian parents had no permanent right to their own children if whites wanted to take them. State officials argued that this was for the benefit of native children, who could be uplifted and civilized by white parents, but in fact the statute gave slave traders the opportunity

When the U.S. Senate refused to ratify the eighteen treaties negotiated with California Indians, non-Indians stole Indian lands with impunity. Rose Emerson, her son (Lee), and many California Indians lost their landed estates.

legally to take native children and sell them. In addition, white justices of the peace had jurisdiction over cases involving Indians, and Indians were not permitted to testify against whites in court. The same justices could resolve contracts and contract disputes between Indians and whites, and they could sentence Indians to jail for buying or consuming alcohol.

Justices of the peace in California also levied fines against Indian offenders or allowed non-Indians to pay the fine and force the Indians into bondage for specified periods of time. In this way, ranchers, farmers, merchants, and miners could pay a fine and force a native person into bondage. The same could happen to Indians who ventured into town without money in their pockets, because town and county sheriffs picked them up for "loitering" or "vagrancy" and placed them in jail. If they were convicted, they could be bonded to white employers for a four-month term. California revised these laws in 1860, but many justices of the peace, sheriffs, and government officials continued to use these laws against Indians until the 1870s. The federal government became more involved in Indian affairs in California during the 1860s and 1870s due to open resistance by many Native Americans in northern California.

Rather than investigate the causes of conflicts between whites and Indians, the federal government increased its effort to assert jurisdiction over the tribes and establish reservations among them.

Throughout American history, from the framing, to the Articles of Confederation, to the present, there has been tension between county-state law and federal law regarding legal issues involving Native Americans. Most often, the federal government asserted its supremacy in these issues, with the notable exception of allowing Georgia, Mississippi, and Alabama to force the southern tribes from their borders. However, in the case of California, officials of the U.S. Army, U.S. Marshal's Office, and Office of Indian Affairs were complacent–if not criminal–in their negligence in addressing the wanton extermination of thousands of California Indians and the enslavement of thousands more.

CALIFORNIA INDIAN TREATIES AND RESERVATIONS

In part, federal officials allowed the state to execute its own Indian policies, because eighteen federal treaties that had been negotiated with California's native people were scuttled in the Senate. However, this was another example of the strong racial, economic, and political agenda that was afoot in early California and was detrimental to Native Americans. In 1850, Congress had passed an act authorizing three commissioners to negotiate treaties with the Indians of California. Dr. Oliver M. Wozencraft, George W. Barbour, and Redick McKee negotiated eighteen treaties that affected 139 diverse bands and tribes. In all the treaties, the native people agreed to end wars, cede their lands to the United States, acknowledge the jurisdiction of the United States, and accept reservations where agents would provide provisions for the tribes. At one time, California's Indians held all the land in California, but under the terms of the treaties, they secured for themselves a mere 7,488,000 acres, or about 7½ percent of state land. The Senate voted against ratification of the treaties, largely because of Senators John B. Weller and William M. Gwin.

In 1853, Superintendent Edward F. Beale established the modern reservation system, with five reservations of twenty-five thousand acres each, including one at Tejon in the Tehachapi Foothills. His purpose was to "civilize" Indians through agriculture, ranching, and crafts–in the manner of Spanish missions and Puritan plantations. In 1854, Beale lost his political position through the spoils system, and the first reservation system fell into ruin. But it was to prove a successful failure, because other Americans carried on the idea and implemented a reservation system among most Native Americans during and after the Civil War. As for California Indians, they lost a great deal of land and resources between the 1850s and 1870s. Neither the United States nor the state of California recognized native land rights, so whites continued to steal Indian land, "legally" claiming it as their own through titles and the enforcement of "law." Already by the 1850s this process had been repeated many times, and the process would repeat itself during and after the American Civil War.

On the eve of the American Civil War, Native Americans had suffered the brutal effects of American Indian policies and the callused treatment of people who resettled former Indian lands. In the American West, farmers, ranchers, mayors, and miners changed the land, converting prairie into agricultural lands and ranging thousands of cattle across the open spaces. Miners dug into the bosom of the earth for gold, silver, and lead. They used hydraulic pressure to force millions of gallons of water at the face of mountains, hills, creek beds, and slopes, disfiguring the earth in their quest for gold. Miners murdered Native Americans, enslaved them, drove them from their homes, raped native women, and kidnapped their children. White politicians sanctioned the racism as a means to clear the land of "heathens" and "savages," while military officials complacently allowed state and county law enforcement officials and officers of the court to rob native people and neglect their rights as human beings.

Whites negotiated directly with native people who were willing to deal and ignored traditional leaders who spoke for the majority of their people. By 1860, many Indians were outcasts in their own lands, and many whites hated Native Americans for surviving the holocaust and looked forward to the day when American Indians would become "Vanished Americans." Racism, theft, murder, rape, kidnapping, and chaos accelerated with each year, and the American Civil War provided white military, civilian, and political figures an opportunity to destroy native power and steal more lands, resources, and pride. The American Civil War was a catalyst for the extension of hatred and a justification for the conquest of many native peoples.

Selected Readings and Bibliography

Native American history from 1800 to 1860 was significantly influenced by the expansion of white Americans from, and immigrants to, the United States. Trafzer's *Yuma: Frontier Crossing of the Far Southwest* deals with Quechan Indians of southern California. Phillips's, *The Enduring Struggle: Indians in California History,* and Rawls's, *Indians of California,* were both helpful in framing the discussion of Native American history in California before the Civil War.

American Friends Service Committee. *Uncommon Controversy.* Seattle: University of Washington Press, 1970.

Bakeless, John. *Lewis and Clark.* New York: W. Morrow, 1947.

Bancroft, Hubert H. *History of Oregon*. San Francisco: The History Company, 1888.

——. *History of Washington, Idaho, and Montana*. San Francisco: The History Company, 1890.

Carrico, Richard L. *Strangers in a Stolen Land: American Indians in San Diego, 1850–1880*. Newcastle, Calif.: Sierra Oaks, 1987.

Chittenden, Hiram M. *A History of the American Fur Trade of the Far West*. 2 volumes. Stanford: Academic Reprints, 1954.

Cohen, Felix S. *Handbook of Federal Indian Law*. Albuquerque: University of New Mexico Press, 1971.

Dale, Edward E. *The Indians of the Southwest*. Norman: University of Oklahoma Press. 1949.

Davidson, Gordon C. *The North West Company*. Berkeley: University of California Press, 1918.

Drury, Clifford M. *Henry Harman Spalding*. Caldwell, Idaho: Caxton, 1936.

——. *Marcus Whitman*. Caldwell, Idaho: Caxton, 1936.

Faulk, Odie B. *Destiny Road*. New York: Oxford University Press, 1973.

Forbes, Jack. *Warriors of the Colorado*. Norman: University of Oklahoma Press, 1965.

Fuller, George. *History of the Pacific Northwest*. New York: Knopf, 1931.

Galbraith, John S. *The Hudson's Bay Company as an Imperial Factor, 1821–1861*. Berkeley: University of California Press, 1957.

Gibbs, George. *Indian Tribes of Washington Territory*. Fairfield, Wash.: Ye Galleon Press, 1972.

Gibson, Arrell Morgan. *Oklahoma: A History of Five Centuries*. Norman: University of Oklahoma Press, 1965.

Heizer, Robert. *Treaty Making and Treaty Rejection by the Federal Government in California, 1850–1852*. Socorro, N.M.: Ballena Press, 1978.

Heizer, Robert, and Alan F. Almquist. *The Other Californians*. Berkeley: University of California Press, 1971.

Howard, Harold P. *Sacajewea*. Norman: University of Oklahoma Press, 1971.

Howard, Oliver O. *Nez Perce Joseph*. Boston: Lee and Shepherd, 1881.

——. *My Life and Experiences among Our Hostile Indians*. Hartford: A. D. Worthington, 1907.

——. *Famous Indian Chiefs I Have Known*. New York: Century, 1907–1908.

Jessett, Thomas E. *Chief Spokan Garry*. Minneapolis: T. A. Dennison, 1960.

Josephy, Alvin M. *The Nez Perce Indians and the Opening of the Northwest*. New Haven: Yale University Press, 1965.

Kip, Lawrence. *Army Life on the Pacific*. New York: Redfield, 1859. Reprinted, Clifford E. Trafzer, introduction, *Indian Wars of the Pacific Northwest*. Lincoln: University of Nebraska Press, Bison Books, 1999.

——. *Indian Council at Walla Walla*. Seattle: Facsimile Reproduction, Shorey Bookstore, 1971.

Macall, Dorman H. *A New Mexico in 1850*. Norman: University of Oklahoma Press, 1968.

Manring, B. F. *Conquest of the Coeur d'Alene, Spokanes, and Palouses*. Spokane, Wash.: Inland Printing, 1912.

McWhorter, L. V. *Tragedy of the Whak-Sham.* Fairfield, Wash.: Ye Galleon Press, 1958.

Meinig, Donald W. *The Great Columbia Plain.* Seattle: University of Washington Press, 1968.

Mooney, James. "The Ghost Dance Religion and the Sioux Outbreak of 1890." *Fourteenth Annual Report to the Bureau of American Ethnology* 14. Washington, D.C.: U.S. Government Printing Office, 1892–1893.

Moulton, Gary, ed. *The Journals of the Lewis and Clark Expedition.* Lincoln: University of Nebraska Press, 1988.

Phillips, George. *Chiefs and Challengers: Indian Resistance and Cooperation in Southern California.* Berkeley: University of California Press, 1975.

Rawls, James J. "Gold Diggers: Indian Miners in the California Gold Rush." *California Historical Quarterly* 55 (1976): 28–45.

Relander, Click. *Drummers and Dreamers.* Caldwell, Idaho: Caxton, 1956.

Richards, Kent. *Isaac I. Stevens: Young Man in a Hurry.* Provo, Utah: Brigham Young University Press, 1979.

Ronda, James P. *Lewis and Clark among the Indians.* Lincoln: University of Nebraska Press, 1984.

Ruby, Robert H., and John A. Brown. *Half-Sun on the Columbia: A Biography of Chief Moses.* Norman: University of Oklahoma Press, 1965.

——. *The Cayuse Indians.* Norman: University of Oklahoma Press, 1972.

——. *Indians of the Pacific Northwest.* Norman: University of Oklahoma Press, 1981.

——. *John Slocum and the Indian Shaker Church.* Norman: University of Oklahoma Press, 1996.

Schwartz, E. A. *The Rogue River Indian War and Its Aftermath, 1850–1880.* Norman: University of Oklahoma Press, 1997.

Trafzer, Clifford E. *The Kit Carson Campaign: The Last Great Navajo War.* Norman: University of Oklahoma Press, 1982.

——. "Washington's Native American Communities." *Peoples of Washington.* Sidney White and S. E. Solberg, eds. Pullman: Washington State University Press, 1989.

——. *The Nez Perce.* New York: Chelsea House Publishers, 1992.

Trafzer, Clifford E., and Joel Hyer, eds. *"Exterminate Them": Written Accounts of Murder, Rape and Enslavement of Native Americans during the California Gold Rush.* East Lansing: Michigan State University Press, 1999.

Trafzer, Clifford E., and Richard D. Scheuerman. *Renegade Tribe: The Palouse Indians and the Invasion of the Inland Pacific Northwest.* Pullman: Washington State University Press, 1986.

Trennert, Robert A. *Alternative to Extinction: Federal Indian Policy and the Beginnings of the Reservation System, 1846–1851.* Philadelphia: Temple University Press, 1975.

Utley, Robert M. *Frontiersmen in Blue: The United States Army and the Indian, 1848–1865.* New York: Macmillan, 1967.

Weber, David J. *The Mexican Frontier, 1821–46.* Albuquerque: University of New Mexico Press, 1982.

Chapter 10

AMERICAN INDIANS DURING THE CIVIL WAR

The American Civil War significantly changed the lives of thousands of Native Americans living in the West, in large part because the war enabled states and territories to muster large standing armies of regular and volunteer forces that were used to conquer Indians and reduce their landed estates. The 1860s provided Native Americans an opportunity to extend their resistance movements against white soldiers, miners, mail drivers, ranchers, town builders, and the like. It was a time when many American Indians came to understand the extreme danger brought by whites who entered their countries through several trails, depicted in American history as the routes that brought civilization to the wild, untamed, virgin West. It also was a time of great national tragedy for Indians and non-Indians alike because of the Civil War.

CIVIL WAR IN INDIAN TERRITORY

Throughout the United States, its territories, and Indian Territory, tensions arose over African-American slavery and the extension of slavery into the trans-Mississippi. Historian Ralph Crowder has shown that many Native Americans living in present-day Kansas, Nebraska, and Oklahoma were drawn into the heated national controversy for two major reasons. First, many Native Americans distrusted the United States because of its national Indian policies. Second, some Indians, mainly those removed from southern states, owned African-American slaves, while others from the South, aspired to own slaves. The southern Indians also had a natural attachment to the region, so when the Civil War began, many sided with the Confederacy. However, regardless of their stance for or against slavery and the extension of slavery into the West, all Native Americans were affected by the conflict, either directly or indirectly.

Before Union and Confederate soldiers fired at each other at Fort Sumter on April 12, 1861, and eleven states seceded from the United States to form the Confederate States of America, Native Americans were drawn into the conflict. During the 1850s, the struggle over slavery erupted in outright combat in "Bleeding Kansas," the home of thousands of Native Americans, many of whom had been removed there. Tribal leaders became concerned after the presidential election of 1860, because William Seward, who had worked tirelessly for Abraham Lincoln and became his secretary of state, had wooed the so-called Free Soilers by suggesting that the government buy up lands in Indian Territory and open them to white settlers. Specifically, Seward had recommended the acquisition of lands belonging to Cherokees, Choctaws, Chickasaws, Seminoles, and Muscogees—the "Five Civilized Tribes." This recommendation had a familiar ring to it for the thousands of Indians from the North and South who had been forced to relocate to Indian Territory.

It appeared to many Native Americans that the Lincoln administration—like former ones—was willing to steal Indian lands for the benefit of white Americans. Between the 1830s and 1860s, Native Americans had made many improvements, establishing farms and ranches that produced cattle, hogs, horses, cotton, and grains. Some wealthy southern Indians had reestablished plantations in Indian Territory with the labor of African-American slaves. In addition, Native Americans had developed a hide industry, producing leather and leather goods for the nation. They had also opened mines that produced the lead from which bullets and other ammunition were made. Although the southern tribes had been banished from Georgia, Mississippi, and Alabama, many Indians were culturally tied to their old region and still had family in the South. Native Americans living in Indian Territory often felt an affinity toward the South, blaming Andrew Jackson and the Union for removal.

The tribes blamed the United States when contractors stole thousands of dollars while providing the tribes with rancid meat, spoiled flour, rotten corn, and inadequate rations. They also blamed the United States for not providing adequate transportation as promised in their removal treaties. The government had guaranteed the tribes help in relocation and resettlement for a year after removal, including adequate protection from Kiowas, Comanches, and Osages who resented eastern interlopers who had invaded their domain. The government ordered a commission led by Major Ethan Allen Hitchcock to investigate, and he easily uncovered neglect, corruption, profiteering, forgery, bribery, perjury, and fraud. Hitchcock prepared an exhaustive report and submitted it to the secretary of war. The report and its one hundred exhibits disappeared from the files of the War Office and have never been found.

NATIVE AMERICANS AND THE CONFEDERACY

Native Americans in Indian Territory did not need a government report to confirm that they had been swindled of millions of dollars by unscrupulous whites. Indians assessed these losses in terms of human life, because everyone lost loved ones during the removals. Government officials and contractors contributed significantly to the misery, starvation, disease, and deaths of thousands of men, women, and children who were forced onto the various trails of tears of the 1820s–1840s. When the Civil War broke out, many Indian nations from the North and South sided with the Confederacy over the Union, but not all. Still, southern government and military officials quickly took advantage of Native American sentiments toward the United States by drawing the tribes in Indian Territory into the southern sphere of influence. Jefferson Davis, president of the Confederacy, commissioned Arkansas attorney Albert Pike to negotiate treaties with native nations.

Pike primarily concentrated on the Cherokees, Choctaws, Chickasaws, Seminoles, and Muscogees, although he also negotiated with Caddoes, Comanches, Kiowas, and others. Pike established formal relations with all of these Indian nations and framed treaties with each. Under the terms of these treaties, the tribes ended their formal relationship with the United States and created a new bond with the Confederacy. The new relationship included raising Indian troops to fight the Union under the command of Pike and Confederate Indian Agent Douglas Cooper. Cherokees committed to raising two regiments, while the combined forces of Choctaw-Chickasaw and Seminole-Muscogee would raise one regiment each. In return, Pike committed the Confederacy to paying annuities owed to the tribes by the United States and protecting the Indian nations from attacks by other Indians or whites.

Although most Choctaws and Chickasaws agreed to abide by the Pike treaties, Cherokees, Seminoles, and Muscogees were divided among themselves. Mixed bloods and full bloods had fought over the sale of their eastern homelands and removal, and the Confederate treaties created more tension between these two groups. Many mixed bloods favored the Pike treaties, whereas full bloods often opposed them, because white leaders in the southern states had forced the people to move. Opothleyoholo, the great Muscogee leader who felt he had been forced to sign the Treaty of Washington of 1832 because of pressure brought to bear on the Muscogees by Alabama, opposed the treaties and refused to meet with Pike. He called a general council of Native Americans in Indian Territory, where he denounced those who supported either side. Opothleyoholo urged Indians to maintain neutrality.

But Indians in present-day Kansas and Oklahoma were hard pressed to stay out of the war. Opothleyoholo tried his best to remain neutral, moving about eight thousand Indians to a secluded settlement in the Muscogee Nation along Deep Fork River. Not content that Opothleyoholo wished to remain neutral, other Confederate Indians determined to force him to join their side. Indian cavalrymen under Agent Cooper, commissioned as a Confederate colonel, attacked Opothleyoholo at the Battle of Round Mountain on November 19, 1861, and the Battle of Chusto Talasah on December 9. Although Opothleyoholo and his followers won these battles, the blood of native people had been shed in the Civil War. Cooper's cavalry requested reinforcements from Fort Smith and Fort Gibson, both forts having been abandoned by Union forces at the outbreak of war, and they received sixteen hundred new pony soldiers in mid-December.

On December 26, 1861, Cooper's Confederate army attacked Chustenalah, where Opothleyoholo was camped with his followers. Muscogees fought gallantly but lacked supplies and ammunition. They fled the field of battle and faced a driving snow as they moved north into Kansas. Opothleyoholo visited Union officials in Kansas and soon committed his followers to the Union. He and his followers formed the First and Second Union Indian Brigades and volunteered to fight the Confederacy. In addition, several thousand Cherokees and Seminoles also joined the war on the side of the North. Opothleyoholo and his Indian Brigades joined forces with Wisconsin and Ohio volunteer cavalry to invade the Cherokee Nation and capture its capital of Tahlequah. They also took Cherokee Chief John Ross, forcing him to return with them to Kansas. Muscogee and Seminole troops also operated with General James Blunt in 1863 when he recaptured Fort Gibson on behalf of the Union Army. From this base of operation, Muscogees, Seminoles, and Cherokees loyal to the Union attacked Confederates in Indian Territory and its border areas.

Some of these Indians participated in the Battle of Pea Ridge on the territory's border with Arkansas on March 6–7, 1862. This was a bloody affair and cost the lives of many Native American soldiers on both sides. But the Confederates suffered the most casualties at Pea Ridge and were dealt a significant blow. The battle was the beginning of the end for the Indian Confederates in Indian Territory, but there would be more fighting before the end of the war. Indian soldiers on both sides distinguished themselves during the Civil War. Cherokee Colonel Stand Watie and his Cherokee Mounted Rifles held the line against the Union troops at the end of the Battle of Pea Ridge. This action allowed the Confederates to fall back and fight again. On July 17, 1863, Confederate forces advanced from Fort Smith toward Fort Gibson but were met by Blunt's troops at the Battle of Honey Springs. Colonel Watie fought with and against his own people, but Confederate troops were no match for the better-armed Union forces.

At the Battle of Honey Springs, the Union army used artillery to break down the Confederates, who had to retreat hastily. Many Indian troops fought during this battle as well as Blunt's offensive. Not satisfied at sweeping the Confederates from the field of battle, Blunt continued the attack, pushing Cooper's Indian forces east to the Choctaw Nation. They opened the road to Fort Smith, Arkansas, and took the Confederate post without much effort. Although the Battle of Honey Springs and capture of Fort Smith ended the major fighting in Indian Territory during the Civil War, Native American forces continued to fight. This was particularly true of Stand Watie, who was promoted to brigadier general and commanded the Indian Cavalry Brigade. Watie and his Indian horsemen fought throughout the Civil War, even after General Robert E. Lee surrendered to Ulysses S. Grant at Appomattox Court House, Virginia, on April 9, 1865. Watie was the last Confederate general to surrender, which he did on June 23, 1865.

RECONSTRUCTION AND NATIVE AMERICANS

The Civil War was disastrous for Native Americans in the West, including those living in Indian Territory. When the war ended in Indian Territory, Senators Samuel Pomeroy and James Lane of Kansas pushed hard to punish all Native Americans whether they had sided with the South or North or remained neutral. They represented the white population of Kansas, and they wanted Indian lands in present-day Kansas and Oklahoma. Therefore, in 1863, they managed a bill known as the "Reconstruction Program for Indian Territory," which authorized the president to void all treaties between the United States and the Cherokees, Choctaws, Chickasaws, Seminoles, and Muscogees so that the government could steal more lands belonging to these tribes. In addition, the bill called for the removal of all Indians from Kansas to Indian Territory, thereby opening thousands of acres in the state for white settlement.

Commissioner of Indian Affairs Dennis N. Cooley convened a meeting at Fort Smith during the summer of 1865 with representatives of several diverse tribes. Cherokees, Choctaws, Chickasaws, Seminoles, Muscogees, Wyandots, Quapaws, Senecas, Osages, Wichitas, Caddoes, Shawnees, and others attended the meeting to hear what the United States had planned for them. Much to their dismay, they learned that the government wanted the tribes living in Kansas to move to Indian Territory (Oklahoma) and that all the tribes in Indian Territory were to surrender lands to make room for the people from Kansas. These were the central points of the forthcoming agreements, although Cooley confirmed that he wanted peace between all the tribes and the United States.

He also ordered the Indian nations to abolish slavery and allow freed men and women to become a formal part of their native nations.

The Cherokee delegation split between followers of the Union Party under John Ross and the Confederate Party under Stand Watie. As a result, all the tribes used this split to argue against making a final decision about the American proposals. Realizing that his thirteen-day conference was nearing its end, Cooley signed pacts of peace with the tribes and instructed them to reconvene in Washington, D.C., where they could make final agreements for reconstruction. Negotiations continued in 1866, in the nation's capital, between the United States and the Cherokees, Choctaws, Chickasaws, Seminoles, and Muscogees. The results greatly reduced native lands and influence, opening vast areas for settlement by farmers, ranchers, merchants, freighters, saloon keepers, and others. All the tribes lost thousands of acres, the United States dictating terms that provided tribes with paltry sums for vast acres. Seminoles, for example, sold the lands of their entire nation of over two million acres for 15¢ per acre and were forced to purchase two hundred thousand acres for their new home for 50¢ per acre.

Under the terms of the Reconstruction treaties, native nations in Indian Territory had to permit rights of way through their lands, and within a short time, railroads moved east-west and north-south across Indian lands, opening the region to further exploitation. Most of the tribes living in Kansas moved south into Indian Territory, and whites resettled their Kansas estates. All the tribes in Kansas and Indian Territory agreed to abolish African-American slavery, and every nation except the Chickasaws eventually consented to adopting freed men, women, and children into their tribes. Nevertheless, African Americans continued to live within the borders of the Indian nations, intermarrying with members of the tribes or living as freed people. Many African-Americans today trace their ancestry to the Indian nations of Indian Territory and beyond. They are part of the incredible mix of people in present-day Oklahoma that has brought a rare cultural richness to the region.

Native Americans in Indian Territory were not the only Indians to be affected by the Civil War. In fact, Indians throughout the West were affected by the war. Numerous native nations became involved in conflicts with the United States. Fights between Indians and whites in the West during the Civil War are too numerous to detail, but a few may illustrate the ever-growing storm between the two peoples and the complexity of events surrounding the era. At the beginning of the war, regular army troops from numerous western posts withdrew to fight Confederates. Territories mustered volunteer troops to fight Confederates, and they also used these troops to fill the gap left by the departing federal troops. Several former soldiers, veterans of Indian wars in the East and the war with Mexico, offered their services to fight Indians.

SHOSHONI, PAIUTE, AND DAKOTA RESISTANCE

For example, in the Utah District, Northern Shoshonis, Bannocks, Utes, and Paiutes struck whites in an attempt to rid themselves of the invaders. Indians attacked miners, mail carriers, stages, stage stations, and settlers. They cut telegraph lines and impeded travel on the Oregon Trail. Colonel Patrick Edward Connor and three hundred soldiers surprised a Shoshoni camp under Bear Hunter on January 27, 1863, killing over 225 people, including Bear Hunter. Shoshonis fought valiantly during the Battle of Bear River, trying to hold off Connor's men until the women and children could escape. But the soldiers overran the village, capturing 160 women and children as well as 175 horses. Connor followed up with attacks on Utes and Gosiutes, and within months, Bannocks and Paiutes asked for peace with the United States. By the autumn of 1863, most Indians in the Utah District ended their fights with Americans, but they continued to resist the conquest of their lands and cultures by whites.

In areas of the West where Confederates were no longer a threat, volunteer and federal troops were used to expand the nation's agenda of defeating recalcitrant Indians. With large standing armies, military officers and territorial governors used troops to fight Indians. The use of volunteer troops against the tribes during the Civil War became commonplace in the 1860s, including in Minnesota, where Dakota people known also as Santee Sioux starved because the government failed to fulfill its treaty obligations to provide them food. By 1862, the government had taken nearly all Dakota lands in Minnesota, except a ten-mile strip that ran along the Minnesota River for 150 miles. As Ojibwe historian Rebecca Kugel has shown in her book, *To Be the Main Leaders of Our People,* at one time the Anishinaabe (Chippewa or Ojibwe) had controlled nearly all of present-day Minnesota (with Dakota people), but by the 1860s, whites had taken their traditional lands through treaties and outright thefts. Many Dakota had left the region for the Great Plains, sometimes insulting their Minnesota relatives.

The government had divided the Santee Sioux Reservation into Upper and Lower agencies, distributing supplies, food, and cash to these Dakotas from Fort Ridgely, situated approximately fifteen miles below the Lower Agency. In 1862, some of the food and supplies had arrived at the post and was placed in a warehouse, but the agent refused to distribute the goods until he had the rest of the shipment as well as the money. So the Sioux waited and waited, patiently. Meanwhile, white Indian traders who usually extended credit to native people cut off their supplies, and during the summer months the Sioux waited for the rations and did not hunt buffalo, fearing that if they left the agency to hunt they would forfeit their annuity, goods, and food. They remained at the agency all summer, waiting. Returning from a small hunt along the Mississippi River, a few young men challenged each other to stand against white settlers. To prove themselves, four young Sioux killed two women and three men then returned home to report their deeds.

Anger, animosity, resentment, and frustration ran high among the Santee Sioux. Little Crow spoke for peace, but the consensus of the people was for war. Little Crow held his leadership position by guiding the warriors against German and other white settlers living in Minnesota. The Sioux struck hard and fast, attacking homes where they killed men, women, and children. They took women and children prisoners, enslaving and raping some of them. Other Sioux, particularly Christian Indians, rescued and saved the lives of sixty-two white men, women, and children. Meanwhile, Sioux warriors looted homes and businesses before attacking Fort Ridgely. Unsuccessful at taking the fort, they moved on to New Ulm, burning most of the town. Whites living in New Ulm held their ground, and Sioux warriors returned to their sanctuary at the Upper Agency. In mid-September 1862, former Governor Henry Sibley had raised an army of sixteen hundred men, which was on its way to engage the Santee Sioux. With the army bearing down on them, Chief Wabasha protected the 269 white captives and returned them to Sibley.

Most of the hostile Dakotas under Little Crow joined their brother and sister Sioux on the Great Plains, while the others remained at the Upper Agency to meet Sibley. Most of these people had not participated in the war, but Sibley dutifully rounded up around two thousand of them before separating four hundred suspects and trying them for murder, rape, and theft. Sibley's court convicted people who had helped whites and were not a part of the fighting, and the court sentenced 306 people to hang. Sibley chained another sixteen people, sentencing them to prison for stealing. He sent all other Dakotas remaining on the reservations to Fort Snelling. Several whites, including survivors of the war, protested Sibley's unjust actions, and Reverend Henry Whipple appealed to President Lincoln for leniency, which saved the lives of 268 people. The soldiers sent them to Mankato and then to Rock Island, Illinois.

As punishment for the war, the government destroyed the Santee Sioux Reservation in Minnesota, including the Upper Agency, which had remained neutral during the war. These were the people who had saved the lives of white settlers. Nevertheless, the government ultimately removed the people to a new reservation in northeastern Nebraska. Some Dakotas remained in Minnesota, but most moved to the Nebraska Reservation or onto the Plains to live with their relatives. On December 26, 1862, Union soldiers simultaneously hanged thirty-eight men, including innocent men who had not taken part in any wrongdoing. Little Crow moved some of his people into Canada, but during a foray into Minnesota, the Dakota leader ambushed and killed whites who were berry picking. The Dakota War in Minnesota had repercussions throughout the

Great Plains. Fearful of a general outbreak, territorial governors mustered more troops and used their large standing armies to prepare for war. In addition, the army sent some of its volunteer units back to the West to do battle with the tribes.

RESISTANCE ON THE SOUTHERN PLAINS

At the outbreak of the Civil War, Indian attacks along western trails to Montana, Colorado, New Mexico, and California decreased due to the withdrawal of soldiers from the forts. But with the Minnesota troubles and rumors that Native Americans planned new attacks on whites, the number of soldiers grew in the West, some coming from the East and others from volunteer units mustered in the West. And with increased numbers of soldiers came more Indian attacks, with Cheyenne, Arapaho, and Sioux dominating the Northern Plains and Cheyenne, Arapaho, Kiowa, and Comanche controlling the Southern Plains. Cheyenne and Arapaho resented whites using their lands in Colorado, where towns like Denver emerged overnight to support the booming silver and gold mines. They disliked ranches that dotted the vast plains east of the Rocky Mountains, because under the terms of the Horse Creek Treaty of 1851 and Ft. Laramie Treaty of 1851, Cheyenne and Arapaho people controlled the region. Sensing trouble, American agents negotiated the Treaty of Fort Wise (Lyon) on February 18, 1861, committing the two tribes to a small reservation in southern Colorado.

Chiefs Black Kettle, White Antelope, and Little Raven and other Cheyenne and Arapaho leaders signed the treaty, even though they had no interpreter and reportedly "did not know what it was." Other Indians severely chastised them for signing, and these leaders refused to settle on this reservation or acknowledge the treaty. Still, the U.S. Senate ratified the treaty, and the president signed it. The government also formalized the Colorado Territory on February 28, 1861, and appointed John Evans governor. Tensions over the new treaty, territorial government, and increased number of troops erupted into minor incidents between whites and Indians throughout the Great Plains. General Samuel R. Curtis, commanding Colorado and Kansas, sought to punish Indians, and he was encouraged in his view by Colonel John Chivington, commanding the Colorado District. Chivington was a Methodist minister and an Indian hater who stirred up trouble with the Indians for his own political gain.

According to scholar Donald Berthrong, Governor Evans feared that the federal government was being too conciliatory with White Antelope, Black Kettle, Lean Bear, and other Cheyenne leaders. In 1863, these leaders and a few Arapaho chiefs visited Washington, D.C., where they committed themselves to peace with the Untied States. Evans worried that the government might recommend an expanded Indian reservation for them and that Indians might be able to secure for themselves a portion of their former homelands. Evans and Chivington wanted them completely out of Colorado Territory, so the two officials spread lies and rumors, an old technique used by whites to create trouble. Evans informed General Curtis that all the Plains Indians planned a general uprising against whites and that the army should move against them at once. The report was unfounded but seemed reliable to Curtis, particularly after Chivington reported on April 7, 1864, that Cheyennes had rustled 175 head of cattle.

Cattle had drifted onto the Plains where Cheyennes had rounded some up, but they had not raided for them. Chivington lied in order to justify military action against the Cheyenne and Arapaho. Chivington ordered his Colorado volunteers into action, striking four Indian villages, killing men, women, and children. His soldiers stole Indian livestock, set fire to their tipis, and brought the region closer to war. Chivington lied again, claiming that these Cheyenne had been stealing property from settlers. Then, on May 26, 1864, Lieutenant George S. Eayre approached a large Cheyenne camp of 250 tipis and several hundred people. Lean Bear, one of the peace chiefs who had recently visited Washington, D.C., rode out to explain to Eayre that the Indians living in the camp were friendly. Eayre ordered his men to fire, murdering Lean Bear. Then the soldiers raced back to Fort Larned while Black Kettle urged the warriors not to retaliate.

Some young men could not resist and initiated raids on white establishments, wagon trains, mail carriers, horse traders, cattle herds, and the like. Bands from other tribes from across the Great Plains joined in this war. Governor Evans ordered all Indians friendly to the United States to camp near the forts, while at the same time ordering volunteers to attack hostile Indians. He proclaimed open season on Native Americans. An inspector general for Curtis commented that soldiers "do not know one tribe from another" and that bluecoats "will kill anything in the shape of an Indian." He prophesied correctly that it would take only a few mistakes and the murder of innocent people to trigger a full-scale war. Arapaho Chief Left Hand made a good-faith effort to negotiate at Fort Larned but was rebuffed by the post commander. At that point Chief Satank of the Kiowa Nation ran off with the post's horse herd. When Left Hand approached the fort to offer his assistance in recapturing the horses, the soldiers fired on him.

The soldiers were poor shots and missed the Arapaho delegation. Left Hand and his band reversed their position and attacked whites whenever possible. They joined in a growing native resistance movement across the Great Plains with Cheyenne, Sioux, Comanche, Kiowa, and Kiowa-Apache. Raiding parties struck from every direction throughout western Kansas and eastern Colorado. One party of warriors attacked the Hungate ranch near Denver, murdering the family and mutilating the bodies. George Bent, a half-blood Cheyenne chief, and Major Edward W. Wynkoop used their diplomatic skills to bring some calm to the storm. They invited Black Kettle, White Antelope, and five other chiefs to visit Governor Evans near Denver. At the meeting, they agreed to make peace and to move closer to Fort Lyon. Curtis was not happy about the turn of events. "I want no peace," the general proclaimed, "till the Indians suffer more." Curtis was to have his way.

The peaceful Cheyenne and forty-seven Arapaho under Left Hand established a camp near the post on the banks of Sand Creek. Along the small creek, women set up about one hundred tipis for approximately 750 people. Arapaho Chief Little Raven also moved his band to the mouth of Sand Creek, not far from the Cheyenne village. Meanwhile, Chivington convinced General Curtis to replace Wynkoop as commander at Fort Lyon and to appoint Major Scott Anthony to the position, a request that Curtis accepted. Then Chivington moved to Fort Lyon with a force of about seven hundred men and advanced to the Sand Creek encampment on November 29, 1864. Black Kettle was not alarmed to see the soldiers but ran up an American flag and a white flag on a pole in front of his tipi. Black Kettle, his wife, and White Antelope stood under the flag to await the visitors. Chivington ordered his men to attack the Indian horse herd so the Cheyenne and Arapaho could not escape. Then he ordered his men to attack.

Stan Hoig has detailed the events surrounding Sand Creek, describing in gruesome detail the carnage there. Bluecoats charged the Indian camp at Sand Creek, killing men, women, and children. White Antelope ran out to stop the soldiers, frantically waving his hands, but when the shooting started, he stood his ground, singing his death song, his arms folded defiantly over his chest. Soldiers shot him to death, cut off his ears, nose, and testicles. A soldier reportedly made a tobacco pouch out of his scrotum. About one hundred Indians ran up Sand Creek, some stopping to dig holes in the ground from which to fight and hide. They put up a limited resistance because they lacked arms and because most of them were women and children. Soldiers rode after them, slaughtering them, including nursing mothers and infants. Soldiers shot people for sport, taking aim at small children crying out in the confusion. They murdered women holding their children, screaming for mercy. Silas Soule and other soldiers protested the slaughter but to no avail.

After shooting all the Indians they could find, many soldiers butchered the people, cutting off scalps, heads, hands, and fingers to display in Denver. Soldiers disemboweled people, cutting out the ovaries and fallopian tubes of women and using reproductive parts for hat bands. They cut off penises and testes, keeping them for souvenirs. John Smith witnessed the massacre, saying the Indians were "scalped, their brains knocked out; the men used their knives, ripped open women, clubbed little children, knocked them in the head with their guns, beat their brains out, mutilated their bodies in every sense of the word." Chivington announced that his men "All did nobly." The former Methodist minister proclaimed that it was "right and honorable to use any means under God's heaven to kill Indians." That included the murder of women and children. Chivington damned "any man that was in sympathy with Indians," and his condemnation of those who criticized him likely extended to women.

The carnage at Sand Creek was tremendous because Chivington and many of his men believed that the Indians were less than human and deserved the butchering. Racism was a powerful element at Sand Creek. The Indians had believed they would be safe living near Fort Lyon. Cheyenne and Arapaho leaders had trusted the words of white men and had complied with the American request to move near the military post. They had chosen to live in peace with whites. The result of following the "peace policy" was disaster and death. Soldiers murdered approximately 137 Cheyenne and 43 Arapaho. Of the Cheyennes slaughtered at Sand Creek, 109 (80 percent) were women and children; 28 were men. Only four Arapaho lived through the harrowing experience, but Black Kettle survived and found his wife alive but with eight bullets in her body.

After Sand Creek, Chivington tried to surprise Little Raven's Arapahoes, but they had learned of the attack and left their village. The colonel and his troops returned to Denver heroes, displaying the body parts they had hacked from the dead and wounded. Not all whites viewed Chivington's deed so positively. Some of his men criticized him, as did some citizens of Denver. Colonel Kit Carson called Chivington a dog. A joint congressional committee convened to investigate the war in Colorado and concluded that Chivington "deliberately planned and executed a foul and dastardly massacre which would have disgraced the very savage among those who were the victims of his cruelty."

The month of November 1864 was important to other Native Americans, including Kiowas and Comanches. During the Civil War, warriors from both tribes moved like prairie fires across the southern Great Plains, striking wagon trains, freight wagons, ranches, and towns. They fought Confederates in Texas and Union sympathizers in Kansas, stealing supplies, killing whites, and disrupting the flow of traffic across the Santa Fe Trail. As a result, General James H. Carleton, commander of all forces in New Mexico, assigned Colonel Kit Carson to move offensively against the Kiowas and Comanches. In the autumn, Carson collected an army of 350 cavalrymen and seventy-five Ute scouts at Fort Bascom in eastern New Mexico. On November 12, the army traveled south along the Canadian River into Texas with two mountain howitzers. Carson had previously learned from Comancheros who traded with the Kiowas, Comanches, and Kiowa-Apaches that Indians had camped near the adobe ruins of William Bent's old trading post. Carson headed toward the camp spoiling for a fight.

At dawn on November 25, four days before Chivington surprised the Cheyennes and Arapahoes at Sand Creek, Carson attacked a large Kiowa and Kiowa-Apache camp with 150 tipis. Chief Little Mountain led the camp, which included the noted Kiowa warrior Satanta. The attack caught the Kiowas off guard, with men, women, and children scurrying for safety down the Canadian River to join their Comanche allies. Women and children escaped, while the men moved downstream before regrouping to launch a counterattack at Adobe Walls with a force of about one thousand. Carson's pony soldiers dismounted and fought for several hours from sand hills, ridges, and ruins. The Indians were some of the greatest cavalry fighters of all time, and they pressed hard against Carson, his soldiers, and the Ute scouts. However, Carson used the howitzers effectively against the Indian cavalry, so that Comanche and Kiowa horsemen could not penetrate the defensive position.

The Indians kept up the pressure until the afternoon, when Carson retreated back to the Kiowa camp, which had been reoccupied by women and children. They left the camp while some of the soldiers stole everything they could carry and set the tipis aflame. Warriors pursued Carson, who fought a rear-guard action and made his way onto the open plains. By December 10, he was back at Fort Bascom, and he thought himself fortunate to have lived through the Battle of Adobe Walls. Kiowas, Comanches, and Kiowa-Apaches gathered their belongings and moved, but the fight did not end their determination to defeat white settlers, soldiers, freighters, or ranchers. The war continued on the Southern Plains as Kiowas, Comanches, Arapahoes, and Cheyennes raided wayfarers on the Santa Fe Trail through the Southwest and Smoky Hill Trail of eastern Colorado and western Kansas. Whites and Indians struck a tenuous peace through a series of treaties in 1865, but none of these created a lasting peace. Not all Indians agreed to the treaties, and not all whites adhered to their provisions.

APACHE AND YAVAPAI RESISTANCE

Foolish tactics on the part of a few individuals often triggered Indian wars, and this was certainly true of whites dealing with volatile Chiricahua Apaches and their allies. Apaches were composed of many diverse bands, including Coyoteroes, Chiricahuas, Mescaleros, Jicarillas, San Carlos, Ojo Calientes, Mimbres, Mogollons, and others. Like many Indians, Apache bands preyed on other Indians and non-Indians for part of their livelihood. Stealing from Spanish, Mexican, and American merchants and ranchers was honorable and right in the minds of many Indians, because these interlopers had invaded native lands and killed Indians. Apaches had raided others Indians as well, principally Pimas and Tohono O'odhams (Papagoes), stealing their food and animals. Apaches enslaved people from time to time, just as whites and other Indians did.

In October 1860, a band of Coyoteroes captured a six-year-old mixed-blood Apache boy living on a ranch in the Sonoita Valley in southern Arizona with his Mexican mother and his stepfather, John Ward. In years to come, the boy became a famous scout named Mickey Free. In addition to the boy, the Coyoteroes ran off several head of oxen down the San Pedro River and disappeared into the valley. Ward tracked the Apaches and rode to Fort Buchanan to report the raid to Colonel Pitcairn Morrison. Ward claimed that Chiricahuas under Cochise had made the raid, so Morrison ordered Lieutenant George N. Bascom to visit the famous leader to retrieve the stolen livestock and boy. On February 4, 1862, Cochise rode into Bascom's camp with his brother, two nephews, a woman, and a child. Through an interpreter, Bascom accused Cochise of the raid on Ward's ranch, but Cochise denied it. Bascom seized the Indians, but Cochise escaped.

Since 1858, the Overland Mail Company of John Butterfield had driven stages through Apache Pass without incident, but after the Bascom Affair, Cochise captured James F. Wallace, a Butterfield employee, and two travelers. Bascom refused to exchange prisoners without the return of Ward's child and livestock—in the possession of Coyoteroes, not Chiricahuas—so Cochise unleashed a series of reprisals. He attacked soldiers and civilians alike, captured a small wagon train and burned the teamsters to death by tying them to the wagon wheels and setting them on fire. Cochise executed Wallace and the travelers, struck at a Butterfield stage, and slipped into Mexico. In retaliation, Bascom hanged three Chiricahuas and three Coyoteroes from the limb of a scrub oak tree. As a result of mistaken identity by Ward, Morrison, and Bascom, northern Mexico and the Southwest were thrown into a series of Apache wars from 1861 to 1886.

The war between the United States and the Apaches was likely inevitable, however, particularly after American, German, and French miners began working gold mines at Pinos Altos in present-day New Mexico. Miners invaded the home of several Apache bands, collectively called Gila Apaches. They included those Apaches who followed Mangas Coloradas. When the Civil War began, the United States abandoned nearby Fort McLane, and Mangas increased his effort to discourage mining by killing, wounding, and exiling miners from Apache lands. On July 15, 1862, Mangas joined Cochise in an ambush of Captain Thomas L. Roberts at the Battle of Apache Pass. Fierce fighting ensued, but the use of artillery saved many bluecoats and ended the lives of sixty-three Apaches. After the fight, General Carleton ordered the construction of Fort Bowie, in the heart of Apache Pass, on a hill overlooking the vital Apache Spring.

Apache men, women, and children lived in small bands and moved about the Southwest "like the wind." Spanish, Mexican, and American soldiers relentlessly pursued Apaches, and nonnative settlers hunted them down like animals. As seen here, Apaches lived in wickiups and were well armed to defend themselves and resist encroachment.

Mangas and Cochise continued their campaigns against the whites, raiding in New Mexico and Arizona. They controlled a vast region of deserts and mountains from the Rio Grande to central Arizona. They raided along the Jornada del Muertos, striking non-Indians at will. In January 1863, Carleton ordered General Joseph R. West to establish Fort West near Los Pinos and to pursue Mangas. On January 18, Captain E. D. Shirland and his cavalry rode into old Fort McLane with Mangas Coloradas, who had been invited into Shirland's camp with a white flag of truce. Shirland had ordered his men to capture the Apache and had brought him to General West. Soldiers tortured Mangas, placing their bayonets into the fire and then laying the hot blades against his feet. The soldiers shot Mangas to death while he was trying "to escape," or so West reported.

In spite of the execution of Mangas Coloradas, Apaches continued to fight, engaging Shirland and Captain William McCleave on two occasions. Both soldiers reported killing forty-eight Apaches, and Captain James H. Whitlock nearly wiped out Mangas's old band in an ambush in February 1864. In spite of these setbacks, Apache resistance continued. Victorio led one band of Ojo Calientes, raiding the famous Jornada from El Paso north for ninety miles. Apaches stole thousands of horses, cattle, sheep, and mules, including those belonging to the U.S. Army. They attacked soldiers and civilians, including Captain Albert H. Pfeiffer, his wife, child, and servant, who were taking a bath in some hot springs not far from Fort McRae. Pfeiffer was the only person to escape and was later important in the last Navajo campaign.

In the spring of 1865, Victorio, Nana, Rinyon, and other leaders asked Superintendent Michael Steck to negotiate peace with them, but before Steck acted on the request, Carleton asserted his superior position and refused, saying that the United States would negotiate only if Apaches agreed to remove to the Bosque Redondo Reservation in eastern New Mexico, where Carleton had recently removed Mescaleros and Navajos. Carleton ordered Colonel Nelson H. Davis to negotiate with these Apaches, but the Indians refused to meet the colonel, remembering the fate of Mangas. Victorio and the other Apaches continued to fight throughout the remainder of the 1860s, and they were joined by Yuman-speaking Yavapai Indians of central Arizona, who were often identified as Tonto Apaches or Yuma Apaches. Like the Athabascan-speaking Apaches, Yavapais adopted the Apache style of fighting on horseback and intermarried with Apaches.

Yavapais became skillful raiders and were responsible for killing Royce Oatman and his wife in 1850 and capturing his daughters, Mary Ann and Olive. Mary Ann died, but Henry Grinnel and a Quechan Indian named Francisco rescued Olive from Mojave Indians living along the Colorado River. Yavapais lived along the Verde and Salt rivers, farming the bottom lands of the streams. Some of the people raided white ranchers and settlements, stealing livestock and supplies. In January 1864, King S. Woolsey and his volunteer army enticed thirty Yavapais into their camp with promises of food, tobacco, and liquor. The whites fell on the Yavapais, killing twenty-four of them. Woolsey reflected the views of many whites in Arizona when he proclaimed, "I fight on a broad platform of extermination."

General Carleton encouraged Woolsey, and he urged his soldiers to strike in Indian fashion against various bands who threatened miners, settlers, ranchers, merchants, and soldiers. He asked Pueblos, Pimas, Maricopas, and other Indians to join with whites to rub out the Apaches. His order of 1864 called for a "general rising." Captain Thomas T. Tidball, a veteran of the Apache campaign, responded by killing fifty Apaches in Aravaipa Canyon in May 1863 and struck the Apaches again in 1864. On May 29, Tidball surprised an Apache village in the Mescal Mountains south of present-day Coolidge Dam, killing and capturing over forty people. Other soldiers and volunteers attacked the Apaches, never discriminating between friends or foes. Whites considered all Apaches—and Yavapais—hostile, and they hunted them like animals.

Carleton's campaign of 1864 against Apaches and Yavapais did not end hostilities but rather inflamed the Southwest. Soldiers killed a sufficient number to anger the Indians, encouraging them to continue their wars and strike whenever possible. Historian Robert Utley has written that Carleton's campaign against the Apaches and Yavapais was "an un-qualified failure." The Apaches and Yavapais kept up the fight for the next two decades, in part because Carleton concentrated his efforts on the Mescalero Apaches and Navajos. Carleton lost interest in continuing the dangerous and difficult Apache wars, which he left for another American to handle. As a result, the various Apache bands of Jicarillas, Ojo Calientes, Mimbres, Mogollons, Copper Mines, Chiricahuas, Pinals, Aravaipas, San Carlos, Coyoteroes, and others became stronger, striking at will between 1865 and 1870. In fact, bands of Apache and Yavapai be-came so strong that the War Department created a separate Department of Arizona and assigned General George Stoneman to launch the Peace Policy among the Apaches, believing that it was easier to feed Indians than kill them.

Apaches living in central Arizona were generally called Pinal and Ar-avaipa Apaches, and many of them settled near the lower San Pedro River not far from Camp Grant, where government agents issued food. Eskiminzin led a large band of these Apaches. He grew to trust Lieu-tenant Royal E. Whitman, commander at Camp Grant, and moved his band close to the fort. In an attempt to strike back at Apaches in general and to further many political careers, a few whites in Tucson assembled a militia force of Tohono O'odham warriors and Mexicans—all of whom hated Apaches—and attacked Eskiminzin's band. They launched a sur-prise attack on the friendly Apaches living in a village not far from Ara-vaipa Canyon, raping, killing, and butchering between 86 and 150 Apache people, most of whom were women and children. They killed everyone they could, except twenty-nine children, whom they took to sell or keep as slaves. Historian Jean Keller has shown that although the American public was outraged and some participants were tried for the atrocities, not one person was convicted of a crime, and every person who participated in the Camp Grant Massacre rose in stature within the region, territory, and city.

Arizona Governor Anson P. K. Safford used the slayings at Camp Grant to get rid of General Stoneman and replace him with Colonel George Crook. President Ulysses S. Grant hand-picked Crook for the assignment. At the same time, the Office of Indian Affairs assigned Vin-cent Colyer of the Board of Indian Commissioners to institute the Peace Policy among the Apaches. Crook and Colyer tried to stay out of each other's path, each pursuing policies for his own success. Colyer's Indian policies included the establishment of reservations and "civilization" of the Indians. He was helped in his work by General Oliver O. Howard, the Bible-toting Christian general who had earned a reputation as a hu-manitarian for his work with the Freedman's Bureau, which aided African-Americans after the Civil War.

Between 1871 and 1872, Colyer and Howard established several reservations, including the Chiricahua, Tularosa, San Carlos, and Date Creek reservations. Through negotiations, they tried to convince Apaches and Yavapais to leave their traditional homes and move onto one of the reservations. Although some Apaches moved onto the reservations, many more did not, and even when they did move onto the reservations, they often left to make their raids and returned to their reservation sanctuaries. The most significant element of Colyer and Howard's peace initiative was negotiating an end to Cochise's war. When Howard learned that Thomas Jeffords had established a personal relationship with Cochise, the general asked Jeffords to arrange a meeting with the Apache leader.

By 1872, Cochise had already sent out peace feelers and contemplated an end to his war against whites. Cochise agreed to the dramatic meeting with Howard that has been dramatized many times in books, magazines, movies, and television. With Jeffords by his side, Howard met Cochise at his stronghold in the Dragoon Mountains of southern Arizona. The two agreed to peace and a new reservation for the Chiricahua in southeastern Arizona. In spite of the fact that Cochise did not war on Americans, his men occasionally slipped into Mexico to raid. These raids increased considerably after Cochise died in June 1874 and Jeffords lost his authority among the divisive bands that emerged. Cochise's sons, Nachez and Taza, could not consolidate the Chiricahuas as their father had, and raids by Chiricahuas increased significantly after 1874.

Even though the truce negotiated by Cochise and Howard brought an element of peace to Arizona, other Apache bands were not as eager to lay down their arms. Between 1871 and 1872, when the peace initiative was active, Apaches reportedly killed forty-four people, wounded sixteen more, and ran off five hundred horses, cattle, and mules. Crook made plans to launch an offensive against the Apaches. In 1867 and 1868, Crook had successfully executed the Paiute Indian War using Shoshoni Indian scouts. He had kept his men in the field pursuing the Indians but had kept their morale high throughout the arduous conflict. Crook had negotiated personally with Old Weawea, the Paiute leader who replaced Pauline, and he had forced the Paiutes to resettle at Fort Harney and latter at the Klamath or Malheur River reservations. By 1872, Crook had convinced himself that the only way to defeat Apaches was to use native scouts, keep his men confident, and supply his troops well with food, ammunition, and goods through the use of large mule trains.

On November 15, 1872, Crook began his first Apache campaign, known as the Tonto Basin War. He used Apache scouts effectively and found his adversaries because these scouts knew their own people so well. Crook's scouts and troops moved rapidly through the Apache-Yavapai country, engaging the people in twenty fights. Captains James

Burns and William H. Brown killed two hundred Yavapais along the Salt River during the Battle of Skull Cave, and south of Camp Verde, Captain George Randall killed twenty-three others at Turret Peak. By the spring of 1873, after a difficult winter campaign launched against them, Apaches and Yavapais drifted into the forts and reservations. Lieutenant John G. Bourke had fought with Crook, and he recorded that when Yavapai leader Chalipun surrendered, he explained that he had to give up because the Americans had used Indian scouts who kept the warriors from sleeping, hunting, and cooking. Without fires the people were cold and hungry. The army promoted Crook to general, but the Apaches wars were far from over.

NAVAJO AND MESCALERO APACHES

Diné (the People), or Navajos, had fought the United States since 1846, when General Kearny and his Army of the West had invaded New Mexico. In spite of repeated treaties and wars, Navajos had refused to surrender. Following Canby's campaign of 1860–1861, Navajos had agreed to a reservation in their own homeland, but the Civil War and use of volunteer troops spoiled the peace. When New Mexicans renewed their raids against the Navajos in search of slaves, Navajo warriors reciprocated with raids on the New Mexican villages and ranches for horses, cattle, and sheep. Navajos struck with increased fury, eliciting demands by New Mexicans that the Navajos be crushed once and for all. General Carleton had lived and worked in the Southwest and was fairly well acquainted with Navajos when he arrived to command New Mexico and Arizona. As a result, he decided to destroy Navajos and Mescaleros, using them in a grand scheme that would alter American Indian policies.

General Carleton intended to end raids by Mescalero Apaches and Navajos and at the same time save their souls. It was also his intention to solve the "Indian problem" by creating a reservation system to destroy that which was native and replace it with white "civilization." He planned to do this by removing Mescaleros and Navajos to the Bosque Redondo in eastern New Mexico along the Pecos River, where whites would uplift their native brothers and sisters with new beliefs, values, ethics, economies, and laws. As Carleton pointed out, he planned to "collect them together, little by little, on to a reservation" to "be kind to them; there teach their children how to read and write."

The general wanted to "teach them the truths of Christianity" as well as "the arts of peace" so that one day they would "acquire new habits, new ideas, and new models of life." He envisioned a day when "the old Indians will die off, and carry with them all latent longings for murdering and robbing." In this way, young people would be raised "without these longings, and thus, little by little, they will become a happy and contented people." Already Edward Fitzgerald Beale had established a reservation system among California Indians at Fort Tejon, but Carleton refined the reservation system so that it would serve as a purgatory for Indians so that they could make the transition from "savage" to "civilized." And although Carleton's experiment at Bosque Redondo ultimately failed, his idea became the hallmark of American Indian policy after the Civil War. In this sense, Carleton's reservation system was a successful failure.

Carleton was a Massachusetts-born Christian who believed that his medicine was bitter for Indians but would save them in this life and the next. The reservation at Bosque Redondo would be like a beacon for other policy makers, "a city upon the hill" that would illuminate the way for future Native American policies. Reservations would help to assimilate Indians into the broader American society. In this way, as opposed to Chivington's, Native Americans would become a part of the country. They would learn basic education, in English, leave their cultures, societies, religions, and languages behind. In order to accomplish these lofty objectives, Carleton proposed forcibly removing Native Americans to a place where they could be trained in agriculture, the work ethic, and Christian beliefs. Upon these principles, Carleton believed, Native Americans would become productive people.

Kit Carson did not share Carleton's views about civilization and Christianization, but he agreed to act as Carleton's field commander. He led campaigns against the Mescaleros and Navajos. The two men were old friends from the days when they had fought Jicarilla Apaches. Carleton and Carson had also known each other when the latter was a Ute agent. Carleton knew that he could control Carson, who admired the general as a learned man and a successful Indian fighter. During the Civil War, Mescaleros and Navajos had taken advantage of troop withdrawals and had launched a series of successful attacks on New Mexican ranchers. In August 1862, the Mescalero Indian agent reported that these Apaches had killed forty men and six children and taken others captive. They also stole many horses, cattle, and mules. Carleton responded by sending Carson, Captain William McCleave, and Captain Thomas L. Roberts to engage the Mescaleros.

Carleton's orders regarding Mescaleros and Navajos to Carson and others were plain. "There is to be no council held with the Indians," Carleton announced, "nor any talk." He proclaimed that the soldiers should not kill women and children but that they "may be taken prisoners." Native American "men are to be slain whenever and wherever they can be found." Carson could not make a peace agreement with the Indians. "If they beg for peace, their chiefs and twenty of their principal men must come to Santa Fe to have a talk here." Carleton ordered Carson to remain in the field and kill Indians until he was told to end hostilities. Some

Known by many names during his life, Chief Manuelito became "the Warrior Who Grabs Enemy" after killing a Spanish soldier. He led his band of Navajos against the United States and New Mexican volunteers. Note the bullet wound on his chest.

Mescaleros moved south into the Guadalupe Mountains; others remained in their homelands near the Sacramento Mountains of New Mexico. When Manuelito and José Largo tried to discuss peace with Captain William Graydon, the soldiers opened fire, killing both chiefs, a woman, and nine warriors. Within a matter of weeks, Mescalero Chiefs Chato, Estrella, Cadete, and others sued for peace, traveling to Santa Fe with Agent Lorenzo Labadi to council with Carleton.

By the time the group reached Santa Fe, Carleton had selected a dry, windy plain upon which to resettle Mescaleros and Navajos. The new reservation, known as the Bosque Redondo, was situated near the Pecos River in southeastern New Mexico, where the army built Fort Sumner to guard the Indians. By March 1863, Carleton had removed four hundred Mescaleros to the Bosque Redondo Reservation, where he hoped to make farmers and Christians of them. In April 1863, Carleton met Navajo Chiefs Barboncito and Delgadito, telling them that if they wished to remain at peace with the United States, they had to remove to Bosque Redondo. Barboncito, a civil leader and holy man, explained that he could not go to the reservation because it was located far from his homeland. This was his way of explaining that the reservation was beyond the boundaries of Dinétah, sacred lands of Navajo people marked by four principal mountains made of earth from the third world–the former world inhabited by ancestors of the people. White bureaucrats cared nothing about Native American spiritual beliefs or economic way of life and gave their secular orders to the Navajos to move to the Bosque Redondo or fight. The Navajos chose to fight.

LAST NAVAJO WAR

When Navajos refused to relocate, Carleton ordered Carson to invade Navajo country and crush "the aggressive, perfidious, butchering Navajos." Carleton ordered Carson to establish Fort Canby and use it as his headquarters to keep after the Indians "not in big bodies, with military noise and smokes, and the gleam of arms by day, and fires, and talk, and comfortable by night." Rather, Carleton advised "in small parties moving stealthily to their haunts and lying patiently in wait for them." Carson was to hunt down Navajos like animals, follow their tracks, lie in wait, ambush, and kill them. Carleton told Carson "never to lax the application of force with a people that can no more be trusted than the wolves that run through the mountain." Carleton had no trust in Navajos, and the Navajos had no trust in the Bilagáana (white people). In July 1863, Navajos began their resistance against bluecoat troops led by Carson (Bi'éé' Lichíí'íí or Red Clothes).

After reestablishing Fort Defiance and renaming it Fort Canby, Carson began his summer scout against the Navajos. Throughout the summer and fall of 1863, Carson was in the saddle with his troops riding in many directions in search of the people. While he was gone from Fort Canby, Navajo warriors attacked the horse herd, making it difficult for Carson's cavalry to remain in the mountains, mesas, and deserts of Dinétah. Navajos also attacked mail riders and freighters hauling supplies to the post. Meanwhile, Carson tried unsuccessfully to find the Navajos. Carson kept the people on the run, not permitting them to care for their livestock, hunt, gather, or raise many crops. Whenever he found small plots of corn, he gathered it for his own use and that of his animals. The people began to starve and freeze to death, because they feared that Carson would catch them in their hogans. So they melted into their sacred lands, many going to Tséyi or Canyon de Chelly.

As winter approached, Carson planned to return to his wife and home in Taos, but Carleton insisted that Carson attack those Navajos holing up in the Canyon de Chelly. So Carson executed a winter campaign, an operation generally not undertaken by the army because of the lack of forage for horses. Carson sent Captain Albert Pfeiffer north into the Chuska Mountains, while the main body of soldiers headed west toward present-day Gando. Carson planned to attack from the west end of the canyon, while Pfeiffer was to attack from the east. The whites believed that Canyon de Chelly was one large canyon, running east-west. Navajo knew that the canyon had three large branches and several smaller ones. Navajos hid in the natural wonder of sandstone cliffs rising twelve hundred feet in some places, a place dotted with spectacular ruins of ancient pueblo dwellers, the home of Red God and other holy people who kept Navajos spiritual life in order.

Pfeiffer rode north into deep drifts of snow, making camps and eating a meager diet by the warmth of camp fires. Navajo women and children, starving and freezing to death, walked into the camps. The soldiers shared some of their food, clothing, and bedding. Through signs and Spanish, Pfeiffer told them to surrender at one of the posts. He and his men did not harm these people, in spite of the fact that Apaches had killed Pfeiffer's own wife and baby. Some women and children returned to the forests near Wheatfield Lake and urged others to join them as they reappeared in the soldiers' camp. Pfeiffer missed the first entrance into the canyon but located the gentle entrance into the northern branch of the canyon known as Canyon del Muerto. At Tsaile (the Place Where the Water Enters the Canyon), the soldiers rode into the canyon followed by several Navajo people. They moved quickly through the canyon, constantly fearing ambush and killing people who resisted.

Meanwhile, Carson and a small detachment moved north to Canyon de Chelly, riding along the southern branch to Spider Rock. Carson had a clear view of the narrow canyon floor where a small stream snaked through red and yellow sandstone walls. He was convinced that Pfeiffer had been ambushed, because he was nowhere in sight. But Pfeiffer was in the northern branch of the canyon and reunited with Carson at the mouth of the canyon near present-day Chinle, Arizona. Carson reported that he told the Navajos that the war was over and to surrender at Fort Canby or Fort Wingate. Carson claimed that he explained to the people that they would be removed to the Bosque Redondo, but Navajo oral accounts have always denied any knowledge of removal prior to the departure for the Bosque.

Teddy Draper Sr., a Navajo born into his mother's Salt People clan and his father's Water Flowing Together clan, reported that "About 20 of our warriors had died. They were buried on the west end of the flat rock. The soldiers stayed for another five or six days after the poles had been pulled up from the trail." Willard Draper stated that one of his relatives had to sleep quietly in a tree all night when Pfeiffer's soldiers made a camp underneath the tree. And Betty Shorthair recorded that "Two girls who went into a cave in the cliff were shot down, and they were hanging out from the cliff. As my mother's group was running along, there was a woman walking toward them with blood flowing from her hip. She had been shot by the soldiers." Whereas soldiers claim to have shot only a few people, Navajo accounts emphasize that numerous men, women, and children were shot during the canyon campaign and that far more died during the removal.

Pfeiffer's and Carson's men may have shot these people during their operations through the canyon in January 1864. It is also possible that volunteers—New Mexicans, Utes, and Paiutes—attacked Navajos after Carson had left the region. In any case, there is no doubt that soldiers attacked and killed several people in 1864–1865, the majority of whom were not involved in raiding. Nevertheless, all Navajos suffered from the war and many from removal. After the canyon campaign, approximately ten thousand Navajos surrendered, while another ten thousand or so moved north and west above the Hopi mesas to escape the Bilagáana. Some Navajo families were not removed to the Bosque Redondo, but many made the Long Walk to Hwééldi (Fort Sumner, New Mexico) in 1864 and 1865. Those who were removed included the Diné Ana'aíí (Enemy Navajos) who had served as scouts for the United States since 1846. The government repaid their loyalty by sending its own scouts into exile at the Bosque Redondo.

In a classic study of the era, Navajo scholar Ruth Roessel presents many original oral narratives about the last Navajo campaign and removal in *Navajo Stories of the Long Walk Period.* Roessel offers the only comprehensive Navajo voice about the Kit Carson campaign and removal. As a Navajo speaker and skilled translator, she interviewed forty Navajo about the subject and allows these native people to speak for themselves, their clans, and families. The result is a brilliant book, one of the few of its kind. And one of the finest tribal histories of the period is presented by Howard W. Gorman, an elder from Chinle and member of the Bitter Water clan. According to members of Gorman's family, his "ancestors were on the Long Walk with their daughter, who was pregnant and about to give birth." Just west of the Rio Grande, "the daughter got tired and weak and couldn't keep up with the others or go any farther because of her condition."

When the pregnant woman's family asked the soldiers to hold up and allow her to give birth, the soldiers refused. The girl could not travel, so she remained behind while her family pushed forward. "Not long after they had moved on," Gorman reported, "they heard a gunshot from where they had been a short time ago." Family members never saw the young woman again, but they watched as soldiers rode past them and believed that a soldier had shot her to death. Every family that made the Long Walk has stories about the killing of civilians who fell behind. Only two military reports of the removal have survived, and both are short.

Neither report mentions that New Mexican volunteers killed civilians, but Navajos recorded the killings and have not forgotten.

Between 1864 and 1868, Navajos languished at Hwééldi, where the U.S. Army expected twenty-five hundred Navajos and received between eight thousand and ten thousand. The soldiers at Fort Sumner did not have enough food, medicine, housing, or supplies to meet the needs of thousands of Indians forced on the Long Walk. Navajos dug holes in the earth, living in pits until they could build other quarters. They arrived too late in 1864 to plant crops, but they worked hard in the years that followed to construct irrigation systems and farms. They were plagued by salty water from the Pecos River, destructive winds, grasshoppers, arid soil, and lack of knowledge regarding agriculture. Soldiers infected Navajos with syphilis, and other diseases swept through the poverty-ridden people. Malnutrition and pneumonia killed children and elders, destroying the immediate future of the people and the collective memory and wisdom of the Navajo.

Comanches, Utes, and Kiowas attacked Navajos living on the Bosque Redondo Reservation, stealing what little they had. Navajo warriors pursued their enemies, and their oral accounts remember some of these lively engagements. In spite of their attempt to raise crops and become "civilized" in accordance with Carleton's plan, the Navajo experiment known as Fair Carletonia was an abysmal failure. Superintendent of Indian Affairs Michael Steck had predicted as much, telling Carleton that the Office of Indian Affairs opposed the removal to eastern New Mexico, 350 miles from Dinétah, where the Indians were unfamiliar with the environment and large-scale agriculture. He and others had advocated a reservation like that proposed by Canby in 1861, along the Little Colorado River near present-day Winslow, Arizona. Carleton refused such an idea and forced Navajos to live with their enemies, the Mescalero Apaches. The results were disastrous for Navajos, who suffered and died.

During their incarceration at Hwééldi, Navajos survived in large part because of the strength of their spiritual beliefs and the work of medicine men. Like many other native people, in times of calamity the Indians turned to their spiritual leaders and songs, prayers, rituals, and philosophies. In April 1868, Barboncito, Manuelito, and other leaders traveled to Washington, D.C., to meet President Andrew Johnson, who informed them that a peace commission led by William Tecumseh Sherman would determine their future. Before arriving, Sherman had learned of the dire Navajo situation and had decided to allow them to return home, provided they treated him with respect and deference. Navajo leaders did not know this, but they gathered under the leadership of Barboncito to conduct a sacred ritual called Coyote Way to learn what the Holy People had in store for them.

Navajo oral accounts and military records indicate that the people formed a huge circle on the Plains, captured a coyote who played possum, and that Barboncito placed a white shell bead in its mouth. When the people backed up, the coyote trotted off in a northwesterly direction, indicating that the people were going home. When the Navajos met with General Sherman, Barboncito spoke for everyone, saying he wanted to return to his home in the West where the clouds would come and clean the earth, renew the people, and allow the Navajo to survive. When Sherman suggested that the Navajos might move to Indian Territory and live there, Barboncito politely declined the offer. War leaders like Manuelito said nothing, allowing Barboncito to negotiate with the Bilagáana. Barboncito represented the people well, saying that "the cause of so much death among us and our animals" had been the removal from their sacred lands, a violation of Navajo spiritual law.

"We have all declared that we do not want to remain here," Barboncito proclaimed. He told Sherman that he wanted to see the place of his birth, told him that he hoped "to God you will not ask me to go to any other country except my own." He told Sherman: "I am speaking to you now as if I was speaking to a spirit." Sherman was moved by Barboncito's words and dignity. Sherman agreed to a new treaty on May 29, 1868, and it was ratified on August 12. It permitted Navajos to return home and secure for themselves a small portion of their traditional lands in New Mexico and Arizona. As with other Indians, the government did not "give" the people land but rather recognized only a small portion of their former homelands. In mid-June 1868, Navajos began their long walk home.

Manuelito's band of Navajos left the Bosque Redondo in June, moving as quickly as possible to the Rio Grande. As they approached Albuquerque and looked west, they saw Mount Taylor, a sacred mountain to Navajo people. His group "wondered if it was our mountain, and we felt like talking to the ground, we loved it so." The people were so moved by reentering Dinétah that "some of the old men and women cried with joy." After a prolonged war, forced removal, and imprisonment, the Navajo returned home. Navajo dealings with the Peace Commission had ended well for Navajo people, but this was not the case for all Native Americans in the West. In fact, the Peace Policy of the U.S. government led to the final military conflicts between Native American nations and the United States.

The Peace Policy also led to divisions among the tribes over whether it was best for the people to fight or negotiate with the United States. Schisms among the tribes were deep and permanent, and these schisms—well over a century old—continue to divide many tribes today. In the post–Civil War era, some Native Americans believed that it was in the best interest of their community to negotiate treaties, whereas others wanted to fight at any cost. Conflict between native nations and the United States did not end as a result of the Peace Policy. In fact, between 1865 and 1890, Indians from many regions and many tribes fought for their people in a series of resistance movements that ended in tragedy. The result of the Indian wars was confinement onto reservations where disease and death took their daily tolls. Yet, remarkably, Native Americans survived and resisted, just as they had during those years prior to the 1860s. Survival was the hallmark of the late nineteenth century, a fact that native people celebrate to this day.

Selected Readings and Bibliography

Native American involvement in the Civil War plays an extremely significant role in Native American history. Previously cited works that deal with native participation in the war include Woodward's *The Cherokees,* Debo's *Rise and Fall of the Choctaw Republic* and *The Road to Disappearance,* Akers's *Living in the Land of the Dead,* Gibson's *The Chickisaws,* and McReynolds's *The Seminoles.* Gibson's books, *Oklahoma, The Kickapoos,* and *The Chickisaws,* contain general information about native involvement in the Civil War and the ill effects of Reconstruction on all the tribes in Indian Territory. The information on Bannocks, Paiutes, and Shoshonis is from Ruby and Brown in *Indians of the Northwest,* but Trafzer and Scheuerman's *Renegade Tribe* also contains information pertinent to the era. Trafzer's *Kit Carson Campaign: The Last Great Navajo War* also deals with the military defeat of the Navajo during the Civil War, and Utley's *Frontiersmen in Blue* addresses several tribes during the war.

Abel, Annie H. *The American Indian as a Slaveholder and Secessionist.* Cleveland: Arthur H. Clark, 1915.

——. *The American Indian under Reconstruction.* Cleveland: Arthur H. Clark, 1925.

Bailey, Lynn R. *The Long Walk.* Los Angeles: Westernlore Press, 1964.

Bearss, Edwin, and Arrell Morgan Gibson. *Fort Smith.* Norman: University of Oklahoma Press, 1969.

Berthong, Donald. *The Southern Cheyennes.* Norman: University of Oklahoma Press, 1963.

Carley, Kenneth. *The Sioux Uprising of 1862.* St. Paul: Minnesota Historical Society, 1976.

Chaput, Donald. "Generals, Indian Agents, Politicians: The Doolittle Survey of 1865." *Western Historical Quarterly* 3 (July 1972): 269–282.

Colton, Ray. *The Civil War in the Western Territories.* Norman: University of Oklahoma Press, 1959.

Dale, Edward E., and Gaston Litton, eds. *Cherokee Cavaliers.* Norman: University of Oklahoma Press, 1939.

Danziger, Edmund J. *Indians and Bureaucrats.* Urbana: University of Illinois Press, 1974.

Dunlay, Thomas. *Wolves for the Blue Soldiers.* Lincoln: University of Nebraska Press, 1982.

Faulk, Odie B. *John Robert Baylor.* Tucson: Arizona Historical Society, 1963.

——. *The Geronimo Campaign.* New York: Oxford University Press, 1969.

Fischer, LeRoy H., ed. *The Civil War Era in Indian Territory.* Los Angeles: Lorrin L. Morrison, 1974.

Franks, Kenny. *Stand Watie.* Memphis: Memphis State University Press, 1975.

Gibson, Arrell M. *The Life and Death of Colonel Albert Jennings Fountain.* Norman: University of Oklahoma Press, 1965.

Hauptmann, Laurence M. *Between Two Fires: American Indians in the Civil War.* New York: Free Press, 1995.

Hoig, Stan. *The Sand Creek Massacre.* Norman: University of Oklahoma Press, 1961.

Hunt, Aurora. *Major General James H. Carleton.* Glendale, Calif.: Arthur H. Clarke, 1958.

Jones, Robert H. *The Civil War in the Northwest: Nebraska, Wisconsin, Iowa, Minnesota and Dakotas.* Norman: University of Oklahoma Press, 1960.

Josephy, Alvin M. Jr. *The Nez Perce Indians and the Opening of the Northwest.* New Haven: Yale University Press, 1965.

——. *The Civil War in the American West.* New York: Knopf, 1991.

Kelly, Lawrence. *Navajo Roundup.* Boulder, Colo.: Pruett Press, 1970.

Kerby, Robert L. *The Confederate Invasion of New Mexico and Arizona, 1861–1862.* Los Angeles: Westernlore Press, 1958.

Madsen, Brigham D. *The Shoshoni Frontier and the Bear River Massacre.* Salt Lake City: University of Utah Press, 1985.

Mayhall, Mildred P. *The Kiowas.* Norman: University of Oklahoma Press, 1962.

McNitt, Frank. *The Navajo Wars.* Albuquerque: University of New Mexico Press, 1972.

McPherson, James M. *Ordeal by Fire.* New York: McGraw-Hill, 1982.

——. *Battle Cry of Freedom.* New York: Oxford University Press, 1988.

McReynolds, Edwin C. *The Seminoles.* Norman: University of Oklahoma Press, 1957.

Meyer, Roy W. "The Canadian Sioux: Refugees from Minnesota." *Minnesota History* 41 (1968): 13–28.

Monaghan, Jay. *Civil War on the Western Border,* 1854–1865. Boston: Little, Brown, 1955.

Moulton, Gary E. *John Ross: Cherokee Chief.* Athens: University of Georgia Press, 1978.

Nevins, Allan. *Ordeal of the Union.* 8 volumes. New York: Charles Scribner's Sons, 1971.

Schultz, Duane P. *Over the Earth I Come: The Great Sioux Uprising of 1862.* New York: St. Martin's Press, 1992.

Thompson, Gerald. *The Army and the Navajo: The Bosque Redondo Reservation, 1863–1869.* Tucson: University of Arizona Press, 1976.

XThrapp, Dan. *The Conquest of Apacheria.* Norman: University of Oklahoma Press, 1967.

Trafzer, Clifford E. "Mr. Lincoln's Army Fights the Navajos, 1863–1864" *Lincoln Herald* 77 (1975): 148–158.

Waldrip, William I. "New Mexico during the Civil War." *New Mexico Historical Review* 28 (1953): 163–182, 251–290.

Wallace, Ernest, and E. Adamson Hoebel. *The Comanches: Lords of the Southern Plains.* Norman: University of Oklahoma Press, 1952.

Woodward, Grace S. *The Cherokees.* Norman: University of Oklahoma Press, 1963.

Wright, Muriel H. *A Guide to the Indian Tribes of Oklahoma.* Norman: University of Oklahoma Press, 1951.

CHAPTER 11

WAR, PEACE, AND CONFINEMENT

The end of the Civil War brought no peace for Native Americans. Conflicts continued after 1865 as American Indians across the West were significantly affected by the war. Indians received no relief from white encroachment and pressures during Reconstruction. In fact, the U.S. Army applied its "Force Policy" with renewed vigor in 1865–1866. Yet the national attitude toward Indians immediately after the Civil War was changing, in large part because of the horrible bloodshed experienced during the war and in part because of shrinking budgets to support large standing armies. Throughout the nation, many people began questioning the army's policy of using guns and rifles rather than words and treaties. Powerful people began urging reforms in Americans Indian affairs, and the result was a national investigation into American Indian affairs that contributed to a new reform attitude toward native people.

THE DOOLITTLE COMMISSION AND THE PEACE POLICY

Senator James R. Doolittle, chair of the Senate Committee on Indian Affairs during the administration of President Andrew Johnson, led an investigation into native people. The investigators, commonly called the Doolittle Commission, researched many aspects of Native American life in relation to the United States. Doolittle's efforts culminated in 1867 in the formidable *Report on the Condition of the Indian Tribes,* commonly called the *Doolittle Report.* It touched off a national debate about American Indian policies, pitting the army and its Force Policy against advocates for the Peace Policy. The report pointed out that Native Americans faced major difficulties as a direct result of the Civil War and white invasion of their land. Many Indians lived in abject poverty, particularly those in Indian Territory.

The Doolittle Commission found that malnutrition, smallpox, measles, cholera, and other diseases had caused high death rates among the tribes, although specifics about the number of Indians dying and the effects of epidemics on Indians were not recorded because the government did not track populations, births, or deaths. But even without exact documentation, the *Doolittle Report* stated that native populations were declining from infectious diseases, warfare, and the lack of food. Whites also took lands formerly controlled by Indians where natural foods–roots, berries, seeds, grains–had been harvested and where game and fish had once flourished.

The *Report on the Condition of the Indian Tribes* also argued that the U.S. Army was at fault for pursuing policies detrimental to the Indians. Commissioner of Indian Affairs Lewis V. Bogy entered the fray in favor of the Peace Policy, which promoted negotiated settlements with the tribes and the establishment of a reservation system. Although the United States had known reservations prior to the 1860s, the modern reservation system emerged fully after the Civil War. The *Doolittle Report* urged the government to end white encroachment onto Indian lands, including that of heavy-handed military officers who sought national recognition and professional promotions through Indian warfare. President Andrew Johnson and President Ulysses S. Grant supported the peace makers, but General William Tecumseh Sherman, who led the postwar army, stated in 1866 that the military should kill the Lakota, "even to their extermination, men, women, and children." Yet, even Sherman slowly, grudgingly began leaning toward the reservation system as a possible solution to the Indian wars. He had to admit that the campaigns of 1865–1866 had been unsuccessful in ending the "Indian problem." In any case, the national mood favored reform, not war.

In 1866, President Johnson appointed Methodist minister Nathaniel G. Taylor as commissioner of Indian affairs. He advocated the recognition of two huge reservations, one for the Northern Plains tribes north of Nebraska and one for the Southern Plains tribes south of Kansas. Congress leaned toward a negotiated settlement with the tribes, so both houses supported the creation of a Peace Commission, to identify and resolve problems between whites and Indians using the reservation system. Commissioner Taylor headed the Peace Commission, composed of Senator John B. Henderson, Samuel F. Tappan, John B. Sanborn, General William S. Harney, General Alfred H. Terry, and Colonel Christopher C. Augur. Eventually, General Sherman also became a member of the Peace Commission.

When Grant became president, he continued the Peace Policy. He met with a group of Quakers–members of the Society of Friends–as well as clerics from other denominations. He was so impressed with the delegation of religious leaders that he invited members to serve as bureaucrats in the Office of Indian Affairs, and act as agents on various reservations.

Grant and others believed that Native Americans would respond well to the honest and moral examples provided by the religious leaders serving as agents. The Grant administration primarily appointed Protestant men to posts within the Indian office, although some Catholics and Jewish superintendents served as well. Most of these men were committed to civilization, assimilation, and Christianization of Indians. Grant believed Christian agents to be honest men, a refreshing change from many corrupt agents who had bilked the tribes out of millions of dollars through shady contracting and outright theft.

All Indian agents were white, not Native Americans. Quakers predominately served as agents during the era, including Laurie Tatum, who worked as Comanche-Kiowa agent and wrote *Our Red Brothers* (1899). Other Quaker agents of note included Hiram W. Jones of the Quapaw Agency, who worked with Quapaws, Modocs, Nez Perces, Senecas, Wyandots, and others, as well as Osage Agent Isaac T. Gibson. Some Indian agents were Methodists, including James H. Wilbur, assigned to the Yakama Agency, which consisted of fourteen different tribes and bands speaking the four languages of Sahaptin, Salishan, Chinookan, and Shoshonian. "Father" Wilbur ran the reservation with an iron fist, dictating policies of assimilation to his charges and treating them like children. Wilbur organized an Indian police force, and an Indian court enforced his laws, punishing Indians who refused to conform to his mandates by administering whippings, jailing people, and withholding food rations.

In the late 1860s and early 1870s, the Peace Commission negotiated with several tribes and created reservations throughout the West. In 1869, Congress created a Board of Indian Commissioners, composed of prominent white men, to monitor agents and reservations, attempting to remove corruption in Indian affairs. The board also advised the secretary of interior and commissioner of Indian affairs. The Board of Indian Commissioners served as one of the few advocates for native people, but its duties were too great and budgets too small to effectuate permanent positive change. It functioned simultaneously with the Peace Commission and continued throughout the century. Sometimes the good intentions of these white bureaucrats worked against the tribes. After making their tour of the tribes inhabiting the American West, members of the Peace Commission urged the United States to end its treaty making with all Indian nations.

The Supreme Court supported the end of treaty making. In 1870, the Supreme Court ruled in the *Cherokee Tobacco* decision that congressional laws were superior to Indian treaties and that treaties with foreign nations were superior to those made with Indian nations. A year later, Congress passed an act providing that Indian nations would no longer "be acknowledged or recognized as an independent nation, tribe, or power with whom the United States may contract by treaty." Long before the Declaration of Independence or ratification of the Constitution, Indian nations had been recognized as sovereign. Even the Cherokee cases had recognized that the tribes had a unique legal status as domestic dependent nations. But in 1870, the Supreme Court tried to redefine the status of tribes, and the federal act of 1871 ended treaty making. The two actions questioned Indian sovereignty, but native peoples never intentionally surrendered sovereignty.

REDUCTION OF INDIAN TERRITORY

The continual erosion of Indian power was evident in Indian Territory, where the United States punished the Cherokee, Choctaw, Chickasaw, Seminole, and Muscogee nations for their involvement with the Confederacy. Even though several Native Americans had fought for the Union, Reconstruction politicians eagerly punished all the tribes in an effort to destroy Indian power, economies, land bases, and resources. This was equally true of Native Americans who had been forcibly removed to the northern half of Indian Territory in present-day Kansas. Politicians used the war as an excuse to steal Indian lands and resources, then forcibly remove thousands of Indians from Kansas into present-day Oklahoma, onto lands vacated by the Five Civilized Tribes. Under the terms of the Reconstruction Treaties of 1866, Cherokees, Choctaws, Chickasaws, Seminoles, and Muscogees lost thousands of acres of land upon which the government relocated most tribes living in Kansas. Consolidation of native populations into war-torn Indian Territory proved disastrous for the people.

During the 1870s, the United States carved out several new Indian agencies from lands previously owned by Cherokees, Choctaws, Chickasaws, Seminoles, and Muscogees. White citizens wanted to purge Kansas of Native Americans. One newspaper editor characterized Indians in Kansas as "a set of miserable, dirty, lousy, blanketed, thieving, lying, sneaking, murdering, graceless, faithless, gut-eating skunks" who should be exterminated. Instead of killing them immediately, the United States moved the Kansas (Kaws) to the northwestern portion of Indian Territory and Osages east, onto lands known as the Cherokee Outlet. Some Osages chose to remain in Kansas on allotments assigned to them by the United States, but within a short time Kansans attacked them, murdering, burning, and driving them out of their homes. Those who survived joined Osages in Indian Territory.

The United States forced Pawnees, Otoes, Missouris, Tonkawas, and Poncas onto the Ponca Agency, located west of the new lands inhabited by Kansas and Osages. These lands were drained by the Chikaskia and Arkansas rivers and were the home of many diverse Native American nations. Between 1879 and 1885, the United States also forced Nez Perce and Palouse Indians under the leadership of Chief Joseph, Yellow Bull, and Husishusis Kute to live on the Ponca Agency until they surrendered their rights to lands in Indian territory from the Ponca Reservation and returned to their native Northwest. Other Native Americans from Kansas, including Potawatomis, Sac, Fox, Absentee Shawnees, and Kickapoos, moved to the Sac and Fox Agency located west of the Seminole Nation. The Iowas from the border of Kansas and Nebraska ultimately settled nearby on a reservation between the Deep Fork and Cimarron rivers.

These were not necessarily the permanent homes of these tribes, because many found that the government had already assigned multiple tribes to the same lands. As a result, Tonkawas, Pawnees, Delawares, and others found themselves living on newly assigned reservations. For example, a group of Delawares and a band of Shawnees relocated among Cherokees. The Cherokees even adopted the Delaware people, bringing them into their nation. Not far from the Cherokee capital of Tahlequah was the Quapaw Agency. Located in the northeastern portion of Indian Territory, this agency included Wyandots, Quapaws, Senecas, Shawnees, Pawnees, Peorias, Miamis, and Ottawas. And after the Modoc War of 1873, the government exiled some Modocs from California to Indian Territory, where they settled at the Quapaw Agency. The government relocated Caddoes, Wichitas, and others onto the Wichita-Caddo Agency and Kiowas, Comanches, Kiowa-Apaches, and, much later, some Chiricahua Apaches onto an agency in southwestern Indian Territory known as the Leased District, former lands of Choctaws and Chickasaws.

Like many regions controlled by the Confederacy, Indian Territory was in ruin by the end of the Civil War. Native Americans spent a good deal of the late 1860s and early 1870s rebuilding homes, barns, towns, churches, schools, and businesses. Soldiers and raiding parties of outlaws had laid waist to Indian Territory, destroying property, bridges, fences, and entire communities. The territory had become a hideout for former soldiers who had used their military might to rob, rape, burn, and terrorize native and nonnative peoples in Kansas, Texas, Colorado, Arkansas, Missouri, Louisiana, and Indian Territory. Indian and non-Indian rustlers stole cattle and horse herds, while whiskey peddlers, prostitutes, gamblers, and gunmen preyed on the general population of Indian Territory. Furthermore, some freedmen from the Indian Nations turned on their former masters, stealing, burning, and destroying property in retaliation for years of enslavement. All the tribes reacted negatively to their former African-American slaves, particularly after Reconstruction politicians tried to force the Native American nations to provide land and resources to former slaves. However, some native people of mixed African-American ancestry continued to live congenially within the nation.

In reaction to many forms of postwar violence, tribes in present-day Kansas and Oklahoma formed vigilante posses to hunt down and punish criminals, and some of the tribes used their tribal court systems (e.g., Cherokee Going Snake Courthouse) to address outlawry with limited success. Tribal pleas for federal help against outlaws were answered in 1871, when the government appointed Isaac Parker to the Western Arkansas Federal District Court. He soon earned a reputation as "Hanging Judge Parker," using U.S. marshals to bring renewed order to Indian Territory. Before the Civil War, all the tribes in Indian Territory had functioned through government councils that worked well for the people; but the war had disrupted government among the Indian nations. They used the era of Reconstruction to heal schisms and begin government anew under the watchful eye of federal agents who actively sought to erode tribal sovereignty.

During Reconstruction, most tribes of the Great Plains, Rocky Mountains, Northwest, and Southwest were learning how the United States conducted its Indian policies. By the 1870s, Native Americans in Indian Territory had dealt with white Euro-Americans for years and well knew that the United States would take from them as much as it could, including tribal lands, resources, and power. For political and economic reasons, native nations in Indian Territory opposed the creation of a unified territorial government, believing that this would be a major step toward the destruction of tribal sovereignty. In addition, tribes would lose land and resources because the government would require them to surrender lands to railroad companies for rights of way through Indian Territory. They would be forced to grant to non-Indian companies lands and all the resources associated with these lands, including timber needed to build railroads.

To placate the United States, Indians living in Indian Territory began holding intertribal meetings; but the pressure from non-Indian sources to "open" Indian Territory became so great in 1870 that Senator Benjamin F. Rice of Arkansas offered a bill to organize the Territory of Oklahoma. Native nations in Indian Territory moved quickly through an emergency session of the Intertribal Council held at Okmulgee, drafting the Okmulgee Constitution, calling for a unified Indian Territory and future Native American state. William P. Ross (Cherokee) authored the Okmulgee Constitution, which the council ratified and sent to Congress. Politicians in Washington, D.C., refused to adopt the constitution because it recognized Native American sovereignty in some areas of government. Rice's activities in 1870 were significant because they launched Indian Territory on a path that would culminate, in 1907, with the merging of Indian Territory with Oklahoma Territory to form the state of Oklahoma.

NATIVE RESISTANCE ON THE
SOUTHERN PLAINS

In October 1865, a federal peace commission headed by Central Indian Superintendent of Indian Affairs Thomas Murphy and General William S. Harney met representatives of the Kiowa, Kiowa-Apache, Comanche, Cheyenne, and Arapaho on the Little Arkansas River near present-day Wichita, Kansas. Black Beaver (Delaware) and Jesse Chisholm (Cherokee) supported the two commissioners and helped them arrange and conduct the meeting. Not all the bands joined the council, but a number of distinguished Cheyenne and Arapaho leaders negotiated with the commissioners, including Black Kettle, Little Raven, Little Robe, and Seven Bulls. Wolf Sleeve, Black Eagle, Stinking Saddle Blanket, Iron Shirt, and Poor Bear represented the Kiowa-Apaches, whereas Buffalo Hump, Ten Bears, and Rising Sun represented the Comanches. Indian leadership among most of the Plains tribes consisted of band leadership, not "tribal" leadership. Thus, within any one tribe there were several chiefs of bands, each of whom spoke for his own group but none other. Women often influenced the leaders informally, particularly those with personal political or religious power, but on the whole, male chiefs made most decisions affecting their bands. This was also true of chiefs in the Rocky Mountains, Great Basin, and Columbia Plateau, although women asserted power in a variety of ways throughout the western tribes.

Male leaders among the Southern Plains tribes negotiated in good faith at the Little Arkansas River, and they concluded a series of treaties with the United States that relinquished their claims to lands north of the Arkansas River. Under the terms of the treaties, Kiowas and Comanches were to settle onto one reservation and Cheyennes, Arapahoes, and Kiowa-Apaches onto another reservation, located south of the Arkansas River in present-day western Kansas, Oklahoma, and the Texas Panhandle. Although the United States agreed to enforce the treaties, the army did not prevent hundreds of settlers from moving across Indian lands. Traders, whiskey peddlers, surveyors, soldiers, and others violated treaty rights and traveled across native lands. Whites built ranches, stage stations, and other structures on Indian lands, generally encroaching on treaty-assigned Indian lands, which destroyed the agreements and triggered war.

The treaties made at the Little Arkansas River were well intended, but they collapsed into a destructive war that pitted the Southern Plains tribes against white civilian and military population. The Senate never ratified these treaties, and the army did virtually nothing to prevent white invasion of tribal lands and the destruction of buffalo herds. As a result, Indians fought most whites, trying to drive them from their homes on the Great Plains. White settlers demanded more land on the Plains, and railroad businessmen lobbied Congress to open up Indian lands across the Great Plains. Even before Congress gave permission to do so, railroad companies surveyed western lands and complained bitterly when Native Americans attacked them. Railroad agents cried even louder for the defeat, removal, and confinement of the Plains people.

White ranchers, farmers, businessmen, and immigrants all had a voice in the American system. They wrote to representatives or former representatives, demanding that the United States confine the tribes to smaller and smaller domains. Eastern Indians forced west by the same demands shook their heads in dismay, because they had seen the same dangerous process unfold again and again in the East. But many tribes on the Great Plains believed they could resist and endure the invasion by standing strong against whites. They spread war with lightning speed, striking wagon trains, stages, ranches, trading posts, and the like. As a result, politicians and soldiers heard the public outcry to do something about the warring Indians. Of course, whites blamed Native Americans, who stood in the way of progress, business, and civilization.

Cheyenne-Arapaho Agent Edward W. Wynkoop and Kiowa-Comanche Agent Jesse H. Leavenworth both respected Indian people and did their utmost to end the violence. Some Indians responded to their pleas for peace, but others ignored them. Like so many tribes, Native Americans of the Southern Plains did not comprise a single "tribe" with a single "chief." Instead, the tribes were composed of many diverse bands who followed several leaders, including war chiefs, civilian leaders, and shaman. For convenience, white agents and soldiers often selected a single male leader and designated him as "chief," but in reality, there were always many leaders within tribes. The designation of a single "head chief" by white officials caused many difficulties for Indians and whites, because these designations were contrary to tribal "law." Within most tribes, no one leader could control all the people. Indeed, Native Americans usually followed leaders who were to their liking. If a leader had a plan of action that appealed to the people, they followed him. If they did not like his plans, they could join another group and follow that group's leader. Thus, some Comanches followed Ten Bears, whereas others followed Buffalo Hump. Agent Leavenworth was not able to communicate with both leaders all the time or convince them to remain on the reservation. Native American leaders followed their own destinies, not those determined by whites. As a result, neither Leavenworth nor Wynkoop could prevent Native American leaders from taking their people into battle against the whites, so the war continued.

In 1867, General Winfield Scott Hancock determined to end Indian attacks on whites throughout the Southern Plains and clear the western trails of resistance fighters. General Hancock informed Leavenworth and Wynkoop of his intent to lead a military expedition onto the Great Plains

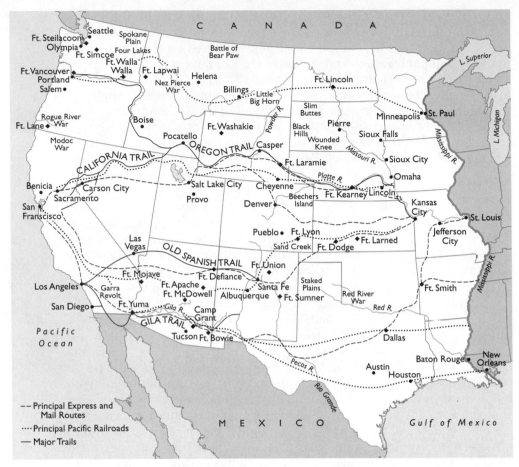

Selected routes, towns, and forts of the American West.

to awe the Indians into submission. He reported that he wanted to parley with chiefs, but if they wanted to fight, he would engage them. Hancock led his cavalry and infantry units into western Kansas, where he met a few Oglala Sioux and Cheyenne leaders at Pawnee Fork near Fort Larned. Not far away, Cheyenne and Arapaho leaders had established a large village of over 250 lodges, and the people would have remained to negotiate with Hancock had he not ordered his men to advance on the village.

Hancock later argued that his troops had no ill intent, but none of the Indians was convinced. They knew what had happened at Sand Creek, and none of them remained in the village to participate in another slaughter. The Indians had not rushed to negotiate with Hancock because they were engaged in a sacred rite, renewing their medicine arrows. They could not be distracted from this rite, but Hancock assumed they were stalling him. Some Cheyenne and Arapaho warriors retaliated for Hancock's march, believing the soldiers meant to destroy the people. Cheyenne and Arapaho warriors attacked whites along the Smoky Hill Road in western Kansas, so Hancock used the attacks as an excuse to torch the Indian village. His men burned all the lodges, destroying tipis, lodge poles, bedding, parfleches, food, and many other items. Hancock then pushed Kiowas and Arapahoes into war by delivering his ultimatum of war or peace.

Kiowas, Comanches, Arapahoes, Cheyennes, and Kiowa-Apaches rose in a general war against the bluecoats because of Hancock's campaign. Warriors attacked whites with renewed vigor, and they closed trails leading west. Surveyors for the Kansas Pacific Railroad could not advance because of the war, knowing that to survey across Indian lands would be deadly and foolhardy. Kiowa leader Satanta and Lakota leader High Back Bone (Miniconjou Sioux) joined in the general effort by many Plains tribes to strike railroad workers, stages, freight wagons, way stations, and whites in general to encourage them to leave the Great Plains forever. Hancock sent Colonel George Armstrong Custer to punish the Lakotas, but he could not find them.

Throughout the summer of 1867, the army campaigned against the Kiowas, Comanches, Kiowa-Apaches, Cheyennes, and Arapahoes. The tribes kept up their raids, but the army pressured them sufficiently that by October, even the fiercest fighters agreed to talk peace. Satank, Satanta, Stumbling Bear, Ten Bears, Wolf Sleeve, Black Kettle, and Tall Bears were among many leaders who agreed to a truce in the autumn of 1867. Over seven thousand Indians joined in a large council held in southwestern Kansas at Medicine Lodge, a grand assemblage with hundreds of tipis, barking dogs, fine horses, and hope. However, by October, the Indians had heard rumors that whites wanted them to end their freedom of movement across the Plains and settle onto a reservation. Buffalo herds had declined, and constant pressure from whites was taking its toll among the people. They came to Medicine Lodge to give their views of the white invasion and to listen to the peace commissioners.

Commissioner of Indian Affairs Nathaniel Taylor led the delegation at Medicine Lodge, joined by Samuel Tappan, John Sanborn, and John Henderson. The other commissioners were the military contingency of the Peace Commission, including Generals Alfred Terry, William S. Harney, and Colonel Christopher Augur. The commissioners presented their arguments in terms of American Indian policies of the day, telling the Indians that whites were numerous beyond words and could not be prevented from moving west. They told the Indians that the buffalo would soon be gone and that farming was the only means of native survival. They urged Native Americans to end their way of life and settle peacefully onto reservations where the government would provide food, housing, medical care, education, and "civilization."

The Native American leaders at Medicine Lodge responded to the white men, and their voices addressed the origin of conflicts, the importance of freedom among the people, and the sacredness of the land. Comanche Chief Ten Bears said the war "was not begun by us" but rather resulted because whites "sent out the first soldier." He pointed out that "blue-dressed soldiers and the Utes [with Carson] came from the night when it was dark and still, and for campfires they lit our lodges." Ten Bears said he wanted nothing to do with reservations or gifts from whites because he "was born upon the prairies, where the wind blew free, and there was nothing to break the light of the sun." Reservations were no place from which to draw "a free breath," so he wanted to live "like my fathers before me." However, he wanted peace with whites and "no blood upon my land to stain the grass."

Satanta, "a tall man and good-looking, with plenty of long shiny black hair," set his "dark piercing eyes" on the commissioners and explained that "All of the land south of the Arkansas belongs to the Kiowas and Comanches" and that he did not plan "to give away any of it." He expressed his love for the land and buffalo, saying he did not want to be confined to a reservation. He pointed out that whites cut down trees and slaughtered buffalo along the Arkansas River, "and when I see that it feels as if my heart would burst with sorrow." He had no interest in receiving anything from whites, saying that the "building of homes for us is all nonsense. We don't want you to build any for us." Satanta reminded the commissioners that the Kiowas were a free and independent people who had survived on the Plains for years without white men.

Like other Native Americans, the Indians of the Southern Plains had a spiritual relationship with their land, with all animate and inanimate objects within the land, and with the streams and rivers, ponds, and lakes. Their Indian law came from oral tradition; sacred narratives from the time of creation when plants, animals, places, and people interacted with each other. This oral tradition established a way of life for the Southern Plains people that had existed for eons. When whites asked Indian leaders to affix their marks to treaties negotiated at Medicine Lodge Creek, the native people were committing themselves to far more than just a surrender of land or an agreement to live in a confined geographical area. Treaties and reservations meant a reordering of life for Native Americans and created a new and unnatural situation for the various tribes. In accordance with Indian "laws," as set forth in the ancient stories, the people affected by the Medicine Lodge Treaty were to hunt, raid, and move across the Southern Plains to special places that had meaning to them. However, confinement on reservations meant an end to self-determined travel, including travel to sacred places to sing, dance, and conduct ceremonies. Confinement meant spiritual and economic restrictions that changed the yearly activities of the tribes. Military and civilian agents of the government–foreign people to Indians–began dictating the movement and activities of native people. These agents used treaties and reservations as a means to restrict Indians, and fundamentally altered the way of life for Plains people and prevented them free access to holy places that had long been a part of their lives. The change did not occur immediately or completely, but a major alteration began in October 1867 for Kiowas, Comanches, Kiowa-Apaches, Cheyennes, and Arapahoes.

Under the terms of the treaties made at Medicine Lodge, Kiowas, Comanches, and Kiowa-Apaches agreed to move onto a reservation in the Leased District, on lands formerly assigned to Choctaws and Chickasaws, in the southwestern corner of present-day Oklahoma. Cheyennes and Arapahoes were to relocate onto a reservation bounded by the Cimarron and Arkansas rivers in the old Cherokee Outlet, but they moved to a more desirable spot on the Canadian River—a reservation recognized by the United States in 1869 by executive order. However, not content with this designation, the United States, in 1872, reduced the executive order reservation of the Cheyenne and Arapaho, colonizing Texas tribes such as Keechis, Anadarks, Ionis, and Wacoes as well as Caddoes, Wichitas, and Absentee Delawares onto these lands.

Before the Kiowas and Comanches would sign the treaty, they insisted on securing their right to hunt on all land south of the Arkansas River. And the Cheyenne and Arapaho would not sign until the commissioners agreed they could continue to hunt between the Platte and Arkansas rivers. All the Indians had to agree that white settlers could use the trails west without molestation and that federal troops could build new forts on the Southern Plains. Although all the tribes were represented at the Medicine Lodge Council, not all leaders signed or agreed with the provisions. The peace commissioners assumed that the treaties bound all the Indians, but this was not the native view. Still, at the conclusion of the council, Satank rode up to the commissioners and announced that he had "come to say that the Kiowas and Comanches have made you a peace, and they intend to stick to it." He said that he was "old and will soon join my fathers, but those who come after me will remember this day."

None of the tribes forgot the agreements made at Medicine Lodge, but the government forgot to fulfill its agreement to deliver food and supplies to Indians living peacefully on the two reservations. Although Kiowas and Comanches stole Chickasaw horses and raided into Texas, most Cheyennes and Arapahoes remained on the reservation for a time. Resentment arose rapidly, however, particularly among young Cheyenne and Arapaho men, who rode off to hunt buffalo and raid Indian and white settlements for cattle, horses, and other valuables. They raided into Kansas, Nebraska, and Texas, triggering a new conflict. General Alfred Sully organized an expedition to the North Canadian River, but after spotting a large Kiowa and Comanche village, turned back to Fort Dodge without firing a shot. He notified other commanders in the region, who planned a winter campaign. General Philip Sheridan ordered his aide, Major George A. Forsyth, to organize a group of volunteers to operate against Cheyenne, Arapaho, and Oglala Sioux warriors. Forsyth chose fifty seasoned plainsmen, former Union and Confederate soldiers, who followed an Indian trail up the Arikara Fork of the Republican River. On September 17, 1868, they ran headlong into Cheyenne Dog Soldiers under Tall Bull, Bull Bear, and White Horse, as well as Lakota under Pawnee Killer. The Indians pinned down the soldiers on Beecher's Island for eight days, killing six and wounding fifteen others. While the volunteers hunkered down in foxholes dug into the sand, two soldiers slipped out to get reinforcements. Their lives were saved by superior weapons and plenty of ammunition, as well as the arrival of the Tenth Cavalry composed of African-American or Buffalo Soldiers who rode to their rescue.

The Battle of Beecher's Island was of little consequence, except to notify the Indians on the southern and northern prairies that the army intended to pursue them throughout the Great Plains. Indeed, in the winter of 1868, troops from Colorado and Kansas converged on Fort Supply, Indian Territory, using it as their base for a winter campaign. General Sheridan planned the expedition and ordered the soldiers to strike boldly. Colonel Custer led the Seventh Cavalry south from Fort Supply with the help of two Osage scouts and one man named California Joe. They traveled across a cold plain of blowing snow until their scouts reported finding a village of fifty-one tipis.

Custer caught Black Kettle and his band of Cheyenne off guard in the predawn hours of November 27, 1868. Situated near the banks of the Washita River in western Indian Territory, the Cheyenne village had no scouts to guard it. The people failed to notice Custer's advance to their very door. On this occasion, Custer followed orders but moved rapidly against the Cheyenne without reconnoitering the area. Custer killed 102 men, women, and children. Custer later claimed to have killed 103 warriors, but the Cheyenne say that this number, like Custer's ego, was inflated. Cheyenne warriors set up a line of defense behind a few trees and logs near the river and tried to shield their families so they could escape down river where many more Indians had camped. Some of the Indians made their way down river to alert others about the attack, but many died, including Black Kettle and his wife.

According to Kiowa elder Harding Big Bow, the night before the attack, two Kiowas, Big Bow and White Bear, were returning to their village and made camp. One man had a premonition that something dangerous was about to happen, so the men made no fire and hobbled their horses close to camp. Early the next morning they heard gunfire, so they gathered their bedding and raced off in the direction of the gunfire. Not far away they found Black Kettle's village under attack, so Big Bow rode in one direction around the outside of the soldiers, while White

Bear did the same in the other direction. Big Bow and White Bear killed and wounded soldiers as they raced around the circle. When they met each other, White Bear asked Big Bow if he had seen a soldier wearing a metal mask. Big Bow said that he had not seen such a bluecoat, but if he did, he would try to kill him.

Off they raced again in a wide circle, and this time Big Bow found the masked soldier and charged him. The soldier knocked Big Bow from his horse, but by the time Big Bow recovered his footing on the ground, he had placed an arrow into his bow and fired point blank at the soldier. Big Bow's arrow flew through a slot in the mask, through the soldier's eye, and into his brain. Big Bow mounted again and rode off to fight more soldiers and help some Cheyenne escape the carnage. Later that day, Big Bow and White Bear were joined by Kiowa, Comanche, Cheyenne, and Arapaho warriors who came to challenge Custer. However, by nightfall Custer began a march toward the Indian villages, so many returned home to protect their families. Custer quickly turned out of the Washita Valley and onto the plains leading to Fort Supply. The soldiers called this fight the Battle of the Washita, but most Native Americans refer to it as the Massacre of the Washita.

Custer killed eight hundred Cheyenne horses and burned all fifty-one of the tipis before leaving the Washita. He took fifty-three women and children captive, a warning to other Indians of the Southern Plains that they would lose their loved ones if the war continued. General Sheridan considered Custer's campaign the opening phase of a war that would destroy the power of Native Americans on the Southern Plains, and he set out in a blizzard on December 7, 1868, with fifteen hundred men. He returned to the Washita, buried some soldiers, and talked with Kiowa leaders Lone Wolf and Satanta, taking them prisoner for not agreeing outright to move their villages to Fort Cobb. Sheridan threatened to hang them both, but enough Kiowas came into Fort Cobb to placate the young general. On Christmas Day, some of Sheridan's men surprised a Kiowa and Comanche village at Soldier Springs, destroying the village and serving notice that no village was safe from attack unless it was located near an American fort.

By the end of December, most Arapaho, Kiowa, Comanche, and Kiowa-Apache had surrendered at Fort Cobb. Although some Cheyenne had ended the fight, far more remained west of the Wichita Mountains, moving freely and avoiding the soldiers. Some Comanches belonging to the Quahada band led by Quanah Parker, the son of Peta Nocona and Cynthia Ann Parker, remained free on the Llano Estacado (Staked Plains). In January 1869, many Indians moved south from Fort Cobb to the eastern edge of the Wichita Mountains, where Colonel Benjamin Grierson and his famous Tenth Cavalry of African-American soldiers built Fort Sill. For a time, several Kiowas, Comanches, and Kiowa-Apaches settled down on the reservation, after Sheridan's devastating winter campaign.

Quanah Parker and one of his wives stand on the front porch of their ranch house. After leading the Quahada Comanche band during the Red River Wars, Quanah became an important reservation leader, maintaining elements of his culture. He is credited with bringing the Peyote religion to the Southern Plains.

Soldiers continued to patrol the region, venturing out now and then in an attempt to round up those native people who refused to join the others on the reservation, including Comanches and Cheyennes and others who left the reservation in search of freedom on the Great Plains. When several Cheyenne told Custer they would surrender at Fort Cobb, the elite warrior society of Dog Soldiers moved north to join the Lakota in their war effort. However, not all Indians remained on the reservations. In 1870, the lack of food forced many people to leave the reservations. The people returning to the Plains found thousands of bloating carcasses of buffalo, slaughtered only for their hides by infamous buffalo hunters.

Native Americans considered the buffalo to be sacred, an animal person who played an important role in the oral narratives, rituals, and ceremonies of many tribes. Plains Indians lived because buffalo sacrificed themselves for the people, but the animal meant far more to them than food. The buffalo was central to Plains Indian religion, history, culture, literature, and economy. A buffalo had brought the sacred pipe to several tribes, offering the pipe as a gift from the Creator, a link between the secular and the spiritual worlds. Indian people wondered what manner of human being would exterminate so many animals just for their hide and not for their meat. They wondered how native people would fare under the thumb of white people who had no respect for buffalo. And they wondered what repercussions they might suffer as a result of the buffalo slaughter, not only in terms of food and diet but also in terms of spirituality. Clearly white men had severely threatened the sacred circle of the earth and the spiritual world.

With renewed vigor, Indians struck white settlements, stealing horses, cattle, and weapons. Kiowas, Cheyennes, Comanches, Arapahoes, and others attacked, killing or wounding anyone who stood in their way. Kiowa leaders Satanta, Big Tree, and Satank struck Jacksboro, Texas, destroying a wagon train and killing some drivers. White officials arrested them on the reservation and sent them in shackles to Texas for trial, even though they were "wards" of the federal government, not the state government. Soldiers placed them in a wagon, and Satank sang the death song of his warrior society.

> *O sun you remain forever*
> *but we Ko-eet-senko must die.*
> *O earth you remain forever*
> *but we Ko-eet-senko must die.*

Satank slipped the shackles from his hands, grabbed a concealed knife, stabbed a guard, and tried to fire a rifle. Before it discharged, a soldier shot him to death.

Satanta and Big Tree arrived in Texas, where a jury of white males in Jacksboro sentenced them to hang. The governor commuted their sentences to life in prison. Kiowas appealed to the federal government to return their leaders, which the bureaucrats agreed to do after Kiowas and Comanches promised to remain on the reservation in Indian Territory. Their arrival back on the reservation did not end conflict but rather seemed to prolong it. Several Indians left the reservation, spreading war across the Southern Plains. This was their last stand, their last attempt to drive white invaders from their lands and live as their grandfathers and grandmothers before them.

As in the past, the Indians struck whites wherever and whenever they could. According to Kicking Bird, a group of Kiowas found a survey party "making lines, setting up sticks and stones with marks on them." The Indians did "not know what it means, but we are afraid it is not for our good." After pulling up a survey stake, Kiowa warrior Mamnti told the others that whites "make this medicine over all the land" and that it was "bad medicine." He knew that the stakes meant that whites "will take the land away from us, just as they have already taken our hunting grounds." The Kiowas, having interpreted the white man's medicine correctly, killed the surveyors.

The major fights of the Red River Wars on the Southern Plains were between native and cavalry units, both moving rapidly from place to place for months. General Nelson A. Miles tried to defeat Native Americans of the Southern Plains, and the Indians resisted. Several cavalry units moved against the Indians, and those under Colonel Ranald Mackenzie were most effective in keeping the pressure on the Quahada band of Comanches. Between August and December 1874, the army prosecuted a vigorous war, riding in many directions in pursuit of bands until every one of them surrendered. A few white men walked into Quanah Parker's camp and urged him to surrender. Not long afterward, the Comanche leader surrendered. His was the last band to come in, but Quanah Parker continued his resistance on the reservation for the rest of his life.

In the aftermath of the Red River Wars, the military sought to punish most native leaders. The oral histories of Kiowas and Comanches describe how leaders were disarmed, stripped naked, and placed into cramped stables at Fort Sill and Fort Reno, where soldiers fed them raw meat and slop. Soldiers took everything the leaders owned, including horses, weapons, and pipes. The soldiers placed the men in shackles and treated them as prisoners of war. The army sent thirty-three Cheyennes, twenty-six Kiowas, nine Comanches, and two Arapahoes to prison at Fort Marion in St. Augustine, Florida. Lieutenant Richard H. Pratt took charge of these prisoners, earning the respect of the Indian prisoners by protecting and caring for them. Those Indians who lived through epidemics of tuberculosis and other diseases returned to their people in 1878. Pratt went on to establish Carlisle Indian School in Pennsylvania, where many native children died of tuberculosis and pneumonia.

Although the military defeat of the Kiowas, Comanches, Kiowa-Apaches, Arapahoes, and Cheyennes ended the Red River Wars, there were other resistance movements on the Southern Plains. One of the more unusual and least known was that of Kickapoos, Mescalero Apaches, and Lipan Apaches who fled the long arm of the United States. Elements of these tribes had moved into Coahuila and Chihuahua, Mexico, across the Rio Grande from Texas and New Mexico. After moving from Indiana and Illinois into Missouri and Kansas, a large group of Kickapoo had moved into Texas and Mexico in 1852 and become known as the Mexican Kickapoo. In 1865, Texans crossed the border and attacked the Mexican Kickapoo village on the Concho River, triggering a bloody campaign. Between 1865 and 1873, Kickapoos killed hundreds of Texans, kidnapped children, and stole anything of value from the Texans. Some Mescalero and Lipan Apaches also joined the war. In 1873, the U.S. Army invaded Mexico and attacked the Kickapoos in the Battle of Remolino.

Colonel Ranald Mackenzie led the Fourth Cavalry into Mexico, striking and burning several Kickapoo and Apache villages and killing and wounding people. African-American cavalrymen and Seminole–African-American scouts attacked Indians south of the border. Mackenzie extended his fight against Lipan and Mescalero Apaches. The attacks caused a minor controversy as the United States violated the border of another nation. Eventually, Mexico and the United States worked out an agreement whereby each could ask permission to cross the other's border in pursuit of Indians. The agreement would be refined in the years ahead to allow Generals George Crook and Nelson A. Miles to chase Apaches into the Sierra Madres.

During the Battle of Remolino, Mackenzie and his soldiers killed men, women, and children. Robert Utley has written that "Remolino is one of the rare instances in which the Regular Army stands convicted of warring purposely, rather than incidentally or accidentally, on women and children." And in the aftermath of the raid, Mackenzie took hostages–fifty women and children. He forced them to Fort Gibson, sending a message to Kickapoo warriors that if they wanted to reunite with their wives, mothers, and children, they had to surrender in Indian Territory. A total of 317 Kickapoos moved to Indian Territory immediately, and another 115 joined their people two years later when they relocated on the Sac and Fox Reservation. At least another four hundred Kickapoos remained in Mexico, and some of them settled on a reservation in the Santa Rosa Mountains of eastern Chihuahua. By 1876, the Indian wars had ended on the Southern Plains, but Native Americans on the Northern Plains continued to resist through armed conflict.

NATIVE RESISTANCE ON THE NORTHERN PLAINS

Hancock's war of 1867 stirred up Indian resistance across the Great Plains and complicated negotiations with several tribes on the Northern Plains. Transportation to and through the region was an issue of utmost importance in the United States during Reconstruction. Transportation systems were a significant element of manifest destiny as the United States redirected its attention away from the devastation of the Civil War and reoriented itself toward nation building. In 1864, Congress had passed a bill reducing government interest rates on loans to railroads, increasing land grants to transcontinental railroad companies, and increasing to one million the number of shares that the companies could sell. Money flowed into the Central Pacific and Union Pacific railroad companies and others. But a major issue was rights of way through Indian lands, so commissioners set out to negotiate with the Northern Plains tribes.

In 1865, federal negotiators, including General Grenville Dodge, approached some Lakota and Cheyenne about a peace agreement that would include rights of way through their lands. Not enough leaders attended the council, so another was held in 1866. Oglala and Brule Sioux led by Red Cloud met commissioners at Fort Laramie, but they refused to discuss rights of way through Lakota country until the soldiers withdrew from and ended white use of the Bozeman Trail, which ran northwest from Fort Laramie along the Powder River and Big Horn Mountains. The trail moved across the Yellowstone River, over Bozeman Pass, and into the new mining town of Virginia City, Montana. This was prime buffalo-hunting grounds for the Lakota, and the Indians wanted whites out of the region. Red Cloud warned whites to stay off the Bozeman Trail, and he refused to negotiate further until whites withdrew.

The army ignored Red Cloud's warnings. Colonel Henry B. Carrington led a force of cavalry and infantry into the Powder River region to protect white miners, merchants, and travelers on the Bozeman Trail. His men built Fort C. F. Smith, Fort Phil Kearny, and Fort Reno along the trail. To the Indians, this was an invasion of their land and a flagrant disregard for native rights, so they responded with hostility. Lakota warriors under Red Cloud and other leaders attacked whites attempting to use the Bozeman Trail, as well as soldiers sent to protect the miners. Between 1866 and 1868, they were often able to close all traffic on the Bozeman Trail, literally choking off access to the road for weeks at a time.

In December 1866, between fifteen hundred and two thousand warriors prepared to strike hard at the U.S. Army stationed at Fort Phil Kearny in northern Wyoming. On December 21, a young Lakota warrior named Crazy Horse rode toward the post, inviting the soldiers to come out and fight, while another group attacked a military wagon train out gathering wood. Captain William J. Fetterman led eighty troopers after Crazy Horse and a few other warriors, riding pell mell over a ridge right into an Indian ambush. This was an old decoy trick, one that generally did not work, but on this occasion, it worked perfectly. A Lakota holy man had predicted that one hundred soldiers would die, and he was nearly correct. Lakotas killed Fetterman and all his men, scalping and mutilating their bodies.

The soldiers called the disaster the Fetterman Massacre, whereas Native Americans usually call it the Fetterman Fight. The Fetterman battle touched off a national debate over American Indian policy. The great generals of the time—Philip Sheridan, William Sherman, John Pope, and others—wanted to destroy the Indians militarily. Sherman urged the United States to "act with vindictive earnestness against the Sioux, even to their extermination, men, women, and children." Reformers such as Senator Doolittle disagreed and wanted to negotiate with the tribes. Han-

*Red Cloud led his people against the United States
and refused to negotiate with the soldiers until they
agreed to remove troops from the Powder River
region.*

cock's campaign was a complete failure for the army on the Northern and
Southern Plains, and the general's bullying techniques—like the murdering actions of Chivington—triggered more killings and war. Hancock's
war and the presence of whites in Indian country contributed to a continuation of conflict.

After Fetterman's defeat, soldiers did not withdraw from forts guard-
ing the Bozeman Trail. However, in spite of their presence, the bluecoats
were not in control of the Northern Plains. Lakota warriors and their
Cheyenne and Arapaho allies had the upper hand. They attacked travelers and soldiers at will after the Fetterman Fight, although not always as
effectively. On August 1, 1867, for example, warriors attacked soldiers
and civilians working at a hayfield not far from Fort C. F. Smith. Their intent was to drive the soldiers from the fort by attacking a vulnerable

group of whites. According to historian Joel Hyer, during the Hayfield Fight, whites effectively resisted the large Indian assault because of superior firepower and large quantities of ammunition. The Civil War had given birth to modern warfare and weapons, and repeating rifles were far more efficient at killing and wounding than were arrows, clubs, and lances. Technological advances in armaments and ammunitions contributed to the decline of the Plains tribes.

The Lakota retreated after the Hayfield Fight, only to regroup and attack a detachment from Fort Phil Kearny the very next day. On August 2, 1867, Lakota warriors attacked woodcutters from Fort Phil Kearny and once again were repulsed because of superior weapons and ample ammunition. During the Wagon Box Fight, Captain J. N. Powell fought from a mule corral made of discarded wooden wagons, turned on their sides and arranged in a circle. From this barricade, Powell's men fought off frontal assaults and sniping. He had learned from the Fetterman Fight not to leave the wagon boxes and pursue small bands of warriors. Powell waited for reinforcements from Fort Phil Kearny, and troops ultimately rescued him.

By the spring of 1868, the Lakota leadership returned to Fort Laramie to talk with whites. In April, Lakota and Cheyenne met with the Peace Commission to negotiate treaties acceptable to Native Americans and whites. The commissioners agreed to Red Cloud's demand of 1866 to remove travelers and forts from the Bozeman Trail. Essentially, the federal government agreed to close the road and recognize Lakota rights to hunt buffalo along the Powder River and Big Horn Mountains. Lakota and Cheyenne agreed to move onto reservations within the borders of Montana, Wyoming, and Dakota territories. They could return to their buffalo grounds to hunt, in this way maintaining their sovereignty and economy. Native leaders agreed to end their conflict with the United States and permit wagon roads and railroads to be built across the Northern Plains. Historian Angie Debo claimed that this provision was "slipped in" and that Native Americans did not understand the phrase "other works of utility and necessity."

In any case, this provision permitted roads, surveys, and railroads and caused great conflict as whites opened new transportation routes across the Northern Plains. The growth in roads, railroads, and telegraph across the Great Plains also facilitated the rapid movement of troops from one point to another. Well-traveled roads enabled cavalry units to ride from place to place with maps designating important landmarks, water holes, and areas of danger. The army could move troops far more rapidly by railroad than by horseback, and soldiers could send messages by telegraph, requesting reinforcements, supplies, arms, and ammunitions. New technology on the Great Plains contributed to the success of whites and the destruction of Plains Indian cultures.

Although the Lakota and Cheyenne secured for themselves a good portion of their lands and their hunting grounds, the Fort Laramie Treaty of 1868 did not end conflict. If anything, the treaty opened the Northern Plains to greater expansion and triggered a series of clashes between Indians and whites. Settlers, surveyors, miners, freighters, traders, workmen, and others invaded the region. As railroad construction moved across the plains north of the Platte River, an entourage of gamblers, whiskey salesmen, prostitutes, and other entrepreneurs tagged along to tempt soldiers, scouts, and Indians to engage in closer social contact. Inevitably, trouble arose, and most often whites took the side of other whites, standing collectively against what historian Ray Allen Billington called the "Indian Barrier."

Lakota, Cheyenne, and other native people argue that whites violated the treaty, trespassed onto Indian lands, stole native livestock, destroyed water holes and natural resources, and violated Indian rights. Also important to the Indians was the destruction of the northern buffalo herd. Like Native Americans living on the Southern Plains, those on the Northern Plains revered the buffalo and used it as their source of food, shirts, blouses, dresses, coats, bedding, blankets, and tipi covers. They used the hides for leather, which they fashioned into pipe bags, tobacco pouches, parfleches, shields, moccasins, rattles, winter counts (hide drawings depicting historical events), gun cases, saddle blankets, belts, boots, leggings, dolls, headdresses, reins, ropes, saddles, and a host of other items. They used buffalo bones for whistles, hoes, awls, needles, knives, and scrapers. The buffalo were significant to the physical and spiritual well-being of Plains Indians, and the destruction of the buffalo harmed them psychologically.

As railroad workers moved west across the Northern Plains, they hired hunters to feed hungry work crews. Railroad companies employed full-time hunters who shot hundreds of buffalo. In addition, as trains moved west, travelers used huge rifles to kill buffalo casually grazing near the tracks. They shot buffalo from seats through windows in the train cars, or they stepped onto the prairie to blast them. Even more destructive were professional buffalo hunters who roamed the plains following the herds so they could slaughter the buffalo, skin the animals, and secure great quantities of hides, which they hauled to railheads and shipped east to be processed into leather. Military and civilian officials of the U.S. government encouraged the extermination of buffalo herds as a means of destroying Native American cultures and resistance.

Without the buffalo, the Plains Indians would starve, and white politicians, Indian agents, and professional soldiers knew it. They encouraged buffalo hunting in spite of the fact that white hunters violated Indian treaty rights and the sacred link between Native Americans and the buffalo. The latter was of no importance to most whites, who little appreciated native religions. Between 1868 and 1874, Indians on the Northern Plains and whites occasionally clashed with one another; but the major turning point in Indian and white relations on the Northern Plains occurred in 1874. For years whites had speculated that they would find gold in the Black Hills of the Dakotas, and some miners claimed to have braved the Lakota and found gold in the heart of Lakota lands.

Lakota call the Black Hills the Pah Sapa, and the mountains are sacred. Although Indian people traveled to the Black Hills to cut lodge poles for their tipis, they did not violate the sacred mountains. The Black Hills were located in the heart of the Sioux Reservation, as set forth in the Fort Laramie Treaty of 1868. But formal agreements such as treaties rarely prevented the exploitation of natural resources such as gold. So the U.S. Army organized a large expedition to penetrate the Sioux Reservation and investigate the rumors of gold in the Black Hills. On July 2, 1874, Colonel Custer led one thousand men of the Seventh Cavalry and two companies of infantry from Fort Abraham Lincoln, accompanied by miners, engineers, cartographers, and reporters.

Miners found color, and Custer wrote glowing newspaper dispatches about the potential of the Black Hills for farming, ranching, and forestry. Game, fish, and water abounded in the hills, and Custer's reports invited whites to invade the Sioux Reservation. Although President Grant promised to prevent whites from entering Lakota lands, "no army on earth can keep the adventurous men of the west out of them." The editor of the *New York Tribune* was correct. By the summer of 1875, approximately eight hundred miners worked the placers in the Black Hills. The federal government tried to purchase the Black Hills for $6 million, but to many Lakota, the amount of money was not at issue. The government could have offered $600 billion and received the same answer from the Lakota, who despised the duplicity of the government and whites who violated the treaty and spiritual beliefs of the people.

In November 1875, President Grant hosted a meeting at the White House, including Secretary of Interior Zachariah Chandler, Secretary of War William W. Belknap, Commissioner of Indian Affairs E. P. Smith, and Generals George Crook and Sheridan. Although they kept no minutes of their meeting, they decided to abrogate part of the Treaty of Fort Laramie by withdrawing troops from the Black Hills and allowing miners into the region. They also determined to force Lakota bands onto the reservation where the army could control them. When the troops left the Black Hills, the population of miners swelled to roughly fifteen thousand. The Northern Pacific Railroad snaked steadily westward from Minneapolis, and Lakota people felt pressured from all sides. Indian runners warned Lakota leaders to settle onto the reservation by February 1, 1876, or face the army. Most Lakotas ignored the ultimatum, and many left the reservation when they learned of the threat. The United States pushed the Lakota into war.

Generals Sherman, Sheridan, Crook, and Terry anticipated war. They knew that the chances of the Lakota backing down from their right to protect their lands and obeying an order of the United States to move onto the reservation were slim to none. So they used the winter of 1875–1876 to plan their upcoming campaign. It did not surprise them that the February deadline for the Lakota to move onto the reservation came and went without compliance, so they set their troops into motion. At the same time, the Lakota and their Cheyenne and Arapaho allies began preparations for war. Crazy Horse of the Oglala, Sitting Bull, Black Moon, and Gall of the Hunkpapa group of Teton Sioux, and Lame Deer and Hump of the Miniconjous gathered their men and discussed the coming conflict. Cheyenne under Charcoal Bear, Lame White Man, and Dirty Moccasins joined the discussions, as remnants of Brule, Yanktonais, and Santee Sioux joined in the war effort with Sans Arc and Blackfeet.

The Hunkpapas held their annual sun dance in June 1876 on Rosebud Creek, where Sitting Bull had a vision of several bluecoat soldiers "falling right into our camp." When the sacred rite concluded, the Indians moved closer to the Little Bighorn River, where they soon learned that Colonel Crook was operating close by, on the Rosebud. In March 1876, Crook had left Fort Fetterman along the Bozeman Trail and had twice engaged Lakota warriors and destroyed over one hundred tipis, setting fire to the lodges. On June 16, Crook met his match as the Lakota and their allies engaged his soldiers in the Battle of the Rosebud. The warriors mauled the soldiers so badly that Crook retreated to Fort Fetterman, where he waited for reinforcements. Crook was not operating by himself, however, because he was part of a much larger military movement.

General Alfred Terry moved west from Fort Abraham Lincoln to the Big Horn River, where the army believed it would find and engage the Lakota. Terry's column included Colonel Custer's Seventh Cavalry. Colonel John Gibbon led a third column that marched east from Fort Ellis, Montana. Columns under Crook, Terry, and Gibbon were to meet at the confluence of the Yellowstone and Powder rivers. Crow, Arikara, and Shoshoni scouts confirmed that the Sioux had gathered at a huge village on the Little Bighorn River. Terry ordered Custer and his mobile Seventh Cavalry to ride quickly to the south end of the Little Bighorn Valley to prevent the Indians from retreating. Gibbon and Terry would move toward the same valley, and the three groups planned to trap their enemy. Custer was to come down the Rosebud and help bottle up the warriors and at the same time prevent their escape.

On June 24, 1876, Custer turned west on a broad Indian trail and did not continue on the Rosebud. The next day, his Indian scouts located a large Indian village from the "Crow's Nest," although Custer said he could not see it. Custer divided his column into four groups and led one of them with 225 men along the Little Bighorn River toward the village that lay in front of him. The Lakota part of the village extended three miles, until it reached the Cheyenne circle of lodges. There were likely between fifteen hundred and three thousand warriors in the village, far more than the entire Seventh Cavalry combined. When warriors received word of advancing troops, they painted themselves and their horses. They gathered their horses and weapons, which now included repeating rifles, including new Winchesters. Off they went to meet their enemy, killing Custer and every one of his men. They also pinned down the other three groups of soldiers, killing and wounding several. On June 27, the warriors withdrew because Terry and Gibbon arrived, saving the lives of half the Seventh Cavalry.

Lakota, Dakota, Cheyenne, and Arapaho participants in the Battle of the Little Bighorn sang and celebrated their victory, but only for a short time. Between 1876 and 1881, the army pursued these people relentlessly, striking them whenever possible and keeping up the pressure until they fled into Canada or removed to the reservation. With the buffalo gone, the people began to starve and freeze to death. Diseases such as measles, smallpox, and whooping cough decimated the people. One by one the leaders surrendered with the hope that the government would abide by its treaty promises to provide Native Americans with food, housing, and medical treatment. Even Crazy Horse and Sitting Bull ultimately had to surrender, but both these men—like so many Native American leaders—continued to resist whites in other ways.

Agents and soldiers considered Crazy Horse an "incorrigible wild man," and some Indians would have agreed. In 1877, Crook feared that Crazy Horse would leave the reservation and organize the younger men into another resistance movement in the Powder River country. Crook ordered Colonel Luther P. Bradley to arrest Crazy Horse, and when a group of soldiers and Indians tried to disarm him, the great Oglala leader was stabbed to death, some say by whites, others say by Indians or his own knife. Years later a similar fate befell Sitting Bull after he was arrested. The wars on the Northern Plains resulted in confinement and cultural calamity for thousands of native people who were forced onto reservations, where they had to contend with disease, starvation, inadequate housing, Christian missionaries, and bureaucratic agents. Life would never be the same for them or their children. Their hearts fell to the ground, but they survived.

This was true of most Native Americans confined to reservations whether or not they had fought the U.S. Army. Hardships were certainly true for Ute Indians who had loyally served as scouts against several different tribes, including the Navajos. By 1876, approximately thirty-six hundred Utes were living peacefully on the White River Reservation in western Colorado when whites decided to liquidate the reservation so that they could steal the land and natural resources. Although Ouray, their leader, encouraged the Utes to acculturate and become more like whites, non-Indians threatened to take their reservation. When Agent

Amos Bad Heart Bull painted this representation of the Battle of Little Bighorn around 1898. On June 25, 1876, Lakota, Cheyenne, and Arapaho warriors defeated Lieutenant Colonel George A. Custer, killing over 250 men to the shock of the citizens of the United States.

Nathan Meeker moved to reduce their lands, an old warrior named Douglas revolted, killing Meeker and eleven other white men. The Utes successfully fought federal and state forces, but in the end agreed to move to the Uinta Reservation in Utah. However, some Utes remained in Colorado. Many forms of Indian resistance emerged in the late nineteenth century, on and off the reservations.

Selected Readings and Bibliography

Since the nineteenth century, historians and writers have been fascinated by Indian warfare, and in the twentieth century, movies depicted the conflicts for a broad audience. Films, books, and new scholarship have captured the imagination of authors who have written extensively about the Indian wars. Several works previously mentioned deal with warfare, including Utley and Washburn's *The Indian Wars,* Utley's *Frontiersmen in Blue,* Berthong's *The Southern Cheyennes,* and Trafzer and Scheuerman's *Renegade Tribe.* These four works survey the era and offer useful details: Champagne, *The Native North American Almanac;* Francis,

Native Time; Gibson, *The American Indian;* and Debo, *History of the Indians of the United States.* Billington's *Westward Expansion,* Mayhall's *The Kiowas,* and Trafzer's *Kit Carson Campaign* were helpful in writing this chapter, as were Dunlay's *Wolves for the Bluecoats,* Harmon's *Sixty Years of Indian Affairs,* and Trennert's *Alternatives to Extinction.*

Andrist, Ralph A. *The Long Death.* New York: Macmillan, 1964.

Berthrong, Donald J. *The Southern Cheyennes.* Norman: University of Oklahoma Press, 1963.

Billington, Ray A. *The Far Western Frontier, 1830–1860.* New York: Harper, 1956.

Doolittle, James R. *Report on the Condition of the Indian Tribes.* Washington, D.C.: U.S. Government Printing Press Office, 1867.

Grinnell, George B. *The Cheyenne Indians.* 2 volumes. New Haven: Yale University Press, 1923.

Hafen, LeRoy R., and Francis M. Young. *Fort Laramie and the Pageant of the West.* Glendale, Calif.: Arthur H. Clark, 1938.

Hagan, William T. "How the West Was Lost." *Indians in American History.* Frederick E. Hoxie, ed. (Arlington Heights, Ill.: Harlan Davidson, 1988) pp. 179–202.

Horsman, Reginald. *Race and Manifest Destiny.* Cambridge: Harvard University Press, 1981.

Hyde, George E. *Red Cloud's Folk.* Norman: University of Oklahoma Press, 1957.

——. *Spotted Tail's Folk.* Norman: University of Oklahoma Press, 1961.

Lavender, David. *Bent's Fort.* Garden City, N.Y.: Doubleday, 1954.

Liberty, John, and Margot Liberty. "Stands in Timber": *Cheyenne Memories.* New Haven: Yale University Press, 1967.

Merk, Fredrick. *Manifest Destiny and Mission in American History.* New York: Knopf, 1963.

Montejano, David. *Anglos and Mexicans in the Making of Texas, 1836–1986.* Austin: University of Texas Press, 1987.

Moore, William Haas. *Chiefs, Agents and Soldiers: Conflict on the Navajo Frontier, 1868–1882.* Albuquerque: University of New Mexico Press, 1994.

Olson, James C. *Red Cloud and the Sioux Problem.* Lincoln: University of Nebraska Press, 1965.

Phillips, George H. *Indians and Intruders in Central California, 1769–1849.* Norman: University of Oklahoma Press, 1993.

——. *Indians and Indian Agents: The Origins of the Reservation System in California, 1849–1852.* Norman: University of Oklahoma Press, 1997.

Rohrbough, Malcolm J. *The Trans-Appalachian Frontier.* New York: Oxford University Press, 1978.

Sandoz, Mari. *Crazy Horse.* Lincoln: University of Nebraska Press, 1961.

Unruh, John D. *The Plains Across.* Urbana: University of Illinois Press, 1979.

Utley, Robert M. *Frontier Regulars: The United States Army and the Indian, 1866–1891.* New York: Macmillan, 1982.

——. *The Indian Frontier of the American West, 1846–1890.* Albuquerque: University of New Mexico Press, 1984.

Weeks, Phillip. *Farewell, My Nation.* Arlington Heights, Ill.: H. Davidson, 1990.

Wooster, Robert. *The Military and United States Indian Policy, 1865–1903.* New Haven: Yale University Press, 1988.

Worcester, Donald E. *The Apaches: Eagles of the Southwest.* Norman: University of Oklahoma Press, 1979.

NATIVE AMERICAN RESISTANCE

Between the middle and end of the nineteenth century, several tribes in the American West made their last stands against the U.S. Army, territorial and state militia forces, and white settlers. Fights occurred in every part of the West. Although Native Americans won a series of battles, they lost the larger war against the United States and paid a heavy price. However, native resistance did not end with the Indian wars but rather has continued to the present day. New warriors emerged among many Indian peoples—men and women who continued to resist domination by white settlers, Indian agents, and local law enforcement officials. Native American resistance was and is grounded in a strong tradition that has transcended military conquest because it has always been an integral part of native character and culture. In the last half of the century, elements of many tribes—too numerous to name—fought foreign forces bent on conquest of Native America.

MODOC WAR

During the 1840s and 1850s, miners overran large portions of northern California and southern Oregon, lands belonging to a number of Indian tribes, including the Modoc. Whites not only mined the region, but also established farms, ranches, and towns. In 1851, miners built the small town of Yreka, which was about fifty miles west of Tule Lake, the home of most Modocs. Whites opened transportation systems through the region and encouraged commerce, which brought more whites and threatened the Modoc. When trouble between whites and Modocs increased, the Indian office decided to move the Modoc from northern California to southern Oregon, onto the Klamath Reservation, the home of Klamath Indians, enemies of Modocs. In 1864, the federal government forced Kenitpoos (Captain Jack) and Old Schonchin to move

Modoc bands to the Klamath Reservation. Within a year, Captain Jack and his followers returned to Lost River to find whites inhabiting their homelands.

Captain Jack and the Modocs remained at their home on Lost River until 1869, when whites demanded the government to force Modocs back onto the Klamath Reservation. Oregon Superintendent of Indian Affairs A. B. Meacham, with the help of some drunken soldiers, convinced the Modoc to return to the reservation before whites exterminated them. They remained on the reservation until April 1870, when Captain Jack and seventy followers returned to their homes on Lost River. They bolted because of internal fights with Klamaths and remained in their homeland until T. B. Odeneal received permission from the Office of Indian Affairs to force the Modoc back onto the Klamath Reservation. General Edward R. S. Canby was not eager to force the Modocs from their homes, believing that such an action could trigger war, but in 1872 he authorized his soldiers to aid in the Modoc removal.

When the superintendent and soldiers tried to force the Modocs to move, the Indians fought back, moving to the south end of Tule Lake to take cover in the natural fortress provided by black lava beds. Bands of Modocs under Hooka (Hooker Jim) and Shacknasty Jim joined Captain Jack. Regular and volunteer soldiers fought the Modocs from November 1872 until April 1873, when Captain Jack and other leaders negotiated with the whites. Various Modoc leaders coerced Captain Jack into murdering Canby, calling Captain Jack a coward and poking fun at him until he agreed to assassinate the general. On April 11, Captain Jack met with a peace commission composed of Canby, Meacham, and Methodist minister Eleasar Thomas. During the negotiations, Captain Jack pulled out a pistol and shot Canby in the face while other leaders shot Meacham and Thomas. Canby and Thomas died, but Meacham recovered from seven gunshot wounds.

The Modocs fought in the lava beds until June, when they surrendered. A military commission found Captain Jack and other Modocs guilty of murder and sentenced them to be hanged. On October 3, 1873, the army hanged Captain Jack, Schonchin John, Boston Charley, and Black Jim. The government did not permit Modocs who had participated in the Modoc War to return to the Klamath Reservation but instead exiled them to Indian Territory as punishment for their "crimes." Government officials forced 153 Modocs to be shipped out of northern California to the Quapaw Agency in Indian Territory, where they remained until 1909, when they were allowed to return to the Klamath Reservation. Some Modocs returned to the Oregon reservation, but others remained in Oklahoma, where their descendants live to this day. The groups of Modocs communicate with one another and share a heritage linking them to northern California.

Modoc leader Kenitpoos was better known as Captain Jack. He was one of many chiefs who resisted white encroachment of their lands in northern California and removal to a reservation. Kenitpoos was the only native leader to kill a general of the U.S. Army.

NEZ PERCE AND THE THIEF TREATY

All Native Americans in the West faced the pressures of the white invasion, including Nez Perce. For years the Nez Perce had maintained good relations with whites, helping Lewis and Clark and inviting Spalding to establish a mission at Lapwai. Most Nez Perce remained peaceful during the Cayuse Indian War and Plateau Indian War. During the treaty of 1855, Nez Perce had agreed to a treaty and reservation, securing for themselves a large portion of their traditional homelands in Oregon and Idaho. However, Nez Perce problems with whites blossomed after Ellias D. Pierce and Seth Ferrell invaded their lands without permission and discovered gold in the Bitterroot Mountains of Idaho.

In 1860, Pierce and other whites began mining on the Nez Perce Reservation, and the Indians complained to their agent that whites were illegally mining and establishing towns such as Lewiston, Elk City, and Florence on Indian land in violation of the Nez Perce Treaty of 1855. The Office of Indian Affairs agreed that it would remove the miners from the reservation, and Superintendent of Indian Affairs Calvin Hale and peace commissioners S. D. Howe and Charles Hutchinson met with the Indians during the Lapwai Council of 1863. Several prominent chiefs met with the commissioners, including Old Joseph, White Bird, Eagle from the Light, and Koolkool Snehee. Hale proposed to shrink the reservation by nearly seven million acres, thus liquidating Indian title to all but one-tenth of the reservation.

Hale's proposal was folly to Nez Perce leaders, who refused to surrender an inch of ground. They reminded Hale that they had negotiated the Nez Perce Treaty in good faith and were not going to cede any of their lands. That said, all the leaders from many diverse bands left the Lapwai Council, except a local leader named Lawyer, a Christian Nez Perce who negotiated with Hale. On June 9, Lawyer and fifty-one male members of his band signed a new Nez Perce Treaty that ceded 6,932,270 acres for 8¢ an acre to the United States. The other bands of Nez Perce labeled this the "Thief Treaty" and refused to acknowledge it. Years later Young Chief Joseph reflected the position of most Nez Perce leaders in this parable that appeared in the *North American Review* in 1879:

> Suppose a whiteman should come to me and say, "Joseph, I like your horses, and I want to buy them." Joseph would respond, "my horses suit me, I will not sell them." When Joseph responded that he was not interested in selling his horses, the white man goes to my neighbor, and says to him: "Joseph has some good horses. I want to buy them, but he refuses to sell." My neighbor answers, "Pay me the money, and I will sell you Joseph's horses." The white man returns to me and says, "Joseph, I have bought your horses, and you must let me have them." If we sold our lands to the Government, this is the way they were bought.

Nez Perce leaders who refused to sign the Thief Treaty became known as the nontreaty bands, and most of them renounced Christianity, returning to their native faith. Young Joseph, known to his people as Hinmahtooyahlatkekht (Thunder Rising over Loftier Mountain Heights), led one band of the nontreaty Nez Perce. He promised his dying father never to sell the bones of his parents and ancestors. With the help of Nez Perce Agent John Monteith and Oregon Superintendent of Indian Affairs Odeneal, Commissioner of Indian Affairs H. R. Clum encouraged President Grant to recognize Joseph's claim to land in the Wallowa Valley of northeastern Oregon. On June 16, 1873, Grant issued an executive order to provide the Wallowa band title to its land.

Unfortunately, bureaucrats mistakenly recognized the lower end of the valley as Indian land rather than the upper end of the valley where the Nez Perce lived. Whites had settled the lower end of the valley and were angry at the president's executive order. Rather than clear up the mistake, Grant listened to poor advice from politicians who did not want the government to recognize any Nez Perce lands in the Wallowa Valley.

On June 10, 1875, Grant rescinded his own order. General Oliver O. Howard, commander of the Department of the Columbia, ordered a quick study of the Nez Perce situation and concluded that "it is a great mistake to take from Joseph and his band of Nez Perces Indians that valley." Howard then ordered Major Henry Clay Wood to investigate the Nez Perce legal claim to the land. In his report, *Joseph and His Land Claims, or Status of Young Joseph and His Band of Nez Perce Indians,* Wood wrote that "The non-treaty Nez Perces cannot in law be regarded as bound by the treaty of 1863" and "its provisions are null and void."

Howard, Monteith, Odeneal, and others supported the nontreaty Nez Perce claim that the Thief Treaty was an illegal document and believed that the nontreaty Nez Perce had been misrepresented in the 1863 treaty. Still, they could not prevent the executive branch from forcing the non-reservation Indians onto the reservation. The federal government did not aggressively move to force the nontreaty Nez Perce onto the Idaho reservation until 1876, when Lakota, Cheyenne, and Arapaho warriors wiped out Custer. The Battle of the Little Bighorn during the centennial year of American independence brought a national cry to round up all non-reservation Indians and force them to reservations before more soldiers lost their lives fighting Indians. In 1876, the War Department ordered General Howard to force the nontreaty bands of Nez Perce onto the reservation. Regardless of his own views, Howard had to comply with the order or resign.

GENERAL HOWARD "SHOWS THE RIFLE"

In November 1876, Howard convened a council at Fort Lapwai to order the Nez Perce onto the reservation. According to Nez Perce warrior Yellow Wolf, this was when Howard showed the people the rifle and threatened to kill the people if they did not move onto the reservation. During the Lapwai Council of 1876, Chief Joseph told Howard that "The Creative Power, when he made the earth, made no marks, no lines of division or separation on it." He explained that the earth was his mother and that he "was made of the earth and grew up on its bosom." The earth, Joseph said, is "too sacred to be valued by or sold for silver or gold." Although Howard had been supportive of the Nez Perce claim, the "Christian general" did not like "Indian Joseph and his malcontents," who practiced a "new-fangled religious delusion" practiced by "wizards" and "magicians." Joseph refused to give up his land, saying, "We will not sell the land. We will not give up the land. We love the land; it is our home."

The Lapwai Council of 1876 ended with no resolution. Joseph remained patient and sure that reason would prevail. Howard prepared for war, ordering troops and supplies up the Columbia River to Fort Walla Walla. Howard and Monteith also made plans to force the nontreaty Indians to Indian Territory. Through his brother Ollocot, Joseph asked for another meeting with Howard. On May 3, 1877, the nontreaty people–including Nez Perce and Palouse–met with Howard at the second Lapwai Council. The Indians appointed a holy man named Toohoolhoolzote to speak for them because they were addressing issues relating to the earth. Toohoolhoolzote spoke long and eloquently about Indian law and the "chieftainship of the earth." Howard became angry at the "cross-grained growler," a man the general described as an "ugly, obstinate savage of the worst type."

Toohoolhoolzote explained that he had "heard of a bargain, a trade between some of these Indians and the white men concerning their land" but that he had never sold his land and never would. For hours the Nez Perce leader laid out the special relationship of man and earth, until Howard replied: "Twenty times over you repeat that the earth is your mother, and about the chieftainship of the earth. Let us hear it no more, but come to business at once." Howard told the Indians that they had no choice but to move onto the reservation or face war. Toohoolhoolzote replied that "The earth is part of my body, and I never gave up the earth." When Howard persisted with his demand for removal to the reservation, Toohoolhoolzote asked, "What person pretends to divide the land, and put me on it?" Howard fired back, "I am that man. I stand here for the President, and there is no spirit good or bad that will hinder me. My orders are plain, and will be executed."

Toohoolhoolzote warned Howard that he was "trifling with the law of the earth" and concluded by saying that the others "may do what they like, but I am not going to the reservation." Howard stepped forward with Captain David Perry to arrest Toohoolhoolzote. The old man asked, "Do you want to scare me in reference to my body?" Howard replied that "I will leave your body with Captain Perry." The soldiers took Toohoolhoolzote to jail, and Howard turned to the Nez Perce leaders and asked if they were going to comply with his order. Joseph later said that Howard was like the grizzly bear and the Indians were like the deer. Joseph's nephew, Yellow Wolf, said that Howard had "showed the people the rifle." Every nontreaty leader in attendance reluctantly agreed to move peacefully onto the reservation, including two Palouse Indian leaders, Husishusis Kute and Hahtalekin.

Nez Perce and Palouse returned to their home to gather their belongings, horses, and cattle and begin moving to the reservation. Before surrendering at the agency headquarters at Lapwai, many bands gathered for a last taste of freedom, on the Camas Prairie near present-day Grangeville, Idaho. Everyone was upset and depressed about leaving the lands of their grandparents, leaving the lands that held the bones of their ancestors, but they could not avoid it without war. Younger men spoke out for war, painting themselves and their horses, parading about the camp in mock preparation for war. One teenager, Wahlitits, joined in the parades and was berated by a man and his wife when his horse trampled camas roots they had set out to dry in the sun.

The man and his wife scolded Wahlitits for pretending to be a warrior, saying that if he were really a warrior he would avenge his father's murder at the hands of a white man. The year before, Larry Ott had murdered the young man's father, Eagle Robe. Before dying, Eagle Robe had implored his family not to seek revenge. Now, distraught over this reprimand, Wahlitits avenged his father's death. With two other boys, Swan Necklace and Red Moccasin Tops, Wahlitits rode off to kill Ott. When they could not find Ott, they killed three white men and wounded another who had harassed the Nez Perce. Young men from White Bird's band learned of these deeds and joined in the killing. War resulted.

NEZ PERCE RESISTANCE

When word reached the Camas Prairie that war had started, all the leaders packed their belongings and moved. Some of them criticized Joseph for his patience and belief that he could reason with whites. While the others rode off to join other bands, Joseph and Ollocot remained in their camp to discuss their course of action. Both men believed that war was futile and that women and children needlessly would die. Yet they could not walk away from the other nontreaty bands. In a council they decided to join the war effort and moved into White Bird Canyon, where they planned negotiations with the bluecoats who would surely come.

Much has been written about Chief Joseph as a great war leader, and some white historians have dubbed him the Red Napoleon. Students have stated that his war tactics are taught at military schools, including West Point. Chief Joseph participated in the entire war of 1877, using a rifle at times to protect his people and resist the soldiers. But he was not an Indian general or a war chief. Joseph was an articulate civilian leader who watched over elders, women, and children, using his innate wisdom to resolve conflicts and negotiate with people. When Captain David Perry rode into White Bird Canyon on June 17, 1877, Joseph was standing near a white flag hoping to talk, but fighting began when mounted Idaho volunteers fired on the Indians. The Nez Perce struck hard during the Battle of White Bird Canyon, killing thirty-four men, wounding others, and chasing the soldiers back to Fort Lapwai.

Between June and October, the Nez Perce and Palouse fought the soldiers many times as they took the Lolo Trail over the Bitterroot Mountains into Montana and decided to join the Crows on the Great Plains. When the Nez Perce and Palouse reached Montana, they could have easily traveled north through the Bitterroot Valley to the Flathead Indian country and moved north into the Grandmother Country of Canada.

However, Looking Glass was leading the people, and he had spent a lot of time hunting and camping with the Crows. He believed the Crows to be his friends and reasoned that because the whites wanted Nez Perce land and now had possession of it, the whites would allow the Nez Perce and Palouse to live on the plains. Looking Glass could not have known that his reasoning was flawed. The United States not only wanted Indian lands but also wanted to punish the people for resisting.

From the eastern end of the Lolo Trail, the Nez Perce and Palouse traveled south to Big Hole, Montana, where they rested at an old campground they had used many times on their way to the buffalo country. Wootolen, an elder, told the people that he had dreamed of soldiers coming right into camp. Many people urged Looking Glass to send scouts back along the trail, but he refused. "All right, Looking Glass," Five Wounds said, "You are one of the Chiefs! I have no wife, no children to be placed fronting the danger that I feel coming to us. Whatever the gains, whatever the loss, it is yours." Early on the morning of August 9, 1877, Hahtalekin left his tipi to check his horses and heard soldiers about. He sounded the alarm, and soldiers shot him to death. His son, Five Fogs, came out of the tipi, standing his ground and firing his arrows. Soldiers shot him down.

In the middle of the night, Colonel John Gibbon and his men crawled forward to the edge of the village. In the gray predawn hours, the Battle of the Big Hole began. Chaos ensued as women and children ran for cover and men grabbed their weapons. Wounded Head reported that the fight played out "Hand to hand, club to club. All mixed up, warriors and soldiers fought. It was a bloody battle." Women hid their children in buffalo robes and blankets. Some burned to death when soldiers set fire to the tipis, while others survived. Eelahweemah (About Asleep), or David Williams, later reported that "Seven of us—five women, my little brother, and myself—were in the shallow gully where my father had directed us. It was not deep, and when the soldiers saw us they began shooting at us." He watched the soldier shoot his mother, Tumokult (I Block Up), and when he looked up, "All the other four women lay dead or bad wounded!" He and his brother ran for their lives while "soldiers fired at us."

Pahit Palikt was also there and "saw and heard lots of Indian men and women crying. Oh, lots of them crying! Crying loud, mournful." He saw "so many women and children lying on the ground. I wondered if they were sleeping so. Afterward I understood." His parents carried him away, and they joined Chief Joseph, who quickly organized the escape of women, children, elders, and wounded, while warriors beat back the soldiers and charged their mountain howitzer. The people lost between sixty and ninety dead and many more wounded at the Big Hole. They buried as many as possible and mourned in their own way.

From the Big Hole, the Nez Perce and Palouse entered Yellowstone National Park. Lean Elk led the people after the battle, moving into Crow country only to learn that the Crows wanted nothing to do with their troubles. In council, the Indians determined to flee to Canada, and many hoped that Sitting Bull, who had escaped into Canada, would come south to help them. The people moved rapidly, fighting a few engagements but always escaping. Along the way they purchased goods from white store-keepers and gave no one any trouble unless they tried to impede the escape. Howard followed the Indians into Montana and was sorely criti-cized for not capturing the Nez Perce and Palouse. Newspaper corre-spondents dogged the general, asking him when he would capture Joseph. Howard replied that he would have his man "the day after to-morrow." When a few Nez Perce read the newspaper account, they laughed and began calling Howard "The Day after Tomorrow."

SURRENDER AT THE BEAR PAW

As the Nez Perce neared the Canadian border, Looking Glass gained the leadership of the group. Scouts had reported that Howard was far behind them, so the people felt safe in camping briefly at the Bear Paw Moun-tains in northern Montana, just forty miles away from the Canadian bor-der. The people were cold, sick, and exhausted, so they rested. They did not know that Howard had telegraphed a message to Nelson A. Miles at Fort Keogh, telling him to cut off the Nez Perce retreat. With Cheyenne scouts, Miles rode pell mell and found the Indian village at Bear Paw. He attacked immediately and engaged in a bloody battle. He pinned down the Indians and arranged a council with Joseph on October 1, 1877. Miles demanded an unconditional surrender, and Joseph negotiated for a con-ditional surrender that would allow the men to keep their weapons and permit everyone to return to the Nez Perce Reservation without punish-ment for the war.

Joseph and Miles agreed to disagree. Howard arrived at Bear Paw on October 5, and almost immediately Meopkowit (Old George) and Jokais (Captain John), two treaty Nez Perce serving as scouts for Howard, rode into Joseph's camp and announced that the soldiers wanted "no more war!" This information provided the Nez Perce an honorable way to end the war, because the army asked for peace. "We were not captured," Yel-low Wolf later reported. "It was a draw battle." The Indians believed that they were making a conditional surrender whereby they would return to Idaho. During negotiations with Miles, the colonel stated, "If you will come and give up your arms, I will spare your lives and send you back to the reservation."

On October 5, Joseph told his people—numbering 87 men, 184 women, and 147 children—that "Our people are out on the hills, naked and freezing. The women are suffering with cold, the children crying with the chilly dampness of the shelter pits." Joseph concluded that "For myself I do not care. It is for them I am going to surrender." Rather than surrender, some people fled quietly into Canada, including Chief White Bird and Joseph's nephew, Yellow Wolf, who left with Joseph's twelve-year-old daughter. Ollocot, Looking Glass, Hahtalekin, Rainbow, Toohoolhoolzote, Lean Elk, and other leaders were dead. Many others, particularly women, children, and elders, were dead.

Ollocot's wife, Wetatonmi, survived to flee into Canada. Years later she told L. V. McWhorter: "Husband dead, friends buried or held prisoner. I felt that I was leaving all that I had but I did not cry. You know how you feel when you lose kindred and friends through sickness-death. You do not care if you die. With us it was worse. Strong men, well women, and little children killed and buried. They had not done wrong to be so killed." On the night of October 6, with others by her side, Wetatonmi wept as she "walked silently on into the wintry night." Their departure from the Bear Paw "was with heavy hearts, broken spirits." Late the next day, Joseph surrendered.

Before sundown on October 7, Joseph mounted a black horse and rode up a small hill to meet Miles and Howard. His hair was in braids, and a gray blanket riddled with bullet holes draped his shoulders. He rode slowly with his hand crossed over the pommel of his saddle. When he reached the two soldiers, Joseph swung off his horse, offering his rifle to Howard, who waved him over to Miles, who accepted the weapon. Yellow Wolf witnessed the surrender and said that "Chief Joseph said, 'Now we all understand these words, and we will go with General Miles.'" Then Miles told Joseph, "No more battles and blood! From this sun, we will have good time on both sides, your band and mine. We will have plenty time for sleep, for good rest. We will drink good water from this time on where the war is stopped."

Howard told Joseph, "You have your life. I am living. I have lost my brothers. Many of you have lost brothers." Yellow Wolf watched as "chiefs and officers crossed among themselves and shook hands all around. The Indians lifted their hands towards the sky, where the sun was then standing." Then the Indians said, "No more battles! No more war!" Yellow Wolf reported that this "was all I saw and heard of chiefs' and generals' ending the war." Lieutenant Charles Erskine Scott Wood provided a newspaper with Joseph's surrender speech, creating a myth that Joseph delivered the eloquent speech attributed to him. Although Joseph's heart was "sick and sad" and he wanted to "fight no more forever," he did not give the speech so often quoted in books and films.

The Nez Perce and Palouse who surrendered at Bear Paw gave up their weapons and gathered their belongings. Soldiers escorted them to Fort Keogh, where they were to spend the winter before returning the next spring to Lapwai. However, General Sherman ordered Miles to take the Indians to Fort Abraham Lincoln, so the soldiers loaded the people onto flatboats that floated down the Yellowstone River to the wide Missouri, which they took to Bismarck, North Dakota. The people of Bismarck treated Joseph as a celebrity, inviting him "to dine with us at the Sheridan House." Sherman ordered Miles to take his hostages by rail to Fort Leavenworth, Kansas, where they arrived on November 24. Miles settled "the 400 miserable, helpless, emaciated specimens of humanity" on the banks of the Missouri River, where they died of malaria. For Miles, the scene brought back visions and "the horrors of Andersonville."

LIFE IN EEKISH PAH

In July 1878, the army turned the people over to the Quapaw Agency, where they remained until the agent transferred them to the newly established Ponca Agency. The Nez Perce and Palouse called the region Eekish Pah, the Hot Place, where they died of disease, depression, and starvation. While they were exiled in Indian Territory, Nez Perce and Palouse leaders visited Washington, D.C., to plead their case. Joseph, Yellow Bull, and Husishusis Kute went to the nation's capital in January 1879, and the first two leaders returned the following March. Joseph met with President Rutherford B. Hayes, Commissioner of Indian Affairs Ezra Hayt, various congressmen, and secretaries who did nothing to effectuate the conditional surrender made at Bear Paw.

Joseph gave an interview to the *North American Review* that appeared in the April issue under the title, "An Indian's View of Indian Affairs." The interview passed from Joseph to interpreter Ad Chapman to the editor, who may have changed the wording. Still, the essence of the article was Joseph's, and it moved many people. The article is one of the best representations of Joseph. "Good words will not give me back my children," Joseph said. "Good words will not make good the promises of your War Chief, General Miles. Good words will not give my people good health and stop them from dying." Words would not bring back the dead or give the Nez Perce "a home where they can live in peace and take care of themselves."

Between 1879 and 1885, several people, including Mrs. James A. Garfield, Senator Henry L. Dawes, and Lieutenant Wood, worked to have Congress return the Nez Perce to the Northwest. Churches, women's groups, and wives of prominent politicians pressured Congress to pass an act on July 4, 1884, authorizing the Interior Department to allow the people to return home. On April 29, 1885, Commissioner of Indian Affairs John D. Atkins ordered the removal home. Nez Perce and Palouse leaders ceded their right to land in Indian Territory and traveled by rail to Walula Junction on the Columbia River. Their only regret was to leave the remains of so many loved ones, so many children, in Kansas and Indian Territory. When they arrived in Washington Territory, Special Agent

Chief Joseph and his band of Nez Perce reluctantly joined in the war against the United States in 1877. Joseph was not a "Red Napoleon," but rather a charismatic civilian leader and statesman who tried to negotiate in the best interests of his people. He died on the Colville Reservation, far from his home in the Wallowa Valley.

W. H. Faulkner split the people into two groups, forcing Joseph to take 150 with him to the Colville Reservation and assigning Husishusis Kute to take 118 people to the Nez Perce Reservation. People in Idaho had issued arrest warrants for Joseph and other Nez Perce, so the Indian office refused to allow him to return to Lapwai.

Although the Nez Perce and Palouse had returned home to the Northwest, they were confined to a reservation. Joseph tried to purchase portions of his former homelands, but whites in the Wallowa Valley wanted to remember the Indian past only by their "Chief Joseph Days," not by allowing Nez Perce to live near them. Joseph visited his home in the Wallowas, said his prayers in the land of his mother and father. He traveled to Washington, D.C., and New York City, but he lived out the rest of his life on the Colville Reservation, where he died on September 21, 1904. Much of the Nez Perce memory is being studied by historian Rob McCoy, and British scholar Mick Gidley has pointed out that although Joseph clinically died of "heart failure," doctor Edward H. Latham, Joseph's friend and physician, wrote that "Chief Joseph died of a broken heart." The Nez Perce leader died, in part, from depression brought on by military conquest, forced removal, and confinement to a reservation far from his own land. Joseph's dream of returning to the Wallowas has never died, and in 1997, Nez Perce people negotiated the use of traditional land and returned to the earth that holds the bones and blood of their ancestors.

SHOSHONI, BANNOCK, AND PAIUTE RESISTANCE

The Nez Perce War overshadowed hostilities that broke out in 1878 and 1879 between whites and numerous Native Americans in the Rocky Mountains and high plateaus of southern Idaho. Several diverse and independent bands of Shoshonian-speaking Indians known as Paiutes, Bannocks, Agaidikas (Salmon Eaters), and Tukuarikas (Bighorn Sheepeaters) and many others were often identified in documents as "Snake Indians." Like other western tribes, these people faced a growing and continual onslaught of immigrant roads, stage coaches, wagon trains, telegraph lines, military posts, trading establishments, whiskey salesmen, farms, towns, ranches, and railroads. Bands of Paiutes, Bannocks, and Shoshonis attacked whites who invaded their lands, stole their resources, disturbed hunting areas, destroyed root grounds, and resettled Indian lands, claiming them as their own.

In an attempt to control Shoshonis, Bannocks, and Paiutes who lived on vast regions of Wyoming, Idaho, Oregon, Nevada, Utah, and California, the United States consolidated them onto reservations, often some distance from their homelands. In this way, the Office of Indian Affairs could dictate Indian policy to them and open thousands of acres of their land to white exploitation, transportation systems, and resettlement. Notable leaders such as Buffalo Horn, Winnemucca, Egan, Washakie, Pocataro (Pocatello), Oytes, and Taghee resisted white invasion of their lands. Although some of their people resettled onto reservations, far more lived free. Reservation and nonreservation people often hunted, fished, and gathered off the reservations. A favorite gathering area was the Camas Prairie southeast of Boise, land guaranteed them in the Treaty of 1868 but land where whites grazed hogs, which threatened starvation for hundreds of native people. War broke out when a Bannock shot and wounded two white men.

Some Indians returned to the reservation at Fort Hall, while Bannocks, Shoshonis, Paiutes, and Umatillas united under Buffalo Horn, spreading terror across the region. Some of these same people had served as scouts for the U.S. army during the Nez Perce War. In 1878, they found themselves facing bluecoat soldiers commanded by Howard and Captain Reuben F. Bernard. Throughout most of the war, Paiute Sarah Winnemucca served as an interpreter and intermediary. Troops pursued the warring bands throughout Idaho and northeastern Oregon, engaging in a major fight at Birch Creek, before following a large group of warriors onto the Umatilla Reservation. Captain Evan Miles chased the warriors and surrounded the agency buildings, driving the Indians toward the Blue Mountains. A group of Umatilla warriors pretended to join the Bannocks and Paiutes, but after joining them, the Umatillas turned on them, killing Egan. Miles cut off Egan's head and gave it to the Medical Museum in Washington, D.C.

General Howard, Colonel Frank Wheaton, Colonel James W. Forsyth, and Miles continued the chase. Soldiers under Nelson Miles engaged a band of Shoshonis east of Yellowstone National Park, and other Shoshonis, Paiutes, and Bannocks considered riding to Canada to join Sitting Bull. But in the end, many bands gave up and moved to reservations or military posts to demonstrate their intention to end the war. Indians surrendered at the Malheur Agency and Forts Hall, Brown, Keogh, and McDermit.

When the government closed the Malheur Reservation to save money, federal officials moved six hundred Paiutes to the Yakama Reservation in Washington Territory to live with their enemies, a fact noted in the Yakama Census and in oral histories. By September 1878, the war ended, but not all Indians moved to the forts or reservations. Some Paiutes, Shoshonis, and Bannocks remained off government-controlled lands and on the so-called public domain. They tried hard to avoid most white people, believing that trouble often resulted from their interaction with whites. Over the years, however, most of these people moved to one of several reservations, where their descendants live today.

LAST APACHE WARS

At the conclusion of General George Crook's campaign against Apache and Yavapai raiders in 1873, Crook commented that he had "finally closed an Indian war that has been waged since the time of Cortez." His comments were premature, because the war died down momentarily but did not end. Small bands of Apaches and Yavapais in the Tonto Basin continued to resist, and this was true of Apaches in other parts of Arizona and New Mexico. But the government recognized Crook for "ending the war" and transferred him, giving the command of Arizona to Colonel August V. Kautz. According to historian Andrew Wallace, Kautz blamed the "Tucson Ring" for Apache troubles because this group of business- men, contractors, and politicians was eager to perpetuate the Apache wars in order to make money and rise politically. Although there was truth to this view, the wars continued because of government Indian policies and internal factors among Apaches.

In an effort to save money and better control the movement of Indi- ans, the Indian office decided to destroy the reservations at Camp Grant, Camp Verde, Chiricahua, and Fort Apache, moving thousands of Indians onto the San Carlos Reservation. The government's concentration policy created more problems than it solved. Among the various groups of Apaches and Yavapais, serious divisions emerged as they broke up into groups who favored peace or war. Many Apaches moved to San Carlos to live, whereas others moved into the mountains to avoid whites. Others left their homelands to live with friends and relatives in the Sierra Madre Mountains of Mexico. Geronimo, Juh, Nachez, and Victorio favored re- sistance over submission, and they led their followers—men, women, and children—on raids in the United States and Mexico.

In 1874, John P. Clum became Indian agent at San Carlos. He was twenty-three, full of himself, confident, and bombastic. But he was gen- erally an honest agent who did not steal from Indians or subscribe to kickbacks from lucrative government contracts. Like Crook, Clum hired Apaches to support his policies. Clum started the Indian police force at San Carlos to coerce and manage Apaches, without the army. Clum shrewdly divided the Apaches further by favoring his police with uni- forms, guns, salaries, leadership, and freedom. Indian police used their positions to feed their families and fill the void in native leadership cre- ated by the reservation. They became the "power" on the reservation, implementing Clum's directives and controlling approximately five thousand diverse Apaches and Yavapais. Clum used his Indian police to force other Apaches onto the San Carlos Reservation.

With orders to destroy the Ojo Caliente Reservation and move the Warm Springs (Ojo Calientes), Mimbres, Gilas, and Mogollon Apaches onto San Carlos, Clum arrived at the reservation in western New Mexico on April 20, 1877. Geronimo and other Apaches from the Ojo Caliente and Chiricahua bands came to the reservation to talk. Instead, the brash agent used his superior force of policemen and element of surprise to ar- rest Geronimo and sixteen other leaders. He threw them into jail, shack- led them, and forced them along with 110 Chiricahuas and 343 Ojo Calientes to move to San Carlos. Not long after, Clum resigned in a huff because of bureaucratic and internal difficulties. He left San Carlos, and so did disgruntled Apaches. Victorio, the Ojo Caliente who had suc- ceeded Mangas Coloradas, bolted the reservation in September 1877 with 310 men, women, and children. Victorio's departure was the first of many, because the government had forced so many Indians from their homes to live in poverty, filth, liquor, disease, and desperation.

Victorio wanted to live at his home near Ojo Caliente, but the government refused. His band moved about for two years while soldiers and Apache police chased them. They ultimately surrendered at Fort Wingate, New Mexico, and the army resettled them at Ojo Caliente for a year before deciding to transfer them back to San Carlos. Victorio had lived in peace at his home, but he bolted before the soldiers forced him back to San Carlos. He tried to remain at his home but then traveled to the Tularosa Agency to live with Mescaleros. Not long after his arrival, rumors circulated among the Indians that whites were planning to arrest or hang Victorio, so he left the reservation with Ojo Caliente, Chiricahua, and Mescalero followers. This time, Victorio declared war by killing eight guards and stealing the cavalry's forty-six horses. He fought forces from the United States and Mexico, including bluecoats, in the Battle of Hembrillo Canyon in April 1880. When soldiers tried to disarm Mescalero Apaches at the Tularosa Agency, even more Apaches joined Victorio.

Ojo Calientes and their allies raided from Texas to Arizona, striking deep into Mexico and eluding most soldiers. On two occasions, Victorio ran headlong into African American soldiers of the Tenth Cavalry commanded by Colonel Benjamin H. Grierson and had to retreat into Mexico. In a joint operation of American and Mexican troops, the two countries worked together to destroy Victorio. Colonel Joaquin Terrazas combed the mountains, locating Victorio in October 1880 in the Tres Castillos Mountains, where the band was participating in a sacred rite and was unable to leave until it was completed. Terrazas attacked Victorio, killing sixty warriors and eighteen women and children. A Tarahumara Indian scout shot Victorio, and the battle ended, but the conflict continued.

Years later, a surviving member of Victorio's band told historian Angie Debo that the cause of the war was the government's removal policy to San Carlos. The people wanted to live in the land of their grandparents, and federal officials pushed them into war. "That was our country. The government didn't give it to us. It had always been our home. And we had been peaceable. We were not to blame for what Geronimo did." In 1880–1881, in retaliation for the treatment of Apache people, Nana rode across the Southwest with fifteen warriors armed to the teeth and spoiling for a fight. The army chased them into Arizona, where Nana joined Geronimo. Like other Apaches, Geronimo lived at San Carlos until 1878, when he joined Juh, leader of the Nednhis band, in the Sierra Madres. Geronimo and Juh raided Mexican settlements, preying on Mexican horses, cattle, grains, and goods and killing anyone who stood in their way.

In 1880, Geronimo and Juh felt increased pressure from Mexican troops and returned to San Carlos, using it as a sanctuary just as they had the Ojo Caliente Reservation in the past. They lived in peace at the reservation, which had grown in numbers with the arrival of many Apache and Yavapai bands. Increasingly, Chiricahua, San Carlo, Ojo Caliente, Coyotero (White Mountain), Yavapai, Pinal, Aravaipa, and others feared the growth of the white settlements. They moved to the reservation for sanctuary as well because whites could murder Apaches without punishment. However, after they were on the reservation, they resented the loss of their freedom. General Crook recognized this dilemma: "These tigers of the human race, resented anything like an attempt to regulate their conduct, or in any way to interfere with their mode of life."

Depression became epidemic at San Carlos, just as it did on most reservations. Many people lost hope and gravitated to the teachings of Nakaidoklini, an Apache holy man who preached a reordering of the earth, an apocalypse in which whites would disappear and the dead would return to a world the Indians had known before white contact. Nakaidoklini's doctrine was similar to that of the Ghost Dance religion among Paiutes and Shoshonis in the 1870s and 1880s, giving hope to desperate people who wanted to rid themselves of white overlords. The new Apache religion spread quickly, even among Indian scouts and policemen. It frightened and threatened whites, including San Carlos Agent J. C. Tiffany and Colonel Orlando B. Willcox, who ordered Colonel Eugene Carr, commander of Fort Apache, to arrest Nakaidoklini.

On August 30, 1881, Carr, eighty-five soldiers, and twenty-three Apache scouts rode to Cibicu to arrest Nakaidoklini. Carr arrested the holy man, much to the displeasure of his followers, who trailed Carr and attacked him. Apache scouts turned against Carr, and two soldiers shot Nakaidoklini trying to escape. Carr slipped back to Fort Apache that night but lost seven men in the ill-conceived affair. The fight triggered new unrest at San Carlos, and another war. The army sent reinforcements to San Carlos and other points in Arizona. Juh, Nachez, Chato, and Geronimo raced off to the Sierra Madres, spreading terror in Arizona, New Mexico, and Mexico. They shot, killed, and robbed along the way and sent soldiers on both sides of the border scurrying after them. Bluecoats crushed Natiotish's band of Coyotero in the Battle of Big Dry Wash, but they were less successful chasing Ojo Calientes and Chiricahuas. So the War Department reassigned General Crook to Arizona.

In 1882, Crook assessed the situation quickly, deciding to bring the Apaches at San Carlos under direct military control and destroy the Apaches in the Sierra Madres using Apache scouts. Crook assigned three of his most trusted officers, who had experience dealing with Apaches, to control the people at San Carlos. He assigned two of them to recruit and train scouts. Meanwhile, Geronimo, Chihuahua, Chato, and Benito raided Mexico and the United States, bringing a public outcry to destroy all Apaches. Crook used the railroad to move quickly from Arizona to Albuquerque, where he planned his Sierra Madres campaign with Ranald Mackenzie. He used the railroad to move troops and supplies into position. He used 350 pack mules to haul supplies south into Mexico. He was aided in his preparations by Lieutenants Britton Davis, Charles Gatewood, and Emmet Crawford, who organized the Apache scouts.

Apache scouts led the campaign and were a key to its success. Tzoe, or "Peaches," guided the army. He had recently raided with Chato and knew the trails, village sites, and water holes of the natural fortress of the Sierra Madres. On May 15, 1883, Apache scouts operating with Crawford fought for several hours against Chato and Benito, killing nine men and setting fire to thirty wickiups. Through the scouts, a captured girl told Crook that many Apaches wanted to return to San Carlos, so he let her go to urge the people to surrender. Chato, Benito, Loco, Nachez, Nana, Chihuahua, Kaytennae, and Geronimo negotiated with Crook, asking to go back to San Carlos. Crook agreed. Then Geronimo asked Crook to trust him to return to San Carlos on his own after rounding up his people, who were scattered throughout the mountain. Crook agreed, returning to Arizona with Loco, Nana, and 325 Apaches. By March 1884, Geronimo, Nachez, Mangas, and Chato had returned to San Carlos with their people.

Gatewood, Crawford, and Davis settled these bands of Apaches in remote areas surrounding San Carlos. Most of the problems surrounding these people centered around making and drinking tizwin (native corn beer) as well as spousal abuse. When Kaytennae challenged the soldiers, Davis and the police arrested him, and an Apache jury sentenced him to two years' imprisonment at Alcatraz. However, in time most of the people who surrendered grew tired of reservation life and challenged the army. Geronimo, Nana, Nachez, Chihuahua, and Mangas bolted. Chato remained at San Carlos, but the others raced back to the Sierra Madres, with Crook and the Apache scouts in hot pursuit during the Sierra Madres campaign of 1885.

Josanie took a band of Apaches and raided successfully across Arizona and New Mexico. Secretary of War William C. Endicott sent General Sheridan to tell Crook to remove all Chiricahuas and Ojo Calientes out of Arizona, likely to Indian Territory. Crook and Crawford disagreed vehemently, saying that such a plan would turn the scouts against the campaign. Sheridan and Endicott were not impressed with Crook's use of scouts, but Crook argued his point sufficiently to stall any decision. Crawford, Davis, and the scouts followed Geronimo into the Sierra Madres, where they ran into Mexican soldiers who shot and killed Crawford. In the aftermath of this fight, Geronimo, Nana, Nachez, and Chihuahua counciled with Lieutenant Marion Maus, saying they wanted to discuss terms of surrender with Crook.

Known to Apache people as Goyathlay, he is known to nonnatives as Geronimo. Goyathlay was a fierce, sometimes ruthless, fighter who led the Apaches on their last major campaign against the United States. The government exiled Goyathlay, never permitting him to return to Arizona. Descendants of his band live primarily in Oklahoma and New Mexico today.

Apache leaders met on March 25, 1886, with Crook, at Canyon de los Embudos, where the general demanded their surrender, removal to Florida for two years as punishment, and their safe return to San Carlos. The leaders and their families were to go to Florida. At a second meeting, the Indians surrendered and began breaking camp for the journey back to San Carlos. Overjoyed, Crook hurried to Fort Bowie to telegraph Sheridan that he had secured a surrender. However, as Geronimo and the others moved north, they fell in with whiskey peddlers who told them they were going to be hanged. According to historian Dan Thrapp, the peddlers likely spread a rumor initiated by the infamous Tucson Ring. The rumor was not true, and the result was a continuation of war that brought a good deal of money into the local economy, which benefited members of the Tucson Ring.

APACHE SURRENDER AND REMOVAL

On April 1, Crook asked to be relieved of his command, and the next day, Sheridan ordered Nelson A. Miles to take over. Miles appointed Captain Henry W. Lawton to lead his Sierra Madres campaign of 1886. While Lawton labored over deserts and mountains in pursuit of Geronimo and the others, Miles removed Chiricahuas and Ojo Calientes under Nana, Josanie, and Chihuahua from San Carlos to Fort Marion, Florida. The army herded 382 Apaches to Holbrook, Arizona, and placed them in cattle cars, like animals. Once a day, whites threw slop to them and used high-powered hoses to blow out the feces and urine from the cars. Miles banished most loyal Apache scouts on this journey to Florida, in spite of their service to the U.S. Army.

Miles did not support the use of Apache scouts at the beginning of his campaign, but two of them—Martine and Kayitah—worked with Lieutenant Gatewood in the Sierra Madres. They bravely entered Geronimo's camp and arranged a meeting between the Apache leader and Gatewood. On the banks of the Bavispe River, Gatewood walked into Geronimo's camp. On August 24, through the Apache scouts, Gatewood conveyed Miles's message. The Indians had to surrender and agree to go to Florida with their families until the president decided what to do with them. There were no other terms. Geronimo agreed to surrender but only to Miles, who reluctantly agreed to accept Geronimo's surrender at Skeleton Canyon on September 4, 1886.

Four days later, at Fort Bowie Station, the army loaded the Apache prisoners onto railroad cars and sent them to Florida. Before departing, a photographer took a picture of a few men, women, and children of Geronimo's band. The somber faces stare blankly at the photographer, but the people must have wondered what lay ahead for themselves and their people. A total of 509 Apaches reached Florida in 1886. The army separated out the leaders, including Geronimo, Chihuahua, Josanie, Nachez, and others, confining them to Fort Pickens in Pensacola, Florida. The other adults—including Kayitah and Martine, the Apache scouts who had arranged Geronimo's last surrender—remained at Fort Marion. In the spring of 1887, the government allowed the adults to join at Mount Vernon Barracks in Alabama. But not their children. The government kidnapped the Apache children and forced them into Carlisle Indian School, where 119 died of depression and disease.

Crook and Howard joined the Indian Rights Association and crusaded to have the Chiricahua Apaches returned to Arizona. They both died trying. Lawton died in the Philippines, and Gatewood sank into obscurity, never gaining rank or receiving recognition for his bravery. Miles won the Congressional Medal of Honor for bringing in Geronimo, although, in his insightful study, *The Geronimo Campaign*, historian Odie B. Faulk has shown that Gatewood should have won the medal and honor. The Apaches died in Florida and Alabama. In 1894, Congress passed a bill that allowed most Apaches to move to Fort Sill, Indian Territory; but not all. Some had to remain at Mount Vernon Barracks. Geronimo and his people arrived at Fort Sill in October, 1894, numbering only 296. Their total number had dropped from 509 due to low birth rates and high death rates. Initially, the people did not prosper in Indian Territory. In 1913, the Apache population in Oklahoma numbered only 261, and in that year, two-thirds of them moved to the Mescalero Reservation. Descendants of the Chiricahua still live in Oklahoma and New Mexico. None of the Apaches has lost the will to resist, however. People from the various bands continue to work within their communities and within the larger society on behalf of their people. Many continue to sing and pray in the old way and preserve that which they consider sacred. None of them has forgotten the wars, but they use their collective memories to face the future.

As for Geronimo, he lived out his days at Fort Sill, sometimes drinking to forget his woes. He traveled with Pawnee Bill's Wild West Show, attended rodeos and fairs, and sold souvenirs to tourists. Geronimo continued his work as an advisor and healer. He was a medicine man and holy man throughout his life and continued to heal people with songs, prayers, and rituals at Fort Sill. He also retained his psychic abilities, which had informed him of ambushes and troop movements. He wanted to die a free man and be buried in the mountains of Arizona. Instead, Geronimo died a prisoner of war in 1909, held captive at Fort Sill, where he was buried in the post graveyard with an elaborate headstone monument capped with a metal eagle. When Geronimo had surrendered to Crook in 1886, he had said, "I give myself up to you. Do with me what you please. I surrender. Once I moved about like the wind." Perhaps his spirit moved like the wind back to the mountains of southern Arizona and northern Mexico, but regardless, he is remembered by his people in Oklahoma, New Mexico, and Arizona as a defender of Apache people and the native way of life.

Selected Readings and Bibliography

Native American resistance of white expansion is well documented in American history, particularly in accounts of the violent encounters between native fighters and the regular and volunteer armies. General works previously cited and used for this chapter are Champagne's *The Native North American Almanac,* Utley and Washburn's *Indian Wars,* Ruby and Brown's *Indians of the Pacific Northwest,* Francis's *Native Time,* and Gibson's *The American Indian.* Robert Utley's two volumes, *Frontiersmen in Blue* and *Frontier Regulars,* were most helpful in framing the major conflicts. Books on the Apache Wars used were Thrapp's *The Conquest of Apacheria* and Faulk's *The Geronimo Campaign.* Madsen's *The*

Shoshoni Frontier and the Bear River Massacre discusses Shoshoni resistance to aggressors, and Murray's *The Modocs and Their War* informs the discussion of the Modoc struggle against the United States. Trafzer and Scheuerman's *Renegade Tribe* provide information on the Nez Perce War in general and Palouse participation in particular. Josephy's *The Nez Perce Indians* and Haines's *The Nez Perces,* serve the discussion of the Nez Perce War.

Ambrose, Stephen E. *Crazy House and Custer.* New York: Doubleday, 1975.

Barrett, S. M. *Geronimo's Story of His Life.* New York: Duffield, 1906.

Beal, Merrill D. *"I Will Fight No More Forever."* Seattle: University of Washington Press, 1963.

Betzinez, Jason. *I Fought with Geronimo.* Harrisburg, Penn.: Stackpole, 1959.

Brown, Dee Alexander. *The Galvanized Yankees.* Urbana: University of Illinois Press, 1963.

——. *The Fetterman Massacre.* Lincoln: University of Nebraska Press, 1976.

Carriker, Robert C. *Fort Supply, Indian Territory: Frontier Outpost on the Plains.* Norman: University of Oklahoma Press, 1970.

Crook, George. *General George Crook: Autobiography.* Norman: University of Oklahoma Press, 1946.

Crum, Steven J. *The Road on Which We Came: A History of the Western Shoshoni.* Salt Lake City: University of Utah Press, 1994.

Davis, Britton. *The Truth about Geronimo.* New Haven: Yale University Press, 1929.

Debo, Angie. *Geronimo.* Norman: University of Oklahoma Press, 1976.

Emmett, Robert. *The Last War Trail: The Utes and the Settlement of Colorado.* Norman: University of Oklahoma Press, 1954.

Evans, Steven Ross. *Voice of the Old Wolf: Lucullus Virgil McWhorter and the Nez Perce Indians.* Pullman: Washington State University Press, 1996.

Ewers, John. *The Blackfeet: Raiders of the Northwest Plains.* Norman: University of Oklahoma Press, 1958.

Fritz, Henry E. *The Movement for Indian Assimilation, 1862–1890.* Philadelphia: University of Pennsylvania Press, 1965.

Gibson, Benson. *Survivors of the Bannock War.* Duck Valley Indian Reservation, Owyhee, Nev.: privately printed, 1990.

Gidley, Mick. *Kopet: A Documentary Narrative of Chief Joseph's Last Years.* Seattle: University of Washington Press, 1981.

Gray, John S. *Centennial Campaign.* Norman: University of Oklahoma Press, 1988.

Hampton, Bruce. *Children of Grace: The Nez Perce War of 1877.* New York: Henry Holt, 1994.

Hopkins, Sarah Winnemucca. *Life among the Piutes, Their Wrongs and Claims.* Boston: Cupples, Upham, 1883.

Hoxie, Frederick E. *Parading though History.* Cambridge: Cambridge University Press, 1995.

Hurtado, Albert. *Indian Survival on the California Frontier.* New Haven: Yale University Press, 1988.

Johnson, Dorothy M. *The Bloody Bozeman.* New York: McGraw-Hill, 1971.

Jones, Douglas C. *The Treaty of Medicine Lodge.* Norman: University of Oklahoma Press, 1966.

Joseph, Young Chief. "An Indian's View of Indian Affairs." *The North American Review* 128 (1879): 412–433.

Leckie, William H. *The Military Conquest of the Southern Plains*. Norman: University of Oklahoma Press, 1963.

——. *The Buffalo Soldiers*. Norman: University of Oklahoma Press, 1967.

Martin, Lucille. "The Modoc in Indian Territory." *The Northwestern Tribes in Indian Territory*. Clifford E. Trafzer, ed. Sacramento: Sierra Oaks, 1987.

McWhorter, L. V. *Yellow Wolf*. Caldwell, Idaho: Caxton, 1940.

——. *Hear Me, My Chiefs!* Caldwell, Idaho: Caxton, 1952.

Murray, Keith A. *The Modocs and Their War*. Norman: University of Oklahoma Press, 1968.

Nye, Wilbur S. Carbine, and Lance Nye. *The Story of Old Fort Sill*. Norman: University of Oklahoma Press, 1937.

Ogle, Ralph H. *Federal Control of the Western Apaches, 1848–1886*. Albuquerque: University of New Mexico Press, 1940.

Olson, James C. *Red Cloud and the Sioux Problem*. Lincoln: University of Nebraska Press, 1965.

Prucha, Francis Paul. *American Indian Policy in Crisis*. Norman: University of Oklahoma Press, 1976.

Sandoz, Mari. *Cheyenne Autumn*. New York: McGraw-Hill, 1953.

Shoemaker, Nancy, ed. *Negotiators of Change: Historical Perspectives on Native American Women*. New York: Routledge, 1995.

Smith, Sherry. *The View from Officers' Row: Army Perceptions of Western Indians*. Tucson: University of Arizona Press, 1990.

Taylor, William O. *With Custer on the Little Bighorn*. New York: Viking, 1996.

Thrapp, Dan. *Al Sieber*. Norman: University of Oklahoma Press, 1964.

Trafzer, Clifford E. "The Palouse in *Eekish Pah*." *American Indian Quarterly* 9 (1985): 169–182.

——. *Chief Joseph's Allies*. Newcastle, Calif.: Sierra Oaks, 1992.

——. "Earth, Animals and Academics: Plateau Indian Communities, Culture and the Walla Walla Council of 1855." *American Indian Culture and Research Journal* 17 (1993): 81–100.

——, ed. *Indians, Superintendents, and Councils: Northwestern Indian Policy, 1850–1855*. Lanham, Md.: University Press of America, 1986.

Trafzer, Clifford E., and Margey Ann Beach. "Smohalla, the Washani, and Religion as a Factor in Northwest Indian History." *American Indian Quarterly* 9 (1985): 309–324.

Trenholm, Virginia Cole, and Maurine Carley. *The Shoshonis*. Norman: University of Oklahoma Press, 1964.

Utley, Robert M. *The Last Days of the Sioux Nation*. New Haven: Yale University Press, 1963.

Vaughn, J. W. Indian Fights: *New Facts on Seven Encounters*. Norman: University of Oklahoma Press, 1966.

Walker, Deward E. *Conflict and Schism in Nez Perce Acculturation*. Pullman: Washington State University Press, 1968.

White, Richard. "The Winning of the West: The Expansion of the Western Sioux in the Eighteenth and Nineteenth Centuries." *Journal of American History* 65 (September 1978): 319–343.

CHAPTER 13

RESERVATIONS, CIVILIZATIONS, AND ALLOTMENT

The concept of forcing Native Americans to live on reservations was not new in the nineteenth century. Human beings had herded other human beings onto specified lands with forced boundaries and rules of behavior for centuries. The reservation system that emerged in the United States during the second half of the nineteenth century was built on past experiences, drawing on two models of colonial policies of the French, Spanish, and English. Although the reservation system owed some of its origin to the Catholic mission systems of the Spanish and French, it owed far more to that of the Puritans of the seventeenth century.

THE RESERVATION SYSTEM

After the Pequot Indian War, Puritans removed Native Americans from their homelands and relocated them onto confined reservations where whites controlled them. Puritan fathers argued that they created towns of praying Indians for the benefit of Native Americans, who would be uplifted in this life and the next by God's earthly agents. Puritan reservations were institutions designed to regulate many aspects of Native American life, including work, recreation, law, trade, hunting, farming, family, education, and religion. Puritan magistrates (agents) controlled towns of praying Indians, overseeing the social and commercial intercourse between "Christian Indians" and those not living on Puritan reservations. Puritans created laws by which native people lived, set up churches and sanctioned Puritan doctrines, meted out punishments, regulated commerce, established social and behavioral rules of conduct, and dictated policies to Native Americans. While Puritans executed their plan, Indians continued to exercise their own resistance, preserving aspects of their cultures, languages, and laws.

Puritans asserted their will at the expense of Native American power and land, but many Indians recognized the white objective of rounding up people onto a single land base. Metacom and other Indian leaders saw through the Puritan reservation system, arguing that the system had more to do with control and land than it did religion and civilization. Besides, many Indians had little or no interest in becoming assimilated or Christian. Some Puritans were well meaning in their interest in converting the Indians of New England, but Puritan policies helped clear lands of native people, concentrating them onto small plots of land where non-whites could control them while many others stole native lands. In this way, God's "chosen people" could resettle Indian lands, exploit natural resources owned by native people, and prosper at the expense of Native Americans suffering from disease, depression, and death.

In colonial Virginia and the southern colonies, whites pushed Indians from their traditional homes, creating continuously moving boundaries between Native Americans and whites. Indians often chose to escape the pressures of white expansion by voluntarily moving away from white settlements. This became the pattern in the western part of the country, as white settlers moved to regions of the vast West. For a time, most Native Americans stayed away from encroachers or tried to drive them from their lands. But whites took more and more lands and most often urged territorial, state, and federal delegations to remove Indians to confined areas that whites did not then desire. Then white settlers resettled former Indian lands. By the late nineteenth century, this was an old process, but one that gave impetus to the reservation system. Instead of exterminating Indians or simply pushing them west, the government determined to follow the advice of humanitarian reformers and create reservations where Indians could be colonized, civilized, and Christianized. Reservations became the purgatorial mechanisms by which whites could begin to assimilate Indians.

A fully developed reservation system emerged between 1867 and 1887 in most parts of the American West. Alaskan natives—who came under the influence of the United States after 1867, when the United States purchased Alaska from Russia—were not forced into the reservation system, because so few whites lived in Alaska and natives controlled vast regions of their traditional homelands. Other Native Americans came under intense pressure from the U.S. Army and civilian Indian agents and commissioners to leave their old ways and move onto reservations where they could be "cared for" and "civilized." Not many Indians were interested in white civilization or a reservation life controlled by whites, but they were interested in securing a portion of their former lands before whites stole all Indian property. Indians were generally interested in establishing permanent boundaries between themselves and whites, but clearly few Native Americans understood the full meaning of reservations, "civilization," and Americanization plans. Little in their experiences prepared them for confinement and white rule.

HUMANITARIANS AND ACCULTURATION

California Superintendent of Indian Affairs Edward Fitzgerald Beale used a portion of his $100,000 appropriation of 1852 to begin the first "modern" reservation in the United States at Fort Tejon at the southern end of the San Joaquin Valley. Beale eventually relocated seven hundred Indians onto the reservation, where they farmed and ranched. Thomas Henley replaced Beale and expanded the reservation system to Nome Lackee (Round Valley), Medicino, and Fresno. Both superintendents lavished praise on themselves, pronouncing their reservations huge successes. In 1864–1865, James Carleton had praised his own experiment at the Bosque Redondo Reservation in eastern New Mexico, where he had relocated Navajos and Mescaleros. Reservations had their problems, but white administrators put the best spin on their handiwork, claiming they were teaching Indians to become productive, self-sufficient workers who would eventually become part of the larger American society.

The reservation system was a secular purgatory for Native Americans, a place where strict and zealous humanitarians often began the process that would lead Indian people–they believed–to higher levels of existence. In Indian purgatory, Native Americans would die and be reborn after they had atoned for their "sins" against whites. White agents used the reservation as a place to kill "savage" Indian cultures and replace them with those of a superior civilization where Indians learned about the one true God and Christ's teachings. Christians had long held that Native Americans were "Red Devils" and "Satan's Children," and the reservation experience offered native people an opportunity to expiate Satan and follow the Jesus Road.

Policy makers treated diverse native populations as if they were homogeneous groups. Most of these policy makers knew little about Native Americans, formulated their own intellectual model of Native Americans, and fit all native peoples into that model. Few white bureaucrats and politicians knew much about complex Native American cultures, beliefs, and languages. They formulated Indian policy based on their own cultural assumptions and prejudices, ignoring cultural components of native nations.

The first element of the reservation system was isolation of reservation Indians from off-reservation Indians, who would lead the reservation people astray. Furthermore, policy makers wanted Indians isolated from gamblers, prostitutes, whiskey, guns, and other negative influences. With Indians confined to the reservation, Christian missionaries could control their flocks and redirect the lives of Indians toward Christianity. On the reservation, missionaries and agents tried to prevent Native Americans from practicing their native religions and performing rituals, ceremonies, dances, and music. White teachers instructed adults and children alike in reading, writing, science, and arithmetic as well as vocational, industrial, and domestic arts. Through education and Christianity, Indians would learn new laws, particularly property rights and rules of law about material items.

Finally, the reservation experience would teach Native Americans to become hard-working yeoman farmers and to contribute to society, national growth, and the economic progress of humanity. The reservation system was intended to make Indians self-sufficient farmers (and later ranchers) so they could earn a living. Self-sufficiency, as interpreted by whites, did not include a traditional native life based on hunting, fishing, and gathering. It did not include a life based on agriculture performed by women and children. Based on their hermeneutics, whites considered these economic approaches primitive and inferior. White policy makers fully believed that the reservation system would enable Indians to learn a better way of life, and because they had the political and military might to do so, white politicians executed their policies to change native people in a radical manner.

Many white reformers and advocates of the reservation system were sincere individuals who believed in their cause. Only a few, including Alfred B. Meacham and Thomas A. Bland, editors of *Council Fire Magazine* and members of the National Indian Defense Association, believed in Indian self-determination and the value of preserving Native American cultures. Most white Americans, including many Friends of the Indians, believed that Indians should be acculturated into mainstream American society. That is, the Friends and others felt that Native American cultures should give way to white culture. The eminent Minnesota Episcopal bishop, Henry B. Whipple, favored this position, as did most Christian officials. In fact, during the late nineteenth century, presidents, secretaries, commissioners, superintendents, and agents shared this position. They worked with congressmen, governors, and legislators to destroy Indian cultures, languages, religions, and societies. They put their power and resources behind this great cause, but Indian cultures survived in spite of the new assault.

The assault on Native American cultures did not originate among American Indians or agents working on the reservations. Acculturation and assimilation emerged on a national level and filtered down from congresses and presidents to commissioners of Indian affairs to superintendents of Indian affairs to agents. However, agents executed policies in the manner they saw fit. Often agents ran reservations like big city bosses, dictating nearly every aspect of life and controlling land, water, mineral, timber, livestock, grazing, and other resources. They doled out patronage to their friends and punished their enemies. Agents gave some Indians jobs, leadership positions, food, and clothing. They withheld food, clothing, and housing from enemies or rounded them up and sent them to prisons. Without due process of law, agents sent Indians to Alcatraz Island, Arizona Territorial Prison, Fort Marion, and Fort Leavenworth.

American Indians were not citizens of the United States, states, or territories. They had no rights as citizens, so the Constitution and Bill of Rights did not apply to them. Agents ruled reservations as virtual sovereigns, and agents executed their own rulings and directives of the Office of Indian Affairs through Indian police forces. On nearly all reservations, agents selected native men to work for them as their own militia forces. Agents referred to these men as Indian policemen, but they often did the bidding of agents, sometimes using force. Policemen arrested recalcitrant Indians living on and off reservations On most reservations, policemen arrested Indians for rustling, robbery, burglary, beatings, and drinking.

Indian policemen held prisoners in agency jails until Indian courts convened to determine what course of action would be taken against the prisoners. In most cases, Indian courts held no trials. Policemen brought prisoners charged with offenses into an Indian court, where one to three Indian judges ruled on their cases. Prisoners had no advocates, unless someone spoke in their behalf. Witnesses spoke for and against individuals, usually speaking in their native languages. Judges made their rulings on evidence provided by policemen and witnesses. If the judges found individuals guilty, prisoners paid a fine, served time in jail, or both. At times, judges drew on their own tribal traditions to mete out punishments, ordering Indians on the Yakama Reservation, for example, to provide two horses to repay the damaged party for the one good horse they had killed. Judges used common sense in their rulings, trying to settle minor offenses, whereas U.S. marshals generally dealt with murder and serious federal cases.

Indian policemen and judges helped agents institute their programs of acculturation. They executed plans and policies formulated by the Indian office and agencies. White Americans defined and determined true culture and civilization. Major cultural elements of white society during the late nineteenth and early twentieth centuries in the United States became the standard for civilization. Whites determined that the English language, formal education in schools, agriculture, materialism, and Christianity were all important elements of free civilization. Laws and institutions that governed white people and legal traditions, with their roots in Greece, Rome, and elsewhere in Europe, were deemed superior to those of Native Americans. Whites judged Native American cultures and civilizations to be nonexistent or inferior, so they tried to destroy Native American languages, religions, rituals, foods, oral narratives, warfare, housing, and economies. Most policy makers and missionaries saw little in Native American life worthy of preservation.

The Bureau of Indian Affairs attempted to destroy Native American cultures, religions, and identities through boarding schools. In 1912 Yakama school children participated in a flag ceremony at Fort Simcoe Indian School, Washington.

On reservations, whites actively worked to change nearly every aspect of Native American life, and such an environment was very destructive to native people, even those who survived the attempts at cultural genocide. No longer able to hunt and gather, Native Americans were encouraged to give up their traditional forms of food, dress, dance, music, and religion. Native people became dependent on whites for their clothing or made their clothes from flour sacks or cloth. Indians no longer had sufficient leather for lodges, moccasins, and leggings, and thus purchased shoes, boots, and clothes from traders in "border towns," adjacent to reservations, that stimulated local economies but intensified insidious racial tensions between whites and Indians, in spite of the fact that whites drew their living, in part, from the sale of goods and services to Native Americans.

Agents often forced native men to cut their long hair, and students at Indian schools lost their hair. Whites considered long hair a symbol of traditionalism and savagery, a form of defiance, an affront to whites who demanded that civilized people wear their hair short. Agents referred to Native American men with long hair as "long hairs" or "blanket Indians," both derogatory labels. Most Indian agents and Christian missionaries despised native independence and pride, seeking to break the spirit of young and old alike. They often changed Indian names that they did not like or could not pronounce, eliminating family names such as Crane, Going Snake, Kelilamand, Nalt' Sos Nez Begay, Night Walker, Curly Mustache, Yellow Knee, Blue Horse, No Horns on Her Head, Nightingale, and replacing them with names such as Smith, Henry, Child, McDonald, or Day. Agency census rolls demonstrate the transition from native names, written in English to conform phonetically with their Indian names, to common English, German, Spanish, and French names easily recognized by non-Indians. A person's name was not sacred to whites. It was a means to assimilate one's identity from Native American to white American.

EDUCATION AND CHRISTIANIZATION

Native Americans had their own systems of education long before whites came to the Americas. They had their own intellectuals and scholars who instructed people with enlightenment and wisdom. Families, clans, and tribes had their own educators who taught children each day. Clan mothers, grandfathers, grandmothers, uncles, fathers, and others taught native literature, history, geography, religious studies, medicine, botany, zoology, soil science, astronomy, political science, law, and manual skills such as making dresses, lodges, bows, and arrows. Professional storytellers shared ancient histories with children and adults alike, reconstructing the world through words and providing sacred oral texts that held the body of law that guided tribes in secular and spiritual matters. All Native Americans had educational systems before Columbus, and all native societies valued learning and wisdom.

Indian models of formal education did not conform with those used by Europeans, so with an air of superiority, whites deemed Indian education nonexistent. Because Indian education centered around an oral tradition—not a written tradition—Europeans determined that traditional Indian learning was flawed and unreliable. And because native education focused on a spiritual understanding of humans as being a part of nature, not above nature, Europeans discredited native education. For numerous reasons, Europeans, and later, Americans, declared that Native Americans had no education, government, or religion. Such a state mattered little to officers sent to defeat Indians, but it mattered a great deal to missionaries and reformers who wanted to uplift their brothers and sisters with the light of the one true civilization. European-American education became the mechanism through which humanitarians wanted to accomplish the transformation of Native Americans to civilized humans.

Although Harvard University admitted some Indians in the seventeenth century, and Dartmouth's charter stated that one of the goals of the institution was "civilizing and christianizing the children of pagans," these institutions had little interest in Native American students or curriculum based on American Indian-related subjects. Most public schools in the United States denied Indians admission, and native parents had little interest in sending their children to white schools. This attitude changed in the early nineteenth century when several Eastern Woodlands tribes—especially Wyandots, Delawares, Choctaws, and Cherokees—sent their children to white schools as a survival strategy. In mission schools, and later in public schools, Indian children learned to read, write, and speak English. Knowledge of the English language led native children to learn about politics, economics, military strategies, and diplomacy.

In a sense, Native Americans turned the power of the English language to their own advantage, using it to defend their people against white settlers and government agents. At the same time, eastern tribes placated whites who wanted the people to learn a "civilized" language. Some of the tribes, including Choctaws, used English as the basis to write their own languages phonetically. They communicated with each other in their own languages through letters and other documents that whites and some other Indians could not read. Choctaw historian Donna Akers has shown that Peter Pitchlyn communicated many times with his relatives through letters written in his tribal language. While he was in Washington, D.C., representing the Choctaw Nation, Pitchlyn wrote letters that could be read only by Choctaws who understood English and Choctaw.

Although some tribes valued public education in English, most tribes considered the system foreign. In the early years of the reservation system, agents confined most of their educational goals to industrial education provided by agricultural teachers, blacksmiths, masons, and mechanics. On some reservations, Native American men had knowledge of agriculture, but on others, they had no tradition in agriculture. Many Native American nations, particularly those from the Eastern Woodlands, had farmed for generations, but among most of these people, women did the farming. As a result, agents and agricultural instructors sought to alter traditional gender roles, forcing men to farm and women to remain within the home.

During the reservation era, vocational teachers taught men to clear lands, plow with harnesses and mules, and sow seeds. Teachers taught native men to harvest crops and prepare them for food or for sale off the reservation. They could not teach native men how to fend off grasshoppers and drought to ensure successful crops. They could not provide men with a new sense of worth because they were no longer hunters, fishers, or primary providers. Some vocational teachers were well meaning, but they watched the people starve when crops failed and government rations did not appear in sufficient quantities. Agents sometimes hired masons, mechanics, wheelwrights, carpenters, blacksmiths, bakers, harness makers, and other tradesmen to teach Indians and attend to the needs of the agency. If an agent needed a mason to build a brick building, he contracted with a mason to do the work and supplied Indian labor to help him. In the process, the natives learned masonry but received little or no remuneration.

Agents generally allowed missionaries to offer native children formal education, which always included a liberal sprinkling of Christian education. Missionaries established schools on reservations and were often associated with the American Board of Commissioners for Foreign Missions (supported by public and private funds). On most reservations, agents eventually established government schools or contracted with Christian missionaries for educational opportunities–all in English. Teachers presented lessons in English on reading, writing, history, and math. The curriculum on reservations focused on learning the three *R*s and agricultural-home economics education. This was the same model followed at American Indian boarding schools located off the reservations, where teachers and administrators had total control over Indian pupils. The development of formal education for Native Americans is presented in Margaret Connell Szasz's *Education and the American Indian* and in her pathbreaking article, "Listening to the Native Voices," in *Montana* (1989). Szasz shows the transition of Indian education; from the boarding schools to Indians' changing philosophies about formal education, Szasz offers an understanding of the dynamic culture of native peoples and education.

In 1879, Captain Richard Henry Pratt established the first American Indian boarding school off a reservation at Carlisle Barracks, Pennsylvania. He founded a school based on a military model that required students to wear military uniforms, march from place to place, and adhere to strict discipline. Although teachers instructed students in many disciplines, the major curriculum focused on industrial-vocational education so that students could leave school with a trade in sewing, cooking, housekeeping, ranching, agriculture, printing, baking, masonry, and so forth. Boys and girls worked for their keep, milking cows, baking bread, cooking meals, butchering cattle, raising vegetables, cleaning grounds, and repairing dormitories. Whites tried to make schools self-sufficient, forcing students to participate in the programs. Matrons, teachers, and disciplinarians at Carlisle punished children for infractions by whipping them, confining them, forcing them to work, shaming them, and withholding food.

At Carlisle and later Indian boarding schools, administrators and teachers punished native children for speaking their first languages. A teacher of a Navajo first-grader heard the boy speak Diné Bizzad (he spoke in Navajo, asking a girl for a pencil) and forced him to come forward and lie face down on the floor in front of the teacher's desk. He remained there all day without food or water, urinating and defecating on himself, and sobbing throughout the day as a result of his embarrassment. A Delaware girl spoke Lenape and was forced to scrub mortar between bricks of a building with a toothbrush, soap, and water. Many times, school officials tried to whip the language out of children. Such a beating is described by Ojibwe author Gordon Henry in "The Prisoner of Haiku," a fiction story that appeared in *Earth Song, Sky Spirit.*

> A few teachers in the school didn't like the way he continuously spoke his own native language in school, so they punished him. Two strong men with the force of God and Jesus who knows what else dragged him outside on a bitter wind-chilled Minnesota day and tied him to an iron post. They left him then without food, without water, through the night.

The other boys at the school heard the young boy "screaming in defiance all night, defending the language, calling wind, calling relatives, singing, so he wouldn't forget." When the teachers untied the boy, he could speak no more, except silent words that floated in the air and rested in the ears of native listeners, who heard what he was saying without sound, without spoken words.

The U.S. government supported Indian boarding schools as institutions through which to destroy Native American cultures, languages, arts, and identities. Indian agents, soldiers, and Indian policemen rounded up children age five and above on reservations, forcing parents to give up their children or face prison terms at Alcatraz or other federal penitentiaries. In 1907, several Hopi Indian families hid their children and refused to allow whites to take their children to boarding school. Agents ordered fathers to be arrested and sent them to Alcatraz. Native American parents hated to lose their children, fearing whites would pollute them, destroying their minds, bodies, and spirits. Several children died at Indian schools, from smallpox, measles, cholera, tuberculosis, and pneumonia. Others died of sickness brought on by severe depression, loneliness, and abuse.

When children became ill at a boarding school, white doctors and nurses treated them in the school infirmary or sent them home to die. When the children of Navajo leader Manuelito contracted measles at Carlisle, officials sent them home, where they infected their father, who died of the disease. In his classic autobiography, Don Talayesva (Hopi) details his own case of pneumonia while he attended Sherman Indian Institute in Riverside, California. Nurses first assigned him to one ward of the school infirmary and then the second ward, which contained the most serious cases. Nurses believed he was going to die, so they ordered his coffin. Talayesva explained that he saw Hopi boys watching him from

As with Native American children everywhere in the United States, the government forced Pima girls and boys to attend an Indian school in Sacaton, Arizona. Government administrators, teachers, and matrons worked to assimilate native children into white society through formal education and work. Here Pima girls are peeling vegetables for a meal.

the door before seeing a Hopi man standing near his bed dressed in traditional ceremonial outfit.

According to Talayesva, the man explained that he was a guardian spirit and would teach the boy a lesson by sending him to the land of the dead. Talayesva had an "afterlife" experience closely associated with his own culture before returning to the ward to hug his own cold body and return to life. He recovered from pneumonia, but other children died at boarding schools and were buried in the schools' cemeteries. No one knows how many children died at the boarding schools, because a detailed study of mortality among native students at each of the schools has not been conducted. Works by historians Robert Trennert, Muscogee Tsianina Lomawaima, and Jean Keller discuss the deep emotion felt by parents who lost their children at the boarding schools.

According to Chippewa historian Brenda Child, author of *Boarding School Seasons,* native parents often wrote letters to school officials, reminding whites to feed, clothe, and care for their children properly so that their children could remain healthy. Native American parents lost a part of their lives when they lost their children to boarding schools, where whites forced them to remain for one to eight years, sometimes without visits home.

Pratt and others tried to instill the Protestant work ethic in children through the school curriculum and Outing Programs that placed native boys and girls into the homes and workplaces of whites, who trained them in trades and helped "civilize" them through their close familial and professional associations. Often, native children lived with white host families who reportedly taught Indian "values," including the work ethic, thrift, religion, and family. At Sherman Indian Institute, the Outing Program primarily placed boys at work temporarily on ranches at low incomes and did little except provide cheap labor for white employers. Nevertheless, many native people enjoyed the work experience away from the school. Robert Levi, a Cahuilla who attended Sherman, once commented that he thought the Outing Program was positive because it provided children with an opportunity to earn money, which was scarce for native students.

Carlisle Indian School became the model for other off-reservation Native American boarding schools, such as Haskell, Hampton, Phoenix, Sherman, Albuquerque, Chemawa, and Chilocco. By 1900, the government boasted 148 Indian boarding schools and 225 Indian day schools. And by 1900, the government had enrolled approximately twenty thousand Native American students each year in its various schools. The number of boarding schools and reservation schools grew during the twentieth century, and some public school systems located adjacent to reservations accepted native students, in part to capture contracts provided by the federal government. However, public schools generally pushed Indians into vocational education. A counselor once explained to a Wyandot youth, "Your mother's an Indian, your father's an upholsterer, and let's face it, you're not smart enough to go to college so you'd better stick with wood shop and carpentry."

Curricular emphasis for Native Americans at boarding schools, reservation day schools, and public schools remained on industrial-vocational education during most of the twentieth century. In large part, whites selected the curriculum for Native Americans and continued to destroy Indian languages, history, art, music, and so forth until the 1930s and 1940s, when white policy makers began to reexamine the value of traditional Indian curriculum. In addition, whites began to reconsider the value of higher education among Native Americans, although this transformation was not universal and gradually materialized over the course of the twentieth century. During the century, Indian education became an important issue among Native Americans living on and off reservations, in part because many native peoples realized that formal education was a survival tactic, a mechanism through which to assert self-determination.

INDIAN HEALTH ON RESERVATIONS

Health among Native Americans changed as a result of the reservation system. American Indians had always been concerned about their health, and every tribe had doctors. Medicine men and women were not "witch doctors" as portrayed in books, movies, and some documents written by white observers. Among their own people, medicine people used their innate or acquired power to do good or harm to others. They had knowledge of plants, animals, and natural substances that served as agents of healing. They knew the correct songs and prayers, the right graphic representations to make on rocks, soil, or people to be healed. They knew how to treat people for physical, mental, and spiritual sicknesses, generally approaching their patients in a holistic manner. Midwives had knowledge of prenatal and postnatal care as well as birthing. However, their traditional training did not prepare them to deal with "white man's diseases" such as smallpox, measles, influenza, tuberculosis, cholera, malaria, pneumonia, whooping cough, and meningitis, which ravaged reservation people.

If funds and personnel were available, a reservation agent could hire a doctor or nurse, or both. The Indian office sometimes hired incompetent physicians who could not find employment in other places. However, this was not always the case, because some doctors and nurses working for the army or the medical division of the Office of Indian Affairs were truly committed to their work and did the best job they could without facilities, budgets, medicines, personnel, and equipment. Some doctors called their native counterparts fakes, frauds, and charlatans. But some of them respected native healers and studied their techniques. In general, reservations had inadequate health-care systems, even though some physicians, including Charles Eastman (Dakota), Edward Latham, Washington Matthews, Margaret W. Koenig, Carlos Montezuma (Yavapai), and James Walker, genuinely worked for the well-being of native people.

Reservations also lacked health facilities such as clinics and hospitals. Often doctors, nurses, agents, and missionaries cried out to the Indian office to build health facilities, but budgets prevented their construction. On the Yakama Reservation, for example, agents asked for a hospital to be built in the 1870s and 1880s, but funding for a hospital did not materialize until 1928, and even then the agency had only enough money to renovate a building at old Fort Simcoe. On a few reservations, the government built health clinics or hospitals, but this was rare, regardless of provisions set forth in treaties to provide Native Americans with medical care. Few reservations had tuberculosis sanatoriums, and officials sent ill patients hundreds of miles to sanatoriums where they convalesced or died.

If the army occupied a fort near a reservation, the post doctor sometimes treated Native Americans. Dr. Washington Matthews practiced medicine at Fort Defiance, near the Navajo Agency headquarters, and he treated Navajos as well as military personnel. In fact, because he greatly respected his Navajo counterparts, native medicine people invited Matthews to study their work among Navajo patients. The result was important studies of Navajo Nightway, Mountain Chant, songs, stories, and prayers. For years Dr. James Walker worked among Lakota people and was accepted by medicine men, who taught him some of the most sacred body of knowledge known to the people. Dr. Margaret Koenig worked among the Ho-Chunk (Winnebago) in Nebraska, treating the people for tuberculosis and composing one of the most insightful treatises on the disease among the people. She demonstrated how Ho-Chunk traditional practices of giving away blankets, pillows, pipes, cups, and so forth after a person's death contributed to the spread of tuberculosis.

Non-Indians living and working with native people often identified health issues on reservations long before bureaucrats in Washington considered widespread problems. For example, doctors, agents, and missionaries recognized that they had a full-blown epidemic of tuberculosis among native peoples of the West in the 1890s and tried to convince the commissioner of Indian affairs of the fact. Finally, in 1903, the commissioner sent a survey to the agencies and was shocked to receive verification of the epidemic. The commissioner reported the results of his national survey in his *Annual Report of the Commissioner of Indian Affairs* in 1904. The commissioner acted on the information, although he blamed Indians for the disease because they lived in poverty and squalor—refusing to follow the white road of cleanliness, progress, and economic development. He failed to acknowledge that the United States had created the conditions that brought about tuberculosis on the reservation.

Congress refused to increase health funding for Indians sufficiently to fight tuberculosis. Native Americans died in large numbers as a result of the disease and suffered from high death rates in comparison to rates for other races in states and territories where reservations were located. Tuberculosis was the most prevalent and deadly malady on the reservations in the late nineteenth and early twentieth centuries. Tuberculosis killed Native Americans of all ages, but it particularly killed young people from roughly fifteen to thirty years of age. This was the Native American workforce and the age group of people who created the next generation of native families. Between 1924 and 1944, tuberculosis killed more females than males, most likely because females took care of their families, including those who became ill, exposing themselves to tubercular bacilli through coughing, sneezing, spitting, and bleeding.

Several conditions on the reservations contributed to the spread of tuberculosis, pneumonia, meningitis, whooping cough, and influenza. On the reservations, Native Americans had increased contact with non-Indians, who introduced pathogens into their rural populations. Bacteria and viruses, so common among whites, African-Americans, and Asian-Americans, were new to Native Americans. By the late nineteenth century, several non-Indians came in contact with Indians through the railroads, wagon roads, steamboats, trade, commerce, and military and civilian personnel working at the reservations. Non-Indians introduced bacteria and viruses onto the reservations, or Native Americans who had traveled away from the reservations and returned brought them home with them. The spread of new bacteria and viruses was the major cause of disease on the reservations, but the pathogens spread rapidly on reservations for several reasons.

Bacteria and viruses found wonderful hosts on the reservations: people who had few or no natural immunities. By the end of the nineteenth century, many Indians had already suffered severely from epidemics of smallpox and measles, but most native people had not been introduced to tuberculosis and other diseases. Many Native Americans were malnourished as a result of confinement to the reservations and the destruction of native foods by hunters, farmers, ranchers, and lumbermen. Scientists debate the role of nutrition in rendering people susceptible to disease, but Native Americans believe that the deprivation of traditional Indian foods made them vulnerable to disease. There is no way to quantify the effects of malnutrition as a contributing factor in disease and mortality among Native Americans historically, but given what is known today, it is plausible that the destruction of native foods was one factor affecting the spread of disease.

In the rush to confine Native Americans to reservations, government officials failed to realize the far-reaching significance of their actions in terms of food. On the Great Plains, the government had actively encouraged the destruction of the buffalo. At the beginning of the nineteenth century, roughly thirteen million buffalo roamed the West. Between 1872 and 1874, hunters killed three million. By 1878, white hunters had exterminated the southern herd, and by 1883, whites had wiped out the buffalo on the Northern Plains. In 1903, the government counted thirty-four buffalo in the United States. White hunters had destroyed the main source of food for most tribes of the plains and the Rocky Mountains. And what happened on the Great Plains was mirrored in many areas of the West, where native foods of salmon, roots, berries, game, and grains fell victim to white hunters, farmers, ranchers, railroads, and towns. White settlement destroyed plant and animal habitats, reducing native foods and inviting malnutrition.

White hunters depleted the deer, antelope, bear, rabbit, geese, ducks, and other game. In California, Oregon, Washington, Idaho, Montana, and Wyoming, farmers and ranchers destroyed millions of nutritious roots, berries, grains, and other fruits and vegetables harvested by Native Americans. Farmers tilled the soil, planting corn, beans, tomatoes, potatoes, and others. Many times, these plant foods had far less nutritive value than those plant foods destroyed by farming at a considerable expense in terms of human labor and production costs. Ranchers grazed thousands of head of cattle, hogs, horses, mules, and sheep, which ate the very plants once eaten by Native Americans.

After they were confined to reservations, native people became dependent on government rations that rarely came in sufficient amounts to sustain reservation populations. Even in those rare cases where government rations were plentiful, the bodies of Native Americans had a difficult and sometimes impossible time breaking down this food because it was foreign to their systems. As a result, Native Americans became malnourished, making their bodies more susceptible to infections. Over the course of the twentieth century, the consumption of native foods declined more with each passing year, and the result has been the rise of diabetes among Native Americans whose "thrift genes" have caused them to store calories from processed foods. Native Americans have contracted diabetes Type 2, which contributes to mortality related to heart disease, hypertension, amputations, renal disease, and others.

Also, the loss of freedom caused depression among Indian people. No one can measure the effects of this form of extreme stress on Native Americans living on reservations in the nineteenth century. However, today medical researchers have confirmed that stress affects a person's health, and stress contributed to deaths on reservations. In 1878, Shoshoni Chief Washakie pointed out that in addition to starvation, Native Americans suffered from "fits of desperation." By the beginning of the twentieth century, many Native Americans had been defeated by the army, and most had been forced onto reservations or consolidated onto Indian lands apart from whites. Native American prisoners of war lived under military guard, while reservation Indians lived under the watchful eye and heavy hand of the Office of Indian Affairs.

The Office of Indian Affairs contributed significantly to native depression. The office actively sought to destroy tribal governments, sovereignty, religions, languages, and arts. It set up schools to destroy Native American culture and to replace it with white civilization. Whites continually reminded Indians that they were "inferior" people, heathens who had no future and would become the "vanished" Americans. This notion gave rise to a field of anthropology and linguistics designed to preserve ethnographies and languages of native people before all American Indians died, taking with them tribal knowledge that would be lost forever. White Americans became obsessed about "The Last" person of a particular tribe—like Ishi the Yahi—while ignoring the surviving Native Americans languishing on the reservations. Many whites believed that Indians had no future, no hope. Some Indians gave up as well, dying of social anomie or turning to alcohol to drown their depression, which increased their despair and set up a dangerous cycle that has not yet been broken. Others persevered, turning to their spiritual beliefs for supplication.

Native American housing and patterns of habitation also changed, and contributed to ill health, as a result of the reservation system. Many Indians had lived in temporary housing, moving from place to place during certain times of the year. Others had moved about in pursuit of the buffalo, following herds across vast regions of the plains. Still others had raided from one region to the next, moving rapidly on horseback. Native Americans from the Columbia Plateau of Washington, Oregon, and Idaho generally had lived in A-framed log and mat lodges during the winter months. In the spring of the year, they had dismantled their mat lodges and moved onto the plateau to gather roots and hunt small game. When they left their permanent village sites near inland rivers, they lived in tipis that they covered either with buffalo hides or tule mats. The destruction of buffalo limited their use of tipis. Apaches and some Paiutes lived in wickiups, making the small lodges wherever they went and leaving them when they traveled.

Comanches, Kiowas, Cheyennes, Lakotas, Dakotas, Crows, Blackfeet, Shoshonis, and many other tribes generally lived in tipis. Native Americans in California lived in a variety of houses, setting them up and taking them down whenever they moved to gather foods. Other Indians, like Hopis, Zunis, and Lagunas, lived in pueblos or unit houses tied together like apartments. In every case, Native Americans had devised methods to keep their homes clean. Each time they moved, they settled in a clean area, free from an accumulation of garbage, feces, and other impurities. As a result of movement and settlement patterns, Native Americans rarely suffered from unsanitary conditions. Confinement on reservations meant that Indians did not live in their old styles of homes. During the nineteenth century, some reservation Indians continued to live in hogans, wickiups, mat lodges, plank homes, earthen lodges, and tipis. However, people often became separated from the natural resources needed to sustain such housing, and their permanent settlement on the reservation obviated a more permanent home built with materials available on the reservation.

Most Indian people on the reservations eventually lived in miserable shacks of one or two rooms with dirt floors. Their new homes were stationary structures, often built with lean-to kitchens so people could cook outside. The homes were poorly heated and ventilated, and they were drafty in winter when winds whipped through the reservations. Hamlin Garland remarked that Indians he met lived in "small, badly-ventilated log or frame hovels of one or two rooms" and that tuberculosis "is very common among them because of their unsanitary housing during cold weather." Before the reservation era, Native Americans had not shared their living quarters with so many microorganisms, and they were not accustomed to using soap and water to kill unseen enemies. They had no concept of bacteria, even after Robert Koch discovered bacteria under a microscope in 1882, and they did not know how to protect themselves against bacteria and viruses that multiplied rapidly in native shacks and traveled by way of hands, fingers, mouths, foods, water, dust, sputum, and blood. Indian homes on reservations became lively breeding grounds for pathogens that thrived on their new hosts.

Armies of microorganisms on reservations killed far more Indians than soldiers did, although the exact count is not known because the Office of Indian Affairs did not keep accurate vital statistics, even though Congress authorized it to do so in 1884.

Indian families did not have general knowledge about pathogens because agencies provided little education to inform them. Indeed, the general public had little understanding of public health until the first half of the twentieth century, and Native Americans had even less knowledge. During the early twentieth century, the Office of Indian Affairs provided a few seminars, including some to help new mothers care for their babies, but most Indians spoke limited English and had a great distrust of white people. Native Americans did not know to isolate patients within the home, so adults and children with tuberculosis, pneumonia, meningitis, whooping cough, and other diseases shared their sicknesses with family and friends.

Adults who contracted diseases often turned to sweat lodges, which were holy and spiritual places, to purge themselves of their ailments and sing for cures. Those persons who joined these sick people in small sweat lodges shared the sick people's pathogens, passing them on to others. Adults and children alike visited Indian doctors, who eradicated diseases by using their ancient methods, including sucking the disease-causing spirit from the person. This procedure likely helped spread disease from patient to doctor and doctor to other patients. During a tuberculosis epidemic among the Quechan of southern California, an Indian doctor dreamed his soul traveled to Avékwame, a sacred mountain, and there spoke to a powerful spirit named Ƙumastmo, who had the doctor suck blood from his chest and taught him to be a sucking doctor who could cure tuberculosis. The doctor returned to his people saying that he could destroy the evil disease.

Many whites discounted such assertions by Indian medicine men and women, but Quechans and other native people kept their faith in traditional medicine people, although some also sought aid from white physicians and nurses. In addition to other changes occurring on reservations, Native Americans had to make the transition from linking disease and death to natural and spirit-soul causes—including forms of witchcraft—to linking disease and death to white man's diseases caused by viruses and bacteria. This transition was not easy or sudden but rather developed over time and with considerable self-evaluation. On the Navajo Reservation, for example, Annie Dodge Wauneka worked

After Native Americans fought an unsuccessful war, the government forced recalcitrant warriors in prisons. A Native American prisoner painted this representation of Fort Marion in St. Augustine, Florida. American Indians in prisons and on reservations contracted many diseases, particularly pneumonia and tuberculosis.

tirelessly among her people to convince them that tuberculosis emerged from invisible bugs that traveled in the air and in their bodies, destroying the body. She used her knowledge of Navajo beliefs about positive and negative forces within Diné cosmology to help people understand how the bacteria works.

Health has been an important issue among native people throughout the twentieth century. Native Americans and whites knew that health among native peoples was poor, even though most Native American populations continued to grow throughout the twentieth century. High fetal and infant mortality rates plagued most Indian nations until the 1950s, and Native Americans suffered from some of the highest crude death rates in the United States, as a result of tuberculosis, pneumonia, gastrointestinal disorders (including dysentery and diarrhea), whooping cough, and accidents. As Cherokee scholar Russell Thornton has demonstrated, the Native American population in the United States reached its nadir in 1890, and most observers of American Indians knew that Native

Americans were suffering severely in the 1880s and 1890s as a result of confinement to reservations. Conscientious white reformers witnessed the ill effects of the reservation system and sought to help their native brothers and sisters by destroying most reservations–dividing them into parcels and providing individuals with their own land.

Selected Readings and Bibliography

General works dealing with the reservation system and allotment include Francis's, *Native Time;* Champagne, *The Native North American Almanac;* Gibson, *The American Indian;* Debo, *History of the Indians of the United States;* and Hoxie, ed., *Indians in American History*. Histories cited earlier that deal with the reservation experience and allotment are Gibson's *The Kickapoo,* Martin's *The American Indian and the Problem of History,* Utley's *The Indian Frontier of the American West, 1846–1890,* Mayhall's *The Kiowas,* Trafzer and Scheuerman's *Renegade Tribe,* Crum's *The Road on Which We Come,* Debo's *Geronimo,* Tyler's *A History of Indian Policy,* Sheehan's *Seeds of Extinction,* and Washburn's *Red Man's Land, White Man's Law*. In addition, oral interviews with historian Jean Keller, who is completing a study of student health at Sherman Indian Institute, informs the section on the varied student perspectives of Indian schools and on the minds of some reformers in terms of human lives. This topic is also addressed in Thornton's *American Indian Holocaust*. The early reservations in California and their role in national Indian policies is addressed in Rawls's *Indians of California,* Carrico's *Strangers in a Stolen Land,* Hurtado's *Indian Survival on the California Frontier,* and Phillips's *Indians and Indian Agents*. Other helpful sources include Hoxie's *The Final Promise,* Weeks's *Farewell, My Nation,* and Danzinger's *Indians and Bureaucrats*.

Bee, Robert L. *Crosscurrents along the Colorado: The Impact of Government Policy on the Quechan Indians*. Tucson: University of Arizona Press, 1981.

Berthrong, Donald J. *The Cheyenne and Arapaho Ordeal*. Norman: University of Oklahoma Press, 1976.

Burt, Larry. *Tribalism in Crisis*. Albuquerque: University of New Mexico Press, 1982.

Child, Brenda. *Boarding School Seasons*. Lincoln: University of Nebraska Press, 1998.

Carlson, Leonard A. *Indians, Bureaucrats and Land: The Dawes Act and the Decline of Indian Farming*. Westport, Conn.: Greenwood Press, 1981.

Controneo, Ross R., and Jack Dozier. "A Time of Disintegration: The Coeur d' Alene and the Dawes Act." *Western Historical Quarterly* 5 (1974): 405–419.

Deloria, Vine Jr. *Custer Died for Your Sins*. New York: Macmillan, 1969.

——, ed. *American Indian Policy in the Twentieth Century*. Norman: University of Oklahoma Press, 1985.

Fey, Harold E., and D'Arcy McNickle. *Indians and Other Americans*. New York: Harper, 1959.

Fritz, Henry E. *The Movement for Indian Assimilation, 1860–1890*. Philadelphia: University of Pennsylvania Press, 1965.

Hagan, William T. *Indian Police and Judges.* New Haven: Yale University Press, 1966.

——. *United States-Comanche Relations: The Reservation Years.* New Haven: Yale University Press, 1976.

——. *The Indian Rights Association.* Tucson: University of Arizona Press, 1985.

Holdford, David M. "The Subversion of the Indian Land Allotment System, 1887–1934." *Indian Historian* 8 (Spring 1975): 11–21.

Hoxie, Frederick E. "The Curious Story of Reformers and the American Indian." *Indians in American History.* Frederick E. Hoxie, ed. Arlington Heights, Ill.: Harlan Davidson, 1988.

Jackson, Helen Hunt. *A Century of Dishonor.* New York: Harper & Brothers, 1881.

Josephy, Alvin M. Jr. *The Indian Heritage of America.* New York: Knopf, 1968.

Keller, Robert H. *American Protestantism and United States Indian Policy,* 1869–1882. Lincoln: University of Nebraska Press, 1983.

Mardock, Robert W. *The Reformers and the American Indian.* Columbia: University of Missouri Press, 1971.

McDonnell, Janet A. *The Dispossession of the American Indian,* 1887–1934. Bloomington: Indiana University Press, 1991.

McNickle, D'Arcy. *Native American Tribalism.* New York: Oxford University Press, 1973.

Miner, H. Craig. *The Corporation and the Indian: Tribal Sovereignty and Industrial Civilization in Indian Territory,* 1865–1907. Columbia: University of Missouri Press, 1976.

Otis, D. S. *The Dawes Act and the Allotment of Indian Lands.* Francis Paul Prucha, ed. Norman: University of Oklahoma Press, 1973.

Patterson, James. *America's Struggle against Poverty, 1900–1954.* Cambridge: Harvard University Press, 1986.

Price, Monroe E. *Law and the American Indian.* Indianapolis: Bobbs-Merrill, 1973.

Prucha, Francis P. *The Great Father.* Lincoln: University of Nebraska Press, 1984.

Simmons, Leo W., ed. *Sun Chief.* New Haven: Yale University Press, 1942.

Sweeney, Edwin R. *Cochise, Chiricahua Apache Chief.* Norman: University of Oklahoma Press, 1991.

Szasz, Margaret Connell. *Education and the American Indian: The Road to Self-Determination since 1928.* Albuquerque: University of New Mexico Press, 1977.

Trafzer, Clifford E. *Death Stalks the Yakama: Epidemiological Transitions and Mortality on the Yakama Indian Reservation, 1888–1964.* East Lansing: Michigan State University Press, 1997.

Unrau, William E. *The Kansa Indians.* Norman: University of Oklahoma Press, 1971.

Washburn, Wilcomb E. *The Assault on Indian Tribalism: The General Allotment Law (Dawes Act) of 1887.* New York: J. B. Lippincott, 1975.

CHAPTER 14

SURVIVAL THROUGH PEYOTE, GHOST DANCE, AND RELIGIOUS REVITALIZATION

Forced removal to reservations and confinement on specific tracts of land were devastating for Native Americans. The people generally suffered anomie on the reservations, a form of societal depression that led some people into despair, substance abuse, and suicide. However, many Native Americans survived American Indian policies designed to destroy their cultures. Tribes, bands, villages, clans, families, and individuals drew on strengths of their cultures to preserve portions of their heritage, and they used the power of their cultures as the key means of physical survival.

CULTURAL STRESS, SURVIVAL, AND WORK

Native American cultures had been under assault for years, but the second half of the nineteenth century was a remarkably difficult time for them. Many American Indians suffered severe stress, but there is no way to measure scientifically the degree of depression suffered by the people during the reservation era—except to listen to native voices of the period. Native Americans had suffered military conquest, land loss, relocations, governance by white agents, establishment of churches and schools, disease, and death. During the bleak era of the reservation, Native Americans survived the holocaust and lived to nurture the next generations through the strength and tenacity of groups and individuals. Contrary to popular stereotypes of lazy and drunken Indians, many native men and women persevered, working hard for their communities and ensuring their families' survival. Whenever possible, women continued their age-old practice of providing for their families. They gathered natural foods, planted peas, beans, squash, corn, and melons.

301

Men hunted and fished to supplement the family diet, and women and children hunted and fished, sharing the work of cleaning, drying, and smoking meat for winter. By hunting, fishing, and gathering, people maintained some measure of the old ways, traveling in groups, re-creating traditional bonds between one another and observing rituals, prayers, songs, and ceremonies to ensure success and continuance. In the 1940s, Charlie Williams, a Nez Perce living on the Colville Indian Reservation, reported in his diary that Mrs. Snake River Kamiakin often gathered bushel baskets of camas and kouse, sharing her bounty with Palouse, Nez Perce, and others living in Nespelem, Washington. Even in the 1990s, Mary Jim, a Palouse Indian living on the Yakama Reservation, gathered camas and kouse, cooking and mashing kouse, creating biscuits by squeezing it in her hands and leaving it in the sun to dry. She also collected moss that she cooked in deep earthen pits.

Another form of survival revolved around ceremonies and rituals of thanksgiving. All tribes had traditions of giving thanks to the Creator, plants, animals, water, and earth for providing for the people. Many tribes gave thanks for fish, game, roots, berries, acorns, wild rice, maple syrup, and other foods. Those gathering fruits, vegetables, and grains often followed culturally specified procedures, songs, words, and prayers before, during, and after gathering. This included speaking to the plants and giving thanks to the Creator. In the same fashion, hunters had prescribed rituals to follow in preparing for hunts, including a clean state of mind, sweat bathing, hunting songs, sacrifices, prayers, and procedures of walking and talking. Some hunters held bows in one hand and arrows in the other, standing in single file and singing the same song. After they purchased rifles, these same men each held a rifle in one hand and bullets in the other. Although hunting weapons changed, hunting rituals often remained intact, illustrating a dynamic form of acculturation. In similar fashion, Indian farmers offered prayers of thanksgiving to the Creator for plants during seasons of planting, growing, and harvesting.

Northwestern Indians from many tribes and bands held salmon ceremonies after the first catch, singing praises to the Creator and salmon people for their sacrifice to preserve human beings. The "law" directing humans to perform salmon ceremonies emerged at the time of creation, and humans had a spiritual obligation to perform the ceremonies. At one ritual, women sat on one side of the lodge and men on the other, following a leader who sang praise and prayers for salmon and water. The people ate salmon and drank water in holy communion, continuing a sacred bond that began at the beginning of time. During the ceremony, all participants ate salmon and traditional Indian foods in a lively feast that ended with song and prayer. At the conclusion of the salmon ceremony, people placed the remaining salmon bones, with head facing upriver, back into the river from which it had been taken to ensure another salmon run. Native Americans living throughout the Northwest performed salmon ceremonies without the permission of agents, and many continue salmon ceremonies today.

Indians worked at various jobs on and off the reservation to earn money for their families. Men, women, and children worked in family gardens, raising fruits and vegetables. They also raised horses and cattle, provided they had sufficient grazing lands to support livestock. They sold cattle and horses to earn money, and they butchered their own cattle for beef. During the 1880s, Snake River Kamiakin raised hundreds of fine horses in the canyons and plateaus adjacent to Snake River, but white settlement forced him onto the Colville Reservation. He drove his horses north along the Columbia River to Colville, where he quietly moved his family to Nespelem. However, he allowed his horses to graze on reservation and nonreservation lands, selling them to supplement his hunting, his wife's gathering, and their paltry reservation rations. Other Indians did the same to support themselves during the difficult times.

Many Indians worked for white farmers and ranchers living near reservations or traveled some distances to pick apples, hops, and cherries or harvest wheat, hay, and oats. In many regions of the West, Native Americans were the farm laborers during the late nineteenth and early twentieth centuries, traveling from place to place. Humishuma (Mourning Dove) recalled the time when her family and village starved, and her father left the tipi to seek work among whites. She did not know if he would ever return, and she grew so hungry she hated the song birds living in the trees above her lodge. Humishuma's mother found work in a nearby town, washing clothes for a prostitute. Her father returned, and both parents saved the family from starvation by their work. Other Indian families worked for food or wages. Some took jobs with railroads, building bridges, mending track, or repairing engines and cars at roundhouses. Women sold their rugs, baskets, bead work, dolls, and pottery at railway stations, sitting in shaded areas near the tracks where travelers milled about.

Native American men sometimes loaded wood, water, coal, and freight onto the trains while their wives sold goods. Along the Missouri, Colorado, and Columbia rivers, Native American men worked on steamboats, loading and unloading cargo. Quechans, Cocopas, and Mojaves cut wood to fuel the steam engines and stacked it on the decks of boats that plied the lower Colorado River. Coastal Indians worked in the fishing industry as sailors cruising lakes and oceans. Indians throughout the West loaded flatboats, barges, and wagons with freight in order to earn money for their families. Anson Damon, a trader and freighter working on the Navajo Reservation in the 1880s, married a Navajo woman whose children and grandchildren carried on Damon's freighting business. Today, Chancellor Damon and his brothers operate the largest truck line owned by Navajos, hauling freight on and off the reservation because of rights established by his ancestors. Other Indians worked in trading establishments, buying and selling items and finding markets for them. Some Indians worked for non-Indians who owned trading posts, dealing successfully with neighbors because they spoke native languages and understood native cultures.

Native Americans worked for the Office of Indian Affairs at various agencies, taking a variety of jobs. Some became policemen, clerks, janitors, and cooks, whereas others worked as secretaries, maids, cowboys, and interpreters. Agencies hired some Indians, providing native people with their first in-depth exposure to white bureaucracy, political maneuvering, administrative inaction, polemics, and rhetoric. The army continued to hire Indians as scouts during the late nineteenth century and employed Native Americans in a variety of jobs at military posts. Indians worked in the entertainment industry, which exploited the American and European fascination with Native Americans. From the 1880s into the twentieth century, white entrepreneurs hired Indians to ride, dance, sing, shoot, and attend fairs, rodeos, stock shows, and various celebrations. Presidents and other politicians paid Indians to attend their inaugurations, and business leaders paid native people to promote their products. Several Indians joined the Wild West shows, working for freedom and money.

Historian George Moses has provided the most enlightening treatment of Native Americans in the Wild West shows. The shows were contrived extravaganzas created by William F. Cody, or Buffalo Bill, Gordon Lillie, or Pawnee Bill, and others. Each show hired fifty to one hundred Indians—mostly men—who painted and dressed like Plains Indians and "attacked" soldiers and wagon trains to the delight of audiences worldwide. Because Indians performed in relatively small arenas under big tents, they often raced around and around their enemies, giving the popular impression that Indian warfare consisted of foolishly exposing oneself while white settlers hid behind wagon boxes firing at foolish fiends racing around the wagons. In many towns, Native Americans set up tipi villages so that tourists could enter real Indian villages and see real Indians. For a price, photographers took pictures of Native Americans or staged meetings between tourists and Indian employees. Sitting Bull, Geronimo, and other noted Indians worked for the Wild West shows, and many Indians traveled throughout the United States, Canada, and Europe with the troupes.

Even more Indians secured employment with medicine shows, traveling in the employ of snake oil salesmen who moved from town to town selling tonics that allegedly cured everything from heart disease to baldness. Native Americans entertained whites by dancing, drumming, and singing while decked out in their finest outfits. They held mini-powwows, made bows and arrows, and displayed beaded and leather crafts to draw people to the medicine show, where white salesmen extolled the virtues of their bottled products. Medicine show salesmen spun their lies shamelessly, telling crowds that their products were based on secret Indian ingredients and had curing powers beyond the imagination. Eastern manufacturers made most of these concoctions, which usually contained a fair amount of alcohol and did customers little good. Still, medicine shows were a very popular form of entertainment and revenue. They provided Indians a few jobs and a chance to escape the boredom of the reservation.

In 1881, John Healy and Charlie Bigelow began the Kickapoo Medicine Show, the largest medicine show company, which, at its peak, included thirty separate troupes. Healy and Bigelow hired about twenty Indians to travel with each troupe, although their numbers varied. Native Americans working with the medicine shows made $30 per month plus food, lodging, and transportation. They primarily worked during the summer in the eastern states, where most whites shared romantic images of noble savages but had little contact with Native Americans. White crowds came to see stereotypical Indians, like the ones they had read about in dime novels or seen in woodcuts and photographs. The evolving perception that all Indians looked like Plains Indians had its origins with Wild West and medicine shows. Motion pictures solidified this perception in the early twentieth century. Several Indians, including Chief Joseph's nephew, Yellow Wolf, earned extra money making headdresses and clothing worn by Indians in the movies.

SURVIVAL THROUGH TRADITION AND CHANGE

Native Americans survived reservation, allotment, and other governmental policies, in part through their own efforts to work during the era to make the best life possible for themselves and their families. The stereotypical perception that lazy Native Americans lived off the government dole belies the fact that Native Americans worked hard to survive. They also continued to use traditional medicines, gathering medicinal herbs to help the people. Dorothy Joseph, a Paiute-Shoshoni woman from Lone Pine, California, grew up chewing and eating early shoots of poison oak that made her people immune to the plant. Tohono O'odham gathered tiny leaves of creosote plants, and Cahuilla took white sage, both using the plants in medicinal teas. In the 1950s, Mary Lou Henry gathered sassafras root to give to her children as medicine when they suffered from colds or flu. Native Americans retained traditional knowledge of medicinal plants, although this knowledge was not as diffused among the people as it had been in years past. Still, parents and grandparents taught children and grandchildren about Indian medicines, preserving an aspect of their culture that agents and missionaries tried to destroy.

The result of traditional education is best illustrated by Katherine Saubel, a Cahuilla elder born on the Los Coyotes Reservation in southern California. She was raised in a traditional fashion, traveling about the deserts and mountains with her father and other tribal elders who taught her the ethnobotany of the region. "They didn't have textbooks on these things," she said in 1997. "They carried the knowledge in their head and used this knowledge to teach me about the plants." Saubel, one of two Native American women initiated into the National Women's Hall of Fame, is a national treasure, in part because of her work in preserving her language and knowledge about medicinal and edible plants. She has written books about the ethnobotany of southern California and helped numerous native and nonnative scholars understand the relationship of the people to plants.

Native Americans also strengthened community ties by studying plants and animals of their regions. Wyandot elder Eleonore Sioui, for example, uses plants and animals as a means to teach history, culture, and religion. They held onto traditional values and material items, thereby preserving their cultures in many ways. Cultural preservation was a conscious survival tactic, one that is still employed. People perpetuated their arts, including basketry, beadwork, bow making, pottery, painting, textiles' lithics, leather work, drawing, and dress making. They sometimes changed their arts, using new designs and materials, but they maintained their Indian identity through their art. On the Great Plains, Gourd Dancers used tin cans and stones to make their rattles, and southwestern Indians used cow hide to make moccasins, shields, and belts. Navajo women adopted rug designs from Persia and used wool made in Germantown, Pennsylvania.

Native women everywhere adopted small manufactured beads with which to decorate pendants, hair pieces, belt buckles, wallets, purses, watch fobs, dresses, and sheathes. Some Kiowa artists continued to paint on hides, whereas others moved to canvas as a new form of expression. Hopis like Paul Coochyamptewa continued the ancient tradition of carving wooden figurines called kachinas, given to girls during ceremonies. They used new carving knives, new paints, and found a market for their "dolls." Eloise Coochyamptewa also offered innovations, creating earrings and pendants in the form of tiny kachinas. In some ways, native arts changed—as most elements of culture change with time—but much remained rooted in tradition and formed a means of cultural survival. Sports and gambling were traditional among Native Americans, and Indians gravitated to both during the reservation era, in spite of objections by agents. Racing, throwing, jumping, and leaping had been a part of Native American cultures for generations, and during the reservation era, Indians continued to enjoy track and field activities. Sac Fox Jim Thorpe excelled in all sports, winning Olympic gold in the decathlon and being voted the best athlete of the first half of the twentieth century. Thorpe was great at football, baseball, and track, playing college and professional sports. Other Indians found joy in horse racing, canoe racing, swimming, and other competitions. Native American "cowboys" became famous in rodeo events that featured calf roping, steer wrestling, saddle and bareback bronco riding, and bull riding. Cherokee actor Will Rogers was a world-class roper and documented his abilities in the film *The Roping Fool.* Kumeyaay cowboys like Charlie and George Poncheti made their marks in rodeo, as did numerous other Indian cowboys.

Begaataway (lacrosse) and shinny (field hockey) also survived, as did other ball games played by native people. Lacrosse is a sacred game that continues to be played and is an important element of survival among people of the Six Nations. It is played on every educational level, at schools and universities from New York to California. New games played by whites, such as baseball and football, were added to the games played by American Indians. By the early twentieth century, most reservations had baseball and football teams that competed with others' community teams. Indian schools fostered the growth of baseball, football, and other sports, encouraging students to excel in sports of all kinds. Sports had always been a source of pride among Native Americans, and they contributed to cultural survival of native people during the reservation era. Such great athletes as Jim Thorpe, Anishinaabes Charles Bender and Joseph N. Guyon, Arapaho John Levi, Cahuilla Jon Meyers, Penobscot Louis F. Sockalexis, and Hopi Louis Tewanima helped revitalize their cultures through sports. In later years, Lakota Billy Mills and Narragansett Tarzan Brown distinguished themselves as world-class athletes. Teams at Carlisle, Haskell, Pembroke, and other institutions emphasized sports and provided native peoples with opportunity and pride through sports excellence. In addition, native peoples continued to play a host of guessing games, including stick games, moccasin games, and peone, an all-night game of chance accompanied by songs and laughter. All these games are still played today, and usually native people place bets on the games. In southern California, Cocopa, Quechan, Cahuilla, Luiseño, Kumeyaay, and others play peone.

Music, song, and dance continued on the reservations in spite of agents who sought to stamp out these aspects of Native American culture. Cherokee ethnomusicologist Charlotte Heth has presented several examples in her work, *Native American Dance.* Her study demonstrates native continuity through time from the prereservation era to the present. In the case of the Kiowa Tonkonga, or Black Legs Military Society, the people temporarily ended the Black Leg ceremony, but Kiowa Gus Palmer Sr. renewed it in 1958 to commemorate the death of his brother, Lyndreth Palmer, and other Kiowas killed during World War II. Since then, Kiowa people remember their war dead of the distant past and recent past through the Black Leg Dance. The Black Leg Dance is celebrated only among the Kiowas, but other tribes and bands perform other

In 1950, the Associated Press named Jim Thorpe the greatest football player during the first half of the twentieth century. Thorpe won Olympic gold and has become a symbol for many Native American athletes who have excelled in sports.

dances. The powwow became a celebration centered around singing, dancing, and drumming that was shared by many tribes. Eastern Woodlands people and plains people had joined in powwows for years, dancing and singing to the beat of drums.

On reservations, and in urban areas, Indians continue powwows, gathering for song and dance, sharing and laughter. Powwows offer a time for people to socialize in a positive fashion and forbid tension and conflicts between participants. During powwows, people are supposed to set aside their anger and animosity so that the community at large may enjoy the celebration of being Indian. If dancers lose feathers or other items from their outfits, the communal message is that a person or group attending the powwow has brought to the celebration negative power that must be tempered through prescribed procedures that restore harmony. Powwows fostered Native American identity and culture, and the drum represented the heart and soul of communities that beat time and time again to ensure life for the people. Songs of the powwow represent the continual voice of the people to keep alive the heart of communities, the link between past and present, secular and spiritual.

Hopi Snake Dances are another ceremony that contribute to cultural survival, although the Moqui Agency tried to suppress them. Antelope and Snake societies offered the Snake Dance to fulfill an obligation and remember with reverence the need for rain. The people hold Snake Dances at pueblos in August every year as a prayer for rain to help their crops survive the final stages of growth. Snake Dances link the people with spirits who control the elements and make possible physical survival of the people. Antelope and Snake dancers and singers spend several days in an underground ceremonial chamber called a kiva preparing for the final phase of the ceremony, which is conducted in the plaza of a pueblo (a conglomerate of unit houses). With rattles moving in time and voices raised in chant, the Antelope Society sings in unison as Snake Dancers hold the midsection of snakes in their mouths, dancing with them and setting them in the plaza until the end of the dance, when men gather the snakes into bags and release them.

In 1976, the Snake Dance at Mishongnovi, Second Mesa, Arizona, opened with clear, blue skies. At the conclusion of the dance, the sky was filled with dark rain clouds except for a small rainbow that appeared above the pueblo. It began to rain, an answer to Hopi prayers. In the same year, Navajos living near Tsaile, Arizona, held a Nightway Ceremony. The sing had survived the same sort of suppression inflicted by agents of the Bureau of Indian Affairs. However, as with the Snake Dances and several other ceremonies, Navajos held their sings in remote areas and continued to dance, pray, and chant for the health and renewal of Diné. During the course of Nightway, medicine men related the origin story of the ceremony. After Navajo Holy People had traveled through three worlds and arrived in the Fourth or Glittering World–the present world–Holy People explained to their relatives, the Earth Surface People (Diné), that they were going to disappear into rocks, mountains, streams, woods, and water but would always be close by if they were needed. Earth Surface People could call on the Holy People through ceremonies to heal people.

Not long after the Holy People disappeared, twins were born to a Navajo family. One boy was blind, and the other could not walk. The family cared for the boys for some years but found them to be such a burden that they banished them from their home. The boys had heard that Holy People living in Canyon de Chelly at White House Ruin could heal them, so they went to that place to pray for help. The blind boy carried his brother on his back, and together they traveled to White House Ruin, where they were magically drawn into the sheer red rock towering above

Cherokee scholar Charlotte Heth has spent her life documenting Native American dance and music; art forms that reflect continuity and change within diverse Native American cultures. A leading authority on these performing arts, Heth is a professor at the University of California–Los Angeles and assistant director of the National Museum of the American Indian.

the ruin. They passed through three rooms and entered the fourth, where they met several gods. Red God approached the boys, asking what business they had among the gods. The boys explained their health problems, and Red God asked if they had goods with which to pay for a curing ceremony. The boys did not, and Red God explained that curing ceremonies were not performed at this place but at other places and by other gods.

The twins traveled from sacred place to sacred place, speaking with the Holy People living in these places. Each time, Holy People said that they did not conduct curing ceremonies that would help the boys. After the twins traveled a great distance, Holy People told them to see Red God at White House Ruin because he was the specialist who could cure them. So they returned to White House Ruin, where they saw an indignant Red God. Yeibitchai, the Grandfather, pulled Red God aside and asked if he knew who the boys were. Red God admitted that he did not, and Yeibitchai responded that the boys were Red God's kin. Learning this, Red God empowered the boys to dupe Hopis out of many valuables, which the boys used for their ceremony. Red God and the other Holy People held the first Nightway up the canyon from White House Ruin, and Diné have participated in the ceremony each winter since Red God and the Stricken Twins performed the first ceremony, after the first frost and the end of autumn lightning.

RESISTANCE THROUGH RELIGION

Individuals and groups resisted cultural genocide on reservations in subtle ways. Some people continued to use feathers with their prayers, offering feathers to the wind, water, trees, and foods. Feathers carry prayers skyward, sending prayers in many directions, where they are received by invisible hosts. Some Native Americans hang prayer feathers in their homes and place them in trees and bushes outside their homes. Some people attach prayer feathers to sticks, placing them in the ground as offerings, while others hang prayer feathers on other people, pipes, bows, dolls, and baskets. Agents and missionaries admonished Indians for using prayer feathers and tried to prevent their use. Whites confiscated feathers and tried to end the ritual killing of eagles, hawks, turkeys, and other birds. They did not understand the native belief that with the death of a bird comes the rebirth of many. Native Americans did not thoughtlessly kill birds for feathers. It was done in a prescribed and sacred manner to ensure the continuation of species.

Native people used feathers for headdresses, baskets, jewelry, and hair pieces. In 1990, one native person involved with the reburial of Native American remains at Mission San Diego placed several prayer feathers in a cemetery to honor the dead and to use as prayers for the people whose bones had been desecrated by their removal. A Lakota person sent another Indian a hawk prayer feather to thank that person for his good work on behalf of native people. Feathers served as honors and prayers, symbols of a bond between the people and the spirit. However, Cahuilla elder Katherine Saubel explained that among her people, common folk never handled feathers because they were too powerful. She explained that only medicine men could touch feathers because they knew how to handle them. Feathers have never lost their significance or power among native people. Throughout the reservation ordeal, Native Americans continued to use feathers in spite of government bans on their use.

Native Americans also continued to use sacred plants in their prayers, including tobacco, sage, cedar, and sweetgrass. Use of these plants was another subtle way in which native people continued their cultures and resisted white rule. They made offerings with these plants, placing them in bundles and hanging them in homes and on objects. Tobacco bundles continued to be a major element of prayer. People also tossed pinches of tobacco into fires or sprinkled tobacco in the four cardinal directions. Throughout Indian country, Native Americans use plants in their prayers. Iroquoian and Algonquian people, from New York and Canada to Minnesota and Oklahoma, still use tobacco offerings with their prayers. Some Indians use tobacco and sacred pipes that were given to their communities as gifts, while others light sweetgrass, cedar, sage, and tobacco in rituals, drawing the smoke to them with their hands or feathers and "bathing" their bodies with smoke. Some place plant material as offerings. For example, in the late 1990s, a Luiseño visiting a sacred site in southern California, known as Piedras Pintadas, placed sage in ancient grinding holes. In addition to plant offerings, some Native Americans have given offerings of coins, bullets, flutes, and other goods. The practice of making offerings with prayer continued throughout the reservation era and remains common today.

Other ancient and common practices that were discouraged but that have survived the reservation era are sweat baths and visions. Sweat baths are far more than mere baths or mechanisms by which to clean the body. They symbolically permit Native Americans to enter the bosom of the earth through the tiny sweat lodge and experience a transformation. During the time spent in the sweat, people open themselves to the spiritual world, clear their minds of evil thoughts, and invite positive goodness to come into their minds, spirits, and bodies. Sometimes sweats stimulate visions that can speak to people. Individuals and groups also seek visions outside the sweat lodge, praying in remote spots to induce a better understanding of their lives and those of their people. Among many Native Americans, boys and girls sought visions when they reached puberty. Adults also sought visions, as pointed out by Black Elk, the Lakota holy man who detailed such religious practices to John Epse Brown in *The Sacred Pipe*.

MOURNING AND NATIVE AMERICAN REMAINS

Another form of resistance revolved around funeral and mourning complexes. Native Americans had many cultural practices regarding the dead, and they preserved elements of their ancient practices. Some of these practices changed over time, particularly as more Indians became Christian; but elements of ritual, ceremony, song, prayer, and practices remained the same or slightly modified. At one time, several tribes practiced interment and reinterment of the dead, cleaning the bones of the dead and placing them in leather bags to be reburied. At the time of reburial, people offered memorial ceremonies for their loved ones and the ancient dead. During the reservation era, some Native Americans cleaned the bones of their relatives or hired bone pickers to do the job, reburying people quietly, away from the influences of Christians and agents.

Among most people, this portion of the practice gave way to memorial services and cries when loved ones gathered to remember. Each summer Palouse Indians gather at a park on the Snake River to remember their relatives buried under the water of Lake Sacajewea. Such memorials are common throughout Indian country, but they take many forms. The Kumeyaay of southern California gather to remember the dead in Karook Ceremonies. In recent years, Kumeyaay at the Sicuyan Reservation hosted a Karook Ceremony. They sang songs accompanied by gourd rattles, danced with two dolls representing men and women who had died, and burned the effigies after the all-night ceremony. During the ceremony, people played peone games and placed bets on players. An Indian approached an elder before the ceremony and asked if the elder knew what had happened to an old school friend. The elder said that the young man in question had died during the Vietnam War, but the elder added, "don't be sad about this, because that boy will be with you tonight, dancing right here, so have good thoughts for him."

RELIGIOUS REVITALIZATION AND CULTURAL SURVIVAL

The reservation system threatened native peoples from the outset because whites sought to destroy the spiritual basis of native cultures. Native people responded to white rule in numerous ways, seeking to revitalize their cultures through new religious movements or elaboration of their old religions. During the 1850s, Smohalla ventured to the mountain of Lalac along the Columbia River, where he "died" and traveled to the Sky Above, where he met Nami Piap (Elder Brother) who told Smohalla to tell the people to return to the old ways of giving thanks and worship, in a prescribed and formal manner in the longhouse. The Wanapum Indian prophet Smohalla returned from the "sky world" to the earth, where he gathered his followers of the Washat at Priest Rapids. There, his followers worshipped each Sunday and held traditional food feasts to commemorate the sacred bond between Nami Piap, the Indian people, and the sacred foods of roots, berries, game, and fish.

After his daughter's death Smohalla had a far more dramatic religious experience, in which he learned more songs and procedures from Nami Piap, which he shared with many Plateau Indians at Water Swirl Place on the Columbia. Smohalla's doctrine spread far and wide, touching the hearts of many Indian people living on the Umatilla, Nez Perce, Colville, Yakama, Warm Springs, and other reservations. Smohalla's teachings of passive resistance altered the lives of native people as they sought solace in their religion. Smohalla urged people to remain off reservations because no person had the right to mark the earth or force others onto designated lands. He urged his followers to be true to their native beliefs regarding hunting, fishing, and gathering. He told them to refuse to work like white men, accumulating wealth that kept Indians from keeping their hearts and minds focused on the Creator and the creation, of which Native Americans were a part. Although government officials tried to force Smohalla onto the Yakama Reservation, the yanchta (religious leader) refused, living out his life on the Columbia River.

Smohalla's religion focused on praying, singing, and dancing to perpetuate the faith. He revitalized the old Washani religion and enriched it with ritual and ceremony. However, Smohalla's Washat and its many derivatives were not healing religions. In the Pacific Northwest, two spiritual traditions emerged that blended traditional native beliefs with new revitalization movements among the people of the coast and plateau. John and Mary Slocum, Squaxin Indians, created one of these healing traditions through the American Indian Shaker Church. In November 1882, John Slocum (Squasachtun) was near death at his home on Skookum Bay of Puget Sound. Slocum said that he died and spoke with angels who took him to heaven and hell. He was given a chance to return to his people, end his drinking, and preach a native form of Christianity that drew heavily on native beliefs but also acknowledged the divinity of Jesus. Slocum's wife, Mary Thompson (Whe Bulehtsah), witnessed Slocum's transformation and helped him spread the religion. The Indian Shaker Church spread among Indians from Canada to northern California and from the Pacific Coast to Idaho. Shaker healers traveled throughout the West, healing patients and spreading their religion. Shakers were best known for healing the sick, exorcising demons, and empowering native people to stop drinking alcohol. During the late nineteenth and early twentieth centuries, Indian agents tried to eradicate the Indian Shaker Church from their reservations. Some agents complained that Shakers howled like animals and knew nothing of prayers or Christ. They spread rumors that Shaker meetings promoted diseases among Indians because the parishioners kicked up dust in their churches, allowing viruses and bacteria to spread through the respiratory system. However, during the early twentieth century, some agents changed their minds about stamping out the Shaker Church because they found that members of the church ended alcohol use and became model citizens on most reservations.

Still another revitalization movement that survived the reservation system was the Waptashi, or Feather religion. Like the Indian Shaker Church, it emerged in the Northwest and was a healing religion. Jake Hunt (Titcam Nashat) received the religion in a vision, which he experienced while mourning the death of his wife, Minnie, and his son. Hunt was a Klickitat who grew up in the Washani and Shaker faiths. During his vision, he saw Lishwailait, the old Klickitat Prophet, who appeared on a round disc that held the prophet's soul. Lishwailait wore buckskin clothing and carried a hand drum. Hunt urged the people to return to their old beliefs of spiritual power, including a strong belief in the power of eagles and their feathers in worship. The Feather religion survived throughout the twentieth century and is practiced on several northwestern Indian reservations. On the Warm Springs Reservation of Oregon, Geraldine Jim and her family are leaders of the faith, and they are teaching songs, prayers, and rituals of the religion to their son, Wendell Jim, a brilliant young man and head of education on the reservation.

Across the Great Plains, Indian agents worked tirelessly to end the Sun Dance held by Crow, Blackfeet, Lakota, Cheyenne, and Hidatsa. Whites often pointed to the Sun Dance as an example of Native American savagery and heathenism because of the self-sacrifice required of initiates. Held in the spring or early summer, the Sun Dance was a renewal for all the people, a blessing of the interconnections between people, plants, animals, and spirits, all of which worked in a great cycle to keep their nations alive and in motion. Sun Dances celebrated survival and thanksgiving, offering a time to reflect on one's own contribution to the tribe, band, community, and family. Sun Dances brought people together through ritual, song, and prayer, ending in a moving ritual in which they sacrificed themselves for the benefit of the whole, cutting their own flesh and placing skewers through the slits. Most often, initiates attached themselves to a sacred tree and danced about it, keeping their minds fixed on the prayers about which they were a part.

There were (and are) variations of the Sun Dance. Women participated in the Sun Dance by cutting and painting the tree and offering sacrifices and gifts of their own, which included strips of their own flesh. Sun Dancing demonstrated great commitment of individuals to the people and brought the spiritual sphere and temporal sphere together. Annual renewal ceremonies, including the Sun Dance, continued on reservations. In Indian Territory, Wyandots, Senecas, Cherokees, Choctaws, Chickasaws, and Muscogees performed Green Corn Ceremonies. In other parts of Indian country, Native Americans continued their ceremonies. The Cheyenne, for example, renew their Sacred Arrows each year and remember their prophet, Sweet Medicine. A good deal that is known about this sacred rite comes from native oral histories, preserved in writing by scholar Peter Powell. The Cheyenne believe that Sweet Medicine gave the people Mahuts, the great person-bundle. Stories involving sacred rites, religious doctrines, and the performances of annual rites are "laws" to Native Americans, higher laws than those given by agents of the United States or by Christian missionaries. As a result, Native Americans often ignored government bans on performing sacred ceremonies and in defiance have quietly held their renewal rites, sung their songs, and given their prayers for the benefit of their communities.

The Office of Indian Affairs also tried to suppress the use of peyote by Native Americans. Peyote buttons are the fruit of a cactus, *Lophophora williamsi,* that grows primarily in northern Mexico and was dried and chewed in religious rituals by some bands of Apaches and others before being adopted by Comanches and Kiowas, spreading north into Indian Territory in the 1880s. The Peyote religion emerged as another response to the oppressive reservation system, providing native people another way to cope with their lives and survive the future. The Peyote religion was not tribally specific but rather drew members from many tribes, forming a brotherhood and pride in being native. The church emphasized positive thoughts and actions among Native Americans, prohibition of alcohol, and cooperation.

Quanah Parker, the Comanche leader, is credited with introducing many Native Americans to the church. Indeed, the church emerged strong among Comanches, Kiowas, Cheyennes, Arapahoes, and Kiowa-Apaches in present-day southwestern Oklahoma and soon spread to Caddoes, Delawares, Ho-Chunks, Osages, and other Native Americans living on the Southern Plains. Since the nineteenth century, the Peyote religion, or Native American Church, has spread throughout the West to many tribes. Navajo members of the Native American Church modified the altar and enriched the religion with their own peyote songs. In California, Kiowa roadman Tim Redbird holds meetings of the Native American Church for urban and reservation Indians from many tribal traditions. Today, the Native American Church is a pan-Indian movement that survived bureaucratic, legislative, and legal assaults. It is a living religion that empowers people to deal with a radically changing world.

PROBLEMS AND RESPONSES

In spite of the fact that Native Americans tenaciously preserved elements of their cultures and survived the reservation system, monumental problems faced them every day. Dull Knife and his band of Cheyenne fled Indian Territory and made their way to Montana, where they chose to live. Their flight, memorialized in a book by Mari Sandoz, ended with death and tragedy. However, the federal government established a new reservation for these "Northern Cheyenne," on the Tongue River of Montana. Several other groups of Indians were sick at heart over their relocation to and confinement in Indian Territory. They felt like animals confined to small wildlife refuges where they could live out their days under the thumb of game wardens. The United States forced sixty-seven tribes onto reservations in Indian Territory, including the Poncas.

In 1877, the government forced 680 Siouian-speaking Ponca Indians to move from Nebraska to Indian Territory, which they shared with

Otoes, Missouris, Pawnees, and Nez Perce. In 1879, the small son of Chief Standing Bear died, and the chief decided to inter his son's remains in the land of his birth. Standing Bear and thirty followers traveled to Nebraska to bury the boy. Standing Bear traveled in a wagon carrying the remains, and the slow-moving party frightened whites, who circulated rumors that Standing Bear was leading a war party intent on killing them. Standing Bear and his people joined the Omahas in Nebraska and buried the boy. Meanwhile, General George Crook received orders to arrest Standing Bear. The general and his soldiers tracked down Standing Bear and confined the Poncas to an Omaha jail to await deportation to Indian Territory.

When white settlers in Omaha learned the true nature of Standing Bear's journey, they became outraged. Newsmen had a field day championing the Poncas, and many non-Indians joined in the movement to free Standing Bear. Whites far and wide shared the injustice of jailing a man who was simply trying to bury his son in his native soil. Whites hired legal counsel for Standing Bear who sought a writ of habeas corpus in a federal district court. When the federal court convened to hear the case, the room was filled with supporters of Standing Bear. Government attorneys argued that Standing Bear had no standing as a person under the Constitution and could not legally petition for a writ of habeas corpus.

The judge stated that never in all his years as an officer of the court had he dealt with a case that "appealed so strongly to my sympathy." The judge ruled in favor of Standing Bear, saying that "an Indian is a 'person' within the meaning of the laws of the United States" and that Standing Bear had a right to personal freedom and civil rights. Standing Bear won great fame, and he traveled throughout the East speaking about the condition of the tribes and the injustice of the reservation system. Some whites hoped he would be able to take his case to the Supreme Court and free other Indians confined to reservations, but in the end, Standing Bear received what he wanted most. He and his followers moved to a new reservation in Nebraska, although most Poncas remained in Indian Territory. Both groups of Poncas lived on reservations designated by the United States, and both groups had to cope with the General Allotment Act that traumatized tribes and cost them thousands of acres.

The court decision in *Standing Bear v. Crook* (1879) ruled that Native Americans are people, but it did not immediately or permanently alter the way in which the federal government dealt with Indians. Federal officials had little regard for native people and primarily used their authority to divest Indians of additional lands, even at the violation of treaties they had negotiated with the tribes. Whenever treaties became obstacles to the objectives of American Indian policies, whites found ways to circumvent the treaties. Muscogee historian C. B. Clark has detailed a classic case in which the federal government ignored its own treaty with Kiowas to effectuate its policy of allotment. The Supreme Court case became known as *Lone Wolf v. Hitchock* (1902) and began after the federal government chose to ignore treaty provisions previously negotiated with the Kiowa tribe.

In 1867, Kiowas, Comanches, and Kiowa-Apaches signed the Treaty of Medicine Lodge, which included a provision stating that the Indians could not sell any portion of the reservation without the approval of three-fourths of the adult male Indians. Lone Wolf filed a lawsuit on behalf of several Indians after the United States allotted the Kiowa, Comanche, Apache, Kiowa-Apache Reservation without the approval, as stipulated in the treaty. The government sold off excess lands not allotted to the Indians. Supported by the Indian Rights Association, the case was argued before the Supreme Court in October 1902. The Supreme Court ruled against Indian people, stating that "The power exists to abrogate the provisions of an Indian treaty, though presumably such power will be exercised only when circumstances arise which will not only justify the government in disregarding the stipulations of the treaty, but may demand, in the interest of the country and the Indians themselves, that it should do so." The court determined that Congress had "plenary authority over the tribal relations of the Indians."

Drawing on Felix S. Cohen's *Handbook of Federal Indian Law,* Russell Lawrence Barsh has surveyed several cases involving American Indians and the government in *The Native North American Almanac,* edited by Anishinaabe scholar Duane Champagne. These works demonstrate that the twentieth century was an important era in Native American legal history when individuals and tribes used federal courts to adjudicate legal matters pertaining to Indian and white relations. Land, water, religion, and treaty rights were the key issues facing Native Americans as they attempted to cope with the reservation system, allotment, land loss, government control of native people, and loss of valuable natural resources. What emerges from these cases is a sense of tension and apprehension on the part of Indian people, who had to face rapid and destructive cultural change. In order to cope, Native Americans often turned to their religions. Some were Christians and turned to Catholic, Protestant, Episcopal, and Russian Orthodox churches for succor. Others turned to their native religions or dynamic revitalization movements for help. This was the case of many Native Americans who took up the Ghost Dance.

GHOST DANCE AND WOUNDED KNEE

During the 1870s, many Native Americans felt the crushing pressures of white encroachment on their lands and the threat to their cultures. Wodziwob, a Paiute holy man living on the Nevada-California border, preached that the world would soon end and that whites would be removed from Native America by the Creator. Tavivo helped Wodziwob elaborate the first Ghost Dance, encouraging Native Americans to pray and sing in order to hasten the apocalypse. When the world did not end, Native Americans in California and Nevada ended their active movement to pray for an end of the earth, but native people say that the Ghost Dance did not die in the 1870s but rather was dormant and subtle for some years, waiting to be reawakened by a new prophet. Tavivo's son, Wovoka, grew up in the Ghost Dance religion but was also influenced by Christianity and by other native spiritual beliefs.

As a young man, Wovoka traveled extensively in California, Nevada, Oregon, and Washington, learning from others about Smohalla's religion and the Indian Shaker Church. He witnessed first hand the ill effects of white settlement. He likely began his own public ministry in the mid-1880s and had heard voices for some time. On January 1, 1889, Wovoka had his first major revelation while he was seriously ill with fever. An eclipse of the sun marked this New Year's Day when Wovoka died and traveled to heaven to meet the Creator. Wovoka told anthropologist James Mooney that "he saw God, with all the people who had died long ago engaged in their old-time sports and occupations, all happy and forever young." After showing Wovoka many things, "God told him he must go back and tell his people they must be good and love one another, have no quarreling, and live in peace with the whites; they must work, and not lie or steal; that they must put away all the old practices that savored of war."

Wovoka learned many things from the Creator and received a great promise that native people would "be reunited with their friends in this other world, where there would be no more death or sickness or old age" if the people promised to obey faithfully the instructions of the Almighty given to them through the Paiute Prophet. For Native Americans suffering under the weight of white rule on reservations and from the devastating effects of epidemics and starvation, Wovoka's message offered hope and promise. The Creator gave Wovoka "the dance which he was commanded to bring back to his people." He told Wovoka that his people should perform "this dance at intervals for five consecutive days each time" and that through it "they would secure this happiness to themselves and hasten the event." After receiving divine instructions, Wovoka returned to earth to spread the good word and new dance that would hasten the Indian apocalypse. Whites called the new ceremony the Ghost Dance because dancers participating in the ceremony for five days appeared ghostlike, dancing and singing until they were exhausted.

Native delegations from many tribes visited Wovoka to learn of his vision. He gave all the delegations a letter, explaining the major tenets of the religion and offering that "Jesus is now upon the earth. He appears like a cloud. The dead are all alive again. I do not know when they will be here." Wovoka urged all American Indians "to dance every six weeks.

Make a feast at the dance and have food that everybody may eat. Then bathe in the water." In 1889, a Lakota delegation led by Kicking Bear visited Wovoka and returned to the Great Plains the following spring. By the summer of 1890, Lakota people began the Ghost Dance. Whites had long feared the fighting abilities of the Lakota, and many whites believed that the Ghost Dance was another avenue that would lead to renewed war. Some Lakota Ghost Dancers made special shirts and talked openly of their invincibility to bullets. They used the Ghost Dance as a resistance movement, but talk of war against whites was not widespread. Newspaper journalists portrayed Lakota people as devils, demons, and fiends, spoiling for a fight through the Ghost Dance religion. Lies, rumors, and innuendo sold newspapers, and agents, soldiers, and settlers bought newspapers with the unfounded stories.

Fearing an Indian conspiracy and an outbreak among Lakota living on several reservations, agents banned the Ghost Dance in November 1890. Native Americans living on the Sioux reservations ignored the order to stop dancing and increased the number of Ghost Dances, particularly after agents requested troops to suspend the ceremony. Agents and soldiers who were determined to stamp out the Ghost Dance among the Lakota ordered several leaders arrested, including Sitting Bull. On December 15, 1890, two Indian policemen at Standing Rock Reservation moved to arrest Sitting Bull, but in the confusion, one of them shot and killed Sitting Bull. Shock and anger swept across the cold Dakota plains, and rumors circulated that the army planned to round up Ghost Dancers or possibly kill them, to prevent them from performing their ceremonies. Several hundred Ghost Dancers, including men, women, and children, under Miniconjou leader Big Foot, fled into the Bad Lands.

Soldiers serving in Custer's old unit, the Seventh Cavalry, intercepted the Indians northeast of the Pine Ridge Reservation, to which Big Foot's band was migrating in order to surrender. On December 28, 1890, soldiers moved the people to Wounded Knee Creek. Big Foot had pneumonia and told his people to surrender, particularly after the soldiers surrounded the village and set up three Hotchkiss guns above the village. The next day, Colonel George Forsyth ordered Lakota men to come out of their tipis and sit on the ground while soldiers separated women and children and rummaged through their lodges looking for weapons. Over one hundred Lakota men complied with the order, and most came out wearing their Ghost Shirts. The situation grew more tense with every minute, as women and children cried out from the tipis. When an officer tried to take a concealed weapon from Yellow Bird, the warrior would not give up the weapon, and as they wrestled, the gun fired, killing the officer. Shooting began from all directions, and shells from the Hotchkiss guns exploded among the people.

Black Elk, the famous Oglala spiritual leader, saw the terrible carnage at Wounded Knee. "Dead and wounded women and children and

The U.S. Army called Wounded Knee a victorious battle, but Native Americans have always considered it a massacre. Soldiers and civilians proudly watch the burial of men, women, and children. "The women and children ran . . . the soldiers shot them as they ran."

little babies were scattered all along there where they had been trying to run away." Black Elk could see that "soldiers had followed along the gulch, as they ran, and murdered them in there. Sometimes they were in heaps because they had huddled together, and some were scattered all along." He saw several people who had been "torn to pieces where the wagon guns [Hotchkiss] hit them. I saw a little baby trying to suck its mother, but she was bloody and dead." When Black Elk saw many dead Lakota, "I wished that I had died too, but I was not sorry for the women and children. It was better for them to be happy in the other world, and I wanted to be there too." Approximately three hundred people, mostly women and children, died that December day in 1890. Black Elk reported that the Wounded Knee Massacre occurred on "a good winter day" filled with sun but that a "wind came up in the night. There was a big blizzard, and it grew very cold."

The killings at Wounded Knee have long served as a metaphor for the entire reservation era of Native American history, a cold, desolate, and bleak era, in which native people died from disease, depression, starvation, and neglect. The United States created the reservation system to destroy native power and cultures as well as to open millions of acres to white settlers. During the nineteenth century, the Native American population dropped dramatically. According to Cherokee demographer Russell Thornton, the American Indian population declined from roughly 600,000 in 1800 to 250,000 between 1890 and 1900. Government policies, war, and disease decimated Native American populations, and the reservation system contributed mightily to this decline.

The United States had made many promises through its treaties, offering Native Americans food, shelter, health care, education, and "civilization." The government broke most of its promises, in large part because Congress refused to appropriate sufficient funds and the Office of Indian Affairs mismanaged the money provided. Reservations were cesspools of disease, despair, and death. Conditions were made worse in the early twentieth century because of allotment and resettlement of former reservation lands by whites. Still Native Americans persevered and recovered, in large part because of their spiritual strengths and sense of community. Although the killings at Wounded Knee ended a chapter in Native American history, they did not end the Ghost Dance. Native Americans still sing the songs, and some meet to dance and sing for the sacred renewal of their people. Perhaps the late nineteenth century is best summed up with the words of an Arapaho Ghost Dance song recorded by Mooney: "Father, have pity on me, Father, have pity on me; I am crying for thirst, I am crying for thirst; All is gone–I have nothing to eat, All is gone–I have nothing to eat."

Selected Readings and Bibliography

Ceremonies, rituals, and religions are of paramount importance in Native American cultures. Indian religions and religious movements are critical factors historically, and they have influenced Indian history since creation. During the late nineteenth and early twentieth centuries, traditional native religions, Christianity, and pluralistic beliefs affected the course of native history. Aspects of native religion are dealt with in Champagne, *The Native North American Almanac;* Francis's, *Native Time;* and Gibson's, *The American Indian.* Native religions and the importance of Christianity are addressed in Berthong's *The Cheyenne and Arapaho Ordeal,* Hagan's *United States-Comanche Relations,* Mardock's *The Reformers and the American Indian,* Tyler's *A History of Indian Policy,* Josephy's *The Nez Perce Indians,* Trafzer and Scheuerman's *Renegade Tribe,* Ruby and Brown's *John Slocum and the Indian Shaker Church,* and Thornton's *American Indian Holocaust.*

Aberle, David F. "The Prophet Dance and Reactions to White Contact." *Southwestern Journal of Anthropology* 15 (Spring 1959): 47–83.

——. *The Peyote Religion among the Navaho.* Chicago: University of Chicago Press, 1982.

——. "The Indian Shaker Church." *Handbook of North American Indians, Northwest Coast*, 7. Wayne Suttles, ed. Washington, D.C.: Smithsonian Institution, 1990, pp. 633–639.

Allen, Paula G. *The Sacred Hoop: Recovering the Feminine in American Indian Traditions.* Boston: Beacon Press, 1986.

Bailey, Paul D. *Wovoka, The Indian Messiah.* Los Angles: Westernlore Press, 1957.

Barnett, Homer G. *Indian Shakers: A Messianic Cult of the Pacific Northwest.* Carbondale: Southern Illinois University Press, 1957.

Basso, Keith H. *Western Apache Witchcraft.* Anthropological Papers of the University of Arizona, no. 15. Tucson: University of Arizona Press, 1969.

Bean, Lowell John, and Katherine Siva Saubel. *Temalpakh: Cahuilla Indian Knowledge and Usage of Plants.* Banning, Calif.: Malki Museum Press, 1972.

Bean, Lowell John, and Sylvia Brakke Vane. "Cults and Their Transformations." *Handbook of North American Indians, California*, 8. Robert F. Heizer, ed. Washington, D.C.: Smithsonian Institution, 1978, pp. 662–672.

Beck, Peggy V., and Anna L. Walters. *The Sacred: Ways of Knowledge, Sources of Life.* Tsaile, Ariz.: Navajo Community College, 1977.

Berkhofer, Robert F. Jr. *The White Man's Indian: Images of the American Indian from Columbus to the Present.* New York: Knopf, 1978.

Black Elk. *The Sacred Pipe: Black Elk's Account of the Seven Rites of the Oglala Sioux.* Joseph E. Brown, ed. Norman: University of Oklahoma Press, 1953.

Bowden, Henry W. *American Indians and Christian Mission: Studies in Cultural Conflict.* Chicago: University of Chicago Press, 1981.

Brown, Donald N. "The Ghost Dance Religion among the Oklahoma Cheyenne." *Chronicles of Oklahoma* 30 (1952–1953): 408–416.

Champagne, Duane. *American Indian Societies: Some Strategies and Conditions of Political and Cultural Survival.* Cambridge, Mass.: Cultural Survival, 1985.

——. "The Delaware Revitalization Movement of the Early 1760s: A Suggested Reinterpretation." *American Indian Quarterly* 12 (1988): 107–125.

Clifton, James A. *The Prairie People: Continuity and Change in Potawatomi Indian Culture, 1665–1965.* Lawrence: Regents Press of Kansas, 1977.

Collins, John James. *Native American Religions.* Lewiston, N.Y.: Edwin Mellen Press, 1991.

Deloria, Vine Jr. *God Is Red.* New York: Grosset & Dunlap, 1973.

DeMallie, Raymond J. "The Lakota Ghost Dance: An Ethnohistorical Account." *Pacific History Review* 51 (1982): 385–405.

DeMontravel, P. R. "General Nelson A. Miles and the Wounded Knee Controversy." *Arizona and the West* 28 (1989): 23–44.

Fritz, Henry E. *The Movement for Indian Assimilation, 1860–1890.* Philadelphia: University of Pennsylvania Press, 1965.

Gill, Sam D. *Native American Religions: An Introduction.* Belmont, Calif.: Wadsworth, 1982.

——. *Mother Earth: An American Story.* Chicago: University of Chicago Press, 1987.

Green, Jerry, ed. *After Wounded Knee.* East Lansing: Michigan State University Press, 1996.

Greene, Jerome A. "The Sioux Land Commission of 1889: A Prelude to Wounded Knee." *South Dakota History* 1 (1970): 41–42.

Harrod, Howard L. *Renewing the World: Plains Indian Religion and Morality.* Tucson: University of Arizona Press, 1987.

Hertzberg, Hazel W. *The Search for an Indian Identity: Modern Pan-Indian Movements.* Syracuse: Syracuse University Press, 1971.

Hitakonanu'laxk, *The Grandfathers Speak.* New York: Interlink Books, 1994.

Hultkrantz, Ake. *Conceptions of the Soul among North American Indians.* Stockholm: Ethnographical Museum of Sweden, 1953.

——. *The Religions of the American Indians.* Berkeley: University of California Press, 1979.

Hunn, Eugene S. *Nch'i-Wana "The Big River": Mid-Columbia Indians and Their Land.* Seattle: University of Washington Press, 1990.

Hyde, George E. *A Sioux Chronicle.* Norman: University of Oklahoma Press, 1956.

Hymes, Dell. *"In Vain I Tried to Tell You": Essays in Native American Ethnopoetics.* Philadelphia: University of Pennsylvania Press, 1981.

Jensen, Richard E. "Big Foot's Followers at Wounded Knee." *Nebraska History* 71 (1990): 194–212.

Johnson, V. W. *The Unregimented General: A Biography of Nelson A. Miles.* Boston: Houghton Mifflin, 1962.

Kehoe, Alice B. *The Ghost Dance. Ethnohistory and Revitalization.* New York: Holt, Rinehart and Winston, 1989.

Knight, Oliver. *Following the Indian Wars.* Norman: University of Oklahoma Press, 1960.

La Barre, Weston. *The Ghost Dance: Origins of Religion.* Garden City, N.Y.: Doubleday, 1970.

——. *The Peyote Cult.* Norman: University of Oklahoma Press, 1989.

Leckie, William H. *The Buffalo Soldiers.* Norman: University of Oklahoma Press, 1967.

Meighan, Clement W., and Francis A. Riddell. *The Maru Cult of the Pomo Indians: A California Ghost Dance Survival.* Los Angeles: Southwest Museum, 1972.

Morrison, Kenneth M. "Baptism and Alliance: The Symbolic Mediations of Religious Syncretism." *Ethnohistory* 37 (1990): 416–437.

Moses, L. G. "Jack Wilson and the Indian Service: The Response of the BIA to the Ghost Dance Prophet." *American Indian Quarterly* 5 (1979): 295–316.

Moses, L. G., and Margaret C. Szasz. "'My Father, Have Pity on Me!' Indian Revitalization Movements of the Late-Nineteenth Century." *Journal of the West* 23 (1984): 5–15.

Neihardt, John G. *The Sixth Grandfather: Black Elk's Teachings Given to John Neihardt.* Raymond J. DeMallie, ed. Lincoln: University of Nebraska Press, 1984.

Olson, James C. *Red Cloud and the Sioux Problem.* Lincoln: University of Nebraska Press, 1965.

Ortiz, Alfonso. *The Tewa World: Space, Time, Being and Becoming in Pueblo Society.* Chicago: University of Chicago Press, 1969.

Paper, Jordan. *Offering Smoke: The Sacred Pipe and Native American Religion.* Moscow: University of Idaho Press, 1988.

Powell, Peter H. *Sweet Medicine: The Continuing Role of the Sacred Arrows, the Sun Dance, and the Sacred Buffalo Hat in Northern Cheyenne History.* 2 volumes. Norman: University of Oklahoma Press, 1969.

Powers, William K. *Oglala Religion.* Lincoln: University of Nebraska Press, 1975.

Prucha, Francis P. *The Churches and the Indian Schools, 1888–1913*. Lincoln: University of Nebraska Press, 1979.

Ruby, Robert H., and John A. Brown. *Dreamer-Prophets of the Columbia Plateau: Smohalla and Skolaskin*. Norman: University of Oklahoma Press, 1989.

Shipek, Florence C. "History of Southern California Mission Indians." *Handbook of North American Indians, California*, 8. Robert F. Heizer, ed. (Washington, D.C.: Smithsonian Institution, 1978) pp. 610–618.

Slotkin, James S. *The Peyote Religion: A Study in Indian-White Relations*. Glencoe, Ill.: Free Press, 1956.

Slagle, Al Logan. "Tolawa Indian Shakers and the Role of Prophecy at Smith River, California." *American Indian Prophets: Religious Leaders and Revitalization Movements*. Clifford E. Trafzer, ed. Sacramento: Sierra Oaks, 1986.

Spier, Leslie. *The Sun Dance of the Plains Indians: Its Development and Diffusion*. Anthropological Papers of the American Museum of Natural History, no. 16. New York: the trustees, 1921.

Stewart, Omer C. *Peyote Religion: A History*. Norman: University of Oklahoma Press, 1987.

Tedlock, Dennis, and Barbara Tedlock, eds. *Teachings from the American Earth: Indian Religion and Philosophy*. New York: Liveright, 1975.

Trafzer, Clifford E., ed. *American Indian Prophets: Religious Leaders and Revitalization Movements*. Sacramento: Sierra Oaks, 1986.

Trennert, Robert. *White Man's Medicine: Government Doctors and the Navajos, 1863–1955*. Albuquerque: University of New Mexico Press, 1998.

Utley, Robert M. *The Lance and the Shield: The Life and Times of Sitting Bull*. New York: Henry Holt, 1993.

Voget, Fred W. *The Shoshoni-Crow Sun Dance*. Norman: University of Oklahoma Press, 1984.

Wallace, Anthony F. C. "Handsome Lake and the Great Revival in the West." *American Quarterly* 4 (1952): 149–165.

——. "The Dekanawidah Myth Analyzed as the Record of a Revitalization Movement." *Ethnohistory* 5 (1958): 118–130.

——. *The Death and Rebirth of the Seneca*. New York: Knopf, 1970.

Williams, Walter L. *The Spirit and the Flesh: Sexual Diversity in American Indian Culture*. Boston: Beacon Press, 1986.

Wooster, Robert. *Nelson A. Miles and the Twilight of the Frontier Army*. Lincoln: University of Nebraska Press, 1993.

CHAPTER 15

INDIANS AND PROGRESSIVES

The late nineteenth and early twentieth centuries were a bleak era in Native American history, but one that brought significant changes for Indian people. During most of this era, Native Americans were recovering from the ill effects of treaties, wars, reservations, starvation, death, and depression. It was also an era in which the government and white Americans divested Native Americans of nearly all their remaining landed estates, including natural resources worth a fortune. Native American populations began to recover after 1890, but the process was slow and uneven. Some tribes grew faster than others, but the increase was in part the result of nonreservation Indians moving off the "public domain" or Indian homesteads and resettling onto reservations where government agents assigned allotments.

TOWARD ALLOTMENT

During the 1870s and 1880s, some whites questioned Native American "ownership" of reservations, because whites wanted to open vast acres set aside as reservations. Cattlemen, lumbermen, miners, farmers, and others wanted more Indian lands. To fight the loss of land, some Native Americans filed Indian homesteads on their traditional lands to work their own places. Wolf Necklace, a Palouse Indian from the Columbia Plateau, filed a homestead on lands at the junction of the Snake and Columbia rivers and owned the largest horse ranch in Washington Territory. County sheriffs harassed Wolf Necklace, taking horses that strayed onto other lands and forced him to surrender his private enterprise. Simply put, Wolf Necklace was too successful for white competitors. Another Palouse, a religious and village leader named Thomásh, filed a legal homestead for his land on Snake River, but his relatives lost the land when the Corps of Engineers condemned it in order to build a dam on the river and create Lake Sacajewea.

Eventually, Thomásh and Wolf Necklace, along with their families, moved to reservations. This was the fate of many nonreservation Indians, even those who filed homesteads. However, their residences on reservations were not secure because of white interest in breaking up the reservations. In 1885, the secretary of interior ruled that Indians merely "occupied" their reservations, like tenants, but did not own the land upon which they lived. Soon after, reformers and capitalists joined forces to end communal ownership of reservations lands. They were aided in their quest by the publication of Helen Hunt Jackson's *Century of Dishonor* (1881), which chronicled American abuses against Native Americans and the failures of American Indian policies. Reformers argued that reservations were never intended to be permanent and that acculturation and education of Native Americans could not fully transform Indians into civilized people without the cornerstone of Euro-American civilization— private ownership of real estate.

Many non-Indian men and women worked tirelessly to enhance life for American Indians, but non-Indians at the national level of reform, not Indians, nearly always determined, through American Indian policy, what was in the best interest of Indians. Such paternalism, no matter how well intended, sometimes harmed Indian people. At other times, positive consequences emerged from the reform. In 1883, Christian women established the Women's National Indian Association in Philadelphia. They worked tirelessly to inform members of Congress, the president, and the Office of Indian Affairs about circumstances on the reservations. These and other women were instrumental in advancing the cause of Chief Joseph and the Nez Perce and Palouse people who had conditionally surrendered to the United States in 1877 but were forced to Indian Territory. Women and men joined in the chorus, which resulted in a congressional act authorizing the government to allow the Nez Perce and Palouse to return to the Pacific Northwest in 1885.

In the same year Thomas Bland formed the National Indian Defense Association, publishing an influential magazine, *Council Fire.* Unlike most reform groups, the National Indian Defense Association favored Indian self-determination, believing Native Americans to be intelligent human beings who could decide for themselves which elements of white culture to incorporate into their own cultures and when to do so. Although favoring acculturation and assimilation, the group believed that ultimately the decision to become more like whites rested with Indians. This was not mainstream American thinking, however, because most white reformers, such as Captain Richard H. Pratt, Bishop Henry B. Whipple, Secretary of Interior Carl Schurz, Thomas A. Bland, Helen Hunt Jackson, and Alfred B. Meacham, believed they knew what was best for Indians and acted accordingly.

In 1879, a group of Christians in Boston formed the Indian Protective Committee to ensure that white settlers did not cheat Indians out of their reservation lands. Like other reform groups, the Indian Protective

Committee favored allotment and citizenship, but its impact as a reform group was overshadowed by the Indian Rights Association, which began in Philadelphia in 1882 and was led by Herbert Welsh and Henry B. Pancoast. The Indian Rights Association was far more effective than other Indian reform organizations, creating branches in many cities throughout the country. It investigated Indian issues, collected evidence against ineffective agents, and published numerous pamphlets on Indian affairs. The Indian Rights Association became the most influential of the early reform organizations and was one of the few vehicles through which Native Americans had a national voice to air their views about land, water, food, disease, and policies.

During the late nineteenth century, reformers sought to solve the so-called Indian problem by dividing portions of reservations into individual allotments that whites believed would transform American Indians into hard-working farmers. During this era, other whites engineered new ways to extinguish native title to the land and take Indian lands rapidly through legal and illegal means. At this time, an ironic, unusual, and unintended alliance developed between well-meaning reformers and selfish capitalists. White ranchers, farmers, miners, merchants, and others living in the West joined in the reform chorus to allot reservations. This odd association of whites caused Native Americans irreparable harm. For many generations white settlers had driven Native Americans from their lands through war, encroachment, and treaties, forcing thousands of native people to resettle in the West. Wherever whites moved in the grand American West, they demanded that their government confine Indians onto smaller and smaller parcels.

Not long after the government had placed most Native Americans onto reservations through treaties and executive orders, reformers demanded the destruction of reservations, clamoring that the United States should "save" native people by breaking up reservations, assigning them individual allotments, and offering them U.S. citizenship. Then reformers led the nation toward a change in Indian policy. Some "do-gooders" were well intended, but most knew little about Native American people or communities and held a romantic attachment to the concept of "noble savages." They generally believed that with benevolent Christian kindness and stern formal schooling, Native Americans would progress along the path toward civilization and assimilation.

GENERAL ALLOTMENT IN SEVERALTY

In 1883, white reformers known as Friends of the Indian met at Albert A. Smiley's resort hotel at Lake Mohonk, New York, and helped frame the General Allotment Act. Smiley, a Quaker member of the Board of Indian Commissioners, surrounded himself with reformers, including Henry L. Dawes, a senator from Massachusetts and chair of the Senate Committee on Indian Affairs. Dawes favored individual allotment and citizenship for Indians. According to Larry Burgess, director of the Smiley Library in Redlands, California, and biographer of Albert Smiley, Smiley and other reformers sought to bring Native Americans into the mainstream by broadening their world. Smiley and the other reformers believed that allotment would enable Native Americans to become farmers and that through private ownership of the land, they would naturally flow into the mainstream of American life, become citizens, and learn the value of hard work and wage earning. Reformers believed that dividing reservations into individual allotments would magically provide the incentive for Native Americans to abandon their communal beliefs about land use and to favor private ownership, which they would work to develop to its fullest potential.

Merrill E. Gates, president of Amherst and another member of the Board of Indian Commissioners, spoke for many reformers when he said that whites had an obligation to kill "savagery" and usher Indians "into citizenship" by making them "more intelligently selfish" and making them desire property of their own. Reformers believed that in order to survive, Native Americans had to become materialistic and individualistic. They wanted to end tribal attachments, divide reservations into individual allotments, educate young people in the arts of "civilization," and make Indians citizens. During the 1880s, the reform movement gained momentum when Dawes introduced a bill in the Senate calling for "Allotment-in-Severalty." Native Americans across the United States denounced the "Dawes Act," and many tried to visit Washington to present their opposition. However, Commissioner of Indian Affairs J. Atkins ordered all agents to arrest all native persons who tried to leave the reservation to voice their views on allotment. Lone Wolf, a Kiowa leader, and Jake, a Caddo, went to Washington anyway. They arrived too late.

In 1887, both houses of Congress passed the General Allotment Act (a.k.a. the Dawes Act), and the president signed it into law. The act and the consequences of allotment have been skillfully detailed in Frederick Hoxie's scholarly study, *A Final Promise: The Campaign to Assimilate Indians, 1880–1920*. Hoxie points out that the act was devastating for Native Americans, because it authorized the president to order the survey of reservations, creation of tribal allotment rolls, and division of reservation lands into individual allotments, usually of 160 acres for heads of families, 80 acres for single people eighteen years old and older and orphans, and 40 acres for Indians under eighteen years of age (the actual amount of land varied among reservations). Babies born after the close of allotment did not receive a portion of the tribal estate and were dependent on their families for a portion of the family allotment. The government did not "give" allotments to Indians. Agents assigned allotments from lands already held by Native Americans.

Under the terms of the act, government officials were to hold allotments in trust for twenty-five years until Indians adjusted to private ownership of the land, and during this time, governments could not tax Indian allotments. Final allotment rolls were made and lands divided by special allotting agents, reservation agents, and allotting commissions, including the infamous Jerome and Dawes commissions headed by David H. Jerome and Henry Dawes, which coerced most of the tribes into allotting and surrendering the remainder of their lands. Although these commissions and allotting agents argued that they were working in the best interests of Native Americans, tribal leaders protested the destruction of tribal lands, knowing that this was a continuation of the white campaign to destroy tribal governments, native sovereignty, land claims, and treaty rights. Tribal leaders were confused about the particulars of the law, but many understood the gravity of the General Allotment Act.

After federal officials determined the number of Indians to receive allotments, location of the land, and the amount on a particular reservation, surveyors divided the land. Indians could select their allotments, or agents could assign them. Often Indians selected allotments on lands that had held villages or had spiritual meaning to them, not necessarily the most productive farm lands. In the Pacific Northwest, Nez Perces living in Idaho had traditionally lived in villages along rivers, and they selected allotments along these magnificent streams rather than the rolling hills above the rivers. When Indians did not select allotments on the hills, the government sold them to white farmers and ranchers. These are some of the most productive farmlands in Idaho, and nearly all the property is owned today by whites. The government paid for all excess lands on reservations not taken up by allotments, offering prices from 30¢ to $1.50 per acre, which was not given to individuals but rather to the Office of Indians Affairs to be used for education and civilization. In this way the government defrauded Native Americans of much of their remaining estates.

Senator Henry M. Teller warned reformers that within forty years, the General Allotment Act would destroy the Indian land base and allow whites to take millions more acres out of the hands of Indians. Senator Teller asserted that "the real aim of this bill is to get at the Indian lands and open them to settlement." He maintained that if this had been "done in the name of greed, it would be bad enough; but to do it in the name of humanity and under the cloak of an ardent desire to promote the Indian's welfare by making him like ourselves . . . is infinitely worse." Teller was correct, and Indians lost most of their remaining lands. In 1500, Native Americans living within the borders of what became the United States owned approximately three billion acres, but by 1887, whites had reduced their land base to 150,000,000 acres. By the time the United States repealed the General Allotment Act, Native Americans controlled a mere forty-eight million acres.

The General Allotment Act opened the reservations and cost Native Americans over one hundred million acres of land sold for very little. Much of it contained billions of dollars' worth of oil, uranium, lead, zinc, coal, gas, timber, water, and other valuable resources. The government altered the original General Allotment Act many times during the late nineteenth and early twentieth centuries and used special legislation to enable white farmers, ranchers, miners, railroad builders, lumber magnates, and other non-Indians to divest Native Americans of their property rights at a much accelerated pace. Originally, mixed-blood Indians of white and African-American ancestry sought allotment, as did non-Indians who were "adopted" into the tribes, married native women, or adopted native children. Some non-Indians defrauded the tribes and secured allotments, whereas some Indians living away from tribal lands never received an allotment. Most Native Americans were confused about the General Allotment Act, as government officials or Indians working in the employ of the government told tribal leaders that they had to allot their reservations or they would lose everything.

Through lies, coercion, cheating, and conspiracies, the government secured allotment agreements with numerous tribes in the West, although a few escaped allotment, including New York Senecas, North Carolina Cherokees, Florida Seminoles, Zunis, Hopis, Navajos, Mescaleros, Tohono O'odhams, Maricopas, and others. The government allotted most reservations, to the lasting detriment of native people, who lost their lands, resources, and futures. Whites purchased thousands of acres of land that had been part of reservations, and they often dominated regions that had once been solely Indian country. The General Allotment Act originally provided U.S. citizenship for Indians who accepted allotment, although the federal government reneged on this aspect of the bill, passing the Burke Act in 1906, which delayed citizenship until the end of the twenty-five-year trust period. The Burke Act and other legislation and acts of the executive branch dropped certain restrictions associated with allotments so that Indians could sell their property to whites. Businessmen used every means possible, legal or illegal, to divest Indians of their allotments and resources.

In the chaos and uncertainty created by the reservation system, allotment, laws, and directives associated with American Indian policy, many Indians turned inward, toward their own holy people or prophets from other native communities, to help them survive change. Some whites foresaw this calamity, including Senator Pendleton of Ohio, who in 1881 had stated, "Our villages now dot their prairies; our cities are built upon their plains; our miners climb their mountains and seek the recesses of their gulches; our telegraphs and railroads and post offices penetrate their country in every direction; their forests are cleared and their prairies are plowed and their wildernesses are opened up."

Pendleton recognized that Indians could no longer fish, hunt, or gather as they once had, saying that Native Americans "must either change their modes of life or they will be exterminated." In discussing Pendleton's statements, Confederated Salish and Kootenai scholar D'Arcy McNickle pointed out that Pendleton and other policy makers failed to ask Native Americans what they thought of allotment, property rights, or other reforms designed to benefit them. The reason is simple: Policy makers believed they knew what was best for Indians, and many believed Indians were not bright enough to make important decisions. Furthermore, reformers knew that most Native Americans opposed allotment, but this was not the message whites wanted to hear, so they chauvinistically ignored native peoples.

Reformers, capitalists, and federal officials were not deterred by Indian voices opposing allotment. Reformers did not prevent other whites from alienating Indians from more lands through legislation. In 1898, Congress passed the Curtis Act, and President William McKinley signed it into law. Under the terms of this act, the government allotted land to members of the so-called Five Civilized Tribes in Indian Territory. The act abolished tribal governments and tribal courts in Indian Territory, a step toward forcing native people to end their organized resistance to allotment and prepare for Oklahoma statehood. Rather than the government paying tribal governments for land, the act allowed the government to pay individuals directly. Some Progressives protested the Curtis Act, but powerful interests against the government's continued assaults on Native Americans did not emerge again until the 1910s and 1920s. By then it was too late to save the Native American estate.

Reformers seemed oblivious to the fact that they contributed to the destruction of native people by supporting allotment. They pushed Congress and the president until they won passage of the General Allotment Act of 1887, and then they lost interest in Indian reforms, believing they had found the solution to the "Indian problem." Some reformers hung on to the Indian reform movement, but their zeal quieted considerably in the 1890s. Reformers ignored the wishes of Native Americans and considered those who opposed allotment to be backward savages who had no concept of the positive civilizing influences of allotment. Some Indians openly opposed allotment. Muscogee leader Chitto Harjo and Keetoowah elder Red Bird Smith stood fast against allotment, punishing other Indians for accepting allotments. In 1901, federal marshals and soldiers ran down Harjo and his supporters, ending the so-called Snake Uprising in Indian Territory. Nevertheless, Keetoowahs and Choctaws rose against allotting agents, making their jobs difficult and encouraging people not to accept allotments.

The division of reservations and sale of excess Indian lands opened millions of acres for white settlement and ushered in a great feeding frenzy in which land sharks devoured Indian lands. By 1900, the government had created 53,168 allotments, consisting of nearly five million acres of former reservation land. In the late nineteenth century, the Native American estate declined considerably. In 1881, western tribes had held 155,632,312 acres, but by 1900, their lands had shrunk to 77,865,373 acres. In less than twenty years, Native Americans had lost 77,766,939 acres or nearly half their landed estate. And the land grab did not end in 1900 but, indeed, accelerated from 1900 to 1934. Between 1887 and 1934, the Native American estate declined by almost two-thirds.

Ranchers, farmers, lawyers, mayors, real estate speculators, miners, lumbermen, oilmen, and other opportunists bought Indian allotments when they became available. These same business interests had supported allotment in order to plunder the Native American estate, and government agents, bankers, and congressmen helped them accomplish their goal. Under the terms of the General Allotment Act, the government held Indian lands in trust for twenty-five years, but special interest groups worked diligently on congressmen and the president to lessen the time after which Indian allotments could be bought by non-Indians. Soon politicians made it easier for business interests to wrest native lands from Indians at a much more rapid pace.

EXPLOITING NATIVE AMERICAN RESOURCES

In response to white demands, the secretary of interior acted to remove restrictions on the sale of Indian allotments. The secretary and his staff could proclaim Indians to be "competent" and allow them to sell their allotments before twenty-five years had ended. The government defined *competent* as being able to cope with the white man's world. In 1917, Secretary of Interior Franklin Lane expedited the competency of thousands of Indians by establishing a Competency Commission that traveled from house to house declaring Indians to be competent. Between 1917 and 1920, the commission declared thousands of Indians to be competent, issuing twenty thousand land patents to Indian allottees, who could then sell their land.

Commissioner of Indian Affairs Cato Sells was delighted, and he set to work establishing the competency of thousands of Indians. Lane and Sells rushed to declare Native Americans of mixed ancestry competent so that they could have full control of their property, and soon after, the two wanted to issue land patents to all Indians on all but forty acres of their land so that the people could have enough property for a home site. Between 1906 and 1916, the government had issued only 9,894 fee simple patents, but between 1917 and 1920, it issued 10,956 fee-simple patents.

Some reformers rose up against Lane and his "blanket competency" program, so the Interior Department ended Lane's scam in 1920, but it did not end competency decrees. Instead, the Office of indian Affairs, which became known as the Bureau of Indian Affairs in the 1930s, slowed the process by which competency was given and declared fewer Indians to be competent. Nevertheless, thousands of acres fell out of Indian hands, as whites "legally" plundered the Indian estate. A common scenario unfolded as white ranchers, farmers, bankers, and other business interests offered to purchase Indian allotments for cash, promising the owners that they could live on the land throughout their lives. Whites purchased and developed most of the allotments, often allowing former allottees to live in their place until their deaths. Then the businessmen evicted the children and grandchildren of the original owners. In Oklahoma, politicians, businessmen, and bankers conspired to declare children wards of white citizens, then defrauded Indian people of all ages of their lands, "legally" transferring title to thousands of acres from Indians to whites.

In Oklahoma, whites established an unprecedented record for cheating Indians out of their land, and these acts against the native people are chronicled in a illuminating piece of historical fiction titled *Mean Spirit*, by Chickasaw writer Linda Hogan. In 1907, Oklahoma became a state, and politicians wanted a greater tax base from which to run their government. In response, Congress passed a bill commonly known as the "Crime of 1908," which gave thousands of Indians in Oklahoma patents to their lands. The government targeted mixed bloods and full bloods as well as African-American freedmen. Within a few years, 90 percent of these patents had been sold to whites. In addition, the secretary of interior ended his involvement in probating Indian estates belonging to members of the Choctaw, Cherokee, Chickasaw, Seminole, and Muscogee nations. This function was turned over to local courts, who took full advantage of the power to take lands away from native people, particularly children, whose "guardians" stole thousands of acres from them.

The government also took possession of Indian lands on behalf of the National Park Service and U.S. Forest Service. The U.S. government stole the Canyon de Chelly in northern Arizona in the name of conservation. The land belonged to the Navajo tribe, but the government determined that it would protect the natural environment and the Anasazi (ancient Pueblo) ruins and material culture found within the canyon. So the government took the Canyon de Chelly from the Navajo Nation and continues to control access and use of the great natural wonder. Navajo families still live in the Canyon de Chelly and have access to their homes, but the National Park Service controls the canyon and determines who may enter. The government took thousands of acres from the larger Native American estate, shamelessly withdrawing lands set aside for the tribes by treaties and executive orders. No land assigned to Native Americans was safe from exploitation or outright theft.

LUMBER AND MINERALS

President Theodore Roosevelt alienated other reservation lands in the name of conservation, for the U.S. Forest Service. Two days before leaving office, Roosevelt issued eight executive orders placing 2,500,000 acres of reservation lands into the hands of the Forest Service, stripping Indian tribes of millions of acres of forested land worth millions of dollars. The Forest Service issued contracts to lumber companies for very little money, so that lumber companies could legally exploit the great wealth of native peoples. Pomo scholar Larry Myers has pointed out numerous times at meetings of the California Native American Heritage Commission that officials of the Forest Service liked to "use" the earth and its bounty, so they invited lumber companies to log vast acres that were once the domain of several western Indian tribes. The tribes received nothing because the land had been alienated by Roosevelt's orders. Eventually, the United States restored some timber lands to the tribes in order to conserve the forests that had been badly managed by the Forest Service. However, the exploitation of tribal forests by non-Indians was in keeping with the time, and private companies worked closely with the government to extract as much money as possible from Native American lands.

Repatriation of Native American remains and grave items is an important issue among Indian people. Larry Myers, a Pomo man, has been a strong advocate for the reburial of remains. As executive secretary of the California Native American Heritage Committee, he has worked closely with Indian people, legislators, and governors, including Governor Gray Davis.

The federal government created other ingenious schemes to rob Native Americans of their natural resources. White Americans had a lengthy history of defrauding Indians of their mineral wealth, and they continued to do so in the twentieth century. By this time much of the gold and silver discovered in the West, off reservations, had been mined, but a new rush developed for minerals on reservations, including coal, gas, oil, and uranium. Under federal law, citizens of the United States had the right to enter public lands and stake out claims on lands believed to hold valuable minerals. Miners began entering Indian reservations and staking out claims, saying that those reservations created by executive orders were public lands. Officials of the Interior Department, representing business interests within the United States, agreed. They upheld the 1885 ruling of the secretary of interior that Indians had only a right of occupancy like that of tenants. He argued that minerals, timber, and other resources belonged to the owner—the federal government.

In the twentieth century, the Interior Department extended this ruling to executive order reservations, often allowing whites to exploit the mineral wealth on reservations without compensation to Indians. White miners moved onto several reservations, staking claims and exploiting mineral wealth. When they tired of mining, they staked out claims on choice ranches and farms run by Indians. In the 1880s, white miners encroached upon the Colville Indian Reservation in north central Washington Territory. Their political clout was sufficient that the government reduced the Colville Reservation, slicing off the upper part that bordered Canada. Like miners in the Northwest, businessmen in Oklahoma used their influence to take oil from the Osage Reservation. In 1902, the secretary of interior issued his first oil and gas lease on Indian lands located within the boundaries of the future state of Oklahoma. By 1908, the secretary had issued approximately twenty-two thousand oil and gas leases on lands belonging to numerous Indian tribes.

Exploitation of oil and gas in Oklahoma is synonymous with the Osage Nation, which controlled vast acres of oil-rich land with subsurface rights. Potawatomi historian Terry Wilson has explored Osage oil in his *Underground Reservation.* He details the exploitation of oil by Indians and non-Indian "guardians" and the violence brought to Osage people as a result of their wealth. During the 1920s, Osage oil earned approximately $20 million each year, and each Osage person received a headright, some of which unscrupulous whites channeled into their own pockets, plundering the Osage of their minerals and money. In the process, some unknown person or persons murdered twenty-four Osage between 1921 and 1924, creating a national scandal. In 1925, Congress passed the Osage Guardianship Act, which tempered the violence over oil that was visited on the reservation but did little to heal the divisions among Osage people over the right to profit from their oil reserves. Excesses in Oklahoma were reflected in other regions of the American

West, where whites took advantage of many techniques to acquire title to Indian lands.

In 1917, white ranchers raced across the lands of the Tohono O'odham, known as the Papago Reservation, setting up mining claims around major watering places on the reservation. Whites took control of range land in this arid desert region, in spite of the fact that Tohono O'odham had worked years as loyal scouts for regular and volunteer troops chasing the Apaches. When the wars ended, whites turned on their former allies because they had choice grazing lands and precious water resources that whites desired. Exploitation such as that on the Papago Reservation occurred throughout the West, as the demand for water and resources increased. The two are intimately linked, regardless of the enterprise pursued. Ranching, farming, mining, lumbering, and other businesses required land and water. During the twentieth century, water became more and more important as the general population grew and demand for water increased. Whites schemed to capture as much water as humanly possible to foster growth and development of rural and urban lands, and in the process, whites took water previously used or controlled by Indians.

NATIVE AMERICANS AND WATER

Miners established claims on several reservations for mineral and water exploitation. Water had always been the key to survival and prosperity in the West, and some whites established "mining" claims on Indian lands to control lakes, rivers, streams, and springs. They used mining claims to enter reservations and divert the flow of water from Native Americans, sometimes selling water to non-Indians. Water struggles in the West between Indians and non-Indians characterized much of the twentieth century as ongoing legal battles deprived native people of precious water. On the Quechan Reservation of southern California, the U.S. Bureau of Reclamation built Laguna Dam to divert water from the Colorado River and channel it south into the Yuma Valley on the Arizona side of the river. In order to do this, the government forced the Quechan to sign an agreement that, in part, allowed the government to build a canal through the reservation to a giant siphon that took water in a huge tube underneath the Colorado River into canals running into Yuma Valley, where white farmers prospered.

The Quechan received no water from the canal running through their reservation from Laguna Dam. And after the Bureau of Reclamation built Imperial Dam just above Laguna Dam, the Quechan received no water from the All American Canal, which ran from the Colorado River west into the Imperial Valley, where white farmers used the water to irrigate thousands of acres and make millions of dollars. Meanwhile, irrigation projects on the Gila River also decreased the amount of water flowing into the Colorado River and through the Quechan Reservation. As a result of water projects, Quechans received little of the water that had nourished their crops and mesquite trees growing near the river. Traditionally, Quechans farmed corn, squash, beans, and melons along the Colorado River, using the natural flooding of the Gila and Colorado rivers to irrigate their crops. Dam projects ended the natural irrigation and helped destroy plant and animal habitats on the lower Colorado River. Starvation, disease, and death resulted as malnutrition opened the door to a host of new bacteria and viruses brought to Indian country by non-Indians.

Officials of the Bureau of Indian Affairs, Bureau of Reclamation, and Bureau of Land Management allowed ranchers to graze cattle and horses along the rivers, and the animals ate the same natural foods—chia, screw beans, mesquite beans, and tule roots—that the Quechan ate. As a result, the Quechan—particularly children—starved or died of malnutrition. They also died of tuberculosis, pneumonia, and gastrointestinal disorders. According to an analysis of death registers kept on the reservation, malnutrition was the foremost cause of death among infants and children at the Fort Yuma Indian Agency between 1915 and 1920. This fact suggests that adults as well as children were undernourished because mothers of infant children were unable to provide their babies with sufficient nutrients from breast milk. Adults also starved as a result of the diversion of water and destruction of native foods.

Issues of Indian water led Secretary of Interior Hubert Work to investigate. In 1927, he assigned Porter Preston of the Bureau of Reclamation and C. A. Engle of the Bureau of Indian Affairs to investigate Indian water rights and irrigation systems. The following year the investigators released their findings in the *Preston-Engle Irrigation Report.* The report recommended that the government reorganize the Indian Irrigation Service, end ineffective projects, and transfer Indian irrigation projects to the Bureau of Reclamation. During the administration of President Herbert Hoover, Secretary of Interior Ray Lyman Wilbur decided to follow the last recommendation of the *Preston-Engle Irrigation Report* and transfer Indian irrigation projects to the Bureau of Reclamation. However, Commissioner of Indian Affairs Charles J. Rhoads blocked the move and kept the water projects within the Bureau of Indian Affairs, believing that water belonging to or serving native people would be best protected by the Indian office than by the Bureau of Reclamation. As a result, water issues and irrigation projects associated with Native Americans remained with the Bureau of Indian Affairs.

Indian water rights emerged as a significant issue in the nineteenth century, when whites began expanding in large numbers into the trans-Mississippi West. However, the legal status of water was not litigated by the U.S. Supreme Court until 1908, when the court ruled in *Winters v. United States.* The case determined that Indians living on reservations retained the right to water for their farming projects and other business ventures. However, state and federal governments, settlers, and various water districts largely ignored the court ruling and did not enforce it on behalf of the Quechans or thousands of other Indians living on reservations. Whites deprived Native Americans of their water, which contributed to poverty, ill health, and mortality on reservations, even after 1909 when the Supreme Court ruled that federal treaties had provided water rights to Native Americans and that states could not deprive Indians of water. The "Winters Doctrine" was not applied to Native Americans until the 1950s, and by then, millions of acre-feet of water had been stolen from rivers flowing through reservations, depriving Native Americans of their water rights. Application of the Winters Doctrine was as harmful as application of the General Allotment Act. The federal government passed the Dawes Act to make farmers out of Indians and then ignored a high court ruling involving water rights that would have aided Indians in their agricultural and ranching enterprises. Whites took Indian lands through the allotment system, and after they had secured ownership of former reservation lands, whites wanted water so that they could make the lands productive. In handling Indian water, the government acted on behalf of whites, not Indians.

PUEBLO LANDS AND REFORMERS

In New Mexico, thousands of non-Pueblo Indians settled lands that had been claimed by the indigenous population for hundreds of years. The various Indian pueblos attempted to evict squatters but were unsuccessful because state, county, and law enforcement agencies and courts refused to acknowledge Pueblo Indian land rights. In order to help squatters gain further access to Indian lands and secure land titles, Congress passed a special act to enable white squatters living on Pueblo Indian lands in New Mexico to keep lands they had stolen. In 1922, Congress proposed the Bursum Bill, but in November of that year, representatives of all the Indian pueblos met at Santo Domingo pueblo to voice their united opposition to the Bursum Bill. The bill had the support of Secretary of Interior Albert B. Fall and conservative business interests in the House, Senate, and White House. Under the terms of the bill, Pueblo Indian communities would have had to prove ownership.

The bill provided that the various pueblos had to prove legal ownership of the land or recognize twelve thousand non-Indians' claims to lands near the pueblos. Normally courts required squatters to prove ownership of lands, but the government went out of its way to recognize squatters' rights. If the Pueblo Indian communities could not prove prior ownership to the satisfaction of the government, then ownership of real

During the Progressive Era of American history, national attention focused on many avenues of reform, including reform of federal Indian policy. In Indian country, Native Americans concentrated on other matters, including cultural preservation. Using ancient designs, Hopi potter Nampeyo revitalized an art form that is prized throughout the world.

estate parcels would be vested in non-Indians. President Harding and Secretary of Interior Fall supported the squatters over the Indians, but they met their match in John Collier, executive secretary of the American Indian Defense Association. Collier supported the Pueblo Indians, and he zealously organized opposition to the Bursum Bill, which was never passed or signed into law. However, Collier's fight against the bill added a new flare to the reform movement, providing momentum that continued for many years.

Collier urged many reform organizations to back the Pueblos and other Indians. As a result they received financial, media, and moral support from numerous groups, including the Indian Rights Association, General Federation of Women's Clubs, and artists-writers such as D. H. Lawrence, Mary Austin, Zane Grey, Carl Sandburg, Oliver LaFarge, and Carlos Vierra. Pueblo delegations traveled across the country, making their case and visiting officials in Washington, D.C. From their meeting at Santo Domingo pueblo, these diverse and autonomous Native Americans worked collectively through the All-Pueblo Council, a confederated group that had been created in 1680 during the Pueblo Revolt. The

Indians worked closely with thousands of non-Indian people, who forced a constipated Congress into action. Reformers made magnificent use of newspapers and magazines to support their cause. *Current History, Sunset Magazine, The Survey, The Forum,* and other periodicals carried articles decrying the theft of Native American lands in New Mexico.

The efforts of Indians and non-Indians working together resulted in new legislation that recognized Pueblo land titles, the establishment of a Pueblo Land Board to investigate ownership issues, and funds to pay nonnative settlers found to have title to Pueblo lands. Organized resistance in the Southwest added impetus to the national Indian reform movement. The movement owed much to past efforts of reformers, but a new vitality emerged out of the 1910s and 1920s as native people and Progressive reformers challenged the government's Indian policies. Like most reformers of the past, the new nonnative reformers were sometimes paternalistic, believing they knew what was best for native people, but they questioned their own past support of allotment and other policies that they had believed would be beneficial to native people. A new awareness of past mistakes brought broader-minded reformers who worked more closely with native people and listened to native voices—even if these reformers ultimately rejected those voices.

INVESTIGATIONS AND CHANGES

Changes in Native American policies during the 1920s emerged out of past reform efforts; many of the suggestions for improving native people had been suggested before but had been ignored by the Bureau of Indian Affairs, president, and Congress. But issues such as the Bursum Bill coalesced a new awareness about native people and a demand to improve conditions for them. Many Native Americans had urged the government to change its policies. These people included hundreds of native leaders who had traveled to Washington, D.C., during the late nineteenth and early twentieth centuries to speak with officials who often listened and did nothing. However, these native delegations introduced Native Americans to Washington politics and the difficulties involved in dealing with the U.S. government. The visits also gave politicians and bureaucrats an opportunity to hear Indian voices and consider the value of their words, stories, and ideas.

Native American delegations to Washington provided a foundation for native reformers. On Columbus Day in 1911, leaders from eighteen tribes met at Columbus, Ohio, at the invitation of sociologist Fayette McKenzie, of Ohio State University, to form a pan-Indian organization, the Society of American Indians. Included in the group was Carlos Montezuma, or Wassaja (Signaling), a Yavapai and Apache. He had been captured by Pima Indians and sold for $30 to a traveling photographer named Carlos Gentile, who settled in Chicago, where Montezuma spent most of his youth. A graduate of the University of Illinois at age seventeen, the brilliant Yavapai earned his medical degree from Chicago Medical College of Northwestern University at the age of twenty-one. Montezuma became a major figure within the Indian reform movement, supporting Americanization through acculturation and education. Montezuma considered native traditions to be an impediment to "progress."

In addition to Montezuma, the meeting drew Arthur C. Parker, the prominent Seneca anthropologist who shared Montezuma's vision that American Indians should be integrated into the larger American society without forfeiting their identities as native people. Other notable participants included Henry Roe Cloud, a Ho-Chunk (Winnebago) leader and teacher, Laura Cornelius, the Oneida reformer, Gertrude Bonnin, Yankton Sioux writer and educator, John Oskisson, Cherokee writer, and Thomas L. Sloan, Omaha attorney. The participants also included Charles Eastman, Dakota medical doctor, and his brother, Reverend John Eastman. These and other Native Americans who met in Columbus were a virtual *Who's Who* of Native American "intellectuals" and reformers. However, most of them would have been quick to assert that there were many intellectuals among all the tribes, although few of the traditional tribal leaders would have agreed with the goals of the Society of American Indians that pan-Indianism was more important than tribalism or that Native American traditions should give way to Americanization.

Members of the Society of American Indians favored formal education for the Indian. They saw this form of education as an "enlightenment which leaves him as a free man to develop according to the natural laws of social evolution." They favored vocational and industrial education for Indians, even though most of them had benefited from an academically oriented education. They supported the Anglo-American work ethic, emphasizing self-help, hard work, and self-determination. The organization's by-laws called for the abolition of the Bureau of Indian Affairs, an agency that, members argued, promoted Indian servitude and denigration. Many native reformers opposed the use of peyote and favored Christianity. Most members supported assimilation and acculturation, speaking out against the perpetuation of Native American dance, music, art, and cultural traditions. In his biography of Montezuma, historian Peter Iverson has demonstrated that Montezuma was one of the most zealous Indian reformers, using his publication, *Wassaja*, to berate the Bureau of Indian Affairs and denounce the Society of American Indians for advocating a gradual process of Americanization—Montezuma supported rapid Americanization of native peoples.

Members of the Society of American Indians dissolved into several other reform programs during the 1920s. Regardless of their personal

Dr. Carlos Montezuma, one of the most outspoken Native American activists of the twentieth century, called for the destruction of the Bureau of Indian Affairs and the integration of Indian people into American society. The Yavapai man graduated from medical school and dedicated his life to the health and well being of native peoples.

beliefs about the best means to achieve improvement, all these reformers continued their efforts to improve conditions for Native Americans. Most Native American reformers had advocated citizenship for all native people. The United States had granted citizenship to selected Native Americans throughout the nineteenth century as a result of removal treaties, allotment, and congressional acts. In 1901, Congress granted citizenship to all native people in Indian Territory but delayed citizenship to Indians in all areas of the United States by the Burke Act of 1906. In 1916, the Supreme Court ruled in *United States v. Nice* that U.S. citizenship could be granted to tribal people or those who were living with guardians. Three years later, the United States granted U.S. citizenship to Native Americans who had served in the armed services during World War I.

Finally, in 1924, the federal government conferred citizenship to all Native Americans, although some states withheld state citizenship. Arizona and New Mexico were the last states to grant citizenship to Native Americans, in 1948. On July 7, 1924, an editor for the *New York Times* wrote that Native Americans "may receive the news of their new citizenship with wry smiles. The white race, having robbed them of a continent, and having sought to deprive them of freedom of action, freedom of social custom, and freedom of worship, now at lasts gives them the same legal basis as their conquerors." No doubt American citizenship meant a good deal to some Native Americans, but to others, life changed little as a result of the federal law. Instead, most native people in the 1920s were more closely connected to their tribal communities on and off reservations, identifying more with their tribe, band, village, clan or family than with the United States of America.

During World War I, several Native Americans had served with distinction during the terrible fighting in Europe, and some died for the United States. Teachers and administrators at the Indian boarding schools kept records of those former students who sailed to Europe to fight and those who died in the war. During the war, the army used Choctaw, Cherokee, and other Native American speakers to communicate messages from one point to another so that German soldiers could not decipher the messages. The major problems were having a sufficient number of native speakers spread out across a field of battle and having sufficient words within the language to describe types of weapons, movements, and equipment. Native American communicators in World War I spoke in their native languages, not in a code devised from their languages. In any case, these and other native soldiers served gallantly "to make the world safe for democracy" but returned home to find little democracy in their relationship with the United States.

During the 1920s, Native American leadership on reservations began to change because of veterans returning from World War I. Many of these soldiers had been willing to lay down their lives for the United States, and they returned home to make changes in their lives and those of their people. Some of these returning soldiers became reformers on their own reservations, and some of them joined the national Indian reform organizations sweeping the country in the 1920s. Some of them became involved in the fight against the Bursum Bill, and many demanded that the Interior Department investigate the Bureau of Indian Affairs. In 1923, the secretary of interior asked the Committee of One Hundred, a national advisory committee on Indian affairs, to investigate the Bureau of Indian Affairs. The committee included many distinguished people, such as Henry Roe Cloud, Thomas D. Sloan, Arthur C. Parker, Sherman Coolidge, William Jennings Bryan, Frederick W. Hodge, Clark Wissler, Alfred L. Kroeber, John J. Pershing, Warren K. Moorehead, and Mark Sullivan.

William Jennings Bryan, the loser of presidential campaigns and always the liberal Christian, described Indians as "a race of primitive, untutored, nature-worshippers." He proposed to "shove the Christian religion down the throat of every Indian." But other reformers were more interested in issues important to the welfare of native people; in

December 1923, the committee offered its report, which urged the government to improve Indian education, health, and economic conditions. Significantly, the committee recommended that the government establish a tribunal of judges to litigate native claims against the government so that Indian claims did not have to be addressed by Congress or by lengthy and expensive legal cases in the courts. Although the Committee of One Hundred had little immediate impact on Indian policies, it contributed to furthering the impetus toward real reform that was developing from this and other reform efforts.

MERIAM REPORT, 1928

Native and nonnative reformers continued their demand for an investigation into American Indian affairs. Once again Secretary Work responded to public pressure and asked the Board of Indian Commissioners to investigate the Indian office. In January 1926, the board recommended that a "non-government, disinterested organization, with a field force of experts" investigate the condition of Indian tribes controlled by the Bureau of Indian Affairs. This was one of the most significant recommendations in American history, an event that led to a thorough and honest evaluation of the Bureau of Indian Affairs and American Indian policy in general. In June 1926, Secretary Work asked Director W. F. Willoughby of the Institute of Government Research to investigate Indian affairs in the United States. Willoughby received a grant from John D. Rockefeller Jr. to fund the study and soon after appointed a well-known scholar, Lewis Meriam, to lead the investigation.

When Lewis Meriam selected his staff, he chose people dedicated to a thorough investigation. He appointed Henry Roe Cloud to serve as an expert on the commission. The Ho-Chunk scholar was a major contributor of the report that emerged from a committee composed of several nationally known experts in health, education, economics, and Indian policy. Some of these people were Mary Louise Mark, William Spillman, W. Carson Ryan, Edward Everett Dale, Emma Duke, Fayette McKenzie, and Herbert Edwards. In 1927, the experts spent seven months in the field, focusing on specific reservations and examining as much data as humanly possible. The committee also reviewed documents at Indian boarding schools and day schools and evaluated conditions at schools, health clinics, and agency offices. The results of its exhaustive work were published in 1928 as *The Problem of Indian Administration* and is better known as the *Meriam Report.*

The *Meriam Report* was a landmark document chronicling many problems among Native Americans, stemming from poverty and the loss of land. The report deemed the allotment system and Indian education, which focused on assimilation and acculturation, to be failures. The *Meriam Report* urged Congress to protect the remaining Native American estate and to create loans for Indian enterprises to foster economic development. Meriam found that most Indians had an annual income of $100 to $200 in a country that had an average annual income of $1,350. In terms of education, the report urged Congress and the Bureau of Indian Affairs to abandon Americanization as a primary educational goal and to focus on a broader curriculum, better facilities, and more qualified teachers. The report recommended that the Indian office emphasize day schools on or near reservations (federal, public, or private) rather than overcrowded boarding schools. The report suggested that schools serve more nutritious foods and end child labor.

Perhaps the most revealing element of the *Meriam Report* was its analysis of Indian health, which was deplorable. According to the report, "taken as a whole practically every activity undertaken by the national government for the promotion of the health of the Indians is below a reasonable standard of efficiency." In addition, Meriam noted that "The health work of the Indian Service falls markedly below the standards maintained by the Public Health Service, the Veterans' Bureau, and the Army and the Navy, and those prescribed to the states by the national government in the administration of the . . . Maternity and Infancy Act." One of the gravest problems faced by the investigation committee was the lack of vital statistics. In 1884, Congress had passed a law requiring the Bureau of Indian Affairs to keep vital statistics on reservations, but most superintendencies and agencies ignored the order. As a result, the data provided the committee were incomplete. Nevertheless, the data obtained by Meriam were sufficient to indict the medical division of the Bureau of Indian Affairs.

Meriam noted that "for many years" the Bureau of Indian Affairs "had rules and regulations requiring the collection and tabulation of vital statistics," but the committee found that "accurate figures based on reasonably complete records are not yet secured." Indian deaths often went unrecorded by county officials or agents assigned to keep death registers. Unfortunately for the tribes and commission, agents had not enumerated deaths or recorded causes, secondary causes, age, occupation, gender, or other variables pertinent to the deceased. In spite of these limitations, Meriam reported that Indians suffered extremely high death rates in comparison to whites, other nonwhites, and the general populations of states where Indians resided. Meriam suggested that these death rates were the result of tuberculosis, pneumonia, gastrointestinal disorders, influenza, and accidental deaths.

Native Americans suffered from high fetal and infant mortality rates–much higher than those of nonnative populations. Meriam pointed out that Native Americans had an infant mortality rate of 190.7 per 1000 live births, whereas whites in the United States had a rate of 70.8 and

African-Americans a rate of 114.1. On some reservations, including the Yakama Reservation, the infant mortality rate was even higher. In *Death Stalks the Yakama*, the author provides averages of infant mortality per one thousand live births from, 1920 to 1964, and compares these with whites, other nonwhites, and the population of Washington. The years from 1925 to 1929 provided the most striking infant mortality data, with Yakamas experiencing a rate of 497 per 1,000 live births. During the same years, whites in the United States had an infant mortality rate of 65, non-whites averaged 105, and the people of Washington had a rate of 51. The averages from these populations demonstrate that Yakamas had a higher average infant mortality rate in every year from 1920 to 1964, although the rate was never again as marked as it was in the late 1920s.

In large part, Indians experienced high death rates because of abject poverty, poor housing, lack of sanitation and public health programs, and the absence of food. Malnutrition was rampant on reservations, weakening native people and inviting bacteria and viruses to destroy their bodies. In Arizona, the Native American death rate from tuberculosis was seventeen times that of the country in general. On the Yakama Reservation in 1930, the Indian death rate from pneumonia was twenty times that of whites in the United States. In addition, Meriam confirmed findings that Native Americans had extremely high rates of trachoma, a blinding disease caused by chlamydia, which the Indian office had been treating through radical and unproven eye surgery that left many native people blind.

Meriam discovered that the Bureau of Indian Affairs spent approximately 50¢ per Indian per year on health care, in spite of the fact that most treaties guaranteed native people health care. In fact, Meriam learned that reservations employed few doctors and nurses, enjoyed few hospitals or clinics, and had little medical equipment. The researchers found that the government forced Native American children to boarding schools, where they contracted diseases spread by poor sanitation, lack of medical care, and poor food. When students became ill, administrators often sent them home so that they did not die at school. In the process, students infected their families and friends, spreading disease to native communities. Meriam argued that many health problems suffered by Native Americans would be improved if the federal government would work more closely with state and county health agencies. In 1929, as a direct result of the *Meriam Report*, the secretary of interior ordered agents to allow state and county health officials to enter reservations and work with Indian people. State and federal officials signed contracts improving Indian health, but cooperation between government agencies remains an impediment to Indian health today.

According to historian S. Lyman Tyler, the *Meriam Report* "was not a revolutionary document. Many of the recommendations made were not original with the survey team, but were present in earlier studies, annual reports, and recommendations to Congress." But for the first time, the report brought together a great deal of data in a comprehensive study "that all who were interested in the Indian were able to rally behind: the Congress, the Bureau, the reformers, and the general public." The *Meriam Report* became the foundation for the next level of Indian reform and changed Native American history for the remainder of the twentieth century.

Selected Readings and Bibliography

The history of Indians during the Progressive era of American history is part of the transitional period when Indians had to cope with dispossession, disease, assimilation, reservation life, allotment, and anomie. Previously cited books that proved helpful for this chapter include Gibson's *Oklahoma,* Trafzer's *Yuma,* Bee's *Crosscurrents along the Colorado,* Burt's *Tribalism in Crisis,* Prucha's *American Indian Policy in Crisis,* Tyler's *History of Indian Policy,* Szasz's *Education and the American Indian,* Hoxie's "The Curious Story of Reformers" and *A Final Promise,* Mardock's *The Reformers and the American Indian,* and Trennert's *White Man's Medicine.* Also helpful were Aberle, *The Peyote Religion among the Navajo;* Berthong, *The Cheyenne and Arapaho Ordeal;* Cohen, *Handbook of Federal Indian Law;* La Barre, *The Peyote Cult;* Debo, *And Still the Waters Run;* Deloria, *American Indian Policy in the Twentieth Century;* Hertzberg, *The Search for American Indian Identity;* and Miner, *The Corporation and the Indian.*

Brayer, Herbert O. *Pueblo Land Grants of the Rio Abajo.* Albuquerque: University of New Mexico Press, 1939.

Carlson, Leonard A. *Indians, Bureaucrats and Land: The Dawes Act and the Decline of Indian Farming.* Westport, Conn.: Greenwood Press, 1981.

Collier, John, and Ira Moskowitz. *Indians of the Americas.* New York: W. W. Norton, 1947.

———. *From Every Zenith.* Denver: Sage Books, 1963.

———. *American Indian Ceremonial Dances.* New York: Bounty Books, 1972.

Downes, Randolph. "A Crusade for Indian Reform, 1922–1934." *Mississippi Valley Historical Review* 32 (1945): 331–354.

Fiske, Turbese Lummis, and Keith Lummis. *Charles F. Lummis.* Norman: University of Oklahoma Press, 1975.

Gessner, Robert. *Massacre: A Survey of Today's American Indian.* New York: J. Cape and H. Smith, 1931.

Iverson, Peter. *Carlos Montezuma and the Changing World of the American Indian.* Albuquerque: University of New Mexico Press, 1982.

Kelly, Lawrence. *The Navajo Indians and Federal Indian Policy, 1900–1935.* Tucson: University of Arizona Press, 1968.

Lee, R. Alton. "Indian Citizenship and the Fourteenth Amendment." *South Dakota History* 4 (1974): 196–221.

Lundquist, G. E. E. *The Red Man in the United States.* New York: George H. Doran, 1923.

Meriam, Lewis. *The Problem of Indian Administration.* Baltimore: Johns Hopkins University Press, 1928.

Moses, L. G. *Wild West Shows and the Images of American Indians, 1889–1933.* Albuquerque: University of New Mexico Press, 1996.

Roy, Chunilal. "Indian Peyotists and Alcohol." *American Journal of Psychiatry* 103 (1973): 329–330.

Stein, Gary. "The Indian Citizenship Act of 1924." *New Mexico Historical Review* 47 (1972): 257–274.

Trafzer, Clifford E. "Horses and Cattle, Buggies and Hacks: Purchases by Yakima Indian Women, 1909–1912." *Negotiators of Change.* Nancy Shoemaker, ed. New York: Routledge, 1994, pp. 176–192.

——. "Invisible Enemies: Ranching, Farming, and Quechan Indian Deaths at the Fort Yuma Agency, California, 1915–1925." *American Indian Culture and Research Journal* 21 (1997): 83–117.

Trafzer, Clifford E., Luke Madrigal, and Anthony Madrigal. *Chemehuevi People of the Coachella Valley.* Coachella, Calif.: Chemehuevi Press, 1997.

Wilson, Raymond. *Ohiyesa: Charles Eastman, Santee Sioux.* Urbana: University of Illinois Press, 1983.

CHAPTER 16

INDIAN NEW DEAL

The election of 1932 brought Franklin D. Roosevelt to the White House and Democrats to the Congress. Roosevelt offered a New Deal to the nation and to Native Americans. The president appointed to his administration two men who had long supported Native American causes. He chose Harold Ickes as secretary of interior and John Collier as commissioner of Indian affairs. Ickes had been a charter member of the American Indian Defense Association, which Collier had directed. Their appointment to the executive branch inaugurated a new day for Native Americans, one that has been viewed by Indian people as both positive and negative. Like millions of other Americans, native people had been adversely affected by the Great Depression and sought relief from the long-term effects of reservations and allotment. Ickes and Collier continued the progress made by Commissioner Rhoads during the administration of Herbert Hoover, but the new administration accelerated the rate of change and diversified efforts to correct problems pointed out in the *Meriam Report.*

LAUNCHING THE INDIAN NEW DEAL

Collier and Ickes were men of great energy and conviction, and they initiated their plans of action even before taking office in 1933. In January 1933, Collier published "Details of the Reorganization on Which the Indians Wait" in *American Indian Life,* which outlined some of his thinking on native affairs. The executive director of the Indian Defense Association and future commissioner suggested that he wanted to reverse several policies of the Indian office by encouraging Native Americans to reestablish tribal councils so that the people could govern themselves and enjoy a degree of self-determination. Collier did not recommend abolition of the Bureau of Indian Affairs, but he wanted Indians to have a greater voice in political and economic matters facing the tribes. He suggested that tribes form corporations through which they could manage their own resources and foster economic development. To this end, Collier also recommended that the federal government provide credit to tribes so that they would have seed money with which to launch business enterprises.

President Roosevelt, Secretary of Interior Ickes, and Commissioner Collier engaged in Indian policy making from the outset of the new administration. Democrats in Congress also contributed to the new energy brought to the Bureau of Indian Affairs, supporting orders and legislation that forever changed the way the Indian office conducted business with Native Americans. William F. Zimmerman became the assistant commissioner of Indian affairs, and Felix Cohen emerged as the leading legal counsel guiding the Indian New Deal. A team of committed bureaucrats met regularly to devise and direct new policies. The team set about to hire more Indians to work in the Bureau of Indian Affairs. Collier immediately accelerated former Commissioner Rhoads's program of transferring students from Indian boarding schools to day schools located on or near reservations, and he ordered employees of the Bureau of Indian Affairs to end the Americanization program that had characterized the Indian office since 1867. To this end, the Interior Department ended the Board of Indian Commissioners, the symbol of white rule, and encouraged Indians to participate in the new reform period.

Through circulars, letters, and verbal instructions, Commissioner Collier made it clear to agents, superintendents, school administrators, and government teachers that the "cultural history of Indians is in all respects to be considered equal to that of any non-Indian group." He was quick to state that he had no "intention of interfering unduly with intelligent and devoted mission effort on the part of Catholic or Protestant workers in the Indian field" while at the same time instructing his employees to end their interference "with Indian religious life or expression." For years the Office of Indian Affairs had actively attempted to destroy Native American religions, ceremonies, rituals, dance, and music. Agents, soldiers, marshals, and Indian police had violated sacred ceremonies and prevented native people from openly practicing their religions because Christians considered them to be heathen or satanic. Agents had arrested medicine men and women as well as native dancers, drummers, and singers. They had disrupted Indian traditions and created difficulties among native people for years.

In 1933, Collier called for a reversal of this policy, encouraging Hopis to hold their annual Snake and Kachina Dances, Lakotas to perform Sun Dances, Palouses to offer their First Food Feasts, and all of the tribes to conduct traditional ceremonies. Christian agents, school administrators, and missionaries had interfered with native religions for over a century, but Collier's orders promoted native religious practices. For the first time since Native Americans had been confined to reservations, the commissioner advocated freedom of expression, speech, and religion for all

Cahuilla, Mojave, Hualapai, Quechan, Cocopa, and other Indians of southern California and western Arizona sing Bird Songs. Cahuilla singer Luke Madrigal and Robert Levi (right) carry on an ancient tradition through song and dance, frequently speaking to young people and sharing the tradition.

native people. Certainly not all employees of the Indian office agreed with Collier's decree, but they risked losing their jobs if they continued to harass Indians for practicing their traditional religions. Collier also abolished the government's requirement for students at Indian boarding schools to attend Christian worship services or face punishment. The commissioner's stand on Native American religious freedom was a radical departure for the Indian office and one that brought Collier severe criticism from Indians and non-Indians alike who agreed with Joseph Bruner, a Muscogee Indian, who stated that Collier and his programs were "dangerous, Christ-mocking, communistic aiding, [and] subversive."

Bruner and others criticized Collier for encouraging Native Americans to wear long hair—a symbol of traditionalism—and to "return to the blanket." He supported natives' use of their own medicine men and women who employed traditional Indian medicines and rituals. Although some Native Americans had used white physicians employed by the Interior and War Departments, most had continued to use Indian medicine. However, as non-Indians introduced more varieties of viruses and bacteria, Indians found that their traditional medicines were not sufficient to destroy new diseases. Suffering from tuberculosis, influenza, gastrointestinal disorders, and pneumonia, Native Americans sought relief through white doctors. Oftentimes, doctors on reservations were ill prepared to minister to the medical needs of native people. Historian Todd Benson has graphically detailed the trachoma campaign launched by the Office of Indian Affairs between 1924 and 1927, when doctors operated on over twenty thousand Native Americans, cutting out infected follicles on the inner eyelid or surgically removing the tarsal plate between the eyelid and upper eye in a futile, untried, dangerous, and ineffective attempt to end trachoma in a swift and inexpensive manner.

Before the trachoma campaign, Native Americans had started seeking out white physicians and nurses for medical help, while agency employees sought to discredit traditional medicine men and women. Letters from various agencies urged the Indian office to stamp out medicine men and women because they considered native healers to be fakes, frauds, and charlatans who led people away from scientific cures. On the Yakama Reservation, agents protested the Indian Shaker Church, saying that the church services stirred up a great deal of dust that caused diseases. Slowly, however, Yakama agents learned that the Indian Shaker Church forbade its members from drinking alcohol and that agency police had little difficulty dealing with members of the church. In the 1920s, agents reassessed their opinions of the Indian Shaker Church and began supporting the movement. In like fashion, agents who had opposed the Native American Church and the use of peyote as its central sacrament found that members of the church often shied away from alcohol and that the service actually helped its membership remain clean and sober. In 1933, Collier ordered agents not to molest Native American healers and to allow them to practice their healing arts for the benefit of their communities.

Collier also ended the federal government's practice of destroying Native American languages and denigrating native people for speaking their own languages. The commissioner wrote that "it is desirable that Indians be bilingual—fluent and literate in the English language, and fluent in their vital, beautiful, and efficient native languages." Federal officials had spent over one hundred years trying to destroy Native American languages, forcing native people to speak English on reservations. In part, the government had established boarding schools as a means of separating children from their friends and relatives who spoke native languages. Administrators, disciplinarians, teachers, and other employees of Indian boarding schools had worked diligently to tear native languages from the minds and tongues of students, severely punishing children for speaking their own languages.

Americanization among Native Americans had been detrimental to their fine arts, theater, dance, and music. Collier announced that Native American "arts are to be prized, nourished and honored." Native Americans had always been creative, imaginative people with numerous and varied art forms. They were noted worldwide for dance, music, and theater, which they performed for themselves and for nonnative audiences. However, some government agents decided that native forms of art were barbaric, uncivilized, and savage. So they denigrated native art forms, discouraging native people from creating traditional arts such as head-dresses, dolls, dresses, jewelry, hair roaches, moccasins, gloves, bows, arrows, shields, tomahawks, knives, flutes, rattles, textiles, baskets, pot-tery, and many other items. Many white workers on reservations had de-valued or outlawed material culture of Native Americans, saying that na-tive material items were representations of backward cultures that had to give way to civilized items that represented progress. Collier ended Americanization and supported Native American cultures in many ways, which led to his being accused of being a communist and an atheist.

In August 1933, Secretary Ickes ordered the end of the sale of Indian allotments. He also recommended against the U.S. government issuing future fee patents to native people for their lands. In sum, Ickes ended the allotment system that had devastated Native Americans and divested them of millions of acres. White ranchers, farmers, oilmen, and other business interests in the West were outraged by Ickes's order, because the secretary took away the possibility of purchasing more native lands and further exploiting native resources. But many people, including politicians, argued that excesses by the business community had caused the Great Depression and that it was time to push policies that ended economic exploitation of poverty-stricken people, including Native Americans. Collier agreed with Ickes that the sale of allotments must end, and he further developed the theme of native lands as he worked with Felix Cohen to compose the first draft of the Indian Reorganization Act (or Wheeler-Howard Act).

INDIAN REORGANIZATION ACT, 1934

In 1933 and early 1934, Collier and Cohen crafted the Indian Reorga-nization Act. The legislation was the culmination of several reform movements, congressional investigations, scholarly studies, tuberculosis reports, trachoma studies, and the *Meriam Report*. Rarely in Native American history had representatives of the U.S. government asked In-dians their opinion about matters affecting them. Collier altered the old approach of creating policy and applying it to native people without lis-tening to a single Native American voice. The Indian office sent a draft of the legislation to tribes, Native American leaders, and employees of the Bureau of Indian Affairs, soliciting input from many sources while build-ing support for the bill. Collier organized a series of meetings with Native American leaders at regional conferences to discuss the bill and possible ways to implement it.

Collier championed self-determination by allowing each tribe to vote on whether or not to become an "IRA" tribe. If a tribe accepted the act, tribal members had to follow the mandates of the act in order to receive the benefits of tribal organization under the act. The original bill did not include American Indians living in Oklahoma or Alaska, but a supplement to the bill in 1936 included them. Although Collier consulted with Native American leaders and supported their right to vote on whether to accept the Indian Reorganization Act, he had already framed the legislation and knew what policies he believed were in the best interest of Indian people. Collier was an opinionated politician who had worked with native peoples for years, but he was obstinate, arrogant, self-righteous, and paternalistic. Worst of all, Collier was impatient.

Collier had spent a decade working for change in American Indian affairs, almost always criticizing actions or inactions of others. When Collier became commissioner, he was anxious to implement changes that he considered vital for the benefit of native people. He overlooked the fact that decision making among Native Americans differed considerably but that in general, native people took time and patience to reach decisions, often coming to important collective decisions through consensus, not majority votes. Collier had spent his life gauging public sentiment, and he believed that his proposal was so important and beneficial to native people that it had to be implemented as quickly as possible before the political climate of the nation changed.

So, in 1933–1934, he pushed native people and Congress to enact the Indian Reorganization Act. Scholars debate whether Collier was right or wrong in his approach to American Indian policies, but the fact remains that his accelerated drive for the act created many problems for the act and the well-meaning commissioner. Collier's impatience cost him support among some native groups, but some native peoples did not support the Indian Reorganization Act because they feared the loss of their allotments. In 1934, Native Americans were weary of government bureaucrats who had wonderful plans that would benefit them.

Between the 1830s and 1930s, Native Americans had experienced forced removals, wars, reduction of their estates, confinement to reservations, punitive imprisonment, government by white fiat, theft of water, timber, minerals, and other valuable resources, the allotment system, epidemics, and chronic depression. Whereas Collier was ready for rapid change, native people pondered the long-term implications of the Indian Reorganization Act. At public hearings held in California, South Dakota, Oregon, and Oklahoma, Native American leaders wisely voiced their decision that they would not commit their people to the legislation until they learned more about it and could inform their people of its full implications.

During congressional hearings, Collier admitted that he did not know if the Indian Reorganization Act would work. He was unsure because such legislation and such an approach to American Indian policy had never been tried, but he urged the nation's representatives to consider making a major change in the way the government dealt with native people. Collier spent a good deal of time explaining to Indians and non-Indians the components of the bill. Collier had already ordered his employees to implement elements of the Indian Reorganization Act, including self-determination. The act proposed to return elements of home rule to native people, but not complete home rule because the United States still assumed jurisdiction over the tribes. However, Collier used the act to extend to the tribes freedom of religion as well as the right to maintain cultural identities through language and literature.

The Indian Reorganization Act sought to improve Indian education and health. In 1934, Congress passed the Johnson-O'Malley Act, which authorized the Office of Indian Affairs, commonly called the Bureau of Indian Affairs by the 1930s, to expand its contracts to states to offer education, social services, and medicine to Native Americans. Over the years more native students had attended public school financed by the federal government through states and counties. The Johnson-O'Malley Act fostered greater cooperation between federal and state governments; but the Indian Reorganization Act sought to further the educational experience of native students through improved funding, broader curriculum, and emphasis on day schools near native communities rather than on boarding schools. The Indian Reorganization Act also proposed improvements in Indian health, focusing on medical treatment and public health on reservations and within boarding schools.

In January 1933, Collier outlined his plan to form tribal business corporations that could acquire business loans from the federal government for ranching, farming, forest products industry, arts and crafts, and light manufacturing. The act provided funds to support tribal businesses, with revolving credit (in which funds were paid out as credit, paid back, paid out again, and so on) to help tribes finance economic development. Collier had conceived this idea before he took office. He also created the Emergency Conservation Work project for Native Americans, a public works project program that became the Indian Civilian Conservation Corps (CCC). Indian individuals and families moved to one of seventy-two CCC camps in fifteen western states to live while adults worked on diverse programs, including reseeding range lands, reforesting, building check dams, creating reservoirs, clearing forests of underbrush, establishing trails, cleaning water holes, digging wells, terracing hillsides, and a host of other conservation projects. Government schools at CCC camps educated adults and children alike, offering native people some social, economic, health, and educational opportunities.

Collier drew Native Americans into other alphabet programs of the New Deal. He secured for several tribes lands from the Resettlement and Farm Security Administration, along with equipment by which native farmers could cultivate marginal lands surrounding or adjacent to their reservations. He also encouraged Indians to develop these new lands for ranges to support cattle and sheep, which could be sold to outside markets. Collier secured funding from the Works Project Administration (WPA) so that Indians could become a part of the national effort to put people to work by conducting public projects. He received $100 million to hire Indians to build roads, bridges, and public buildings, as well as supplemental funding through the CCC for soil and water conservation programs. Collier found resources in many areas to fund projects that helped Native Americans find work and earn wages during a difficult time.

Collier's concentration on conservation of the Native American environment became one of the themes of his administration, after passage of the Indian Reorganization Act. He and his agents had discussed many aspects of the bill with American Indians and congressional leaders. Collier took to heart some of the advice he received, but for the most part, he maintained his own vision of Indian reform. Collier and other bureaucrats continued the age-old paternalism that Native Americans had criticized for years. On June 18, 1934, the bill passed the two houses of Congress, and President Roosevelt quickly signed it into law. Collier then took the legislation to the tribes to convince them to vote for it and become part of the new program. A total of 181 tribes voted to become IRA tribes, whereas 78 rejected the IRA. Some of the most populous tribes with large land areas voted against the act, including Crows, Navajos, and Klamaths. A total of 135 Native American communities drafted tribal constitutions, creating tribal governments with formal documents by which to govern themselves. Although the large and powerful Navajo tribe refused to join in the Indian Reorganization Act, it and all other Native American Nations were profoundly and permanently affected by the act and the administration of John Collier.

The Indian Reorganization Act was a watershed in Native American history. The act reversed specific aspects of American Indian policy, and it influenced the course of native history from 1934 forward. The act encouraged tribal self-determination in many areas of Indian life. It ended allotment and gave tribes the right to reacquire lands to add to tribal estates and some funds with which to accomplish the process immediately. Between 1935 and 1937, native tribes added 2,100,000 acres to their estates, and this amount grew as a result of the Indian Reorganization Act, altering the trend begun in the colonial period when Native Americans began losing millions of acres to non-Indians. The act also permitted tribes to purchase resources, water rights, and surface rights.

The Indian Reorganization Act helped Indians find employment, including jobs offered through the civil service, which employed native peoples in many government jobs, including those within the Bureau of Indian Affairs. Native Americans received hiring preferences for a variety of jobs on the reservations, including work on construction projects that built bridges, hospitals, government offices, roads, schools, and homes. Indians also worked for the government to fight soil, wind, and water erosion. Under the act, the secretary of interior was authorized to manage forests and range lands on reservations. The secretary could "restrict the number of livestock grazed on Indian range units to the estimated carrying capacity of such ranges" and could "promulgate such other rules and regulations as may be necessary to protect the range from deterioration, to prevent soil erosion, to assure full utilization of the range." This section of the Indian Reorganization Act caused great stress and economic loss to some Indians, including tribes that did not vote to become IRA tribes.

The Indian Reorganization Act encouraged tribes to reconstitute their governments and manage numerous aspects of tribal affairs through majority rule. The act specified that an Indian tribe "shall have the right to organize for its common welfare, and may adopt an appropriate constitution and bylaws." The act authorized tribes to create Indian courts to handle minor offenses. In the past, Indian agents had ruled reservations with more power than big city bosses. They could also order Indian policemen to arrest recalcitrant Indians and have them confined to federal penitentiaries without tribal juries or due process of any sort. Agents also had appointed native people to serve as judges, but under the new act, Native Americans could elect judges for specified terms of office. The act empowered the secretary of interior to "make loans to Indian chartered corporations for the purpose of promoting the economic development of such tribes." The loans were to "be credited to the revolving fund" so that other tribes could draw upon the money for future projects. As a result, Native Americans established tribal business enterprises in agriculture, ranching, forest industries, and others.

The legislation also focused on improving Native American education. It provided tribes with approximately $250,000 per year "for loans . . . for the payment of tuition and other expenses in recognized vocational and trade schools" and another $50,000 to be used for loans to native students to attend high school or college. In this way, the federal government encouraged native people to seek higher education. A subsequent bill of 1935 created the Indian Arts and Crafts Board "to promote the development of Indian arts and crafts and to create a board to assist" native people to benefit from their varied art forms. The board was established "to promote the economic welfare of the Indian tribes . . . through the development of Indian arts and crafts and the expansion of the market for the products."

Through these acts and several executive orders of Collier, the government sanctioned the use and development of Native American art, culture, history, religion, and language. The acts did not end discrimination against native peoples, their cultures, or languages by government and nongovernment people, but they set the country on a new course toward accepting the cultural diversity native to "Turtle Island," including that part known as the United States. Under Collier, the Indian office attempted to nurture native culture, rather than destroy it, and to preserve the remainder of the Indian estate, adding more land and resources whenever feasible. These two elements of the Indian New Deal drew heavy criticism from Indians and non-Indians alike. Most of the critics were business and banking interests eager to plunder additional native resources and continue the great land barbecue. Collier's reforms also infuriated conservative Christians who believed that the commissioner was leading Indians back down the path of heathenism, barbarism, and savagery. Several people believed that Collier was an agent of Satan, sent to destroy the work of Christ among native people.

ASSESSMENT OF THE INDIAN REORGANIZATION ACT

Business and religious interest groups had always been powerful forces within the United States and were skilled politically at executing their agendas. Some Native Americans, including people who shared religious or business views with whites, joined together to attack the Indian New Deal. Some native people cooperated with those living at Laguna and Acoma pueblos regarding stock reduction to preserve ranges, but government agents did not adequately consult Navajo people. Through a number of oral interviews, Navajo scholar Ruth Roessel has shown that government range riders rode across the vast stretches of the Navajo Reservation without the permission of the people, shooting herds of sheep and goats without explaining their purpose or reimbursing Navajos for their losses. The government acted to preserve limited range on the Navajo Reservation, but government agents did not take the time to discuss the problem with the elder women who "owned" the sheep, cattle, and horses. As a result of the government's assault on the herds, Navajos disliked and distrusted Collier's people. They have never forgotten that they lost thousands of animals—their wealth—due to John Collier, and the stories of stock reduction are woven into the oral memory of the Navajo. Although stock reduction was a negative result of the Indian New Deal, the government's action helped create a new era for tribal governments.

Many Native Americans believed that the IRA created more divisions among the people, and this belief compelled them toward inaction. Rather than cause more internal strife through their actions, several native leaders stalled and did nothing. Some scholars have argued that Indians did not know how to act after power had been given to them, but this is not true. Native American leaders knew how to act and use power, but they chose not to assert power because it was detrimental to their communities to be divided over reforms thrust on them by white bureaucrats. Many native people opposed Collier and the reforms, including Alice Lee Jemison, a Seneca proassimilationist who felt that the Indian New Deal was taking Indians "back to the blanket," and Delos K. Lone Wolf, a national leader of the Peyote religion who believed that the Indian Reorganization Act was divisive and destructive.

Other Native Americans simply came to believe that if they supported the IRA they would lose their allotments or lands. Given the government's record for "protecting" the interests of Indians, their concerns were well founded. Among Indians it just made sense not to trust the federal government, and it seemed to many native people that the Indian Reorganization Act was just the most recent in a series of "good ideas" set forth by the federal government for their "benefit." They were skeptical of Collier and the Indian New Deal. As a result of many forces and factors, native and nonnative people urged their congressmen to investigate the Bureau of Indian Affairs.

The Senate Committee on Indian Affairs had been investigating the Indian office since 1928, when Lewis Meriam published his report. And throughout the 1930s, the Senate investigated Indian affairs with different committee chairs, including Burton K. Wheeler of Montana, the coauthor of the Wheeler-Howard Act, which launched Collier's reforms, and Elmer Thomas of Oklahoma, a conservative representing business. After years of investigations and supplements to the various reports, the Senate produced a mammoth document of over twenty-three thousand pages. In 1943, the Senate offered the *Survey of Conditions of the Indians of the United States.* An analysis of the document provides many details regarding American Indian policy in transition, but a few points become very clear. The Bureau of Indian Affairs was riddled with problems, and many policy makers felt that the office should be abolished.

The Senate report offered American Indians a small voice regarding policies. Native Americans had many complaints about the Indian office and the U.S. government. They demanded that the government settle native claims against the United States for the theft of millions of acres and billions of dollars' worth of natural resources. They wanted the government to honor its treaty obligations and trust responsibilities by improving health and education among the tribes. Native Americans also demanded that the government improve Indian education by providing day schools, vocational schools, and college opportunities. They wanted greater employment opportunities so they could care for their families, and they wanted the personnel makeup of the Indian office to include Indians.

The Senate report satisfied few people and was a ponderous document. Rather than act on it, members of the House of Representatives in 1944 concluded that they should investigate American Indian affairs. Led by Congressman Karl E. Mundt of South Dakota, the House committee recommended that the government downsize the Bureau of Indian Affairs and end the special status of Native Americans, forcing them to assimilate and acculturate immediately. Mundt wanted to abolish the Bureau of Indian Affairs altogether. After several witnesses gave testimony, the House committee composed its own report, which indicated that many House members were eager for native peoples to govern themselves and pay their own way without significant federal funding. They recommended the creation of an Indian Claims Commission to end tribal claims against the federal government and clear future litigation between the government and the tribes. In this way, conservatives could claim to have been fair to Native Americans and to have provided them with seed money to launch a future for themselves without further federal aid.

The House committee concluded that the Indian Reorganization Act had cost too much money for so little reform, and several members of the House felt that funding for Native Americans should be cut. The House committee report reflected the ebb and flow of American Indian affairs. During World War II, many House members believed the time had come for the country to decrease its emphasis on native people and for them to become "mainstreamed." For over a decade, Collier had led American Indian affairs, and some government leaders wanted to end his influence and reverse the course of the Indian office. Some traditional Indians added that the new forms of government created by the Indian New Deal were foreign to them and proved divisive among the people, and progressive Indians argued that Collier had set back Native American assimilation by encouraging people to conduct their old ceremonies, speak native languages, and return to ancient art forms. Leaders of the Indian Rights Association and the National Council of Churches joined in the chorus against Collier for his support of cultural pluralism rather than assimilation and acculturation.

Several observers noted this philosophical and political change emerging in the nation's capital, including Scudder Mekeel, who wrote a perceptive essay in *The American Indian*. In 1944, Mekeel wrote that the renewed "hard-boiled" mood had "just cropped up in Congress," where House members had decided that "Indians ought to be turned loose immediately even if it means starvation for large numbers." He noted that members of the House had had enough of Indian reform and wanted Indians to shift for themselves without federal funding. In part, this was a reaction to Collier's innovative and controversial policies. It was also a reaction to domestic spending, which conservatives wanted to reduce. Mekeel believed that congressmen were threatening Collier's "new and more constructive policy which seeks to reorganize Reservation societies on an economically sound basis." He believed that "this is not [the] time to abandon the whole effort," but some policy makers disagreed and continued to push their agenda to end and reverse Collier's reforms.

By 1945, Collier was tired and disillusioned, having fought numerous battles against Indian and non-Indian foes. However, an assessment of Collier's New Deal programs includes many considerations that may be deconstructed in a number of ways. The Indian Reorganization Act ended allotment, and Collier actually added four million acres to the native estate and secured additional resources through purchases and conservation. For the first time in American history, the government encouraged Native Americans to preserve their cultures. Although some Native Americans criticized Collier for preserving native culture and establishing (or reestablishing) tribal governments, the act brought Native American communities together and encouraged self-determination.

The U.S. government had spent 153 years seeking to destroy native self-determination, and the Indian Reorganization Act sought to provide natives with some say in their lives. In addition, Indian health improved during the New Deal era, in part because of improved education about sanitation and public health, but also because of increased earnings and better health programs that lowered some of the highest death rates of any population within the United States. Vine Deloria Jr., the eminent Lakota scholar from Standing Rock, and Clifford Lytle sum up Collier's contributions by arguing that "the man engineered a complete revolution in Indian affairs" that was to influence native policies and Indian people for the remainder of the twentieth century. In spite of shortcomings, the Indian New Deal benefited most Native Americans, changed the course of American Indian policies, and led the way to future changes that provided native people greater self-determination.

INDIAN CLAIMS COMMISSION

In February 1945, Collier resigned, but his influence on American Indian affairs was apparent on many levels for years to come. One of Collier's accomplishments passed Congress after his resignation: the creation of the Indian Claims Commission. Before the Claims Commission, individual tribes had to petition Congress for permission to sue the United States in the Court of Claims. Tribes had to specify their grievances and note the violations in terms of their treaties and agreements with the federal government. In the past, Congress had not been eager to allow tribes to sue the United States, but in 1945, the House committee investigating Indian affairs had recommended an Indian Claims Commission. Because members of the House had made the most recent recommendation for an Indian claims commission, members of that body were more enthusiastic about supporting it. Even more important, some members of the House suggested ending the legal relationships between the United States and the tribes and resolving outstanding claims against the government in the hope of eventually concluding all government affairs with Native Americans.

Various studies of Indian affairs during the 1920s and the *Meriam Report* had recommended a claims commission. These studies had mentioned that many tribes had legitimate claims against the federal government for lands and resources stolen from them as well as for obligations that the government had failed to fulfill. Commissioner Rhoads had recommended a special commission to consider Indian claims against the government because the U.S. Court of Claims could not hear all Indian cases in one hundred years of work. In 1929, Representative Scott Leavitt introduced a bill to establish an Indian court of claims, but the bill never got out of committee. During Collier's administration, he was never able to persuade Congress to pass a bill enabling an Indian claims commission. In 1945, members of the House introduced two bills for the creation of an Indian claims commission, held hearings on these bills, and established a joint congressional committee to investigate a claims commission.

In 1946, the House and Senate passed the Indian Claims Commission Act, and on August 13, President Harry S Truman signed it into law. The act allowed Native Americans in the United States and Alaska to file a claim against the government directly with the Claims Commission, regarding claims "in law or equity arising under the Constitution, laws, treaties . . ., and Executive orders" that dealt with "fraud, duress, unconscionable consideration, mutual or unilateral mistake, whether of law or fact, or any other ground cognizable by a court of equity." Attorneys for the government and tribes could use "all records, hearings, and reports made by the committees of each House of Congress" and "any official letter, paper, document, map, or record in the possession of any officer or department, or court." Under the terms of the act, the government paid for the attorneys and witnesses on both sides, but the act limited plaintiffs' attorneys to no more than 10 percent of the final judgment. Originally, the Indian Claims Commission of three judges (later changed to five) was to function for ten years; but the commission operated until 1978.

By 1978, the commission had adjudicated 285 of the 850 cases filed and awarded more than $800 million. Awards averaged $3 million, and individuals usually received about $2,000. One of the largest cases involved California Indians who received a combined award of over $29 million plus interest, but when the money was distributed, each person received $668.51 in compensation for millions of acres containing billions of dollars in gold, lumber, water, and choice real estate. As the cases worked their way through the system, some native peoples clamored to be enrolled formally with their tribe, a matter that had meant little to them before they learned of possible claims awards. Of course, the rush to enroll became a hotly debated issue among tribes. Most of the awards were for lands, and tribes received the fair market value of land at the time it was taken from them, minus any funds already offered to the tribes for those lands. When the Confederated Tribes of the

Colville and Yakama nations won a combined award for Palouse Indians who lived on their reservations, they received 50¢ an acre for some of the most productive farm land in all of the United States—worth billions of dollars today. When the Claims Commission made awards, it did so in money, not land or resources, and after the government made an award, a tribe waived its right to sue the government over the claims ever again.

The Indian Claims Commission made awards to tribes, bands, and other native groups. These entities could provide per-capita payments to individuals or disperse the funds in whatever manner they deemed appropriate. Some government officials were eager to conclude this aspect of Indian-white relations, so that the government would no longer have to deal with the issue of native claims. Other politicians believed that the government was giving America back to the Indians and wasting taxpayer dollars. Some Native Americans were anxious to litigate their claims against the United States, because many of their claims were long-standing. The Confederated Salish and Kootenai tribes of the Flathead Reservation of Montana—tribes organized under the Indian Reorganization Act—filed claims against the government for lands ceded under the Flathead Treaty of 1855. They filed another claim (Docket 156) for erroneous boundary surveys, their trust funds, settlement of their reservation by non-Indians, and other losses of land and water. The water issues stemmed from the fact that water was taken from Hell Roaring Creek and used to create electricity for Polson, Montana, and to supply reservation lands, which, in addition, had been stolen for the site of the power plant. Furthermore, the Flathead Irrigation Project of 1908 had taken water from Flathead Lake without just compensation. The confederated tribes won a number of awards, totaling over $22 million, and the tribal council determined the disposition of the funds.

Sometimes the Indian Claims Commission consolidated claims by several tribes into fewer related dockets. This was the case for the Shoshoni-Bannock tribes of the Fort Hall Reservation of Idaho and several other groups of Shoshonis, Bannocks, and some Paiutes. Through Docket 326, all the Shoshoni, Bannock, and Shoshoni-Bannock groups petitioned to recover funds for multiple claims. Some of the many bands that joined in the litigation included the Pohogwe, Cache Valley, Bear Lake, Bannock Creek, Lemhi, Boise, Bruneau, Wind River, Washakie Shoshoni, Western Shoshoni of Nevada, and Gosiute. In addition to filing for lost lands, they petitioned the Indian Claims Commission for mismanagement of funds and loss of grazing, gold, timber, water, and other resources. Litigation took years and was extremely complicated because so many groups had lost land and resources in a large area over more than one hundred years. The Claims Commission made awards for Dockets 326-D, E, F, G, and H for $15,700,000 as well as separate judgments for Docket 326-I of $4,500,000.

*Mary Jim is a Palouse elder who identifies as Naa'hum
(People of the River). Currently living on Yakama
Reservation, Mary shares her tribe's history and has
helped to create an account of the history of the
Palouse people.*

In July 1951, the Nez Perce tribe of Idaho filed three petitions with
the Indian Claims Commission, including Docket 175 for lands taken
without compensation under the Nez Perce Treaty of 1855. At the same
time, the Colville Confederated Tribes of Washington filed Docket 180 for
compensation of the same lands. Nez Perce lived on both reservations,
and both had legitimate claims to the lands lost to non-Indians. On February 27, 1953, the Indian Claims Commission collapsed both claims into
Docket 175 and did not render a decision in the case until 1971, when the
commission awarded $3,550,000, of which the Nez Perce on the Idaho
reservation received over 86 percent of the award. The two groups of Nez
Perce split other awards, including that of 1974 for $725,000 for lands lost

in the Wallowa Valley of Oregon when in 1873 the president had re-scinded his executive order creating a reservation in the valley among Chief Joseph's band. Of this amount, the Nez Perce on the Colville Reservation received $406,542.07.

The Nez Perce filed Docket 175-A for lands taken by the United States through the "Thief Treaty of 1863." Between 1861 and 1863, white miners had invaded the Nez Perce Reservation and mined gold in the Bitterroot Mountains. Miners built towns on the reservation, desecrated Indian burials, and stole horses and cattle while committing general mayhem. When Nez Perce leaders demanded that the government remove miners from their land, commissioners resolved the problem by shrinking the reservation to one-tenth its original size. All Nez Perce leaders refused to sign a new treaty except Lawyer, but the Nez Perce Treaty sailed through the Senate, and President Lincoln signed it into law. The Nez Perce lost thousands of acres of land rich with timber, gold, and other minerals. They also lost access to fishing areas, villages, and sacred sites. The Indian Claims Commission awarded Nez Perce people a paltry $4,650,000 for loss of 6,924,843 acres of land, or $1.49 per acre.

The Indian Claims Commission and U.S. Court of Claims made other awards to Nez Perce people. Like other Native Americans across the United States, tribes sometimes issued per-capita payments and used some funds for economic development, educational programs, housing programs, water-sewer development, and health clinics. The money benefited some tribes in several ways, but to many Indians cash was not land or water. Settlements through the Indian Claims Commission could not return old villages, desecrated grave sites, or plants and animals from their former homelands. When the Claims Commission awarded Taos pueblo $10 million for Blue Lake and surrounding lands, the people refused, explaining that the lake was their church, a sacred place where all life begins and where dead spirits dwell. As Paul Bernal put it, "We cannot sell what is sacred."

When a relative of Mary Jim, a Palouse elder living on the Yakama Reservation, tried to hand her a wrapped stack of greenbacks, she threw it at him, telling him that "money is not my land, not my Snake River." She told her relative that she would not take the money because whites would say she sold her land and river. She vowed never to sell, never to take money for land. Mary Jim proudly says that she is Naa'hum, a person of Snake River, a woman born at Tasawicks who knows that Indian law prohibits her from selling the earth that holds the bones of her mother and father. In her mind, her claim for her land and river will never be settled until the white man returns her home to her. When asked about this incident again in 1981, she did not know what happened to that money, but in her mind, she never accepted it. Mary Jim believes that the government must keep its money and settle with her and her people by returning lands that whites stole from her.

On another occasion Mary Jim walked along an irrigation ditch that runs beside her home on the Yakama Reservation, lamenting the loss of her land. She explained that the ditch was not her Snake River, and she cried when she remembered the sound of the river running past her former home. "My Snake River," she explained, "made music to me, sang to me—so sweet." In an attempt to recover her land along Snake River, which the Corps of Engineers had condemned for a dam site, Senator Henry Jackson of Washington agreed to use his influence to settle Mary Jim's claim. He died shortly after making the commitment, but she still dreams of returning to her home along Snake River. Dakota scholar John Rouillard once commented that the native objection to the Indian Claims Commission was simple. Reflecting Mary Jim's feelings, he said that the Claims Commission settled native claims with money, which is the way of white culture, not traditional native culture. No amount of money could replace land, water, minerals, fish, or other resources because native "law" would not permit a person or group to sell the gifts of the creation. It was simply not the Indian way.

Native American objection to the Indian Claims Commission and awards made by the U.S. Court of Claims was not concerned with the amounts awarded but rather the fact that money was not land or resources. Money could not return sacred places that have more meaning to the people than money. To traditional Nez Perces, the fact that the people received $1.49 an acre for lands stolen in the Thief Treaty of 1863 was not at issue. As Carol Bull, a Nez Perce from Idaho, once explained, the commission could have awarded $1,000 per acre or $1,000,000 per acre. It made little difference. To accept any amount of money would have been wrong. However, this was only one view within native communities. Other Native Americans believed that the awards made by the Indian Claims Commission and Court of Claims were the best that native people could ever expect from the United States, so they accepted them and used the money for the benefit of the tribes. Through it all, Native Americans maintained their attachments to their lands, the waters that flowed through them, and plants and animals sharing the land with them. They have never forgotten their sacred places and the cemeteries that held the remains of their ancestors.

Selected Readings and Bibliography

Major changes in Indian history occurred during the New Deal era, when the government of the United States altered many of its policies toward native peoples. General sources previously cited that offer information on the Indian New Deal include Champagne's *The Native North American Almanac*, Francis's *Native Time*, Gibson's *The American Indian*, Fey and McNickle's *Indians and Other Americans*, Wise's *The Red Man in the New World Drama*, Debo's *And Still the*

Waters Run and *History of the Indians of the United States,* Tyler's *A History of Indian Policy,* Washburn's *Red Man's Land, White Man's Law,* Spicer's *A Short History of the Indians of the United States,* and McNickle's *They Came Here First.* A good deal of the information on reforms pertaining to native education is from Szasz, *Education and the American Indian;* specifics about native law are from Cohen, *Handbook of Federal Indian Laws.* Information regarding Indians of the Northwest is taken from Ruby and Brown's *A Guide to the Indian Tribes of the Pacific Northwest* and Trafzer and Scheuerman's *Renegade Tribe.* Other recommended books on Indians of the twentieth century are Hertzberg, *The Search for an American Indian Identity;* Deloria, *American Indian Policy in the Twentieth Century;* Kelly, *The Navajo Indians and Federal Indian Policy;* Brayer, *Pueblo Land Grants on the Río Abajo;* Collier, *From Every Zenith* and *Indians of the Americas.*

Barsh, Russel L., and James Y. Henderson. *The Road: Tribes and Political Liberty.* Berkeley: University of California Press, 1980.

Biolsi, Thomas. *Organizing the Lakota: The Political Economy of the New Deal on the Pine Ridge and Rosebud Reservations.* Tucson: University of Arizona Press, 1992.

Deloria, Vine Jr., and Clifford Lytle. *American Indians, American Justice.* Austin: University of Texas Press, 1983.

——. *The Nations Within.* New York: Pantheon Books, 1984.

Downes, Randolph. "A Crusade or Indian Reform, 1922–1934." *Mississippi Valley Historical Review* 32 (1945): 331–354.

Hauptman, Laurence M. *The Iroquois and the New Deal.* Syracuse: Syracuse University Press, 1981.

Kelly, Lawrence. *The Assault on Assimilation.* Albuquerque: University of New Mexico Press, 1983.

Kelly, William H. *Indian Affairs and the Indian Reorganization Act: The Twenty Year Record.* Tucson: University of Arizona Press, 1954.

——, ed. "The Indian Reorganization Act: The Dream and the Reality." *Pacific Historical Review* 44 (1975): 291–312.

Koppes, Clayton R. "From New Deal to Termination: Liberalism and Indian Policy, 1933–1953." *Pacific Historical Review* 45 (1977): 543–566.

Lowitt, Richard. *The New Deal and the West.* Bloomington: Indiana University Press, 1984.

Nash, Jay B., ed. *The New Day for the Indians: A Survey of the Working of the Indian Reorganization Act of 1934.* New York: Academy Press, 1938.

Parman, Donald L. "The Indian and the Civilian Conservation Corps." *Pacific Historical Quarterly* 40 (1971): 39–56.

——. *The Navajos and the New Deal.* New Haven: Yale University Press, 1976.

Philip, Kenneth R. *John Collier's Crusade for Indian Reform, 1920–1954.* Tucson: University of Arizona Press, 1977.

Prucha, Francis P., ed. *Documents of United States Indian Policy.* Lincoln: University of Nebraska Press, 1975.

Schrader, Robert F. *The Indian Arts and Crafts Board: An Aspect of New Deal Indian Policy.* Albuquerque: University of New Mexico Press, 1983.

Shipek, Florence Connolly. *Pushed into the Rocks: Southern California Indian Land Tenure, 1769–1986.* Lincoln: University of Nebraska Press, 1987.

Strickland, Rennard. *Fire and the Spirit: Cherokee Law from Clan to Court.* Norman: University of Oklahoma Press, 1975.

Taylor, Graham D. *The New Deal and American Indian Tribalism.* Lincoln: University of Nebraska Press, 1980.

Wilkinson, Charles F. *American Indians, Time and the Law.* New Haven: Yale University Press, 1987.

Wright, Peter M. "John Collier and the Oklahoma Indian Welfare Act of 1936." *Chronicles of Oklahoma* 50 (1972): 347–371.

Zimmerman, William. "The Role of the Bureau of Indian Affairs since 1933." *Annals of the American Academy of Political and Social Science* 102 (1957): 31–40.

——. "Tribal Self-Government and the Indian Reorganization Act of 1934." *Michigan Law Review* 70 (1972): 955–986.

CHAPTER 17

NATIVE AMERICANS AND WORLD WAR II

On December 7, 1941, Japanese fighter planes and bombers struck Pearl Harbor. It was a day that "will live in infamy" for all Americans, including Native Americans. When word reached American Indian communities that the United States had declared war on the Axis Powers, native men turned out in large numbers to "report for duty." Throughout Indian country, Native Americans grabbed their rifles, handguns, and ammunition, while others sharpened hunting and butcher knives, hatchets and axes, sickles and shovels, all in preparation for the Japanese invasion of the mainland. Native Americans considered the Japanese attack on Pearl Harbor an attack on their land, a threat to their country. In spite of years of discrimination and innumerable problems with the U.S. government, native people loved the land and considered the Japanese, Germans, and Italians a threat to their homes, families, tribes, and country.

NATIVE AMERICANS AND EARLY WAR EFFORTS

Native Americans were, and are, patriotic Americans, and many had supported the United States during World War I when approximately ten thousand Indians had served in the armed forces. At that time only half of the native population were considered citizens of the United States, but Congress had granted blanket citizenship in 1924, in part because of the native participation in the war to end all wars. In 1940, when the United States began conscripting men into the armed forces, Native Americans were citizens. At that time, four thousand Indians already were in the various branches of service. By the end of World War II, about twenty-five thousand Native Americans had served in the military. Service in the U.S. Army was not new for Native Americans. Since the American Revolution, Native Americans had served in the army, often as scouts, but in other capacities as well.

Many Native American tribes had warrior traditions that contributed to enlistment and support for World War II. Some of these tribes had fought alongside American troops at various times, whereas others–Lakota, Dakota, Modoc, Comanche, Kiowa–had fought against the United States. In both cases, the tribes had warrior traditions that contributed to an interest in supporting the country during World War II in a military capacity. Wyandot, Delaware, Mohawk, Seneca, Cherokee, Choctaw, and others had fought with the United States against the British. Apache, Pawnee, Crow, Arikara, Cheyenne, Navajo, Nez Perce, Ute, Osage, Shoshoni, Cahuilla, and many other people served as scouts and troops for the army during the nineteenth century. Several others sent men into battle in Belgium and France during the First World War and encouraged their young men to fight for the United States after Pearl Harbor. War was one mechanism through which young men could prove themselves in the twentieth century, as their fathers and grandfathers had before them.

Another factor that contributed to an outpouring of support for the United States during World War II was the school experience of native people. By 1941, many Native American men and women had attended boarding schools and day schools operated by the Bureau of Indian Affairs. They learned about patriotism toward the United States through history lessons, Fourth of July celebrations, speeches, flag days, and other programs. Furthermore, part of the school curriculum centered around military training, particularly physical training. One soldier said, "we had been exposed to it [military life] in some respects during the old boarding school days in the Bureau of Indian Affairs." While he was in boarding school, this person "marched to wherever we went to, school or to classroom or to the dining hall or to churches in formation. We knew how to drill." During the late nineteenth and early twentieth centuries, school officials dressed children in military uniforms and marched them from place to place. Children learned to drill and march with wooden rifles. Over the years, some of these children joined the military, but nearly all students of government schools were influenced by patriotic and military programs. When World War II began, former students supported their country and Indian nation by taking up arms or working in various ways to win the war.

NATIVE AMERICAN SOLDIERS, SAILORS, AND DEFENSE WORKERS

Before Native Americans left their homeland to fight in the war, tribal elders and medicine people prayed over them to keep them safe. Many conducted similar ceremonies to purify the warriors after they returned from the war. Among the Pomo of California, Esie Parish used a ceremony called the Bole Maru to protect Pomo men who had gone off to fight. Pomo-Coast Miwok scholar Greg Sarris has written that the ceremony emerged from a wellspring of traditional medicine that enabled Parish and Pomo women to pray for their boys and enjoin the power to protect them during combat. A Lakota woman cut pieces of her flesh and placed them into a bundle as a sacrifice for her son's safe return, whereas women from other tribes set out feathers and tobacco bundles as prayers for their young men. Many native soldiers received similar blessings from elders who sent their prayers up with the use of smoke from sweetgrass, tobacco, and sage. Smoke bathed the young men, as holy people used eagle feathers to surround their bodies in prayers and blessings. Other tribes used more formal ceremonies to protect their soldiers from physical danger or the ill effects of killing someone and to cope with the ghosts of enemy soldiers. Delawares in Dewey, Oklahoma, held three Round House Rite Ceremonies during the war to protect their soldiers, and Navajos performed Enemy Way ceremonies for three days, moving the site from place to place.

After the war, one Navajo Code Talker explained that during the first night of Enemy Way, the people prepared "for an excursion for a war party, and they formed a drum . . . they take the raw materials and make a drum out of it and then they dance just a little bit." The former marine explained that "they go into simulated battle, like the old days, and they go to the enemy, and the first night there they have a contact with the enemy, and then they get this prayer stick, they take this prayer stick over there—it's more or less like a war club, with feathers and other vegetation that's attached to it." The ceremonial party returned to the place of the first night's activities during the second night. On the last night of Enemy Way, the ceremonial party "come rushing back into camp just like they were coming back from the war party or contact with the enemy, and they shoot off guns and . . . arrows, whatever they may have." During the last night of the ceremony, young, unmarried women dance with partners who have to pay a small fee for the honor.

Over two hundred native women served in the army as WACs and in the Navy as WAVEs, while others served as nurses, clerks, and supply supervisors. Native American women worked for the Red Cross and Women's Voluntary Service, sometimes serving overseas in war zones. Still other Native American women supported the war effort from their reservations by raising victory gardens, tending sheep and cattle, collecting scrap metal and rubber, and launching blood drives, selling war bonds, and caring for elders and children. Native American women wrote letters and sent food to soldiers and sailors. They gave food and drink to soldiers traveling through their reservations on trains bound for action, and they worked at defense plants off the reservations. By 1943, over twelve thousand Native American women were working off the reservations, making guns, munitions, tanks, ships, bombs, airplanes, uniforms, canned foods, and other items necessary for the war effort. Some Native American women were "Rosie the Riveters," working in many jobs for their families, nations, and country.

JAPANESE INTERNMENT ON RESERVATIONS

Some native women worked for the government at prisons maintaining German, Japanese, and Italian prisoners of war. The Bureau of Indian affairs hired native women and men to work on the Colorado River Indian Reservation at Poston, Arizona, and the Gila River Indian Reservation south of Phoenix, Arizona, where the War Relocation Authority removed Japanese-Americans to internment camps. Commissioner of Indian Affairs John Collier fully supported this endeavor because the Bureau of Indian Affairs had a great deal of experience "handling a minority group." He also wanted the Bureau of Indian Affairs to increase its funding and participate in the war effort in a manner that would satisfy congressional members. As usual, the commissioner did not inform Indians living on these two reservations about the removal and relocation of Japanese onto their homelands. Government agents told the tribes about the relocation programs after the decision had been made.

Historian Niki Chang has shown that the Indian office dealt with Japanese-Americans in much the same manner as it had Native Americans. Policies forced on Japanese-Americans mirrored American Indian policies, although the Japanese received better health care and rations. The government isolated the Japanese based on race, passed legislation harmful to the people without their input, and executed removal and relocation at public expense. The government argued that Japanese-Americans, like Native Americans, posed a threat to national security. The government also responded to demands of non-Japanese people interested in having their neighbors removed. In part, non-Japanese people genuinely feared that Japanese-Americans were in league with officials in Japan. Others used removal and relocation to steal productive farms and businesses owned by Japanese-Americans, a justification for "legally" taking Japanese-American land, resources, and property. As with Native Americans, the government forced Japanese-Americans to develop raw land that had never been farmed. Government agents also forced Japanese-Americans to attend schools to learn about white culture and civilization. As with native people, the government isolated and confined them to reservations where white agents controlled them.

NATIVE WAR EFFORTS

While the government removed Japanese-Americans and confined them to internment camps, Native Americans enlisted in all branches of the service. Most native people served in the army. Of the twenty-five thousand Native Americans who served in the armed forces, 21,767 served in the army, 1,910 served in the navy, 874 in the Marine Corps, and 121 in the Coast Guard. Native American soldiers and sailors served in all theaters of war. They fought from island to island in the Pacific, and they participated in the invasion and conquest of North Africa, Sicily, Italy, France, and Germany. Native American sailors sailed on warships, cargo ships, and cutters in oceans around the world. Unlike African-American and Japanese-American soldiers who served in segregated units, Native Americans served in integrated units with non-Indians. The War Department integrated Native American soldiers, perhaps in an effort to assimilate them into the dominant society.

Many Indians gave their lives, limbs, and minds to protect the United States during the war, whereas others came through the war unscathed. Leaford Bearskin, chief of the Wyandotte tribe of Oklahoma, was decorated many times for his service and bravery. Like Bearskin, each Native American survivor of the war has his or her own history to share, but Alison R. Bernstein has chronicled the contributions of some of these people in *American Indians and World War II*. Robert LaFollette Bennett, an Oneida born near Green Bay, Wisconsin, served in the Marine Corps from 1943 to 1945. Like many veterans, after the war he took advantage of the G.I. Bill and earned his degree. After the war, Bennett worked as area director of the Bureau of Indian Affairs in Juneau, Alaska, where he protected native rights and claims. As a result, in 1962, Bennett received the Indian Achievement Award, and in 1966, he received the Outstanding American Indian Citizen Award. That same year, President Lyndon Johnson appointed Bennett as Native American commissioner of Indian affairs.

Edward P. Dozier was born at Santa Clara pueblo, New Mexico, in 1916, and served with distinction in the U.S. Army Air Corps during the war. He fought in the Pacific campaigns before returning home to continue his education at the University of New Mexico. He completed his Ph.D. at the University of California, Berkeley, in 1952, and published his first of five books, *The Hopi-Tewa of Arizona*, with the University of California Press. Dozier became an eminent professor of anthropology at the University of Arizona, where he offered outstanding undergraduate education and trained numerous graduate students. Another Native American who distinguished himself during World War II was Raymond Nakai, a Navajo who became tribal chair. Born at Lukachukai, Arizona, under the towering red bluffs of the Chuska Mountains, Nakai attended schools at Fort Wingate and Shiprock, New Mexico. In 1941, Nakai joined the navy and served in the South Pacific during most of the war. When he returned home, he worked successfully to benefit his people through agriculture, business, and tourism.

Barney Old Coyote was born in 1923 on the Crow Reservation of Montana. A leader of the Crow Nation, he also served in the war. It was natural for Old Coyote to join the armed forces when the war began, because he was the descendant of several generations of Crow warriors, including Mountain Sheep and Big Forehead. After Pearl Harbor, Old Coyote "joined the Army Air Corps to get back at the Japs." During his five years in the Army Air Corps, he flew over fifty missions and once crash landed in Puerto Rico. He was lucky to escape with his life. As it did so many other Native American soldiers, the army decorated Old Coyote for his service. He received the Air Medal and fourteen oak clusters, but even more important, members of the Crow Nation honored him through their war ceremonies. The elders drew him into a new circle of responsibility by giving Old Coyote a sacred pipe that was traditionally bestowed on Crow warriors. Certainly Old Coyote had measured up to the status of war leader, and he has carried the banner well for years. At the end of the war, Old Coyote worked for the Bureau of Indian Affairs, served as the first president of the American Indian National Bank, and became professor and director of Native American studies at Montana State University.

David Risling was another university professor who served with distinction during World War II. Born on April 10, 1921, in Weitchpec, California, Risling grew up on the Hoopa Reservation in northern California. He started college but quit when the war began. Between 1943 and 1946, Risling served in the Naval Reserves as a lieutenant commander. When the war ended, he became the first Native American from California ever to receive a bachelor's degree. In 1970, he became the first director of Native American studies at the University of California, Davis, and helped found D-Q University, a community college focused on Native American and Chicano studies.

Like Risling and Old Coyote, Joe Sando of Jemez pueblo is an internationally recognized scholar of Native American history and a veteran of World War II. In 1943, Sando began his freshman year of college but dropped out to join the navy. He saw action during the invasion of the Gilbert and Marianas islands in the Pacific and was promoted to petty officer second class. The navy awarded Sando the Pacific Campaign Ribbon with four stars. In his book, *Nee Hemish: The History of the Jemez Pueblo*, Sando writes that he was "fortunate that I survived World War II to take advantage of the G.I. Bill, which opened up a new world for me."

Ben Reifel was born on the Rosebud Reservation in South Dakota in September 1906. He attended South Dakota State University, majoring in chemistry and dairy science. When World War II began, Reifel was working as an organizational field agent in five states on the Great Plains. He quit his job to join the army and was commissioned a second lieutenant. During most of the war, he remained in the states, serving with the military police. But after the Allies won their victory in Europe, the army transferred him to Europe to retrain selected soldiers as military policemen who maintained order during the chaotic months after the war. The army recognized Reifel's work by promoting him to major, but in 1946, he resigned his commission and returned to the United States to work for the Bureau of Indian Affairs. Between 1961 and 1971, Reifel served four terms in Congress, as its first member from the Sioux Nation.

One of the most famous heroes of World War II was Ira Hamilton Hayes. Born on January 12, 1923, in Sacaton, Arizona, Hayes grew up on the Pima Reservation in the southern part of the state. When the war began, Hayes joined the marines and served quietly but efficiently until February 23, 1945, when he participated in the invasion of Iwo Jima. During the fighting, the marines fought a bloody campaign to form a beachhead and gain the highest ground on the island at Mount Suribachi. During the heat of battle, six marines planted an American flag in the rocky terrain, with the wind blowing violently and the sound of intense gunfire ringing out all around. Ira Hayes helped plant the Stars and Stripes while photographer Joe Rosenthal captured the event on film. Hayes lived through the moment, whereas Japanese soldiers killed three of the six marines who raised the flag.

The marines recalled the three surviving members of the group that had raised the flag and sent them to the United States to meet President Roosevelt. Because of their national fame, the marines sold war bonds and made public appearances. Hayes was embarrassed about his notoriety, feeling that he had done nothing more than any other marine would have done. The thought of his comrades slain during combat and the flag raising troubled Hayes the rest of his life, and he hated attending parades, dinners, speeches, and parties commemorating the event. The flag raising had become a national symbol, memorialized on a postage stamp and a magnificent bronze statue in Washington, D.C. While Hayes sold war bonds, everyone wanted to buy him drinks, and soon he drank to excess. Hayes asked the marines to reassign him to combat, but with the war winding down, he remained in the States and, at war's end, returned to the Pima Reservation. He traveled around the country from job to job, became alcoholic, and was arrested many times. He lived a lonely, depressed life, never readjusting to a civilian life. On January 24, 1955, Hayes died of exposure in his homeland and was buried with full honors in Arlington National Cemetery. He was thirty-two years of age.

Carl Nelson Gorman was one of 375 to 420 Navajos who served as Code Talkers during World War II. He joined the marines in 1942 and fought in many campaigns in the Pacific, including Guadalcanal,

Tarawa, Saipan, and Tinian. Gorman returned to the Navajo Nation after the war and used the G.I. Bill to attend the Otis Art Institute in Los Angeles, where he graduated in 1951. He became well known for his art while he worked for the tribe as head of the Navajo Arts and Crafts Guild, Navajo Culture Center, and Navajo Health Authority. He became a professor of Native American art at the University of California, Davis, and professor of Navajo and Native American history and culture at Diné College (Navajo Community College) and the University of New Mexico, Gallup. In 1990, the University of New Mexico awarded him a doctorate for his achievements. Gorman was known internationally as an artist and lecturer, and he often spoke about the Navajo Code Talkers. He was a leader of surviving Code Talkers and was a "Living Treasure" of Arizona.

NAVAJO CODE TALKERS AND NATIVE WARRIORS

When World War II began, many Navajos and people associated with Diné people eagerly joined the war effort. One such person was Philip Johnston, an engineer working in Los Angeles, who had grown up on the Navajo Reservation and spoke Navajo. His father had been a missionary, and young Philip had learned Diné Bizzad as a child. Early in 1942, the U.S. military experienced grave problems as a result of Japanese cryptographers who decoded secret messages. When Johnston learned of this, he conceived of using the Navajo language as a code for use by the military. He drove to Camp Elliot, a marine base situated near the present-day naval air station at Miramar in San Diego. Johnston convinced a reluctant Major General Clayton B. Vogel to allow him to bring some Navajos to the base and demonstrate the transmission of military messages in a Navajo code.

"With the cooperation of four Navajos residing in the Los Angeles area," wrote Benis M. Frank of the History and Museums Division of the U.S. Marine Corps, "the experiment worked so well that Vogel ordered the beginning of a program to train Navajo Code Talkers." In April 1942, the marines selected thirty young men to initiate the program, although one of them could not join his cohorts because of a sports injury. Frank interviewed several Navajo Code Talkers at their reunion in Window Rock on July 9–10, 1971, offering one of the finest documents ever to address the action, destruction, contribution, and significance of the now-famous Navajo Code Talkers.

Philip Johnston and twenty-nine Navajos devised the first Navajo code, which was never broken by the Japanese during World War II. Code Talkers Carl Gorman and Teddy Draper Sr. have pointed out that Navajo marines changed the code in the field of battle from time to time, so that words used to describe dive bombers, fighter planes, battleships, or submarines would not be overused and decoded by the Japanese. They also devised an alphabet to spell out difficult words not commonly

Navajo Code Talkers served in World War II throughout the Pacific theater. The Japanese never broke the Navajo code, and these Navajos saved thousands of American lives.

used, for example *Mount Suribachi*. Although Navajo Code Talkers changed the alphabet designations from time to time, a general working alphabet emerged:

A	Wollachee	Ant
B	Shush	Bear
C	Mósi	Cat
D	Be	Deer
E	Dzeh	Elk
F	Ma-e	Fox
G	Klizzie	Goat
H	Kléé	Horse
I	Tin	Ice
J	Tkelechogi	Jackass
K	Klizzie-Yazzie	Kid

L	Debe-Yazzie	Lamb
M	Naastsosi	Mouse
N	Neshchee	Nut
O	Neahshah	Owl
P	Bisodih	Pig
Q	Cayeilth	Quiver
R	Gah	Rabbit
S	Dibeh	Sheep
T	Thanzie	Turkey
U	Nodaih	Ute
V	Akehdiglini	Victor
W	Gloeih	Weasel
X	Alanasdzoh	Cross
Y	Tashaszih	Yucca
Z	Beshdogliz	Zinc

In addition to the alphabet, Code Talkers created hundreds of words to be used to designate military intelligence. The Navajo word for *hawk* might indicate a fighter plane for a period of time before the Code Talkers changed the word for *fighter plane* to be the Navajo word for *eagle*. At times, Navajo Code Talkers used their word, *besh-lo* (iron fish), to designate a submarine, *tsidi-ney-ye-hi* (bird carrier) to describe an aircraft carrier, and *neasjah* (owls) to report observation planes. Although the words sometimes changed, Code Talkers used their Navajo words for *turtle* to describe tanks, *potatoes* for hand grenades, *buzzards* for bombers, and *whales* for battleships. According to Jimmy King Sr., "Staff Sergeant Johnston's role, as we understood it, he was a bridge between the Navajo and the Marine Corps." King also asserted that "Johnston played a very important role in establishing this secret communication" and that the Code Talkers had thanked Mr. Johnston very much.

Other Code Talkers have argued that although Johnston got the system under way, Navajo marines devised, developed, refined, and executed the code on the mainland and overseas. As John Benally pointed out in July 1971 in an interview with Benis M. Frank, "the original outset of the code was done by the 29 men independently from Mr. Johnston. He may have . . . initiated the program to the Marine Corps and got it accepted, but the actual code in itself was developed by these boys, the original 29 men." Navajo Code Talkers created and enriched the code with their own innovations, working as a team to ensure precision performance of the code each time they used it. As a result, they saved thousands of American lives.

One mistake in transmitting or receiving the code could cost soldiers and sailors their lives, but Navajo Code Talkers excelled at their work. During the Battle of Iwo Jima, Navajo Code Talkers fought alongside the other marines but also operated six radios for two days straight. "During the first forty-eight hours," Major Howard M. Conner of the Fifth Marine Division remembered, "while we were landing and consolidating our shore positions," Code Talkers sent and received "over eight hundred messages without an error." According to Teddy Draper Sr., a Navajo from Canyon del Muerto, Arizona, as soon as the flag went up on Mount Suribachi, Navajo Code Talkers sent word of the event to the ships at sea and on to San Francisco, where another Navajo interpreted it. The Code Talkers translated the following words from the Navajo code to English to communicate the fact that marines had taken Suribachi: *sheep, uncle, ram, ice, bear, ant, cat, horse, itch.*

In 1976, Dillon Story, a non-Indian marine who had fought at Iwo Jima, remembered that Code Talkers "were 100 percent effective, 100 percent. Without them a lot more boys would have died taking those islands." While he related his account, Story's eyes welled up with tears, remembering the men shot and wounded on the shores of many islands. He recalled that Navajo Code Talkers fought beside him as friends and comrades. In boot camp he had met John Benally, reporting that this young Navajo man was one of the best athletes that Story had ever met and that the two young men had become friends. "We were in the war together, in the same unit, fighting in the same battles and we both lived through it," Story said. "If you ever see Benally or his family," Story told the author, "tell him I haven't forgotten him and never will." Some time later the author met Benally and communicated the message from his old friend. "They were great fighters," Story concluded, "everyone of them, and they saved our lives through their code which they could send within seconds bringing us support and supplies, ordering men, artillery bombardments, and aerial strikes." Story confirmed that the Japanese never broke the Navajo Code, which saved his life many times. This sentiment is shared by several surviving soldiers who fought during the Pacific campaigns.

Story's old friend Benally maintained that "the Navajo code, the Navajo language itself was indecipherable, and the code therefore, the code within a code, within the language, would have been totally indecipherable."

Judge W. Dean Wilson remembered that "in between the actual combat operations, we did a lot of message sending" so that the Code Talkers would "be up to snuff" when they reentered "the real operation." Jimmy King asserted that the Navajo code was flexible so that "We could change it. We could keep it as long as we wanted. But you had to live with it from day to day, week to week, month to month, in order to make it as effective and as speedy and as secure as it was." After the Battle of Peleliu, the Marine Corps sent the Code Talkers back to Guadalcanal, where the high command sent them into the Coconut Grove, where King was ordered to "reschool them." King was a leader among the Code Talkers, a man of mixed Navajo and Kiowa blood who guided the men through many campaigns.

When he got the Code Talkers together at Guadalcanal, he asked them to discuss "what problems they had run across, and from your standpoint, how the new improvements, how you should do it at the next operations—speedier, more effectively and efficiently." As a result, the Code Talkers altered parts of the code and added words. King contacted Johnston, back in the States, to let him know "what was happening at the forward echelon, so that they could keep abreast with what was happening out there." Navajo Code Talkers also changed the code "under actual battle conditions, actually under fire." They revised the code because they "learnt things under fire, under battle, actual battle conditions, and we employed those new ways of sending, quicker and faster, and we had to adopt new names, place names, because of changes of geographical locations, different islands, and the Navy devised different ships, different ways, had different weapons and how to use these."

Navajos and other Native Americans who fought in the Pacific theater had to be careful not to be mistaken for Japanese soldiers or infiltrators. From time to time, soldiers from the army and marine units unfamiliar with Native Americans mistook the men for Japanese soldiers. During intense fighting, soldiers on both sides shot prisoners and infiltrators, so Navajos and other native soldiers had to talk their way out of such situations. When they were threatened by other Americans, they demanded that someone contact headquarters to verify their status as soldiers fighting for, not against, the United States. Sometimes American soldiers fired on a group of native soldiers, not realizing that they were Americans. At other times, war dogs confused Japanese soldiers with American Indian soldiers. All combat personnel were subject to the violence around them, but Native American soldiers had an added danger because some looked similar to Japanese soldiers, particularly in the heat of battle.

One dark, rainy night on Cape Gloucester, white marines captured Jimmy King and nearly shot him because they thought he was a Japanese soldier dressed in a marine's uniform. "It was raining," King recalled, "Monsoon, you know, strikes there, and rains all through the night." During the "black, dark, feeling your way around," King "ran into one fellow, and he asked me for the password." King knew that the password was "Lame Duck," but his pronunciation of *lame* was not exactly correct because of the nature of the Navajo language, King's first language. So the soldier exclaimed, "You son of a bitch," before sticking "a bayonet right in my back, ready to kill me." As King walked forward with the bayonet in his back, he fell into a foxhole, "and in this foxhole there happened to be a man that I knew whose name was Sergeant Curtis. He was from Kalamazoo." Curtis asked what was going on, and King replied, "They think I'm a Jap. They want to kill me." Because of Curtis, King survived. To protect them, the Marine Corps tried to send white marines with the Code Talkers whenever they moved about among soldiers unfamiliar with the native radio men. However, sometimes the worst occurred to Navajo marines.

On the island of Peleliu, Japanese soldiers captured Tom Singer, who was from Teec Nos Pos. The Code Talker refused to divulge anything about the code to his captors. When King and others found Singer, his "throat had been cut right from under the ear almost to the other end of his neck here, only that white cord [spinal cord]" could be seen. King reported that Singer's "head was back, just bleeding to death, as if he had lassoed a wild horse and you pulled on the rope until it was so tight he would suffocate." King lamented that he couldn't reach him but believed that Singer "had given the supreme" sacrifice. All the Navajo Code Talkers saw a good deal of action as "riflemen, machine gunners, everything–wherever we were needed," and as a result, they saw a great many men die. During the landings, they watched the dead "slowly . . . washed ashore." They lived in harm's way all the time, sometimes volunteering for dangerous assignments. At Iwo Jima, Paul Blatchford led his platoon through a mine field and told a nineteen-year-old boy from Ohio and all his men to follow him into battle. Blatchford followed the armored vehicles and warned the young man not to take "souvenirs," but the eager Buckeye "got off my trail and picked up something, I guess it was that booby trap, and when I saw him he was going 50 feet up in the air, and when he came down he was just nothing but hamburger."

Marine commanders did not spare Navajo Code Talkers from deadly fire. Navajo marines landed and fought beside other Leathernecks in many campaigns, making the landings sometimes in the first waves. All the Code Talkers who lived through the war realized their contribution to the war effort. John Benally reported in 1971 that they appreciated "the opportunity we had to serve our country, and there's no doubt that we helped the Marine Corps and the United States for that matter." He acknowledged that Navajo marines also appreciated "the opportunity we had to serve in this capacity, as our own basic language that we used [sic], we were very happy that we could serve in some respect." In November 1946, Philip Johnston wrote Representative Norris Poulson complaining about policies of the government that were detrimental to native people. Johnston noted that during the war, Navajo Code Talkers had provided "a service that materially shortened our war against Japan, saved thousands of American lives, and billions of American dollars." He reminded his representative that "Many of those Navajo Marines made the supreme sacrifice on the battlefield to uphold the principles of international morality and impartial justice."

When Navajo Code Talkers returned home from the war, the government prohibited them from talking about their code. Information about the code remained classified until 1969, when the Fourth Marine Division met in Chicago to discuss the code and honor some Code Talkers, and Philip Johnston, with bronze medallions. As a result of this gathering, Navajo Code Talkers formed their own association with headquarters in Gallup, New Mexico.

When the war ended, Teddy Draper Sr. remained in the marines and worked in Japan. He learned the Japanese language and became friends with several former Japanese soldiers against whom he had fought. All the Japanese told him how frightened they had become whenever they heard the Navajo code on the radio. They never knew exactly what was being communicated, but they knew that it was something detrimental to the Japanese cause. German and Japanese soldiers told Native American soldiers that they were particularly fearful of Native American soldiers because of their famous fighting abilities.

NATIVE AMERICAN CONTRIBUTIONS AND CHANGES

Navajo Code Talkers were not the only Native Americans to be decorated during and after the war. Native Americans won two Congressional Medals of Honor, the nation's highest military award for bravery. They won fifty-one Silver Stars and forty-seven Bronze Stars. Many Native Americans served as pilots, navigators, and gunners in the Army Air Corps, the precursor of the air force, and these men won seventy-one Air Medals. Native Americans lost at least 550 dead and about 700 wounded in a war that forever changed world history. Through all the misery and fighting, Native Americans and nonnative Americans developed a greater respect for each other, in spite of the fact that nonnative personnel often referred to their Indian comrades as "chief" and teased them about drumming, war dances, and rain dances.

Contemporary native writers have explored the significance of World War II in the lives of Native Americans. Most noteworthy is Laguna writer Leslie Marmon Silko, whose acclaimed novel, *Ceremony*, focuses on Tayo, a Laguna man who returns from fighting in World War II much troubled by his experiences. The protagonist has a difficult time returning home to family and friends, and the book follows his journey back into life at Laguna pueblo. He reenters his native world by undergoing a ceremony that makes him "whole" and prepares him to face the horrors of his past experiences overseas and the challenges of life on the reservation. The war affected native men and women in diverse ways and continues to influence the lives of Native Americans today.

Most important, American Indian men and women who left reservations and tribal lands for the war entered a far broader world. Native

American factory workers and residents of reservations had purchased $12,600,000 in war bonds and contributed to the war effort every day by saving gasoline, growing food, and recycling tin cans, scrap metal, and paper. Combat soldiers put their lives on the line for the United States, and they had no inclination to return to the status quo where government bureaucrats ruled native people without permitting them much voice in their own affairs.

Former soldiers and defense workers demanded a voice on their own reservations, and the franchise that local and state governments had long denied them. New Mexico and Arizona continued to deny Native Americans the right to vote, so native people sued the states while urging Congress to investigate this form of discrimination. In 1948, courts in both states ruled that laws denying native people the franchise were unconstitutional. In like fashion, federal laws prohibited the sale of alcohol to Indians and severely restricted them from buying firearms. In 1953, Congress enacted legislation permitting native people to purchase liquor and firearms on and off reservations. Although Native Americans asserted their self-determination after the war and attempted to acculturate and participate more in the nonnative world, they also became more conscious of preserving that which was truly native to this land. This duality of cultural purposes is best illustrated by historian Gerald Nash, who has pointed out that the war strengthened "acculturation of some Indians," while "it also had the effect of strengthening various aspects of Indian traditionalism."

Some Native Americans returned home determined to continue their education or find employment near their homes. Others moved to urban areas to find jobs and raise their families where they believed their children would have advantages over those of reservation children. One Navajo Code Talker moved to Riverside, California, where he and his Navajo wife raised their family. One of their children excelled in school, earned a master's degree from Harvard, and was awarded a Ph.D. from Claremont Graduate School. However, in spite of these advantages, the children of this Navajo Code Talker cannot speak Diné Bizzad and have been criticized by other Navajos for not knowing more about native culture. Still, this became a trend after World War II. In 1941, twenty-four thousand Native Americans lived in urban areas, but by 1950, fifty-six thousand lived in urban areas, creating a major transition for native people that continues to influence them to the present.

When Native Americans returned home after the war, they found themselves and their people changed, just as American society in general was changed. Because of the unique relationship of native people to the federal government, American Indians watched

At the conclusion of World War II, Native American men and women returned to their reservations with a renewed appreciation for their culture. Famed Hopi artist Paul Coochyamptewa preserves the ancient tradition of Kachina carving.

with interest as politicians in Washington shaped new policies that affected every native person. Because Indian soldiers, sailors, and factory workers had melded so well with other Americans, some politicians determined to end the legal relationship of the United States with native peoples. Besides, many politicians had had enough of Roosevelt, Collier, and Democrats. Some determined to save tax dollars and end the Indian New Deal. The political pendulum was swinging back toward the right, and some white politicians emphasized acculturation and assimilation. This was an old path taken many times in the past–and a destructive path for Native Americans.

Selected Readings and Bibliography

The participation of Native Americans in World War II and the effects of the war on Native American history are facts that are generally unknown to the average U.S. citizen. The war was a watershed for native people who fought for the United States or who worked to win the war in defense plants, civic organizations, and government jobs. An outstanding overview of native people and the war is in the first chapter of Rawls's *Chief Red Fox Is Dead.* Other general works dealing with the war are Champagne's *Native North American Almanac* and Spicer's *A Short History of the Indians of the United States.*

Adair, John. "The Navajo and Pueblo Veteran." *The American Indian* 4 (1947): 5–11.

Adair, John, and Evon Vogt. "The Returning Navajo and Zuni Veteran." *American Anthropologist* 46 (1947): 10–39.

——. "Navajo and Zuni Veterans." *American Anthropologist* 51 (1949): 547–568.

Bernstein, Alison R. *American Indians and World War II.* Norman: University of Oklahoma Press, 1991.

Bushnell, John. "From American Indian to Indian American." *American Anthropologist* 70 (1968): 1106–1116.

Champagne, Duane. *Native America: Portrait of the Peoples.* Detroit: Visible Ink, 1994.

Chang, Niki. "The Normal Fabric of American Life: The Internment of Japanese Americans on the Colorado River Indian Reservation." Unpublished manuscript. Author's office, University of California, Riverside, History Department.

Collier, John. "The Indian in a Wartime Nation." *The Annals of the American Academy* 223 (1942): 31–34.

Cropp, Richard. "A History of the 147th Field Artillery Regiment." *South Dakota History Collections* 30 (1980): 506–508.

Davis, Mary, ed. *Native America in the Twentieth Century.* New York: Garland Publishing, 1994.

Dozier, Edward. *The Hopi-Tewa of Arizona.* Berkeley: University of California Press, 1954.

Fixico, Donald L. *Termination and Relocation.* Albuquerque: University of New Mexico Press, 1986.

Frank, Benis M. *Marine Corps Navajo Code Talkers.* Washington, D.C.: History and Museums Division, U.S. Marine Corps, 1976.

Hauptman, Laurence M. *The Iroquois Struggle for Survival: World War II to Red Power.* Syracuse: Syracuse University Press, 1986.

Holm, Tom. "Fighting a White Man's War: The Extent and Legacy of American Indian Participation in World War II." *Journal of Ethnic Studies* 9 (1981): 69–81.

Ickes, Harold. "Indians Have a Name for Hitler." *Colliers* (1944): 41–45.

Indians in War, 1945. Chicago: Department of the Interior, Bureau of Indian Affairs, 1945.

Iverson, Peter. *"We Are Still Here": American Indians in the Twentieth Century.* Wheeling, Ill.: Harlan Davidson, 1998.

——, ed. *The Plains Indians of the Twentieth Century.* Norman: University of Oklahoma Press, 1985.

Johnson, Broderick H., ed. *Navajos and World War II*. Tsaile, Ariz.: Navajo Community College Press, 1977.

Malinowski, Sharon, and George H. J. Abrams, eds. *Notable Native Americans*. New York: Gale Researchers, 1995.

McCoy, Ron. "Navajo Code Talkers of World War II." *American West* 18 (1981): 67–73.

Murray, Paul T. "Virginia Indians in the World War II Draft." *The Virginia Magazine of History and Biography* 95 (1987): 215–231.

Nash, Gerald D. *The American West Transformed: The Impact of the Second World War*. Bloomington: Indiana University Press, 1988.

Paul, Doris A. *The Navajo Code Talkers*. Bryn Mawr, Penn.: Dorrance, 1973.

——. *They Spoke Navajo*. Philadelphia: Dorrance, 1974.

Sando, Joe. *Nee Hemish: The History of the Jemez Pueblo*. Albuquerque: University of New Mexico Press, 1982.

Silko, Leslie Marmon. *Ceremony*. New York: Viking Press, 1977.

They Talked Navajo: The United States Marine Corps Navajo Code Talkers in World War II. Window Rock, Ariz.: Navajo Tribal Museum, 1977.

Trafzer, Clifford E. Interview with Dillon Story. May 1976. Yuma, Ariz.

——. Interview with John Benally. July 1976. Tsaile, Ariz.

Washburn, Wilcomb, ed. *History of Indian-White Relations, Handbook of North American Indians*. 4 volumes. Washington, D.C.: Smithsonian Institution Press, 1988.

CHAPTER 18

TERMINATION AND SELF-DETERMINATION

World War II transformed all Americans, and the United States emerged from the war a superpower. The world would never be the same, as colonialism began to break down and people in Africa, Southeast Asia, the Philippines, the United States, and elsewhere asserted self-determination. Postwar powers divided Germany, eastern Europe, and Korea into spheres of influence. The Soviet Union dominated one sphere, whereas the United States and its allies dominated the other. In 1954, France lost its colony in Vietnam, and soon after politicians divided the nation until the Vietnamese could hold free elections. World War II was also a watershed in Native American history, in part because native people entered a new era with a great deal of practical experience gained through the New Deal and war. In the wake of World War II emerged a Cold War, waged on many fronts in many new ways. It was a period of American history that significantly affected Native Americans, just as it did all Americans. Politicians built a postwar economy on an arms race with the Soviet Union, offering jobs for former native soldiers in Chicago, Los Angeles, Seattle, and other large cities. Politicians also began a witch hunt for communists, pointing their fingers at anyone who did not fit their definition of American.

NATIVE AMERICANS IN POSTWAR AMERICA

The postwar era brought new directions to American Indian policies, based on the genuine interests of some people to end segregation of Native Americans and allow them into mainstream America. Some politicians believed that because American Indians had fought gallantly and effectively beside other Americans during the war, they should share equally in the benefits of citizenship. It seemed to some whites that Native Americans had nearly assimilated during the war, fighting with troops overseas or working domestically in defense plants. Because Native Americans had adapted so well, some whites argued that they should be drawn fully into the economic, social, and cultural fabric of the United States. In this way, Native Americans could enjoy full civil rights granted under the Constitution and Bill of Rights. Some whites wanted to end the rural ghettos dotting the American West, the reservations that bred disease, poverty, death, and despair. Some well-meaning whites wanted to free Native Americans from reservation bonds, whereas others had different agendas.

Several politicians were angry at John Collier for his policies that encouraged Indians to return to the days of "savagery" and "heathenism." During the 1930s and 1940s, conservatives branded Collier a communist and his policies communistic. Collier had favored communal ownership of the land by tribes rather than individual ownership, and some whites labeled such a policy downright un-American. Besides, bankers and other business interests wanted to open Indian lands to exploitation once again and remove Collier's barriers to gaining access to native lands and resources. Business interests argued that Collier's protection of Indian lands through communal ownership was communistic and dangerous to national security. And this view of the Indian New Deal fit well into Senator Joseph McCarthy's campaign to root out and destroy communists in government.

Conservative members of Congress sought to reverse Collier's New Deal reforms even before he resigned office, and they desired to redefine Indian policy to terminate federal relations with some tribes. Such a change reflected the national mood of intolerance toward cultural diversity and the desire to trim the federal bureaucracy created by the Roosevelt administration. Conservative congressmen vowed to reduce federal spending by withdrawing services to Native Americans. Some congressmen determined that it was in the best interest of Native Americans to phase out their tribal governments along with any trust responsibilities of the federal government. In this way, Congress would lift its protection of native lands and invite business to develop Indian resources. Congressmen maintained that Indians would assimilate faster if they owned their lands outright and were allowed to sell them to anyone. In this way, states could tax Indian lands so that Native Americans might help pay for public services.

TERMINATION

Noted historian Donald L. Fixico of Creek, Seminole, Shawnee, Sac, and Fox ancestry has asserted in his pathbreaking book, *Termination and Relocation: Federal Indian Policy, 1945-1960,* that termination was an intentional policy designed by politicians to withdraw federal services specified in treaties, laws, and agreements. He maintains that the attempt to "desegregate Indian communities and to integrate Indians into the rest of society" was also intended as "the ultimate destruction of tribal cultures and native life-styles." Collier's successors, William Brophy and John Nichols, were not equal to the task of fending off assaults by conservative congressmen, and Dillon S. Myer, chosen by President Harry S Truman to head the Bureau of Indian Affairs in 1950, favored termination. Myer had been director of the War Relocation Authority, which had forcibly removed Japanese-Americans from their homes onto internment camps. Myer managed the rural relocation of thousands of people. Throughout the war, Myer believed that Japanese-Americans and others should be assimilated into the dominant society and thereby reduce racial conflicts.

When Myer became commissioner, he believed that Native Americans should be assimilated rapidly into the broader American society, and to this end, he launched a major counterrevolution against Collier's policies. Myer believed that Native American cultures were oxymorons, because he argued that native people had no "legitimate cultures." He felt that the government had no business encouraging native languages, arts, literatures, and governments. He ordered his employees to end cultural preservation programs and emphasis on "cultural pluralism." Myer had no interest in diversity or tolerance. He deemphasized day schools near reservations and enlarged boarding schools, ordering teachers and administrators to assimilate native students. When Dwight D. Eisenhower won the presidency in 1952, Myer realized he would have no place in the new administration. Therefore, he volunteered his services and helped Glenn Emmons, the new commissioner of Indian affairs, compose a document to Congress endorsing termination.

By the time Emmons assumed the post of commissioner of Indian affairs in 1953, the Indian office had already advocated termination as the "new" national Indian policy. Neither Myer nor Emmons considered it appropriate to seek Native American advice in formulating the new policy, and white administrators initiated the policy very rapidly before native people could respond to the new threat. Emmons was a former banker from New Mexico, a state with a large Native American population and business interests eager to reopen reservation lands to exploitation. Emmons and Senator Arthur V. Watkins of Utah, chair of the Senate Committee on Indian Affairs, championed termination as a way of abolishing the tax-exempt status of tribes. Conservative Republicans chaired Committees on Indian Affairs in both houses, and they shepherded the "valuable and salutary Congressional measure" of termination through Congress so that by August 1, 1953, Congress unanimously passed House Concurrent Resolution 108.

The resolution stated that Congress wanted Indians to be "subject to the same laws and entitled to the same privileges and responsibilities" as other Americans. It abolished the status of native peoples as "wards" and listed tribes in California, New York, Wisconsin, Oregon, Montana, Kansas, Nebraska, Florida, and Texas that were prepared to have federal services ended. Flatheads, Klamaths, Potawatomis, Menominees, and California Indians headed the list. Although House Concurrent Resolution 108 was not law, it guided congressional Indian policy and that of the Bureau of Indian Affairs. It had the full support of Emmons and the Bureau of Indian Affairs and signaled the beginning of an official congressional termination policy. Two weeks later, both houses of Congress passed Public Law 280 (PL 280), and the president signed it into law, noting that Congress had not included a provision asking for native consent in the law. The law placed Indian lands in Minnesota, Wisconsin, California, Nebraska, and Oregon under the criminal and civil jurisdiction of the states. It also invited other states to assume jurisdiction over their Indian lands.

Public Law 280 smacked of the discriminatory laws passed by Mississippi, Georgia, and Alabama against Native Americans in the 1820s and 1830s. It also mirrored the series of laws passed by California in the 1850s to legalize state control of native lands and people. Historically, politicians had acted on American Indian policies without consulting native peoples, and PL 280 perpetuated this process while ignoring Collier's more recent policy of consulting tribes. To their credit, congressmen knew that most Indians would oppose termination after they understood the implications, so the congressmen chose not to consult them about the matter. In 1954, the Indian Affairs Committees of the House and Senate met to craft legislation that they submitted almost simultaneously and moved through both houses rapidly, effectively terminating federal relations with particular tribes. The legislation also ended tribal governments and constitutions, forcing Indian people to be subjects of states and counties because they had lost their trust relationships with the federal government.

Through termination, the United States ended services to some Native Americans and could legally ignore treaties and agreements that the government had made with the tribes. In this way, the United States got out of the "Indian business" and ordered states and counties to deal directly with tribes and individual Indians. Tribes could either sell lands and resources held in common and offer their former tribal members a per-capita payment, or they could transfer title to common lands to a trustee. Individual Native Americans who owned property were given title to their lands so they could sell them, just as they did during the allotment period in the days before the Indian Reorganization Act. Most Native Americans learned of termination after 1954, and they were greatly confused about termination and PL 280. However, some Native

Americans recognized the danger inherent in termination, and several tribal councils passed resolutions opposing it.

NATIVE AMERICAN VOICES AND TERMINATION

The National Congress of American Indians (NCAI), an organization founded in 1944 by eighty Indians in Denver, mobilized opposition to termination in 1953. Joseph Garry, a former marine and chair of the Coeur d'Alene tribe of Idaho, led the national fight against termination. The National Congress of American Indians argued that only Native Americans, not Congress, could terminate their relationship with the United States, and in 1958, this view prevailed. However, not before the government had terminated some tribes. Blackfeet elder Earl Old Person spoke out against termination, noting that the native translation for *termination* is "wipe out" and "kill off." He asked federal policy makers, "How can we plan our future when the Indian Bureau threatens to wipe us out as a race?" He pointed out that planning that future with the threat of termination was like cooking "a meal in your tipi when someone is standing outside trying to burn the tipi down."

In the Northwest, Lucy Covington of the Colville Confederated Tribes fought fearlessly against termination. When some members of the tribal council waivered in favor of terminating the tribe, Covington took the lead to defeat such action. The blood of Chief Moses of the Mid-Columbia River tribes flowed through her veins, and, as one tribal member put it, "Lucy Covington single-handily stopped the Colvilles from terminating." Covington also fought Senator Henry Jackson of Washington state, who vigorously attempted to terminate the people of the Colville tribe. With the help of Commissioner of Indian Affairs Philleo Nash, she successfully prevented termination in 1966. But this was not the fate of some tribes targeted by the House for termination. Congress terminated 109 tribes and bands or 3 percent of federally recognized tribes owning 3.2 percent of the native estate. This number included forty-one reservations in California, the largest number from any state. In 1958, Congress passed the "rancheria bill, which severed the trust relationship of the United States with several native California people in one mighty act." Congress also terminated several bands in western Oregon. Indians in California and Oregon owned small parcels of land that were coveted by land-hungry whites. Congress also terminated Wyandots, Peorias, and Ottawas in Oklahoma as well as larger tribes such as the Klamaths of Oregon and Menominees of Wisconsin.

In 1954, Congress passed the Klamath Termination Act, which ended federal trust responsibilities among the various tribes and bands living on the Klamath Reservation in Oregon. The Klamath Reservation had rich forests, and lumber companies had long desired to cut them. White businessmen saw board feet when they envisioned termination, whereas some tribal leaders saw the woods as their legacy. Wade Crawford, a tribal member who lived off the reservation, led the campaign to terminate, whereas such leaders as Dibbon Cook, Boyd Jackson, Seldon E. Kirk, and Jesse L. Kirk Sr. led the campaign against termination. The Klamath Termination Act allowed the Indians the option of remaining with the tribe and allowing the unsold part of their reservation to be placed into trust or severing their relationship with the tribe and federal government. Those people who ended their tribal membership received a share of tribal assets. Klamath termination experienced several difficulties during the four-year transition period, until 1958, when Congress authorized the sale of forests to private lumber companies through bids equal to or above fair market value.

The government made other specific provisions with Klamath people in 1958, but most important, 1,659 Klamaths (77 percent) voted to terminate and receive a one-time per-capita payment of $43,000. In order to pay these people for severing their relations with the federal government, agents sold 717,000 acres, leaving 145,000 acres to the 474 (23 percent) who voted to retain their tribal status. In 1974, these people voted to withdraw from the Klamath tribe and to terminate their relationship with the government for a per-capita payment of $173,000. However, in spite of termination, Klamaths continued to identify as Indians and function informally as a tribe. In 1975, Klamath people readopted their tribal constitution and formally functioned as the Klamath Tribe of Oregon. They asserted their water, hunting, and fishing rights as provided in their treaty with the government and lobbied Congress to restore them as a federally recognized tribe. In 1978, Congress recognized the Klamath and restored their federal status.

As with the Klamath, in 1954, the government targeted the Menominee of Wisconsin for termination. In 1961, the government executed the Menominee Termination Act, but in the interim period, the people tried to prepare for termination and cope with the ill effects of the federal mandate. Some Menominee people were confused about the meaning of *termination*, voting in favor because they believed they were agreeing to accept a per-capita payment for outstanding claims or believing that the Indian office would withdraw services unless they voted in favor of termination. Clearly some Menominee understood the meaning of *termination* and voted in favor of the measure because they believed that it was in their best interests. Of the 3,254 members of the tribe, only 200 (6 percent) voted, and they voted unanimously in favor of termination. People opposed to termination demonstrated their disdain for the measure by not voting at all, a circumstance common among native peoples.

Termination proved disastrous for Menominees. Between 1954 and 1961, the people spent nearly all their tribe's cash reserves kept by the U.S. Treasury, which caused the Menominee to close their tribal hospital. Tuberculosis, which had been on the decline, surfaced again among the people. In 1965, one-third of the tribe tested positive for the disease, while in the same year, Menominee suffered an infant mortality rate 200 percent higher than the national average. Menominee drained their resources trying to pay for schools, municipal governments, road maintenance, and other services. Menominee children were no longer recognized as "Indian" because tribal rolls had closed in 1954. People with employment opportunities elsewhere left the area, causing a brain drain, and those who remained had little hope for the future. In 1961, the people created Menominee Enterprises Incorporated to operate their lumber mill and lands. They also created Menominee County out of the old reservation, where unemployment rose to 25 percent. Facing economic calamity by the late 1960s, Menominees sold land to whites along lakes and rivers in prime hunting and fishing areas. For generations the people had fished and hunted for subsistence, but termination and PL 280 brought them into the jurisdiction of Wisconsin law enforcement officials. State game and fish authorities arrested native people for fishing and hunting out of season. When non-Menominees moved into the area threatening native political power and self-determination, some Menominees became activists. In 1970, they formed the Determination of Rights and Unity for Menominee Shareholders (DRUMS). Ada Deer, a former tribal chair, led DRUMS, arguing that the federal government had created the trust relationship for Menominees and should restore this responsibility as soon as possible in order to reverse the negative effects of termination. On December 22, 1973, President Richard M. Nixon signed the Menominee Restoration Act by which the government recognized the tribe and reestablished nearly all of the former reservation. The act signaled an end to termination.

Once again federal Indian policy had cost Native Americans their lands and resources. Lumber, mining, farming, and ranching interests in the West profited from termination by capturing land and resources they had wanted for years. But the loss of land and resources was not as significant as the physical and psychological damage to Native Americans brought about by terminating tribes, taking away from the people a sense of being Indian. Severing the trust relationships with the tribes and liquidating tribal lands cut the tie between many people and their pasts. Poverty increased among terminated tribes as the federal government withdrew services. However, the government neither saved money through termination nor got out of the Indian business. Between 1953 and 1973, the Bureau of Indian Affairs grew in budget and staff. Instead of saving money, the government spent vast sums on welfare, public health, and Social Security. Scholars maintain that termination was a failure in terms of both money and assimilation. In spite of termination, Native Americans did not blend into the melting pot. If anything, termination helped ignite a new activism of self-determination among Indians. Self-determination also emerged because of the growing number of urban Indians, including those the government encouraged to relocate to urban centers.

RELOCATION

Following World War II, an estimated sixty-five thousand to one hundred thousand Native American veterans and workers sought employment. Politicians in Washington, D.C., believed this was a positive development for Native Americans, a mechanism through which native people could be assimilated into society. However, some political leaders worried that Native Americans would not find enough work on their reservations to match their expectations. During the depression and war, Native Americans had gained work experiences through factory and management positions, military training and administrative duties, construction, and management of soil, water, animal, timber, and range resources. The problem facing the nation was the lack of jobs for native men and women who had contributed to the war effort. Some policy makers feared that veterans and workers would return home in despair due to the lack of opportunities on their reservations.

Commissioner Collier had recognized this fear in 1941 when he wrote in his annual report that "Indians will be among the first to be affected by the shrinkage of employment opportunities subsequent to the war." He prophesied correctly that with inadequate job opportunities on the reservations, "a means of livelihood for each of the returning soldiers and workers will prove a staggering task." Collier also noted that after the war American industries would "continue to offer employment opportunities" and that "many Indians will undoubtedly choose to continue to work away from the reservations." In this way, Native Americans would "take their places among the general citizenry and . . . become assimilated into the white population." In 1946, Commissioner William Brophy wrote in his annual report that Native Americans were experiencing "a profound change in fortunes" as wages vanished and salaries "sent home by servicemen and women began to dwindle." He noted a "downward trend in family incomes," which the Bureau of Indian Affairs had to address.

Congress established the G.I. Bill for veterans so that they could continue their educations, including college and vocational school. The government established on-the-job training programs and special loans for veterans. This included commercial loans for Native Americans so they could purchase farms, ranches, livestock, farm equipment, dairies, construction machinery, and small businesses. Still, employees of the Bureau of Indian Affairs reasoned that these actions were not sufficient to provide employment to all Native Americans after the war, and so they sought innovative approaches to find employment for them. The commissioner worked with the U.S. Employment Service to locate jobs for Indians and established a job placement service for Navajos in 1948. The bureau established a pilot program among Navajos to employ them in Los Angeles, Denver, and Salt Lake City—three urban areas with expanding economies.

The government set up placement offices for Native Americans in these cities and expanded the program in the autumn of 1950 to help Indians "who wished to seek permanent employment opportunities away from the reservations." In 1951, Congress passed a bill to fund a job placement and relocation program in California, Colorado, Arizona, Oklahoma, New Mexico and Utah. The Bureau of Indian Affairs opened a field relocation office in Los Angeles, Salt Lake City, Denver, and Chicago to serve all tribes; by 1952, the relocation program was under way. In the years that followed, the Bureau of Indian Affairs established other field relocation offices in Phoenix, St. Louis, Oakland, San Francisco, San Jose, Dallas, Cleveland, Oklahoma City, Tulsa, and Albuquerque. Relocation, under the Employment Assistance Program, received a boost in 1956 when Congress enacted funds to provide vocational and industrial training specifically for Native Americans. Unlike in the past, the government did not forcibly remove Native Americans from their homes, but rather used well-designed posters and brochures as well as persuasive agents to encourage Indians to relocate to urban areas.

The program was voluntary, and the government provided funds to help native people travel to urban areas, obtain housing, sustain themselves for a month, and receive job training at no cost. While they were relocating, the program offered Native Americans free medical services off of the reservations as well as free placement service after completing their training. The relocation program attracted many Native Americans who wanted economic opportunities available in cities and the lucrative inducement offered by the government to move and be trained in exciting urban centers. Younger men and women relocated and took job training, but many found urban life and job routines to be distasteful. Jobs in urban areas meant far less freedom than that found on reservations and an aggressive, accelerated, and impersonal life. In urban areas, Native Americans often found higher crime rates, racial hatred, layoffs, and poor-paying jobs with no future. Alcoholism and ill health increased, and promised medical care disappeared after a time.

According to San Carlos Apache artist Earl Sisto, who participated in the relocation program, some Indians believed that relocation would create economic opportunities, whereas others believed that whites had designed the program to separate Native Americans from their lands and people. Suspicion ran high in some native communities that the relocation program was an extension of termination. Both programs, some native critics argued, were designed to steal land and resources by alienating people from the land. In addition, both programs aimed at assimilating native peoples into the dominant society by separating them from their families, elders, traditions, languages, and ceremonies. Between 1945 and 1960, approximately one hundred thousand Native Americans left their tribal homes for urban areas, but only thirty-three thousand of these were part of the government's relocation effort. Many Native Americans who participated in relocation—between 30 and 75 percent, depending on the tribe—returned to their reservations.

The relocation program did little to assimilate Indians. Native scholar Donald Fixico has maintained that most Native Americans who moved to urban areas retained a link with their home communities and continued to maintain their cultures in urban settings. Native Americans in nearly all the major cities established urban Indian centers where people held meetings regarding employment opportunities, job counseling, substance abuse, and personal problems. These centers served as gathering places for powwows, arts and craft shows, language and dance instruction, fellowship meetings, pot lucks, and sports—particularly basketball. Many Native Americans returned home to participate in ceremonies, powwows, traditional medicine, funerals, and family gatherings. Most American Indians living in urban areas resided in native neighborhoods. Some set up small businesses, bringing native arts and foods into the urban areas and introducing non-Indians to elements of native culture.

Some politicians had hoped to save money through termination and relocation programs. Some thought that these two programs would prove to be the "final solution" to the so-called Indian problem. Still others thought that termination and relocation would magically assimilate Native Americans. Politicians had also thought this about removal, reservations, and allotment. They never seemed to learn from the past or understand the strength that had so characterized Native American people. The new policies failed to save money, assimilate Indians, or solve Indian problems. If anything, these policies complicated matters for Native Americans, introducing them to urban areas and often sinking them deeper into poverty and ill health. As usual, Native Americans survived termination and relocation. Like Ada Deer, John James, Henry Duro, Earl Old Person, Leaford Bearskin, Lorena Dixon, Eleonore Sioui, Clarence Brown, Ben Reifel, Raymond Nakai, Katherine Saubel, and hundreds of other Native Americans leaders, American Indians asserted themselves in the interest of their own people and brought about their own self-determination and continued sovereignty.

PATERNALISM TO PARTNERSHIP

The phrase "Native American self-determination" describes an era that emerged in the 1960s and continues to the present. "Self-determination" suggests that Native Americans exercised their right to govern themselves and make decisions affecting their own lives and people. This is particularly true in determining issues involving land, water, hunting, fishing, mining, repatriation, and gaming. Native American self-determination is also tied to international laws that assert that all people have the right to choose their own government and control their own future. In 1959, the United States admitted Alaska to the Union, but before the state could define "state lands," Secretary of Interior Stewart Udall insisted that Native Alaskans determine their boundaries and rights. Alaskan Natives had anticipated statehood and had rallied to protect their rights. By 1964, Alaskan Natives claimed more than three hundred million acres and formed local and regional village associations to protect their lands and resources.

In 1965, native people in Alaska organized a powerful statewide group known as the Alaska Federated Natives to protect land claims and native community interests. After a decade of dedicated work, the Alaska Federated Natives led the fight for the Alaska Native Claims Settlement Act in 1971. Under the terms of this act, Alaskan Natives preserved for themselves forty-four million acres and received $962 million for their claims on the remaining land in the state. Native Alaskans used the funds to finance many economic ventures. Like Alaskan Natives, other Native Americans demonstrated their commitment to self-determination. In the 1960s and 1970s, Indian activists, tribal leaders, and government officials used the term *self-determination* to describe native decisions regarding economic development, education, land use, treaty rights, health programs, social services, and other issues.

Ideally, the core meaning of self-determination is tribal sovereignty, which arises out of the tribal past, not policies or legislation issued by the United States, Canada, Mexico, or any other foreign country. Native Americans have always had their own sovereignty, a birthright given to them at the time of creation. The ancient oral narratives of all Native Americans explain the law and spirit that define tribal sovereignty and self-determination. Laws and rights vary from tribe to tribe and region to region, but all Native American tribes received their laws long before the arrival of nonnatives. Throughout the nineteenth and twentieth centuries, Native Americans asserted some measure of self-determination and sovereignty in spite of policies placed upon them by the United States. In the face of treaties, agreements, executive orders, and so forth, Native Americans never relinquished their right to, or use of, self-determination. Assertion of tribal sovereignty and self-determination had been a form of native resistance, one that native people asserted more forcefully after World War II.

Cherokee scholar Ward Churchill has argued that Native Americans asserted self-determination throughout the 1950s and 1960s, but termination and relocation strengthened self-determination among Native Americans. Through political adversity, individuals, tribes, and Indian organizations mobilized politically so they could more fully influence policies affecting them. By the 1960s, Indians had learned how to deal with the political system and skillfully maneuver within the bureaucracy of the United States. Several tribal leaders had completed high school, college, professional schools, and vocational schools. Many had fought in World War II and Korea or worked in defense plants, where they gained valuable experience dealing with whites on many levels. Native Americans had worked with the U.S. government for years—including the Bureau of Indian Affairs—learning practical political lessons. They understood the power of organization, and to this end in 1961, native representatives of ninety tribes met at the Chicago Indian Conference to mobilize against termination and chart a new course for greater self-determination. Their agenda emphasized economic development, job training, business loans, health initiatives, educational funding, and housing.

In 1961, the National Indian Youth Council also asserted self-determination but criticized the Indian Rights Association, Christian churches, and National Congress of American Indians for not being sufficiently active and aggressive. Activism and self-determination mounted when Cahuilla Indian scholar and activist Rupert Costo and Jeanette Henry Costo began the American Indian Historical Society. In 1964, they published the first issue of *The Indian Historian*, a historical journal that reflected the changing times and determination of native people to have a voice in their own history. In addition, the Indian Historian Press began a series of publications on a variety of subjects, including a criticism of American history textbooks that depicted Native Americans as crude savages with little foresight and less ability. The Costos altered the way in which scholars studied native people and were among the earliest "new Indian historians."

In 1960, the nation elected President John F. Kennedy, who had campaigned to preserve the Indian estate but offered few details of his American Indian policy. Still, Kennedy's few years in the White House proved pivotal, because his administration offered a "New Trail" that would lead away from termination and toward self-determination. In addition, President Kennedy and Vice President Lyndon B. Johnson gave Native Americans a greater voice in their lives, through programs designed to achieve a small degree of economic opportunity, social justice, and tribal development. Kennedy was careful not to offend conservative Democrats or Republicans by openly opposing termination, but shortly after his election, he appointed an American Indian task force to investigate Indian affairs. Clearly, Kennedy anticipated making Indian affairs a minor part of his New Frontier.

Principal Chief of the Cherokee Nation W. W. Keeler headed the task force, which solicited Native American opinions. After extensive hearings, the task force learned that Native Americans opposed termination and wanted the government to focus on a "New Trail" of economic development and equal rights as citizens. In part because of the task force and because of his own background in Arizona, Secretary of Interior Udall opposed the "so-called termination policy" of the Eisenhower administration and promoted "Indian development" in order to "win the cooperative response from our Indian citizens which is the keystone of a successful program." President Kennedy believed that defeating grinding poverty among Native Americans was a key solution to the so-called Indian problem. Kennedy and Johnson focused on ways to provide greater economic opportunities and more self-determination for Native Americans through federal programs they initiated through the New Frontier and Great Society.

Newly appointed Commissioner of Indian Affairs Philleo Nash put Kennedy's and Udall's views into action. He favored greater native participation in the political process and believed programs should be initiated for the welfare of tribes. In 1961, several hundred tribal leaders voiced their view that the administration should permit Indians a greater role in designing and executing programs, budgets, and evaluations of programs. Nash drew Native Americans into the Area Redevelopment Act (ARA), which provided resources for economic development in depressed areas. Certainly reservations qualified, and the commissioner provided assistance for economic development to fifty-six reservations and four regions with populations of Native Alaskans. Native Americans also took advantage of the Manpower Development and Training Act of 1962, which enabled them to set up eighty-nine public works projects and employment training programs on reservations. Building on the economic emphasis, Nash formed the Division of Economic Development within the Bureau of Indian Affairs, which initially attracted twenty-six small industrial plants onto or near reservations, where employers hired Indians and encouraged corporate investment in native peoples.

JOHNSON YEARS

President Johnson expanded these economic efforts after Kennedy's assassination in 1963 and brought Native Americans into the larger goals of the War on Poverty and the Economic Opportunity Act, which created the Office of Economic Opportunity (OEO). The legislation creating the OEO included a special Indian Office to handle programs designed to defeat poverty among Native Americans, and many native people supported the act. In May 1964, the National Congress of American Indians met in Washington, D.C., and aggressively lobbied Congress to pass several programs, including the Community Action Projects, programs designed to provide training, employment, and economic development within minority communities. Other departments within the executive branch responded to Native American voices calling for more participation in government decisions involving Indians. Within the Labor Department, officials established an Indian office to handle Manpower Administration and Work Incentive Projects. The same occurred in the Departments of Health, Education, and Welfare; Agriculture; and Housing and Urban Development—where Native Americans developed projects and programs tied to housing, sanitation, commodities, electricity, forestry, education, Social Security, and others.

In 1968, President Johnson delivered his address, "The Forgotten American," which called for an end to termination and sanctioned self-determination. Johnson strengthened the movement toward Indian self-determination by establishing the National Council on Indian Opportunity, which was another task force that investigated Indian affairs. Headed by Vice President Hubert Humphrey of Minnesota, the council conducted a series of hearings and concluded that Native Americans should have a greater role in decisions affecting their lives. In the same spirit, in 1968 South Dakota Senator George McGovern guided a resolution through Congress repudiating termination, and although the resolution did not repeal House Concurrent Resolution 108, it encouraged Indians and non-Indians alike to demand an end to termination. A month after Johnson delivered his address on "The Forgotten American," Senator Sam Ervin of North Carolina sponsored the Indian Civil Rights Act, which increased the power of tribal governments and allowed them to decide whether a state could apply Public Law 280 on their lands. The law also strengthened the power of tribal police and courts.

Senator Robert Kennedy and, after his death, Senator Edward Kennedy provided a comprehensive report detailing the "disastrous effects" of assimilationist policies on Indian education. The report was supported by a study of the U.S. Office of Education between 1967 and 1971, which offered the *National Study of American Indian Education* by Robert J. Havighurst and Estelle Fuchs. These two scholars used data in the study to offer *To Live on This Earth: American Indian Education*, which revealed educational problems facing Indians. Their studies helped pass the Indian Education Act of 1972, the Indian Self-Determination and Education Assistance Act of 1975, and Title XI of the Education Amendments of 1978—all of which provided funding and a native voice in Indian education. Equally important was Task Force Five of the American Indian

Policy Review Commission, which demanded increased funding for Indian education. Native Americans also benefited from the Head Start and Follow Through programs as well as the Elementary and Secondary Education Act of 1965. President Johnson supported these and similar programs that empowered Indian education and Indian educators.

NIXON YEARS

Many Native Americans feared that the election of Richard Nixon would mean a return to the days of termination and relocation that had emerged under Republican rule while Nixon served as Eisenhower's vice president. But this was not to be the case, as Nixon became a strong advocate of self-determination and tribal sovereignty. He appointed Louis R. Bruce, a man of Mohawk and Sioux ancestry, as commissioner of Indian affairs. Bruce argued that "the Indian future is determined by Indian acts and Indian decisions" and that "self-determination has become a vital component of the thinking of Indian leadership," which "is an irreversible trend, a tide in the destiny of American Indians." Through self-determination, Bruce maintained, all Americans would "recognize the dignity and human rights of Indian people." The president echoed such views in a nationwide speech on July 8, 1970, in which he asked Congress to "renounce, repudiate and repeal the termination policy." Although Congress did not officially end termination and embrace self-determination until the passage of the Indian Self-Determination and Education Assistance Act of 1975, termination effectively died in 1970.

Powhatan and Lenape scholar Jack Forbes has criticized Nixon in his cutting-edge book, *Native Americans and Nixon: Presidential Politics and Minority Self-Determination, 1969–1972,* arguing that Nixon outwardly favored self-determination as a defense against Indian activism and as a means of harnessing natural resources controlled by Indians. Other scholars point to the many ways in which Nixon's policies fundamentally and permanently moved American Indian policy toward greater tribal sovereignty and self-determination. Not long after giving his "Indian Self-Determination" speech, Nixon expanded Indian influence in the Bureau of Indian Affairs and Office of Economic Opportunity and backed legislation returning Blue Lake and forty-eight thousand acres to Taos pueblo. With Nixon's help, Paiute, Yakama, Havasupai, Warm Springs, and other tribes secured a portion of their traditional lands that the United States had stolen from them. Nixon cleared the way for the passage of the Alaska Native Claims Settlement Act and federal recognition of tribes that the government had terminated, including Menominee, Wyandotte, Modoc, Ottawa, Paiute, Peoria, and others. Nixon supported

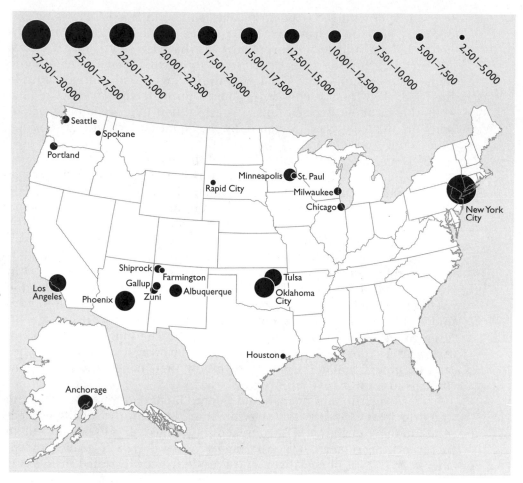

27,501–30,000
25,001–27,500
22,501–25,000
20,001–22,500
17,501–20,000
15,001–17,500
12,501–15,000
10,001–12,500
7,501–10,000
5,001–7,500
2,501–5,000

Seattle
Spokane
Portland
Minneapolis
St. Paul
Rapid City
Milwaukee
Chicago
New York City
Shiprock
Farmington
Gallup
Albuquerque
Los Angeles
Phoenix
Zuni
Tulsa
Oklahoma City
Houston
Anchorage

Native American Populations, 1990s.

the creation of tribal governments among Cherokee, Choctaw, Chicka-saw, Seminole, Muscogee, and others.

Nixon encouraged Congress to pass the Indian Financing Act, which provided more capital for Indian businesses. He supported the American Indian Policy Review Commission, which made over two hundred recommendations to the government on how to improve Indian affairs. Nixon's resignation during the Watergate scandal did not end Indian reforms, as President Gerald Ford continued the process of self-determination, signing into law the Indian Self-Determination and Education Assistance Act of 1975. However, a notable change occurred after Nixon left office because the rate of change in Indian policy slowed considerably within the executive and legislative branches. And the sphere of change in Indian policies shifted to federal courts, which became far more assertive in rulings generally favoring self-determination and tribal sovereignty. In the case *Santa Clara Pueblo v. Martinez,* the Supreme Court ruled that Santa Clara pueblo could deny membership to the child of a woman who had married outside the tribe, even though children of men who married outside of pueblo could be enrolled. Because this was a tradition that predated the Constitution, the tribe was not bound by the equal protection clause of the Fourteenth Amendment.

This and many other cases marked the era of the 1970s and 1980s; but the administration of President Jimmy Carter did little in the way of Indian affairs, with the notable exception of two important issues. The first involved upgrading the position of commissioner of Indian affairs to an assistant secretary of interior for Indian affairs. Forrest J. Gerard was a Blackfeet administrator working within the Bureau of Indian Affairs and the first assistant secretary to fill this position. Gerard played an important role in urging Congress to pass the Indian Child Welfare Act in 1978. As noted historian Troy Johnson has demonstrated, before the welfare act, state and county courts often placed Indian children in non-Indian homes, often giving non-Indians preference so that native children could be assimilated into white families. The Indian Child Welfare Act restricted the placement of native children away from Indian families and permitted Indian parents to withdraw their consent to allow non-Indians to adopt native children.

Presidents Ronald Reagan and George Bush continued to adhere to the principles of Indian self-determination, but they drastically cut federal funding to tribes and encouraged states and tribes to pay for Indian programs. Secretary of Interior James Watt referred to tribal governments as a form of socialism, and President Reagan stated in Moscow that it was a mistake for the United States to "maintain Indian cultures" in what he characterized as "primitive lifestyle." Reagan and Watt were assimilationist and unsupportive of Native American sovereignty. Although President Bill Clinton supported Indian self-determination and sponsored a White House conference of Native Americans in 1994, he did little to further American Indian sovereignty during his two terms. Clinton favored open communications with the tribes and set up "Indian Listening Conferences," but overall the budget for Indian affairs did not increase. Two noteworthy efforts of his administration were his choice of Menominee leader Ada Deer to head the Bureau of Indian Affairs and his executive order in 1998 to increase appropriations to encourage Indian children to finish high school and attend college. Throughout the Clinton years, Native American leaders such as Katherine Saubel, Anthony Pico, John James, Mark Macarro, Dean Mike, Peterson Zah, and Wilma Mankiller urged the administration to protect tribal sovereignty and provide more federal resources to fight poverty, ill health, and poor education.

Several native leaders encouraged the government to support Indian gaming as a means of economic sovereignty. Overall, Clinton's administration did little to further the cause of Native Americans.

NATIVE AMERICAN EDUCATION

Native American education was a national disgrace during the 1950s and 1960s, and in spite of some gains by native people after 1970, Indian education remained substandard during the last half of the twentieth century. However, the era after 1970 was characterized by greater Native American involvement in education and substantial efforts by native educators to improve education. Day schools, public schools, boarding schools, and mission schools offered educational opportunities to most Indians, although some Indian families continued traditional forms of education through stories, songs, dances, and arts. Native American families continued to teach young people about agriculture, architecture, fishing, hunting, gathering, and medicine. These traditional forms of education declined among some native peoples, but after the 1960s, a renaissance developed in education–built on the efforts of elders, past administrators, and teachers–that emphasized the place of Indian people in American art, culture, literature, and history.

In part, the renewal of traditional forms of Indian education emerged because Native Americans had a greater voice in education after 1933. W. Carson Ryan and Willard Beatty of the Education Division of the Bureau of Indian Affairs revolutionized Indian education in the 1930s and 1940s by emphasizing American Indian subjects in the curriculum. Ryan published curriculum guides, books, and training manuals that featured Native American topics, people, and languages. For the first time, the government offered bilingual and bicultural education. Missionary educators of Native Americans had provided such material in native languages earlier, but the government did not promote bilingual education until the New Deal era. In 1949, the Education Division of the Bureau of Indian Affairs published *Coyote Tales* as part of the Navajo Life Series, which included a bilingual book for second- and third-graders and offered traditional stories collected and translated by William Morgan and Robert Young, adapted into English by Heldegard Thompson.

The use of bilingual texts declined within the Bureau of Indian Affairs during the era of termination and the emphasis on assimilation, but it gained strength again in the 1960s and 1970s. In her classic work, *Education and the American Indian*, Margaret Connell Szasz details these transitions in Native American education, including the influence of self-determination among native peoples. During the administrations of Kennedy and Johnson, Indians served greater roles on education advisory committees and designed their own programs through the Office of Economic Development. On the Navajo Reservation, the people created their own Indian-controlled school at Rough Rock with instruction in Navajo and English. Students attending Rough Rock Demonstration School learned Navajo language, literature, history, and culture. They read books written in Navajo and English, including *Stefanii dóó Ma'ii/Stephannie and The Coyote* by Jack L. Crowder. In addition, students at Rough Rock Demonstration School learned their own tribal history through Ethelou Yazzie's work, *Navajo History*, which offers a traditional view of history, beginning with the stories of creation of the earth, animals, holy people, clans, and ceremonies.

Following the example of Rough Rock Demonstration School, Navajos at Ramah and Borrego Pass, New Mexico, established Indian-controlled schools that emphasized bilingual-bicultural education. Chippewas and Crees in Montana took over the Rocky Boy School, featuring curricula that included native language, culture, history, and literature. In southern California, Robert Brown established the Viejas Indian School, which featured preschool training for native children, free breakfasts and lunches, and after-school educational programs for children from kindergarten through high school. The curriculum at the Viejas Indian School featured oral traditions, reading, art, and writing about Native Americans and was used to prepare children for success in the public schools in Alpine, California. In addition to schools located on or near reservations, Native Americans established schools in urban areas such as the successful community school in Milwaukee, Wisconsin. In Minneapolis, the large urban Indian population created the Heart of the Earth School, while native people in St. Paul set up the Red School House.

In California, Native American scholars Rupert Costo and Jeanette Henry Costo advocated the classroom teaching of Native American history that accurately portrayed the invasion, conquest, and exploitation of American Indians throughout American history. In 1967, Hupa and Yurok educator David Risling brought many Native Americans together in a common cause to support native education through the creation of the California Indian Education Association. Risling was strongly supported in his effort by members of his family, including Lois Risling, and Jack Norton, who helped establish the Indian Education Program at Humboldt State University. In the mid-1960s, Navajos began developing a comprehensive plan to fund and build Navajo Community College, the first Indian-owned and -operated college in North America. In January 1969, Navajo Community College opened classes in Many Farms, Arizona, before the Navajo Nation built a permanent campus at Tsaile, Arizona. The main campus and its branch campuses offer a curriculum rich in Native American history, literature, arts, language, and

*N. Scott Momaday pro-
foundly influenced American
literature with* House Made
of Dawn, *his Pulitzer-Prize-
winning novel. Momaday's
work affected the way people
thought about Native Americans intellectually, politically,
and socially. He also helped
create a new generation of
American Indian writers who
provide new voices in literature, art, and history.*

government. The college offers courses to enable students to continue
their schooling at a university or to learn a vocational skill in automobile
mechanics, welding, nursing, or drafting.

In 1971, Congress passed the Navajo Community College Act providing funding for the college, and five years later, the college received
accreditation from the North Central Association of Colleges and
Schools. As part of the curriculum, Navajo Community College (re-
named Diné College) encouraged all students to preserve their native
culture and language, strongly emphasizing the Navajo studies and
history component of the curriculum. Students from other tribes from
around the Americas studied at the college, many choosing to attend
in order to learn Navajo arts, including silversmithing, rug making,
moccasin making, and herbology. Diné College is truly a reservation
institution with a board of regents composed of Navajo people and a
strong link to the community through lecture series, ceremonies, animal sciences, and educational outreach programs. Tribal elders, including tribal historian Curly Mustache and medicine men like Ray
Winnie and Charlie Benally, often participate in educational programs
at the college. Ned Hatathli became the first president of the college,

and he has been succeeded by other Navajo presidents who shared his vision that the college was "an Indian owned and an Indian operated institution, and we certainly don't want any people other than Indians to dictate to us what is good for us."

This same vision of Indian-owned and -operated colleges inspired new community colleges, including Sinte Gleska College (South Dakota), D-Q University (California), Oglala Lakota College (South Dakota), Turtle Mountain College (North Dakota), Blackfeet Community College (Montana), Salish Kootenai College (Montana), Lac Courte Oreilles Ojibwa College (Wisconsin), and Fond du Lac Community College (Minnesota). One of the most successful colleges has been Northwest Indian College, spearheaded by the Lummi tribe of Washington. Lummi leaders Theresa Mike and Bernie Thomas were two of many leaders involved in establishing the college, and in 1999, Mike launched an effort with Gloria Wright to begin an Indian college to benefit native people in California, Arizona, and Nevada.

The tribally controlled colleges vary in size, course offerings, degrees, certificate programs, and facilities. C. Patrick Morris and Michael O'Donnell have noted in "Education," a chapter within Chippewa scholar Duane Champagne's *The Native North American Almanac*, that the "list of tribal colleges is evidence that something remarkable is happening in Indian higher education. For the first time, Indians have control over the college education of their tribal members." They point out that in spite of funding problems, Indian community colleges continue to offer educational opportunities for thousands of Native Americans, many of whom receive advanced degrees. Between 1988 and 1989, 3,954 Native Americans received bachelor's degrees, 1,086 received master's degrees, and 85 received doctorates.

Morris and O'Donnell point out that to be successful, American Indian community colleges have to "support and implement Indian cultural values, and this must be coupled with a clear statement from the institution's administration that NAS [Native American Studies] and other Indian student support programs have a legitimate academic role in higher education." Their argument also applies to many colleges in North America that offer Native American studies. In the late 1960s and early 1970s, Native American college students joined the chorus of African-American, Latino, Asian-American, and other students to demand a curriculum and scholarship that addressed their experiences. Anthropology departments had taught courses regarding Native Americans for years, and some history departments offered courses in the American West that dealt with native peoples. However, such courses often depicted Native Americans as primitive people, and the writings of noted historians like Frederick Jackson Turner and Ray Allen Billington often characterized Indians as "savages."

Native American students demanded more rigorous community-based scholarship by individuals who knew something about native peoples and their cultures.

Thus, in addition to the issues of intellectual exclusion, Native American students asked for sound scholarship in research and teaching. They demanded classes by Native Americans about Native Americans. Some Native American students were interested in issues of American Indian identity, but equally important were academic programs within institutions of higher education that presented native studies in a rich and diverse manner based on knowledge of native communities. Professors and administrators agreed, often grudgingly, to establish Native American studies as an academic discipline. Some of the earliest Native American studies units emerged in the 1970s at the University of California at Berkeley, Davis, and Los Angeles, University of Minnesota, University of New Mexico, San Diego State University, Palomar College, Pembroke State University, University of Montana, South Dakota State University, University of Oklahoma, and others. By 1985, 107 Native American studies programs existed in the United States, offering numerous degree programs and courses, including Native American history, contemporary literature, oral narratives, community development, governments, Indian policies, and regional native studies such as plains Indians, southwestern Indians, northeastern Indians, and northwestern Indians.

Some Native American studies programs offered language courses in Ojibwa, Dakota, Lakota, Navajo, Kumeyaay, Luiseño, and Hupa. The faculties of Native American studies units supported the publication of recent scholarship in the field through such scholarly journals and publications as *American Indian Culture and Research Journal, The American Indian Quarterly, Wicazo Sa Review, Ethnohistory,* and various books, such as those published by the University of California at Riverside and Los Angeles, San Diego State University, and Pembroke State University. Edward Castillo, Henrietta Whiteman, John Rouillard, N. Scott Momaday, Charlotte Heth, Vine Deloria Jr., Delores Huff, Roger Buffalohead, Cheryl Metoyer-Duran, Jack Norton, Ruth Roessel, Dillon Platero, David Risling, Joy Harjo, Jack Forbes, Michael Dorris, Linda Oxendine, Carter Blue Clark, Simon Ortiz, Beatrice Medicine, Richard Glazier-Danay, Elizabeth Cook-Lynn, Darryl Wilson, Patricia Dixon, Dean Chavers, Duane Champagne, William Willard, and many other Native American scholars were in the forefront of establishing and nurturing Native American studies as academic units within colleges. For some of these Native American professors, their field of study is an important link between Native American communities and the academy. Native American studies empower Indians with knowledge about the contributions of Indian people in many fields of study.

NATIVE AMERICAN HEALTH

Academic programs provided Native Americans a voice in their own affairs, and they brought much-needed funding to projects designed for and by native people. Some native leaders criticized tribal governments for focusing so heavily on obtaining federal dollars, while others eagerly initiated projects intended to fight poverty, ill health, substandard housing, inadequate education, staggering unemployment, and a host of other problems. All the national reports regarding Native Americans, from the 1950s through the 1970s, emphasized that conditions among American Indians were far worse than among any other group in the United States, and social geographer John Weeks has pointed out that Native American populations appeared more like "Third World Nations" than a population within the United States. Infant mortality rates were the highest within the United States, and life expectancy was low. Native Americans suffered high death rates resulting from heart disease, pneumonia, gastrointestinal disorders, accidental deaths, alcohol-related deaths, suicides, and diseases stemming from diabetes.

In 1954, Congress passed the Transfer Act, moving the responsibility of health services among Native Americans from the Bureau of Indian Affairs to the Indian Health Service, a division of the Public Health Service. Health services among Native Americans improved appreciably after 1955, as demonstrated by lower crude death rates from many diseases, lower fetal and infant mortality rates, and a dramatic decline in tuberculosis cases and deaths. The Indian Health Service, of the Public Health Service, offered new programs designed to prevent diseases and high mortality rather than provide only reactive medicine to address native health issues. The transfer of health services from the Bureau of Indian Affairs to the Public Health Service positively affected Indian health, but high mortality and morbidity continued to exist on reservations. Blackfeet scholar Raymond Butler has argued that withdrawing Indian health services from the Bureau of Indian Affairs was one component of termination, but one that worked to the advantage of native people. Between 1955 and 1975, the budget for the Indian Health Service grew from roughly $34 million to $200 million and the number of employees increased from twenty-nine hundred to seventy-four hundred. Nevertheless, the government did not fund the Indian Health Service sufficiently to tackle the diverse problems facing Native Americans—layers of health problems involving infants, children, and adults—that had been growing for years and were largely ignored in the past.

Still, as Robert Trennert has demonstrated in *White Man's Medicine*, the Indian Health Service used innovative ways to address health problems on reservations and in urban areas, although the primary focus of Indian health remains on reservation Indians—not urban Indians. After

1955, the Indian Health Service made remarkable strides fighting tuberculosis, pneumonia, trachoma, and other infectious diseases by focusing on health education, nutrition, sanitation, water and sewer problems, housing projects, waste disposal systems, and other health initiatives. On some reservations, teams of paraprofessional health workers visited homes and offered training programs to small groups of Indians. The daughter of Henry Chee Dodge, Annie Dodge Wauneka, became one of the premier health workers for the Indian Health Service among Navajo people. Because she knew the language, culture, and religion of the Navajo, she was able to communicate with the people, explaining to them about bacteria and viruses, which invade and kill the body like the monsters of Navajo oral traditions. She initiated her own radio program and traveled on and off the reservation, providing new knowledge about health, diseases, and preventive care. In 1964, President Johnson awarded her the Presidential Medal of Freedom, which encouraged Dr. Wauneka to continue her campaign to improve health among all Native Americans.

In addition to increasing the number of health facilities, nurses, programs, and doctors on reservations, the Indian Health Service funded several urban Indian health centers in San Diego, Los Angeles, San Francisco, Sacramento, Portland, Seattle, Denver, Phoenix, Chicago, Minneapolis, and other cities. These centers offered a wide range of services for Native Americans, including open clinics for medical help, immunization programs, prenatal care, nutritional programs, dental services, AIDS prevention programs, and substance abuse programs. Some clinics offered family counseling, whereas others offered basic programs on traditional Indian health practices. Urban Indian health centers, like those on reservations, practiced preventive medicine through public health, sanitation, nutrition, and so forth. The approach at some health centers was more holistic than that found in the general population and included programs associated with self-esteem and Indian identity. Some clinics sponsored Native American cultural programs, powwows, public exhibits, lecture series, publications, plays, storytellings, and other cultural components that linked people through native culture. Ralph Forquera, Carmella Ignacio, Anna Puzz, Jane Dumas, and Edna Kidwell are among the native health leaders who emphasize the cultural connection in Indian health.

In spite of improvements, since World War II an increasing number of Native Americans have suffered from degenerative diseases, including heart disease, cancer, and diabetes. Gregory Campbell has conducted some of the most innovative work on diabetes and has demonstrated that before 1940, Native Americans suffered very little from diabetes. His research is suggestive in terms of heart disease and cancer because the 1940s marked the era in which Native Americans obtained better employment, and with jobs came cash incomes, which resulted in new diets of processed foods high in short-chain carbohydrates and fiber and high in fats. In 1996, noted medical anthropologist Diane Weiner of the American Indian Center at the University of California, Los Angeles, detailed the implication of diabetes among Luiseño Indians in southern California. Like many Native Americans, these people believed that their disease was caused by several factors, including diet. During the post-World War II era, Native Americans seemed to receive less exercise, as many factors prohibited them from moving across the land and waterways as they had done in the past.

Thus, Native Americans developed diabetes after the war for several reasons. These reasons, combined with what geneticist James Neel has labeled a "diabetes gene," have resulted in an epidemic of diabetes among Native Americans. Before the 1940s, most Native Americans had relied heavily on natural foods that their bodies could digest easily and from which they could take nutrition. However, by the 1940s, Native Americans had lost access to fish, game, roots, nuts, berries, and grains that had for centuries been the basis of their diets. As a result, disease developed among the people, as their biological systems struggled to adjust to this new world. Diabetes emerged as an important health problem among Native Americans after 1940 and contributed to cancer, heart disease, and other degenerative diseases brought about by human activities.

During the 1980s, Native Americans faced another health threat as a result of human immunodeficiency virus (HIV) and acquired immunodeficiency syndrome (AIDS), deadly conditions that plagued reservation and urban Indians. HIV and AIDS have caused a number of deaths among Native Americans and have contributed to mortality resulting from pneumonia, cancer, influenza, heart ailments, and other diseases that attack the weakened immune system of infected individuals. The new epidemic also has been responsible for suicides and mortality described in death certificates as alcohol-related or accidents. In addition, HIV and AIDS have contributed to a new outbreak of tuberculosis among Native Americans. In 1993, the Indian Health Service reported that tuberculosis mortality among Native Americans was seven hundred times greater than it was among the general population. In spite of these trends, the National Institute of Health and University of California's Office of AIDS Research have largely ignored the rise of AIDS among Native Americans.

American Indians have created their own initiatives to fight the disease. During the 1990s, Choctaw-Kaskaskia-Chickasaw administrator Ron Rowell led the National Native American AIDS Prevention Center in Oakland, California, providing research information on native peoples and HIV-AIDS. Several Indian health centers supported AIDS projects or independent Indian AIDS programs. In 1990, the San Diego American Indian Health Center published *Coyote's Penis*, a modern coyote story that encouraged young people to use condoms and reminded them that substance abuse could be deadly in many ways. In 1991, native students in Minneapolis used the story as the basis of a traveling play that radiated out into Indian country in several directions. In addition to such programs and native initiatives to fight HIV and AIDS, Native Americans received important funding from the federal government, including the Indian Self-Determination and Education Assistance Act of 1975 and the Indian Health Care Improvement Act of 1976, which encouraged tribes to contract with the government to provide their own health programs.

By the 1990s, Indians operated over three hundred health centers, health clinics, and hospitals. In his original volume, *American Indian Holocaust and Survival,* Cherokee scholar Russell Thornton carefully analyzes the effects of improved health among Native Americans while pointing out problems that remain. In 1997, Michigan State University Press published *Death Stalks the Yakama: Epidemiological Transitions and Mortality on the Yakama Indian Reservation, 1888–1964,* which uses death certificates and birth certificates to illustrate graphically the decline of mortality resulting from infectious diseases after the 1940s but points out the rise of human-made degenerative diseases among the fourteen tribes and bands living on the Yakama Reservation from the 1940s to the 1990s. Like other recent studies of Indian health during the post-World War II era, *Death Stalks the Yakama* details the rise of murder, suicide, diabetes, accidents, and alcohol-related deaths among the diverse people of the Confederated Tribes and Bands of the Yakama Nation.

On reservations like the Yakama, and in the nation's cities, the era from 1950 to the present has been marked by an increasing number of deaths caused by suicide, murder, substance abuse, and accidents. In addition, fetal alcohol syndrome (FAS) emerged as a significant problem among Native Americans after World War II, a problem well known to Native Americans but made known to the general public by Modoc scholar Michael Dorris in *The Broken Cord.* In 1997, health officials on the Yakama Indian Reservation labeled suicides and alcohol-related deaths "epidemic" and argued that the Confederated Tribe was losing its young people and with them the future of the tribe. In 1991, the Indian Health Service clinic in Toppenish, Washington, reported the age-adjusted mortality rate from suicide per one hundred thousand population to be forty among Yakama, nineteen among other Native Americans, and thirteen among the general population. The clinic also reported that "there is excessive mortality from unintentional injury as well as from homicide and suicide." Like other Native Americans, those living on the Yakama Reservation experienced a deadly trend toward the end of the twentieth century.

In border towns surrounding Indian reservations and in urban areas with large concentrations of Americans Indians, there was an alarming number of murders or suspicious "accidental deaths." Native Americans reported rampant police abuse in Minneapolis, Los Angeles, and Chicago. Indians living on reservations near nonnative border towns such as Gallup, Farmington, Browning (Montana), Rapid City, Reno, Spokane, San Diego, and Tulsa had their own special problems. Young whites doused Indians with gasoline and set them on fire. One Navajo reported that police in one border town had taken his brother into custody on a charge of drunk and disorderly conduct, and when his brother refused to stop crying out for help, the police kicked the young man to death. Such atrocities were not uncommon in border towns and are woven into the fabric of Native American history. Racism against American Indians did not end with World War II but rather continued throughout the twentieth century, sometimes increasing as Native Americans asserted their sovereignty, self-determination, and civil rights.

Yet racism never deterred Native Americans from resisting injustices that have long been a part of American history.

Selected Readings and Bibliography

The era from the 1940s to the 1960s was a pivotal period for Native Americans. They were forced to deal with a conservative government bent on destroying tribal sovereignty and with ending the federal relationship with native nations. Several general works deal with this era, including Gibson, *The American Indians,* Champagne, *The Native North American Almanac;* Debo, *History of the Indians of the United States;* Tyler, *A History of Indian Policy;* Szasz, *American Indian Education;* Burt, *Tribalism in Crisis;* Thornton, *American Indian Holocaust;* and Trafzer, *Death Stalks the Yakama.* Other helpful books include Bernstein's *Native Indians and World War II,* Deloria's *Custer Died for Your Sins,* Fixico's *Termination and Relocation,* Francis's *Native Time,* Rawls's *Chief Red Fox Is Dead,* Davis's *Native America in the Twentieth Century,* and Malinowski and Abrams's *Notable Native Americans.*

Brophy, William A., and Sophie D. Aberle. *The Indian: America's Unfinished Business.* Norman: University of Oklahoma Press, 1966.

Cahn, Edgar, ed. *Our Brother's Keeper: The Indian in White America.* Washington, D.C.: New Community Press, 1969.

Costo, Rupert, and Jeanette Henry. *Indian Treaties.* San Francisco: Indian Historian Press, 1977.

Crowder, Jack. *Stefanii doo Ma'ii /Stephanie and the Coyote.* Translation by William Morgan Sr. Bernalillo, N.M.: privately published, 1969.

Dorris, Michael. *The Broken Cord.* New York: Harper and Row, 1989.

Fixico, Donald L. *Urban Indians.* New York: Chelsea House, 1991.

Forbes, Jack D. *Native Americans and Nixon: Presidential Politics and Minority Self-Determination, 1969–1972.* Los Angeles: American Indian Studies Center, University of California, Los Angeles, 1981.

Fuchs, Estell, and Robert J. Havighurst. *To Live on This Earth: American Indian Education.* Garden City, N.Y.: Anchor, 1972.

Getches, David J., and Charles F. Wilkinson. *Federal Law.* St. Paul: West Publishing, 1986.

Harmer, Ruth Mulvey. "Uprooting the Indians." *Atlantic Monthly* 197 (1956): 54–57.

Hasse, Larry J. "Termination and Assimilation: Federal Indian Policy, 1943–1961." Ph.D. dissertation. Washington State University, 1974.

Henry, Jeanette, and Rupert Costo, eds. *Textbooks and the American Indian.* San Francisco: Indian Historian Press, 1970.

Herzberg, Stephen J. "The Menominee Indians: Termination to Restoration." *American Indian Law Review* 6 (1978).

Holms, Tom. *Strong Hearts, Wounded Souls: Native American Veterans of the Vietnam War.* Austin: University of Texas Press, 1996.

Hood, Susan. "Termination of the Klamath Tribe in Oregon." *Ethnohistory* 19 (1972).

Johnson, Tim. *Spirit Capture: Photographs from the National Museum of the American Indian.* Washington, D.C.: Smithsonian Institution Press with the National Museum of the American Indian, 1998.

LeDuc, Thomas. "The Work of the Indian Claims Commission under the Act of 1946." *Pacific Historical Review* 26 (1957): 1–16.

Lurie, Nancy O. "The Indian Claims Commission Act." *The Annals of the American Academy of Political and Social Science* 311 (1957): 56–70.

Moses, L. G., and Raymond Wilson, eds. *Indian Lives.* Albuquerque: University of New Mexico Press, 1985.

Neils, Elaine. *Reservation to City: Indian Migration and Federal Relocation.* Chicago: University of Chicago, Department of Geography, 1971.

O'Brien, Sharon. *American Indian Tribal Governments.* Norman: University of Oklahoma Press, 1989.

Orfield, Gary. *A Study of the Termination Policy.* Denver: National Congress of American Indians, 1965.

Parman, Donald L. *Indians and the American West in the Twentieth Century.* Bloomington: Indiana University Press, 1994.

Peroff, Nicholas C. *Menominee DRUMS: From Tribal Termination to Restoration, 1953–1973.* Norman: University of Oklahoma Press, 1982.

Rosenthal, Harvey D. "Their Day in Court: A History of the Indian Claims Commission." Ph.D. dissertation. Kent State University, 1976.

Udall, Stewart L. "The State of the Indian Nation–An Introduction." *Arizona Law Review* 10 (1968).

"Ute Indians Hit a $31.7 Million Jackpot." *Life Magazine* 29 (1950): 37–40.

Work, Susan. "The 'Terminated' Five Tribes of Oklahoma: The Effect of Federal Legislation and Administrative Treatment on the Government of the Seminole Nation." *American Indian Law Review* 6 (1977): 81–141.

Yazzie, Ethelou. *Navajo History.* Many Farms, Ariz.: Navajo Community College Press, 1971.

CHAPTER 19

ACTIVISM, ALCATRAZ, AND WOUNDED KNEE

Activism and Native American resistance did not emerge suddenly in the 1960s but rather have been a part of American Indian history since the beginning of time. Native American creation stories encourage human beings to be activist, attempting to do what is right for their communities. Ancient narratives of native people tell of numerous culture heroes who battle enemies of various sorts to protect the people. Throughout Native American history men, women, and children resisted colonization, enslavement, imperialism, and removal. Indian people actively resisted European and American domination and never surrendered their right to fight injustice or address issues that influenced their well-being. The great prophets of native people taught that it was their duty to care for each other and fight collectively against common enemies. The Iroquois Peacemaker urged the people to consider all questions carefully and to make their decisions with foresight because their words and actions would affect future generations.

RECENT NATIVE AMERICAN ACTIVISM

During the nineteenth century, Native Americans made a strong effort to preserve their lands and cultures in the face of American Indian policies designed to expand from shore to shore, isolate Native Americans onto specified lands, concentrate as many tribes as possible onto small parcels of land, and assimilate Indians into white society through removal, reservations, allotment, boarding schools, and other programs. Men and women under the leadership of Red Cloud, Big Bow, Standing Bear, Quanah, Manuelito, Geronimo, Kamiakin, Joseph, Captain Jack, and many others resisted the white invasion and American Indian policies. Sarah Winnemucca, Lozan, Colestah, Bright Eyes, and thousands of other Native American women joined resistance movements and kept their activism alive after the government had placed them on reservations. During the early part of the twentieth century, the same spirit of resistance that had sustained Native Americans since the beginning of time continued to survive throughout Indian country. In many simple but profound ways, Native Americans fought for survival and betterment of their people.

However, because of tribalism and divisions among tribes, Native Americans often had divided voices over important matters. For example, whereas many Indians favored the Indian Reorganization Act and campaigned in favor of it, Muscogee Joseph Bruner heatedly opposed it, labeling it communistic and un-American. Intertribal and intratribal division had always been a part of the Native American experience and continue to influence policies today. Some scholars and politicians have pointed to tribal divisions to criticize Indian people for forming factions. Cahuilla and Luiseño scholar Edward Castillo has been quick to respond that "when whites have political differences, they call it democracy, but when we have differences, they call it factionalism." Native Americans have been extremely democratic and outspoken about differences among and within native nations. This element of native culture has contributed to a disunited voice at times, but it has also encouraged activism for or against numerous issues.

In 1919, a number of Cahuilla and Luiseño Indian activists met at the home of Jonathan Tibbet in Riverside, California, and formed the Mission Indian Federation to challenge federal Indian policies and demand greater control of tribal affairs by Indian people. They were particularly alarmed that the Bureau of Indian Affairs opened Indian lands to non-Indians and permitted non-Indians access to Indian water. Many Cahuilla, Kumeyaay, Luiseño, Serrano, Juaneño, and Gabrielleno people joined the activist movement, including those like Cahuilla scholar Rupert Costo, who demanded the abolition of the Bureau of Indian Affairs and total tribal control of decisions and resources. The Mission Indian Federation proved so effective that the villages of Walpi and Supai in Arizona joined the federation. Native Americans controlled the organization and elected Cahuilla and Luiseño Adan Castillo as president. He served in this post from 1920 to his death in 1953. To voice their disgust of the BIA, members of the Mission Indian Federation published a newsletter entitled *The Indian.*

Over the years the goals of the federation changed, but in general the membership favored abolition of the BIA, tribal control of land and water, law and order, resurveying of reservation boundaries, and self-determination. In the early years, members of the Mission Indian Federation formed their own police force to protect Indian people from harassment at tribal political, cultural, and spiritual events. The bureau was seriously threatened by this police force and arranged to have the Justice Department arrest fifty-seven members of the Mission Indian Federation for "conspiracy against the government." Indians and non-Indians rallied in support of the Mission Indian Federation and convinced the Justice Department to drop the charges. The Mission Indian Federation fought the implementation of the General Allotment Act and Indian Reorganization Act in southern California, arguing that both were attempts by the government to extend its control over Indian people. The federation functioned until 1963, when the leadership split, and the federation totally disbanded in 1967.

The Mission Indian Federation had a lasting effect on Native American history. Tribes in southern California often consider their actions in terms of objectives set forth by members of the federation and attempt to act in a way that would be in conformity with federation goals. Central to the Mission Indian Federation was self-determination, and the words of Adan Castillo published in *The Indian* in 1945 best sum up this sentiment:

> To say that the records of the Indian wardship is disgraceful is an understatement. With rare interludes, it has been disgraceful through administrations. The past is irrevocable. The present and future lie in our hands. The bonds of Indian wardship must be broken forever.

Some tribal leaders of the Mission Indian Federation joined in the national effort to form the National Congress of American Indians (NCAI) in 1944, but others did not because they believed that NCAI was not aggressive enough and did not share the views of the more activist elements of the Mission Indian Federation. Some scholars have characterized NCAI as an activist organization that challenged federal Indian policies such as termination, relocation, and Public Law 280. As historian Gerald Nash has pointed out, several leaders of the NCAI were veterans of World War II or women who had contributed to the war effort in many ways. Lakota Robert Burnette, tribal chair of the Rosebud Reservation, became executive director of NCAI and a vocal opponent of federal Indian policies. Burnette was an activist, to be sure, and he furthered the agenda of NCAI with his outspoken denunciation of the Bureau of Indian Affairs.

Some members of NCAI were Iroquois, but members of the Six Nations did not wait for the lead of the pan-Indian group to address the destruction and desecration of Iroquois lands by the United States. During the 1950s, the federal government planned to dam the Allegheny River in western Pennsylvania and New York on lands belonging to the Seneca and containing a cemetery with over three thousand graves, including that of famed Chief Cornplanter, a friend of George Washington. To the Iroquois, the land was sacred, particularly that part holding the remains and grave goods of their people. Seneca spokesperson Harriet Pierce explained that members of the Haudenosaunee "have a spiritual tie with the earth." She maintained that Six Nations people opposed the destruction of ten thousand acres of their land because Native Americans had "a reverence for it that whites don't share and can hardly understand." In 1958, a federal court ruled against the Seneca and permitted the forced removal of over seven hundred people and exhumation of three thousand graves.

Like the Senecas, Tuscaroras in upstate New York fought to protect over one thousand acres of reservation land from a government dam project. Tuscarora leader Wallace Anderson, commonly called Mad Bear, led the movement against the dam proposal. Mad Bear became one of the foremost leaders of the Indian movement that emerged after World War II and spent his life fighting for the betterment of Native Americans everywhere. In the 1950s, he mobilized opposition after New York offered to compensate the Tuscaroras $3 million. Mad Bear reminded state officials that land could not be sold because the earth is the mother of all humankind. In 1958, men, women, and children blocked surveyors, and they harassed the workers with gunfire and firecrackers. When law enforcement officials tried to intervene, Indians wrestled county and state police to the ground. Mad Bear took his protest to Washington, D.C., where he and over three hundred followers tried to place the secretary of interior under arrest. The protest resulted in an investigation in which a federal commission ruled in 1959 that the government of the United States could not force the Tuscaroras to sell their land for the dam project.

Native Americans throughout the United States and Canada eagerly watched the Tuscaroras and other Iroquois stand against the federal government. Some native people learned valuable lessons about the importance of media attention and direct confrontations with federal officials. During the 1950s and 1960s, various Native Americans spoke at the United Nations, explaining treaty and human rights violations of the United States and Canada to representatives from around the world. Often they wore traditional dress and formally met with delegates, including representatives of the Soviet Union. They also maximized their visits to New York City by staging press conferences to outline their grievances. In spite of criticisms by officials of the U.S. government and suggestions that the government would not be influenced by such tactics, Native Americans gained ground in the court of public opinion because their arguments were sound, resonating within the public a sense of humanity and justice.

In various regions of the United States, Native Americans actively challenged federal and state laws as well as construction projects that severely affected them. In 1953, members of the Cheyenne and Arapaho tribes of Oklahoma protested the draining of Canton Lake, an area in western Oklahoma where the Indians hunted and fished—not simply for recreation but also for food for their families. In 1960, a group of Utes in Utah seceded from the United States, proclaiming itself the True Ute. This new native "nation" used the media to protest the control of tribal mineral wealth and leases to corporations by the Bureau of Indian Affairs rather than Ute people. In Washington state, Wanapum and Palouse Indians protested construction of the Priest Rapids Dam because of the destruction of the rapids and canyon walls surrounding the dam site and the desecration of Indian burial sites throughout the area. Native Americans throughout the Northwest voiced their concern that this dam and others prohibited runs of salmon and steelhead, and these concerns escalated as various states attempted to prevent Indians from fishing at all "usual and accustomed areas" as provided in oral narratives and specified in several treaties.

FISH-INS

For many Native Americans, fishing was, and is, a way of life. Native Americans from the Atlantic Seaboard to the Pacific Ocean and from Alaska to the Gulf of Mexico have fished for a portion of their livelihoods. Native Americans living near the Great Lakes and the streams throughout the United States have fished. Many native people have a spiritual relationship with fish and mammals associated with oceans, bays, rivers, and lakes. This relationship emerged during the time of creation, and knowledge of this relationship was passed down through oral traditions from generation to generation. Among Chinookan, Sahaptian, and Salishan Indians living along the banks of the Columbia River, Coyote became a salmon chief when he broke the fish dam created by five monsters known as Tah Tah Kleah. Coyote led the salmon up the Columbia River and determined which tributaries the salmon would travel, giving those people who were kind to Coyote better access to the fish than those who did not supply him with food and wives.

At the time of creation, the Creator instructed human beings to give thanks for salmon, roots, and berries in communal ceremonies with elaborate songs and rituals. Salmon Ceremonies have been conducted ever since, and Native Americans in the Northwest still give thanks to the Almighty through First Salmon Ceremonies, rituals of communion with the fish and water. The act of fishing and the assertion of fishing rights are more than economic, social, or political. They are also spiritual, part of traditional law that guides Native American people. In 1854 and 1855, Washington Territorial Governor Isaac Stevens and Oregon Superintendent of Indian Affairs Joel Palmer concluded several treaties with native peoples of the Northwest. All these treaties included provisions for native people to continue to fish, gather, and hunt at all usual and accustomed places. As with land, the United States did not "give" Native Americans fishing rights. Rather, Native Americans secured for themselves rights they had been given by the Creator. This point was graphically depicted in an exhibit titled "Remembering Medicine Creek" (1998), curated by Maria Pasqually of the Washington State Historical Society. In part, the exhibit focused on Article III of the treaty: "The right of taking fish at all usual and accustomed grounds and stations is further secured to said Indians in common with all citizens of the Territory."

During treaty negotiations at Medicine Creek and throughout the Northwest, whites and Indians alike understood that Native Americans could always hunt, fish, and gather on and off the reservation. However, the United States ratified these treaties at a time when few whites wanted to fish commercially or for sport. Indians continued their age-old practices of fishing, hunting, and gathering until game and fish officials in various states demanded that Native Americans purchase licenses and take game in season as specified by the states. Native Americans in Oregon, Washington, Idaho, California, Wisconsin, Minnesota, and other states argued that their treaties with the United States superseded state law and that they did not have to follow state regulations. States arrested, convicted, and imprisoned Native Americans for exercising their spiritual, natural, and treaty rights to fish at all usual and accustomed grounds. State law enforcement officials aggressively impounded fishing boats, nets, and other gear as evidence. They prevented Native Americans from procuring food necessary for their spiritual, physical, and mental well-being. They deprived Native Americans of their rights and freedoms.

In 1954, Washington state prosecuted and convicted Puyallup and Yakama fisherman Robert Satiacum for fishing and possessing steelhead with fixed gill nets out of season. Satiacum appealed his case to the Supreme Court, and in 1957, the court dismissed the case in a split decision that left the issue of fishing rights unresolved. Native Americans argued that they had a right to take fish whenever and wherever they wanted. They maintained that they had always fished with gill nets and would continue to do so regardless of state regulations. State law enforcement officials in Washington and Oregon argued that gill nets used by Native Americans were illegal and would damage fish runs and spawning. Native people countered that they had fished for thousands of years with nets and had never harmed the fish runs and that if whites were concerned about the fish runs, whites should stop damming rivers, polluting waterways, and fishing commercially or for sport. Native Americans, they argued, fish for economic and spiritual survival.

In an attempt to exert state power, hunting and fishing authorities in several states, but primarily in the Pacific Northwest and Great Lakes, arrested native men and women, claiming power to regulate fishing under Public Law 280. Native Americans from other parts of the United States and Canada joined the struggle to preserve Indian fishing, hunting, and gathering rights. In the 1950s, many members of NCAI supported fishing rights, and members of the National Indian Youth Council (NIYC), formed in 1961 in Gallup, New Mexico, actively joined in the struggle to fight states opposing native treaty rights in the 1960s. Led by Herbert Blatchford (Navajo), Clyde Warrior (Oklahoma Ponca), Melvin Thom (Nevada Paiute), and Shirley Hill Witt (Akwesasne Mohawk), the NIYC criticized conservative native leaders and NCAI, labeling them Uncle Tomahawks and Apples (red on the outside and white on the inside). These young native leaders formed a bond with tribal elders and fought collectively for Indian rights. In 1963, the Washington Supreme Court ruled in *Washington v. McCoy* that the state had the right to regulate Indian fishing on the basis of conservation. Slade Gorton, now a U.S. senator from Washington state, was attorney general in Washington during the fish-ins, when Indians fished in defiance of state laws in an attempt to assert sovereign tribal and treaty rights. Gorton became a symbol of whites who ignored Indian fishing rights and tried to end or curtail the major livelihood of many northwestern Indians. On a much broader scale, the conservative senator continues to ignore Indian rights and actively seeks to destroy American Indian sovereignty throughout the United States, most particularly in Washington state.

The Makah Tribal Council in Washington responded to the McCoy decision by inviting members of the NIYC to demonstrate in support of Makah tribal fishing rights. Before acting, the NIYC met with tribal elders from forty diverse tribes to seek their advice, and "fish-ins" emerged from these discussions. Native Americans launched fish-ins as acts of civil disobedience, similar to sit-ins among African-Americans. Native and nonnative fishers defied state laws, while hundreds of Indian people lined the rivers of the Northwest to watch state game and fish authorities, arrest those fishing. In 1964, Washington wardens arrested Robert Satiacum again and hundreds of other Indians, as well as nonnative supporters such as Marlon Brando and Dick Gregory. Although native fishers received support from nonnatives, they also watched the rise of renewed racism from political, judicial, and commercial forces in Washington and Oregon. This development is best exemplified by a statement by one prosecutor in Washington: "We had the power and force to exterminate these people from the face of the earth, instead of making treaties with them." He mused that "Perhaps we should have! We certainly wouldn't be having all this trouble with them today."

Before the fish-ins, the branches of the U.S. government generally did not actively support Indian fishing rights as outlined in federal treaties. The executive branch and the president did not become involved either directly or through the Bureau of Indian Affairs. Congress did not pass legislation in support of Indian fishing, hunting, or gathering rights. In 1966, the Justice Department under President Johnson began to support Indian fishing rights and agreed to back the Puyallup people in a case known as *Puyallup Tribe v. Department of Game* (1968). The Supreme Court ruled in favor of Indian fishing rights as outlined in the

Medicine Creek Treaty, but it did not deal with all the questions involved with the fishing issue. However, after this case, the federal courts actively supported native fishing rights in a series of decisions. Most important was a ruling in 1974 by Judge George H. Boldt of the Ninth U.S. District Court, commonly called the Boldt decision. The decision reaffirmed Indian treaty and fishing rights. It upheld the right of Indians to fish at all usual and accustomed areas on and off the reservation and ruled that fishing in common with other citizens meant that Native Americans would be legally entitled to 50 percent of the harvestable catch.

RED POWER AND ALCATRAZ ISLAND

The fish-ins in the Pacific Northwest were part of a larger national movement with many local expressions of "Red Power." National Native American organizations such as the NIYC, NCAI, and National Indian Education Association (NIEA) had members in many parts of Indian country. They helped frame new and assertive agendas that were best expressed by Standing Rock Sioux Vine Deloria Jr. As executive director of the NCAI in 1966, Deloria told an enthusiastic audience at the annual meeting that "Red Power means we want power over our own lives . . . the political and economic power, to run our own lives in our own way." A new spirit stirred Native Americans living on reservations and in urban areas, as larger numbers of them challenged the status quo and demanded improvements in health, housing, education, economic development, funding, and administration of governance. Native Americans of every age group exerted greater self-determination, and tribal governments strengthened their own sovereignty. New national organizations emerged during the 1960s, including the National Council on Indian Opportunity (NCIO) and the National Tribal Chairmen's Association (NTCA), both of which were mainstream organizations.

In every part of the country, Native Americans found ways to express their opinions and make changes in the system. At urban Indian centers and on tribal lands, many people organized to effectuate change and have a voice. In Minneapolis, Anishinaabe activists Dennis Banks, George Mitchell, and brothers Clyde and Vernon Bellecourt joined forces in 1968 to form the American Indian Movement (AIM). Originally established to monitor the treatment of Native Americans by Minneapolis police, AIM became a national organization with many chapters with well-known leaders such as Oglala Lakota Russell Means. However, AIM became a national organization only after Native Americans took over Alcatraz Island in 1969. AIM had many local and national concerns and became the militant arm of the Red Power movement. Often AIM leaders openly criticized tribal chairs and councils for complying with the federal government and not asserting strong self-determination. They urged Native Americans to remember that the letters *BIA* (as in Bureau of Indian Affairs) stood for "Bossing Indians Around" and that Indians must stand united against white dominance, oppression, and racism.

Through AIM or independently, Native Americans across the country became involved in the Red Power movement. In 1968, Mohawk people blockaded the Cornwall International Bridge to protest the fact that Canada had failed to honor Jay's Treaty of 1794 and had assessed members of the Six Nations tolls and duties for using the bridge and bringing goods into Canada from the United States. Under the terms of Jay's Treaty, Iroquois people secured their right of free movement across the border. The blockade and arrest of Indian people served as a catalyst for other movements, including the formation of the White Roots of Peace and North American Indian Traveling College, both of which encouraged native people to learn and teach traditional values, languages, and arts. In 1969, Canada agreed to follow Jay's Treaty, and the same year, the White Roots of Peace visited San Francisco State University at the invitation of Mohawk activist Richard Oakes.

In his classic book, *The Occupation of Alcatraz Island,* historian Troy R. Johnson has shown the relationship between the blockade of the Cornwall Bridge and Indian activism in the San Francisco Bay area. He has demonstrated that Oakes and other young Indians living in the Bay Area were motivated by presentations of Iroquois members of the White Roots of Peace. The mood of these young Indian activists was communicated by activist Lehman Brightman in 1968 through his Bay Area newspaper, *Warpath:*

> The "Stoic, Silent Redman" of the past who turned the other cheek to white injustice is dead. (He died of frustration and heartbreak). And in his place is an angry group of Indians who dare to speak and voice their dissatisfaction at the world around them. Hate and despair have taken their toll and only action can quiet his smoldering anger that has fused this new Indian movement into being.

Johnson illustrates how this new attitude among numerous native people influenced the course of Indian activism in the Bay Area in comparison to the first Native American takeover of Alcatraz Island in 1964. The importance of the second takeover of Alcatraz is remarkable given the few years between the two occupations. The second landing was significant to Native American history. It was in 1969, an era of protest movements across the United States, that native history took a new turn toward pan-Indian activism.

In the early morning of November 20, 1969, eighty-nine Native Americans from many tribal backgrounds landed on Alcatraz Island in San Francisco Bay. By right of discovery they claimed the island. The

"Indians of All Tribes" offered a Proclamation to the Great White Father and All His People, stating that they reclaimed "the land known as Alcatraz Island in the name of all American Indians." With tongue in cheek, participants in the takeover offered to purchase Alcatraz for $24 in glass beads and red cloth, the amount paid for Manhattan Island. Young students taking the island offered to hold a portion of the land for whites "in trust by the American Indian Government—for as long as the sun shall rise and the rivers go down to the sea." The land was to be administered by the Bureau of Caucasian Affairs (BCA), and the Indian government offered to help whites "achieve our level of civilization" so that the Native Americans could raise "their white brothers up from their savage and unhappy state." They pointed out that Alcatraz was an appropriate site for an Indian reservation because it was isolated, had no fresh water source, no sanitation, no minerals or industry, no employment, no educational facilities, and no productive soil. Because the former residents on Alcatraz were held as prisoners, the island certainly qualified as an appropriate site for a reservation.

John Trudell, LaNada Boyer, Richard Oakes, Dorothy Lone Wolf Miller, Edward Castillo, Adam Nordwall (Fortunate Eagle), Grace Thorpe, Earl Livermore, Wilma Mankiller, Darryl Wilson, Dennis Hastings, Lanada Means, Stella Leach, and many other Native Americans lived on Alcatraz during the eighteen-month occupation. These individuals inaugurated the new Indian movement, which took an activist stand against federal Indian policies, racism, and hatred. As Troy Johnson has pointed out, "the general public who follow Indian issues frequently and incorrectly credit this new Indian activism to the American Indian Movement," but, he explains, only "after visiting the Indians on Alcatraz Island and realizing the possibilities available through demonstration and seizure of federal facilities did AIM actually enter into the national activist role." Thus, he argues that "It was on Alcatraz . . . that the flint first met the steel and young Indian college students stood toe to toe with the federal government for nineteen months and did not bend" until June 11, 1971, when FBI agents and U.S. marshals heavily armed with handguns, shotguns, and rifles removed six men, four women, and five children from Alcatraz Island, ending the occupation.

Native Americans who occupied Alcatraz stated that they wanted a cultural center built there to preserve native religion, languages, material culture, and ecology. They did not achieve this goal, but they succeeded in focusing national attention on American Indian issues and served as a catalyst for the new activism, self-determination, and change that has characterized Native American history since 1969. They triggered a pan-Indian movement in many areas of the United States, Canada, and Mexico that brought together native people from diverse backgrounds and experiences. As Choctaw scholar Michelene Pesantubbee has argued, "Indian people were aware of, and in some cases, a part of the protest movements of the 1960s and 1970s," but most "Indians were actually engaged in a separate, but parallel protest." She maintains that Native Americans "on Alcatraz were trying to publicize the economic and social plight of Indian people." The Indian movement was part of the larger civil rights movement, but separate from it because of the unique historical and legal relationship native peoples had with the United States.

BROKEN TREATIES AND WOUNDED KNEE

This unique relationship between Native Americans and the United States was noted in two critical studies of the Bureau of Indian Affairs: historian Alvin Josephy Jr.'s national study, *The American Indian and the Bureau of Indian Affairs, 1969: A Study with Recommendations,* and Edgar S. Cahn's *Our Brother's Keeper: The Indian in White America.* Both are critical of the federal government for its handling of Indian affairs, specifically lack of housing, high unemployment, high disease and death rates among Indian populations, termination, relocation, and the absence of quality education among Indians. More emotionally charged were Vine Deloria Jr.'s *Custer Died for Your Sins* and Dee Brown's *Bury My Heart at Wounded Knee.* Both books were timely. Although Brown's book was a best-seller and made millions of dollars, Deloria's book became an immediate classic among Native Americans who could relate to Deloria's humor, satire, and accusations against bureaucrats, anthropologists, and professional politicians who knew little or nothing about Native Americans.

These studies stirred a response among native people, but the Indian occupation of Alcatraz sparked Native American takeovers of and demonstrations at several federal facilities. Native American activists took over a communications base near Davis, California, that became D-Q University (a community college for Native American and Chicano students), Fort Lawton and Fort Lewis in Washington, a lighthouse on the shores of Lake Superior, Lassen National Park in California, Plymouth Rock and *Mayflower II* in Massachusetts, Mount Rushmore in South Dakota, offices of the Bureau of Indian Affairs, and many others. In the Pacific Northwest, fish-ins grew violent after Tulalip Janet McCloud led sixty Indians on a protest march to a federal court building. In January 1971, two white sports fishermen walked up to Assiniboine and Sioux activist Hank Adams, stuck a rifle to his stomach, and fired. Adams survived and participated in the "Trail of Broken Treaties," bringing with him a fifteen-point plan to change federal Indian policy that served as the basis of the twenty demands offered by AIM in Washington, D.C., in November 1972.

Many native protests linked young native people to tribal elders and medicine people. Together, they forged cultural and spiritual revitalization movements that emphasized strength through unity with each other and with tribal traditions that tied humans to place, plants, animals, rocks, rivers, mountains, and other holy places. In one meeting between activists and elders, Robert Burnette explained his idea of gathering hundreds of Indians on the Trail of Broken Treaties, and soon Vernon Bellecourt organized the march. Many Native American protesters learned about the Trail of Broken Treaties through telephone, radio, television, and other native voices such as *Wassaja, Akwesasne Notes, Newsletter of the American Indian Movement,* and *Indians of All Tribes Newspaper.* On November 3, 1972, over five hundred Indian activists arrived in Washington, D.C., and assembled in the auditorium at the Bureau of Indian Affairs Building. Lower-level bureaucrats but not the commissioner or secretary of interior agreed to meet with the people. Activists had no housing, so when guards attempted to force them from the building, they barricaded themselves in the BIA building and occupied it.

Discrimination and abuse against Native Americans did not end in the nineteenth century with the conclusion of the Indian wars, but rather negative stereotypes and segregation continued well into the twentieth century. In 1973, the American Indian Movement (AIM) took over Wounded Knee, South Dakota, and took a strong stand against the United States and even a few tribal officials.

For five days activists held the building, receiving food, supplies, and support from sympathizers who included Stokley Carmichael and Benjamin Spock. Several members of AIM were in the building, including the Bellecourts, Hank Adams, Russell Means, Mad Bear Anderson, and Dennis Banks. All the participants knew that federal law enforcement might break through their barricades at any moment and end the occupation in violence. According to Robert Burnette, on November 6 tensions ran so high that some of Indian protesters "ran amok with clubs and hammers, smashing windows, shattering toilet bowls, and ripping files of records to shreds." Something snapped among the native protesters, perhaps the blood memory of generations of frustrations in dealing with the bureau. In any case, within minutes, "the BIA central office was littered with paper and chunks of broken furniture." The next day protesters and federal officials negotiated a tentative agreement, in which the government promised to consider twenty demands made by the protesters and provide $66,500 for transportation costs of the people back to their homes. The occupation ended on November 8, 1972, but the Red Power movement continued.

Protesters from the Trail of Broken Treaties had demanded that the government reestablish treaty relations or nation-to-nation relationships with the tribes. A special task force that was formed to investigate the twenty demands of the protesters rejected such an idea. Indeed, the task force rejected every demand of the protesters, which, of course, outraged native activists everywhere. Meanwhile, protests continued in several parts of the country, and shortly after the task force issued its findings, a white man murdered a Lakota Indian named Wesley Bad Heart Bull in Buffalo Gap, South Dakota. White authorities charged the suspected murderer with second-degree manslaughter, not first-degree murder, and national focus shifted to the Great Plains, where AIM mounted a demonstration on February 6, 1973, at the Custer County Courthouse. Violence erupted between local police and Indians, and the demonstration spread to Rapid City. In Custer City and Rapid City, Indians and police fought street battles that ended in several arrests and injuries. National media covered the skirmishes. The nightly news offered stark footage of burning buildings, fistfights, baton-wielding police, and rock-throwing demonstrators.

Traditionalists on the Pine Ridge Reservation (Sioux) urged the protesters to confer with them about problems on the reservation. Several traditionalists believed that tribal chair Richard Wilson was corrupt and that he did not represent their interests or those of Sioux people. They wanted him out of office, and they wanted a new form of government created by the people—not the Bureau of Indian Affairs—that returned power to the people. In *American Indian Activism*, three noted scholars of Native American studies have put it succinctly: "Wilson was viewed as a corrupt puppet of the BIA by some segments of the tribe, including those associated with AIM."

Sioux traditionalists suggested that the protesters take their stand against injustice at the little reservation town of Wounded Knee, where the U.S. Seventh Cavalry had murdered men, women, and children in 1890 and buried them in a common grave on the site.

The conflict began between divisions on Pine Ridge long before Russell Means and Dennis Banks led 250 AIM supporters onto the reservation. But the arrival of activists became the immediate cause of hostilities between AIM and Wilson. Of course, Wilson, his supporters, and the BIA found the proposal to establish a new tribal government at Pine Ridge to be preposterous and revolutionary. Wilson had created a "goon squad" to protect him and to attack his opponents physically. On February 26, 1973, the goons attacked Russell Means, and the next day two hundred protesters took over the town of Wounded Knee. Armed with rifles, shotguns, and dynamite, Indian activists held Wounded Knee against FBI agents and U.S. marshals armed with machine guns, M-16s, armored personnel carriers, and other sophisticated weapons. The standoff was characterized by gunfights, roadblocks, demonstrations, negotiations, and visitations. Native Americans moved fairly easily in and out of Wounded Knee, bringing supplies and ammunition to the protesters.

On March 11, Native Americans participating at Wounded Knee proclaimed the new Oglala Nation, a nation totally independent of the United States, the Bureau of Indian Affairs, and Chairman Wilson. They planned to send representatives directly to the United Nations and swear in new citizens of the native nation. Protesters at Wounded Knee pointed out that their movement was far more than political, however. It had a spiritual core. Three years after the takeover at Wounded Knee, two Lakota participants discussed the religious dimensions of the protest at a seminar at Diné College. They argued that every native person who participated at Wounded Knee was fundamentally touched by a spiritual revitalization movement that was at the center of the movement. They explained the importance of the sweat lodge and pipe ceremony as well as their strong connection with traditional Lakota elders and medicine people. They maintained that the spiritual element of Wounded Knee affected people who were neither Lakota nor from the Great Plains because they prayed and worshipped in their own ways.

Leonard Garment represented President Richard Nixon during the negotiations at Wounded Knee. He had negotiated with native protesters during the takeover of the BIA Building, and in May 1973, he arranged an end to the deadly standoff at Wounded Knee. Federal agents had killed two Native Americans, Frank Clearwater and Lawrence Lamont. And one federal agent was shot and paralyzed. According to the negotiated agreement, Native Americans agreed to disarm and leave. Those who had warrants against them agreed to surrender voluntarily. The United States promised to investigate the administration of Richard Wilson and to discuss the implications of the Fort Laramie Treaty of 1868 with Lakota people. When federal agents moved into Wounded Knee, they found 129 participants left at the site. Nevertheless, the government managed to arrest 238 Indians who allegedly participated in the Wounded Knee protest. Although government officials faithfully met traditional Lakotas at the home of Frank Fools Crow on May 17, 1973, the meeting amounted to nothing when Garment informed the protesters by letter that "treaty making with the American Indians ended in 1871, 102 years ago." And federal accountants assigned to investigate corruption of Chairman Wilson found financial records in such disarray that they claimed they could discover no wrongdoing.

Another incident occurred at Pine Ridge Reservation in 1975, when FBI agents exchanged gunfire with AIM members. During the firefight, Joe Killsright and FBI agents Jack Coler and Ronald Williams were killed. Government agents arrested four AIM members but tried only Leonard Peltier for murder. He fled to Canada but was arrested and returned to Fargo, North Dakota, where a jury convicted him of murdering the two FBI agents. He received two consecutive life sentences and is serving time in a high-security prison in Marion, Illinois. Many Native Americans and people outside the United States consider Peltier a political prisoner. Many people feel that the government singled out Peltier for punishment and believed they had their best chance of convicting him over the others. Although federal agents admitted making initial false reports about the shooting, Peltier was convicted. Writer Peter Matthiessen has uncovered evidence, which he has presented in *Nation,* that casts doubt on Peltier's participation in the shootings and may clear Peltier. However, the government remains unwilling to reconsider its case against the AIM leader.

Although the imprisonment of Leonard Peltier was a setback for the Red Power movement, Native Americans across the United States continued the struggle for self-determination and tribal sovereignty. In July 1978, Native Americans marched on Washington, D.C. This was the culmination of the Longest Walk, a protest march against federal Indian policies that began in February. From San Francisco, native protesters had walked to the nation's capital to remind the world that the United States had forced Native Americans off their lands and onto confined areas throughout American history. The Longest Walk also occurred in reaction to the negative backlash against Native Americans that had emerged in local, state, and national government. Two congressmen from Washington had submitted in the House the "Indian Equal Opportunity Act," a bill that would have abrogated all federal treaties. Conservative members of the House and Senate floated such bills to appease white constituents who wanted to end the Red Power movement and gain access to resources.

The Indian movement encouraged Seneca, Juaneño, Chemehuevi, Coeur d'Alene, Spokane, San Carlos Apache, Paiute, Shoshoni, Luiseño,

Chumash, and many other tribes to push their own tribal agendas. A major controversy arose in the early 1970s when the federal government proposed to build a road through the Siskiyou Mountains of northern California in an area containing native sites such as burial grounds and sacred places. The Gasquet-Orleans Road (G-O Road) became a rallying point for Indians in northern California, including Yuroks, Karuks, Tolowas, Hupas, Pit Rivers, Wintus, Miwoks, and Pomos. Using the California Wilderness Act of 1980 and evidence provided by the Forest Service, Native Americans won a federal court injunction in 1983 halting construction. However, in 1988, the U.S. Supreme Court overruled the injunction, with Sandra Day O'Connor writing the majority opinion. The ruling was a setback for all Native Americans who wished to protect sacred sites and remains of their ancestors. The case flew in the face of the American Indian Religious Freedom Act of 1978, which guaranteed the right of native people to practice their traditional religions and protect holy places. However, most law enforcement agencies—local, state, and federal—did not enforce the law or understand the issue of sacred rights guaranteed by traditional native law.

In spite of such setbacks Native American affairs after Alcatraz changed forever. Indians initiated their own agendas and effectuated their own change, often challenging the government. A'Ani historian George Horse Capture has stated that the Indian landing on Alcatraz Island was like the landing of marines on the Pacific islands during World War II. The marines were simply the first wave, just as the Indians on Alcatraz were the first wave. After Native Americans had secured a beachhead on Alcatraz, there was no stopping them. From that day forward they asserted renewed self-determination and tribal sovereignty. Horse Capture summed up the significance of the first Red Power movement, and his words offer a means of understanding the importance of the movement. "It suddenly occurred to me that this was a key point in Indian history. No matter what happened, the Indian world would never be the same after this. Indian people were declaring their independence, challenging the status quo, taking chances, being committed, being warriors; none of these things is new to our race," Horse Capture wrote in 1994, "but they have been absent of late, or forgotten."

The trail from Alcatraz to the Longest Walk and beyond led to a new era in Native American history, one that has been characterized by assertive self-determination and the demand for tribal sovereignty. The lessons learned from this era have permeated Indian country from 1969 to the present and have influenced every Indian person. The Red Power movement launched a new era in the 1970s and 1980s, when tribes applied to the BIA to regain federal recognition. It ignited a new pride in native history, music, literature, religion, and rights. By 1995, the United States had recognized 550 tribes, including two hundred village groups in Alaska. But this was just the beginning of many manifestations of self-determination that emerged among Indian tribes. To solidify political gains made during the 1970s, many tribes concentrated on economic development during the decade and beyond, believing that economic well-being would lead to tribal sovereignty in cultural, educational, health, and social matters.

SELF-DETERMINATION

In spite of the backlash against the civil rights movement in general and the Red Power movement in particular, Native Americans asserted their self-determination with persistence and confidence. Tribes throughout the United States consolidated power within their tribal governments and hired experts to help them develop economically, educationally, culturally, linguistically, and politically. Several tribal leaders understood that the future of their people depended on political and economic power to control their own destiny. Author Robert H. White has discussed the various ways in which tribes have asserted their economic self-determination in *Tribal Assets: The Rebirth of Native America.* He describes several tribal projects throughout the West, where tribes have taken control of their natural resources to better the economic, social, and cultural conditions of people. He demonstrates that economic development has not solved poverty and unemployment on the reservations, but it has provided native people with cash, confidence, and opportunities.

On the Yakama Reservation, the tribe demanded and received control of its forests along the eastern slopes of its sacred mountain, Pahto (Mount Adams). This is the largest commercial forest on Indian lands in the United States, and the Yakama Nation has managed its forests so that they produce 90 percent of tribal income on the reservation. The Yakama started a furniture manufacturing company and invested heavily in agriculture through the extensive Wapato Project, which diverted water to 150,000 acres. Like other tribes, the Yakama invested in banking, livestock, and fishing. They established Camp Chaparral on their reservation, a summer academy for Yakama students. They have also established Heritage College, a four-year liberal arts college, and the Stanley Smartlowit Education Center, led by Dr. Martha B. Yallup, the first Yakama person to earn a Ph.D. The Yakama Nation Cultural Center in Toppenish, Washington, includes a restaurant, gift shop, tribal library, theater, and museum. The cultural center is much like the heart of the reservation, preserving the language and values of the people.

During the late 1970s and early 1980s, the Confederated Tribes of the Colville Reservation offered an extensive cultural program in tribal art, dance, story, and history, through funds provided by Johnson O'Malley. In addition, the people at Colville demanded that teachers dealing daily with Native American children must be grounded in native history and culture. In terms of economic development, Colville negotiated the lease of land for a massive molybdenum mine, which operated for a short time before closing. However, the tribe took control of its forests and has initiated reforestation and constructed a state-of-the-art sawmill. Like other tribes in the Northwest, the people of Colville have also taken control of their fishing and hunting resources. In like fashion, Quinaults, Chinooks, Makahs, Klallams, and native people of Puget Sound took control of their fishing rights, developing companies, cooperatives, and hatcheries that helped maintain the fish and provide employment for native fishers.

The Muckleshoot of western Washington had taken a lead role in the fish-ins and determined that fishing was their life and their economic future. In 1976, the Muckleshoot began the Keta Creek Rearing Station on Green River. The salmon hatchery succeeded and grew sufficiently that in 1981, the Muckleshoot expanded their hatchery so they could manage approximately fifty thousand fish at one time. As a result of expansion, the Muckleshoot raise chinook, coho, and chum salmon as well as steelhead, golden, and eastern trout. The tribe releases the fish back into the rivers and donates the trout for distribution to lakes and streams throughout King County. Muckleshoot Enterprises also includes the White River Hatchery, which supported 650,000 springer salmon in 1993. It also supports an Indian "smoke shop," which includes a liquor and convenience store. In 1985, the Muckleshoot started their own bingo hall, which held nearly fifteen hundred people, and planned a full-scale casino. In spite of many advances, the Muckleshoot reported an unemployment rate of 75 percent in 1993, a problem that still plagues reservations.

Among the Blackfeet, the unemployment rate in the 1980s was 50 to 55 percent, in large part because of the lack of employment on or near the Blackfeet Reservation. Over the years the Blackfeet started a sawmill and the American Calendar Company, but both enterprises failed. However, the tribe's Blackfeet Writing Company, which makes pencils and pens, has been a success. Most of the tribe's income is derived from leasing lands for grazing, oil, and gas. Significantly, the Blackfeet have established the Blackfeet National Bank in Browning, Montana, an enterprise that has expanded small business opportunities to tribal people. In the 1980s, several Blackfeet contributed to an unusual revitalization project when they helped produce a unique book, *The Reservation Blackfeet*. The book began as a classroom project for students in Browning, Montana, who were studying American history. Rather than study history simply from a textbook, students brought in photographs from family albums for an exhibit based on the images. Students also helped create one of the finest representations of Native Americans through a photo-based book published by the University of Washington Press.

The Northern Cheyenne Reservation has determined to limit its economic development as a strategy to maintain culture. Although 53 percent of the people living on the Northern Cheyenne Reservation were unemployed in 1988, the tribe determined not to mine twenty-three billion tons of coal located on the reservation because to dig in the earth would be contrary to the cultural and spiritual values of Tse-tsehes-staestse Cheyenne people. In addition, the Cheyenne stopped construction of a coal-fired power plant on their reservation with the help of the Council of Energy Resource Tribes (CERT). The tribe was convinced that the plant would harm the air and earth, violating the sacred relationship of the people to their environment. However, tribal members have taken jobs with the Montana Power Company, Western Energy Company, Betchel Power Company, Morning Star Construction, the Forestry Division of the BIA, and the federal government. The Northern Cheyenne tribe also hires a number of people. This is also the case for the Cheyenne and Arapaho tribes of Oklahoma, which also suffers from high unemployment, with an average annual income on the reservation in 1990 of approximately $3,000. The tribe is involved in ranching, wheat farming, and oil and gas leasing. Both tribes have decided for themselves which forms of economic development they wish to pursue. They will continue to make their own decisions in the future.

Anishinaabe people live throughout the Northern Plains and Great Lakes, from Montana to Michigan. Many of the leaders of the activist movements of the 1960s and 1970s were Anishinaabe, and they certainly have exerted considerable self-determination. But even before the new Indian movement began in 1969, Anishinaabe people pushed their own forms of self-determination. In fact, as early as 1929 the people of the Red Lake Reservation in northern Minnesota established the Red Lake Fisheries Association, a cooperative for Red Lake's fishermen to market fish. In similar fashion, the people on the White Earth Reservation established Manitok Incorporated, which is a company that processes wild rice and other natural products. In recent years, many Anishinaabe communities and reservations have turned to gaming as the "new buffalo." Some of the casinos include the Shooting Star at White Earth, Fortune Bay at Bois Forte, and High Stakes Bingo and Grand Portage Casino at Grand Portage, all in Minnesota. Anishinaabe people are using resources generated from gaming to stimulate other investments that will have a positive, long-term effect on tribal communities.

In the Southwest, Quechan and Cocopa people have begun to prosper because of gaming. For years the two Yuman-speaking peoples suffered severe deprivation because the government isolated them onto small parcels of land and refused to recognize tribal water rights. At one time, Quechan farmers cultivated the shores of the Colorado for miles, while Cocopas practiced similar agriculture along the shores of the same river in present-day Mexico. However, dams on the Colorado River and urban irrigation water projects of the Bureau of Reclamation ruined native agriculture by diverting water. As a result, Indian agriculture declined dramatically, and death rates from disease and malnutrition soared. The government denied water to Quechans and, after 1907, the Cocopas. Their economies became wage labor and the sale of dolls, pottery, bows, arrows, rattles, and bead work to tourists on Highway 80 and the Southern Pacific Railroad. Since the 1980s, the tribes have developed high-stakes casinos and have attracted thousands of winter visitors who come to the desert Southwest. Quechans and Cocopas now determine for themselves which forms of development they want and have invested in health, education, and business investments for the future.

Chemehuevi, Kumeyaay, Luiseño, and Cahuilla-Serrano Indians of southern California have also invested in gaming. Casinos on the Twenty-Nine Palms, Sycuan, Barona, Viejas, Pechanga, San Manuel, Morongo, Agua Caliente, Cabazon, and other reservations have significantly improved the economic well-being of tribal members. Moreover, casinos have been a boon to the local economies of Alpine, El Cajon, Coachella, Temecula, San Bernardino, Indio, Beaumont, Banning, and many other California communities. Before these reservations had casinos, they depended heavily on government assistance, ranching, farming, and wage labor. The various Luiseño reservations at Pauma, Pala, Rincon, La Jolla, and others also had a long-standing lawsuit against the government and city of Escondido for taking Indian water. According to tribal elder Henry Rodriquez, the Indians thought they had settled the San Luis Rey water case out of court in 1985 for a cash settlement and a promise of sixteen thousand acre-feet of water. In 1993, the government had yet to deliver even one acre-foot of the promised water, and by 1999 the water case had not been settled. The issue of water is also of utmost importance to the Mojave, Chemehuevi, Hopi, and Navajo living along the Colorado River. Indians and non-Indians farm ninety thousand acres on the Colorado River Indian Reservation and depend on water to cultivate cotton, alfalfa, wheat, lettuce, melons, and other crops. The tribe owns a cotton gin, hardware store, and recycling plant. It plans to build the Moovalya Plaza Shopping Center.

Choctaws in Oklahoma own a cattle ranch of nearly three thousand acres and boast light industry, including the Choctaw Finishing Company, which is associated with Texas Instruments. The tribe also owns the Choctaw Travel Center and invests in other enterprises. However, gaming has substantially changed the tribe, allowing members of the Choctaw Nation to determine how to invest its new resources. Those Choctaws who remained in Mississippi have developed diverse enterprises, but not gaming. Under the skilled leadership of Phillip Martin, the Mississippi Band of Choctaw Tribal Council has entered into a number of tribal enterprises that have flourished. In 1969, the tribal council established the Chahta Development Company, a private stock company directed by an unpaid Choctaw board. Chahta reinvests its profits into the company so that the company may initiate more projects and employ more Choctaw people. Chahta initiated construction of a number of projects, including an industrial park. The company also started the Chahta Wire Harness Enterprise, Choctaw Electronics Enterprise, and the Choctaw Greetings Enterprise. This is a thriving, growing tribal enterprise that has significantly changed the lives of Choctaw people in Mississippi.

During the 1970s, Shoshoni people of the Rocky Mountains and Great Basin furthered their self-determination in many ways. Eastern Shoshonis of Wind River, Wyoming, insisted that the administration of the Wyoming Indian High School begin teaching the Shoshonian language as part of its curriculum. Furthermore, they established a Tribal Cultural Center and began offering adult education classes. Shoshonis at Wind River set up a curriculum at their cultural center, including dancing, drumming, and singing. Shoshoni-Bannocks living on the Fort Hall Reservation in Idaho made a study of their own development interests and established a trading post in 1978. It was so successful that the tribe expanded the enterprise to include the Clothes Horse, Teepee Gass and Diesel Filling Station, and Oregon Trail Restaurant. Soon the tourist and truck trade became so important that the tribe constructed the Bannock Peak Truck Stop and Convenience Store on the reservation. With the proceeds from their tribal enterprises, the Shoshoni-Bannock built a tribal museum and steel fabrication business. They used some profits to establish high-stakes bingo in 1991 but have fought the state ever since about gaming on the reservation.

Western Shoshonis of eastern California and western Nevada established several smoke shops during the 1970s. The Shoshonis at Battle Mountain built a convenience store to supplement money earned by individuals from ranching. Shoshonis living on the Duckwater Reservation started a catfish farm, whereas those at the Duck Valley Reservation started a tribal farm. In addition to these elements of economic self-determination, Shoshonis living throughout the West participated in protests against exploitation of tribal lands and resources by non-Indians, particularly the federal government, miners, and white ranchers eager to take what was left of the Shoshoni estate, a vast region that once encompassed millions of acres. Much of this history has been chronicled in Shoshoni professor Steven Crum's *The Road on Which We Came*. The last chapter of this book details the history of western Shoshoni people from 1960 to 1990 and graphically illustrates the power of Shoshoni people to decide for themselves their own destinies through direct and legal action. Professor Crum's book is itself a product of native self-determination by a western Shoshoni person.

Shoshoni and Paiute people of eastern California and western Nevada have both fought against the diversion of water from their traditional homelands. The Newlands Reclamation Project had diverted water from the Truckee River flowing from the Sierra Nevada Mountains. The Newlands project took thousands of acre-feet of water from this vital artery in the arid lands of western Nevada and prevented the Truckee River from feeding Pyramid Lake with the amount of water the lake once enjoyed. As a result, the water level and fish population in Pyramid Lake declined. Paiutes fought the Newlands project through federal courts and after years of litigation won the case in 1981, forcing the "reclamation" project to allow sufficient water from the Truckee River to flow into Pyramid Lake to maintain the lake and its fish. Paiutes also filed a lawsuit to maintain the waters of Walker Lake in Nevada because of the diversion of water flowing into the lake. Paiutes have a spiritual relationship to both lakes, and they have aggressively fought to preserve the natural balance between humans and the environment.

The sacred connection between tribes and their environment is a constant theme in Native American history as Indians assert their self-determination not simply to provide economic benefits but also to protect cultural resources and values. The Passamaquoddies and Penobscots of Maine used an award of $80 million for the theft of their lands by New York to purchase a blueberry farm, cement factory, and other businesses that have economically revitalized the people. Wasco, Warm Springs, and Paiute people on the Warm Springs Reservation of Oregon have combined their energies to develop economically and simultaneously protect the environment. This confederated tribe has established its own forest products industry, a hydroelectric plant, clothing plant, and Nike shoe factory. The tribe is best known for its full-service resort hotel, Kah-Nee-Ta Lodge, which features a four-star restaurant, shops, fishing, horseback riding, swimming pool, golf course, and casino gaming. Kah-Nee-Ta is located high on a steep ridge overlooking the Warm Springs River and a huge expanse of the Columbia Plateau. West of the lodge, the Cascade Mountains rise up, creating a powerful natural scene. Tourism has increased on the Warm Springs Reservation and others, including the Mescalero Apache Reservation of New Mexico.

To encourage tourism, Mescalero Apaches built the Inn of the Mountain Gods, a beautiful resort hotel located on the reservation in the Sacramento Mountains. The Hopi tribe built a smaller hotel at Second Mesa, Arizona, but it offers an excellent restaurant and museum as well as gift shops displaying jewelry, kachinas, pottery, and paintings by Hopi artists. West of the Hopis, the Hualapais living on the western edge of the Coconino Plateau established their own gift shop and hotel on Old Route 66 in Peach Springs, and tribal members serve as big-game guides for non-Indians interested in hunting deer, antelope, and bighorn sheep along the southwestern end of the Grand Canyon. To the east of Hualapais and Hopis are the autonomous Pueblo peoples of New Mexico. Several of the tribes have developed tourism, including San Juan, San Ildefonso, and Taos. Acoma, Laguna, and Zuni, as well as other Pueblo communities, have developed tourism through walking tours, gift shops, camping, and fees for visitors and cameras. White Mountain Apaches have developed a ski resort, whereas Swinomish of Washington have developed a large marina. The Lummi Nation of Washington has a successful fish hatchery and contributes to the economic well-being of the people while maintaining fish runs. Many Alaskan natives have created the Alaska Native Tourism Council to regulate and maximize tourism among Inuit, Aleuts, and American Indians.

Tourism is one of many enterprises initiated by the Navajo Nation, the largest tribe in the United States, numbering approximately 150,000 and ever increasing. Navajos have developed tourism based on the magnificence of the deserts, mountains, and canyons of Dinétah. Canyon de Chelly, Monument Valley, Chuska Mountains, San Juan River, Little Colorado River, Grand Canyon, Sheep Springs, Shiprock, Window Rock, Fort Defiance Mesa, Blue Canyon, Tsaile Butte, Black Mesa, and Wheatfield Lake are just a few of the locations on the reservation that attract thousands of tourists each year. Tourists also visit the reservation to purchase rugs and jewelry made by artists from every corner of Dinétah or to attend the annual Navajo Tribal Fair, which attracts over one hundred thousand visitors each year. The Navajo economy is enriched by tourism, but problems have been caused on the Navajo Reservation and other reservations by nonnative tourists who take photographs and recordings of people and ceremonies, appropriating that which is native without permission.

The Navajo Nation has also expanded its self-determination by taking greater control of natural resources, including coal, gas, oil, timber, and uranium. The U.S. government had removed the people from their homes following the Navajo War of 1864, in part to exploit gold and silver believed to exist in Dinétah. White miners found no veins of gold or silver and failed to recognize the potential of coal, oil, and uranium. These minerals have provided Navajo and Hopi people with both resources and problems. Some Navajo and Hopi favor exploitation of minerals, whereas others insist that mining desecrates the earth and ruins water. Indeed, Peabody Coal Company's 270-mile coal and water slurry line from northern Arizona to southern Nevada threatened the water supply among Hopis and Navajos, leading "traditionalists" who ranched and farmed to protest mineral development. Air and water pollution continues to plague both tribes, but elements of both continue to wrestle with the tension between economic development and preservation.

In order to take greater control of mineral resources, former Navajo tribal Chair Peter McDonald, Comanche activist LaDonna Harris, and Osage leader Charles Lohah formed the Council for Energy Resource

Tribes (CERT) in 1975. In a fine scholarly work, historian Marjane Ambler has detailed the relationship of native people to mineral development in *Breaking the Iron Bonds: Indian Control of Energy Development.* The book details the birth and work of CERT and describes how CERT has been an advocate for the tribes. To enhance its bargaining position, CERT has met with the international oil cartel, OPEC. CERT has stood by the tribes as they deal and renegotiate with Standard Oil, Exxon, Shell, Gulf, Peabody Coal, and other international mineral companies. However, CERT has not been able to settle a major land dispute between Navajos and Hopis over a "joint use" area set aside by the government for Hopis and other Indians and containing millions of tons of coal and other mineral wealth.

But the struggle between Navajos and Hopis over the joint use land area is far more than economic, because it concerns strong spiritual beliefs of Hopis and Navajos who recognize several places in the region as sacred. In addition, generations of Navajos have lived in and were buried in the area. When the federal government attempted to remove them from their homes in the 1970s and 1980s, the people resisted with all the force they could muster, short of war. Some scholars point out that the government and Peabody Coal Company have conspired to pit one tribe against the other so that nonnatives can exploit the resources while the Indians fight with one another. Certainly both the government and the coal company helped create the conflict between the two tribes by dictating unsound Indian policies in the past and, indeed, simply by establishing a mining company bent on extracting as much mineral wealth from the earth as possible while maximizing profits for executives and stockholders.

From the Navajo-Hopi Land Settlement Act of 1974 to the present, Navajos and Hopis have demonstrated their dedication to self-determination, but their stance on the joint use land area has not been solved. As of 1998, approximately 250 Navajo families remain in the area, defying orders to remove. The land, water, and minerals involved in the joint use land area also played a role in the unraveling of a political career. Some Navajo and non-Navajo people had accused Navajo Chairman Peter McDonald of corruption during the 1970s; but in 1989, the Navajo Nation accused him of bribery, conspiracy, and ethical violations. In 1990, a Navajo tribal court convicted McDonald on forty criminal counts and sentenced him to over five years in prison. In 1992, a federal court found McDonald guilty on sixteen additional counts. McDonald's conviction was a setback for tribes everywhere, because some non-Indians asserted that McDonald's record mirrored that of other tribal leaders. However, his conviction did not end self-determination, as tribes continue to assert their sovereignty. During the late 1990s, the application of self-determination was best represented by the tribal fight to offer and keep gaming on reservations.

INDIAN GAMING

Gaming among Native Americans is as old as native creation. Traditional tribal narratives tell of gaming among Animal People–because there are risks involved in doing anything in this life–long before human beings arrived on the earth. The ancients understood this and told stories about guessing games that resulted in certain types of weather, the roles of males and females, the question of life or death, and whether the earth would have perpetual day or perpetual night. In a Navajo story, animals of the night argued with animals of the day, saying that they should change the law and have no day, only night. The Animal People played a moccasin game to determine which it would be, day or night. They played all night, with one side hiding a small rock in one of four moccasins as the other side guessed which moccasin had the rock, until the night animals had scored all the points except one. Fearing they might lose, the day animals sent for Magpie, who was on his honeymoon, and it took four requests before Magpie came to play. He sang his power song over and over until he finally took the pointer and struck Owl on his talon. Owl had hidden the rock in his talon, not in one of four moccasins where it was supposed to be hidden. Rather than become angry, everyone laughed and ran off home. This is why there is still day and night in the world today.

Native Americans placed bets on foot, horse, and canoe races. They bet on bone games, ball games, wrestling matches, archery, and track events. Native people bet on all sorts of competition long before Europeans arrived, and they continued to bet after white contact. Choctaw historian Donna Akers pointed out that in a dispute between Choctaws and Muscogees over ownership of Beaver Pond, the tribes decided to settle the matter in a traditional ball game. People from both sides bet all their goods, and they played "the little war" with great energy and commitment. After days of playing, the Muscogees barely won and insulted the Choctaws by calling them names. Fighting broke out near the shores of Beaver Pond and lasted for days. When the people could fight no more, they counted 178 dead Choctaws and Muscogees. Because they had violated the sacred ball game by their violence, the Creator caused the beaver to move away. Years later, Christian missionaries decided to establish a church near Beaver Pond. Choctaws protested, explaining the dangers of this place, but the Christians considered Choctaws to be heathens filled with foolish stories.

As an act of self-determination, another southern tribe established the first commercial gambling enterprise on a reservation. In 1979, the Seminole tribe in Florida offered prizes of $10,000 or more at its bingo hall. Churches in Florida (and other states) had long offered bingo as a means of raising money, but Seminoles challenged state law that prohibited prizes over $100. Seminoles reasoned that they had a legal relationship with the United States and that Florida state law did not apply to them. Florida law enforcement moved to shut down Seminole gaming, but Seminoles sued in federal court and won. The United States had no prohibition against Indian gaming, so the Seminoles opened four additional bingo parlors. Soon they netted $10 million a year and encouraged Indian tribes throughout the country to establish bingo halls. Over the years, many tribes have turned to gaming to improve life on their reservations. The Mashantuckt Pequot tribe of Connecticut, with its Foxwoods Casino, is the most successful of all tribal gaming operations, but Tohono O'odhams, Muscogees, Choctaws, Mille Lacs, Colvilles, Pascua Yaquis, White Mountain Apaches, and others have also been successful at high-stakes gaming.

During the early 1980s several bands of Indians in southern California established bingo parlors, including Twenty-Nine Palms, Cabazon, San Manuel, Morongo, Rincon, Barona, Viejas, and Sycuan. Others have followed their example, but the sheriff of San Diego County raided the bingo operations on several reservations, and the tribes filed lawsuits against the state and county in federal court. State law enforcement officials also attacked the bingo parlor owned by the Cabazon band of Mission Indians, so tribal officials filed a lawsuit that the Supreme Court reviewed in 1987, ruling that California could not regulate gaming on federal Indian reservations. In the opinion, the Supreme Court stated that California permitted many forms of gambling in the state, including church bingo and its own state lottery. The state could not prohibit the Cabazon tribe from operating its own bingo operation. Another California tribe, the Twenty-Nine Palms band of Mission Indians, under the astute leadership of Dean Mike, has successfully operated the Spotlight 29 casinos in Coachella, California. Chairman Mike, his wife Theresa Thomas Mike, and the tribe's business council have improved income, housing, health, education, and cultural events for tribal members.

Many states have objected to Indian gaming, in part because Native Americans have been very successful at the enterprise and have made considerable money. Furthermore, state officials resented the fact that they could not control tribes. Nevada lost many gamblers to Indian casinos located in nearby California and lobbied congressional delegations and the governor in California to regulate Indian gaming. As a result, in 1988, Congress passed the Indian Gaming Regulatory Act (IGRA), which forced tribes to negotiate agreements with the states, providing guidelines for tribal gaming. By 1997, many states had negotiated agreements with tribes, but in California, Governor Pete Wilson and Attorney General Dan Lungren—both Republicans—refused to negotiate with the tribes except for people living on the Pala Reservation, which did not offer any gaming. Both politicians criticized the tribes and tried to ruin Indian gaming.

Although the rhetoric of Wilson and Lungren was designed to turn the public against the tribes, Indians and non-Indians rallied to support the gaming tribes in California. Gaming tribes successfully placed an initiative called Proposition 5 on the ballot in November 1998 and mounted a professional and well-financed publicity campaign, with actor Chuck Norris and other celebrities championing Indian efforts to use gaming funds in the struggle against poverty, disease, ill health, and poor housing. Luiseño leader Mark Macarro often represented the tribes in television commercials stressing the benefits of gaming for Indians and non-Indians. Lummi Aaron Thomas organized tribes to stand together in favor of Proposition 5. Some Indians filed lawsuits against the government, and the deadline for implementing IGRA came and went in 1997 without the federal government closing Indian casinos in California. In 1998, a federal court ruled that the tribes did not have to follow the Pala Compact, providing a limited victory for California's Indians. At the same time, some tribes signed the compact with the state while hoping that Proposition 5 would pass. In November 1998, Proposition 5 passed with 65 percent of the voting public in California supporting Indian gaming. In the same election, voters elected as governor Gray Davis, a Democrat who supported gaming. Shortly after taking office, he withdrew Governor Wilson's legal opposition to Proposition 5 and has been quietly supportive of gaming. Still, the fate of Indian gaming is tenuous, as federal officials, influenced greatly by funding from Nevada gaming interests and Washington state political leaders, seek to curtail Indian sovereignty and the right to economic development through gaming.

Gaming and other forms of economic development have improved the conditions of tribes that have successfully established casinos. However, grinding poverty, disease, suicides, and despair also exist on reservations, and many people have little concept of the real problems facing reservations. Information provided by the media sometimes suggests that *all* native people are prospering and making millions of dollars from gaming. In the *San Bernardino Sun* on July 21, 1997, Bad River Ojibway Mark Anthony Rolo, editor of *Circle*, a native newspaper in Minneapolis, pointed out that reservations still suffer unemployment that is ten times that of the national average and that most native people live below the poverty level. Reservation and urban Indians still suffer such ills in spite of "a growing perception that Indians are becoming rich off casino profits. Reality is, only about 100 tribes operate casinos, and only a handful of tribally owned casinos take in sizable revenues." As Senator Paul Wellstone of Minnesota began his nationwide tour to study poverty in America, Rolo pointed out that Wellstone forgot to include reservations on his itinerary. "The senator should step foot on tribal land," Rolo remarked, if he would like to "see that poverty is more than a social ill in Indian country; it's an epidemic."

In 1997, the Twenty-Nine Palms band of Mission Indians used some of its proceeds from gaming to initiate a cultural heritage project that included creation of the Native American Land Conservancy, preservation of songs, collection of oral histories, cultural resource management, and a museum program. Under the leadership of Dean and Theresa Mike, the Twenty-Nine Palms band of Chemehuevi Indians has used some of its revenues from the Spotlight 29 Casino to finance a cultural-economic revitalization among the Chemehuevis, and they have expanded their circle to help Indians and non-Indians by contributing to fight diseases, help orphaned and abused children, fund Indian arts projects, establish scholarship funds, and conduct a host of other philanthropic projects. Gaming has provided this change among the Twenty-Nine Palms Nation and tribes throughout North America.

Selected Readings and Bibliography

Self-determination and tribal sovereignty are topics dealt with in several sources, but they were illustrated in an exhibit of the Medicine Creek Treaty at the Washington Historical Society in 1998, curated by Maria Pascually. Some of the previously cited sources that address self-determination and sovereignty are Cahn, *Our Brother's Keeper;* Deloria, *Custer Died for Your Sins;* Crum, *The Road on Which We Came;* and Rawls, *Chief Red Fox Is Dead.* Also see Davis's *Native America in the Twentieth Century,* Francis's *Native Time,* and Champagne's *The Native North American Almanac.* For government policy, see O'Brien's *American Indian Tribal Governments,* Tyler's *A History of Indian Policy,* Forbes's *Native Americans and Nixon,* Deloria and Lytle's *American Indians, American Justice,* Holm's *Strong Hearts,* Fixico's *Termination and Relocation,* and Szasz's *American Indian Education.*

Ambler, Marjane. *Breaking the Iron Bonds: Indian Control of Energy Development.* Lawrence: University Press of Kansas, 1990.

American Friends Service Committee. *Uncommon Controversy: Fishing Rights of the Muckleshoot, Puyallup and Nisqually Indians.* Seattle: University of Washington Press, 1970.

Asch, Michael. *Home and Native Land: Aboriginal Rights and the Canadian Constitution.* Toronto: Methuen, 1984.

Barman, Jean, Yvonne Hebert, and Don McCaskill, eds. *Indian Education in Canada.* 2 volumes. Vancouver: University of British Columbia Press, 1986.

Berger, Thomas R. *Village Journey: A Report of the Alaska Native Review Commission.* New York: Hill and Wang, 1985.

Boldt, Menno, J. Anthony Long, and Leroy Little Bear, eds. *The Quest for Justice: Aboriginal Peoples and Aboriginal Rights.* Toronto: University of Toronto Press, 1985.

Bonney, Rachel A. "The Role of AIM Leaders in Indian Nationalism." *American Indian Quarterly* 3 (1977): 209–224.

Boxberger, Daniel L. *To Fish in Common: The Ethnohistory of Lummi Indian Salmon Fishing.* Lincoln: University of Nebraska Press, 1989.

Bray, Tamara L., and Thomas W. Killion, eds. *Reckoning with the Dead: The Larsen Bay Repatriation and the Smithsonian Institution.* Washington, D.C.: Smithsonian Institution Press, 1994.

Brightman, Lehman. "Stoic, Silent Readman." *Warpath,* San Francisco Bay area newspaper, *1968.*

Brodeur, Paul. *Restitution: The Land Claims of the Mashpee, Passamaquoddy, and Penobscot Indians of New England.* Boston: Northeastern University Press, 1985.

Cadwalader, Sandra L., and Vine Deloria Jr. *The Aggressions of Civilization: Federal Indian Policy since the 1800s.* Philadelphia: Temple University Press, 1984.

Cardinal, Harold. *The Unjust Society: The Tragedy of Canada's Indians.* Edmonton: Hurtig, 1969.

——. *The Rebirth of Canada's Indians.* Edmonton: Hurtig, 1977.

Castille, George P., and Robert L. Bee. *State and Reservation: New Perspectives in Federal Indian Policy.* Tucson: University of Arizona Press, 1992.

Churchill, Ward, and Jim V. Wall. *Agents of Repression: The FBI's Secret Wars against the Black Panther Party and the American Indian Movement.* Boston: South End Press, 1988.

Cornell, Stephen. *The Return of the Native: American Indian Political Resurgence.* New York: Oxford University Press, 1988.

Deloria, Vine Jr. *Behind the Trail of Broken Treaties: American Indian Declaration of Independence.* Austin: University of Texas Press, 1985.

Echo-Hawk, Roger. *Battlefields and Burial Grounds: The Indian Struggle to Protect Ancestral Graves in the U.S.* Minneapolis: Lerner Publications, 1994.

Farr, William E. *The Reservation Blackfeet, 1882–1945.* Seattle: University of Washington Press, 1984.

Gross, Michael P. "Indian Self-Determination and Tribal Sovereignty: An Analysis of Recent Federal Indian Policy." *Texas Law Review* 56 (1978): 1195–1244.

Guillemin, Jeane. *Urban Renegades.* New York: Columbia University Press, 1975.

Hawthorn, Harry B., ed. *A Survey of the Contemporary Indians of Canada: A Report on Economic, Political, Educational Needs and Policies.* 2 volumes. Ottawa: Queen's Printer, 1966–1967.

Hill, Tom, and Richard W. Hill Sr., eds. *Creation's Journey: Native American Identity and Belief.* Washington, D.C.: Smithsonian Institution Press with the National Museum of the American Indian, 1994.

Huff, Delores J. "The Tribal Ethic, the Protestant Ethic, and American Indian Economic Development." *American Indian Policy and Cultural Values.* Jennie R. Joe, ed. Los Angeles: American Indian Studies Center, University of California, Los Angeles, 1986.

Hundley, Norris Jr. "The Dark and Bloody Ground of Indian Water Rights: Confusion Elevated to Principles." *Western Historical Quarterly* 9 (1978): 455–482.

——. "The 'Winters' Decision and Indian Water Rights: A Mystery Reexamined." *Western Historical Quarterly* 13 (1982): 17–42.

Indians of All Tribes. *Alcatraz Is Not an Island.* Berkeley: Wingbow Press, 1972.

Israel, Daniel H. "The Reemergence of Tribal Nationalism and Its Impact on Reservation Resource Development." *University of Colorado Law Review* 47 (1976): 617–652.

Johnson, Tim. *Spirit Capture*. Washington, D.C.: National Museum of the American Indian, 1998.

Johnson, Troy. *The Occupation of Alcatraz Island*. Urbana: University of Illinois Press, 1996.

Jorgensen, Joseph G. "A Century of Political Economic Effects on American Indian Society, 1880–1980." *Journal of Ethnic Studies* 6 (1978): 1–82.

Josephy, Alvin M. Jr. *Red Power*. New York: McGraw-Hill, 1971.

——. *Now That the Buffalo's Gone: A Study of Today's American Indians*. Norman: University of Oklahoma Press, 1989.

Kappler, Charles J., comp. and ed. *Indian Affairs: Laws and Treaties*. Washington, D.C.: U.S. Government Printing Office, 1903–1941.

Klein, Barry T. *Reference Encyclopedia of the American Indian*. New York: Todd Publications, 1986.

Little Bear, Leroy, et al., eds. *Pathways to Self-Determination: Canadian Indians and the Canadian State*. Toronto: University of Toronto Press, 1984.

Matthiessen, Peter. *In the Spirit of Crazy Horse*. New York: Viking, 1983.

Messerschmidt, Jim. *The Trial of Leonard Peltier*. Boston: South End Press, 1983.

Miller, J. R., ed. *Sweet Promises: A Reader on Indian-White Relations in Canada*. Toronto: University of Toronto Press, 1991.

Mission Indian Federation. *The Indian,* newsletter, various issues, 1920s–1940s.

Newton, Nell Jessup. "Federal Power over Indians: Its Sources, Scope, and Limitations." *University of Pennsylvania Law Review* 132 (1984): 195–288.

Orem, Belinda K. "Paleface, Redskin, and the Great White Chiefs in Washington: Drawing the Battle Lines over Western Water Rights." *San Diego Law Review* 17 (1980): 449–489.

Peroff, Nicholas C. *Menominee Dreams: Tribal Termination and Restoration, 1954–1974*. Norman: University of Oklahoma Press, 1982.

Purich, Donald. *Our Land: Native Rights in Canada*. Toronto: J. Lorimer, 1986.

Reno, Phillip. *Mother Earth, Father Sky, and Economic Development: Navajo Resources and Their Use*. Albuquerque: University of New Mexico Press, 1981.

Satz, Ronald N. *Chippewa Treaty Rights: The Reserved Rights of Wisconsin's Chippewa Indians in Historical Perspective*. Madison: Wisconsin Academy of Sciences, Arts and Letters, 1991.

Steiner, Stan. *The New Indians*. New York: Harper and Row, 1967.

Trafzer, Clifford E., ed. *American Indian Identity: Today's Changing Perspectives*. Sacramento: Sierra Oaks, 1989.

Walker, Bryce, and Jill Maynard, eds. *Through Indian Eyes*. Pleasantville, N.Y.: Reader's Digest, 1995.

Weatherford, Jack. *Indian Givers*. New York: Crown, 1988.

——. *Native Roots*. New York: Crown, 1991.

Weaver, Sally M. *Making Canadian Indian Policy: The Hidden Agenda 1968–1970*. Toronto: University of Toronto Press, 1981.

Weibel-Orlando, Joan. *Indian Country, L.A.* Urbana: University of Illinois Press, 1991.

Weyler, Rex. *Blood of the Land: The Government and Corporate War against the American Indian Movement*. Philadelphia: Society Publishers, 1992.

White, Robert H. *Tribal Assets: The Rebirth of Native America*. New York: Henry Holt, 1990.

Wright, Ronald. *Stolen Continents*. Boston: Houghton Mifflin, 1992.

CHAPTER 20

NATIVE AMERICAN
FINE ARTS

During the last half of the twentieth century, Native Americans experienced a dynamic growth in cultural expression. Whereas some Indians have argued that the phenomenal interest in architecture, pottery, painting, sculpture, carving, dry painting, silver jewelry, grillwork, quilts, and ribbon work is a form of cultural revitalization, others have argued that the interest is simply a continuation of an interest in traditional art forms that have developed among native communities since the time of creation. Regardless, American Indian artists have produced varied and numerous art forms that have been acclaimed worldwide. Native American painters, sculptors, carvers, jewelers, and other artisans have contributed significantly to native history and contemporary society, and their role in Indian country will continue to grow.

Fine arts and performing arts are ancient in the Americas. Song, music, dance, painting, narratives, and sculptures set the native world in motion, depicting the creation of the earth, sky, stars, and universe. Plants, animals, rivers, mountains, humans, and a host of other animate and inanimate elements are part of the great creative force that ties Native America with the past and present. Navajo Blessingway Singer Frank Mitchell once commented on the creative force, saying, "It is something that is beyond the power of human beings." He maintained that "Somebody with a higher power, with more force, must have created these things and put them into motion. And we keep the motion going with those songs in the Blessingway." Arts among Native Americans are a living cultural tradition that have never been static but rather adapting and dynamic, taking many forms that reflect the creative force and styles of individuals as well as regions, tribes, villages, and bands. Many Native American artists, dancers, musicians, and writers draw on their own rich heritage or that of other native people to inspire and inform their work.

American Indian artists are quick to point out that non-Indians should not stereotype the work as "Indian art," pointing out that Native American art is part of the larger world. Many Native American artists would agree with Dakota artist Oscar Howe, who said that "Indian Art can compete with any Art in the world, but not as a suppressed Art." Native American dancers, musicians, painters, architects, sculptors, silver workers, beaders, quill workers, and others oppose non-Indians defining artists and their art or determining what is truly "Indian." During a lecture at Washington State University, Seneca artist George Longfish explained that he did not create "Indian art" but rather created art based on his life's experiences. Mohawk painter Richard Glazier Danay pointed out that Native American artists enjoy great diversity in their work and that their own interpretation of that work reflects a variety of ideas. Danay remembered a lecture given by famed Chiricahua Apache sculptor Allan Houser, who maintained that he was not an "Indian artist." Immediately after Houser spoke, his son, Robert Haozous, stood up to announce that he was an American Indian artist, even though his sculptures are very contemporary. Danay stated that Native American artists are as diverse as their work, interpretations, identities, and experiences. This is no less true of native architectural designs and styles.

ARCHITECTURE

Native American architecture is one of the oldest art forms in the Americas. It is extremely diverse and has changed over time but incorporates elements of traditional ideas, architectural designs, and techniques. Many contemporary designs created by Indians and non-Indians are based on ancient architecture, and some native people continue to use traditional native homes and buildings that are at once functional, traditional, and contemporary. On some reservations, Native Americans live in more contemporary dwellings while maintaining traditional dwellings not far away. At times more traditional buildings are used for ceremonies and important gatherings of families, clans, and bands. These traditional buildings might be the homes of elders who prefer to live in old-style homes, or they might also serve as storage. It is not uncommon on and near reservations to find that native families have built sweat lodges near their homes. And urban Indians have also placed sweat lodges in their back yards or in secluded places in rural areas not far from cities.

During the early twentieth century, many Native Americans continued to build and live in traditional forms of housing, including small log houses or rough-hewn wood homes, such as those that Wyandots, Senecas, Cayugas, Lenapes, Ottawas, Peorias, and others used in the East. Those Indians in Kansas and Oklahoma who had previously made homes from sod continued to construct sod homes, including large round structures, such as those of the Pawnee. Cheyennes, Arapahoes, Comanches, Kiowas, Lakotas, Dakotas, Crows, Shoshonis, Blackfeet, and other Plains tribes continued to live in tipis during the early twentieth century, but the number of people continuing to live in tipis declined due to the lack of buffalo hides, canvas, availability of tipi poles, and policies of the BIA. Nevertheless, tipis survived across the Great Plains and Columbia Plateau of the United States and Canada.

From Alaska to the Pacific Northwest to California, Native Americans continued to live in traditional homes, particularly cedar plank homes along the Northwest Coast. Inuits used igloos as temporary homes, especially on hunting and fishing trips away from their main villages. On the Columbia Plateau, Nez Perce, Yakama, Palouse, Wanapum, Wenatchi, Sinkaietk, and others continued to make large A-framed mat lodges, as well as tipis. However, confinement to reservations, along with government policies, led the people to adopt small wooden shacks with dirt floors and poor ventilation, where disease spread rapidly. This became the most common housing form on most reservations, although native peoples did not completely abandon traditional homes.

Paiutes and Shoshonis of the Great Basin, California Indians, and the various Apache groups in New Mexico and Arizona abandoned their wickiups for small rectangular homes that fit the white bureaucrats' image of "civilized" houses. Navajos continued to live in round or octagonal hogans, but as the century progressed, many abandoned their hogans as permanent residences, although they generally maintained hogans for elders, storage, and ceremonies. This continues to be the case today among Tohono O'odham, Pima, Quechan, Yavapai, and others.

Pueblo Indians of Arizona and New Mexico have largely maintained their ancient architecture, and it is commonly copied or modified by non-Indians throughout the West for condominiums, shopping centers, apartments, homes, convenience stores, and government buildings. The All Pueblo Council used traditional pueblo design for its cultural center in Albuquerque, and today pueblo architecture employs adobe bricks, rocks, timbers, cement blocks, and stucco.

During the twentieth century, most Indians preserved their ancient architectural designs but used buildings made by the army and BIA. After World War II, the government added several stucco buildings for Indian schools, clinics, and offices. Some agencies, tribes, and individuals used mobile homes for houses, schools, colleges, offices, clinics, and banks. Mobile homes and temporary buildings are functional and affordable.

Since the 1960s and 1970s, architecture on some reservations has reflected the general trend toward self-determination. Native people planning construction of schools, colleges, community centers, libraries, museums, offices, health centers, and casinos have created buildings based on traditional ideas of architecture. Native architects have formed community committees to discuss designs before drawing their plans, and non-Indian architects working for tribes have become sensitive to traditional architecture. As the National Museum of the American Indian planned for the construction of a world-class museum on the mall in Washington, D.C., Cheyenne Director of the Museum Richard West and a team of his staff traveled throughout Indian country, meeting with native people to elicit ideas about the design of the building. Diversity within Native American groups, particularly in the area of architecture, made designing the building an opportunity and a challenge. The product is a museum design that incorporates traditional and contemporary designs, drawing on the past and looking to the future.

Carol Herselle Krinsky has offered a few examples of innovative Native American architecture, and Hopi architect Dennis Numkena designed the cultural center at Pyramid Lake. Chickasaw designer Neil McCaleb planned the Seneca-Cayuga Tribal Office in Miami, Oklahoma; and Laguna architect Andy Acoya collaborated on the design of the Oke Owe'enge Cultural Center at San Juan pueblo, New Mexico. Sioux and Arikara designer Denby Deegan created the plans for the Four Winds School at Fort Totten Reservation, North Dakota. Because four is the sacred number of native people from the Northern Plains, Deegan designed a large circular building with four pathways leading into four entrances that face to and from the four cardinal directions. Arapaho designer Dennis Sun Rhodes helped create the Native American Center for the Living Arts at Niagara Falls, New York. The building is in the shape of Turtle, upon whose back, many native people believe, the earth was created. The turtle, complete with mouth, eyes, claws, tail, and shell, offers a magnificent building that demonstrates the power of tribal traditions in contemporary society. Pomo builder Delbert Thomas Jr. uses contemporary construction materials and advances in architectural design to create neotraditional ceremonial roundhouses for native California Indians.

Scholars Stephen Jett, Virginia Spencer, Peter Nabokov, and Robert Easton have discussed other native architectural structures that draw on traditions to create contemporary structures. The Hoo-hoogam Ki Museum of the Salt River Pima and Maricopa people in Scottsdale, Arizona, employs traditional native design, construction techniques, and materials. The massive Ned A. Hatathli cultural center stands as a monument on the Navajo Nation. Constructed near the towering Tsaile Butte and in the shadow of the Chuska Mountains, the Hatathli center was constructed with eight sides to resemble a giant hogan and stands six stories tall. Copper-colored glass creates the sides of the building, which overlooks Tsaile Lake and the eastern entrance to Canyon del Muerto. It is located at Tsaile, the place where the water enters the canyon, not far from the Hopi Reservation, where some of the most exquisite native pottery is created.

POTTERY

Before the arrival of the Spanish, Native Americans in the Southeast and Southwest developed excellent pottery. In the Southeast, Catawba, Cherokee, and Pamunkey people were well known for their pottery, and in the Southwest, Hopi, Zuni, Acoma, San Ildefonso, Santa Clara, Jemez, Taos, Laguna, and the several pueblos of the Rio Grande Valley perfected pottery making. Indeed, Native Americans created pottery at least by 2400 b.c. in the Southeast, perhaps earlier. In the Southwest–dating as early as a.d. 200–ancient cultures labeled by anthropologists as Anasazi, Hohokam, and Mogollon made pottery. Designs of these ancient people have influenced the work of contemporary native potters. Native Americans developed utilitarian pottery for plates, bowls, jugs, cups, platters, pipes, and other items. They used some of these items, including clay pipes, for ceremonial purposes.

During the colonial period, Catawba, Pamunkey, Cherokee, and others found that they had a difficult time continuing their pottery, given pots, pans, kettles, cups, and other items introduced by the English and Dutch. Native Americans could easily obtain manufactured items through the fur trade, and as a result, native interest in pottery declined. However, Catawba, Cherokee, and Pamunkey potters persisted, and their pottery is a distinguished art form today. Catawba potters Sara Lee Ayers, Georgia Harris, Nola Campbell, Earl Robbins, Mildred Blue, Catherine Canty, and Evelyn George are among the best-known artists, while Cherokee potters Ella Arch, Kamie Owl Wahnetah, Rebecca Youngblood, and Anna Belle Sixkiller Mitchell also have distinguished themselves. Among Cherokees the Katalsta and Bigmeat families are also well known for their innovative art.

Catawba potters follow the pottery traditions of Mississippian cultures. They burnish their clay with quartz pebbles and cut their clay with ancient motifs that are burned in open fires outside their homes. Catawba pottery emerges red, gray, and black. According to art historian John W. Barry, author of *American Indian Pottery,* incising of their pottery "represents a direct link with the pre-Columbian past." Catawba, Cherokee, and Pamunkey potters are best known for making snake effigy pots, tobacco pipes, water jars, and cooking pots. Oklahoma Cherokee Anna B. Mitchell produces red-on-buff bowls, pitchers, and vases with "step to the mounds" design as well as a "Cherokee scroll" incised design of several circular swirls. In the East, Native Americans have formed pottery groups to revitalize the art. Such groups exists among the Catawba of South Carolina, Cherokee of North Carolina, Pamunkey and Mattaponi of Virginia, and Caushatta of Louisiana. Other native groups have considered organizing to preserve pottery among their people, and this trend bodes well for the art.

Among the Pueblo Indians of the Southwest, pottery has always been an important cultural element. During the Spanish and Mexican periods of southwestern history, the newcomers did not have a well-developed trade system to match that in the Southeast. As a result, Native Americans maintained their pottery, using it in their homes on a daily basis. The art declined in the early twentieth century because of the introduction of so many trade goods, but some potters continued the art and took advantage of the tourist trade. The Santa Fe Railroad and others ran near or through the pueblos, and new roads emerged, bringing tourists west. The Fred Harvey Company and a number of white Indian traders encouraged Pueblo potters to create inexpensive works to sell on trains to tourists or at Harvey Houses along the tracks. In addition to small pottery bowls, vases, plaques, and figurines to be sold to tourists, Harvey's agent Frederick Huckle purchased several fine pieces of Pueblo pottery, which encouraged potters to expand their art. Some traders also encouraged Pueblo potters to expand their art, but the great impetus to create pottery came from the native peoples themselves.

Between 1918 and 1919, Maria and Julian Martinez of San Ildefonso earned the attention of the business, art, and Native American communities by introducing a new technique to Pueblo Indian pottery making. From its small village north of Santa Fe, the Martinez family developed black pottery—matte black on polished black. Family members worked as a team, with Maria making the pottery and Julian creating the designs. The new style of black pottery was an immediate success and has become a prized style of Pueblo pottery. Today, people travel from around the world to visit the large plaza at San Ildefonso and visit the family shops owned by the Martinez family, its friends, and fellow villagers. During the summer, potters from San Ildefonso offer lectures and pottery demonstrations in the shade of the giant trees that sing in the breeze at the old pueblo where Maria and Julian Martinez helped revitalize Pueblo pottery.

Revival of Hopi and other Pueblo pottery owes much to Nampeyo, a Hopi and Tewa potter from First Mesa, Arizona. For some time, Nampeyo and her husband, Lesou, had collected old pottery shards on the mesa tops as well as the sides of the mesas where their ancestors had discarded broken pottery. They studied the shards and created new designs based on them. Lesou worked at an archaeological site of Sikyatki, a fifteenth-century site located near First Mesa, and he and Nampeyo saw intricate motifs painted on red-and-brown pottery with a background of soft yellow. Animals of all sorts as well characterized the beautiful flowing, soft texture of the ancient Pueblo pottery, and Nampeyo began employing these designs on her work. Although encouraged to develop her art, Nampeyo and Lesou did so because of their love of pottery. And this attachment to clay led many potters at San Ildefonso, Santa Clara, Hopi, and other pueblos to create their pieces. Although many potters took their designs from ancient patterns, others received inspiration though dreams and the natural environment.

Margaret Tafoya, Marie Chino, Lucy Lewis, Jessie Garcia, and other Pueblo potters also helped revitalize the art. In their fascinating book, *The Pueblo Storyteller,* Barbara Babcock, Guy Monthan, and Doris Monthan have shown the development of another innovative pottery form among Pueblo people. In the 1960s Cochiti Pueblo potter Helen Cordero created a "Storyteller" fashioned from hand to depict a male storyteller with wide-open mouth telling a tale to small children. Cordero's grandfather had been a great storyteller, so she formed her clay into a likeness of him and set clay figures around his body as if he was speaking to them. Storytellers became a great success, and potters from other pueblos created their own storytellers of humans, animals, clowns, and other characters. Jemez artist Juanita Martinez also presents her storytellers as grandfathers, speaking with a large oval mouth to numerous clay children who cling to the grandfathers' arms, legs, back, and head. Some of the children clutch balls and birds in their hands and appear to be speaking or singing. Storytellers are also presented as drumming and singing, playing cards, reading, eating, or joking.

Pottery among native artists is not limited to the people of the Southeast and Southwest, but these potters are best known. In the Southwest, Quechan, Mojave, Maricopa, Cahuilla, Kumeyaay, Navajo, and other natives have developed fine pottery. In addition to forming pots, jugs, vases, plates, and other utilitarian items, artists among many tribes have used clay to form singers, animals, and human dolls. Rhoda Yuma continued the art form at the Fort Yuma Agency among the Quechan Nation during the early twentieth century, selling her "dolls" to tourists and collectors. Visitors at the bus and train stations in Yuma, Arizona, often bought Mrs. Yuma's pottery figures of humans. Although Yuma produced many dolls over the years, only a few are found in homes and collections today. This is also true of similar dolls made by other Yuman-speaking Native Americans in Arizona. Creation of human, plant, and animal figures has developed among many tribes, including those that did not previously have a strong tradition in pottery. Native American pottery has expanded considerably in recent years, in large part because of the commercial value of the art, but also because of the relationship of native people to the earth.

During a gathering of Native Americans at the Heye Foundation Building in New York City in 1992 to interpret material culture of the National Museum of the American Indian, Santa Clara scholar Rina Swentzel held a huge pottery bowl in her hands and commented that the art reminded her of all the grandmothers who loved the earth and molded clay into pottery. The bowl brought to mind a story about Water Jug Boy. According to the story, a woman went to the side of a river to gather clay, and while she was reveling in the soft clay oozing between her toes, the clay moved up her leg and made love to her. She became pregnant and gave birth to Water Jug Boy. The family was proud of the boy, who grew into a youngster who soon realized that he could not play with the other children because he was too fragile. One day, his father prepared to go hunting, and Water Jug Boy begged to go along, saying he would be no trouble because his father would have to carry him only to the top of hills and could allow him to roll down the other side. After much discussion, the father took his son on the hunt, walking him up every hill and allowing him to roll down the other side. But on a steep hill the boy rolled down too fast, hit a rock, and broke into many pieces. The father raced down the hill, crying and calling out for his beloved son. Holding the shards in his hands, the father heard someone calling him from a nearby rock. It was his son, who had come to life from within the pottery.

To many native potters, the clay, paint, designs, and firing of pottery are alive, like the spirit of Water Jug Boy.

PAINTING

Painting by Native Americans, on bark, rocks, wood, clay, walls, skins, and other surfaces, predates white contact and has been modified many times over the years. Painting is an art that links the past to the present but also provides opportunities for native artists to expand and experiment far beyond that which was once labeled real Indian painting. During the late nineteenth and early twentieth centuries, Native American painting was more traditional, depicting subjects, techniques, and colors used by native artists of the past. Native people painted masks of wood, skin, and basketry as well as elaborate cedar boxes, drums, pipe stems, homes, and many other items. Kiowa, Comanche, Cheyenne, Arapaho, Lakota, and other artists painted drawings on buffalo hides. Winter counts (historical paintings) depict episodes of native history, including the feats of warriors in battle or raids on villages where enemies killed or wounded women, men, and children or set fire to villages. Ledger art sometimes depicts camp movements, buffalo hunts, ceremonies, starvation, and diseases. Plains Indian paintings by Kiowa artist Ohettoint offer decorative renditions of Plains Indian lifestyles and captivity in prisons like Fort Marion, Florida, while Lakota artist Red Hawk offered scenes from Wounded Knee, 1890.

Kiowa artist Paul Zotom, like Ohettoint, had been a prisoner of war confined to Fort Marion, but his paintings attracted the attention of anthropologist James Mooney, who hired Zotom to paint miniature shields and tipis to illustrate designs common to Kiowa people. Ohettoint's younger brother, Silverhorn, also worked for Mooney, painting his

Kiowa interpretation of the Ghost Dance, Sun Dance, Kiowa narratives, Native American Church services, and other subjects. In similar fashion, anthropologist Jesse Walter Fewkes hired Hopi artists to paint the art that appeared as "Hopi Kachinas, Drawn by Native Artists" in the *Annual Report of the Bureau of American Ethnology,* 1899–1900. Native American painters throughout the Southwest—including Crescencio Martinez, Alfredo Montoya, and Alfonso Roybal (also known as Awa Tsireh), from San Ildefonso pueblo—sold their work to collectors, museums, and tourists. During the early twentieth century, several non-Indian artists moved to New Mexico to work, and they took a special interest in native art, which was not well known in other parts of the world. Although many non-Indian artists, collectors, teachers, scholars, and museum directors encouraged native painters, the blossoming of native art came from the talented minds of Indian people.

The Santa Fe Indian School produced a number of noted painters during the 1920s, including Hopi Fred Kabotie, Zia Velino Herrera, and Hopi Otis Polelonema. Elizabeth DeHuff gathered these students into a group and asked them to paint Pueblo dances with all the feelings that the dances conveyed to the young artists. In 1919, DeHuff arranged a showing for these painters at the Museum of New Mexico, which helped launch their careers. These native artists led the way for other Pueblo painters, many of whom were from San Ildefonso, including Tonita Peña, Richard Martinez, Julian Martinez, Romando Vigil, Oqwa Pi, and Wo-Peen. In 1932, teacher Dorothy Dunn established the "Studio" at the Santa Fe Indian School, where she trained native students, including such noted artists as Apache Allan Houser, Navajo Gerald Nailor, Yanktonai Oscar Howe, Navajo Harrison Begay, Navajo Narciso Abeya, Navajo Quincy Tahoma, and Santa Clara Pablita Velarde. Not all these artists continued painting, but all of them were influenced by the realistic, flat color techniques of the Dunn school of art.

During the early twentieth century in Oklahoma Territory, Absentee Shawnee painter Earnest Spybuck and Arapaho artist Carl Sweezy created their work but were not well known outside their own communities. However, by 1918 a growing interest in Native American painting helped open the path for other native artists in Oklahoma. During the 1910s and 1920s, Native American art developed more fully in Oklahoma because of talented native painters—and Susie Peters, who worked on the Kiowa, Comanche, Kiowa Apache Reservation in southwestern Oklahoma. She introduced six young Kiowa artists (Lois Smoky, Monroe Tsatoke, James Auchiah, Spencer Asah, Jack Hoeah, and Stephen Mopope) to art professor Oscar B. Jacobson. Jacobson invited these painters to a workshop at the University of Oklahoma, where they received some instruction from professor Edith Mahier. Art exhibits in several parts of the world showed their work, and these Kiowa painters produced a limited edition folio entitled *Kiowa Indian Art* in France.

In Oklahoma, the Kiowa style of ledger art continued to influence native painters until the 1930s, when a variety of young artists began experimenting. In addition to support provided by the University of Oklahoma, the Indian school at Muskogee, Oklahoma, also furthered native painters and artists in general. In 1935, the elementary and high school at Bacone introduced an Indian art department led by Muscogee artist Acee Blue Eagle, who began an important tradition of allowing the imagination of young native artists to flow from sketches, paints, clay, wood, and other mediums. Muscogee and Potawatomi painter Woody Crumbo and Cheyenne artist Richard West Sr. led the department after Blue Eagle. West guided the department from 1947 to 1970. All three influenced generations of native artists, encouraging them to put their own imprint on their art and allow their paintings to take flight. Today Lenape and Shawnee artist Ruth Blalock Jones leads the art department at Bacone, encouraging painters and other artists to express themselves, drawing on the strengths of the native past to build toward a creative future.

Some of the better-known native artists during the last half of the twentieth century were Cochiti Joe Herrera, Yaktonai Oscar Howe, Cherokee-Muscogee Virginia Stroud, Muscogee-Cherokee Joan Hill, Muscogee-Seminole Jerome Tiger, Luiseño Fritz Scholder, and Kiowa-Caddo T. C. Cannon. Herrera blended traditional Anasazi and Pueblo Indian ceremonial art–from kivas, rocks, and pottery–with modern art. Howe fused parts of traditional native culture with modern art, using surrealism and cubism to convey the depth of American Indian culture, particularly his own Dakota culture. *Head Dancer, Medicine Man,* and *War Dancer* are just three of his paintings that allow viewers to see beyond the mask and into the past. His works are mirrors by which contemporary subjects meet the past. In their work *Shared Visions: Native American Painting and Sculpture in the Twentieth Century,* Osage-Cherokee scholar Rennard Strickland and Margaret Archuleta point out that both Herrera's and Howe's work represent a cross-fertilization of modern and native art. Both painters faced strong resistance to their work because it was modern and innovative. In 1959, Howe's work was rejected as "non-Indian," and in the ensuing controversy, the artist asked, "Are we to be held back forever with one phase of Indian painting, with no right for individualism, dictated to as the Indian always has been, put on reservations and treated like a child, and only the White Man knows what is best for him?" Howe declared that he would not stand for this treatment, would not allow others to suppress his painting.

Luiseño painter Fritz Scholder shared Herrera's and Howe's contempt for other people determining for Native American artists the true nature of Indian art. Scholder taught at the Institute of American Indian Arts and is best known for "unfixing" the image of Native Americans in popular culture by tearing away the stylized romanticism of Native Americans from the nineteenth century. He created a new frame of reference, of Indians without stereotypes, and he passed this idea along to his students. Scholder worked in subjects that Indians and non-Indians had not considered seriously in native art, and he shocked the art world with such paintings as *Indian with a Beer Can* because it did not fit the common image of native painting. In this respect, Scholder, Herrera, and Howe shared an interest in changing the way others viewed Native American painting. Scholder wanted to free himself and other native artists from the confining realm of native art so that it might include modern styles of surrealism, photo realism, cubism, and styles and techniques that had yet to be created.

T. C. Cannon was Scholder's student at Santa Fe, and he expanded on the art produced by Herrera, Howe, and Scholder. As a painter, Cannon made his mark through his abstract expressionism, which brings out the conflict within many native people who live in two worlds, negotiating those worlds while continually being forced to explain their work to both worlds. Often Cannon's subjects speak to viewers on many levels, which elicits confusion among some and understanding among others. This is also true of several contemporary artists, including Mohawk Richard Glazier Danay, Kiowa-Cherokee N. Scott Momaday, Seneca-Tuscarora George Longfish, Lakota David Whitehorse, Aleut Alvin Amason, and Onondaga Eric Gansworth. Their paintings are a blend of modern art and traditional native concepts that reflect a strong desire to paint out of and into the native world. The abstract nature of the new native art is evidenced in works by Cree-Shoshoni Jaune Quick-to-See Smith, Yaqui Anita Endrezze, and Choctaw-Chippewa James Harvard. The expressionism of Anishinaabe painter and sculptor George Morrison has confused critics who cannot see the "Indian" within his paintings. "I've never tried to prove my Indianness through my art," Morrison stated, but "there remains deep within [my work] some remote suggestion of the earth and the rock from which I come." This is the case for many contemporary native painters.

Carl Gorman, the Navajo Code Talker, and his son, R. C. Gorman, are both well-known contemporary artists. With a Navajo tribal scholarship, the younger Gorman traveled to Mexico to study such Mexican painters as Diego Rivera and José Clemente Orozco. As a result of his studies abroad, R. C. Gorman has chosen to concentrate on depicting tranquil women engaged in common tasks such as creating pottery, telling stories, or nursing. His colors reflect pastel reds, pinks, and purples found in the Desert Southwest. In contrast are such California native artists as Nisenan-Maidu Harry Fonseca, Luiseño James Luna, and Wintu-Nomtipom Frank LaPena. Fonseca uses Coyote—the great trickster, teacher, and creator of confusion—to depict stories, humor, lessons, and traditions. *When Coyote Leaves the Res* (1980), *Coyote Koshares* (1983), and *Coyote in the Mission* (1989) are among his best-known paintings. San Carlos Apache Earl Sisto provides neorealism in his paintings of

Apache men, women, and children, as well as other native subjects, such as Cocopa women and children and Menominee animal people, which have been published as cover art for books. James Luna employs painting within his participatory art, often placing himself into the art he creates. Luna's denunciation of Father Serra, the Catholic Church, and the process toward the canonization of Serra is captured in an unusual photo essay that appeared in *Looking Glass*. Frank LaPena is an exceptional artist best known for *Deer Rattle-Deer Dancer* and *Earth Mother*, both of which reflect the painter's personal connection with the earth, animals, and ceremonies. His strong use of red reflects colors common in native Californian headdresses and suggests the importance of blood to life.

SCULPTURE, CARVING, AND DRY PAINTING

Native Americans from many cultures expressed themselves through sculpture and carving of earth, wood, bone, ivory, and stone. Through their desire for beauty and understanding, native sculptors and carvers created an array of art. In the Ohio and Mississippi river valleys, Native Americans formed sculptures from the earth, including the great Serpent Mound in Ohio and towering earthen mounds in several eastern and midwestern states. Native peoples made many other sculptures from natural materials found in their environment. Materials such as bone, wood, earth, stone, and ivory were a part of native communities, not inanimate objects set apart from the people. Therefore, native artists expressed themselves to and through natural materials and viewed these natural media as integral parts of the community. As a result, traditional native sculptors and carvers had a spiritual connection with their materials. The Wyandot artist who carved a wooden ladle once displayed in New York by the National Museum of the American Indian likely asked the tree from which the wood was taken for permission to use the wood for carving. In the same manner, before beginning the work, Onondaga false face carver Gowahenc'da:we likely asked the pine tree for permission to carve a Broken Nose mask.

The special relationship between artists and their materials is as ancient as human habitation of the earth. Carving and sculpting are ancient arts, and many pieces of art carved and sculpted by Native Americans have been unearthed in archaeological sites throughout the Americas. Indeed, as far back as the seventeenth century, non-Indians exploring the Americas noted Native American sculpting and carving, sometimes rendering sketches of the art. Iroquoian and Algonquian peoples throughout the Eastern Woodlands carved sculptures from wood, particularly masks and faces on posts. Iroquois False Face masks are some of the best-known forms of wood carving in the Northeast. Traditionally carved from the trunk of live basswood trees, False Face masks have great significance among Six Nations people. Although False Face masks are sold as commercial art today, they are also sacred art worn by select individuals among the Haudenosaunee or Iroquois people. Only members of the False Face Society may wear the masks or speak the special words of these holy characters. Carving has deep meaning for Iroquois people.

False Face carvings are part of the fabric of ancient oral narratives of Six Nations people, emerging from the creative time when a spirit challenged the Creator over which of them had more power. Sitting near the Atlantic and looking east toward the sea, the Creator challenged the spirit to move the mountains to the east. Try as he might, the spirit failed. When the Creator had his chance, he instructed the spirit not to look, but as the Creator moved the mountains eastward, the spirit turned to watch. The mountains smashed into his face, broke his nose, and disfigured his face. This is why Iroquois mask carvers present Broken Nose with distorted nose and mouth. Humbled by the event, Broken Nose apologized for his challenge, but the Creator rewarded the grandfather of the False Face with power to head a medicine society that comforts and heals members of the Six Nations.

Carving wooden masks is also important among Haida, Tsimshian, Tlingit, Kwakiutl, Bella, Bella Coola, Nootka, and other northwestern people. Kwakiutl carver James Mathew created *Hawk-Man,* a cedar mask with large beak and eyes that peer out from a white painted background accentuated by brown paint. Red is the dominant color of the mask, although portions of the face are white and brown. In 1987, Tsimshian carver Andrew Morrison from Kincolith Nass River in British Columbia created *Bear Speaker* of alder wood. Blue, black, and red are the dominant colors. Bear dominates the entire mask, with a bear image appearing on the forehead just above open eyes and pear-shaped blue paint surrounding the eyes. Morrison paints bear in black, although he presents portions of the face, nose, and ears in red. Bear's nose is wide and flat, his mouth red, in an elongated oval. The carver created a left-handed bear paw of black and blue, pointing downward on the right side of the cheek, while a similar figure, but representing another animal with a large blue and black eye, appears on the left cheek. Kwakiutl carver Stan Matilpi created *Whale* from red cedar, with no open eyes on the mask and two killer whales facing each other with angry and toothy faces dominating the forehead. A dorsal fin rises above these two figures from the top of the mask, with two additional whale faces appearing on each side of the dorsal fin. Chnagmiut Eskimo Larry Beck has enlarged mask making by constructing traditional Eskimo masks and other objects using eating utensils, plates, mirrors, hubcaps, and other commonplace items of the contemporary world.

Beck's use of manufactured items reflects cultural change experienced by native people, and environmental themes have become more important to native artists such as Mohawk Richard Glazier Danay, whose *Chief's Chair* is a wheeled toy with a car phone carrying an ancient Aztec leader. Cherokee Ron Anderson has produced *Car Scaffold Burial,* which features a Mercury Cougar surrounded in a burial shroud and hoisted on a Plains-style burial scaffolding. In 1996, Inuit artist Audrey Powers offered *Igloo with Electric Light* to demonstrate the contradiction between traditional and modern, while Apache-Navajo Bob Haozous created *The Abortionist's Bed* from steel to shock the viewer and question the values of modern society. Santa Clara Rina Swentzel, Cherokee Bill Glass, Comanche Karita Koffey, and Cree-Anishinaabe Glen LaFontaine all work in clay sculpture. Similar to potters and makers of storytellers, these artists have extended their art and offered unique innovations and interpretations. Koffey creates clay masks of fine quality, while Swenzell has produced hauntingly realistic Pueblo figures such as her 1988 work, *The Emergence of the Clowns,* which offers koshare clowns situated close to the earth in awe and wonder.

Totem poles are the best-known form of wood carving in the Pacific Northwest, although the people there are also known for exquisitely carved boxes and plaques with intricate designs. Originally created as a means of honoring the living and dead, commemorating events, and presenting traditional and familial stories, totem poles are best known today among Tsimshian and Haida people, although carvers from other tribes are emerging as a result of an art revitalization. Sometimes totems tell stories of human encounters and relationships with thunderbirds, eagles, bears, whales, beavers, otters, ravens, and other animal people. During the 1950s, Kwakiutl carver Mungo Martin and Haida sculptor Bill Reid teamed up to revitalize the art, inspiring and training young artists in the ancient art form. Northwestern carvers have made a special effort to be true to the techniques and designs of their ancestors rather than emphasize innovations. They established a "school" to teach carvers and have presented demonstrations in museums and other institutions in the United States and Canada. Totem pole carving is an intricate art form that is more common today than at the beginning of the twentieth century.

Throughout the Northwest and other regions of North America, Native American carvers and sculptors are working in wood and stone. Tlingit carver James Schoppert has created a series of wood sculptures that are abstract and surrealistic. Schoppert's art is indicative of a new generation of artists who have introduced innovation in a variety of wood-carving forms. Kwakiutl T. Whonnock of Alert Bay, British Columbia, in 1991 created *Kwakuitl Wolf,* a carefully carved wolf painted black, red, and green with alert eyes, ears, and growling teeth. In 1964, Cherokee Willard Stone produced *Proud Peyote Bird* in walnut with long, slender lines that make the bird appear as though it will take flight. During the 1970s, Hopi kachina carver Paul Coochyamptewa became famous for the color and movement he carved into cottonwood roots to create masterful kachinas. He is among the finest kachina carvers and exhibits a special talent for carving Crow Mother. Cheyenne painter and sculptor Richard West Sr. is also known for his wood carvings, as is a fellow Oklahoman, Cherokee John J. Wilnotty. Ho-Chunk Truman Lowe, Eastern Cherokee Amanda Crowe, Inupiat Eskimo Susie Bevins-Ericsen, and Aleut John Hoover all work in wood and stone, extending and developing traditional sculpture among their people and innovating their art. At the Santa Fe Indian Art Institute, Inuit carver Bekoa Look presented *Inuit Hunter,* a soapstone carving with ivory face and detachable fishing harpoon tied with lengths of string, a sculpture with grace and power.

Chiricahua Apache Allan Houser was the premier native sculptor of the twentieth century. Trained as a painter at the Santa Fe Studio, Houser became an instructor at the Santa Fe Art Institute and influenced hundreds of artists. Native Americans attending the school or other institutions learned a great deal from Houser's moving creations, which offer a sense of splendor and elegance. Houser's 1987 bronze, *Earth Mother,* is a rounded and warm mother nurturing and holding a person within the arms of the earth. A native person within the piece grasps the Earth Mother with the right hand while the Earth Mother reaches out with both arms to envelop the individual and pull that person to her breast. The mother and the person within the mother are at once separate and together. Houser's critics point out that his work overlooks the horrors of the Apache wars, the Apaches' imprisonment in Florida and Alabama, and confinement to a reservation in Indian Territory far from their homelands in New Mexico and Arizona. However, Houser was very much aware of the Apache past but chose to express the beauty of his people and the relationship with positive traditional values that sustained Apache people during the American holocaust.

Positive power is also found in dry paintings of selected tribes from among Uto-Aztecan, Athabascan, Piman, Cahitan, and Pueblo peoples of North America. This is sacred art produced during ceremonies to teach, cure, and determine elements of the future. Native artists traditionally produce dry paintings from sand, earth, ground charcoal, ground shells, plant pollens, and other natural materials. Some people refer to them as sand paintings, earth pictures, sand altars, sand pictures, sand mosaics, and ground paintings. Dry paintings are generally created to do someone good and provide the vehicle through which healing forces help fight disease of the body, mind, and soul. Navajos call sand paintings *iikáah* or "the place where the holy people come and go." During a Navajo curing ceremony, medicine men invite Holy People to the ceremony through songs, chants, prayers, and sand paintings. Patients sit on the dry paintings, and Holy People travel through the paintings to the patients' buttocks, through their spine, and throughout the body, expelling that which has made the patients ill. Although these paintings are intended to do good, they have considerable dangerous power when misused. This is why native people do not encourage school teachers and elementary students to re-create sacred sand paintings.

Cahuilla-Luiseño historian Edward Castillo has emphasized the possible negative power of sand paintings in his research on the Gabrielino people of southern California. He has pointed out that during the Spanish colonial period the Gabrielino died in large numbers from an epidemic that they attributed to two medicine men who had turned the power in a negative direction to harm their community. The Gabrielino cornered the two medicine men, set fire to their home, and killed them. A young boy working with the medicine men told the Gabrielino that the medicine men had created a sand painting on an island off the California coast. He led Gabrielino elders to a cave where they found the sand painting. They ordered the boy to destroy the powerful object, which he did. The elders killed the boy, too, because he was connected to the unholy act that had caused the epidemic. When the Gabrielino returned home they found their community recovering from the disease. The epidemic ended, and Gabrielino attributed this to the destruction of the sand painting. Such powerful sand paintings were made by many native people, most often created for the good of the community, not the destruction of the people. Today, some native artists have changed the process and design of sand paintings and placed them in rugs, paintings, or glued them to wood for commercial art. As with all native art forms, collectors and tourists purchase the art, creating a market.

BASKETS, BEADS, AND TEXTILES

Native Americans have made basketry for over seven thousand years, and many tribes continue to preserve the art. American Indians used baskets as storage containers, water jugs, winnowing baskets, trays, beaters, and baby cradles. Indians used baskets to gather, process, and store nuts, grains, dried meat and fish, and fruits. Until recently, women made most of the baskets found in North America, although some men have learned the art in recent years. Native Americans employed three techniques in basket making: twining, plaiting, and coiling. And they used a variety of materials from which to construct baskets, including stems, leaves, roots, grass, wood, and hair. Cherokees, Choctaws, Chickasaws, and Muscogees plaited cane and oak splint baskets, whereas Chitamachas of Louisiana made cane baskets of narrow splints that they dyed black and orange in order to create rectangular boxes with tight fitting lids. Lumbees of North Carolina, including Mary J. Bell and Hayes Lowry, also made plaited baskets. Iroquoian and Algonquian peoples of the Eastern Woodlands plaited their baskets, often using ash splints to create bowls, trays, and hand baskets. Hidatsas, Mandans, and Arikaras of the Northern Plains also made plaited baskets.

Native Americans living on the Columbia Plateau, Puget Sound, and Pacific Coast also made baskets. In her classic book, *A Time of Gathering: Native Heritage in Washington State,* Robin K. Wright offers chapters dealing with basketry of the plateau and coast. Nez Perce, Palouse, Wanapum, Cayuse, Coeur d'Alene, and many other people of the Columbia Plateau are known for their geometrically designed basket hats, which women make of many colors. These hats have no brim but rise up approximately eight to twelve inches above the head, slowly tapering inward to form a relatively flat top. In addition, women on the plateau, including Palouse elder Mary Jim, make flat twined bags of hemp, corn husk, wool yarn, leather, and cotton cord. Most women incorporate intricate designs into their art, as do the women of the lower Columbia River, coast, and Puget Sound. Chinooks, Quinaults, Makahs, Nisquallies, Lummis, Duamish, and others have a rich tradition in basketry and continue to develop the art form today. On the Pacific Coast as well as in the Puget Sound, native basket makers also construct hats with broad brims to ward off rains. They also twine fine baskets of split spruce root and decorate them with images of whales, salmon, thunderbirds, bears, and other figures. Sometimes the designs tell stories that range from the time of creation to the present.

Shoshoni, Ute, and Paiute of the Great Basin and eastern California also make a variety of baskets, including hooded cradleboards and coiled seed and water jars. During the late nineteenth and early twentieth centuries, basketry among Navajos declined, particularly their unique white, red, and black wedding baskets. As a result, Navajos purchased their own style of wedding baskets from Paiutes living north and west of Dinétah. However, since the 1970s, Navajos have revitalized their basketry, in part because of classes that taught the art at Diné (formerly Navajo Community) College, but also because of contemporary artists who have expanded the art form with new designs. Apache cousins of Navajos also make fine baskets with human, animal, and geometric figures, and Yuman-speaking peoples, including Yavapais, Havasupais, and Walapais, also make coiled baskets with three rod foundations and black geometric designs from splits of devil's claw. Tohono O'odham and Pima also use devil's claw and once used grasses sewn with willow splints. However, today most Tohono O'odham use coils of bear grass sewn with yucca splints, which can be sold at lower prices to collectors and tourists. Hopis on Second and Third Mesas make a variety of colorful coiled baskets from yucca splints over bundles of galleta grass. Hopis on Third Mesa use rabbit brush and sumac in their basketry. Their Pueblo neighbors to the east are known far more for their pottery than their basketry, although ancient Pueblos made some of the first basketry in North America. Some of the Pueblos along the Rio Grande as well as those at Jemez and San Juan also make baskets.

California Indians are known the world over for their diverse and beautiful baskets. From the Kumeyaays, Luiseños, and Chemehuevis of southern California to the Miwuks, Pomos, Wintus, Maidus, and Achumawis of northern California, native women in the region are considered some of the best basket makers on earth. In his pathbreaking volume, *The Fine Art of California Indian Basketry,* Brian Bibby details the development and continuance of basketry in California. He also provides outstanding examples of California Indian baskets, including those of Chumash Maria Marta, which are made of juncus, split sumac shoots, and bulrush roots depicting symbols of castles, lions, and crowns taken from a Spanish coin in about 1822. He offers examples of a Wailaki burden basket, Yurok hopper mortar basket, Washoe tray, Konkow acorn flour-receiving basket, and Yuki utility basket. Some of the best-known basket makers featured in Bibby's study include Konkow Amanda Wilson, Wintu Bertha Mitchell, Tolowa-Karuk Loren Bommelyn, Atsugewi Selena LaMarr, Pomo-Wintu Myrtle McKay Chavez, and Chemehuevi Leroy Fisher. In a recent volume, *Remember Your Relations,* Suzanne Abel-Vidor, Dot Brovarney, and Pomo basket maker Susan Billy detail the revitalization of Pomo basketry by Pomo Elsie Allen, the artist who passed on knowledge of Pomo basket making in order to preserve the art among her people.

Renewed interest in beadwork has characterized this art form since 1970, when schools, tribal centers, urban Indian centers, Title IV and Title V programs, and senior citizens centers offered classes and workshops on beading. Beadwork is another ancient Native American art that began before white contact, when native artists used baked clay beads, shells, teeth, bones, seeds, wood, ivory, stones, gold, silver, and copper for beading. Iroquoian and Algonquian peoples used wampum shells to make beautiful and sacred belts that recorded historical events such as tribal alliances. Wampum belts were highly prized, but Native Americans soon incorporated glass beads brought by Europeans into their cultures, using them to decorate a variety of items. Most beadworkers were women, but recently men have learned the art. In the nineteenth and twentieth centuries, many tribes from many parts of North America sewed glass beads onto shirts, dresses, moccasins, leggings, necklaces, earrings, bolos, belts, bags, wrist bands, and a host of other items. Some tribes have gravitated to certain colors. Many Apaches prefer bold yellows and reds mixed with black, whereas Lakotas prefer greens. A certain shade of pink is commonly called "Cheyenne pink." Native artists on the Northwest Plateau often prefer royal blue, whereas Luiseños prefer browns. In recent years, beaders favor cut beads that catch the light and sparkle. Beaded objects are common in Indian country and highly prized.

Pueblo and Navajo people in the Southwest are best known for their textiles. Ancient Pueblo peoples wove textiles of cotton, rabbit fur, and turkey feathers. They were known for making blankets, skirts, sashes, belts, leggings, and others items from woven cotton. Although Pueblo Indian textile production had declined by 1900, the people revitalized the art in the 1920s with the help of the Santa Fe Indian School, American Indian Arts and Crafts Board, and the School of American Research. Weavers at San Juan pueblo and at Hopi took the lead to renew interest in the art, and by the middle of the twentieth century, most of the pueblos had joined in the efforts to continue the art with wool and cotton. Today, many pueblos make mantas, kilts, sash belts, leggings, and other garments in a variety of colors. Hopi weavers include Roger Nasevaema, Martin Gashweseoma, Louis Josytewa, and Elmer Sequoptewa; and prominent Zuni weavers include Vivian Kaskalla and Herrin Othole. Numerous people at San Juan weave, including Ramoncita Sandoval, Piedad Antoine, Lorencita Bird, Gavrelita Nave, Reyes Abeita, and Geronima Montoya.

For generations Navajos have woven blankets, sashes, saddle blankets, rugs, and dresses. Before the Navajo removal to the Bosque Redondo, women perfected their art using wool. After the Long Walk, white Indian traders such as C. N. Cotton, Juan Lorenzo Hubbell, Anson Damon, Samuel Day, and Thomas Keams encouraged Navajos to weave for the tourist market. Navajos began using new designs and created rugs distinct to their area on the vast Navajo Reservation. Ganado became known for the use of red as the dominant color, accompanied by grays and blacks, whereas rugs from Klahgeto contain red and black with the dominant color gray. Two Grey Hills is known for designs reminiscent of Persian rugs with corners featuring stair steps. Wide Ruin rugs are soft with tans, grays, and whites featured in geometric designs. The Wheelwright Museum, Museum of Northern Arizona, Museum of New Mexico, Denver Art Museum, and many other institutions around the world, as well as collectors, began buying Navajo rugs.

During the twentieth century the growing interest in Native American textiles increased their value and demand. As a result, more Navajo women have learned to weave, from their mothers, grandmothers, aunts, and tribal elders. Bertha Beall of Lukachukai has provided brilliant examples of pictorial rugs, including Yeibitchai rugs, and those of Rose Owens, Amy Begay, Irene Julia Nez, Ason Yellowhair, Sadie Curtis, Mary Lee Begay, Irene Clark, Bessie B. Yazzie, and many others have become well known. General interests in textiles also led the Chilkat Tlingit to revive their art of weaving robes or dancing blankets. The late Maria Miller became one of the foremost weavers among the Tlingit, and her work is highly prized throughout the world. These are exquisite robes made of cedar bark and mountain goat hair with family crests woven into the textiles. Salish-speaking peoples of the

Chilkat robes are made by artists like the late Maria Miller of Haines, Alaska. Here, she is exhibiting a dance apron with a Killer Whale clan robe behind her. She collected the mountain goat wool to make the robe and cleaned, dyed, and wove this prized work of art.

Northwest also renewed their creation of blankets made from mountain goat hair and vegetable fibers. Chilkat and Salish peoples used their weavings in ceremonies and as gifts for potlatches. The Salish also used their blankets for everyday bedding. The Totem Heritage Center in Ketchikan, the Institute of Alaska Native Arts, and the University of British Columbia Museum have encouraged the people to revive their textile art. The results of cooperative efforts have been phenomenal and these efforts have spread to other native nations, where artists are creating their own textile traditions or reviving old ones. Cherokees, Kickapoos, Yakamas, Narragansetts, and other peoples are now producing textiles, and the art is growing. In addition, many native peoples are creating quilts of unique design, including Star Quilts that have spiritual significance to Plains people. This is also the case in Mexico and other Latin American countries, where Native Americans have an ancient tradition in making textiles.

SILVERWORK, QUILLS, AND RIBBONS

Although traditional native artists north of the Rio Grande worked wood, bone, feathers, seeds, clay, ivory, shells, and copper into body ornaments, they used little silver or gold until the arrival of Spaniards. According to scholar Frederick J. Dockstader, Pueblo, Navajo, and Calusa made some jewelry from Spanish coins, but the art of silversmithing did not thrive until the late nineteenth and early twentieth centuries, when materials became more available and techniques for working these metals became common knowledge. In 1853, Navajo artist Atsidi Sani learned silverwork from a Latino ironworker, and Sani shared his knowledge with other Navajo. While in captivity at the Bosque Redondo, Navajos learned blacksmithing and used their knowledge of metal working to form silver items like those they had obtained from Latinos in New Mexico. Navajos, Hopis, and Zunis dominate silversmithing among Native Americans, although in recent years, artisans of the Kiowa, Comanche, Northwest Coast people, and Iroquois have rivaled southwestern silversmiths. For years Navajos were known for casting or handworking silver with large chunks of turquoise, a sacred stone to many southwestern peoples. Today, Frank and Evelyn Chee of Vanderwagon, New Mexico, and an increasing number of Navajo artisans are using gold and silver as well as smaller pieces of stone in their jewelry.

Recent Navajo jewelry is similar to Zuni inlay jewelry that employs intricate patterns of mother of pearl, jet, coral, and turquoise. Zuni artist Robert Tsabetsaye employed enamel in his innovative work, but most Zuni silversmiths use mosaics of the above-mentioned materials. Zuni artisans Robert Kaskalla, Carolyn Bobelu, and Milford Nahohai are a few of the best known jewelry makers from this pueblo. However, it has become a trend at Zuni for families to work as a team to produce fine jewelry. The Calabaza, Quam, Weebothee, and Ondelacy families have taken the lead in jewelry making at Zuni pueblo. At Hopi, Howard Sice has offered a new technique for engraving designs on silver, although the traditional Hopi method of overlay remains dominant. Hopi artists cut animal, plant, and geometric designs on their silver and overlay it onto another surface of silver. This overlay provides a distinctive shadowing effect. However, not all Hopi artisans employ this technique, experimenting instead with techniques used by other Pueblo and Navajo artists or creating their own techniques. The late Charles Loloma was the most renowned of all native artisans who worked in silver or gold. He used a variety of stones in ways that appeared "nontraditional" but had the graceful beauty and symmetry of Hopi jewelry. Numerous jewelry artisans work at Hopi and surrounding cities, including Michael Kabotie, Louis Lomayesva, Robert Lomadapki, Lawrence Saufkie, and Bernard Dawahoya.

The success of silver and gold jewelry among Navajos, Hopis, and Zunis has encouraged other Native American artists to explore jewelry making. Santo Domingo artisans Gail Bird and Charles Lavato work primarily in silver, as do Inuit Ronald Senungetuk, Aleut Gertrude Svarny, and Aleut Denise Wallace. Two Haida artists, Bill Reid and

Robert Davidson, cast and engrave silver and gold. In 1959, Reid produced a cast broach of a frog from gold, while Denise Wallace offered a "Seal Hunt" ring, reminiscent of transformation masks that work on many levels. The late Pawnee silversmith Julius Caesar and his son, Bruce Caesar, offered jewelry made of German silver. Choctaw Robert Kaniatobe works in shell carving, whereas Cherokee Patty Fawn Smith works in ivory.

Many native artists have revived the art of quillwork, but Lakota Alfred Zephier offers jewelry of quills mixed with stones, an unusual combination that sets him apart from most artists working in quills. Unlike silver and gold art, quillwork is ancient to the Americas. Native people from many areas used porcupine quills to decorate moccasins, dresses, shirts, belts, bags, and other items. Today, innovative native artisans use quills on bolos, baseball hats, wallets, earrings, necklaces, and other items.

Native American artists also use ribbon work to decorate shawls, shirts, quilts, moccasins, breechcloths, and dresses. Unlike other native arts, ribbon work is a combination of traditional and contemporary Native American designs and subjects with manufactured cloths. For years Native Americans had painted, beaded, woven, and cut designs and applied the art to objects. With this tradition, Native Americans used manufactured cloth obtained through trade with whites and cut out designs that they applied to various materials, including other cloth. Traditional and contemporary ribbon artists cut fabric into elaborate designs and sew them onto other surfaces. They cut out geometric, floral, and animal designs. The art grew full bloom in the nineteenth century, only to decline in the early twentieth century. Wyandot, Lenape, Osage, Sac, Fox, Kickapoo, and other peoples in Kansas and Oklahoma maintained the art. During the 1950s, Wyandot Mary Louise Henry used ribbon work to decorate a breechcloth and shirt for her son's dance outfit, and in like fashion, women in other parts of the United States and Canada returned to the old technique after the 1930s. By the mid-1970s, ribbon work had become fashionable throughout Indian country, particularly on the powwow circuit, where dancers and participants wore ribbon shirts and where vendors offered ribbon work for sale.

The late twentieth century was a time when many native artists renewed their interests in traditional arts and created their own art forms, drawing on the larger art world as well as their own life experiences as native people. Native self-determination influenced the artistic renewal, although non-Indian traders, collectors, museum curators, teachers, artists, and others encouraged native people to study and renew their ancient art forms and create contemporary art forms. Native American fine arts are an integral part of American Indian history, but no less so than literature and the performing arts.

Selected Readings and Bibliography

Native Americans have always been artists, working with many natural materials and producing beautiful pottery, paintings, masks, clothing, carvings, sculptures, baskets, beadwork, quillwork, and other art forms as well. Some of the works previously cited and used to write this chapter are Johnson's *The Occupation of Alcatraz Island,* Rawls's *Chief Red Fox Is Dead,* Champagne's *The Native North American Almanac,* Ortiz and Erdoes's *American Indian Myths and Legends,* Child's *Boarding School Seasons,* Trafzer and Scheuerman's *Mourning Dove's Stories,* Beavert's *The Way It Was,* Trafzer's *Grandmothers, Grandfathers and Old Wolf,* and Malinowski and Abrams's *Notable Native Americans.*

Abbot, Lawrence, ed. *I Stand in the Center of the Good: Interviews with Contemporary Native American Artists.* Lincoln: University of Nebraska Press, 1994.

Abel-Vidor, Suzanne, Dot Brovarney, and Susan Billy. *Remember Your Relations: The Elsie Allen Baskets, Family & Friends.* Oakland and Berkeley: Grace Hudson Museum, Oakland Museum of California, and Heyday Books, 1996.

Archuleta, Margaret, and Rennard Strickland. *Shared Visions: Native American Painters and Sculptors in the Twentieth Century.* Phoenix: Heard Museum, 1991.

Babcock, Barbara, Guy Monthan, and Doris Monthan. *The Pueblo Storyteller.* Tucson: University of Arizona Press, 1986.

Bad Heart Bull, Amos. A *Pictographic History of the Oglala Sioux.* Text by Helen H. Blish. Lincoln: University of Nebraska Press, 1967.

Berlo, Janet Catherine. "Native North American Visual Arts." *Native North American Almanac.* Duane Champagne, ed. Detroit: Gale Researchers, 1994. pp. 714–721.

Bibby, Brian. *The Fine Art of California Indian Basketry.* Sacramento and Berkeley: Crocker Art Museum and Heyday Books, 1996.

Bonar, Eulalie H. *Woven by the Grandmothers: Nineteenth Century Navajo Textiles from the National Museum of the American Indian.* Washington, D.C.: Smithsonian Institution Press, 1996.

Breeskin, Adelyn D., and Rudy H. Tuck. *Scholder/Indians.* Flagstaff: Northland Press, 1972.

Broder, Patricia Janis. *American Indian Painting and Sculpture.* New York: Abbeville Press, 1981.

Brody, J. J. *Indian Painters & White Patrons.* Albuquerque: University of New Mexico Press, 1971.

Brodzky, Anne Trueblood, Rose Danesewich, and Nick Johnson. *Stones, Bones, and Skin: Ritual and Shamanic Art.* Toronto: Society for Art Publications, 1977.

Bunzel, Ruth L. *The Pueblo Potter: A Study of Creative Imagination in Primitive Art.* New York: Columbia University Press, 1929.

Caduto, Michael J., and Joseph Bruchac. *Keepers of the Earth.* Golden, Colo.: Fulcrum, 1988.

——. *Keepers of the Animals.* Golden, Colo.: Fulcrum, 1991.

——. *Keepers of the Night.* Golden, Colo.: Fulcrum, 1994.

Cinader, Bernhard. *Contemporary Indian Art: The Trail from the Past to the Future.* Peterborough, Ontario: Mackenzie Gallery and Native Studies Programme, 1977.

Coe, Ralph T. *Lost and Found Traditions: Native American Art 1965–1985.* Seattle: University of Washington Press and New York: American Federation of Arts, 1986.

Conn, Richard. *Native American Art in the Denver Art Museum.* Denver: Denver Art Museum, 1979.

Crozier, Lois, and Darryl Babe Wilson, eds. *Surviving in Two Worlds: Contemporary Native American Voices.* Austin: University of Texas Press, 1997.

Douglas, Fredric H., and Rene d'Harnoncourt. *Indian Art of the United States.* New York: Museum of Modern Art, 1941.

Evers, Larry, and Felipe S. Molina. *Yaqui Deer Songs.* Tucson: University of Arizona Press, 1987.

Feest, Christian F. *Native Arts of North America.* London: Thames and Hudson, 1980.

Fletcher, Alice C. *Indian Games and Dances with Native Songs.* Lincoln: University of Nebraska Press, 1994.

Grant, Campbell. *Rock Art of the American Indian.* New York: Crowell, 1967.

Harrison, Julia, et al. *The Spirit Songs: Artistic Traditions of Canada's First Peoples.* Toronto: McClelland and Stewart and Calgary: Glenbow Museum, 1987.

Henkes, Robert. *Native American Painters of the Twentieth Century.* Jefferson, N.C.: McFarland, 1995.

Henningsen, Chuck. *R. C. Gorman. A Portrait.* Boston: Little, Brown, 1983.

Highwater, Jamake. *The Sweet Grass Lives On: Fifty Contemporary North American Indian Artists.* New York: Lippincott and Crowell, 1980.

——. *Ritual of the Wind: North American Indian Ceremonies, Music, and Dance.* New York: A. Van der Marck Editions, 1984.

Horse Capture, George P. *Powwow.* Cody, Wyo.: Buffalo Bill Historical Center, 1989.

Howard, James H., and Victoria Lindsay Levine. *Choctaw Music and Dance.* Norman: University of Oklahoma Press, 1990.

Jacka, Jerry D., Lois E. Jacka, and Clara L. Tanner. *Beyond Tradition: Contemporary Indian Art and Its Evolution.* Flagstaff: Northland Press, 1988.

Kramer, Barbara. *Nampeyo and Her Pottery.* Albuquerque: University of New Mexico Press, 1996.

Marriott, Alice. Maria: *The Potter of San Ildefonso.* Norman: University of Oklahoma Press, 1948.

McLuhan, Elizabeth, and Tom Hill. *Norval Morrisseau and the Emergence of the Image Makers.* Toronto: Methuen, 1984.

McLuhan, Elizabeth. *Altered Egos: The Multimedia Work of Carl Beam.* Thunder Bay, Ontario: Thunder Bay National Exhibition Centre and Centre for Indian Art, 1984.

Mellick, Jill. *The Worlds of P'otsunu: Geronima Cruz Montoya of San Juan Pueblo.* Albuquerque: University of New Mexico Press, 1996.

Nemirodff, D., R. Houle, and C. Townsend-Gault. *Land, Spirit, Power: First Nations at the National Gallery of Canada.* Ottawa: National Gallery of Canada, 1992.

Penney, David W. *Art of the American Indian Frontier: The Chandler-Pohrt Collection*. Detroit: Detroit Institute of Arts and Seattle: University of Washington Press, 1992.

——. "Native North American Arts and Visual Culture." *The Native North American Almanac*. Duane Champagne, ed. Detroit: Gale Researchers, 1994. pp. 722–730.

Perlman, Barbara H. *Allan Houser*. Boston: D. R. Godine, 1987.

Peterson, Susan. *Maria Martinez: Five Generations of Potters*. Washington, D.C.: Smithsonian Institution Press, 1978.

Phillips, Ruth B. "Glimpses of Eden: Iconographic Themes in Huron Pictorial Art." *European Review of Native American Studies* 5:2 (1991): 19–28.

Pollock, Jack, and Lister Sinclair. *The Art of Norval Morrisseau*. Toronto: Methuen, 1979.

Schoolcraft, Henry Roe. *Schoolcraft's Indian Legends*. East Lansing: Michigan State University Press, 1997.

——. *Schoolcraft's Ojibwa Lodge Stories*. East Lansing: Michigan State University Press, 1997.

Seymour, Tryntje V. N. *When the Rainbow Touches Down*. Phoenix: Heard Museum, 1988.

Shadbolt, Doris. *Bill Reid*. Vancouver: Douglas & McIntyre, 1986.

Swann, Brian, ed. *Coming to the Light: Contemporary Translations of the Native Literatures of North America*. New York: Vintage, 1994.

This Path We Travel: Celebrations of Contemporary Native American Creativity. Golden, Colo.: The National Museum of the American Indian, Smithsonian Institution, and Fulcrum Publishing, 1994.

Trafzer, Clifford E., ed. *Looking Glass*. San Diego: San Diego State University Press, Publications in American Indian Studies, 1991.

Vastokas, Joan M. "Bill Reid and the Native Renaissance." *Arts Canada* 32 (1975): 12–21.

——. "Native Art in North America." *The Native North American Almanac*. Duane Champagne, ed. Detroit: Gale Researchers, 1994. pp. 693–701.

Wade, Edwin L. *The Arts of the North American Indian: Native Traditions in Evolution*. New York: Hudson Hills Press, 1986.

Wade, Edwin L., and Rennard Strickland. *Magic Images: Contemporary Native American Art*. Tulsa: Philbrook Art Center and Norman: University of Oklahoma Press, 1981.

West, W. Richard. Foreword. *Stories of the People: Native American Voices*. Washington, D.C.: National Museum of the American Indian, 1997.

Williams, Chuck. *Bridge of the Gods, Mountains of Fire*. Hood River, Ore.: Elephant Mountain Arts, 1993.

Wilson, Darryl Babe. *The Morning the Sun Went Down*. Berkeley: Heyday Books, 1998.

Wright, Robin K. *A Time of Gathering: Native Heritage in Washington State*. Seattle: Burke Museum and University of Washington Press, 1991.

Alvin Amason, an Aleut artist from Kodiak Island, painted Papa Would Like You, which depicts a Kodiak bear studying two salmon. Like all of Amason's work, this painting focuses on animals found in the artist's native land, where the world's largest bears fish the streams during annual salmon runs.
© Alvin Amason.

Wintu-Nomtipom artist Frank La Pena painted Blue Shadow Spirit in 1991. La Pena's paintings reflect the blend of past and present, and they draw on Native American spirituality to illustrate known but unseen power. La Pena uses a modern medium to present ancient ideas.
Frank La Pena. Photo courtesy of American Indian Contemporary Arts.

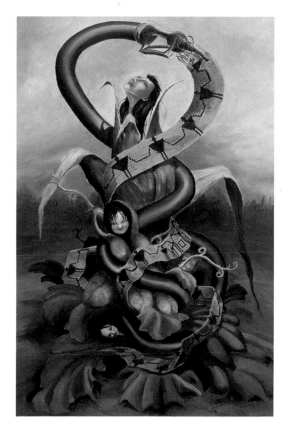

Onondaga artist and writer Eric Gansworth uses paint to depict the importance of corn, squash, and beans in The Three Sisters. These are three staples of Iroquoian peoples and are considered sacred to many Native American people, who conduct ceremonies related to planting, growing, maturing, and harvesting.
© Eric Gainsworth.

Maidu artist Harry Fonseca draws on his heritage in his presentation of Moon Dancers. *Like many native people, Maidus celebrated and prayed through music, song, and dance. Fonseca is best known for his artful portrayal of Coyote, the trickster and creator who helped put the world into motion.*

© Harry Fonseca. Photo courtesy of American Indian Contemporary Arts.

This "Grandmother" mask made by Lilly Kilbear was constructed from caribou hide. Kilbear made the mask in Point Barrow, Alaska, about 1984, forming it by hand from the hide of the animal and stretching it to create the nose, cheeks, and chin. She stitched the hair and fur into the mask before braiding the gray hair of grandmother, giving the mask the face of a tribal elder.

From the Trafzer Family Collection.

Lakota chief Tatanka Yotanka (or Sitting Bull) was a medicine man and warrior of great stature among the Teton Sioux. Here, he is wearing an eagle feather headdress, which denotes his position as a leader among his people.

The Granger Collection, New York.

CHAPTER 21

LITERATURE AND PERFORMING ARTS

Traditional narratives, dance, and music emerged among Native Americans at the time of creation. Many ancient songs are stories of creation and migration, movement from one world to the next, or of characters diving to the bottom of endless seas to bring up mud from which to make the earth. Dance and movement are often a part of storytellings, which may include songs and sounds of wind, cloud, tree, mountain, and river. Many Native American societies do not organize oral narratives, songs, music, and dance into separate categories. Rather, for example, oral narratives may be at once songs and poetry, music and dance. When Cahuilla singers Luke Madrigal, Anthony Madrigal, Alvino Silva, and Robert Levi sing Bird Songs, they sing of creation, migration, and the relationship of people to plants, animals, and places. This is no less true when Larry Eddy and Mat Leivas sing Chemehuevi Indian Salt Songs, which describe the movement of two sisters from the Bill Williams River of Arizona to Las Vegas and from the Mojave Desert of California to the Colorado River. According to Navajo scholar Paul Apodaca, Salt Songs and Bird Songs are music, literature, dance, and history. They emerge from an oral tradition that is kept alive today with the singing of the songs and formal native organizations designed to perpetuate the ancient songs.

ORAL LITERATURE AND AUTOBIOGRAPHY

The first literature of the Americas was Native American oral narratives, which are rich with the events and forces that set the world into motion. Each native group has its own stories of creation, although these stories may be similar with slight variations. Storytellers shared these narratives of plant and animal people, telling of interactions between rocks, rivers, trees, winds, oceans, sky, and stars. Stories often deal with cultural heroes and their triumphs over monsters. Stories are still shared today, but some have been recorded by anthropologists, folklorists, and linguists. These are but a small portion of the vast number of oral narratives passed down from generation to generation. On the La Jolla Reservation in southern California, Luiseño singer and scholar Temet Aguilar worked with the Costo Historical and Linguistics Native American Research Center to capture on video some oral traditions of elder Robert Lofton. Aguilar's project links the past to the present, as does the work of Swhyaylpuh-Okanogan Christine Quintasket, better known as Mourning Dove. Her works, *Coyote Stories* and *Mourning Dove's Stories,* present a few examples of oral stories from the inland Northwest. Mourning Dove pointed out in her papers that elders had told her traditional stories that were "true" and historical, not fairy tales. Like many native people of her time, she believed that these traditional stories held values, reminding humans that love, generosity, fear, responsibility, hunger, humor, greed, sickness, and death came with the creation and remain part of life. These are the motifs found in the sacred oral texts of Native Americans.

Writing from and through the oral tradition has become a genre in native literature. Many tribes throughout the Americas have recorded and published oral narratives that they wish to share with a broader audience. San Juan Tewas Alfonso Ortiz and Richard Erdoes produced a fine collection of traditional stories in *American Indian Myths and Legends,* which offers several tribal stories presented thematically: creation, celestial bodies, heroes and monsters, war stories, love and lust, trickster stories, animal people, ghost and spirit stories, and others. Brian Swann has edited a contemporary oral collection in *Coming to Light: Contemporary Translations of the Native Literatures of North America,* which includes several selections by native writers, including Lushootseed Vi Hilbert, Nez Perce Archie Finney, Mohawk Pauline Johnson, Sioux Charles A. Eastman, and Blackfeet Percy Bullchild. Abnaki author Joseph Bruchac III and Michael J. Caduto have teamed up to coedit and retell the stories of many Indians in *Keepers of the Earth, Keepers of the Animals, Keepers of the Night,* published by Fulcrum Press.

Yakama Virginia Beavert edited several native stories from her reservation in *The Way It Was, Inaku Iwacha: Yakima Indian Legends,* and recently, Michigan State University Press offered other original stories from the Northwest Plateau in Wyandot Clifford E. Trafzer's edited work, *Grandmother, Grandfather, and Old Wolf: Tamánwit Ku Súkat and Traditional Native American Stories from the Columbia Plateau.* Henry Roe Schoolcraft recorded Native American stories in the 1820s and 1830s that have been reprinted by Michigan State University Press as *Schoolcraft's Indian Legends* and *Schoolcraft's Ojibwa Lodge Stories: Life on the Lake Superior Frontier,* both edited by Philip P. Mason. Pit River scholar Darryl Wilson used oral narratives as the basis of his autobiographical story, *The Day the Sun Went Down,* and Tohono O'odham linguist Ofelia

Zepeda has also produced a number of scholarly articles dealing with oral traditions.

Yaqui scholar Felipe Molina and Larry Evers have collaborated on a fascinating bilingual work, *Yaqui Deer Songs/Maso Bwikam,* and Nez Perce historian Alan P. Slickpoo Sr. compiled several stories from his tribe in *Nu Mee Poom Tit Wah Tit.* Anishinaabe writer Kimberly Blaeser explores the meaning of oral traditions in her book, *Gerald Vizenor: Writing in the Oral Tradition.* In addition to these published sources, some tribes and public archives have tape recordings and videotapes of tribal elders singing and storytelling. The Warm Springs tribe of Oregon has collected several stories, and the Yakima City and County Regional Library has a tape recording of Puck Hiya Toot, the nephew of Smohalla. Historian Jean Keller has recently published a guide to the Gerald Smith Collection at Smiley Library in Redlands, California, which includes oral renditions of Serrano stories that have never been reproduced. Libraries and archives across North America contain such treasures, and these oral stories provide a foundation for understanding Native American history.

Native American autobiography was one of the earliest forms of written literature. Some of the most noteworthy of these autobiographical presentations includes Pequot minister William Apess's *A Son of the Forest,* which criticizes settlers for their ill treatment of Native Americans, and Ojibway William Copway's *Life, History, and Travels of Kah-ge-ga-gah-bowh,* which is pro-Christian. This is the same theme offered by Dakota Charles Eastman in *Indian Boyhood* and *From Deep Wood to Civilization,* both of which acknowledge the value of native culture but encourage assimilation. Non-Indian scholars have also written numerous volumes dealing with American Indian people and a variety of subjects. These scholars' contributions have been significant to the study of Native American history. Too often, however, the contributions of native people in writing their own narratives have been overlooked or considered less important than those of nonnatives.

In 1884, for example, Paiute Sarah Winnemucca wrote *Life among the Piutes, Their Wrongs and Claims,* an autobiographical account with tribal history. This approach is also found in *Black Hawk, an Autobiography; Black Elk Speaks; Sun Chief; Lame Deer: Seeker of Visions; Yaqui Woman;* and more recently, *Lakota Woman* and *Mourning Dove: A Salishan Autobiography.* Native autobiographical accounts permit readers to enter the author's world, although some of the accounts are through the lens of nonnative collaborators. The works by Lame Deer, Mary Crow Dog, and Mourning Dove are near original, and the same is true of Osage John Joseph Mathews's *Talking to the Moon,* Kiowa N. Scott Momaday's *The Way to Rainy Mountain* and *Names,* Anishinaabe Gerald Vizenor's *Interior Landscapes,* and Cocur d'Alene-Kootenai Janet Campbell Hale's *Bloodlines.*

Satire, criticism, and humor are found in other writings by Native Americans who address their views of white institutions. Muscogee writer Alexander Posey offered his values in "Fus Fixico Letters" (1902–1908), newspaper articles that have been skillfully edited by Osage Carol Hunter and Cherokee Dan Littlefield. They point out that Fixico uses Muscogee elders as characters and writes in Muscogee Indian dialect of English. Cherokee humorist and satirist Will Rogers wrote a daily column in newspapers, commenting on American politics and sharing his opinions on a variety of subjects. One of his many books is *Rogers-isms: The Cowboy Philosopher on the Peace Conference.* Nez Perce warrior Hemene Moxmox left a classic account of his participation in the Nez Perce War in *Yellow Wolf: His Own Story,* edited by L. V. McWhorter. In recent years literary scholars have criticized McWhorter's work with Mourning Dove, but scholar Steven Evans has pointed out that McWhorter's work with Yellow Wolf carefully represents the warrior's voice. Arnold Krupat and Brian Swann have offered a number of diverse autobiographical accounts of native people in *I Tell You Now* and *Everything Matters,* providing insights into the lives and work of contemporary native writers.

Under the leadership of Tlingit Nora Marks Dauenhauer and Richard Dauenhauer, Tlingit people have published numerous personal accounts through the Sealaska Heritage Foundation and the University of Washington Press. These offer contemporary native voices from Alaska, including *Haa Shuká, Our Ancestors: Tlingit Oral Narratives; Haa Tuwunáagu Yís, for Healing Our Spirit: Tlingit Oratory;* and *Haa Kusteeyí, Our Culture: Tlingit Life Stories.* Other native communities have offered autobiographical presentations of their people through a variety of means, but major publishing houses and university presses have generally ignored native autobiography. Fortunately, Nez Perce elder Horace Axtell published *A Little Bit of Wisdom,* and Eleonore Sioui is finishing an autobiographical community narrative of her Wyandot people.

POETRY

Many contemporary writers compose short stories, novels, and poetry. However, in the era prior to the twentieth century, Native Americans wrote little poetry as the genre is known today, but they did compose a voluminous array of songs, chants, and narratives that are poetic. The traditional "Song of the Earth" of Diné people is poetic, as are the lines of several native songs. Some scholars maintain that traditional oral narratives are "ethno-poetic" and were told traditionally as if they were poems. This is the case in contemporary North America among some storytellers. The first contributions of modern poetry were published by

Mohawk writer E. Pauline Johnson, who offered *Flint and Feather,* and Alexander Posey, whose *The Poems of Alexander Posey* was published posthumously. In 1924, Wyandot Bertrand N. O. Walker offered *Yon-doo-shah-we-ah,* a small body of work that offers narrative poems focusing on people and place.

The most important native poets emerged in the late twentieth century. N. Scott Momaday is best known for his poetry through *Angle of Geese and Other Poems,* and he is known for his ability to read his own work with power and eloquence. His ability to perform his poetry is equaled by that of other native poets, including Anishinaabe Mark Turcotte, Yaqui Anita Endrezze, and Duane Niatum. One of the most talented native poets is Simon Ortiz of Acoma pueblo, who distinguished himself as a master writer in *Going for the Rain, A Good Journey, Howbah Indians, Song, Poetry and Language,* and *From Sand Creek.* Ortiz uses his poetry to affirm the vitality of native people, the attachment of people to the earth, and outrages against Indian people by non-Indian people. Ortiz is a prolific writer, working in many genres simultaneously. Laguna pueblo poet Carol Lee Sanchez is another exceptional poet who has a talent to capture personalities and locations on paper through her colorful and moving *She Poems.* The same is true of Anishinaabe author Gerald Vizenor, who offered native poetry in the Haiku form in *Raising the Moon Vines, Seventeen Chirps,* and *Empty.* Anishinaabe author Gordon Henry has also used Haiku poetry in his novel, *The Light People,* a book that blends poetry and prose.

Laguna poet Leslie Silko has drawn on her own tribal traditions to inform her poetry, some of which appeared in *Laguna Woman* and *Storyteller.* Silko's poetry is varied, drawing on familial experiences as well as the lives of others. Much of her poetry centers on Laguna traditions and characters found within tribal narratives. Fellow Laguna author Paula Gunn Allen is also a prolific poet and has a magical way with words. Some of her work includes *Coyote's Daylight Trip, Shadow Country,* and *Skin and Bones.* Allen's work is provocative, often filled with sadness, which has been an integral part of the native experience. Koyukon Athabaskan poet Mary TallMountain is best known for the spirituality of her work, which draws heavily on her Alaskan roots. Her works include *There Is No Word for Goodbye, Green March Moons, The Light on the Tent Wall,* and *A Quick Brush of Wings.* Two talented and rising Abnaki poets are Carol Snow Moon Bachofner and Cheryl Savageau, who have written several books, including, respectively, *Gluscabi and Wind Eagle* and *Dirt Road Home.*

Blackfeet-Gros Ventre James Welch began his writing career as a poet. Many people consider his book, *Riding the Earthboy 40,* to be a classic because it deals with the cold realism that has characterized the native experience since white contact. Death, disease, desperation, depression, and identity are a part of the past that Welch captures in his writings.

Welch's poetry foreshadowed his critically acclaimed novel, *Winter in the Blood,* and some of his other novels. Osage Carter Revard is a poet who uses narrative lines that draw on Osage traditions and families. His book, *Ponca War Dancers,* deals with his uncle, Gus McDonald, a noted pow-wow fancy dancer. The joy of Revard's work is matched by the sadness in the poetry of Hopi-Miwuk Wendy Rose. She has published several books, including *Lost Copper, Going to War with All My Relations,* and *Bone Dance.*

Navajo Luci Tapahonso was born into a strong poetic tradition of Diné songs used extensively in ceremonies. She is best known for *One More Shiprock Night: Poems* and *Saanii Dahataal, The Women Are Singing: Poems and Stories.* Her imagery and use of words are well crafted, providing readers with vivid descriptions of people, places, and events. The relationship of the poet to her nation is also felt in Oneida poet Roberta Hill Whiteman's *Star Quilt,* which offers elements of history, tradition, and environment. Whiteman's feelings of dispossession, resulting from white intrusions into native life, are as clear as her attachment to family. The significance of family is also woven into the poetry of Wasco-Navajo poet Elizabeth Woody in *Hand into Stone* and *Luminaries of the Humble,* which deal with love, laughter, and home cooking. Like Tapahonso, Whiteman, and other native poets, Woody carefully selects her subjects in a lucid, wise, and wonderful fashion to express depth of feelings. This is also true of Anishinaabe poet Kimberly Blaeser, whose poem, "Sewing Memories: This Poem I've Wanted to Write," beautifully weaves together her lifelong relationship with her mother.

Humorous and serious issues are dualities that appear in poems by many Native American writers, including Mohawk poet Beth Brant, who has published several poems and actively encourages other native writers to compose. Her books include *Mohawk Trail, Food & Spirits,* and *Writings as Witness,* which offer work ranging from light-hearted humor to important issues facing society, including the AIDS epidemic. The strength found in Brant's poetry is equaled by renowned Dakota writer Elizabeth Cook-Lynn, whose poems have appeared widely in journals, magazines, and anthologies. She expresses her defiance of white society while demonstrating the tenacious survival of native people in *Why I Can't Read Wallace Stegner and Other Essays.* Through her writing, she actively stands against oppression while recognizing the contributions of tribal elders. The powerful use of English to convey feelings is also found in Coeur d'Alene writer Janet Campbell Hale's *Custer Lives in Humboldt County and Other Poems.* Physical, emotional, and spiritual abuses are themes found in Hale's writings, which offer a stark contrast to the sweetness found in other native poetry.

Anishinaabe poet Diane M. Burns captures the struggle within many native people regarding fitting and not fitting into society. Her book, *Riding the One-Eyed Ford*, explores individuality and community among contemporary native people. Shawnee poet and composer Barney Bush offers many dualities in his books, short stories, and personal memoirs, but his sense of humor is unmistakable in *My Horse and a Jukebox* and *Inherit the Blood*. Bush has made his mark as a writer, teacher, and activist but also has concentrated on music, making successful CDs that have sold internationally. The poetry of Cherokee writer Gladys Cardiff reads like music, particularly those selections found in *To Frighten a Story*. While unfortunately, Cardiff has not published other works, Abnaki poet Joseph Bruchac III has written hundreds of books, articles, essays, interviews, songs, stories, and other works. Since 1971, when he published *Indian Mountain and Other Poems*, Bruchac has published numerous poems in a variety of motifs but is best known today for his oral and written storytelling and his novel, *Dawn Land*.

Anishinaabe writer Louise Erdrich also started as a poet. Her colorful and skilled use of the language led her to publish *Jacklight: Poems* and *Baptism of Desire: Poems*, which illustrate her imaginative use of words to convey concerns. A cast of characters and situations are found within the poetry of Muscogee poet and musician Joy Harjo, who is best known for *What Moon Drove Me to This?*, *She Had Some Horses*, and *In Mad Love and War*. The award-winning author's book, *The Woman Who Fell from the Sky*, deals with spiritual themes, the innate power of women, and the importance of storytelling. Chickasaw poet Linda Hogan also began her career writing poetry, publishing *Calling Myself Home*, *Eclipse*, and other collections, but, like Erdrich, she is best known for her novels, including *Mean Spirit*, which won several awards and was nominated for a Pulitzer Prize. Cherokee writer Diane Glancy is also known for her poetry, which reflects her love of Oklahoma and the Great Plains as well as tribal traditions. Some of her books of poetry include *Traveling On*, *Brown Wolf Leaves the Res and Other Poems*, and *Lone Dog's Winter Count*.

Native survival is a common theme in the poetry of Klallum Duane Niatum, who uses the theme successfully in *After the Death of an Elder Klallam; Carriers of the Dream Wheel: Contemporary Native American Poetry; Digging Out the Roots;* and *Drawings of the Song Animals: New and Selected Poems*. Niatum often focuses on the relationship of Northwest coastal people to the environment, and he uses the world of his ancestors to paint vivid word images of trees, salmon, canoes, songs, and relatives. Mohawk Maurice Kenny is a master poet who has been contributing since the 1950s, writing over twenty volumes of poetry. This remarkable writer has traveled extensively, drawing on his experience to compose poetry on a wide variety of subjects. However, he is best known for work that expresses his native heritage. He was nominated for a Pulitzer Prize for *Blackrobe* but has used his poetry to portray his own family, members of his tribe, tragedies, and the sacred. Kenny and Niatum are great performers of their art, speaking to thousands of people over the years and moving many to the rhythm of their thoughts and voices.

Mesquakie author Ray Young Bear is a poetic voice of his ancestors. His work focuses on memory, dreams, and blood, which nourishes people in a profound manner. Young Bear's poems are musical to the ear, and he purposely invites his readers to listen to the sounds of the words. He has offered *Winter of the Salamander*; *The Woodland Singers: Traditional Mesquakie Songs* (cassette tape, 1987); and *The Invisible Musician*. Choctaw poet Jim Barnes skillfully deals with a host of topics tying the past to present, including *The American Book of the Dead* and *A Season of Loss*. Mohawk writer Peter Blue Cloud has written numerous poems with several publishers, but his book *Alcatraz Is Not an Island* and his poem "Alcatraz Visions" offer a creative view of an important political event in native history. Award-winning Yaqui poet Anita Endrezze has distinguished herself through her poetry and short stories, publishing *at the helm of twighlight*, while Pawnee poet Glenn McGuire delights audiences with his colorful readings. Cherokee-Quapaw-Chickasaw writer Geary Hobson published an early and significant collection of Native American writings in *The Remembered Earth: An Anthology of Contemporary Native American Literature*, which included mixed genres. His book, *Deer Hunting and Other Poems*, draws the reader into the author's world, which moves in time and space through a variety of subjects. The devastating effects of alcohol and other problems are found in Paiute Adrian Louis's *Fire Water World*.

Journals and magazines around the world publish Native American poetry by many talented, undiscovered writers. It is impossible to mention all these poets, but their work is contributing significantly to the arts. At the University of Arizona, native students offer *Red Ink*, a creative literary magazine. In Tucson, Arizona, the *Arts Reach Literary Magazine* has featured the writings of several native children and has been edited by such notable native people as N. Scott Momaday, Ajumawe Darryl Wilson, Leslie Silko, Simon Ortiz, Tohono O'odham Ofelia Zepeda, Tohono O'odham Christina Zepeda, and Spokane-Coeur d'Alene writer Sherman Alexie, who began his career as a poet. He has offered his perspectives of Christopher Columbus, white oppression, Sand Creek, movies, and reservation life in *The Business of Fancydancing* and *Old Shirts & New Skins*. Another talented poet is Diné author Rex Lee Jim, who has written poetry and plays in his native language, including *Ahí Ni Ni' Nikisheega'ch* and *Saad*.

Like Jim, Anishinaabe author Mark Turcotte is a rising poet whose work has been critically acclaimed. Turcotte's book, *The Feathered Heart*, is filled with energy, honesty, and hope, which are also themes in the poetry of Ajumawe author Darryl Wilson. Born and raised in the Pit River country of California, Wilson has championed the preservation of the sacred Mount Shasta, which holds a basket containing goodness that is shared with the world. Wilson's hope for earth's renewal and native revival appears in his poetry.

> During the ripe-pine-nut season,
> they commanded that all people
> Hurry to the mountain tops,
> And before the silver of first light,
> prepare for a Great Sing
> And so it was and so it will be
> The love song will heal Mother Earth, again.
> It will begin when sister sun
> kisses the tops
> of AkoYet,
> The Great Mountain
> that balances the earth with the universe
> and the universe with forever and ever.

FICTION

Words wove Native American people into being, long before Vikings or Spaniards set foot on Turtle Island. All native nations have a variety of stories. Some were tribal and common knowledge, whereas others belonged to individuals—such as war stories or birthing stories. Other stories belonged to families, clans, villages, or moieties. Elders considered some stories to be history, whereas others were creative tales intended to entertain through humor, tragedy, and drama. Storytellers shared rich oral traditions that developed into written stories, including fiction. Native American fiction has grown each year as diverse writers use pens, pencils, and computers to express native experiences, sometimes using oral narratives, songs, and values while developing new ways to write about nature, identity, injustice, healing, family, witchcraft, and tricksters. Cultural change and images of native people, as well as reconciling past and current dealings with nonnative peoples, are also subjects found in fiction.

Muscogee author S. Alice Callahan was an early native writer of fiction who published her only book, *Wynema: A Child of the Forest,* in 1891. Noted scholar A. LaVonne Brown Ruoff has argued that the book is one of the earliest volumes by a native woman, and it is a book of romance, of condemnation toward the white invasion, and of information about native life and traditions. Callahan's work appeared in the late nineteenth century when few Native Americans wrote, but she was followed by Mohawk writer Emily Pauline Johnson and Colville author Mourning Dove. These women were transitional writers whose work drew heavily on oral traditions. Mourning Dove's work, for example, reflects a detailed knowledge of Chipmunk stories and the lives of other animal people.

Emily Johnson began her writing career in the 1870s by publishing a poem in the Brantford, Ontario, newspaper and soon after published other poems in *Harper's* and *Athenaeum*. She published poetry in *Songs of the Great Dominion* and *The White Wampum* before publishing her essays in *Canadian Born* and traditional narratives in *Legends of Vancouver*. In 1913, Johnson offered *The Moccasin Maker*, a cutting-edge work dealing with mixed-blood native people and white settlers. Mourning Dove published a similar portrayal in her novel, *Cogewea, the Half-Blood: A Depiction of the Great Montana Cattle Range*, and her books of traditional narratives, *Coyote Stories* and *Mourning Dove's Stories*. Osage writer John Joseph Mathews in 1934 offered *Sundown*, which focused on problems arising out of being a mixed-blood Osage who ignored his Indian past but could not adjust to white society, turning instead to liquor. His second work of fiction was *Wah'Kon-Tah*, which detailed forced removal to the reservation but survival through tradition.

Confederated Salish and Kootenai writer D'Arcy McNickle wrote several books, but his fiction included *The Surrounded, Runner in the Sun,* and *Wind from an Enemy Sky*. All of his writing reflects his pride but also emphasizes conflicts within families, communities, and tribes as well as interactions with whites. Cherokee writer John Oskisson was a contemporary of McNickle who wrote *Brothers Tree*, a novel recounting a Cherokee family's fight to preserve its land and heritage. Choctaw Todd Downing wrote nine mysteries that did not emphasize Choctaw themes, including *The Cat Screams*, but his finest work was *The Mexican Earth*. Although written in the 1940s, Lakota writer Ella Deloria's novel, *Waterlily*, was not published until 1988. Deloria's book is a historical novel, tracing the camp life of a Sioux band through several years and incorporating familiar Native American themes. Although Native Americans offered some fiction before the 1960s, the era of native activism brought forth a wealth of fine work that has grown prodigiously since 1968, when N. Scott Momaday published his Pulitzer Prize-winning novel, *House Made of Dawn*.

Momaday's work emphasizes the struggle of contemporary native people to find themselves through tribal traditions, including stories, imagination, creativity, and ceremony. Leslie Silko's *Ceremony* explores similar ground found in Momaday's first book and his novel, *The Ancient Child*. All these works focus on journeys of discovery that take characters through a series of events leading back to ritual and tradition that offer healing and a measure of understanding. Momaday's work *The Way to Rainy Mountain* is many genres in one, including fiction and nonfiction. The book re-creates Kiowa migration and Momaday's own journey of self-identification. Silko offers several short stories and poems in *Storyteller*, but her powerful novel, *Almanac of the Dead*, explores the continued confusion that arises between Indians and non-Indians as they attempt to communicate with each other. Like most native writers, Momaday and Silko write poetry, short stories, and novels using themes of imagination, identity, and survival. Survival and identity are underlying concerns found in the work of many native writers; others explore these and other themes through trickster characters from many diverse cultures.

Anishinaabe author Gerald Vizenor is a trickster, professor, poet, prophet, essayist, and screenwriter. Since the 1960s, he has produced a large body of literature that challenges readers to see the complexities and contradictions of and about Native Americans, stemming from images offered by Indians and non-Indians alike. Vizenor transforms a mixed-blood native into the Chinese trickster in *Griever: An American Monkey King in China* and deals with an entire family of tricksters fighting the system in *Trickster of Liberty: Tribal Heirs to a Wild Baronage at Petronia*. He continues his trickster antics in *The Heirs of Columbus*, which features a "cross-blood" descendant of Columbus who creates his own native nation of confusion, humor, and healing. Vizenor also has written criticism, using his talents as a trickster to enlighten, poke fun at, and expose the difficulties of dealing with the tribal past and present. Making sense out of life is a theme also developed by Laguna-Lakota Paula Gunn Allen in *The Woman Who Owned the Shadows*, a novel of a woman's ritual quest. Allen's work, *The Sacred Hoop: Recovering the Feminine in American Indian Traditions*, explores the significance of women among selected tribes, through native thought, culture, songs, and narratives.

Blackfeet-Gros Ventre James Welch offers a nameless protagonist in search of his Blackfeet background, including a quest to understand his grandmother, in *Winter in the Blood*. He further explores identity issues in *The Death of Jim Loney* and *Indian Lawyer*. His interest in Native American history led Welch to write a historical novel, *Fools Crow*, and an insightful history in *Killing Custer* (with Paul Stekler). Welch uses stark realism, exposing the positive and negative within human character and reservation life. Such realism also is found in *Love Medicine*, *Beet Queen*, and *Tracks*, by Louise Erdrich, who creates characters of strength. She was once married to and worked with Modoc Michael Dorris, who died in 1997. In 1991, they published *The Crown of Columbus*. Dorris is best known for his novel, *Yellow Raft in Blue Water*, and his work of nonfiction, *The Broken Cord: A Family's On-going Struggle with Fetal Alcohol Syndrome*, which was the basis of a documentary film.

Cherokee Robert Conley is best known for his historical novel, *Mountain Windsong*, which explores the love between a couple separated because of the infamous Trail of Tears, and for his collection of short stories, *The Witch of Goingsnake and Other Stories.* Fellow Cherokee author Thomas King creates humorous and satirical characters and situations in his two novels, *Medicine River* and *Green Grass, Running Water.* Powhatan-Lenape writer Jack Forbes explores the meaning of cultural myths regarding Indians in *Only Approved Indians.* Coeur d'Alene Janet Campbell Hale has distinguished herself through her insightful novel, *Jailing of Cecelia Capture,* which deals with the trials of an urban Indian woman who reclaims her life and values. Preserving and celebrating culture are also the theme of Dakota author Elizabeth Cook-Lynn in *The Power of Horses, From the River's Edge,* and *Seek the House of Relatives.* In *Mean Spirit,* Chickasaw writer Linda Hogan explores the Osage oil boom of the 1920s and the tragic results of many forms of exploitation.

Oto-Pawnee author Anna Walters offers a unique theme of ghoulish theft and confinement of Native American remains and patrimony in *Ghost Singer* and demonstrates the depth of her writing through stories in *The Sun Is Not Merciful.* Her husband, Harry Walters, is Diné and has been director of the museum at Diné College for many years. Both Walterses are internationally respected and have offered their research through books, articles, documentaries, and films. Cheyenne writer Hyemeyohsts Storm stirred controversy through his presentation of sacred rites, ideas, and beliefs in *Seven Arrows,* and he wove concepts of Cheyenne religion into fiction in *The Song of the Heyoehkah.* Yaqui writer Martin Cruz Smith uses native characters in *Nightwing* and *Stallion Gate* but is best known for *Gorky Park* and *Polar Star,* which deal with the former Soviet Union and the United States. Native American themes and characters are also found in Cherokee Barbara Kingsolver's *Pigs in Heaven,* which focuses on family. Extended family is an important theme to Richard Van Camp of the Dogrib Nation in the Northwest Territories and Micmac Lorne Simon, both former students of the First Nation's literary institution, the En'owikin Center of Penticton, British Columbia. Before his tragic death, Simon offered *Stones and Switches,* a novel set in the depression and providing details of Micmac life. Van Camp's *Lesser Blessed* is a novel about growing up among Dogrib people, while his book, *What's the Most Beautiful Thing You Know About Horses?,* is a beautiful book for children, with art provided by Cree George Littlechild and published by Harriet Rohmer of the Children's Book Press of San Francisco.

One of the most accomplished novelists in recent years is Choctaw-Cherokee Louis Owens, who has offered several novels that deal with a wide variety of contemporary topics, including identity, cultural maintenance, and the environment. Some of his novels are *Sharpest Sight, Wolf Song,* and *Bone Game.* Owens has also put out a history and analysis of Native American novels in *Other Destinies: Understanding the American Indian Novel.* However, the most complete survey of various genres of native literature is Ruoff's *American Indian Literature: An Introduction,*

Bibliographic Review, and Selected Bibliography. David Seals offered *Pow Wow Highway,* providing a realistic image of contemporary native life that offends some readers but has a powerful message about continued problems facing Native Americans. Onondaga writer and painter Eric Gansworth draws on his own family experiences to create his fiction in *Indian Summer,* a story that ties past to present and offers a realistic representation of Iroquois people in upstate New York. Navajo writer A. A. Carr provides mystery, monsters, and heroes in *Eye Killer,* a novel that explores vampires but draws on Navajo beliefs about witches and negative forces as well as a hero's journey to challenge evil. Nez Perce-Osage writer W. S. Penn skillfully explores family and cultural links with the past in *The Absence of Angels, The Telling of the World,* and *All My Sins Are Relatives.*

In her critical essay on Native American literature, presented in the *Native North American Almanac,* Lakota scholar Kate Shanley points out that by the end of the twentieth century, relatively few Native Americans had written novels but that growth is inevitable. In part this is because of a new interest in native novels by university presses. In the 1980s, the University of Oklahoma Press began a series on Native American literature, publishing several novels by native people. In the 1990s, Michigan State University Press and University of Nebraska Press also began publishing native fiction. During the late twentieth century, collections of native fiction appeared from many quarters, edited by talented writers, including such regional anthologies as Gary Holthaus and the Dauenhauers's *Native Writers, Storytellers and Orators,* Larry Evers's *The South Corner of Time,* Alan Velie's *American Indian Literature,* and Penny Petrone's *First People, First Voices.* Native American women have edited a few collections by and about women, including Paula Gunn Allen's *Spider Woman's Granddaughters* and *Voice of the Turtle,* Cherokee Rayna Green's *That's What She Said,* Dexter Fisher's *The Third Woman,* and Beth Brant's *A Gathering of Spirit.*

In 1991, the talented writer Craig Leslie edited *Talking Leaves: Contemporary Native American Short Stories,* and in 1993, Joe Bruchac compiled an anthology from a native gathering in 1992 of approximately five hundred Native Americans: *Returning the Gift.* Miwok-Pomo Greg Sarris presented several California Indian writers in *The Sound of Rattles and Clappers,* while Clifford Trafzer edited anthologies of short fiction in *Looking Glass, Earth Song, Sky Spirit, Blue Dawn, Red Earth,* and *Whirlwind.* Other anthologies include *Songs from This Earth on Turtle's Back, an Anthology of Canadian Native Fiction,* and *Earth Power Coming, Survival This Way,* and *Luminaries of the Humble.* In addition to these anthologies, Native Americans have published short fiction in *Akwe-kon, The Notre Dame Magazine, Moccasin Telegraph, Cream City Review, Loonfeather, Raven Chronicle, The Chariton Review, The Kenyon Review, Northeast Indian Quarterly, Blue Cloud Journal, Evergreen Chronicle,*

Windmill, Red Ink, and many others. Native Americans find many magazines interested in native literature and are able to place their work with journals interested in new and diverse subjects. As a result, native writers have produced a large body of short fiction that deserves close attention by anyone interested in contemporary native history. Only a sampling is provided to offer an understanding of the wealth of writing produced in the late twentieth century. Without question, new native writers will publish far more in the future and take their place among the best writers of American literature. In 1998, Anishinaabe writer Kimberly Blaeser—herself an accomplished short story writer—compiled a collection of short stories by Anishinaabe authors.

Scott Momaday, Leslie Silko, James Welch, Paula Gunn Allen, Gerald Vizenor, Louise Erdrich, Maurice Kenny, and many other well-known authors have written short stories. But short fiction offers lesser-known Native Americans an opportunity to express themselves through the written word. Lumbee writer Julia Lowry published "Faces," which deals with a young woman upset with her own appearance. When the protagonist peers into a mirror, she sees her native mother looking back at her, so she seeks to change her looks with cold cream, sculpting a new face but all the time knowing the depth of identity lying beneath the mask. In the end, the young woman reconciles with herself and peers deep below the surface of her face to find her identity. Choctaw writer Don Birchfield is extremely versatile, dealing with a variety of topics in his books and short fiction. In his story, "Lost in the Land of Ishtaboli," Birchfield explores a land below the earth known as the Little Choctaw—a nation within a nation found in the womb of the earth. His protagonist is confined there and wants to escape to the upper world so that he may know what life was like before the Choctaw Nation was forced to move into the earth.

Yaqui author Anita Endrezze deals with duality through twin sisters, Darlene and Marlene. In one story, "Marlene's Adventure," the conservative character, Marlene, finds life dull, until her husband nearly dies. Marlene's sister, Darlene, is a wild woman who has a grand time in life and drives a Ford Pinto that she has painted to look like a pinto horse. In "Darlene and the Dead Man," Darlene and Marlene find a dead Indian on the hood of the Pinto and return later to find that someone has moved the body. Endrezze is a masterful storyteller, as is Muscogee Craig Womack, whose stories, "Lucy, Oklahoma, 1911" and "Witches of Eufaula, Oklahoma," allow readers to enter Creek Indian life, which is rarely traveled by non-Indians. Both stories are set in Oklahoma and deal with aspects of witchcraft. A different form of negative power is found in Quinault writer Inez Petersen's "Joseph's Rainbow." Child abuse is the theme of this tragic story, which leads Joseph to report his own mother to Children's Services after she kills little Bobby and beats baby Teena. This is an emotionally charged story similar to that of Mohawk author

Richard Green, who deals with sexual abuse and worse in his story, "A Jingle for Silvy."

Anishinaabe writer Penny Olson also deals with sexual assault of a small girl by a "friendly" in "The Dream," whereas Cherokee-Shawnee writer E. K. Caldwell considers the separation of a couple in "Cooking Woman." Tension and reconciliation between a couple are captured in "Rocking in the Pink Light" by talented Spokane writer Gloria Bird, who deals with the beauty of birthing, holding a child for the first time, and presenting the child to the father. Bird captures the light of the moment when a caring mother holds positive power in the palms of her hands and shares her joy with another. The creative power of women is also a theme found in "The Atsye Parallel" by Laguna writer Lee Francis. When the daughter of a prominent clan leader returns to the reservation to bury her mother, she is obligated to ascend to a position of power within the Rock clan, a difficult and troubling position. However, Francis shows the importance of responsibility toward the community over one's own wishes, and he conveys the internal struggles of his character as she assumes her new position. Coping with responsibility is also a theme in the work of Lenape writer Annie Hansen Linzer in "Sun Offering" and "Spirit Curse," two stories Hansen incorporates into her novel *Ghost Dancing*. Both stories center around the One Rock family, who has moved to the Pacific Northwest and attempts to negotiate life far from the Eastern Woodlands and Oklahoma. Tension characterizes the two stories which are part of a recent novel, *Ghost Dancing*, written under the name of Anna Linzer.

Powerful characters are also found in the fiction of Navajo writer Laura Tohe, whose story, "So I Blow Smoke in Her Face," speaks volumes about native survival and defiance. Although a Navajo girl is under the thumb of a matron who works at the Albuquerque Indian School, the protagonist uses the smoke as a clear message about her feelings. Shoshoni-Bannock writer Ed Edmo exposes many conflicts in his work, "After Celilo." Along the Columbia River, many tribes lived in relative peace until the government sent soldiers, surveyors, and engineers to dam the river. When this occurred, the government destroyed the fish runs and the homes of thousands of people, including Edmo's protagonist, who is forced to live elsewhere and suffer the wrath of whites. Blackfeet author James LaMotte offers a twist to this in "Dreamland." Living on the streets, a veteran of Vietnam comes to the aid of a prostitute being beaten by a pimp. Although immediate conflict subsides in this story, a general confusion remains.

Confusion is also found in "Avian Messiah and Media Mistress" by Anishinaabe writer Andrew Connors. The story has little to do with identity, tragedy, or survival but much to do with contemporary tricksters and fools. Death is a common theme in native writing and rightfully so, given the history of native people. In "Sky Burial," Dogrib author Richard

Van Camp explores the last moments of an elder's life before traveling on to the next world. Unfortunately, the talented Micmac author, Lorne Simon, died in a car wreck trying to miss a deer, but before his death, he offered "Names," a story about a ghost known to his people as Amalegne'j. In a colorfully descriptive manner, Simon tells of children living in a remote cabin with their father while their mother is away in an urban area. Andy sees something unusual outside the cabin and learns that only he can alter the frightening aberration and negative power it portends.

Short fiction is an extension of native storytelling and the long tradition of oral narratives among all tribes. Numerous native authors write stories each day, and only a small number are published. The works of Cherokee writer Ralph Salisbury, Miwok-Pomo Greg Sarris, Cherokee Patricia Riley, Metis writer Misha, Lakota Tiffany Midge, Ajumawe Darryl Wilson, Mohawk Chris Fleet, and hundreds of others have appeared in magazines and books in the United States and Canada, providing a new voice for native people in the world of fiction. A few native writers have concentrated on nonfiction, and these individuals are not widely known. Native American scholars, including historians, sociologists, and anthropologists, have written many works in an attempt to counter interpretations and representations of native people offered by non-Indians. A few of these teachers and scholars have influenced the discourse associated with native studies, a discipline controlled by non-Indian scholars in the past.

NONFICTION

One of the earliest native scholars who focused on Indian history, culture, and contemporary life was D'Arcy McNickle, who wrote fiction and nonfiction, including *They Came Here First*, which dealt with migrations, laws, invasion, war, trade, colonialism, expansion, reservations, allotment, and self-determination. McNickle became the first director of the American Indian segment of the Newberry Library in Chicago, which created the famous D'Arcy McNickle Center for the Study of American Indians in honor of the former director. Seneca scholars Arthur C. Parker and George H. J. Abrams also contributed to native history, and Abrams used his expertise in anthropology to identify and protect the remains of Cornplanter and other Senecas buried at Grant Cemetery, which was threatened by the U.S. Corps of Engineers and the Kinzua Dam. Abrams also participated in the desanctification of the Coldspring Longhouse, removal of its eternal fire to Steamburg on the Allegany Reservation, and the repatriation of remains and patrimony, particularly wampum belts.

Among the Wendat-Huron people of Quebec, members of the Sioui family are keepers of traditions. Eleonore Marie Sioui is considered "the Spiritual Mother" of Huron-Wyandot people, the keeper of the sacred fire and director of the Huron-Wyandot Spiritual and Philosophical Center at the Village-des-Huron Reserve near Quebec City. She was the first First Nations woman to receive a Ph.D., and she is an accomplished writer, having published three books: *Andatha: Femme du Nord, Femme de LIle*, and *Corps A Coeur Eperdu*. Her books on contemporary Wyandot spiritual beliefs will be forthcoming from Michigan State University Press. One of her seven children is the noted Wyandot historian Georges Sioui, professor and former dean at the Saskatchewan Indian Federated College. Like other members of his family, Sioui is a dynamic speaker, activist, and innovative scholar who challenges old paradigms. He has published several works but is best known for his volumes *For an Amerindian Autohistory* and *The Wyandots*. Metis scholar Olive Patricia Dickason is another First Nations historian known for her award-winning book, *Canada's First Nations: A History of the Founding Peoples from Earliest Times*.

Standing Rock Sioux Vine Deloria Jr. is one of the leading scholars in Native American studies. His book, *Custer Died for Your Sins: An Indian Manifesto*, challenges stereotypes and scholars dealing with native culture and history. As a professor at the University of Arizona and University of Colorado, Deloria has influenced thousands of students. He is an activist scholar who has given lectures around the world and authored or edited over twelve books, including *We Talk, You Listen: New Tribes, New Turf; God Is Red: A Native View of Religion; Behind the Trail of Broken Treaties; The Nations Within: The Past and Future of American Indian Sovereignty* (with Clifford Lytle); and *American Indian Policy in the Twentieth Century*. Deloria's activism as a scholar of Indian history is equaled by that of Lakota anthropologist Beatrice Medicine, who has written over sixty articles and book chapters with an emphasis on the history of native women. Her volume, *The Hidden Half: Studies of Plains Indian Women*, edited with Patricia Albers, provides a rare study of Plains women in native history.

Cherokee historian R. David Edmunds has published several important studies dealing with the history of Native Americans from the Old Northwest. His book, *The Potawatomis: Keepers of the Fire*, won the Francis Parkman Award in American History. In 1983, he published *The Shawnee Prophet*, which deconstructed the life of Tenskwatawa and provided a life history of a significant and often misunderstood historical character. The book was nominated for a Pulitzer Prize in history and asserted that Tenskwatawa, not Tecumseh, began the Indian movement during the first decade of the nineteenth century, through religious revitalization. Gros Ventre scholar George Horse Capture has lectured on and researched Native American history throughout the world. As curator of the Plains Indian Museum of the Buffalo Bill Historical Center and as deputy assistant director of cultural resources at the National Museum of the American Indian, Horse Capture has informed millions of people about the history and culture of native peoples through museum exhibits, writings, and lectures. Horse Capture is known for his edited work, *The Seven Visions of Bull Lodge,* and his award-winning documentary, "I'd Rather Be Powwowing."

Cheyenne scholar W. Richard West Jr. shares Horse Capture's zeal for community-based scholarship. As director of the National Museum of the American Indian, West has traveled widely, speaking and researching. His work has led to the publication of several books by his museum, as well as public exhibits of material items. One of the many books published by the museum under the direction of West is *Native American Dance: Ceremonies and Social Traditions* by Cherokee ethnomusicologist Charlotte Heth. The book is a colorful masterpiece that combines the work of several native scholars to portray the power of song, dance, music, and tradition. Heth has worked with Native American communities across the United States and is one of the foremost scholars of native music.

One of the finest Cahuilla singers is also a tribal historian of international note. Katherine Siva Saubel was trained in native history by her father, Juan Siva, but she also learned some of the most sacred songs known to Cahuilla people from her father-in-law. She is a singer, dancer, and storyteller but is best known as a historian, linguist, and museum curator. She helped begin the Malki Museum on the Morongo Reservation, the first museum established on a California Indian reservation. She has published several books, including *Cahuilla Ethnobotanical Notes: The Aboriginal Uses of Oak* (with Lowell Bean), *Cahuilla Ethnobotanical Notes: Aboriginal Uses of Mesquite and Screwbean* (with Lowell Bean), *Temalpakh: Cahuilla Indian Knowledge* (with Lowell Bean), and *I'sniyatam Designs, a Cahuilla Word Book.* She is currently completing a multivolume work on Cahuilla history and culture as well as a volume on her language. Saubel has produced two tapes: *The Cahuilla Creation Story* and *Cahuilla Language.* She has been inducted into the National Women's Hall of Fame and continues her own community-based research.

Saubel's nephew, Ernest Siva, taught Native American ethnomusicology at the University of California, Los Angeles, for over twelve years before returning to the reservation. Siva is also a musician and has worked with church choirs. Another scholar who has used community-based scholarship in his work is Cahuilla-Luiseño ethnohistorian Edward Castillo. He is known for his in-depth knowledge of California's native people and the power of culture as a historical factor. Castillo has published numerous articles and book chapters but is best known for *The Missions of California; Native American Perspectives on the Hispanic*

Throughout Indian country, tribal people have an intense interest in collecting and preserving their culture. Tribal heritage committees exist on many reservations, including the Twenty-Nine Palms Reservation, where Anthony Madrigal, Luke Madrigal, Dean Mike, Theresa Mike, Bernie Thomas, and Joe Benitez lead preservation efforts.

Colonization of Alta, California; The Indians of Southern California; and Indians, Franciscans and Spanish Colonization: The Impact of Franciscan Missionaries on the Indians of California. San Juan Tewa Alfonso Ortiz also wrote about the community, particularly in editing volume 10 of the *Handbook of North American Indians.* Oritz edited and composed several articles, chapters, and books, including *The Tewa World: Space, Time, Being and Becoming in a Pueblo Society; New Perspectives on the Pueblos; and The Pueblo.*

During the last decade of the twentieth century, few scholars equalled the work of Anishinaabe sociologist Duane Champagne. The director of the American Indian Studies Center, Champagne is also editor of the *American Indian Culture and Research Journal* and has produced numerous books, including *Strategies and Conditions of Political and Cultural Survival in American Indian Societies; Social Order and Political Change: Constitution Governments among the Cherokees, the Choctaw, the Chickasaw, and the Creeks; Native North American Almanac;* and *Native America: A Portrait of the Peoples.* And fellow Anishinaabe scholar Basil Johnston has spent his life preserving native culture and history, through *Ojibway Heritage, Moose Meat and Wild Rice, Tales the Elders Told: Ojibway Legends, Ojibway Ceremonies,* and *Indian School Days.*

Lenape-Powhatan scholar Jack Forbes has written nonfiction as well as fiction. He has contributed *Apache, Navaho, and Spaniard; Warriors of the Colorado; Native Americans of California and Nevada;* and *Black Africans and Native Americans.* Wyandot Clifford E. Trafzer published several articles on Navajo history in the 1970s before offering *The Kit Carson Campaign: The Last Great Navajo War,* which provides a voice for Navajo interpretations about the war and Long Walk. He published *Renegade Tribe: The Palouse Indians and the Invasion of the Inland Pacific Northwest* (with Richard Scheuerman), a tribal history that draws on oral sources of Palouse people and won the Governor's Writers Award in 1986. Palouse involvement in the Nez Perce war is presented in *Chief Joseph's Allies,* and Trafzer offers a concise survey of the Nimiipu in *The Nez Perce.* His work on Plateau Indians led him to research mortality on the Yakama Reservation in *Death Stalks the Yakama: Epidemiological Transitions and Mortality on the Yakama Indian Reservation, 1888–1964.* He is currently studying mortality on the Hupa Reservation and deaths on twenty-nine reservations of the Mission Agency in southern California and with Joel Hyer has edited *Exterminate Them: Written Accounts of Murder, Rape, and Enslavement of Native Americans during the California Gold Rush.*

Several scholars have emerged out of the Indian country of Oklahoma. Choctaw-Anishinaabe historian Clara Sue Kidwell is director of American Indian studies at the University of Oklahoma but has also worked for the National Museum of the American Indian. In 1980, she and fellow Choctaw historian Charles Roberts wrote *The Choctaws: A Critical Bibliography,* and in 1995 Kidwell published *Missionaries among the Choctaws.* Like Kidwell and Roberts, Shawnee-Sac-Fox-Creek-Seminole professor Donald Fixico is respected for his teaching and his books, including *Termination and Relocation: Federal Indian Policy, 1945–1960* and his edited book, *An Anthology of Western Great Lakes Indian History.* Potawatomi historian Terry Wilson contributed several articles and chapters over a number of years, but his most important work is *The Underground Reservation.* Muscogee historians Carter Blue Clark and Duane Hale have taught native history at several universities and always conducted community research as part of their academic work. In 1995, Clark produced *Lone Wolf v. Hitchcock,* which explores the immediate and long-term significance of the case to native people.

Cherokee historians Howard Meredith and Tom Holm have distinguished themselves through their research and teaching. Meredith has published several books on native peoples of Oklahoma, whereas Holm is best known for his work on Native American veterans. Cherokee sociologist Russell Thornton has also published widely in the field of demographics, including *American Indian Holocaust and Survival* and *We Shall Live Again.* K. Tsianina Lomawaima is a Muscogee historian who has published on Indian education, including her award-winning *They Called It Prairie Light: Oral Histories from Chilocco Indian Agricultural School, 1920–1940.* Her husband, Hopi scholar Hartman Lomawaima, is internationally known for his own research and work with communities. Anishinaabe scholar Brenda Child has published *Boarding School Seasons: Native Americans and the Government's Boarding School Experience, 1890–1940.* Anishinaabe historian Jean O'Brien has published *Dispossession by Degrees,* dealing with Indians in New England.

In nonfiction writing, Native Americans have been active in a variety of fields. Cherokee scholar Cheryl Metoyer-Duran published *Gatekeepers in Ethnolinguistics Communities,* and Choctaw historian Donna Akers offered *Living in the Land of Dead: Choctaw Nation in the 19th and 20th Centuries.* In 1994, Shoshoni scholar Steven Crum published a history of his people, *The Road on Which We Came,* and Diné scholar Jennie Joe has published extensively on Indian health. Pawnee writer and scholar James Riding In has worked with Pawnees and many other native people to protect and repatriate the remains of Native Americans. This is also the case of Pawnee attorneys John Echohawk, Walter Echo-Hawk, and Roger Echo-Hawk, all of whom have worked with the Native American Rights Fund on behalf of American Indian religious freedom. Issues involving repatriation have been championed by several American Indian newspapers, radio stations, and television programs. Lakota writer and publisher Tim Giago has used his newspaper, *Indian Country Today* (formerly *Lakota Times*), to address issues facing Indian people, including repatriation. This is also true of Shoshoni-Bannock journalist Mark Trahant. Without a doubt, Indians and non-Indians in many fields have written nonfiction that has contributed significantly to furthering knowledge by and about native people.

PERFORMING ARTS

Ceremony, dance, music, song, and storytelling within Native American communities require ritual performance. *Theater* is a word that might convey the performing arts associated with religious and secular presentations of native men and women. Contemporary Native American theater has its origins within communities, but native peoples have adapted some performances to modern stages. The Indian movement of the early 1970s encouraged artists to express themselves through theater, including Kiowa-Lenape playwright and professor Hanay Geiogamah. In his play, *Body Indian* (1972), Geiogamah offers stark realism through an Indian alcoholic whose life is filled with pain, misery, and hopelessness. The next year, he produced *Foghorn,* which deals with problems arising out of Indian and white relations. Geiogamah used his play, *49* (1975), to convey the renewal of Native American cultures, while Nez Perce playwrights John Kaufman and Wayne Johnson offered a native interpretation of history through their play, *The Indian Experience* (1975).

During the 1980s, Cree playwright Tomson Highway presented *The Rez Sisters* (1986) and *Dry Lips Oughta Move to Kapuskasing* (1989), both of which dealt with issues involving women and their relationships with men. Another Cree playwright, Jim Morris, offered a presentation of native oral narratives in their original language in *Son of Ayash* (1990). Traditional narratives regarding Coyote being swallowed by a great monster in Nez Perce literature are the basis for Lenape Danie David Moses's *Coyote City* (1988), and he deals with the relationship of a young woman with her deceased lover in *Almighty Voice and His Wife* (1991). During the 1990s, Native American women played a larger role as actors and playwrights. They addressed women's issues in Saulteaux-Cree-Blackfeet Margo Kane's *Moonlodge* (1990), Kuna-Rappahannock Monique Mojica's *Princess Pocahontas and the Blue Spots* (1992), and Metis Beatrice Culleton's *Night of the Trickster* (1992). Native American theater played in a number of locations and through a number of theater companies, including Red Earth Performing Arts Company (Seattle), Native American Theater Ensemble (Oklahoma), Awasikan Theatre (Winnipeg), Native Earth Performing Arts Company (Toronto), and Spiderwomen Theater (New York).

Mohawk Jay Silverheels, Cherokee Thunder Cloud, Squamish Dan George, and other Native American actors performed in films between 1930 and 1970, but Hollywood generally forced them into stereotypical characters before the 1970s, even though some portrayals of native people were sympathetic. During the 1970s, such films as *Soldier Blue* (1970), *A Man Called Horse* (1970), *Little Big Man* (1971), and *Ulzana's Raid* (1972) attempted to portray native people more accurately, but the focus of the films remained on the thoughts and actions of nonnative peoples. These films suggested that Native Americans were victims and that native leadership had little to say about decisions that were made for their people. *One Flew over the Cuckoo's Nest* (1975) and *Harry and Tonto* (1974) took steps away from victimization and powerlessness, and the strength of native character is portrayed by Muscogee Will Sampson and Dan George. In *The Outlaw Josey Wales*, George played a strong and wise character. *Windwalker* also emphasized the strength of native people and depicted the deep divisions between tribes. The producers cast Trevor Howard, a non-Indian, as the lead because they did not believe that a native actor was sufficiently competent to perform the role.

The ABC television special "I Will Fight No More Forever" and the PBS special "Roanoke" cast several Native Americans, including Will Sampson. Both films strive for balance in their presentations, although the story of Chief Joseph is sweet in places and contains factual errors, including the recitation of the speech, "I Will Fight No More Forever," which Hinmahtooyahlatkekt (Chief Joseph) never made. Nevertheless, like the surrender speech, the film is moving and depicts a tragic episode in American history. In the late 1980s and early 1990s,

Native Americans had a greater say in the making of *Loyalties* (1985), *Powwow Highway* (1988), and *Thunderheart* (1992). Cree-Metis actress Tantoo Cardinal gave a strong performance in *Loyalties*, while Mohawk Gary Farmer played the lead and offered an accomplished presentation in *Powwow Highway*. Oneida Graham Greene (who appeared regularly on the television series *Northern Exposure*) and Menominee-Munsee-Stockbridge Sheila Tousey excelled in *Thunderheart*. Kevin Costner's *Dances with Wolves* (1990) offers a balanced portrayal of Lakota people but casts Costner as the only good white person on earth and depicts Pawnees as savages and Lakotas as nonaggressors. In 1992, Michael Mann offered a remake of James F. Cooper's *Last of the Mohicans* that still portrays the Mohicans as noble people and Hurons as dirty dogs, a stereotype difficult to break when it is the basis of the story.

Walt Disney's Indians have changed significantly since the days of *Davy Crockett* when Chief Red Stick (who never existed) fought hand-to-hand combat with Davy who single-handedly won the Creek Wars. In the recent portrayal of *Pocahontas,* Disney skillfully deals with the relationship of native people to the earth, animals, and environment but presents a buxom teen talent as the heroine roughly twelve years old and married to John Rolfe, not John Smith. Historical accuracy never got in the way of this film or others produced by the Disney studios, although its version of Squanto's life is a minor improvement. Still, Katherine Saubel has pointed out that the strength of the film is portraying the sacredness of the earth, which is still an abiding belief of Native Americans. In reaction to stereotypical presentations of native people in film, several American Indians have produced their own to offer a different view, including Gerald Vizenor's *Harold of Orange* (1983), featuring Oneida comedian Charlie Hill and other warriors of Orange. The film permits Hill and his warriors to secure funding for an orange tree grove on the Northern Plains. Lakota actress Valerie Redhorse works diligently through her portrayals of Indian people to end stereotypes and present a realistic view of contemporary native life.

Muscogee-Seminole Bob Hicks lampoons the dominant society in *Return of the Country*, which features a rediscovery of America by Native Americans who dominate whites through the Bureau of Caucasian Affairs and force them to assimilate into native societies. Since the 1980s, several native people have made films, including Hopi filmmaker Victor Masayesva Jr., who offered *Itam Hakim, Hopiit* (1984), which offers a bilingual interpretation of Hopi history by Hopi people. In *Pott Starr* (1990), Masayesva explores nonnative tourism to Hopi, where thousands of people come to the mesas to see the Indians and get a great buy on native art. Houma Chris Spotted Eagle explores spiritual topics in *The Great Spirit within the Hole* (1983) and *Our Sacred Land* (1984), which deal with religious freedoms of Native Americans in penitentiaries and recovery of the sacred Black Hills by Lakota people. In 1985, Clifford E.

Trafzer and Richard D. Scheuerman wrote the original screenplay for *Everything Changing, Everything Changing* (1985), dealing with the life of Wenatchi Ida Nason. Robert Redford's Sundance Institute has helped some native filmmakers hone their art, and Valerie Redhorse, Greg Sarris, Sherman Alexie, and Tom King have had their works produced into films shown internationally. Playwright and director Hanay Geiogamah has led the movement for authentic native voices in film, theater, and dance. His most recent work includes *Geronimo* (1995) and a Turner Broadcasting special, *The Native Americans* (1997).

Many Native Americans believe that there can be no creation without song, music, and movement. Since the beginning of time, song, music, and dance have been integral elements of Native American societies. People sing to the earth and seeds when planting, and they sing to the animals before hunting. In the creation stories, a variety of characters sing the world into creation. In Maidu creation, Earthmaker and Coyote travel on a raft in an endless blue sea until Earthmaker has a vision of land, mountains, valleys, rivers, lakes, and other features of the natural environment. Only after his vision does Earthmaker poetically sing the world into being with the sacred song of creation.

> Little world, where are you?
> Little world, where are you?
> My world of great mountains,
> where are you?
> My foggy mountains,
> where are you?
> My world,
> where one will travel
> by the valley's edge,
> by great foggy mountain,
> by the zigzag paths
> through range after range.
> I sing of the country
> I shall travel in.
> In this world
> I shall wander.

Songs, music, and dance were central to the creation of native worlds, and songs keep the world in motion today through social and religious dances. Songs, dances, ceremonies, and rituals are integrally related to each other, and they are generally accompanied by flutes, drums, rattles, clappers, bull roarers, whistles, rasps, and other musical instruments. These elements of the performing arts are not something belonging to the past; rather, they are essential to Native American communities today. Some songs, dances, ceremonies, and rituals have changed over thousands of years, but others reflect the time of creation. During the Memorial Day weekend each year, Cahuilla, Quechan, Cocopa, Mojave, Serrano, and other tribes of southern California meet on the dance grounds of the Malki Museum to sing ancient Bird Songs. Bird Songs are creative components of native cultures, and while male singers shake rattles, women dance in time to the music.

Cherokee ethnomusicologist Charlotte Heth has argued that music promotes dance and dance permits music to be visual. Some dances are accompanied only by songs, whereas other dances require music from instruments that may be attached to the dancer's body or clothing, including deer hooves, cocoons, turtle shells, wood, sea shells, metal cones, tin cans, and bird beaks. Native Americans traditionally created music with different kinds of drums, rattles, boxes, hollowed logs, wooden floors, wooden flutes, clappers, wooden rasps, scrapers, bows, rocks, fiddles, and other items. All these are used today, but Native American musicians also play metal flutes, saxophones, guitars, pianos, violins, and other modern musical instruments. Today, the Haudenosaunee dance to their ancient music and songs in the cycles of life. Iroquoian peoples use water drums and hoof rattles during social dances and will use turtle rattles only in sacred ceremonies. When a person becomes ill or is near death, elders may call on the False Face Society to minister to the person with songs, prayers, tobacco, ashes, and rattles that are filled with power. Seneca artist Linley B. Logan shares the morning prayer song that welcomes the day during midwinter ceremonies. In the longhouse these reverent words are sung:

> I love my world
> I love my time
> I love my growing children
> I love my old people
> I love my ceremonies

In the tradition of the Southeast, several tribes conduct Stomp Dances with water drums, street clothing, and little of the fuss and feathers found at powwows. Women wear shackles or rattles of box turtle shell, which they use to keep time. The ancient dance is conducted at night around fires in Oklahoma, Arkansas, Mississippi, and other places in the South where tradition lives. In the Southwest, Cocopa, Quechan, and Kumeyaay conduct Karooks in memorial services that include songs, dance, and music provided by gourd rattles. Native Americans from many areas offer gourd songs, peyote songs, gaming songs, love songs, first food songs, Sun Dance songs, trick songs, and many others. Quechan, Pima, Yaqui, and Tohono O'odham people also do the Chicken Scratch or Waila, which draws on European polkas and schottisches brought to the Southwest by Catholic missionaries and changed to fit the culture of these native people. In addition to these social dances, native people sing songs for specific ceremonies, including those of the Ghost

Dance. And several Native Americans, including Ed Wapp Sr., John Rainer Sr., Kevin Locke, and Ute-Navajo Carlos Nakai, are accomplished on the wood flute.

Pueblos of the Southwest hold numerous dances that employ a variety of songs and dancing styles, including lines of colorfully dressed women and men dancing in time to melodic songs accompanied by drums and rattles. Apaches use water drums and bullroarers in their Gaan, Sunrise, and Crown dances, offering their voices and movement to make the ceremony complete. In 1916, Pliny Goddard published "The Masked Dancers of the Apache," which included this verse from a Crown Dance song:

> Earth was holy,
> Sky was made,
> The Gan young people lighted on the sky four times.
> Their lives, four directions they heard me.
> With pollen speech,
> With my mouth speech,
> It moves within me.
> The holy Gans were in line four times with me.

Navajo people also enjoy a rich musical heritage as well as dance during ceremonies ranging from Nightway to Enemy Way. These are sacred ceremonies filled with ritual, song, dance, and music intended to heal. Navajo people also have social dances, including those at the conclusion of Enemy Way, and these songs are shared outside the hogan where ceremonies occur. The Nimiipu at Lapwai, Idaho, offer a grand celebration of war dances, and other nations in the Northwest–Aleuts, Athabascans, Tlingits, Haidas, Tsimshians, Nootkas, Lummis, Klallums, Nisquallies, Chinooks, Quinaults, Makahs, and others–also hold their annual dances, ceremonies, potlatches, clan gatherings, and tribal celebrations. In northern California, Hupas perform White Deerskin Dances, and their Yurok neighbors conduct Brush Dances.

Powwow songs and dances are the most widespread among Native Americans today, as the powwow traditions of the Great Plains and Western Great Lakes reach every corner of Indian country. Native peoples of the Northern Plains and Southern Plains have developed their own styles, drums, protocols, dances, and songs for their powwows, most consisting of head singers or drums, head male dancers, head female dancers, head boy dancers, and head girl dancers. Singers also drum, and many drums may be present at large powwows. Head dancers lead all the dancers into the arena during the grand entry, which is always colorful. Dancers often carry flags of native nations, the United States, and Canada, posting them with a Flag Song. The master of ceremonies remembers veterans, and elders say prayers. When a powwow is held in Lakota country, singers offer their own Flag Song, which is also the Lakota National

Anthem. Famed ethnomusicologist Lynn F. Huenemann offers this translation of a segment of the song in *Native American Dance*:

> Tunkasilayapi tawapaha kin oihanke sni najin ktelo
> Iyohlate oyate kin wicicagin;
> ktaca, lecamon.
> The flag of the United States will fly forever.
> Under it the people will grow and prosper;
> Therefore have I done this [fought for my country].

Powwows include a number of intertribal dances and songs with traditional and fancy dancers alike. Men and women dance, and each may have specialty dances. Couples dance together in the Oklahoma Two-Step, Owl Dance, Rabbit Dance, and Snake Dance. Often the master of ceremonies will call for a woman's choice during the powwow. The master of ceremonies may also convey to the arena director requests for particular songs, honorings, giveaways, and specials. At one powwow in California, Chumash Indian dancers offered a Crane Dance as a special, and in Arizona, Aztec Indian dancers presented a special dance and song to the delight of spectators. Hoop Dancers display great skill and agility, and they are favorites at powwows. Everyone attending powwows is expected to come with a good heart and set aside all grievances against personal foes. Dancers and singers are required to enter the powwow for their own enjoyment and that of everyone attending. When a feather drops from a dancer's outfit, this is evidence that someone has come with hard feelings.

According to Lakota author David Whitehorse, great emphasis is placed on keeping the powwow filled with goodwill, generosity, and civility. Powwows are free of alcohol and drugs. A powwow is a celebration of being Indian and sharing with others the rich cultural traditions of native people. Although it is not a religious ceremony, it is part of the sacred and ties the people to the Creator through song, dance, music, and fellowship. Generally, numerous vendors attend powwows to sell ribbon shirts, dresses, shawls, drums, rattles, paintings, jewelry, leather goods, T-shirts, beadwork, books, and bumper stickers. Food is also available, including fry bread, tacos, corn, and mutton stew. Following powwows, many people gather away from the arena to sing forty-nine songs, round dance, and court. Some songs are sung in native languages, but others are sung in English: "When the dance is over, sweetheart, I will take you home in my One-eyed Ford."

Cahuilla musician Ernest Siva conducts his own choir in Banning, California, and Quapaw-Cherokee composer Louis Ballard promotes native choirs through lectures, films, and records. Native American choirs have emerged in many schools, including the Institute of American Indian Arts, Bacone College, and Haskell Indian Nation's College. Native American singers include Dakota Floyd Westerman, Cree Buffy Sainte-Marie,

Dakota John Trudell, and Joanne Shenandoah. Some of the notable Native American musical groups include XIT, Redbone, Navajo Sundowners, Wingate Valley Boys, Winterhawk, and Sand Creek. Many tribes, including Quechans and Navajos, have their own bands. Mohawk John Kim Bell is the first Native American to conduct a professional symphony orchestra as conductor of the Toronto Symphony. Muscogee Joy Harjo often plays her saxophone during her lectures and readings, and she is the leader of a highly acclaimed band, Poetic Justice. Dakota John Rouillard played numerous instruments and was known for his musical ability with modern instruments as well as traditional native instruments. As in the past, many other native people are accomplished musicians with traditional and modern musical instruments.

As with music, several Native Americans have distinguished themselves in dance. Osage Maria Tallchief and her sister, Marjorie Tallchief, are ballerinas of international renown. In 1965, Maria won the Capezio Dance Award, and in 1997, President Bill Clinton honored her for her lifelong contribution to dance. Choctaw dancer Rosella Hightower was also a ballerina in France and began her own school of dance there. Hanay Geiogamah helped establish the American Indian Dance Theatre in 1987, emphasizing traditional native dances performed by the finest contemporary dancers. However, like the Tallchiefs, many native dancers have chosen to work within contemporary dance of the larger world, focusing on tap, jazz, ballet, and other modern forms. This is the case for Wyandot dancers Tess, Hayley, and Tara Trafzer, was well as Blackfeet-Anishinaabe Rosalie M. Jones, Cree Rene Highway, Yaqui Juan Valenzuela, and San Juan Pueblo Belinda James, who are in the forefront of modern dance. Native men and women also choreographed "Sacred Woman, Sacred Earth," "The Woman Who Fell from the Sky," "Corn Mother," "Dry Lips Oughta Move to Kapauskasing," and "The Rez Sisters." Other native people listed in the American Indian Registry of the Performing Arts include Cherokee Leilani Taliaferro, Blackfeet-Yokut Michael Meyers, Choctaw Aurorah Allain, and Cherokee Ann Roberts Khalsa.

Dance, song, and music are a major part of Native American cultures, woven into the traditions and transitions of native peoples everywhere. Dance, song, and music can be traditional or innovative. In either case, the performing arts are linked to the past and past influences will affect the future course of these art forms in the twenty-first century.

Selected Readings and Bibliography

Native American literature and performing arts date back to ancient days when life was woven into motion by the forces of the universe. Old stories provide a link between the past and present, informing us about the interrelationship of all things. Stories, songs, chants, dances, music, poems, and prayers keep the native world in motion and offer new creations that have become part of the native world. Champagne's *The Native North American Almanac,* Malinowski and Abrams's *Notable Native Americans,* Davis's *Native America in the Twentieth Century,* and Francis's *Native Time,* all deal with native performing arts and literature. In addition, Rawls's *Chief Red Fox Is Dead* offers important elements of contemporary native culture, including segments on film, literature, and history. Other sources previously cited include West's *Stories of the People,* Oritz and Erdoes's *American Indian Myths and Legends,* Swann's *Coming to the Light,* Trafzer's *Grandmother, Grandfather, and Old Wolf,* McWhorter's *Yellow Wolf,* Trafzer and Scheuerman's *Mourning Dove's Stories,* and Deloria's *We Talk, You Listen, Behind the Trail of Broken Treaties, The Nations Within* (with Lytle), and *American Indian Policy in the Twentieth Century.* Still others include Heth's *Native American Dance,* Champagne's *The Native North American Almanac,* Trafzer and Scheuerman's *Renegade Tribe,* Crum's *The Road on Which We Came,* Clark's *Lone Wolf v. Hitchcock,* and Thornton's *American Indian Holocaust.*

Adamson, Judith. *Graham Greene and Cinema.* Norman: Pilgrim Books, 1984.

Allen, Paula Gunn. *The Sacred Hoop.* Boston: Beacon Press, 1986.

Axtell, Horace and Margo Aragon. *A Little Bit of Wisdom.* Lewiston, Idaho: Confluence Press, 1997.

Black Bear, Ben Sr., and R. D. Theisz. *Songs and Dances of the Lakota.* Rosebud, S.D.: Sinte Gleska College, 1976.

Blaeser, Kimberly M. *Gerald Vizenor.* Norman: University of Oklahoma Press, 1996.

Burton, Bryan. *Moving within the Circle: Contemporary American Indian Music and Dance.* Danbury, Conn.: World Music Press, 1993.

Canfield, Gae Whitney. *Sarah Winnemucca of the Northern Paiutes.* Norman: University of Oklahoma Press, 1988.

Clements, William M. *Native American Verbal Art.* Tucson: University of Arizona Press, 1996.

Cody, Iron Eyes. *Iron Eyes, My Life as a Hollywood Indian.* New York: Everest House, 1982.

Collier, John. *American Indian Ceremonial Dances.* New York: Bounty Books, 1972.

Colonnese, Tom, and Louis Owens. *American Indian Novelists.* New York: Garland Publishing, 1985.

Coltelli, Laura. *Winged Words: American Indian Writers Speak.* Lincoln: University of Nebraska Press, 1990.

Dockstader, Fredrick J. *Indian Art of the Americas.* New York: Museum of the American Indian, Heye Foundation, 1973.

Foss, Phillip, ed. *The Clouds Threw the Light: Contemporary Native American Poetry.* Santa Fe, N.M.: Institute of American Indian Arts Press, 1983.

Frisbie, Charlotte J., ed. *Southwestern Indian Ritual Drama.* Albuquerque: University of New Mexico Press, 1980.

Frisbie, Charlotte J., and David P. McAllester, eds. *Navajo Blessingway Singer: The Autobiography of Frank Mitchell, 1881–1967.* Tucson: University of Arizona Press, 1978.

Hanson, Elizabeth I. *Paula Gunn Allen.* Boise, Idaho: Boise State University, 1990.

Heth, Charlotte. "Traditional and Contemporary Ceremonies, Rituals, Festivals, Music, and Dance." *The Native North American Almanac*. Duane Champagne, ed. Detroit: Gale Researchers, 1944, pp. 701–713.

Keeling, Richard. *Cry for Luck: Sacred Song and Speech among the Yurok, Hupa, and Karok Indians of Northwestern California*. Berkeley: University of California Press, 1993.

——, ed. *Women in North American Indian Music: Six Essays*. SEM Special Series 6. Bloomington, Ind.: Society for Ethnomusicology, 1989.

Laubin, Reginald. *Indian Dances of North America*. Norman: University of Oklahoma Press, 1977.

Lincoln, Kenneth. *Native American Renaissance*. Berkeley: University of California Press, 1983.

Momaday, N. Scott. *American Indian Authors*. Boston: Houghton Mifflin, 1971.

Parins, James W. *John Rollin Ridge: His Life and Works*. Lincoln: University of Nebraska Press, 1991.

Parker, Dorothy R. *Singing an Indian Song: A Biography of D'Arcy McNickle*. Lincoln: University of Nebraska Press, 1992.

Powers, William K. *War Dance: Plains Indian Musical Performance*. Tucson: University of Arizona Press, 1990.

Ruoff, A. LaVonne. *American Indian Literatures: An Introduction, Bibliographic Review, and Selected Bibliography*. New York: Modern Language Association of America, 1990.

Sarris, Greg, ed. *Keeping Slug Woman Alive*. Berkeley: University of California Press, 1993.

——. *The Sound of Rattles and Clappers*. Tucson: University of Arizona Press, 1994.

Schubnell, Matthias. *N. Scott Momaday, the Cultural and Literary Background*. Norman: University of Oklahoma Press, 1985.

Sioui, Georges E. *For an Amerindian Autohistory*. Montreal: McGill University Press, 1992.

Smyth, Willie, ed. *Songs of Indian Territory: Native American Music Traditions of Oklahoma*. Oklahoma City: Center of the American Indian, 1989.

Sweet, Jill D. *Dances of the Tewa Pueblo Indians: Expressions of New Life*. Sante Fe, N.M.: School of American Research, 1985.

Trafzer, Clifford E. *Earth Song, Sky Spirit*. New York: Doubleday/Anchor Books, 1993.

——, ed. *Blue Dawn, Red Earth*. New York: Doubleday/Anchor Books, 1996.

Van Camp, Richard. *What's the Most Beautiful Thing You Know about Horses?* San Francisco: Children's Book Press, 1998.

Velie, Alan R., ed. *American Indian Literature: An Anthology*. Norman: University of Oklahoma Press, 1991.

Wade, Edwin L., ed. *The Arts of the North American Indian: Native Traditions in Evolutions*. New York: Hudson Hills Press and Tulsa: Philbrook Art Center, 1986.

Wiget, Andrew. *Simon Ortiz*. Boise, Idaho: Boise State University, 1986.

——, ed. *Dictionary of Native American Literature*. New York: Garland, 1994.

Wild, Peter. *James Welch*. Boise, Idaho: Boise State University, 1983.

Wilson, Raymond. *Ohiyesa: Charles Eastman, Santee Sioux*. Urbana: University of Illinois Press, 1983.

CHAPTER 22

CONTINUING CIRCLE

At the beginning of the twenty-first century, much has changed within Native American cultures, but much has been retained. Native Americans have not vanished from the earth as some people had prophesied. Instead, Native Americans recovered from the invasions, conquests, removals, reservations, allotments, termination, and relocations. Native Americans had survived their own holocaust and had moved forward to a better day. However, like all cultures, American Indian cultures have changed and experienced transitions, responding to numerous events and conditions inside and outside their cultures. At the beginning of the new millennium, Native Americans have taken control of many aspects of their own lives through self-determination, and they continue to assert tribal sovereignty, treaty rights, and initiatives. The strength and perseverance that have sustained Native American people and communities are the same forces that have enabled them to survive. And the personal and communal integrity that has characterized native peoples for centuries has brought them through a harrowing time and enabled them to triumph through persistent cultural preservation and adaptation.

Hate and racism against Native Americans still exist, but the dignity of tribal elders and native people of all ages has often countered negative stereotypes and offered a realistic image that emphasizes respect, generosity, elders, and cultural preservation. Native Americans today are not "noble savages" or romantic characters, as depicted in some books and films. Indian people are genuine individuals who work hard in many different ways and are a part of contemporary society. However, many native people are concerned about preserving native language, culture, history, literature, and the overall well-being of their communities. Several reservations have taken advantage of the Native American Languages Act of 1990, and such individuals as Chemehuevi anthropologist Yolanda Montijo, Leanne Hinton, and Miwuk Jenifer Bates have helped revive Hupa, Yurok, Mojave, Wintu, and Yowlumni. Katherine Saubel has set out to preserve Cahuilla, and others are making similar efforts among Kumeyaay, Luiseño, Quechan, and Juaneño. Speakers of Native American languages have teamed up with scholars at the University of California to create the Master Apprenticeship Language Learning Program to preserve Chemehuevi, Tubatulabal, Karuk, Washoe, and Hupa languages. California is representative of many other areas in Indian country where native people are working with nonnative people to teach native languages, use them in classrooms, and perpetuate them.

Native American languages are being preserved through stories by many native people, including those on the Warm Springs Reservation, where education tribal leader Wendell Jim heads a project to videotape tribal elders telling stories in their native languages. In addition, Myra Shawaway has coordinated a successful language program on the Warm Springs Reservation, through the tribe's Culture and Heritage Department. The same is occurring on other reservations in the United States, Canada, Mexico, and other Latin American nations. The Wordcraft Circle of Native Writers and Storytellers is also contributing to the preservation of language through storytelling. Members of this international organization also compose poetry and prose in native languages and English. Spearheaded by Laguna pueblo scholar Lee Francis, Wordcraft Circle supports an annual meeting known as Returning the Gift and a mentor program linking elder storytellers and writers with young native people. Wordcraft Circle is composed of diverse people eager to support language, literature, and history. They have organized regional meetings of Wordcraft Circle at the University of California at Riverside, University of New Mexico, Oklahoma Christian College, En'owiken Center of British Columbia, Cherokee national capital in Tahlequah, Oklahoma, University of Arkansas at Little Rock, University of California at Los Angeles, and other sites.

In addition to preserving native languages, the National Museum of the American Indian has published several books in recent years, providing Native American authors an international voice that will touch the lives of millions of people for many years to come. In the foreword of *Stories of the People: Native American Voices*, Cheyenne W. Richard West, director of the National Museum of the American Indian, states that the mission of the museum is to preserve and present Native American life and culture through the voices of American Indians. This book—and all the museum's books—is a graphic example of the manner in which native people represent their own tribes' histories through material culture, stories, and historical interpretation that allow readers to enter native worlds in an accurate, exciting manner. In addition to presenting information about treaties, reservations, starvation, loss of land, and bureaucratic bungling, native writers invite an understanding of religion as a force that is historical and part of a beautiful material culture presented in the book. Cradleboards, baskets, vests, canoes, paddles, photographs, jewelry, harpoons, hats, games, moccasins, masks, and many other items that tie native people to their history and culture are featured in the publications of the National Museum of the American Indian. Native stories about objects demonstrate that history is many things, including community, which is composed of people, places, plants, animals, lakes, rivers, deserts, and other components of the physical and spiritual worlds that are manifested in material culture.

The entire approach of the National Museum of the American Indian is inclusive of diverse native populations, encouraging Indians to interpret native history and material culture. In 1989, when Cheyenne Congressman Ben Nighthorse Campbell introduced a bill to create the National Museum of the American Indian within the Smithsonian Institution, his dream was to establish an institution that would forever change the way people view Native Americans. His goal was to allow native people to tell their own stories and histories. The museum became a reality when Congress authorized it and work began to preserve native artifacts at the Heye Foundation in preparation for the first exhibit of the museum, titled "All Roads Are Good." In order to include native voices, museum officials invited numerous Native Americans to New York to plan the exhibit, including Kiowa elder Harding Big Bow, who was interviewed about material culture surrounding the Peyote religion.

As past president of the Native American Church in Oklahoma and a member of the church since the 1920s, Big Bow was eminently qualified to interpret material culture associated with the Peyote religion. When a Wyandot interviewer asked Big Bow to discuss a peyote fan, Big Bow responded that the fan had belonged to a Kiowa elder named Poolah. When asked how he knew this, Big Bow responded that he could identify the fan made from the wing of an eagle by the intricate beadwork on its handle. The design and colors were distinctly those used by Kiowa elder Poolah. Big Bow had been in many ceremonies where that very fan had been used, and he identified it without difficulty, explaining its function and use during the ceremony. He told stories elicited by objects, and he clarified that the pipe was used in other Kiowa ceremonies but not in services of the Native American Church. Big Bow spent the evening telling traditional and personal stories. The next day he sang peyote songs and answered questions. His voice is a permanent part of the collection at the National Museum of the American Indian, and he shared several sacred thoughts, ideas, songs, and stories so that young people would know the Kiowa traditions he had spent his life learning.

Harding Big Bow was one of hundreds of Native Americans who have participated in programs of the National Museum of the American Indian. This includes planning the new museum, to be built on the mall in Washington, D.C., next to the Air and Space Museum toward the Capitol Building. The staff of the museum traveled to many sites in Indian country to listen to suggestions about the design of the museum, presentation of exhibits, and interpretations of history, artifacts, and cultures of native populations in North, South, and Central America. Native American Studies and the Native American Student Program of the University

Powwows emerged among Great Lakes and Great Plains people and are common among many native peoples today. In 1992, southern Cheyenne participants W. Richard West Sr., W. Richard West Jr., James West, (unidentified), Christina West, and Karin West posed for this photograph.

of California at Riverside hosted such a meeting, drawing on the expertise of California's original people as well as urban Indians to meet with Richard West, Clara Sue Kidwell, George Horsecapture, Paul Apodaca, and others.

Over the years, various museums have collected the remains of thousands of Native Americans, placing bones into boxes and claiming that they owned or controlled them for scientific research. Some forensic scholars have studied these remains and published their findings, but thousands of remains are still in warehouses and basements, where they have never been studied. Some archaeologists have claimed these remains to be their private or institutional property, but Native Americans have protested the desecration of Indian burials, theft of funerary objects, and storage of native remains. An archaeologist in the Northwest Plateau has refused to turn over remains to native nations, claiming the prehistoric remains to be those of a European. Some archaeologists view remains as simply "material" that are to be studied and that have no relationship to contemporary Indians, but this is not the native view.

Native Americans have often asked how whites would feel if Native Americans dug up the remains of Puritans, Pilgrims, or pioneers so they could measure skulls for brain capacities (intelligence), study teeth for wear, or examine bones for fractures and diseases that may have contributed to their demise. As Sioux scholar Vine Deloria and Pawnee historian James Riding In have pointed out, the issue is really a matter of basic human rights and decency.

Repatriation of Native American remains is an emotional issue among those archaeologists who believe they own these "cultural resources" and have no obligation whatsoever to Native Americans. Repatriation is also emotional for Native Americans, who often believe that the souls of the deceased cannot rest until remains are properly cared for by other peoples–generally reburied in the ground or handled in accordance with tribal tradition. Archaeologists often claim that Native American remains are so old that they cannot be directly related to any particular group living today, but Pomo Larry Myers, executive secretary of the Native American Heritage Commission, counters that this does not matter as long as native people determine the disposition of native remains, regardless of their age. To native people the issue of repatriation is a sacred one, not a scientific one, and many Native Americans maintain that if archaeologists wish to work with native communities to conduct scientific research, they may do so, but they cannot dictate policies regarding American Indian remains. Native Americans pressed the issue with Congress in 1990, resulting in the Native American Grave Protection and Repatriation Act (NAGPRA). It required all institutions receiving federal funds to inventory their collections, including the remains of Native Americans, and respond to tribes interested in receiving their patrimony and remains of their ancestors.

Some archaeologists were outraged by NAGPRA. One archaeologist at the University of California called the act "disastrous" because the university would have to return the remains of approximately ten thousand Native Americans. "Some Native Americans claim they believe in spirits," one official stated, "and that's why they want the bones back. But to me, that just isn't good enough. That kind of thinking disappeared in the Dark Ages." Clearly this academic had little knowledge of contemporary Native American cultures, religious beliefs, mourning ceremonies, and after-life. Such marginalization of Native American beliefs is common, but Miwuk Reba Fuller, Serrano Henry Duro, Cahuilla Anthony Madrigal, Lummi Theresa Mike, Navajo Paul Apodaca, and others have continued the struggle to implement NAGPRA with dignity and intelligence. But the law enables many tribes to regain remains stolen from their burials and reclaim grave goods and other patrimony (artifacts) that are of a spiritual nature to their cultures. Whereas many archaeologists and anthropologists opposed NAGPRA, others supported it, including professor Barbara O'Connell of Hamline University in Minneapolis, who urged her colleagues to cooperate with the law. Pawnee scholar James Riding In has argued that the well-being of entire Native American communities depends on the safe and proper return of remains, and he is a native person who has spent his academic life fighting for the dignity of the dead and the living.

Issues surrounding remains and patrimony are as old as European colonization of Native America. Since the colonial era, non-Indians have robbed graves for bones, skulls, and grave goods to keep in private and public collections or sell to worldwide markets interested in owning a piece of Native American history. During the bicentennial celebration of the United States, several Native Americans in California demanded that the state protect remains, grave goods, and village sites. This was an era of great expansion in California, as contractors used massive bulldozers to tear the earth and make ready for housing projects, industry, and freeways. In 1976, Cahuilla Katherine Saubel, Luiseño Henry Rodriquez, Juaneño Steve Rios, Hupa-Yurok David Risling, Powhatan-Lenape Jack Forbes, Cahuilla-Luiseño Edward Castillo, Luiseño Vincent Ibanez, and many other Native Americans in California joined forces to create the Native American Heritage Commission. The result was a commission that created a sacred sites file for the state, evaluated every environmental impact report and forest report, and protected remains, villages, and artifacts being threatened by development.

Pomo administrator Larry Myers has made a profound contribution as administrator of the Native American Heritage Commission by working closely with Native Americans, developers, state agencies, and federal agencies to protect remains, village sites, and artifacts. Through a wide range of projects, the Native American Heritage Commission furthers cultural and historical preservation. For many years Paiute-White Mountain Apache William Mungary has led the commission as chair, while Shoshoni-Mono elder Dorothy Joseph and Cahuilla Katherine Saubel have initiated many changes that strengthen self-determination of native people to decide how to deal with continued growth, development, and construction on former Indian lands. They have also worked tirelessly to protect sites and remains, in spite of nonnative business and governmental interests bent on expanding and exploiting the natural environment.

Ajumawe scholar Darryl Wilson addressed the Native American Heritage Commission in 1990 to inform commissioners that the U.S. Forest Service planned to develop Ako-Yet (Mount Shasta) as a ski resort. He was supported by several native leaders in northern California and southern Oregon. A Wyandot member of the commission introduced a resolution to protect the mountain, knowing all the time that a state agency could not dictate policy to a federal entity. Commissioners met with officials of the Forest Service on the mountain to discuss preserving the sacredness of the area. However, officials of the Forest Service

Gaming among some tribes has brought economic, social, and cultural revitalization. American Indian casinos exist in every part of the United States. In 1994, Chemehuevis of the Twenty-Nine Palms band of Mission Indians built Spotlight 29 on the eastern edge of the Coachella Valley.

emphasized land use rather than spiritual preservation, a dichotomy common in dealings between native and nonnative officials, particularly bureaucrats. The Forest Service postponed the development of Mount Shasta by a former employee and Asian financial backers and in 1998 decided against permitting development on the sacred mountain in accordance with the wishes of native people.

In similar fashion, Kumeyaay, Luiseño, and Cupeño Indians united in 1990 to prevent the Diocese of San Diego from building a fellowship hall on the site of Mission San Diego. The parish decided to build a bingo-fellowship hall on the second mission site, a historical monument visited by thousands of people and listed on the National Register of Historic Sites. To mitigate the impact of construction, the Catholic Church hired archaeologist Richard Carrico to conduct the dig and forced him to sign a gag order not to inform others of his work. However, Carrico would not violate California law, and when he found Native American remains, he informed the county coroner and Native American Heritage Commission. Digging continued until archaeologists had removed and preserved between seventy and one hundred articulated and inarticulated remains. Native Americans from the region protested the desecration of the cemetery, and when contractors determined to destroy remains by drilling huge holes into the earth, an assistant attorney general threatened to file charges against the Church and city. As a result of pressure from Native Americans, politicians, and preservationists, the Church ended construction and negotiated a settlement with Native Americans recognizing the site as a legal cemetery and agreeing to a traditional and Catholic reburial.

The fight to preserve burials at the mission led Kumeyaays to form a Cultural Resource Committee composed of representatives of native people from many reservations. This committee is a leader in implementing NAGPRA. Native Americans throughout the country have taken the initiative to reclaim remains, rebury them, and secure medicine bundles, representations of gods, masks, baskets, carvings, paintings, feathers, fans, prayer sticks, and other items. The struggle of Native Americans to preserve their cultural heritage, patrimony, and remains is integrally tied to spiritual beliefs about the earth and homelands of people. For the Wallowa band of Nez Perce Indians, the sacred ground is the Wallowa River Valley of Oregon and the surrounding mountains, lakes, plants, and animals. In 1997, nonnative residents of the Wallowa Valley invited the Nez Perce to return to their homes, and Nez Perce gained access to 160 acres overlooking the Wallowa River through the Wallowa Band Nez Perce Interpretive Center Coalition. Nez Perce coalition member Joseph McCormack has helped bridge the gap between his people and non-Indians in a joint effort to preserve the environment and provide a place for Nez Perce to gather, sing, pray, dance, and remember. The Wallowa band of Nez Perce has come full circle, back to its traditional home, the land that holds the bones of its relatives, the place of its origins.

As American Indians faced the twenty-first century, they asserted their sovereignty in many ways. They demanded that historical curriculum in schools honestly portray the invasion and conquest. In 1990, California's State Department of Education recommended the acceptance of the Houghton-Mifflin K-8 programs, in part because the publisher had dealt accurately with Native American history in its textbooks. And throughout Indian country, native leaders have determined for themselves other matters pertaining to education, economics, language, law, culture, religion, politics, and health. Perhaps no area of Indian life received as much attention as did sovereignty, particularly as gaming tribes with casinos asserted their sovereignty to operate video slot machines. For the first time since the American conquest, tribes found some measure of self-sufficiency through gaming. Tribes offered thousands of jobs and added millions of dollars to the tax rolls, but this was not sufficient for politicians, particularly those tied closely to gaming interests in Nevada.

In California, Governor Pete Wilson refused to negotiate with gaming tribes to make a compact as dictated by federal law. In response, the Twenty-Nine Palms Band of Mission Indians, Cahuilla, Pechanga, San Manuel, Cabazon, Viejas, Barona, Sycuan, and other native nations led the fight for sovereignty. Dean Mike, Theresa Mike, Mark Macarro, Aaron Thomas, and Anthony Pico were among the leaders standing and fighting for Indian sovereignty. At a congressional hearing in 1998, many native leaders in southern California vowed to spend their lives protecting native sovereignty. Edward Castillo and Lummi Bernie Thomas pointed out that Americans everywhere should be proud of contemporary Indian leaders who have protected Indian rights—and by extension inalienable rights of all Americans. Indian leaders at the beginning of the twenty-first century deserve every bit as much credit as the Indian leaders of the nineteenth century. The nature of the fight has changed, Castillo argued, but the issue of sovereignty remains.

The past has an important relationship to the present and future, whether the issue is gaming, education, repatriation, or representation. Ajumawe scholar Darryl Wilson once illustrated the point by telling a story about tribal elder Craven Gibson. Wilson once asked Gibson to tell him when time began for the Indian people of the Pit River Country. The elder asked Wilson to return in two nights, and when he did, the moon was "Huge. Full. Orange!" By the light of the full moon, in the shadow of Ako-Yet (Mount Shasta), Gibson answered:

> I don't think there was a beginning
> Because there is no ending
> And if there is no ending
> Then there cannot be a beginning

Native American history is a great circle with no beginning and no ending. It is much a part of American history, but no account is capable of describing and interpreting all of native history, particularly the historical record contained in the blood memories of Native Americans. American Indian history is more than a chronicle of human interactions. It is a past related to rivers, rocks, mountains, animals, plants, places, and people. From Maine to Florida and Alaska to New Mexico, the earth holds the historical drama that is a part of the Native American past. Human beings are merely a component of Native American history, which began when the earth was young and brought to life with movement, dance, song, and story. With each telling of historical narratives, the past comes alive and is kept alive with the retelling. For many native people, the past is a continuing circle with no beginning and no ending, an ever-moving and expanding circle where the past is present and the present is prologue.

Selected Readings and Bibliography

The final chapter focuses on the theme of Native American history as a circle in which the past continues to influence the present and will affect the future. Information regarding native language projects is from *News from Native California* and personal information from Wendell Jim, director of education at the Warm

Springs Reservation of Oregon. Material on Wordcraft Circle is from *Moccasin Telegraph*, edited by Lee Francis. Information on the National Museum of the American Indian is from publications by the museum. Repatriation is a sensitive and significant topic among Indians, and the information presented in this chapter is drawn from personal participation with the Native American Heritage Commission and from work implementing the Native American Graves Protection Act among tribes in southern California, particularly the Chemehuevi of the Twenty-Nine Palms Band of Mission Indians. Most of the information in this chapter is from oral interviews taken for personal research during the last three decades.

INDEX

Main headings followed by an asterisk (*) will have variant spellings throughout the book. Page numbers in italics refer to illustrations and maps.

*Main headings followed by an asterisk (*) will have variant spellings throughout the book.

PHOTO CREDITS

Photos courtesy of the author unless otherwise noted.

p. 8 Corbis. **p. 27** Eleanore Sioui. **p. 35** Courtesy of Edward Castillo. **p. 48** Smithsonian Institution, Neg. No. T13409. **p. 57** Peabody Museum of Archaeology and Ethnology, Harvard University. **p. 115** The Granger Collection, New York. **p. 126** National Museum of American Art, Washington, D. C./Art Resource, NY. **p. 130** The Granger Collection, New York. **p. 141** The Granger Collection, New York. **p. 151** Corbis. **p. 155** The Granger Collection, New York. **p. 185** Washington State Historical Society, Tacoma. **p. 186** Washington State Historical Society, Tacoma. **p. 195** Courtesy of the California State History Section, California State Library, Neg. No. 317030. **p. 197** Photo by Rodman Wanamaker. Courtesy Department of Library Services, American Museum of Natural History. **p. 216** Corbis. **p. 222** Corbis. **p. 244** Smithsonian Institution, Neg. No. 1754A2. **p. 249** The Granger Collection, New York. **p. 255** The Granger Collection, New York. **p. 259** Corbis. **p. 268** Corbis. **p. 275** Corbis/UPI. **p. 290** Courtesy of the National Museum of The American Indian, Smithsonian Institution. **p. 298** The Granger Collection, New York. **p. 308** Corbis/UPI. **p. 310** Jeff Tinsley. **p. 321** Corbis/UPI. **p. 335** Larry Myers. **p. 340** Courtesy of the National Museum of The American Indian, Smithsonian Institution. **p. 343** Arizona Historical Society. **p. 352** Luke Madrigal. **p. 365** Richard D. Scheuerman. **p. 378** Corbis/UPI . **p. 407** © Hulton Getty/Liaison Agency. **p. 427** Corbis/UPI. **p. 465** Courtesy of the National Museum of The American Indian, Smithsonian Institution. **p. 489** Twenty-Nine Palms Band of Mission Indians. **p. 504** Courtesy of the National Museum of The American Indian, Smithsonian Institution. **p. 507** Twenty-Nine Palms Band of Mission Indians.